STUDY GUIDE

Richard O. Straub

University of Michigan, Dearborn

with
**Focus on Vocabulary and Language
by *Cornelius Rea***
Douglas College, British Columbia

and

Foreword by
Charles T. Blair-Broeker
Cedar Falls High School, Iowa

Randal M. Ernst
Lincoln Public Schools, Nebraska

to accompany

David G. Myers

Psychology

Eighth Edition

WORTH PUBLISHERS

Study Guide (AP* Edition)
by Richard O. Straub
to accompany
Myers: **Psychology,** Eighth Edition

Printed in the United States of America

ISBN-13: 978-0-7167-6137-2
ISBN-10: 0-7167-6137-8

Sixth Printing

Worth Publishers
41 Madison Avenue
New York, NY 10010
www.worthpublishers.com

Contents

Foreword

You have enrolled in Advanced Placement Psychology, a college-level class. Bravo! If, by chance, you are questioning your ability to successfully complete this rigorous curriculum, you are not alone. True, there is no magic trick that will ensure your success in AP classes, but these suggestions will help you to achieve your goals:

1. Use this Study Guide to help master psychology's fundamental concepts. There is much to learn, but this guide's structure simplifies the learning process.
2. Keep up from the very beginning. It's easy to let one class slide if there is a big project or test in another class. Don't let AP Psychology slip just because you're busy.
3. Prioritize your activities. Sports, jobs, volunteer work, social events, and family responsibilities all compete for your time. One sign of academic maturity is your ability to fit all these important activities into your daily schedule.
4. Listen to your teacher, who knows what it takes to succeed and is your greatest resource. Your teacher has your best interests in mind and wants you to succeed.
5. Actively participate in class. Ask lots of questions.
6. Don't question whether you're smart enough to succeed. You are! The difference between successful and unsuccessful AP students is rarely intelligence. The difference is in *attitude, self-discipline, study skills,* and the *investment of time,* all of which you control. Evaluate where you stand on these four areas, making the adjustments necessary to ensure that you will succeed.
7. Establish a study group of two to four classmates, and meet regularly to discuss course content.
8. Don't freak out about the AP Exam in May. Take one day at a time, focusing on what should be done *today*. Have you completed your reading? Are you using this Study Guide? Have you reviewed material from earlier in the unit? Are you making progress on assignments? Are you following your teacher's suggestions? Take care of business on a daily basis throughout the course, and when May rolls around, you'll be ready.

Unlike many AP courses, AP Psychology is immediately relevant to your life. That is, the content of every AP psychology unit applies to your life in ways that will help you understand yourself and others better than you do now, and the scientific methods of psychology will improve your critical thinking skills. Former students often tell us that AP Psychology was the most valuable course they ever took. Dedicate yourself to this class, and you may find yourself agreeing with so many of our former students!

Charles T. Blair-Broeker
Randal M. Ernst

Preface

This Study Guide is designed for use with *Psychology*, Eighth Edition, by David G. Myers. It is intended to help you to learn material in the textbook, to evaluate your understanding of that material, and then to review any problem areas. Beginning on page ix, "How to Manage Your Time Efficiently and Study More Effectively" provides detailed instructions on how to use the textbook and this Study Guide for maximum benefit. It also offers additional study suggestions based on principles of time management, effective notetaking, evaluation of exam performance, and an effective program for improving your comprehension while studying from textbooks.

The eighth edition of this Study Guide offers many useful features. Each chapter includes three review tests: In addition to the two Progress Tests that focus on facts and definitions, there is a Psychology Applied test that evaluates your understanding of the text chapter's broader conceptual material and its application to real-world situations. This test contains at least 20 multiple-choice questions and an essay question. For all three review tests, the correct answers are given, followed by textbook page references (so you can easily go back and reread the material). In addition, complete explanations are given not only of why the answer is correct but also of why the other choices are incorrect.

The chapter review is organized by major text section. For each section the fill-in and essay-type questions are organized under their relevant learning objectives from the text. All chapters also include a Cross-Check, which provides an engaging crossword puzzle review of chapter terms and concepts. In addition, each chapter includes Focus on Vocabulary and Language, written by Cornelius Rea of Douglas College, British Columbia. This section provides brief, clear explanations of some of the idioms and expressions used by David Myers that may be unfamiliar to some students. They are first listed at the beginning of the relevant section, then explained at the back of the chapter.

General Internet Resources

To obtain general information about psychology-related topics, you might want to consult some of the following Web sites. Russ Dewey's Psych Web is an effort to compile a great deal of information for psychology students and teachers, including self-quizzes, lists of psychology journals on the Web, self-help resources, tip sheets for psychology majors, and psychology departments on the Web. Psych Web is available at the following site:

www.psychwww.com

Deborah Kelley-Milburn and Michael A. Milburn's "Cyberspace: Resources for Psychologists on the Internet" (*Psychological Science*, [1995, July], Volume 6, pp. 203–211) is another excellent resource. This review provides helpful information on Listservs, Usenet groups, electronic journals and newsletters, databases, grant and job information, and library catalogues.

Both the American Psychological Association (APA) and the American Psychological Society (APS) have Internet services. These services provide not only information about their organizations but also selected articles from their main journals, information about current research in the discipline, and links to other science-related sites on the Internet. Their locations are as follows:

APA: www.apa.org/ and APS: http://www.psychologicalscience.org

Finally, and perhaps most important, is Psychtalk, a list for students interested in discussion topics and controversies related to psychology. Topics that have been discussed over the past few years include child abuse, the nature-nurture issue, homosexuality, and pornography. To subscribe, send a message to:

psychtalk-request@fre.fsu.umd.edu

The message should read "subscribe psychtalk (your name)."

Acknowledgments

I would like to thank all the students and instructors who used this Study Guide in its previous editions and provided such insightful and useful suggestions. Special thanks are also due to Betty Shapiro Probert for her extraordinary editorial contributions and to Don Probert for his skill and efficiency in the composition of this guide. I would also like to thank Andrea Musick, Eve Conte, and Stacey Alexander of Worth Publishers for their dedication and energy in skillfully coordinating various aspects of production. Most important, I want to thank Jeremy, Rebecca, Melissa, and Pam for their enduring love and patience.

Richard O. Straub

How to Manage Your Time Efficiently and Study More Effectively

How effectively do you study? Good study habits make the job of being a college student much easier. Many students, who *could* succeed in college, fail or drop out because they have never learned to manage their time efficiently. Even the best students can usually benefit from an in-depth evaluation of their current study habits.

There are many ways to achieve academic success, of course, but your approach may not be the most effective or efficient. Are you sacrificing your social life or your physical or mental health in order to get A's on your exams? Good study habits result in better grades *and* more time for other activities.

Evaluate Your Current Study Habits

To improve your study habits, you must first have an accurate picture of how you currently spend your time. Begin by putting together a profile of your present living and studying habits. Answer the following questions by writing *yes* or *no* on each line.

_____ 1. Do you usually set up a schedule to budget your time for studying, recreation, and other activities?

_____ 2. Do you often put off studying until time pressures force you to cram?

_____ 3. Do other students seem to study less than you do, but get better grades?

_____ 4. Do you usually spend hours at a time studying one subject, rather than dividing that time between several subjects?

_____ 5. Do you often have trouble remembering what you have just read in a textbook?

_____ 6. Before reading a chapter in a textbook, do you skim through it and read the section headings?

_____ 7. Do you try to predict exam questions from your lecture notes and reading?

_____ 8. Do you usually attempt to paraphrase or summarize what you have just finished reading?

_____ 9. Do you find it difficult to concentrate very long when you study?

_____ 10. Do you often feel that you studied the wrong material for an exam?

Thousands of college students have participated in similar surveys. Students who are fully realizing their academic potential usually respond as follows: (1) yes, (2) no, (3) no, (4) no, (5) no, (6) yes, (7) yes, (8) yes, (9) no, (10) no.

Compare your responses to those of successful students. The greater the discrepancy, the more you could benefit from a program to improve your study habits. The questions are designed to identify areas of weakness. Once you have identified your weaknesses, you will be able to set specific goals for improvement and implement a program for reaching them.

Manage Your Time

Do you often feel frustrated because there isn't enough time to do all the things you must and want to do? Take heart. Even the most productive and successful people feel this way at times. But they establish priorities for their activities and they learn to budget time for each of them. There's much in the saying "If you want something done, ask a busy person to do it." A busy person knows how to get things done.

If you don't now have a system for budgeting your time, develop one. Not only will your academic accomplishments increase, but you will actually find more time in your schedule for other activities. And you won't have to feel guilty about "taking time off," because all your obligations will be covered.

Establish a Baseline

As a first step in preparing to budget your time, keep a diary for a few days to establish a summary, or baseline, of the time you spend in studying, socializing, working, and so on. If you are like many students, much of your "study" time is nonproductive; you may sit at your desk and leaf through a book, but the time is actually wasted. Or you may procrastinate. You are always getting ready to study, but you rarely do.

Besides revealing where you waste time, your diary will give you a realistic picture of how much time you need to allot for meals, commuting, and other fixed activities. In addition, careful records should indicate the times of the day when you are consistently most productive. A sample time-management diary is shown in Table 1.

Plan the Term

Having established and evaluated your baseline, you are ready to devise a more efficient schedule. Buy a calendar that covers the entire school term and has ample space for each day. Using the course outlines provided by your instructors, enter the dates of all exams, term paper deadlines, and other important academic obligations. If you have any long-range personal plans (concerts, weekend trips, etc.), enter the dates on the calendar as well. Keep your calendar up to date and refer to it often. I recommend carrying it with you at all times.

Develop a Weekly Calendar

Now that you have a general picture of the school term, develop a weekly schedule that includes all of your activities. Aim for a schedule that you can live with for the entire school term. A sample weekly schedule, incorporating the following guidelines, is shown in Table 2.

1. Enter your class times, work hours, and any other fixed obligations first. *Be thorough.* Using information from your time-management diary, allow plenty of time for such things as commuting, meals, laundry, and the like.

Table 1   Sample Time-Management Diary

Behavior	Time Completed	Duration Hours: Minutes
Monday		
Sleep	7:00	7:30
Dressing	7:25	:25
Breakfast	7:45	:20
Commute	8:20	:35
Coffee	9:00	:40
French	10:00	1:00
Socialize	10:15	:15
Video game	10:35	:20
Coffee	11:00	:25
Psychology	12:00	1:00
Lunch	12:25	:25
Study Lab	1:00	:35
Psych. Lab	4:00	3:00
Work	5:30	1:30
Commute	6:10	:40
Dinner	6:45	:35
TV	7:30	:45
Study Psych.	10:00	2:30
Socialize	11:30	1:30
Sleep		

Prepare a similar chart for each day of the week. When you finish an activity, note it on the chart and write down the time it was completed. Then determine its duration by subtracting the time the previous activity was finished from the newly entered time.

2. Set up a study schedule for each of your courses. The study habits survey and your time-management diary will help direct you. The following guidelines should also be useful.

(a) Establish regular study times for each course. The 4 hours needed to study one subject, for example, are most profitable when divided into shorter periods spaced over several days. If you cram your studying into one 4-hour block, what you attempt to learn in the third or fourth hour will interfere with what you studied in the first 2 hours. Newly acquired knowledge is like wet cement. It needs some time to "harden" to become memory.

(b) Alternate subjects. The type of interference just mentioned is greatest between similar topics. Set up a schedule in which you spend time on several *different* courses during each study session. Besides reducing the potential for interference, alternating subjects will help to prevent mental fatigue with one topic.

(c) Set weekly goals to determine the amount of study time you need to do well in each course. This will depend on, among other things, the difficulty of your courses and the effectiveness of your methods. Many

Table 2 — Sample Weekly Schedule

Time	Mon.	Tues.	Wed.	Thurs.	Fri.	Sat.
7–8	Dress Eat	Dress Eat	Dress Eat	Dress Eat	Dress Eat	
8–9	Psych.	Study Psych.	Psych.	Study Psych.	Psych.	Dress Eat
9–10	Eng.	Study Eng.	Eng.	Study Eng.	Eng.	Study Eng.
10–11	Study French	Free	Study French	Open Study	Study French	Study Stats.
11–12	French	Study Psych. Lab	French	Open Study	French	Study Stats.
12–1	Lunch	Lunch	Lunch	Lunch	Lunch	Lunch
1–2	Stats.	Psych. Lab	Stats.	Study or Free	Stats.	Free
2–3	Bio.	Psych. Lab	Bio.	Free	Bio.	Free
3–4	Free	Psych.	Free	Free	Free	Free
4–5	Job	Job	Job	Job	Job	Free
5–6	Job	Job	Job	Job	Job	Free
6–7	Dinner	Dinner	Dinner	Dinner	Dinner	Dinner
7–8	Study Bio.	Study Bio.	Study Bio.	Study Bio.	Free	Free
8–9	Study Eng.	Study Stats.	Study Psych.	Open Study	Open Study	Free
9–10	Open Study	Open Study	Open Study	Open Study	Free	Free

This is a sample schedule for a student with a 16-credit load and a 10-hour-per-week part-time job. Using this chart as an illustration, make up a weekly schedule, following the guidelines outlined here.

professors recommend studying at least 1 to 2 hours for each hour in class. If your time-management diary indicates that you presently study less time than that, do not plan to jump immediately to a much higher level. Increase study time from your baseline by setting weekly goals [see (4)] that will gradually bring you up to the desired level. As an initial schedule, for example, you might set aside an amount of study time for each course that matches class time.

(d) Schedule for maximum effectiveness. Tailor your schedule to meet the demands of each course. For the course that emphasizes lecture notes, schedule time for a daily review soon after the class. This will give you a chance to revise your notes and clean up any hard-to-decipher shorthand while the material is still fresh in your mind. If you are evaluated for class participation (for example, in a language course), allow time for a review just *before* the class meets. Schedule study time for your most difficult (or least motivating) courses during hours when you are the most alert and distractions are fewest.

(e) Schedule open study time. Emergencies, additional obligations, and the like could throw off your

schedule. And you may simply need some extra time periodically for a project or for review in one of your courses. Schedule several hours each week for such purposes.

3. After you have budgeted time for studying, fill in slots for recreation, hobbies, relaxation, household errands, and the like.

4. Set specific goals. Before each study session, make a list of specific goals. The simple note "7–8 PM: study psychology" is too broad to ensure the most effective use of the time. Formulate your daily goals according to what you know you must accomplish during the term. If you have course outlines with advance assignments, set systematic daily goals that will allow you, for example, to cover fifteen chapters before the exam. And be realistic: Can you actually expect to cover a 78-page chapter in one session? Divide large tasks into smaller units; stop at the most logical resting points. When you complete a specific goal, take a 5- or 10-minute break before tackling the next goal.

5. Evaluate how successful or unsuccessful your studying has been on a daily or weekly basis. Did you

reach most of your goals? If so, reward yourself immediately. You might even make a list of five to ten rewards to choose from. If you have trouble studying regularly, you may be able to motivate yourself by making such rewards contingent on completing specific goals.

6. Finally, until you have lived with your schedule for several weeks, don't hesitate to revise it. You may need to allow more time for chemistry, for example, and less for some other course. If you are trying to study regularly for the first time and are feeling burned out, you probably have set your initial goals too high. Don't let failure cause you to despair and abandon the program. Accept your limitations and revise your schedule so that you are studying only 15 to 20 minutes more each evening than you are used to. The point is to *identify a regular schedule with which you can achieve some success.* Time management, like any skill, must be practiced to become effective.

Techniques for Effective Study

Knowing how to put study time to best use is, of course, as important as finding a place for it in your schedule. Here are some suggestions that should enable you to increase your reading comprehension and improve your notetaking. A few study tips are included as well.

Using SQ3R to Increase Reading Comprehension

How do you study from a textbook? If you are like many students, you simply read and reread in a *passive* manner. Studies have shown, however, that most students who simply read a textbook cannot remember more than half the material ten minutes after they have finished. Often, what is retained is the unessential material rather than the important points upon which exam questions will be based.

This Study Guide employs a program known as SQ3R (*S*urvey, *Q*uestion, *R*ead, *R*ehearse, and *R*eview) to facilitate, and allow you to assess, your comprehension of the important facts and concepts in *Psychology*, Eighth Edition, by David G. Myers.

Research has shown that students using SQ3R achieve significantly greater comprehension of texts than students reading in the more traditional passive manner. Once you have learned this program, you can improve your comprehension of any textbook.

Survey Before you read a text chapter, determine whether the text or the study guide has an outline or list of objectives. *Psychology*, Eighth Edition, includes a number of specific learning objectives for each sec-

tion of the chapter. Read this material and the learning outcomes at the end of each section. Next, read the textbook chapter fairly quickly, paying special attention to the major headings and subheadings. This survey will give you an idea of the chapter's contents and organization. You will then be able to divide the chapter into logical sections in order to formulate specific goals for a more careful reading of the chapter.

In this Study Guide, the *Chapter Overview* summarizes the major topics of the textbook chapter. This section also provides a few suggestions for approaching topics you may find difficult.

Question You will retain material longer when you have a use for it. If you look up a word's definition in order to solve a crossword puzzle, for example, you will remember it longer than if you merely fill in the letters as a result of putting other words in. Previewing the chapter will allow you to generate important questions that the chapter will proceed to answer. These questions correspond to "mental files" into which knowledge will be sorted for easy access. The learning objectives that appear throughout the chapter can easily be reframed into questions for this purpose.

As you survey, jot down several additional questions for each chapter section. One simple technique is to generate questions by rephrasing a section heading. For example, the "Preoperational Thought" head could be turned into "What is preoperational thought?" Good questions will allow you to focus on the important points in the text. Examples of good questions are those that begin as follows: "List two examples of . . . ." "What is the function of . . .?" "What is the significance of . . .?" Such questions give a purpose to your reading. Similarly, you can formulate questions based on the chapter outline.

Read When you have established "files" for each section of the chapter, review your first question, begin reading, and continue until you have discovered its answer. If you come to material that seems to answer an important question you don't have a file for, stop and write down the question.

Using this Study Guide, read the chapter one section at a time. First, preview the section by skimming it, noting headings and boldface items. Next, study the appropriate section objectives in the *Chapter Review*. Then, as you read the chapter section, search for the answer to each objective.

Be sure to read everything. Don't skip photo or art captions, graphs, or marginal notes. In some cases, what may seem vague in reading will be made clear by a simple graph. Keep in mind that test questions are sometimes drawn from illustrations and charts.

Rehearse When you have found the answer to a question, close your eyes and mentally recite the question and its answer. Then *write* the answer next to the question. It is important that you recite an answer in your own words rather than the author's. Don't rely on your short-term memory to repeat the author's words verbatim.

In responding to the objectives, pay close attention to what is called for. If you are asked to identify or list, do just that. If asked to compare, contrast, or do both, you should focus on the similarities (compare) and differences (contrast) between the concepts or theories. Answering the objectives carefully not only will help you to focus your attention on the important concepts of the text but also will provide excellent practice for essay exams.

Rehearsal is an extremely effective study technique, recommended by many learning experts. In addition to increasing reading comprehension, it is useful for review. Trying to explain something in your own words clarifies your knowledge, often by revealing aspects of your answer that are vague or incomplete. If you repeatedly rely upon "I know" in recitation, you really *may not know*.

Rehearsal has the additional advantage of simulating an exam, especially an essay exam; the same skills are required in both cases. Too often students study without ever putting the book and notes aside, which makes it easy for them to develop false confidence in their knowledge. When the material is in front of you, you may be able to *recognize* an answer, but will you be able to *recall* it later, when you take an exam that does not provide these retrieval cues?

After you have recited and written your answer, continue with your next question. Read, recite, and so on.

Review When you have answered the last question on the material you have designated as a study goal, go back and review. Read over each question and your written answer to it. Your review might also include a brief written summary that integrates all of your questions and answers. This review need not take longer than a few minutes, but it is important. It will help you retain the material longer and will greatly facilitate a final review of each chapter before the exam.

In this Study Guide, the *Chapter Review* contains fill-in and brief essay questions for you to complete after you have finished reading the section and have written answers to the objectives. The correct answers are given at the end of the chapter. Generally, your answer to a fill-in question should match exactly (as in the case of important terms, theories, or people). In some cases, the answer is not a term or name, so a word close in meaning will suffice. You should answer these questions several times before taking an exam, so it's a good idea to mentally fill in the answers until you are ready for a final pretest review. Text page references are provided with each section title, in case you need to reread any of the material.

Also provided to facilitate your review are two *Progress Tests* that include multiple-choice questions and, where appropriate, matching or true–false questions. These tests are *not* to be taken until you have read the chapter and completed the *Chapter Review*. Correct answers, along with explanations of why each alternative is correct or incorrect, are provided at the end of the chapter. The relevant text page numbers for each question are also given. If you miss a question, read these explanations and, if necessary, review the text pages to further understand why. The *Progress Tests* do not test every aspect of a concept, so you should treat an incorrect answer as an indication that you need to review the concept.

Following the two *Progress Tests* is a *Psychology Applied* test, which should be taken just prior to an exam. It includes questions that test your ability to analyze, integrate, and apply the concepts in the chapter. Each *Psychology Applied* test includes an essay question dealing with a major concept covered in the chapter. As with the *Progress Tests*, answers for the *Psychology Applied* test are provided at the end of each chapter, along with relevant page numbers.

The core of each chapter concludes with *Key Terms*, which includes not only a list of key terms but also a crossword puzzle. *Writing Definitions* requires that you write definitions of all key terms on a separate piece of paper. *Cross-Check* reverses the process, asking you to complete a crossword puzzle by filling in the terms that apply to the definitions provided. As with the *Chapter Review* learning objectives, it is important that these answers be written from memory, and in your own words. The *Answers* section at the end of the chapter gives a definition of each term, sometimes along with an example of its usage and/or a tip to help you remember its meaning. It also includes answers to the crossword puzzle.

Following the answers is a list of potentially unfamiliar idioms, words, and expressions (*Focus on Vocabulary and Language*), ordered by text page number and accompanied by definitions and examples.

One final suggestion: Incorporate SQ3R into your time-management calendar. Set specific goals for completing SQ3R with each assigned chapter. Keep a record of chapters completed, and reward yourself for being conscientious. Initially, it takes more time and effort to "read" using SQ3R, but with practice, the steps will become automatic. More important, you will comprehend significantly more material and retain what you have learned longer than passive readers do.

Taking Lecture Notes

Are your class notes as useful as they might be? One way to determine their worth is to compare them with those taken by other good students. Are yours as thorough? Do they provide you with a comprehensible outline of each lecture? If not, then the following suggestions might increase the effectiveness of your notetaking.

1. Keep a separate notebook for each course. Use $8^1/_2 \times 11$-inch pages. Consider using a ring binder, which would allow you to revise and insert notes while still preserving lecture order.

2. Take notes in the format of a lecture outline. Use roman numerals for major points, letters for supporting arguments, and so on. Some instructors will make this easy by delivering organized lectures and, in some cases, by outlining their lectures on the board. If a lecture is disorganized, you will probably want to reorganize your notes soon after the class.

3. As you take notes in class, leave a wide margin on one side of each page. After the lecture, expand or clarify any shorthand notes while the material is fresh in your mind. Use this time to write important questions in the margin next to notes that answer them. This will facilitate later review and will allow you to anticipate similar exam questions.

Evaluate Your Exam Performance

How often have you received a grade on an exam that did not do justice to the effort you spent preparing for the exam? This is a common experience that can leave one feeling bewildered and abused. "What do I have to do to get an A?" "The test was unfair!" "I studied the wrong material!"

The chances of this happening are greatly reduced if you have an effective time-management schedule and use the study techniques described here. But it can happen to the best-prepared student and is most likely to occur on your first exam with a new professor.

Remember that there are two main reasons for studying. One is to learn for your own general academic development. Many people believe that such knowledge is all that really matters. Of course, it is possible, though unlikely, to be an expert on a topic without achieving commensurate grades, just as one can, occasionally, earn an excellent grade without truly mastering the course material. During a job interview or in the workplace, however, your A in HTML won't mean much if you can't actually program a computer.

In order to keep career options open after you graduate, you must know the material and maintain competitive grades. In the short run, this means performing well on exams, which is the second main objective in studying.

Probably the single best piece of advice to keep in mind when studying for exams is to *try to predict exam questions.* This means ignoring the trivia and focusing on the important questions and their answers (with your instructor's emphasis in mind).

A second point is obvious. How well you do on exams is determined by your mastery of *both* lecture and textbook material. Many students (partly because of poor time management) concentrate too much on one at the expense of the other.

To evaluate how well you are learning lecture and textbook material, analyze the questions you missed on the first exam. If your instructor does not review exams during class, you can easily do it yourself. Divide the questions into two categories: those drawn primarily from lectures and those drawn primarily from the textbook. Determine the percentage of questions you missed in each category. If your errors are evenly distributed and you are satisfied with your grade, you have no problem. If you are weaker in one area, you will need to set future goals for increasing and/or improving your study of that area.

Similarly, note the percentage of test questions drawn from each category. Although exams in most courses cover *both* lecture notes and the textbook, the relative emphasis of each may vary from instructor to instructor. While your instructors may not be entirely consistent in making up future exams, you may be able to tailor your studying for each course by placing *additional* emphasis on the appropriate area.

Exam evaluation will also point out the types of questions your instructor prefers. Does the exam consist primarily of multiple-choice, true–false, or essay questions? You may also discover that an instructor is fond of wording questions in certain ways. For example, an instructor may rely heavily on questions that require you to draw an analogy between a theory or concept and a real-world example. Evaluate both your instructor's style and how well you do with each format. Use this information to guide your future exam preparation.

Important aids, not only in studying for exams but also in determining how well prepared you are, are the *Progress* and *Psychology Applied Tests* provided in this Study Guide. If these tests don't include all of the types of questions your instructor typically writes, make up your own practice exam questions. Spend extra time testing yourself with question formats that are most difficult for you. There is no better way to evaluate your preparation for an upcoming exam than by testing yourself under the conditions most likely to be in effect during the actual test.

A Few Practical Tips

Even the best intentions for studying sometimes fail. Some of these failures occur because students attempt to work under conditions that are simply not conducive to concentrated study. To help ensure the success of your time-management program, here are a few suggestions that should assist you in reducing the possibility of procrastination or distraction.

1. If you have set up a schedule for studying, make your roommate, family, and friends aware of this commitment, and ask them to honor your quiet study time. Close your door and post a "Do Not Disturb" sign.

2. Set up a place to study that minimizes potential distractions. Use a desk or table, not your bed or an extremely comfortable chair. Keep your desk and the walls around it free from clutter. If you need a place other than your room, find one that meets as many of the above requirements as possible—for example, in the library stacks.

3. Do nothing but study in this place. It should become associated with studying so that it "triggers" this activity, just as a mouth-watering aroma elicits an appetite.

4. Never study with the television on or with other distracting noises present. If you must have music in the background in order to mask outside noise, for example, play soft instrumental music. Don't pick vocal selections; your mind will be drawn to the lyrics.

5. Study by yourself. Other students can be distracting or can break the pace at which *your* learning is most efficient. In addition, there is always the possibility that group studying will become a social gathering. Reserve that for its own place in your schedule.

If you continue to have difficulty concentrating for very long, try the following suggestions.

6. Study your most difficult or most challenging subjects first, when you are most alert.

7. Start with relatively short periods of concentrated study, with breaks in between. If your attention starts to wander, get up immediately and take a break. It is better to study effectively for 15 minutes and then take a break than to fritter away 45 minutes out of an hour. Gradually increase the length of study periods, using your attention span as an indicator of successful pacing.

Some Closing Thoughts

I hope that these suggestions help make you more successful academically, and that they enhance the quality of your college life in general. Having the necessary skills makes any job a lot easier and more pleasant. Let me repeat my warning not to attempt to make too drastic a change in your life-style immediately. Good habits require time and self-discipline to develop. Once established, they can last a lifetime.

STUDY GUIDE

Prologue: The Story of Psychology

PROLOGUE OVERVIEW

Psychology's historical development and current activities lead us to define the field as the science of behavior and mental processes. This Prologue discusses the development of psychology from ancient times until today and the range of behaviors and mental processes being investigated by psychologists in each of the various specialty areas. In addition, it introduces the biopsychosocial approach that integrates the three main levels of analysis followed by psychologists working from the seven major perspectives. Next is an overview of the diverse subfields in which psychologists conduct research and provide professional services.

The Prologue concludes with a Close-Up explaining how to get your study of psychology off on the right foot by learning (and pledging to follow!) the SQ3R study method. This study method is also discussed in the essay at the beginning of this Study Guide.

NOTE: Answer guidelines for all Prologue questions begin on page 10.

PROLOGUE REVIEW

First, skim each section, noting headings and boldface items. After you have read the section, review each objective by answering the fill-in questions that follow it. As you proceed, evaluate your performance by consulting the answers on page 10. Do not continue with the next section until you understand each answer. If you need to, review or reread the section in the textbook before continuing.

Psychology's Roots (pp. 2–8)

> David Myers at times uses idioms that are unfamiliar to some readers. If you do not know the meaning of any of the following words, phrases, or expressions in the context in which they appear in the Introduction and this section, refer to page 14 for an explanation: *peekaboo; grist for psychology's mill; unpack this definition; hunches; down-to-earth; structuralism waned; wise-cracking; "Magellans of the mind."*

Objective 1: Define *psychology*.

1. The author of your text defines psychology as the scientific study of _____ and _____ processes.

2. In this definition, "behavior" refers to any action that we can _____ and _____ , and "mental processes" refers to the internal _____ we _____ from behavior.

3. As a science, psychology is less a set of findings than a way of _____ _____ .

Objective 2: Trace psychology's prescientific roots, from early understandings of mind and body to the beginnings of modern science.

4. In the prescientific era, scholars such as _____ in India and _____ in China pondered the relationship between mind and body.

5. The Greek philosophers _____ and _____ viewed mind and body as _____ (inseparable/separable), and assumed that knowledge is _____ (innate/learned). The Greek philosopher who argued that all knowledge comes from experiences stored in memories is _____ . Unlike his teacher, who derived principles from _____ , he derived principles from careful _____ .

6. In the 1600s, the views of the Greek philosophers were revived by _____ , who believed that some ideas are innate; by Englishman _____ , who became one of the founders of modern science; and by _____ , who believed that knowledge originates in experience. This idea, along with the principle that science flourishes through observation and experiment, is called _____ .

Objective 3: Explain how the early psychologists sought to understand the mind's structure and functions, and identify some of the leading psychologists who worked in these areas.

7. The first psychological laboratory was founded in 1879 by Wilhelm _____ . His student, _____ , introduced the school of _____ , which explored the basic elements of mind using the method of _____ . This method proved _____ (reliable/unreliable), and psychologist _____ introduced the school of _____ , which focused on how mental and behavioral processes enable the organism to adapt, survive, and flourish.

8. The first female president of the American Psychological Association was _____ . The first woman to receive a Ph.D. in psychology was _____ .

Objective 4: Describe the evolution of psychology as defined from the 1920s through today.

9. The historical roots of psychology include the fields of _____ and _____ .

10. Some early psychologists included Ivan Pavlov, who pioneered the study of _____ ; the personality theorist _____ ; and Jean Piaget, who studied _____ .

11. In its earliest years, psychology was defined as the science of _____ life. From the 1920s into the 1960s, psychology in America was redefined as the science of _____ behavior. The author of your text defines psychology as the science of _____ and _____ processes.

12. As a response to Freudian psychology and to _____ , which they considered too mechanistic, pioneers _____ and _____ forged _____ psychology. This new perspective emphasized the _____ potential of _____ people.

13. During the 1960s, psychology underwent a _____ revolution as it began to recapture interest in _____ processes. The study of the interaction of thought processes and _____ function is called _____ .

Contemporary Psychology (pp. 8–14)

If you do not know the meaning of any of the following words, phrases, or expressions in the context in which they appear in the text, refer to pages 14–15 for an explanation: *mushrooming; wrestled with some issues; rekindled the debate; weaves a thread; nature-nurture tension dissolves; "Red in the face" and "hot under the collar"; But there is a payoff; psychoceramics.*

1. Worldwide, the number of psychologists is _____ (increasing/decreasing).

Objective 5: Summarize the nature-nurture debate in psychology, and describe the principle of natural selection.

2. The nature-nurture issue is the controversy over the relative contributions of _____ and _____ .

3. The Greek philosopher who assumed that character and intelligence are inherited is _____ . The Greek philosopher who argued that all knowledge comes from sensory experience is _____ .

4. In the 1600s, the views of the Greek philosophers were revived by _____ , who believed that most knowledge comes in through the senses, and _____ , who believed that some ideas are innate.

5. In 1859, naturalist _____ explained species variation by proposing the process of _____ , which works through the principle of _____ _____ .

Objective 6: Identify the three main levels of analysis in the biopsychosocial approach, and explain why psychology's varied perspectives are complementary.

6. Each person is a complex _____ that is part of a larger _____ _____ and at the same time composed of smaller systems. For this reason, psychologists work from three main _____ of _____— biological , _____ , and _____-_____— which together form an integrated _____ approach to the study of behavior and mental processes.

7. Psychologists who study how the body and brain enable emotions, memories, and sensory experiences are working from the _____ perspective.

8. Psychologists who study how natural selection influences behavior tendencies are working from the _____ perspective, whereas those concerned with the relative influences of genes and environment on individual differences are working from the _____ _____ perspective.

9. Psychologists who believe that behavior springs from unconscious drives and conflicts are working from the _____ perspective.

10. Psychologists who study the mechanisms by which observable responses are acquired and changed are working from the _____ perspective.

11. The _____ perspective explores how our minds encode, process, store, and retrieve information.

12. Psychologists who study how thinking and behavior vary in different situations are working from the _____- _____ perspective.

13. The different perspectives on the big issues _____ (contradict/complement) one another.

Objective 7: Identify some of psychology's subfields, and explain the difference between clinical psychology and psychiatry.

14. Psychologists may be involved in conducting _____ _____ , which builds psychology's knowledge base, or _____ _____ , which seeks solutions to practical problems.

15. Psychologists who help people cope with problems in living are called _____ psychologists. Psychologists who study, assess, and treat troubled people are called _____ psychologists.

16. Medical doctors who provide psychotherapy and treat physical causes of psychological disorders are called _____ .

Close-Up: Your Study of Psychology
(pp. 15–16)

> If you do not know the meaning of the following expression in the context in which it appears in the text, refer to page 15 for an explanation: *spaced practice*.

Objective 8: State five effective study techniques.

1. In order to master any subject, you must _____ process it.

2. The _____ study method incorporates five steps: **a.** _____ , **b.** _____ , **c.** _____ , **d.** _____ ., and **e.** _____ .

List five additional study tips identified in the text.

a. _____

b. _____

c. _____

d. _____

e. _____

PROGRESS TEST 1

Multiple-Choice Questions

Circle your answers to the following questions and check them with the answers beginning on page 10. If your answer is incorrect, read the explanation for why it is incorrect and then consult the appropriate pages of the text (in parentheses following the correct answer).

1. In its earliest days, psychology was defined as the:
   a. science of mental life.
   b. study of conscious and unconscious activity.
   c. scientific study of observable behavior.
   d. scientific study of behavior and mental processes.

2. Who would be most likely to agree with the statement, "Psychology should investigate only behaviors that can be observed"?
   a. Wilhelm Wundt
   b. Sigmund Freud
   c. John B. Watson
   d. William James

3. Today, psychology is defined as the:
   a. scientific study of mental phenomena.
   b. scientific study of conscious and unconscious activity.
   c. scientific study of behavior.
   d. scientific study of behavior and mental processes.

4. Who introduced the early school of structuralism?
   a. Edward Titchener
   b. Wilhelm Wundt
   c. William James
   d. Mary Whiton Calkins

5. Who wrote the early textbook *Principles of Psychology*?
   a. Wilhelm Wundt
   b. Ivan Pavlov
   c. Jean Piaget
   d. William James

6. Psychologists who study the degree to which genes influence our personality are working from the _____ perspective.
   a. behavioral
   b. evolutionary
   c. behavior genetics
   d. neuroscience

7. Which of the following exemplifies the issue of the relative importance of nature and nurture on our behavior?
   a. the issue of the relative influence of biology and experience on behavior
   b. the issue of the relative influence of rewards and punishments on behavior
   c. the debate as to the relative importance of heredity and instinct in determining behavior
   d. the debate as to whether mental processes are a legitimate area of scientific study

8. The seventeenth-century philosopher who believed that the mind is blank at birth and that most knowledge comes through sensory experience is:
   a. Plato.
   b. Aristotle.
   c. Descartes.
   d. Locke.

9. Which seventeenth-century philosopher believed that some ideas are innate?
   a. Aristotle
   b. Plato
   c. Descartes
   d. Locke

10. Which psychological perspective emphasizes the interaction of the brain and body in behavior?

    a. neuroscience

    b. cognitive

    c. behavioral

    d. behavior genetics

11. A psychologist who explores how Asian and North American definitions of attractiveness differ is working from the _____ perspective.

    a. behavioral   **c.** cognitive

    b. evolutionary   **d.** social-cultural

12. A psychologist who conducts experiments solely intended to build psychology's knowledge base is engaged in:

    a. basic research.

    b. applied research.

    c. industrial-organizational research.

    d. clinical research.

13. Psychologists who study, assess, and treat troubled people are called:

    a. basic researchers.

    b. applied psychologists.

    c. clinical psychologists.

    d. psychiatrists.

14. Today, psychology is a discipline that:

    a. connects with a diversity of other fields.

    b. is largely independent of other disciplines.

    c. is focused primarily on basic research.

    d. is focused primarily on applied research.

15. (Close-Up) In order, the sequence of steps in the SQ3R method is:

    a. survey, review, question, read, reflect.

    b. review, question, survey, read, reflect.

    c. question, review, survey, read, reflect.

    d. survey, question, read, review, reflect.

16. Francis Bacon's ideas led most directly to the scholarly view known as:

    a. functionalism.

    b. structuralism.

    c. empiricism.

    d. introspection.

Matching Items

Match each psychological perspective, school, and subfield with its definition or description.

Terms

_____   1. neuroscience perspective
_____   2. social-cultural perspective
_____   3. psychiatry
_____   4. clinical psychology
_____   5. behavior genetics perspective
_____   6. behavioral perspective
_____   7. industrial/organizational psychology
_____   8. cognitive perspective
_____   9. basic research
_____ 10. applied research
_____ 11. evolutionary perspective
_____ 12. psychodynamic perspective
_____ 13. structuralism
_____ 14. functionalism
_____ 15. empiricism

Definitions or Descriptions

a. behavior in the workplace

b. how people differ as products of different environments

c. the study of practical problems

d. an early school of psychology that used introspection to explore the contents of the mind

e. the mechanisms by which observable responses are acquired and changed

f. how the body and brain create emotions, memories, and sensations

g. how the mind encodes, processes, stores, and retrieves information

h. the view that science flourishes through observation and experimentation

i. how natural selection favors traits that promote the perpetuation of one's genes

j. the study, assessment, and treatment of troubled people

k. the medical treatment of psychological disorders

l. the disguised effects of unfulfilled wishes and childhood traumas

m. adds to psychology's knowledge base

n. an early school of psychology that focused on the adaptive value of thoughts and behaviors

o. how much genes and environment contribute to individual differences

PROGRESS TEST 2

Progress Test 2 should be completed during a final chapter review. Answer the following questions after you thoroughly understand the correct answers for the section reviews and Progress Test 1.

Multiple-Choice Questions

1. The first psychology laboratory was established by _____ in the year _____ .

   a. Wundt; 1879   c. Freud; 1900
   b. James; 1890   d. Watson; 1913

2. Who would be most likely to agree with the statement, "Psychology is the science of mental life"?
   a. Wilhelm Wundt
   b. John Watson
   c. Ivan Pavlov
   d. virtually any American psychologist during the 1960s

3. In psychology, "behavior" is best defined as:
   a. anything a person says, does, or feels.
   b. any action we can observe and record.
   c. any action, whether observable or not.
   d. anything we can infer from a person's actions.

4. Carl Rogers and Abraham Maslow are most closely associated with:
   a. cognitive psychology.
   b. behaviorism.
   c. psychodynamic theory.
   d. humanistic psychology.

5. In defining psychology, the text notes that psychology is most accurately described as a:
   a. way of asking and answering questions.
   b. field engaged in solving applied problems.
   c. set of findings related to behavior and mental processes.
   d. nonscientific approach to the study of mental disorders.

6. Two historical roots of psychology are the disciplines of:
   a. philosophy and chemistry.
   b. physiology and chemistry.
   c. philosophy and biology.
   d. philosophy and physics.

7. The Greek philosopher who believed that intelligence was inherited was:
   a. Aristotle.   c. Descartes.
   b. Plato.   d. Simonides.

8. The way the mind encodes, processes, stores, and retrieves information is the primary concern of the _____ perspective.
   a. neuroscience   c. social-cultural
   b. evolutionary   d. cognitive

9. Which of the following individuals is also a physician?
   a. clinical psychologist
   b. experimental psychologist
   c. psychiatrist
   d. biological psychologist

10. Dr. Jones' research centers on the relationship between changes in our thinking over the life span and changes in moral reasoning. Dr. Jones is most likely a:
   a. clinical psychologist.
   b. personality psychologist.
   c. psychiatrist.
   d. developmental psychologist.

11. Which subfield is most directly concerned with studying human behavior in the workplace?
   a. clinical psychology
   b. personality psychology
   c. industrial/organizational psychology
   d. psychiatry

12. Dr. Ernst explains behavior in terms of different situations. Dr. Ernst is working from the _____ perspective.
   a. behavioral   c. social-cultural
   b. evolutionary   d. cognitive

13. Which perspective emphasizes the learning of observable responses?
   a. behavioral   c. neuroscience
   b. social-cultural   d. cognitive

14. A psychologist who studies how worker productivity might be increased by changing office layout is engaged in _____ research.
   a. applied   c. clinical
   b. basic   d. developmental

15. (Close-Up) A major principle underlying the SQ3R study method is that:
   a. people learn and remember material best when they actively process it.
   b. many students overestimate their mastery of text and lecture material.
   c. study time should be spaced over time rather than crammed into one session.
   d. "overlearning" disrupts efficient retention.

16. The biopsychosocial approach emphasizes the importance of:
   a. different levels of analysis in exploring behavior and mental processes.
   b. basic research over pure research.
   c. pure research over basic research.
   d. having a single academic perspective to guide research.

True–False Items

Place a T or an F in the blank next to each statement.

_____   1. Psychology's three main levels of analysis often contradict each other.
_____   2. The primary research tool of the first psychologists was the experiment.
_____   3. The subject matter of psychology has changed over the history of the field.
_____   4. Every psychological event is simultaneously a biological event.
_____   5. Today, most psychologists work within the behavioral perspective.
_____   6. The major perspectives in psychology contradict one another.

_____ 7. (Close-Up) "Spaced practice" promotes better retention than "massed practice."

_____ 8. (Close-Up) "Overlearning" hinders retention.

_____ 9. A major goal of psychology is to teach us how to ask important questions and to think critically as we evaluate competing ideas.

_____ 10. One reason the school of structuralism fell from favor is that the method of introspection was unreliable.

PSYCHOLOGY APPLIED

Answer these questions the day before an exam as a final check on your understanding of the chapter's terms and concepts.

Multiple-Choice Questions

1. Psychology is defined as the "scientific study of behavior and mental processes." Wilhelm Wundt would have omitted which of the following words from this definition?
   a. scientific study
   b. behavior and
   c. and mental processes
   d. Wundt would have agreed with the definition as stated.

2. Jawan believes that psychologists should go back to using introspection as a research tool. This technique is based on:
   a. survey methodology.
   b. experimentation.
   c. self-examination of mental processes.
   d. the study of observable behavior.

3. Dharma's term paper on the history of American psychology notes that:
   a. psychology began as the science of mental life.
   b. from the 1920s into the 1960s, psychology was defined as the scientific study of observable behavior.
   c. contemporary psychologists study both overt behavior and covert thoughts.
   d. all of the above are true.

4. Terrence wants to talk to a professional to help him cope with some academic challenges he's facing. You recommend that he contact a(n):
   a. industrial/organizational psychologist.
   b. developmental psychologist.
   c. counseling psychologist.
   d. psychiatrist.

5. Professor Gutierrez, who believes that human emotions are best understood as being jointly determined by heredity, learning, and the individual's social and cultural contexts, is evidently a proponent of the:
   a. psychodynamic perspective.
   b. biopsychosocial approach.
   c. evolutionary perspective.
   d. neuroscience perspective.

6. The philosophical views of John Locke are to those of René Descartes as _____ is to _____ .
   a. nature; nurture
   b. nurture; nature
   c. rationality; irrationality
   d. irrationality; rationality

7. To say that "psychology is a science" means that:
   a. psychologists study only observable behaviors.
   b. psychologists approach the study of thoughts and actions with careful observation and rigorous analysis.
   c. psychological research should be free of value judgments.
   d. all of the above are true.

8. In concluding her report on the "nature-nurture debate in contemporary psychology," Karen notes that:
   a. most psychologists believe that nature is a more important influence on the development of most human traits.
   b. most psychologists believe that nurture is more influential.
   c. the issue is more heatedly debated than ever before.
   d. nurture works on what nature endows.

9. Dr. Waung investigates how a person's interpretation of a situation affects his or her reaction. Evidently, Dr. Waung is working from the _____ perspective.
   a. neuroscience   c. cognitive
   b. behavioral   d. social-cultural

10. Dr. Aswad is studying people's enduring inner traits. Dr. Aswad is most likely a(n):
    a. clinical psychologist.
    b. psychiatrist.
    c. personality psychologist.
    d. industrial/organizational psychologist.

11. The psychological perspective that places the *most* emphasis on how observable responses are learned is the _____ perspective.
    a. behavioral
    c. behavior genetics
    b. cognitive
    d. evolutionary

12. During a dinner conversation, a friend says that the cognitive and behavioral perspectives are quite similar. You disagree and point out that the cognitive perspective emphasizes_____ , whereas the behavioral perspective emphasizes _____ .
    a. conscious processes; observable responses
    b. unconscious processes; conscious processes
    c. overt behaviors; covert behaviors
    d. introspection; experimentation

13. Concerning the major psychological perspectives on behavior, the text author suggests that:
    a. researchers should work within the framework of only one of the perspectives.
    b. only those perspectives that emphasize objective measurement of behavior are useful.
    c. the different perspectives often complement one another; together, they provide a fuller understanding of behavior than provided by any single perspective.
    d. psychologists should avoid all of these traditional perspectives.

14. (Close-Up) Your roommate announces that her schedule permits her to devote three hours to studying for an upcoming quiz. You advise her to:
    a. spend most of her time reading and rereading the text material.
    b. focus primarily on her lecture notes.
    c. space study time over several short sessions.
    d. cram for three hours just before the quiz.

15. (Close-Up) A fraternity brother rationalizes the fact that he spends very little time studying by saying that he "doesn't want to peak too soon and have the test material become stale." You tell him that:
    a. he is probably overestimating his knowledge of the material.
    b. if he devotes extra time to studying, his retention of the material will be improved.
    c. the more often students review material, the better their exam scores.
    d. all of the above are true.

16. The psychological views of William James are to those of Edward Titchener as_____ is to _____ .
    a. nature; nurture
    b. nurture; nature
    c. structuralism; functionalism
    d. functionalism; structuralism

Essay Question

Explain how researchers working from each of psychology's major perspectives might investigate an emotion such as love. (Use the space below to list the points you want to make, and organize them. Then write the essay on a separate piece of paper.)

KEY TERMS

Using your own words, on a separate piece of paper write a brief definition or explanation of each of the following.

1. psychology
2. empiricism
3. structuralism
4. functionalism
5. humanistic psychology
6. nature-nurture issue
7. natural selection
8. levels of analysis
9. biopsychosocial approach
10. basic research
11. applied research
12. counseling psychology
13. clinical psychology
14. psychiatry

ANSWERS

Chapter Review

Psychology's Roots

1. behavior; mental
2. observe; record; subjective experiences; infer
3. asking and answering questions
4. Buddha; Confucius
5. Socrates; Plato; separable; innate; Aristotle; logic; observation
6. Descartes; Francis Bacon; John Locke; empiricism
7. Wundt; Edward Titchener; structuralism; introspection; unreliable; William James; functionalism
8. Mary Calkins; Margaret Washburn
9. biology; philosophy
10. learning; Sigmund Freud; children
11. mental; observable; behavior; mental
12. behaviorism; Carl Rogers; Abraham Maslow; humanistic; growth; healthy
13. cognitive; mental; brain; cognitive neuroscience

Contemporary Psychology

1. increasing
2. biology; experience
3. Plato; Aristotle
4. Locke; Descartes
5. Charles Darwin; evolution; natural selection
6. system; social system; levels; analysis; psychological; social-cultural; biopsychosocial
7. neuroscience
8. evolutionary; behavior genetics
9. psychodynamic
10. behavioral
11. cognitive
12. social-cultural
13. complement
14. basic research; applied research
15. counseling; clinical
16. psychiatrists

Close-Up: Your Study of Psychology

1. actively

2. SQ3R; a. survey; b. question; c. read; d. review; e. reflect
   a. Distribute study time.
   b. Listen actively in class.
   c. Overlearn material.
   d. Focus on the big ideas.
   e. Be a smart test-taker.

Progress Test 1

Multiple-Choice Questions

1. **a.** is the answer. (p. 7)
   b. Psychology has never been defined in terms of conscious and unconscious activity.
   c. From the 1920s into the 1960s, psychology was defined as the scientific study of observable behavior.
   d. Psychology today is defined as the scientific study of behavior and mental processes. In its earliest days, however, psychology focused exclusively on mental phenomena.

2. **c.** is the answer. (p. 7)
   a. Wilhelm Wundt, the founder of the first psychology laboratory, was seeking to measure the simplest mental processes.
   b. Sigmund Freud developed an influential theory of personality that focused on unconscious processes.
   d. William James, author of the early textbook *Principles of Psychology,* was a philosopher and was more interested in mental phenomena than observable behavior.

3. **d.** is the answer. (p. 2)
   a. In its earliest days psychology was defined as the science of mental phenomena.
   b. Psychology has never been defined in terms of conscious and unconscious activity.
   c. From the 1920s into the 1960s, psychology was defined as the scientific study of behavior.

4. **a.** is the answer. (p. 4)

5. **d.** is the answer (p. 6)
   a. Wilhelm Wundt founded the first psychology laboratory.
   b. Ivan Pavlov pioneered the study of learning.
   c. Jean Piaget was this century's most influential observer of children.

6. **c.** is the answer. (p. 11)

7. **a.** is the answer. Biology and experience are internal and external influences, respectively. (p. 9)
   b. Rewards and punishments are both external influences on behavior.
   c. Heredity and instinct are both internal influences on behavior.

d. The legitimacy of the study of mental processes does not relate to the internal/external issue.

8. **d.** is the answer. For Locke, the mind at birth was a blank tablet. (p. 3)
   a. Plato assumed that much of intelligence is inherited and therefore present at birth. Moreover, he was a philosopher of ancient Greece.
   b. Aristotle held essentially the same viewpoint as Locke, but he lived in the fourth century B.C.
   c. Descartes believed that knowledge does not depend on experience.

9. **c.** is the answer. (p. 3)
   a. Aristotle was a philosopher in ancient Greece who would have agreed with Locke that knowledge comes from experience.
   b. Plato assumed that character and intelligence are inherited.
   d. Locke believed that the mind is a blank slate at birth.

10. **a.** is the answer. (p. 11)
    b. The cognitive perspective is concerned with how we encode, process, store, and retrieve information.
    c. The behavioral perspective studies the mechanisms by which observable responses are acquired and changed.
    d. The behavior genetics perspective focuses on the relative contributions of genes and environment to individual differences.

11. **d.** is the answer. (p. 12)
    a. Behavioral psychologists investigate how learned behaviors are acquired. They generally do not focus on subjective opinions, such as attractiveness.
    b. The evolutionary perspective studies how natural selection favors traits that promote the perpetuation of one's genes.
    c. Cognitive psychologists study the mechanisms of thinking and memory, and generally do not investigate attitudes. Also, because the question specifies that the psychologist is interested in comparing two cultures, d. is the best answer.

12. **a.** is the answer. (p. 12)
    b. & c. Applied and industrial/organizational psychologists tackle practical problems.
    d. Clinical psychologists (and researchers) focus on treating troubled people.

13. **c.** is the answer. (p. 13)
    d. Psychiatrists are medical doctors rather than psychologists.

14. **a.** is the answer. (p. 12)
    c. & d. Psychologists are widely involved in *both* basic and applied research.

15. **d.** is the answer. (p. 14)

16. **c.** is the answer. (p. 3)
    a. & b. Bacon emphasized the importance of orderly observation and experimentation, neither of which was a focal point of these early schools of psychology.
    d. This is a research method used by the early structural psychologists, not a scholarly viewpoint.

Matching Items

1. f (p. 11)
2. b (p. 12)
3. k (p. 12)
4. j (p. 12)
5. o (p. 11)
6. e (p. 11)
7. a (p. 13)
8. g (p. 12)
9. m (p. 12)
10. c (p. 13)
11. i (p. 11)
12. l (p. 11)
13. d (p. 4)
14. n (p. 5)
15. h (p. 3)

Progress Test 2

Multiple-Choice Questions

1. **a.** is the answer. (p. 3)

2. **a.** is the answer. (p. 3)
   b. & d. John Watson, like many American psychologists during this time, believed that psychology should focus on the study of observable behavior.
   c. Because he pioneered the study of learning, Pavlov focused on observable behavior and would certainly have *disagreed* with this statement.

3. **b.** is the answer. (p. 4)

4. **d.** is the answer. (p. 7)

5. **a.** is the answer. (p. 2)
   b. Psychology is equally involved in basic research.
   c. Psychology's knowledge base is constantly expanding.
   d. Psychology is the *scientific study* of behavior and mental processes.

6. **c.** is the answer. (p. 6)

7. **b.** is the answer. (p. 2)
   a. Aristotle believed that all knowledge originates with sensory experience.
   c. Descartes was a philosopher of the seventeenth century.
   d. Simonides was a well-known Greek orator.

8. **d.** is the answer. (p. 11)

a. The neuroscience perspective studies the biological bases for a range of psychological phenomena.
b. The evolutionary perspective studies how natural selection favors traits that promote the perpetuation of one's genes.
c. The social-cultural perspective is concerned with variations in behavior across situations and cultures.

9. **c.** is the answer. After earning their M.D. degrees, psychiatrists specialize in the diagnosis and treatment of mental health disorders. (p. 13)
a., b., & d. These psychologists generally earn a Ph.D. rather than an M.D.

10. **d.** is the answer. The emphasis on change during the life span indicates that Dr. Jones is most likely a developmental psychologist. (p. 12)
a. Clinical psychologists study, assess, and treat people who are psychologically troubled.
b. Personality psychologists study our inner traits.
c. Psychiatrists are medical doctors.

11. **c.** is the answer. (p. 13)
a. Clinical psychologists study, assess, and treat people with psychological disorders.
b. & d. Personality psychologists and psychiatrists do not usually study people in work situations.

12. **c.** is the answer. (p. 12)
a. Psychologists who follow the behavioral perspective emphasize observable, external influences on behavior.
b. The evolutionary perspective focuses on how natural selection favors traits that promote the perpetuation of one's genes.
d. The cognitive perspective places emphasis on conscious, rather than unconscious, processes.

13. **a.** is the answer. (p. 11)

14. **a.** is the answer. The research is addressing a practical issue. (p. 13)
b. Basic research is aimed at contributing to the base of knowledge in a given field, not at resolving particular practical problems.
c. & d. Clinical and developmental research would focus on issues relating to psychological disorders and life-span changes, respectively.

15. **a.** is the answer. (p. 15)
b. & c. Although each of these is true, SQ3R is based on the more *general* principle of active learning.
d. In fact, just the opposite is true.

16. **a.** is the answer. (p. 10)

b. & c. The biopsychosocial approach has nothing to do with the relative importance of basic research and applied research and is equally applicable to both.
d. On the contrary, the biopsychosocial approach is based on the idea that single academic perspectives are often limited.

True–False Items

1. F (p. 11)	**5.** F (p. 11)	**9.** T (p. 2)
2. F (p. 3)	**6.** F (p. 12)	**10.** T (p. 5)
3. T (pp. 2–4)	**7.** T (p. 15)	
4. T (p. 10)	**8.** F (p. 16)	

Psychology Applied

Multiple-Choice Questions

1. **b.** is the answer. (p. 3)
a. As the founder of the first psychology laboratory, Wundt certainly based his research on the scientific method.
c. The earliest psychologists, including Wilhelm Wundt, were concerned with the self-examination of covert thoughts, feelings, and other mental processes.

2. **c.** is the answer. (p. 4)

3. **d.** is the answer. (pp. 6–7)

4. **c.** is the answer. (p. 13)
a. Industrial/organizational psychologists study and advise on behavior in the workplace.
b. Developmental psychologists investigate behavior and mental processes over the life span.
d. Psychiatrists are medical doctors who treat medical disorders. There is no indication that Terrence is suffering from a medical disorder.

5. **b.** is the answer. (p. 10)
a., c., & d. Each of these perspectives is too narrow to apply to Professor Gutierrez's belief. Moreover, the psychodynamic perspective (a.) emphasizes unconscious processes, which Professor Gutierrez has not expressed a belief in.

6. **b.** is the answer. Locke believed that all knowledge comes from experience (nurture). Descartes believed that some ideas are innate (nature). (p. 3)
c. & d. The text does not discuss the views of these philosophers regarding this issue.

7. **b.** is the answer. (p. 2)
a. Psychologists study both overt (observable) behaviors and covert thoughts and feelings.
c. Psychologists' values definitely *do* influence their research.

8. **d.** is the answer. Because both nature and nurture influence most traits and behaviors, the tension surrounding this issue has dissolved. (p. 10)

9. **c.** is the answer. (p. 12)
   a. This perspective emphasizes the influences of physiology on behavior.
   b. This perspective emphasizes environmental influences on observable behavior.
   d. This perspective emphasizes how behavior and thinking vary across situations and cultures.

10. **c.** is the answer. (p. 12)
    a. Clinical psychology is concerned with the study and treatment of psychological disorders.
    b. Psychiatry is the branch of medicine concerned with the physical diagnosis and treatment of psychological disorders.
    d. Industrial/organizational psychologists study behavior in the workplace.

11. **a.** is the answer. (p. 11)

12. **a.** is the answer. (pp. 11–12)
    b. Neither perspective places any special emphasis on unconscious processes.
    c. Neither perspective emphasizes covert behaviors.
    d. Introspection was a research method used by the earliest psychologists, not those working from the cognitive perspective.

13. **c.** is the answer. (p. 12)
    a. The text suggests just the opposite: By studying behavior from several perspectives, psychologists gain a fuller understanding.
    b. & d. Each perspective is useful in that it calls researchers' attention to different aspects of behavior. This is equally true of those perspectives that do not emphasize objective measurement.

14. **c.** is the answer. (p. 15)
    a. To be effective, study must be *active* rather than passive in nature.
    b. Most exams are based on lecture *and* textbook material.
    d. Cramming hinders retention.

15. **d.** is the answer. (pp. 15–16)

16. **d.** is the answer. James emphasized the adaptive value of our thoughts and behaviors (functionalism). Titchener used the method of introspection to examine the basic contents of the mind (structuralism). (pp. 4, 5)
    a. & b. The text does not discuss the views of these psychologists regarding the nature-nurture issue.

Essay Question

A psychologist working from the neuroscience perspective might study the brain circuits and body chemistry that trigger attraction and sexual arousal. A psychologist working from the evolutionary perspective might analyze how love has facilitated the survival of our species. A psychologist working from the behavior genetics perspective might attempt to compare the extent to which the emotion is attributable to our genes and the extent to which it is attributable to our environment. A psychologist working from the psychodynamic perspective might search for evidence that a person's particular emotional feelings are disguised effects of unfulfilled wishes. A psychologist working from the behavioral perspective might study the external stimuli, such as body language, that elicit and reward approach behaviors toward another person. A psychologist working from a cognitive perspective might study how our thought processes, attitudes, and beliefs foster attachment to loved ones, and a psychologist working from a social-cultural perspective might explore situational influences on attraction and how the development and expression of love vary across cultural groups.

Key Terms

1. **Psychology** is the scientific study of behavior and mental processes. (p. 2)
2. **Empiricism** is the twofold view that (a) knowledge comes from experience via the senses (rather than being inborn), and (b) observation and experimentation are the basis of science. (p. 3)
3. Introduced by Edward Bradford Titchener, **structuralism** is the early school of psychology that used self-reflection (introspection) to examine the elemental structure of the mind. (p. 4)
4. Introduced by William James, **functionalism** is the early school of psychology that emphasized how behavior and mental processes enable the organism to adapt, survive, and flourish. (p. 5)
5. **Humanistic psychology** is the branch of psychology that emphasizes the growth potential of healthy people. (p. 7)
6. The **nature-nurture issue** is the controversy over the relative contributions that genes (nature) and experience (nurture) make to the development of psychological traits and behaviors. (p. 9)
7. **Natural selection** is the principle that those traits of a species that contribute to reproduction and survival are most likely to be passed on to succeeding generations. (p. 9)

8. Psychologists analyze behavior and mental processes from differing complementary views, or **levels of analysis.** (p. 10)

9. The **biopsychosocial approach** is an integrated perspective that focuses on biological, psychological, and social-cultural levels of analysis for a given behavior or mental process. (p. 10)

10. **Basic research** is pure science that aims to increase psychology's scientific knowledge base rather than to solve practical problems. (p. 12)

11. **Applied research** is scientific study that aims to solve practical problems. (p. 13)

12. **Counseling psychology** is the branch of psychology that helps people cope with challenges in their daily lives. (p. 13)

13. **Clinical psychology** is the branch of psychology concerned with the study, assessment, and treatment of people with psychological disorders. (p. 13)

14. **Psychiatry** is the branch of medicine concerned with the physical diagnosis and treatment of psychological disorders. (p. 13)

FOCUS ON VOCABULARY AND LANGUAGE

Page 1: Have you ever played *peekaboo* with a 6-month-old . . . ? Peekaboo is a game played in most cultures where a person hides or pretends to hide from a child and then reappears saying "PEEKA-BOO!" The important question for psychologists is, why do infants all over the world react similarly to this game; what are they actually feeling, perceiving, and thinking?

Page 1: Such questions provide *grist for psychology's mill* . . . . The expression *"provide grist for the mill"* derives from the practice in the past where farmers brought their grain (*grist*) to the *mill* (a building with machinery for grinding grain into flour). Today the expression means that a greater volume of work (*grist*) does not present a problem; in fact, it is welcomed. The amount of grain (*grist*) is analogous to the variety of questions asked, and the research conducted to answer them is like the *mill* producing flour from the grist. Thus, psychology is a science that thrives on attempting to answer a variety of questions about how we think, feel, and act through scientific methodology (research).

Psychology's Roots

Page 2: Let's *unpack* this definition. *Unpack* here means to take apart or disassemble. So psychology, defined as the science of behavior and mental processes, is broken down into overt behavior (i.e., observable events) and covert processes (i.e., events hidden within, such as thoughts, feelings, perceptions, beliefs, and so on) and is studied using the scientific or empirical method.

Page 2: . . . psychological science welcomes *hunches* and plausible-sounding theories. In popular usage a *hunch* is an intuitive feeling about a situation or event. Psychology can use subjective ideas to help

formulate hypotheses or predictions which can then be tested empirically or scientifically.

Page 3: . . . *down-to-earth* . . . This means to be straightforward and practical. In Britain, scientists such as Francis Bacon (1561–1626) were concerned with experimentation, experience, and common-sense judgment (they took a *down-to-earth* approach).

Page 5: Alas, structuralism *waned* as introspection *waned.* To *wane* means to fade away or to decline in power. Systematic *introspection* (self-reflective analysis of immediate sensations, thoughts, feelings, etc.) was not a reliable scientific method; as its use decreased (*waned*) so too did **structuralism,** the school devoted to finding the basic elements of mind through introspection.

Page 5: . . . *wise-cracking* . . . William James was well-known for joking and making witty remarks (*wise-cracking*) during his lectures on psychology. He also showed great courage (*displayed spunk*) by admitting Mary Calkins into his graduate seminar despite the objections of Harvard's president.

Page 6: This list of pioneering psychologists . . . *"Magellans of the mind"* . . . . Ferdinand Magellan (1489–1521) was a famous Portuguese navigator who made many discoveries and explored areas of the world previously unknown to his fellow Europeans. Because early psychologists made exciting discoveries and explored unknown frontiers, they were preparing the way (they were *pioneers*) for future psychologists and can thus be considered *"Magellans of the mind."*

Contemporary Psychology

Page 8: . . . *mushrooming* . . . Membership in psychological societies is growing at a rapid rate (*mushrooming*), and psychology is becoming more and more international (*globalizing*).

Page 9: . . . psychology has *wrestled* with some issues . . . . Psychology has struggled (*wrestled*) with a number of debates, the biggest and most enduring of which is the controversy over the relative influence that genes (biology) and environment (experience) have on the development of psychological traits and behaviors (the **nature-nurture issue**).

Page 9: In the 1600s, philosophers *rekindled* the debate [nature-nurture]. *Rekindled* means to restart, as in to restart a fire (*rekindle*). John Locke in the 1600s repeated what Aristotle had said 2000 years before—that humans are born without any knowledge (i.e., that we are blank slates, or blank paper, at birth) and that all knowledge comes from experience (*nurture*). Plato and, later, René Descartes argued that we are born with some innate knowledge (*nature*).

Page 9: The nature-nurture debate *weaves a thread* from the distant past to our time. This simply means that the issue has been of concern to scholars and others from the time of the Greek philosophers right up to modern times. The debate connects the past to the present (*weaves a thread* between the two).

Page 10: Yet over and over again we will see that in contemporary science the nature-nurture *tension dissolves*. The main point is that both sides of the debate have something to offer: Each contributes to the search for the truth. Thus, in modern science the strained relations (*tension*) over this issue diminish (*dissolve*).

Page 11: "*Red in the face*" and "*hot under the collar*" refer to the physical changes that often accompany emotional arousal (e.g., anger). A person's face may become red due to blood rushing to it (blushing), and he or she may feel hot and perspire (*hot under the collar*). Different perspectives (neuroscience, evolutionary, behavior genetics, psychodynamic, behavioral, cognitive, and social-cultural) examine the same event (emotional change) using different levels of analysis. Myers points out that these different perspectives are not necessarily in opposition to each other but, rather, are complementary; that is, each level helps to complete the puzzle of why the event occurs by supplying answers from different points of view (*perspectives*).

Page 12: But there is a *payoff:* Psychology is a *meeting ground* for different disciplines, and is thus a *perfect home* for those with *wide-ranging* interests. Myers points out that there is much diversity in the discipline of psychology (i.e., it lacks unity), but this is beneficial (a *payoff*) because it is a nice place (area) to work in (a *perfect home*) for those who have broad or diverse (*wide-ranging*) interests. Thus, psychology is the ideal meeting place or *meeting ground* for different disciplines.

Page 13: . . . *psychoceramics* (the study of crackpots). This joke derives its humor from the fact that some words or phrases in English have more than one meaning, and it is this "play on words" that makes the joke funny. *Ceramics* is concerned with the work (or art) of making pottery, porcelain, etc. Some of the pots may develop small breaks or splits and consequently would be referred to as "cracked pots." The term *crackpot,* on the other hand, is a colloquial (informal) expression used to describe a useless, impractical, or even a crazy person. Although psychologists engage in a variety of interdisciplinary studies, such as psychohistory, psycholinguistics, and so on, there is obviously no such thing as "*psychoceramics* (the study of crackpots)." Clinical psychologists, of course, assess and treat mental, emotional, and behavioral disorders (mental illness or psychopathology). (Note that Myers confesses in a footnote that he wrote this sentence on April 1st, April Fools' Day, which traditionally involves people playing practical jokes on other people. Did he fool you?)

(Close-Up) Your Study of Psychology

Page 15: One of psychology's oldest findings is that *spaced practice* promotes better retention than *massed practice*. *Spaced practice* refers to studying over a longer period of time, say 2 hours a day over 5 days rather than 10 hours on 1 day (*massed practice* or cramming). Distributing your study time is much better for learning and retention than one long study period (a *blitz*).

1 : Thinking Critically With Psychological Science

CHAPTER OVERVIEW

Chapter 1 explains the limits of intuition and common sense in reasoning about behavior and mental processes. To counteract our human tendency toward faulty reasoning, psychologists adopt a scientific attitude that is based on curiosity, skepticism, humility, and critical thinking. Chapter 1 also explains how psychologists, using the scientific method, employ the research strategies of description, correlation, and experimentation in order to objectively describe, predict, and explain behavior.

The next section discusses how statistical reasoning is used to help psychologists describe data and to generalize from instances. To describe data, psychologists often rely on measures of central tendency such as the mean, median, and mode, as well as variation measures such as the range and standard deviation. Statistical reasoning also helps psychologists determine when it is safe to generalize from a sample to the larger population.

Chapter 1 concludes with a discussion of several questions people often ask about psychology, including why animal research is relevant, whether laboratory experiments are ethical, whether behavior varies with culture and gender, and whether psychology's principles don't have the potential for misuse.

Chapter 1 introduces a number of concepts and issues that will play an important role in later chapters. Pay particular attention to the strengths and weaknesses of descriptive and correlational research. In addition, make sure that you understand the method of experimentation, especially the importance of control conditions and the difference between independent and dependent variables. Finally, you should be able to discuss three important principles concerning populations and samples, as well as the concept of significance in testing difference.

NOTE: Answer guidelines for all Chapter 1 questions begin on page 31.

CHAPTER REVIEW

First, skim each section, noting headings and boldface items. After you have read the section, review each objective by answering the fill-in and essay-type questions that follow it. As you proceed, evaluate your performance by consulting the answers beginning on page 31. Do not continue with the next section until you understand each answer. If you need to, review or reread the section in the textbook before continuing.

The Need for Psychological Science (pp. 19–26)

David Myers at times uses idioms that are unfamiliar to some readers. If you do not know the meaning of any of the following words, phrases, or expressions in the context in which they appear in the introduction to this chapter and in this section, refer to pages 38–40 for an explanation: *to remedy their own woes; winnow sense from nonsense; dresses it in jargon; bull's eye; "Out of sight, out of mind"; "Absence makes the heart grow fonder"; familiarity breeds contempt; drop a course; lackluster predictions; hard-headed curiosity; leap of faith; the proof is in the pudding; auras; crazy-sounding ideas; arena of competing ideas; so much the worse for our ideas; "The rat is always right"; the spectacles of our preconceived ideas; gut feelings; debunked; "play the tape"; sift reality from illusion.*

Objective 1: Define *hindsight bias,* and explain how it can make research findings seem like mere common sense.

1. The tendency to perceive an outcome that has occurred as being obvious and predictable is called the _____ _____ . This phenomenon is _____ (rare/common) in _____ (children/adults/both children and adults).

2. Because it is _____ (after the fact/usually wrong), this tendency makes research findings seem like mere common sense.

Objective 2: Describe how overconfidence contaminates our everyday judgments.

3. Our everyday thinking is also limited by _____ in what we think we know, which occurs because of our _____ to seek information that confirms our judgments.

4. Most people are _____ (better/worse/equally wrong) in predicting their social behavior.

Objective 3: Explain how the scientific attitude encourages critical thinking.

5. The scientific approach is characterized by the attitudes of _____ , _____ , and _____ .

6. Scientific inquiry thus encourages reasoning that examines assumptions, discerns hidden values, evaluates evidence, and assesses conclusions, which is called _____ _____ .

Objective 4: Describe how psychological theories guide scientific research.

7. Psychologists use the _____ _____ to guide their study of behavior and mental processes. They make _____ and form _____ , which are _____ based on new _____ .

8. An explanation using an integrated set of principles that organizes and predicts behaviors or events is a _____ . Testable predictions that allow a scientist to evaluate a theory are called _____ . These predictions give direction to _____ .

9. In order to prevent theoretical biases from influencing scientific observations, research must be reported precisely—using clear _____ _____ of all concepts—so that others can _____ the findings.

10. The test of a useful theory is the extent to which it effectively _____ observations and implies clear _____ .

11. Psychologists conduct research using _____ methods, _____ , and _____ methods.

Description (pp. 26–30)

> If you do not know the meaning of any of the following words, phrases, or expressions in the context in which they appear in the text, refer to page 40 for an explanation: *Numbers are numbing; Anecdotes are often more startling; a thimbleful; snapshot of the opinions.*

Objective 5: Identify an advantage and a disadvantage of using case studies to study behavior.

1. The research strategy in which one or more individuals is studied in depth in order to reveal universal principles of behavior is the _____ _____ .

2. Although case studies can suggest _____ for further study, a potential problem with this method is that any given individual may be _____ .

Objective 6: Identify the advantages and disadvantages of using surveys to study behavior and mental processes, and explain the importance of wording effects and random sampling.

3. The method in which a group of people is questioned about their attitudes or behavior is the _____ .

4. An important factor in the validity of survey research is the _____ of questions.

5. The tendency to overestimate others' agreement with us is the _____

_____ _____ .

6. Surveys try to obtain a _____ sample, one that will be representative of the _____ being studied. In such a sample, every person _____ (does/does not) have a chance of being included.

7. Large, representative samples _____ (are/are not) better than small ones.

8. We are more likely to overgeneralize from select samples that are especially _____ .

Objective 7: Identify an advantage and a disadvantage of using naturalistic observation to study behavior.

9. The research method in which people or animals are directly observed in their natural environments is called _____

_____ .

10. Case studies, surveys, and naturalistic observation do not explain behavior; they simply _____ it.

11. Using naturalistic observation, researchers have found that people are more likely to laugh in _____ situations than in _____ situations. Also, using observations of walking speed and the accuracy of public clocks, researchers have concluded that the pace of life _____ (varies/ does not vary) from one culture to another.

Correlation (pp. 30–36)

> If you do not know the meaning of any of the following words, phrases, or expressions in the context in which they appear in the text, refer to page 40 for an explanation: *naked eye; flipped a coin; "cold hands" . . . "hot hands."*

Objective 8: Describe positive and negative correlations, and explain how correlational measures can aid the process of prediction.

1. When changes in one factor are accompanied by changes in another, the two factors are said to be _____ , and one is thus able to _____ the other. The mathematical expression of this relationship is called a

_____ _____ .

2. Graphs called _____ are often used to depict the relationship between two sets of scores.

3. If two factors increase or decrease together, they are _____ _____ . If, however, one decreases as the other increases, they are _____ _____ . Another way to state the latter is that the two variables relate _____ .

If your level of test anxiety goes down as your time spent studying for the exam goes up, would you say these events are positively or negatively correlated? Explain your reasoning.

Objective 9: Explain why correlational research fails to provide evidence of cause-effect relationships.

4. A negative correlation between two variables does not indicate the _____ or _____ of the relationship. Nor does correlation prove _____ ; rather, it merely indicates the possibility of a _____ -_____ relationship.

5. A correlation between two events or behaviors means only that one event can be _____ from the other.

6. Because two events may both be caused by some other _____ , a correlation does not mean that one _____ the other. For this reason, correlation thus does not enable _____ .

Objective 10: Describe how people form illusory correlations.

7. A perceived correlation that does not really exist is an _____

_____ .

8. People are more likely to notice and recall events that _____ their beliefs. This error in thinking helps explain many _____ beliefs.

Objective 11: Explain the human tendency to perceive order in random sequences.

9. Another common tendency is to perceive order in

_____ _____ .

10. Patterns and streaks in random sequences occur _____ (more/less) often than people expect, and they _____ (do/ do not) appear random.

Experimentation (pp. 36–39)

> If you do not know the meaning of the following word in the context in which it appears in the text, refer to page 40 for an explanation: *recap.*

Objective 12: Explain how experiments help researchers isolate cause and effect.

1. To isolate _____ and _____ , researchers _____ control for other _____ .

2. Research studies have found that breast-fed infants _____ (do/do not) grow up with higher intelligence scores than those of infants who are bottle-fed with cow's milk. To study cause-effect relationships, psychologists conduct _____ . Using this method, a researcher _____ the factor of interest, while _____ _____ other factors.

3. If a _____ changes when an _____ factor is varied, the researcher knows the factor is having an _____ .

Objective 13: Explain why the double-blind procedure and random assignment build confidence in research findings.

4. Researchers sometimes give certain participants a pseudotreatment, called a _____ , and compare their behavior with that of participants who receive the actual treatment. When merely thinking that one is receiving a treatment produces results, a _____ _____ is said to occur.

5. When neither the subjects nor the person collecting the data knows which condition a subject is in, the researcher is making use of the _____ - _____ _____ .

6. An experiment must involve at least two conditions: the _____ condition, in which the experimental treatment is present, and the _____ condition, in which it is absent.

7. Experimenters rely on the _____ _____ of individuals to the experimental conditions.

Objective 14: Explain the difference between an independent and a dependent variable.

8. The factor that is being manipulated in an experiment is called the _____ variable.

The measurable factor that may change as a result of these manipulations is called the _____ variable.

9. The aim of an experiment is to _____ a(n) _____ variable, _____ the _____ variable, and _____ all other _____ .

Explain at least one advantage of the experiment as a research method.

Statistical Reasoning (pp. 39–44)

> If you do not know the meaning of any of the following words, phrases, or expressions in the context in which they appear in the text, refer to pages 40–41 for an explanation: *Off-the-top-of-the-head estimates; national income cake; gauges; data are "noisy."*

Objective 15: Explain the importance of statistical principles, and give an example of their use in everyday life.

1. Researchers use _____ to help them see and interpret their observations.

Objective 16: Explain how bar graphs can misrepresent data.

2. Once researchers have gathered their _____ , they must _____ them. One simple way of visually representing data is to use a _____ _____ . It is important to read the _____ _____ and note the _____ to avoid being misled by misrepresented data.

Objective 17: Describe the three measures of central tendency, and tell which is most affected by extreme scores.

3. The three measures of central tendency are the _____ , the _____ , and the _____ .

4. The most frequently occurring score in a distribution is called the _____ .

5. The mean is computed as the _____ _____ of all the scores divided by the _____ of scores.

6. The median is the score at the _____ percentile.

7. When a distribution is lopsided, or _____ , the _____ (mean/median/mode) can be biased by a few extreme scores.

Objective 18: Describe two measures of variation.

8. Averages derived from scores with _____ (high/low) variability are more reliable than those with _____ (high/low) variability.

9. The measures of variation include the _____ and the _____ _____ .

10. The range is computed as the _____ _____ .

11. The range provides a(n) _____ (crude/accurate) estimate of variation because it _____ (is/is not) influenced by extreme scores.

12. The standard deviation is a _____ (more accurate/less accurate) measure of variation than the range. Unlike the range, the standard deviation _____ (takes/does not take) into consideration information from each score in the distribution.

Objective 19: Identify three principles of making generalizations from samples.

13. It is safer to generalize from a _____ sample than from a _____ sample.

14. Averages are more reliable when they are based on scores with _____ (high/low) variability.

15. Small samples provide a _____ (more/less) reliable basis for generalizing than large samples.

Objective 20: Explain how psychologists decide whether differences are meaningful.

16. Tests of statistical _____ are used to estimate whether observed differences are real—that is, to make sure that they are not simply the result of _____ variation. The differences are probably real if the sample averages are _____ and the difference between them is _____ (relatively small/relatively large).

17. Statistical significance does not necessarily indicate the importance or _____ significance of a difference or result.

Frequently Asked Questions About Psychology (pp. 44–50)

> If you do not know the meaning of any of the following words, phrases, or expressions in the context in which they appear in the text, refer to page 41 for an explanation: *plunge in; To understand how a combustion engine works . . . .; screen; color "the facts."*

Objective 21: Explain the value of simplified laboratory conditions in discovering general principles of behavior.

1. In laboratory experiments, psychologists' concern is not with specific behaviors but with the underlying theoretical _____ . As an example, researchers have found that people who

flexibly cope with _____ stresses also cope flexibly with _____

_____ .

2. Psychologists conduct experiments on simplified behaviors in a laboratory environment in order to gain _____ over the many variables present in the "real world." In doing so, they are able to test _____

_____ of behavior that also operate in the real world.

Objective 22: Discuss whether psychological research can be generalized across cultures and genders.

3. Culture refers to shared _____ ,

_____ , _____ , and

_____ that one generation passes on to the next.

4. Although specific attitudes and behaviors vary across cultures, the underlying _____ are the same. For instance, throughout the world people diagnosed with _____ exhibit the same _____ malfunction. Likewise, similarities between the _____ far outweigh differences.

Objective 23: Explain why psychologists study animals, and discuss the ethics of experimentation with both animals and humans.

5. Many psychologists study animals because they are fascinating. More important, they study animals because of the _____ (similarities/differences) between humans and other animals. These studies have led to treatments for human _____ and to a better understanding of human functioning.

6. Some people question whether experiments with animals are _____ . They wonder whether it is right to place the _____ of humans over those of animals.

7. Opposition to animal experimentation also raises the question of what _____ should protect the well-being of animals.

Describe the goals of the ethical guidelines for psychological research.

Objective 24: Describe how personal values can influence psychologists' research and its application, and discuss psychology's potential to manipulate people.

8. Psychologists' values _____ (do/do not) influence their theories, observations, and professional advice.

9. Although psychology _____ (can/cannot) be used to manipulate people, its purpose is to _____ .

10. (Thinking Critically) The viewpoint called _____ questions scientific objectivity, arguing that most scientific concepts are merely _____ constructs. Psychological scientists _____ (agree/disagree) on whether there is, in fact, a "real world" of psychological principles that science can reveal.

11. (Thinking Critically) People who serve on juries in capital punishment cases _____ (do/do not) represent the greater population. They are _____ (more/less) likely to be minorities and women.

12. (Thinking Critically) States with a death penalty _____ (have/do not have) lower homicide rates.

PROGRESS TEST 1

Multiple-Choice Questions

Circle your answers to the following questions and check them with the answers beginning on page 33. If your answer is incorrect, read the explanation for why it is incorrect and then consult the appropriate pages of the text (in parentheses following the correct answer).

1. After detailed study of a gunshot wound victim, a psychologist concludes that the brain region destroyed is likely to be important for memory functions. Which type of research did the psychologist use to deduce this?
   a. the case study
   b. a survey
   c. correlation
   d. experimentation

2. In an experiment to determine the effects of exercise on motivation, exercise is the:
   a. control condition.
   b. intervening variable.
   c. independent variable.
   d. dependent variable.

3. In order to determine the effects of a new drug on memory, one group of people is given a pill that contains the drug. A second group is given a sugar pill that does not contain the drug. This second group constitutes the:
   a. random sample.
   b. experimental group.
   c. control group.
   d. test group.

4. Theories are defined as:
   a. testable propositions.
   b. factors that may change in response to manipulation.
   c. statistical indexes.
   d. principles that help to organize, predict, and explain facts.

5. A psychologist studies the play behavior of third-grade children by watching groups during recess at school. Which type of research is being used?
   a. correlation
   b. case study
   c. experimentation
   d. naturalistic observation

6. To ensure that other researchers can repeat their work, psychologists use:
   a. control groups.
   b. random assignment.
   c. double-blind procedures.
   d. operational definitions.

7. The scientific attitude of skepticism is based on the belief that:
   a. people are rarely candid in revealing their thoughts.
   b. mental processes can't be studied objectively.
   c. the scientist's intuition about behavior is usually correct.
   d. ideas need to be tested against observable evidence.

8. Which of the following is *not* a basic research technique used by psychologists?
   a. description
   b. replication
   c. experimentation
   d. correlation

9. Psychologists' personal values:
   a. have little influence on how their experiments are conducted.
   b. do not influence the interpretation of experimental results because of the use of statistical techniques that guard against subjective bias.
   c. can bias both scientific observation and interpretation of data.
   d. have little influence on investigative methods but a significant effect on interpretation.

10. If shoe size and IQ are negatively correlated, which of the following is true?
    a. People with large feet tend to have high IQs.
    b. People with small feet tend to have high IQs.
    c. People with small feet tend to have low IQs.
    d. IQ is unpredictable based on a person's shoe size.

11. Which of the following would be best for determining whether alcohol impairs memory?
    a. case study   c. survey
    b. naturalistic observation d. experiment

12. Well-done surveys measure attitudes in a representative subset, or _____ , of an entire group, or _____ .
    a. population; random sample
    b. control group; experimental group
    c. experimental group; control group
    d. random sample; population

13. What is the mean of the following distribution of scores: 2, 3, 7, 6, 1, 4, 9, 5, 8, 2?
    a. 5   c. 4.7
    b. 4   d. 3.7

14. What is the median of the following distribution of scores: 1, 3, 7, 7, 2, 8, 4?
    a. 1   c. 3
    b. 2   d. 4

15. What is the mode of the following distribution: 8, 2, 1, 1, 3, 7, 6, 2, 0, 2?
    a. 1   c. 3
    b. 2   d. 7

16. In generalizing from a sample to the population, it is important that:
    a. the sample is representative of the population.
    b. the sample is large.
    c. the scores in the sample have low variability.
    d. all of the above are observed.

17. When a difference between two groups is "statistically significant," this means that:
    a. the difference is statistically real but of little practical significance.
    b. the difference is probably the result of sampling variation.
    c. the difference is not likely to be due to chance variation.
    d. all of the above are true.

18. A lopsided set of scores that includes a number of extreme or unusual values is said to be:
    a. symmetrical.   c. skewed.
    b. normal.   d. dispersed.

19. Juwan eagerly opened an online trading account, believing that his market savvy would allow him to pick stocks that would make him a rich day trader. This belief best illustrates:
    a. the false consensus effect.
    b. illusory correlation.
    c. hindsight bias.
    d. overconfidence.

20. Which of the following is the measure of central tendency that would be most affected by a few extreme scores?
    a. mean   c. median
    b. range   d. mode

Matching Items

Match each term and concept with its definition or description.

Terms

_____ 1. culture
_____ 2. median
_____ 3. placebo effect
_____ 4. hindsight bias
_____ 5. mode
_____ 6. range
_____ 7. standard deviation
_____ 8. scatterplot
_____ 9. mean
_____ 10. measures of central tendency
_____ 11. measures of variation
_____ 12. false consensus effect
_____ 13. critical thinking
_____ 14. illusory correlation

Definitions or Descriptions

a. the mean, median, and mode
b. the difference between the highest and lowest scores
c. the arithmetic average of a set of scores
d. the range and standard deviation
e. the most frequently occurring score
f. the middle score in a distribution
g. a graphed cluster of dots depicting the values of two variables
h. a measure of variation based on every score
i. shared ideas and behaviors passed from one generation to the next
j. "I-knew-it-all-along" phenomenon
k. reasoning that does not blindly accept arguments
l. experimental results caused by expectations alone
m. overestimating others' agreement with us
n. false perception of a relationship between two variables

PROGRESS TEST 2

Progress Test 2 should be completed during a final chapter review. Answer the following questions after you thoroughly understand the correct answers for the section reviews and Progress Test 1.

Multiple-Choice Questions

1. Which of the following research methods does _not_ belong with the others?

    a. case study
    b. survey
    c. naturalistic observation
    d. experiment

2. To prevent the possibility that a placebo effect or researchers' expectations will influence a study's results, scientists employ:

    a. control groups.
    b. experimental groups.
    c. random assignment.
    d. the double-blind procedure.

3. Which statement about the ethics of experimentation with people and animals is _false_?

    a. Only a small percentage of animal experiments use shock.
    b. Allegations that psychologists routinely subject animals to pain, starvation, and other inhumane conditions have been proven untrue.
    c. The American Psychological Association and the British Psychological Society have set strict guidelines for the care and treatment of human and animal subjects.
    d. Animals are used in psychological research more often than they are killed by humane animal shelters.

4. In an experiment to determine the effects of attention on memory, memory is the:

    a. control condition.
    b. intervening variable.
    c. independent variable.
    d. dependent variable.

5. One reason researchers base their findings on representative samples is to avoid the false consensus effect, which refers to our tendency to:
   a. overestimate the extent to which others share our belief.
   b. falsely perceive a relationship between two events when none exists.
   c. underestimate errors in our judgment.
   d. make all of the above reasoning errors.

6. Which of the following *best* describes the hindsight bias?
   a. Events seem more predictable before they have occurred.
   b. Events seem more predictable after they have occurred.
   c. A person's intuition is usually correct.
   d. A person's intuition is usually not correct.

7. The procedure designed to ensure that the experimental and control groups do not differ in any way that might affect the experiment's results is called:
   a. variable controlling.
   b. random assignment.
   c. representative sampling.
   d. stratification.

8. Illusory correlation refers to:
   a. the perception that two negatively correlated variables are positively correlated.
   b. the perception of a correlation where there is none.
   c. an insignificant correlation.
   d. a correlation that equals –1.0.

9. In generalizing from a sample to the population, it is important that:
   a. the sample be representative.
   b. the sample be nonrandom.
   c. the sample not be too large.
   d. all of the above be true.

10. The strength of the relationship between two vivid events will most likely be:
    a. significant.
    b. positive.
    c. negative.
    d. overestimated.

11. Which of the following is true, according to the text?
    a. Because laboratory experiments are artificial, any principles discovered cannot be applied to everyday behaviors.
    b. No psychological theory can be considered a good one until it produces testable predictions.
    c. Psychology's theories reflect common sense.
    d. Psychology has few ties to other disciplines.

12. Which type of research would allow you to determine whether students' college grades accurately predict later income?
    a. case study   c. experimentation
    b. naturalistic observation   d. correlation

13. In a test of the effects of air pollution, groups of students performed a reaction-time task in a polluted or an unpolluted room. To what condition were students in the unpolluted room exposed?
    a. experimental   c. randomly assigned
    b. control   d. dependent

14. In order to study the effects of lighting on mood, Dr. Cooper had students fill out questionnaires in brightly lit or dimly lit rooms. In this study, the independent variable consisted of:
    a. the number of students assigned to each group.
    b. the students' responses to the questionnaire.
    c. the room lighting.
    d. the subject matter of the questions asked.

15. What is the mode of the following distribution of scores: 2, 2, 4, 4, 4, 14?
    a. 2   c. 5
    b. 4   d. 6

16. What is the mean of the following distribution of scores: 2, 5, 8, 10, 11, 4, 6, 9, 1, 4?
    a. 2   c. 6
    b. 10   d. 15

17. What is the median of the following distribution: 10, 7, 5, 11, 8, 6, 9?
    a. 6   c. 8
    b. 7   d. 9

18. Which of the following is the measure of variation that is most affected by extreme scores?
    a. mean   c. mode
    b. standard deviation   d. range

19. The set of scores that would likely be most representative of the population from which it was drawn would be a sample with a relatively:
    a. large standard deviation.
    b. small standard deviation.
    c. large range.
    d. small range.

20. If a difference between two samples is not statistically significant, which of the following can be concluded?
    a. The difference is probably not a true one.
    b. The difference is probably not reliable.
    c. The difference could be due to sampling variation.
    d. All of the above can be concluded.

Matching Items

Match each term with its definition or description.

Terms

_____ 1. hypothesis
_____ 2. theory
_____ 3. independent variable
_____ 4. dependent variable
_____ 5. experimental condition
_____ 6. control condition
_____ 7. case study
_____ 8. survey
_____ 9. replication
_____ 10. random assignment
_____ 11. experiment
_____ 12. double-blind

Definitions or Descriptions

a. an in-depth observational study of one person
b. the variable being manipulated in an experiment
c. the variable being measured in an experiment
d. the "treatment-absent" condition in an experiment
e. testable proposition
f. repeating an experiment to see whether the same results are obtained
g. the process in which research participants are selected by chance for different groups in an experiment
h. an explanation using an integrated set of principles that organizes and predicts observations
i. the research strategy in which the effects of one or more variables on behavior are tested
j. the "treatment-present" condition in an experiment
k. the research strategy in which a representative sample of individuals is questioned
l. experimental procedure in which neither the research participant nor the experimenter knows which condition the participant is in

PSYCHOLOGY APPLIED

Answer these questions the day before an exam as a final check on your understanding of the chapter's terms and concepts.

Multiple-Choice Questions

1. You decide to test your belief that men drink more soft drinks than women by finding out whether more soft drinks are consumed per day in the men's dorm than in the women's dorm. Your belief is a(n) _____ , and your research prediction is a(n) _____ .

   a. hypothesis; theory
   b. theory; hypothesis
   c. independent variable; dependent variable
   d. dependent variable; independent variable

2. Your roommate is conducting a survey to learn how many hours the typical college student studies each day. She plans to pass out her questionnaire to the members of her sorority. You point out that her findings will be flawed because:
   a. she has not specified an independent variable.
   b. she has not specified a dependent variable.
   c. the sample will probably not be representative of the population of interest.
   d. of all the above reasons.

3. The concept of control is important in psychological research because:
   a. without control over independent and dependent variables, researchers cannot describe, predict, or explain behavior.
   b. experimental control allows researchers to study the influence of one or two independent variables on a dependent variable while holding other potential influences constant.
   c. without experimental control, results cannot be generalized from a sample to a population.
   d. of all the above reasons.

4. Martina believes that high doses of caffeine slow a person's reaction time. In order to test this belief, she has five friends each drink three 8-ounce cups of coffee and then measures their reaction time on a learning task. What is wrong with Martina's research strategy?
   a. No independent variable is specified.
   b. No dependent variable is specified.
   c. There is no control condition.
   d. There is no provision for replication of the findings.

5. A researcher was interested in determining whether her students' test performance could be predicted from their proximity to the front of the classroom. So she matched her students' scores on a math test with their seating position. This study is an example of:
   a. experimentation.
   b. correlational research.
   c. a survey.
   d. naturalistic observation.

6. Your best friend criticizes psychological research for being artificial and having no relevance to behavior in real life. In defense of psychology's use of laboratory experiments you point out that:
   a. psychologists make every attempt to avoid artificiality by setting up experiments that closely simulate real-world environments.
   b. psychologists who conduct basic research are not concerned with the applicability of their findings to the real world.
   c. most psychological research is not conducted in a laboratory environment.
   d. psychologists intentionally study behavior in simplified environments in order to gain greater control over variables and to test general principles that help to explain many behaviors.

7. A professor constructs a questionnaire to determine how students at the university feel about nuclear disarmament. Which of the following techniques should be used in order to survey a random sample of the student body?
   a. Every student should be sent the questionnaire.
   b. Only students majoring in psychology should be asked to complete the questionnaire.
   c. Only students living on campus should be asked to complete the questionnaire.
   d. From an alphabetical listing of all students, every tenth (or fifteenth, e.g.) student should be asked to complete the questionnaire.

8. If eating saturated fat and the likelihood of contracting cancer are positively correlated, which of the following is true?
   a. Saturated fat causes cancer.
   b. People who are prone to develop cancer prefer foods containing saturated fat.
   c. A separate factor links the consumption of saturated fat to cancer.
   d. None of the above is necessarily true.

9. To say that "psychology is a science" means that:
   a. psychologists study only observable behaviors.
   b. psychologists study thoughts and actions with an attitude of skepticism and derive their conclusions from direct observations.
   c. psychological research should be free of value judgments.
   d. all of the above are true.

10. Rashad, who is participating in a psychology experiment on the effects of alcohol on perception, is truthfully told by the experimenter that he has been assigned to the "high-dose condition." What is wrong with this experiment?
    a. There is no control condition.
    b. Rashad's expectations concerning the effects of "high doses" of alcohol on perception may influence his performance.
    c. Knowing that Rashad is in the "high-dose" condition may influence the experimenter's interpretations of Rashad's results.
    d. Both b. and c. are correct.

11. A friend majoring in anthropology is critical of psychological research because it often ignores the influence of culture on thoughts and actions. You point out that:
    a. there is very little evidence that cultural diversity has a significant effect on specific behaviors and attitudes.
    b. most researchers assign participants to experimental and control conditions in such a way as to fairly represent the cultural diversity of the population under study.
    c. it is impossible for psychologists to control for every possible variable that might influence research participants.
    d. even when specific thoughts and actions vary across cultures, as they often do, the underlying processes are much the same.

12. The scientific attitude of humility is based on the idea that:
    a. researchers must evaluate new ideas and theories objectively rather than accept them blindly.
    b. scientific theories must be testable.
    c. simple explanations of behavior make better theories than do complex explanations.
    d. researchers must be prepared to reject their own ideas in the face of conflicting evidence.

13. Which of the following procedures is an example of the use of a placebo?
    a. In a test of the effects of a drug on memory, a participant is led to believe that a harmless pill actually contains an active drug.
    b. A participant in an experiment is led to believe that a pill, which actually contains an active drug, is harmless.
    c. Participants in an experiment are not told which treatment condition is in effect.
    d. Neither the participants nor the experimenter knows which treatment condition is in effect.

14. If height and body weight are positively correlated, which of the following is true?
    a. There is a cause-effect relationship between height and weight.
    b. As height increases, weight decreases.
    c. Knowing a person's height, one can predict his or her weight.
    d. All of the above are true.

15. The football team's punter wants to determine how consistent his punting distances have been during the past season. He should compute the:
    a. mean.   c. mode.
    b. median.   d. standard deviation.

16. Joe believes that his basketball game is always best when he wears his old gray athletic socks. Joe is a victim of the phenomenon called:
    a. statistical significance.
    b. overconfidence.
    c. illusory correlation.
    d. hindsight bias.

17. Esteban refuses to be persuaded by an advertiser's claim that people using their brand of gasoline average 50 miles per gallon. His decision probably is based on:
    a. the possibility that the average is the mean, which could be artificially inflated by a few extreme scores.
    b. the absence of information about the size of the sample studied.
    c. the absence of information about the variation in sample scores.
    d. all of the above.

18. Bob scored 43 out of 70 points on his psychology exam. He was worried until he discovered that most of the class earned the same score. Bob's score was equal to the:
    a. mean.   c. mode.
    b. median.   d. range.

19. The four families on your block all have annual household incomes of $25,000. If a new family with an annual income of $75,000 moved in, which measure of central tendency would be most affected?
    a. mean   c. mode
    b. median   d. standard deviation

20. Dr. Salazar recently completed an experiment in which she compared reasoning ability in a sample of females and a sample of males. The means of the female and male samples equaled 21 and 19, respectively, on a 25-point scale. A statistical test revealed that her results were not statistically significant. What can Dr. Salazar conclude?
    a. Females have superior reasoning ability.
    b. The difference in the means of the two samples is probably due to chance variation.
    c. The difference in the means of the two samples is reliable.
    d. None of the above is true.

Essay Question

Elio has a theory that regular exercise can improve thinking. Help him design an experiment evaluating this theory. (Use the space below to list the points you want to make, and organize them. Then write the essay on a separate piece of paper.)

KEY TERMS

Writing Definitions

Using your own words, on a separate piece of paper write a brief definition or explanation of each of the following.

1. hindsight bias
2. critical thinking
3. theory
4. hypothesis
5. operational definition
6. replication
7. case study
8. survey
9. false consensus effect
10. population
11. random sample
12. naturalistic observation
13. correlation
14. scatterplot
15. illusory correlation
16. experiment
17. double-blind procedure
18. placebo effect
19. experimental condition
20. control condition
21. random assignment
22. independent variable
23. dependent variable
24. mode
25. mean
26. median
27. range
28. standard deviation
29. statistical significance
30. culture

Cross-Check

As you learned in the Prologue, reviewing and overlearning of material are important to the learning process. After you have written the definitions of the key terms in this chapter, you should complete the crossword puzzle to ensure that you can reverse the process—recognize the term, given the definition.

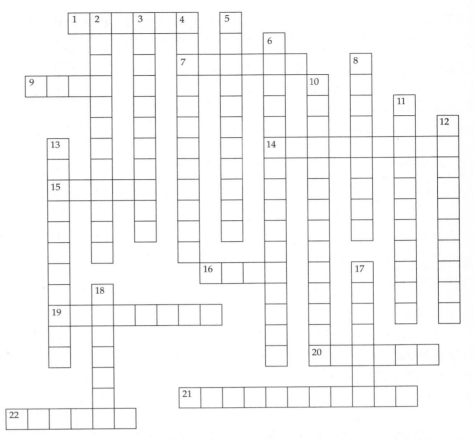

ACROSS

1. Score that falls at the 50th percentile, cutting a distribution in half.
7. Explanation using an integrated set of principles that organizes and predicts behaviors or events.
9. Most frequently occurring score in a distribution.
14. Descriptive research strategy in which one person is studied in great depth.
15. Measure of variation computed as the difference between the highest and lowest scores in a distribution.
16. Measure of central tendency computed by adding the scores in a distribution and dividing by the number of scores.
19. Perception of a correlation between two events where none exists.
20. Descriptive research technique in which a representative, random sample of people is questioned about their attitudes or behaviors.
21. Depiction of the relationship between two sets of scores by means of a graphed cluster of dots.
22. Sample in which every member of the population has an equal chance of being included.

DOWN

2. Experimental condition in which research participants are exposed to the independent variable being studied.
3. In an experiment, the variable being manipulated and tested by the investigator.
4. Research method in which behavior is observed and recorded in naturally occurring situations without any manipulation or control.
5. A precise definition of the procedures used to identify a variable.
6. Careful reasoning that examines assumptions, discerns hidden values, evaluates evidence, and assesses conclusions.

8. The bias in which we believe, after learning an outcome, that we could have foreseen it.
10. Our tendency to overestimate the extent to which others share our beliefs and behaviors.
11. Control procedure in which neither the experimenter nor the research participants are aware of which condition is in effect.
12. Testable prediction, often implied by a theory.
13. Measure that indicates the extent to which one factor predicts another factor.
17. Experimental condition in which the treatment of interest is withheld.
18. When a research participant's expectations produce the results of an experiment, it is called a _____ effect.

ANSWERS

Chapter Review

The Need for Psychological Science

1. hindsight bias; common; both children and adults
2. after the fact
3. overconfidence; bias
4. equally wrong
5. curiosity; skepticism; humility

6. critical thinking
7. scientific method; observations; theories; revised; observations
8. theory; hypotheses; research
9. operational definitions; replicate
10. organizes; predictions
11. descriptive; correlation; experimental

Description
1. case study
2. hypotheses; atypical
3. survey
4. wording
5. false consensus effect
6. random; population; does
7. are
8. vivid
9. naturalistic observation
10. describe
11. social; solitary; varies

Correlation
1. correlated; predict; correlation coefficient
2. scatterplots
3. positively correlated; negatively correlated; inversely
4. strength; weakness; causation; cause-effect

This is an example of a negative correlation. As one factor (time spent studying) increases, the other factor (anxiety level) decreases.

5. predicted
6. event; caused; explanation
7. illusory correlation
8. confirm; superstitious
9. random events
10. more; do not

Experimentation
1. cause; effect; statistically; factors
2. do; experiments; manipulates; holding constant (controlling)
3. behavior; experimental; effect
4. placebo; placebo effect
5. double-blind procedure
6. experimental; control
7. random assignment

8. independent; dependent
9. manipulate; independent; measure; dependent; control; variables

Experimentation has the advantage of increasing the investigator's control of both relevant and irrelevant variables that might influence behavior. Experiments also permit the investigator to go beyond observation and description to uncover cause-effect relationships in behavior.

Statistical Reasoning
1. statistics
2. data; organize; bar graph; scale labels; range
3. mode; median; mean
4. mode
5. total sum; number
6. 50th
7. skewed; mean
8. low; high
9. range; standard deviation
10. difference between the lowest and highest scores
11. crude; is
12. more accurate; takes
13. representative; biased
14. low
15. less
16. significance; chance; reliable; relatively large
17. practical

Frequently Asked Questions About Psychology
1. principles; laboratory; stress in their marriages
2. control; general principles
3. ideas; behaviors; attitudes; traditions
4. principles or processes; dyslexia; brain; genders
5. similarities; diseases
6. ethical; well-being
7. safeguards

Ethical guidelines require investigators to (1) obtain informed consent from potential participants, (2) protect them from harm and discomfort, (3) treat information obtained from participants confidentially, and (4) fully explain the research afterward.

8. do
9. can; enlighten
10. postmodernism; social; agree
11. do not; less
12. do not have

Progress Test 1

Multiple-Choice Questions

1. **a.** is the answer. In a case study one subject is studied in depth. (p. 26)
   b. In survey research a group of people is interviewed.
   c. Correlations identify whether two factors are related.
   d. In an experiment an investigator manipulates one variable to observe its effect on another.

2. **c.** is the answer. Exercise is the variable being manipulated in the experiment. (p. 38)
   a. A control condition for this experiment would be a group of people not permitted to exercise.
   b. An intervening variable is a variable other than those being manipulated that may influence behavior.
   d. The dependent variable is the behavior measured by the experimenter—in this case, the effects of exercise.

3. **c.** is the answer. The control condition is that for which the experimental treatment (the new drug) is absent. (p. 37)
   a. A random sample is a subset of a population in which every person has an equal chance of being selected.
   b. The experimental condition is the group for which the experimental treatment (the new drug) is present.
   d. "Test group" is an ambiguous term; both the experimental and control group are tested.

4. **d.** is the answer. (p. 24)
   a. Hypotheses are testable propositions.
   b. Dependent variables are factors that may change in response to manipulated independent variables.
   c. Statistical indexes may be used to test specific hypotheses (and therefore as indirect tests of theories), but they are merely mathematical tools, not general principles, as are theories.

5. **d.** is the answer. In this case, the children are being observed in their normal environment rather than in a laboratory. (p. 29)
   a. Correlational research measures relationships between two factors. The psychologist may later want to determine whether there are correlations between the variables studied under natural conditions.
   b. In a case study, one subject is studied in depth.
   c. This is not an experiment because the psychologist is not directly controlling the variables being studied.

6. **d.** is the answer. (p. 25)

7. **d.** is the answer. (p. 23)

8. **b.** is the answer. Replication is the repetition of an experiment in order to determine whether its findings are reliable. It is not a research method. (p. 25)

9. **c.** is the answer. (p. 48)
   a., b., & d. Psychologists' personal values can influence all of these.

10. **b.** is the answer. (p. 31)
    a. & c. These answers would have been correct had the question stated that there is a *positive* correlation between shoe size and IQ. Actually, there is probably no correlation at all!

11. **d.** is the answer. In an experiment, it would be possible to manipulate alcohol consumption and observe the effects, if any, on memory. (p. 36)
    a., b., & c. These answers are incorrect because only by directly controlling the variables of interest can a researcher uncover cause-effect relationships.

12. **d.** is the answer. (p. 28)
    a. A sample is a subset of a population.
    b. & c. Control and experimental groups are used in experimentation, not in survey research.

13. **c.** is the answer. The mean is the sum of scores divided by the number of scores. $[(2 + 3 + 7 + 6 + 1 + 4 + 9 + 5 + 8 + 2)/10 = 4.7.]$ (p. 41)

14. **d.** is the answer. When the scores are put in order (1, 2, 3, 4, 7, 7, 8), 4 is at the 50th percentile, splitting the distribution in half. (p. 41)

15. **b.** is the answer. The mode is the most frequently occurring score. Because there are more "twos" than any other number in the distribution, 2 is the mode. (p. 41)

16. **d.** is the answer. (pp. 42–43)

17. **c.** is the answer. (p. 43)
    a. A statistically significant difference may or may not be of practical importance.
    b. This is often the case when a difference is not statistically significant.

18. **c.** is the answer. (p. 41)

19. **d.** is the answer. (p. 22)
    a. This is the tendency to overestimate the extent to which others share our beliefs.
    b. This is the false perception of a relationship between two events.
    c. This is the tendency to believe, after learning an outcome, that one could have foreseen it.

20. **a.** is the answer. As an average, calculated by adding all scores and dividing by the number of scores, the mean could easily be affected by the inclusion of a few extreme scores. (p. 41)

b. The range is not a measure of central tendency.
c. & d. The median and mode give equal weight to all scores; each counts only once and its numerical value is unimportant.

Matching Items

1. i (p. 45)
2. f (p. 41)
3. l (p. 37)
4. j (p. 20)
5. e (p. 41)
6. b (p. 42)
7. h (p. 42)
8. g (p. 31)
9. c (p. 41)
10. a (p. 41)
11. d (p. 41)
12. m (p. 28)
13. k (p. 24)
14. n (p. 33)

Progress Test 2

Multiple-Choice Questions

1. **d.** is the answer. Only experiments can reveal cause-effect relationships; the other methods can only *describe* relationships. (p. 36)

2. **d.** is the answer. (p. 37)
   a., & b. The double-blind procedure is one way to create experimental and control groups.
   c. Research participants are randomly assigned to either an experimental or a control group.

3. **d.** is the answer. Animal shelters are forced to kill 50 times as many dogs and cats as are used in research. (p. 47)

4. **d.** is the answer. (p. 38)
   a. The control condition is the comparison group, in which the experimental treatment (the treatment of interest) is absent.
   b. Memory is a directly observed and measured dependent variable in this experiment.
   c. Attention is the independent variable, which is being manipulated.

5. **a.** is the answer. (p. 28)
   b. This refers to illusory correlation.
   c. This refers to overconfidence.

6. **b.** is the answer. (p. 20)
   a. The phenomenon is related to hindsight rather than foresight.
   c. & d. The phenomenon doesn't involve whether or not the intuitions are correct but rather people's attitude that they had the correct intuition.

7. **b.** is the answer. If enough subjects are used in an experiment and they are randomly assigned to the two groups, any differences that emerge between the groups should stem from the experiment itself. (p. 39)
   a., c., & d. None of these terms describes precautions taken in setting up groups for experiments.

8. **b.** is the answer. (p. 33)

9. **a.** is the answer. (p. 42)
   b. & c. Large, random samples are more likely to be representative of the populations from which they are drawn.

10. **d.** is the answer. Because we are sensitive to dramatic or unusual events, we are especially likely to perceive a relationship between them. (p. 34)
    a., b., & c. The relationship between vivid events is no more likely to be significant, positive, or negative than that between less dramatic events.

11. **b.** is the answer. (p. 25)
    a. In fact, the artificiality of experiments is part of an intentional attempt to create a controlled environment in which to test theoretical principles that are applicable to all behaviors.
    c. Some psychological theories go against what we consider common sense; furthermore, on many issues that psychology addresses, it's far from clear what the "common sense" position is.
    d. Psychology has always had ties to other disciplines, and in recent times, these ties have been increasing.

12. **d.** is the answer. Correlations show how well one factor can be predicted from another. (p. 30)
    a. Because a case study focuses in great detail on the behavior of an individual, it's probably not useful in showing whether predictions are possible.
    b. Naturalistic observation is a method of describing, rather than predicting, behavior.
    c. In experimental research the effects of manipulated independent variables on dependent variables are measured. It is not clear how an experiment could help determine whether IQ tests predict academic success.

13. **b.** is the answer. The control condition is the one in which the treatment—in this case, pollution—is absent. (p. 37)
    a. Students in the polluted room would be in the experimental condition.
    c. Presumably, all students in both conditions were randomly assigned to their groups. Random assignment is a method for establishing groups, rather than a condition.
    d. The word *dependent* refers to a kind of variable in experiments; conditions are either experimental or control.

14. **c.** is the answer. The lighting is the factor being manipulated. (p. 38)
    a. & d. These answers are incorrect because they involve aspects of the experiment other than the variables.

b. This answer is the dependent, not the independent, variable.

15. **b.** is the answer. (p. 41)

16. **c.** is the answer. The mean is the sum of the scores divided by the number of scores (60/10 = 6). (p. 41)

17. **c.** is the answer. When the scores are put in order (5, 6, 7, 8, 9, 10, 11), 8 is at the 50th percentile, splitting the distribution in half. (p. 41)

18. **d.** is the answer. Since the range is the difference between the highest and lowest scores, it is by definition affected by extreme scores. (p. 41)
a. & c. The mean and mode are measures of central tendency, not of variation.
b. The standard deviation is less affected than the range because, when it is calculated, the deviation of every score from the mean is computed.

19. **b.** is the answer. Averages derived from scores with low variability tend to be more reliable estimates of the populations from which they are drawn. Thus, a. and c. are incorrect. Because the standard deviation is a more accurate estimate of variability than the range, d. is incorrect. (p. 43)

20. **d.** is the answer. A difference that is statistically significant is a true difference, rather than an apparent difference due to factors such as sampling variation, and it is reliable. (p. 43)

Matching Items

1. e (p. 25)	5. j (p. 37)	9. f (p. 25)
2. h (p. 24)	6. d (p. 37)	10. g (p. 37)
3. b (p. 38)	7. a (p. 26)	11. i (p. 36)
4. c (p. 38)	8. k (p. 27)	12. l (p. 37)

Psychology Applied

Multiple-Choice Questions

1. **b.** is the answer. A general belief such as this one is a theory; it helps organize, explain, and generate testable predictions (called hypotheses) such as "men drink more soft drinks than women." (pp. 24, 25)
c. & d. Independent and dependent variables are experimental treatments and behaviors, respectively. Beliefs and predictions may involve such variables, but are not themselves those variables.

2. **c.** is the answer. The members of one sorority are likely to share more interests, traits, and attitudes than will the members of a random sample of college students. (p. 28)
a. & b. Unlike experiments, surveys do not specify or directly manipulate independent and de-

pendent variables. In a sense, survey questions are independent variables, and the answers, dependent variables.

3. **b.** is the answer. (p. 38)
a. Although the descriptive methods of case studies, surveys, naturalistic observation, and correlational research do not involve control of variables, they nevertheless enable researchers to describe and predict behavior.
c. Whether or not a sample is representative of a population, rather than control over variables, determines whether results can be generalized from a sample to a population.

4. **c.** is the answer. In order to determine the effects of caffeine on reaction time, Martina needs to measure reaction time in a control, or comparison, group that does not receive caffeine. (p. 37)
a. Caffeine is the independent variable.
b. Reaction time is the dependent variable.
d. Whether or not Martina's experiment can be replicated is determined by the precision with which she reports her procedures, which is not an aspect of research strategy.

5. **b.** is the answer. (pp. 30–31)
a. This is not an experiment because the researcher is not manipulating the independent variable (seating position); she is merely measuring whether variation in this factor predicts test performance.
c. If the study were based entirely on students' self-reported responses, this would be a survey.
d. This study goes beyond naturalistic observation, which merely describes behavior as it occurs, to determine if test scores can be predicted from students' seating position.

6. **d.** is the answer. (p. 45)

7. **d.** is the answer. Selecting every tenth person would probably result in a representative sample of the entire population of students at the university. (p. 28)
a. It would be difficult, if not impossible, to survey every student on campus.
b. Psychology students are not representative of the entire student population.
c. This answer is incorrect for the same reason as (b.). This would constitute a biased sample.

8. **d.** is the answer. (pp. 30–32)
a. Correlation does not imply causality.
b. Again, a positive correlation simply means that two factors tend to increase or decrease together; further relationships are not implied.
c. A separate factor may or may not be involved. That the two factors are correlated does not imply a separate factor. There may, for example, be a

direct causal relationship between the two factors themselves.

9. **b.** is the answer. Psychology is a science because psychologists use the scientific method and approach the study of behavior and mental processes with attitudes of curiosity, skepticism, and humility. (p. 23)
   a. Psychologists study both overt (observable) behaviors and covert thoughts and feelings.
   c. Psychologists' values definitely do influence their research.

10. **d.** is the answer. (p. 37)
    a. The low-dose comparison group is the control group.

11. **d.** is the answer. (p. 46)
    a. In fact, just the opposite is true.
    b. Actually, psychological experiments tend to use the most readily available people, often white North American college students.
    c. Although this may be true, psychological experiments remain important because they help explain underlying processes of human behavior everywhere. Therefore, d. is a much better response than c.

12. **d.** is the answer. (p. 23)
    a. This follows from the attitude of skepticism, rather than humility.
    b. & c. Although both of these are true of the scientific method, neither has anything to do with humility.

13. **a.** is the answer. (p. 37)
    b. Use of a placebo tests whether the behavior of a research participant, who mistakenly believes that a treatment (such as a drug) is in effect, is the same as it would be if the treatment were actually present.
    c. & d. These are examples of *blind* and *double-blind* control procedures.

14. **c.** is the answer. If height and weight are positively correlated, increased height is associated with increased weight. Thus, one can predict a person's weight from his or her height. (p. 30)
    a. Correlation does not imply causality.
    b. This situation depicts a negative correlation between height and weight.

15. **d.** is the answer. A small or large standard deviation indicates whether a distribution is homogeneous or variable. (p. 42)
    a., b., & c. These statistics would not give any information regarding the consistency of performance.

16. **c.** is the answer. A correlation that is perceived but doesn't actually exist, as in the example, is known as an illusory correlation. (p. 33)

a. Statistical significance is a statement of how likely it is that an obtained result occurred by chance.
b. Overconfidence is the tendency to think we are more right than we actually are.
d. Hindsight bias is the tendency to believe, after learning an outcome, that one would have foreseen it.

17. **d.** is the answer. (pp. 41, 42)

18. **c.** is the answer. (p. 41)
    a. The mean is computed as the sum of the scores divided by the number of scores.
    b. The median is the midmost score in a distribution.
    d. The range is the difference between the highest and lowest scores in a distribution.

19. **a.** is the answer. The mean is strongly influenced by extreme scores. In this example, the mean would change from $25,000 to (75,000 + 25,000 + 25,000 + 25,000 + 25,000)/5 = $35,000. (p. 41)
    b. & c. Both the median and the mode would remain $25,000, even with the addition of the fifth family's income.
    d. The standard deviation is a measure of variation, not central tendency.

20. **b.** is the answer. (p. 43)
    a. If the difference between the sample means is not significant, then the groups probably do not differ in the measured ability.
    c. When a result is not significant it means that the observed difference is unreliable.

Essay Question

Elio's hypothesis is that daily aerobic exercise for one month will improve memory. Exercise is the independent variable. The dependent variable is memory. Exercise could be manipulated by having people in an experimental group jog for 30 minutes each day. Memory could be measured by comparing the number of words they recall from a test list studied before the exercise experiment begins, and again afterward. A control group that does not exercise *is* needed so that any improvement in the experimental group's memory can be attributed to exercise, and not to some other factor, such as the passage of one month's time or familiarity with the memory test. The control group should engage in some nonexercise activity for the same amount of time each day that the experimental group exercises. The participants should be randomly selected from the population at large, and then randomly assigned to the experimental and control groups.

Key Terms

Writing Definitions

1. **Hindsight bias** refers to the tendency to believe, after learning an outcome, that one would have foreseen it; also called the *I-knew-it-all-along phenomenon*. (p. 20)

2. **Critical thinking** is careful reasoning that examines assumptions, discerns hidden values, evaluates evidence, and assesses conclusions. (p. 24)

3. A **theory** is an explanation using an integrated set of principles that organizes and predicts behaviors or events. (p. 24)

4. A **hypothesis** is a testable prediction, often implied by a theory; testing the hypothesis helps scientists to test the theory. (p. 25)

   Example: In order to test his theory of why people conform, Solomon Asch formulated the testable **hypothesis** that an individual would be more likely to go along with the majority opinion of a large group than with that of a smaller group.

5. An **operational definition** is a precise statement of the procedures (operations) used to define research variables. (p. 25)

6. **Replication** is the process of repeating an experiment, often with different participants and in different situations, to see whether the basic finding generalizes to other people and circumstances. (p. 25)

7. The **case study** is an observation technique in which one person is studied in great depth, often with the intention of revealing universal principles. (p. 26)

8. The **survey** is a technique for ascertaining the self-reported attitudes or behaviors of a representative, random sample of people. (p. 27)

9. The **false consensus effect** is the tendency to overestimate the extent to which others share our beliefs and behaviors. (p. 28)

10. A **population** consists of all the members of a group being studied. (p. 28)

11. A **random sample** is one that is representative because every member of the population has an equal chance of being included. (p. 28)

12. **Naturalistic observation** involves observing and recording behavior in naturally occurring situations without trying to manipulate and control the situation. (p. 29)

13. **Correlation** is a measure of the extent to which two factors vary together, and thus of how well either factor predicts the other. The correlation coefficient is a statistical measure of the relationship; it can be positive or negative. (p. 30)

    Example: If there is a **positive correlation** between air temperature and ice cream sales, the warmer (higher) it is, the more ice cream is sold. If there is a **negative correlation** between air temperature and sales of cocoa, the cooler (lower) it is, the more cocoa is sold.

14. A **scatterplot** is a depiction of the relationship between two variables by means of a graphed cluster of dots. (p. 31)

15. **Illusory correlation** is the perception of a relationship where none exists. (p. 33)

16. An **experiment** is a research method in which a researcher directly manipulates one or more factors (independent variables) in order to observe their effect on some behavior or mental process (the dependent variable); experiments therefore make it possible to establish cause-effect relationships. (p. 36)

17. A **double-blind procedure** is an experimental procedure in which neither the experimenter nor the research participants are aware of which condition is in effect. It is used to prevent experimenters' and participants' expectations from influencing the results of an experiment. (p. 37)

18. The **placebo effect** occurs when the results of an experiment are caused by a participant's expectations about what is really going on. (p. 37)

19. The **experimental condition** of an experiment is one in which participants are exposed to the independent variable being studied. (p. 37)

    Example: In the study of the effects of a new drug on reaction time, participants in the **experimental condition** would actually receive the drug being tested.

20. The **control condition** of an experiment is one in which the treatment of interest, or independent variable, is withheld so that comparison to the experimental condition can be made. (p. 37)

    Example: The **control condition** for an experiment testing the effects of a new drug on reaction time would be a group of participants given a placebo (inactive drug or sugar pill) instead of the drug being tested.

21. **Random assignment** is the procedure of assigning participants to the experimental and control conditions by chance in order to minimize preexisting differences between those assigned to the different groups. (p. 37)

22. The **independent variable** of an experiment is the factor being manipulated and tested by the investigator. (p. 38)

    Example: In the study of the effects of a new drug on reaction time, the drug is the **independent variable**.

23. The **dependent variable** of an experiment is the factor being measured by the investigator. (p. 38)

    Example: In the study of the effects of a new drug on reaction time, the participants' reaction time is the **dependent variable.**

24. The **mode** is the most frequently occurring score in a distribution; it is the simplest measure of central tendency to determine. (p. 41)

25. The **mean** is the arithmetic average, the measure of central tendency computed by adding the scores in a distribution and dividing by the number of scores. (p. 41)

26. The **median**, another measure of central tendency, is the score that falls at the 50th percentile, cutting a distribution in half. (p. 41)

    Example: When the **mean** of a distribution is affected by a few extreme scores, the **median** is the more appropriate measure of central tendency.

27. The **range** is a measure of variation computed as the difference between the highest and lowest scores in a distribution. (p. 42)

28. The **standard deviation** is a computed measure of how much scores in a distribution deviate around the mean. Because it is based on every score in the distribution, it is a more precise measure of variation than the range. (p. 42)

29. **Statistical significance** means that an obtained result, such as the difference between the averages for two samples, very likely reflects a real difference rather than sampling variation or chance factors. Tests of statistical significance help researchers decide when they can justifiably generalize from an observed instance. (p. 43)

30. **Culture** is the enduring behaviors, ideas, attitudes, and traditions shared by a large group of people and transmitted from one generation to the next. (p. 45)

Cross-Check

ACROSS	DOWN
1. median	2. experimental
7. theory	3. independent
9. mode	4. naturalistic
14. case study	5. operational
15. range	6. critical thinking
16. mean	8. hindsight
19. illusory	10. false consensus
20. survey	11. double-blind
21. scatterplot	12. hypothesis
22. random	13. correlation
	17. control
	18. placebo

FOCUS ON VOCABULARY AND LANGUAGE

Page 19: . . . to remedy their own woes, millions turn to "psychology." In order to alleviate or fix (*remedy*) their misery, anxiety, grief, pain, and suffering (*woes*), people seek help from "psychology." (Psychology is in quotes because Myers wants to point out that not everything you think of as "psychology" is part of scientific psychology.)

The Need for Psychological Science

Page 19: . . . helps *winnow* sense from nonsense. *Winnow* means to separate out and was originally used to describe the separation of chaff (dust, etc.) from the grains of wheat. The scientific method helps sort out, or separate (*winnow*), good ideas from bad ones.

Page 19: Some people think psychology merely *documents* what people already know and *dresses it in jargon.* Some people criticize psychology, saying that it simply reports (*documents*) common sense, or what's obvious to everyone. Instead of stating something plainly, the critics suggest, psychology translates the information into the specialized and obscure vocabulary of the discipline (*dresses it up in jargon*). Myers makes it very clear with some good examples that this criticism is not justified and points out that our intuitions about reality can often be very mistaken (they can *lead us astray*).

Page 20: How easy it is to seem *astute* when *drawing the bull's eye after the arrow has struck.* In the sport of archery the task is to shoot the arrow at the red circle in the center of the target (the *bull's eye*). If we first shoot an arrow, then draw the target so that the arrow is in the center (in the *bull's eye*), we can appear to be very accurate. Myers uses this analogy to illustrate how the hindsight bias (or the *I-knew-it all-along phenomenon*) can lead us to believe that we are shrewd (*astute*) and would have been able to predict outcomes that we have learned after-the-fact.

Page 20: "Out of sight, out of mind" and *"Absence makes the heart grow fonder."* These two sayings, or expressions, about romantic love have opposite meanings. The first one suggests that when couples are apart (*out of sight*) they are less likely to think about each other (*out of mind*) than when they are together. The second saying makes the point that being separated (*absence*) increases the feelings of love the couple shares (*makes the heart grow fonder*). People who are told that the results of a study support the first expression (*out of sight, out of mind*) see this as mere common sense. People told that the results support the second expression (*absence makes the heart grow fonder*) also say this is obviously true. There is clearly a problem here; relying on common sense can lead to opposite conclusions.

Page 21: . . . our intuition may tell us that *familiarity breeds contempt.* . . . This expression and others are based on many casual observations but are often wrong. For example, is it true that the better you know someone (*familiarity*), the more likely it is that you will dislike the person (have *contempt*)? In fact, research shows that the opposite is probably true. (Your text, again and again, will emphasize the fact that our common sense and intuition do not always provide us with reliable evidence.)

Page 22: . . . *drop a course* . . . This means to stop going to class and to have your name removed from the class list.

Page 22: . . . . *lackluster predictions* . . . *Lackluster* originally meant to be deficient in brightness or to be dull. *Lackluster predictions* are forecasts that are usually wrong. As Myers notes, those who made them (those who erred) tended to be overconfident about their ability to foretell the future. Along with hindsight bias, this overconfidence often leads us to overestimate our intuitions.

Page 23: Underlying all science is, first, a *hard-headed curiosity* . . . *Hard-headed* here means to be practical, uncompromising, realistic, or unswayed by sentiment. All science, including psychology, is guided by this realistic desire to know (*curiosity*) about nature and life.

Page 23: . . . *leap of faith.* This is a belief in something in the absence of demonstrated proof. Some questions—about the existence of God or life after death, for example—cannot be answered by science and cannot be scientifically proved or disproved; if a person believes, then it is on the basis of trust and confidence alone (*leap of faith*).

Page 23: . . . the *proof is in the pudding.* This comes from the expression "*the proof of the pudding is in the eating.*" A *pudding* is a sweet dessert. We can test (or prove) the quality of the dessert (*pudding*) by trying

it (*eating*). Likewise, many questions, even if they appear to make little sense (*crazy-sounding ideas*), can be tested using the scientific method.

Page 23: . . . *auras* . . . An *aura* is a bright glow surrounding a figure or an object. Some believe that humans have auras which only those with extrasensory abilities can see. The magician James Randi proposed a simple test of this claim, but nobody who is alleged to have this magical power (*aura-seer*) has taken the test.

Page 23: More often, science relegates *crazy-sounding ideas* to the *mountain* of forgotten claims. . . . The use of scientific inquiry can get rid of or dispose of (*relegate*) non-sensible concepts (*crazy-sounding ideas*) to the large stack or pile (*mountain*) of ridiculous claims no longer remembered.

Page 23: In the *arena* of competing ideas . . . An *arena* is an area where games, sports, and competitions take place. Myers is suggesting that in an area (*arena*) where there is a contest between ideas (*competing ideas*), skeptical testing can help discover the truth.

Page 23: . . . *then so much the worse for our ideas.* This means that we have to give up, or get rid of, our ideas if they are shown to be wrong (*so much the worse for them*). We have to be humble (i.e., have humility).

Page 23: "*The rat is always right.*" This early *motto* (a phrase used as a maxim or guiding principle) comes from the fact that for most of the first half of the twentieth century psychology used animals in its research (especially in the study of learning). The *rat* became a symbol of this research, and its behavior or performance in experiments demonstrated the truth. If the truth, as shown by the rat, is contrary to the prediction or hypothesis, then one has to be humble about it and try another way.

Page 24: We all view nature through the *spectacles* of our *preconceived ideas.* This means that what we already believe (*our preconceived ideas*) influences, and to some extent determines, what we look for and actually see or discover in nature. It's as though the type of eyeglasses (*spectacles*) we wear limits what we can see.

Page 24: . . . *gut feelings* . . . This refers to basic intuitive reactions or responses. Critical thinking requires determining whether a conclusion is based simply on a subjective opinion (*gut feeling*) or anecdote (a story someone tells) or on reliable scientific evidence.

Page 24: . . . *debunked* . . . This means to remove

glamour or credibility from established ideas, persons, and traditions. Myers points out that scientific evidence and critical inquiry have indeed discredited (*debunked*) many popular presumptions.

Page 24: . . . one *cannot* simply *"play the tape"* and relive long-buried or *repressed* memories. . . . This is an example of a discredited (*debunked*) idea that hidden (*repressed*) memories can be accurately and reliably retrieved (*brought back*) intact and complete in the same way that *playing a tape* on a VCR allows us to watch exactly the same show over and over again.

Page 26: . . . a scientific approach helps us *sift* reality from illusion. A scientific (*or empirical*) attitude can separate (*sift*) what's real from what is not and take us beyond the constraints (limits) of our beliefs, experience, intuition, and common sense.

Description

Page 27: Numbers can be numbing . . . and *Anecdotes are often more startling.* We are often overwhelmed and our senses deadened (*numbed*) by the sometimes inappropriate use of statistics and numbers. We are also alarmed or frightened (*startled*) by the strange stories people tell (*anecdotes*).

Page 27: As psychologist Gordon Allport (1954, p. 9) said, "Given a *thimbleful* of [dramatic] facts we rush to make *generalizations as large as a tub*." A *thimble* is a small metal container which fits over the top of the thumb or finger and is used while sewing to push the needle through the material, and a *tub* is a very large container (e.g., a *bathtub*). Allport is saying that given a *small* amount of information (a *thimbleful*), we tend to make very *big* assumptions (*generalizations as large as a tub*).

Page 29: . . . 1500 randomly sampled people, drawn from all areas of a country, provide a remarkably accurate *snapshot* of the opinions of a nation. A *snapshot* is a picture taken with a camera, and it captures what people are doing at a given moment in time. A good survey (*1500 randomly selected representative people*) gives an accurate picture (*snapshot*) of the opinions of the whole population of interest (the *target group*).

Correlation

Page 31: Statistics can help us see what the *naked eye* sometimes misses. When looking at an array of data consisting of different measures (e.g., height and temperament) for many subjects, it is very difficult to discern what, if any, relationships exist. Statistical tools, such as the correlation coefficient and the scatterplot, can help us see clearly what the unaided

(*naked*) eye might not see. As Myers notes, we sometimes need statistical illumination to see what is in front of us.

Page 34: If someone *flipped a coin* six times, which of the following sequences of heads (H) and tails (T) would be most likely: HHHTTT or HTTHTH or HHHHHH? *Flipping a coin* means throwing or tossing the coin into the air and observing which side is facing up when it lands. (The side of the coin that usually has the imprint of the face of a famous person on it—e.g., the president or the queen—is called *heads* (H) and the other side is called *tails* (T).) By the way, all of the above sequences are equally likely, but most people pick HTTHTH. Likewise, any series of five playing cards (e.g., a bridge or poker hand in a game of cards) is just as likely as any other hand.

Page 35: "cold hands" . . . *"hot hands"* . . . In this context, "hot" and "cold" do not refer to temperature. Here, being hot (or having *"hot hands"*) means doing well, and doing well consistently is having a hot streak. Having a run of poor luck is a cold streak. The crucial point, however, is that our intuition about sequences of events (streaks or streaky patterns) often deceives us. True random sequences often are not what we think they should be, and thus, they don''t *appear* to be really random. When we think we're doing well (*"hot hands"*), we're very often not; we are merely noting or overinterpreting certain sequences (*streaks*) found in any random data.

Experimentation

Page 39: Let's *Recap*. Recap is an abbreviation of *recapitulate*, which means to repeat or go over briefly, to summarize. Myers summarizes (*recaps*) the important points in each section of the chapter.

Statistical Reasoning

Page 40: Off the top-of-the head estimates often misread reality and then mislead the public. Without knowing actual data and numbers (statistics), people may guess at the figures (they make *top-of-the-head estimates*), and these guesses do not represent the true nature of things (they often *misread reality*) and consequently can deceive (*mislead*) the public. The figures generated in this manner are often easy to articulate, such as 10 percent or 50 percent (*big round numbers*) and, when repeated (*echoed*) by others, may eventually be believed to be true by most people (*they become public misinformation*).

Page 41: Because the bottom *half* of British income earners receive only a *quarter* of the *national income cake*, most British people, like most people everywhere, make less than the mean. Incomes are not normally distributed (they do not follow a bell-shaped curve when plotted as a frequency distribution), so a better measure of central tendency than the mean (arithmetic average) is either the median (the score in the middle) or the mode (the most frequently occurring score). In Myers' example, half the people account for 25 percent of all the money earned in the country (*national income cake*); in this uneven (*skewed*) distribution, therefore, most people earn below-average wages.

Page 42: It [**standard deviation**] better *gauges* whether scores are packed together or dispersed, because it uses information from each score (Table 1.4). The most commonly used statistic for measuring (*gauging*) how much scores differ from one another (their variation) is the standard deviation (SD). Using this formula, each score is compared to the mean; the result is an index of how spread out (*dispersed*) the scores are. A relatively small SD indicates that most of the scores are close to the average; a relatively large SD indicates that they are much more variable.

Page 44: Data are *"noisy."* Differences between groups may simply be due to random (*chance*) variations (*fluctuations*) in those particular samples. When data have a great deal of variability, they are said to be *"noisy,"* which may limit our ability to generalize from them to the larger population. In order to determine if differences are reliable, we should be sure that (a) samples are random and representative, (b) scores in the sample are similar to each other (have low variability), and (c) a large number of subjects or observations are included. If these principles are followed, we can confidently make inferences about the differences between groups.

Frequently Asked Questions About Psychology

Page 45: . . . plunge in. In this context, *plunge in* means to move ahead quickly with the discussion. (Similarly, when you dive into a swimming pool [*plunge in*], you do so quickly.) Before going on with the discussion of psychology (*plunging in*), Myers addresses some important issues and questions.

Page 46: To understand how a combustion engine works, you would do better to study *a lawn mower's engine than a Mercedes'*. A *Mercedes* is a very complex luxury car, and a *lawn mower* (a machine for cutting grass in the garden) has a very simple engine. To understand the principles underlying both machines, it is easier to study the simpler one. Likewise, when trying to understand the nervous system, it is better to study a simple one (e.g., a sea slug) than a complex one (a human).

Page 48: . . . most universities today screen research proposals through an *ethics committee. . . . Ethics committees* (groups of people concerned with moral behavior and acceptable standards of conduct) subject research proposals to rigorous tests (*screen them*) to ensure that they are fair and reasonable and that they do not harm the participants' well-being.

Page 48: Values can also *color* "the facts." Our values (what we believe is right and true) can influence (*color*) our observations, interpretations, and conclusions ("the facts").

2 : Neuroscience and Behavior

CHAPTER OVERVIEW

Chapter 2 is concerned with the functions of the brain and its component neural systems, which provide the basis for all human behavior. Under the direction of the brain, the nervous and endocrine systems coordinate a variety of voluntary and involuntary behaviors and serve as the body's mechanisms for communication with the external environment.

The brain consists of the brainstem, the thalamus, the cerebellum, the limbic system, and the cerebral cortex. Knowledge of the workings of the brain has increased with advances in neuroscientific methods. Studies of split-brain patients have also given researchers a great deal of information about the specialized functions of the brain's right and left hemispheres.

Many students find the technical material in this chapter difficult to master. Not only are there many terms for you to remember, but you must also know the organization and function of the various divisions of the nervous system. Learning this material will require a great deal of rehearsal. Working the chapter review several times, drawing and labeling brain diagrams, and mentally reciting terms are all useful techniques for rehearsing this type of material.

NOTE: Answer guidelines for all Chapter 2 questions begin on page 59.

CHAPTER REVIEW

First, skim each section, noting headings and boldface items. After you have read the section, review each objective by answering the fill-in and essay-type questions that follow it. As you proceed, evaluate your performance by consulting the answers beginning on page 59. Do not continue with the next section until you understand each answer. If you need to, review or reread the section in the textbook before continuing.

Introduction (pp. 53–54)

> David Myers at times uses idioms that are unfamiliar to some readers. If you do not know the meaning of any of the following words, phrases, or expressions in the context in which they appear in the text, refer to page 68 for an explanation: *to shoot a basketball; an ill-fated theory; a wrong-headed theory.*

Objective 1: Explain why psychologists are concerned with human biology, and describe the ill-fated phrenology theory.

1. In the most basic sense, every idea, mood, memory, and behavior that an individual has ever experienced is a _____ phenomenon.

2. The theory that linked our mental abilities to bumps on the skull was _____ .

3. Researchers who study the links between biology and behavior are called _____

   _____ .

Neural Communication (pp. 54–61)

> If you do not know the meaning of any of the following words, phrases, or expressions in the context in which they appear in the text, refer to pages 68–69 for an explanation: *happy fact of nature; building blocks; a sluggish 2 miles per hour to . . . a breakneck 200 or more miles; rather like manhole covers flipping open; boggles; somewhat like pushing a neuron's accelerator . . . more like pushing its brake; How do we distinguish a gentle touch from a big hug; "protoplasmic kisses"; "runner's high"; They trigger unpleasant, lingering aftereffects; Agonists excite . . . Antagonists inhibit; some chemicals can slither through this (blood-brain) barrier.*

Objective 2: Explain how viewing each person as a biopsychosocial system helps us understand human behavior, and discuss why researchers study other animals in search of clues to human neural processes.

1. We are each a _____ system, composed of _____ that are parts of larger _____ , which are parts of an even larger _____ .

2. Viewing each person in this way allows psychologists to study behavior and mental processes from multiple levels, noting how

   _____ , _____ , and

   _____-_____ systems

   work and interact.

Objective 3: Describe the parts of a neuron, and explain how its impulses are generated.

3. Our body's neural system is built from billions of nerve cells, or _____ .

4. The extensions of a neuron that receive messages from other neurons are the _____ .

5. The extension of a neuron that transmits information to other neurons is the

   _____ ; some of these extensions are insulated by a layer of fatty cells called the

   _____ _____ , which

   helps speed the neuron's impulses.

6. Identify the major parts of the neuron diagrammed below:

   a. _____   c. _____
   b. _____   d. _____

7. The neural impulse, or _____

   _____ , is a brief electrical charge

   that travels down a(n) _____ .

8. The fluid interior of a resting axon carries mostly
   _____ (positively/negatively)
   charged ions, while the fluid outside has mostly
   _____ (positively/negatively)
   charged ions. This polarization, called the
   _____ _____ , occurs
   because the cell membrane is _____

   _____ .

9. An action potential occurs when the first part of the axon opens its gates and _____ (positively/negatively) charged ions rush in, causing that part of the neuron to become

   _____ .

10. During the resting pause following an action potential, called the _____
    _____ , the neuron pumps
    _____ (positively/negatively)
    charged ions outside the cell.

11. In order to trigger a neural impulse,
    _____ signals minus
    _____ signals must exceed a certain
    intensity, called the _____ .
    Increasing a stimulus above this level
    _____ (will/will not) increase the
    neural impulse's intensity. This phenomenon is
    called an _____ -

    _____ -_____

    response.

12. The strength of a stimulus _____ (does/does not) affect the speed of a neural impulse.

Objective 4: Describe how nerve cells communicate.

13. The junction between two neurons is called a _____ , and the gap is called the _____ _____ .

14. The chemical messengers that convey information across the gaps between neurons are called _____ . These chemicals unlock tiny channels on receptor sites, allowing electrically charged atoms (_____) to enter the neuron.

15. Neurotransmitters influence neurons either by _____ or _____ their readiness to fire. Excess neurotransmitters are reabsorbed by the sending neuron in a process called _____ .

Outline the sequence of reactions that occur when a neural impulse is generated and transmitted from one neuron to another.

Objective 5: Explain how neurotransmitters affect behavior, and outline the effects of acetylcholine and the endorphins.

16. Among the neurotransmitters that researchers have pinpointed are _____ , which influences movement, learning, attention, and emotion; _____ , which affects mood, hunger, sleep, and arousal; _____ , which helps control alertness and arousal; _____ , which is an inhibitory neurotransmitter whose undersupply is linked to seizures, tremors, and insomnia; and _____ , which is involved in memory.

17. A neurotransmitter that is important in muscle contraction is _____ .

18. Naturally occurring opiatelike neurotransmitters that are present in the brain are called _____ . When the brain is flooded with drugs such as _____ or _____ , it may stop producing these neurotransmitters.

Objective 6: Explain how drugs and other chemicals affect neurotransmission, and describe the contrasting effects of agonists and antagonists.

19. Drugs that produce their effects by mimicking neurotransmitters are called _____ . Drugs that block the effects of neurotransmitters by occupying their _____ _____ are called _____ . While certain _____ drugs create a temporary "high" by mimicking the endorphins, the poison _____ produces paralysis by blocking the activity of the neurotransmitter ACh.

20. The molecular shape of some drugs prevents them from passing through the _____-_____ _____ by which the brain fences out unwanted chemicals.

21. The tremors of _____ disease are due to the death of neurons that produce the neurotransmitter _____ . People with this condition can be helped to regain control over their muscles by taking _____ .

The Nervous System (pp. 61–65)

> If you do not know the meaning of any of the following words, phrases, or expressions in the context in which they appear in the text, refer to pages 69–70 for an explanation: *Like an automatic pilot, this system may be consciously overridden; yield an ever-changing wiring diagram that dwarfs a powerful computer; information highway; The knee-jerk response . . . a headless warm body could do it; Being human takes a lot of nerve; work groups.*

Objective 7: Describe the nervous system's two major divisions, and identify the three types of neurons that transmit information through the system.

1. Taken altogether, the neurons of the body form the _____ _____ .

2. The brain and spinal cord comprise the _____ nervous system. The neurons that link the brain and spinal cord to the body's sense receptors, muscles, and glands form the _____ nervous system.

3. Sensory and motor axons are bundled into electrical cables called _____ .

4. Information arriving in the central nervous system from the body travels in _____ neurons. The neurons that enable internal communication within the central nervous system are called _____ .

5. The central nervous system sends instructions to the body's tissues by means of _____ neurons.

Objective 8: Identify the subdivisions of the peripheral nervous system, and describe their functions.

6. The division of the peripheral nervous system that enables voluntary control of the skeletal muscles is the _____ nervous system.

7. Involuntary, self-regulating responses—those of the glands and muscles of internal organs—are controlled by the _____ nervous system.

8. The body is made ready for action by the _____ division of the autonomic nervous system.

9. The _____ division of the autonomic nervous system produces relaxation.

Describe and explain the sequence of physical reactions that occur in the body as an emergency is confronted and then passes.

Objective 9: Contrast the simplicity of the reflex pathways with the complexity of neural networks.

10. Automatic responses to stimuli, called _____ , illustrate the work of the _____ _____ . Simple pathways such as these are involved in the _____-_____ response and in the _____ reflex.

Beginning with the sensory receptors in the skin, trace the course of a spinal reflex as a person reflexively jerks his or her hand away from an unexpectedly hot burner on a stove.

11. To perform complex computations, neurons in the brain cluster into work groups called _____ _____ .

The Endocrine System (pp. 65–67)

> If you do not know the meaning of any of the following words, phrases, or expressions in the context in which they appear in the text, refer to page 70 for an explanation: *kindred systems; Conducting and coordinating this whole electrochemical orchestra is that maestro we call the brain.*

Objective 10: Describe the nature and functions of the endocrine system and its interaction with the nervous system.

1. The body's chemical communication network is called the _____ _____ .

This system transmits information through chemical messengers called _____
at a much _____ (faster/slower) rate than the nervous system, and its effects last _____ (a longer time/a shorter time).

2. In a moment of danger, the _____ glands release _____ and
_____ .

3. The most influential gland is the
_____ , which, under the control of an adjacent brain area called the
_____ , helps regulate
_____ and the release of hormones by other endocrine glands.

Write a paragraph describing the feedback system that links the nervous and endocrine systems.

The Brain (pp. 67–92)

If you do not know the meaning of any of the following words, phrases, or expressions in the context in which they appear in the text, refer to pages 70–72 for an explanation: _we live in our heads; neural cartographers; snoop on the messages . . . and eavesdrop on the chatter of billions of neurons; the right side of the body is wired to . . .; Newer windows into the brain . . . Supermanlike; snapshots of the brain's changing activity provide . . . divides its labor; This peculiar cross-wiring is but one of many surprises the brain has to offer; . . . what London is to England's trains; the doughnut-shaped limbic system; reduced fits of rage; magnificent mistake; wrinkled organ, shaped somewhat like the meat of an oversized walnut; neural nannies; spine-tingling thrills; eyes in the back of our head; most widespread falsehoods; frontal lobes ruptured . . . Gage's moral compass; What you experience as . . . the visible tip of the information-processing iceberg; one patient even managed to quip that he had a "splitting headache"; When the "two minds" are at odds; pretzel-shaped finding . . . breadstick-shaped story; appear alike to the naked eye . . . harmony of the whole; southpaws; dwarfs._

Objective 11: Describe several techniques for studying the brain.

1. Researchers sometimes study brain function by producing _____ or by selectively destroying brain cells. The oldest technique for studying the brain involves _____
_____ of patients with brain injuries or diseases.

2. The _____ is a recording of the electrical activity of the whole brain.

3. The technique depicting the level of activity of brain areas by measuring the brain's consumption of glucose is called the
_____ _____ .

Briefly explain the purpose of the PET scan.

4. A technique that produces clearer images of the brain by using magnetic fields and radio waves is known as _____ .

5. By taking pictures less than a second apart, the
_____ _____ detects blood rushing to the part of the cortex thought to control the bodily activity being studied. Using this technique, researchers found that activity increases in the _____
_____ _____ when people experience conflicting
_____ .

Objective 12: Describe the components of the brainstem, and summarize the functions of the brainstem, thalamus, and cerebellum.

6. The oldest and innermost region of the brain is the _____ .

7. At the base of the brainstem, where the spinal cord enters the skull, lies the _____ , which controls _____ and _____ . Just above this part is the _____ , which helps coordinate movements.

8. Nerves from each side of the brain cross over to connect with the body's opposite side in the _____ .

9. The _____ _____ is contained inside the brainstem and plays an important role in controlling _____ . Electrically stimulating this area will produce an _____ animal. Lesioning this area will cause an animal to lapse into a _____ .

10. At the top of the brainstem sits the _____ , which serves as the brain's sensory switchboard, receiving information from all the senses except _____ and routing it to the regions dealing with those senses. These egg-shaped structures also receive replies from the higher regions, which they direct to the _____ and the _____ .

11. At the rear of the brainstem lies the _____ . It influences one type of _____ _____ and memory, but its major function is coordination of voluntary movement and _____ control.

12. The lower brain functions occur without _____ effort, indicating that our brains process most information _____ (inside/outside) of our awareness.

Objective 13: Describe the structures and functions of the limbic system, and explain how one of these structures controls the pituitary gland.

13. Between the brainstem and cerebral hemispheres is the _____ system. One component of this system that processes memory is the _____ .

14. Aggression or fear will result from stimulation of different regions of the _____ .

15. Amygdala lesions, produced by _____ techniques, have been used to treat violent humans. This treatment is controversial and _____ (widely/seldom) used today.

16. Below the thalamus is the _____ , which regulates bodily maintenance behaviors such as _____ , _____ , and _____ . This area also regulates behavior by secreting _____ that enable it to control the _____ gland. Olds and Milner discovered that this region also contains _____ centers, which animals will work hard to have stimulated.

17. Some researchers believe that alcoholism, drug abuse, binge eating, and other _____ disorders may stem from a genetic _____

_____ _____ in the natural brain systems for pleasure and well-being.

Objective 14: Define *cerebral cortex*, and explain its importance to the human brain.

18. The most complex functions of human behavior are linked to the most developed part of the brain, the _____ _____ . This thin layer of interconnected neural cells is the body's ultimate control and _____-_____ center.

Objective 15: Identify the four lobes of the cerebral cortex.

19. The non-neural cells that support, protect, and nourish cortical neurons are called _____ _____ . New evidence suggests that these cells may also play a role in _____ and _____ .

20. Compared to the cortexes of lower mammals, the human cortex has a _____ (smoother/more wrinkled) surface. This _____ (increases/decreases) the overall surface area of our brains.

21. List the four lobes of the brain.

    a. _____   c. _____

    b. _____   d. _____

Objective 16: Summarize some of the findings on the functions of the motor cortex and the sensory cortex, and discuss the importance of the association areas.

22. Electrical stimulation of one side of the _____ cortex, an arch-shaped region at the back of the _____ lobe, will produce movement on the opposite side of the body. The more precise the control needed, the _____ (smaller/ greater) amount of cortical space occupied. Research findings from studies involving _____ _____ , in which recording electrodes are implanted in this area of animals' brains, raise hopes that people who are _____ may one day be able to control machines directly with their _____ .

23. At the front of the parietal lobes lies the _____ cortex, which, when stimulated, elicits a sensation of _____ .

24. The more sensitive a body region, the greater the area of _____ _____ devoted to it.

25. Visual information is received in the _____ lobes, whereas auditory information is received in the _____ lobes.

26. Areas of the brain that don't receive sensory information or direct movement but, rather, integrate and interpret information received by other regions are known as _____ . Approximately

_____ of the human cortex is of this type. Such areas in the _____ lobe are involved in judging and planning, and in some aspects of personality. In the _____ lobe, these areas enable mathematical and spatial reasoning, and an area of the _____ lobe enables us to recognize faces.

Objective 17: Describe the five brain areas that would be involved if you read this sentence aloud.

27. Brain injuries may produce an impairment in language use called _____ . Studies of people with such impairments have shown that _____ _____ is involved in producing speech, _____ _____ is involved in understanding speech, and the _____ _____ is involved in recoding printed words into auditory form.

28. Although the mind's subsystems are localized in particular brain regions, the brain acts as a _____ _____ .

Objective 18: Discuss the brain's plasticity following injury or illness.

29. The quality of the brain that makes it possible for undamaged brain areas to take over the functions of damaged regions is known as _____ . This quality is especially apparent in the brains of _____ (young children/adolescents/adults).

30. Although most severed neurons _____ (will/will not) regenerate, neural tissue can _____ in response to damage. New evidence suggests that adult mice and humans _____ (can/cannot) generate new brain cells in two older brain regions; research also reveals the existence of master _____ cells in the developing fetal brain that can develop into any type of brain cell.

Objective 19: Describe split-brain research, and explain how it helps us understand the functions of our left and right hemispheres.

31. Because damage to it will impair language and understanding, the _____ hemisphere came to be known as the _____ hemisphere.

32. In treating several patients with severe epilepsy, Vogel and Bogen separated the two hemispheres of the brain by cutting the _____ _____ . When this structure is severed, the result is referred to as a

    _____ _____ .

33. In a split-brain patient, only the _____ hemisphere will be aware of an unseen object held in the left hand. In this case, the person would not be able to _____ the object. When different words are shown in the left and right visual fields, if the patient fixates on a point on the center line between the fields, the patient will be able to say only the word shown on the

    _____ .

Explain why a split-brain patient would be able to read aloud the word *pencil* flashed to his or her right visual field, but would be unable to identify a pencil by touch using only the left hand.

34. When the "two minds" of a split brain are at odds, the _____ hemisphere tries to rationalize what it doesn't understand. The _____ hemisphere often acts on autopilot. This phenomenon demonstrates that the _____ mind _____ (can/cannot) control our behavior.

35. Researchers studying undivided brains _____ (have/have not) found evidence of hemispheric specialization, which is also called _____ . For example, pictures are recognized more rapidly when they are

flashed to the _____ (right/left) hemisphere, whereas words are recognized faster and more accurately when flashed to the _____ (right/left) hemisphere.

36. Deaf people use the _____ hemisphere to process sign language.

Objective 20: Discuss the relationships among brain organization, handedness, and mortality.

37. In all cultures of the world, most of the human population is _____ (right/left)-handed. Genetic factors _____ (play/do not play) a role in handedness. This handedness bias is unique to humans and to our nearest _____ relatives.

38. With age, the percentage of left-handers _____ (increases/decreases). One controversial explanation of this difference is that _____ (right/left)-handers die at a younger age than their counterparts.

Identify several health risks that left-handers are more likely to have experienced.

PROGRESS TEST 1

Multiple-Choice Questions

Circle your answers to the following questions and check them with the answers beginning on page 61. If your answer is incorrect, read the explanation for why it is incorrect and then consult the appropriate pages of the text (in parentheses following the correct answer).

1. The axons of certain neurons are covered by a layer of fatty tissue that helps speed neural transmission. This tissue is:
   a. the glia.
   b. the myelin sheath.
   c. acetylcholine.
   d. an endorphin.

2. Heartbeat, digestion, and other self-regulating bodily functions are governed by the:
   a. voluntary nervous system.
   b. autonomic nervous system.
   c. sympathetic division of the autonomic nervous system.
   d. somatic nervous system.

3. A strong stimulus can increase the:
   a. speed of the impulse the neuron fires.
   b. intensity of the impulse the neuron fires.
   c. number of times the neuron fires.
   d. threshold that must be reached before the neuron fires.

4. The pain of heroin withdrawal may be attributable to the fact that:
   a. under the influence of heroin the brain ceases production of endorphins.
   b. under the influence of heroin the brain ceases production of all neurotransmitters.
   c. during heroin withdrawal the brain's production of all neurotransmitters is greatly increased.
   d. heroin destroys endorphin receptors in the brain.

5. The brain research technique that involves monitoring the brain's usage of glucose is called (in abbreviated form) the:
   a. PET scan.   c. EEG.
   b. fMRI.   d. MRI.

6. In a resting state, the axon is:
   a. depolarized, with mostly negatively charged ions outside and positively charged ions inside.
   b. depolarized, with mostly positively charged ions outside and negatively charged ions inside.
   c. polarized, with mostly negatively charged ions outside and positively charged ions inside.
   d. polarized, with mostly positively charged ions outside and negatively charged ions inside.

7. Though there is no single "control center" for emotions, their regulation is primarily attributed to the brain region known as the:
   a. limbic system.   c. brainstem.
   b. reticular formation. d. cerebellum.

8. Which is the correct sequence in the transmission of a simple reflex?
   a. sensory neuron → interneuron → sensory neuron
   b. interneuron → motor neuron → sensory neuron
   c. sensory neuron → interneuron → motor neuron
   d. interneuron → sensory neuron → motor neuron

9. Damage to _____ will usually cause a person to lose the ability to comprehend language.
   a. the angular gyrus
   b. Broca's area
   c. Wernicke's area
   d. frontal lobe association areas

10. Which of the following is typically controlled by the right hemisphere?
    a. language
    b. learned voluntary movements
    c. arithmetic reasoning
    d. perceptual tasks

11. Dr. Hernandez is studying neurotransmitter abnormalities in depressed patients. She would most likely describe herself as a:
    a. personality psychologist.
    b. phrenologist.
    c. psychoanalyst.
    d. biological psychologist.

12. The increasing complexity of animals' behavior is accompanied by a(n):
    a. increase in the size of the brainstem.
    b. decrease in the ratio of brain to body weight.
    c. increase in the size of the frontal lobes.
    d. increase in the amount of association area.

13. Voluntary movements, such as writing with a pencil, are directed by the:
    a. sympathetic nervous system.
    b. somatic nervous system.
    c. parasympathetic nervous system.
    d. autonomic nervous system.

14. A neuron will generate action potentials more often when it:
    a. remains below its threshold.
    b. receives an excitatory input.
    c. receives more excitatory than inhibitory inputs.
    d. is stimulated by a neurotransmitter.

15. Which is the correct sequence in the transmission of a neural impulse?
    a. axon → dendrite → cell body → synapse
    b. dendrite → axon → cell body → synapse
    c. synapse → axon → dendrite → cell body
    d. dendrite → cell body → axon → synapse

16. Chemical messengers produced by endocrine glands are called:
    a. agonists.   c. hormones.
    b. neurotransmitters.   d. enzymes.

17. Following a head injury, a person has ongoing difficulties staying awake. Most likely, the damage occurred to the:
    a. thalamus.   c. reticular formation.
    b. corpus callosum.   d. cerebellum.

18. (Thinking Critically) Based on research, which of the following seems true about the specialized functions of the right and left hemispheres?
    a. They are more clear-cut in men than in women.
    b. They are more clear-cut in women than in men.
    c. Most complex tasks emerge from the activity of one or the other hemisphere.
    d. Most complex activities emerge from the integrated activity of both hemispheres.

19. Cortical areas that are not primarily concerned with sensory, motor, or language functions are:
    a. called projection areas.
    b. called association areas.
    c. located mostly in the parietal lobe.
    d. located mostly in the temporal lobe.

20. In the brain, learning occurs as experience strengthens certain connections in cell work groups called:
    a. action potentials.   c. endocrine systems.
    b. neural networks.   d. dendrites.

Matching Items

Match each structure or technique with its corresponding function or description.

Structures

_____ 1. hypothalamus
_____ 2. lesion
_____ 3. EEG
_____ 4. fMRI
_____ 5. reticular formation
_____ 6. MRI
_____ 7. thalamus
_____ 8. corpus callosum
_____ 9. cerebellum
_____ 10. amygdala
_____ 11. medulla

Functions or Descriptions

a. amplified recording of brain waves
b. technique that uses radio waves and magnetic fields to image brain anatomy
c. serves as sensory switchboard
d. contains reward centers
e. tissue destruction
f. technique that uses radio waves and magnetic fields to show brain function
g. helps control arousal
h. links the cerebral hemispheres
i. influences rage and fear
j. regulates breathing and heartbeat
k. enables coordinated movement

PROGRESS TEST 2

Progress Test 2 should be completed during a final chapter review. Answer the following questions after you thoroughly understand the correct answers for the section reviews and Progress Test 1.

Multiple-Choice Questions

1. The visual cortex is located in the:
   a. occipital lobe.
   b. temporal lobe.
   c. frontal lobe.
   d. parietal lobe.

2. Which of the following is typically controlled by the left hemisphere?
   a. spatial reasoning
   b. word recognition
   c. the left side of the body
   d. perceptual skills

3. When Sandy scalded her toe in a tub of hot water, the pain message was carried to her spinal cord by the _____ nervous system.
   a. somatic
   b. sympathetic
   c. parasympathetic
   d. central

4. Which of the following are/is governed by the simplest neural pathways?
   a. emotions
   b. physiological drives, such as hunger
   c. reflexes
   d. movements, such as walking

5. Melissa has just completed running a marathon. She is so elated that she feels little fatigue or discomfort. Her lack of pain is probably the result of the release of:
   a. ACh.
   b. endorphins.
   c. dopamine.
   d. norepinephrine.

6. Parkinson's disease involves:
   a. the death of nerve cells that produce a vital neurotransmitter.
   b. impaired function in the right hemisphere only.
   c. impaired function in the left hemisphere only.
   d. excess production of the neurotransmitters dopamine and acetylcholine.

7. The technique that uses magnetic fields and radio waves to produce computer images of structures within the brain is called:
   a. the EEG.
   b. a lesion.
   c. a PET scan.
   d. MRI.

8. The myelin sheath that is on some neurons:
   a. increases the speed of neural transmission.
   b. slows neural transmission.
   c. regulates the release of neurotransmitters.
   d. does a. and c.

9. During an action potential, the electrical state of the axon becomes:
   a. polarized, as positively charged ions are admitted.
   b. polarized, as negatively charged ions are admitted.
   c. depolarized, as positively charged ions are admitted.
   d. depolarized, as negatively charged ions are admitted.

10. The neurotransmitter acetylcholine (ACh) is most likely to be found:
    a. at the junction between sensory neurons and muscle fibers.
    b. at the junction between motor neurons and muscle fibers.
    c. at junctions between interneurons.
    d. in all of the above locations.

11. The gland that regulates body growth is the:
    a. adrenal.
    b. thyroid.
    c. hypothalamus.
    d. pituitary.

12. Epinephrine and norepinephrine are _____ that are released by the _____ gland.
    a. neurotransmitters; pituitary
    b. hormones; pituitary
    c. neurotransmitters; thyroid
    d. hormones; adrenal

13. Jessica experienced difficulty keeping her balance after receiving a blow to the back of her head. It is likely that she injured her:
    a. medulla.
    b. thalamus.
    c. hypothalamus.
    d. cerebellum.

14. Moruzzi and Magoun caused a cat to lapse into a coma by severing neural connections between the cortex and the:
    a. reticular formation.
    b. hypothalamus.
    c. thalamus.
    d. cerebellum.

15. Research has found that the amount of representation in the motor cortex reflects the:
    a. size of the body parts.
    b. degree of precise control required by each of the parts.
    c. sensitivity of the body region.
    d. area of the occipital lobe being stimulated by the environment.

16. The effect of a drug that is an agonist is to:
    a. cause the brain to stop producing certain neurotransmitters.
    b. mimic a particular neurotransmitter.
    c. block a particular neurotransmitter.
    d. disrupt a neuron's all-or-none firing pattern.

17. The nerve fibers that enable communication between the right and left cerebral hemispheres and that have been severed in split-brain patients form a structure called the:
    a. reticular formation.   c. corpus callosum.
    b. association areas.   d. parietal lobes.

18. Beginning at the front of the brain and moving toward the back of the head, then down the skull and back around to the front, which of the following is the correct order of the cortical regions?
    a. occipital lobe; temporal lobe; parietal lobe; frontal lobe
    b. temporal lobe; frontal lobe; parietal lobe; occipital lobe
    c. frontal lobe; occipital lobe; temporal lobe; parietal lobe
    d. frontal lobe; parietal lobe; occipital lobe; temporal lobe

19. Following a nail gun wound to his head, Jack became more uninhibited, irritable, dishonest, and profane. It is likely that his personality change was the result of injury to his:
    a. parietal lobe.   c. occipital lobe.
    b. temporal lobe.   d. frontal lobe.

20. Three-year-old Marco suffered damage to the speech area of the brain's left hemisphere when he fell from a swing. Research suggests that:
    a. he may never speak again.
    b. his motor abilities may improve so that he can easily use sign language.
    c. his right hemisphere may take over much of the language function.
    d. his earlier experience with speech may enable him to continue speaking.

Matching Items
Match each structure or term with its corresponding function or description.

Structures or Terms

_____ 1. right hemisphere
_____ 2. brainstem
_____ 3. glial cells
_____ 4. aphasia
_____ 5. plasticity
_____ 6. Broca's area
_____ 7. Wernicke's area
_____ 8. limbic system
_____ 9. association areas
_____ 10. left hemisphere
_____ 11. angular gyrus

Functions or Descriptions

a. controls speech production
b. specializes in rationalizing reactions
c. translates writing into speech
d. specializes in spatial relations
e. brain cells that provide nutrients and insulating myelin
f. language disorder
g. oldest part of the brain
h. regulates emotion
i. the brain's capacity for modification
j. responsible for language comprehension
k. brain areas involved in higher mental functions

In the diagrams to the right, the numbers refer to brain locations that have been damaged. Match each location with its probable effect on behavior.

Location	Behavioral Effect
_____ **1.**	**a.** vision disorder
_____ **2.**	**b.** insensitivity to touch
_____ **3.**	**c.** motor paralysis
_____ **4.**	**d.** hearing problem
_____ **5.**	**e.** lack of coordination
_____ **6.**	**f.** abnormal hunger
_____ **7.**	**g.** split brain
_____ **8.**	**h.** sleep/arousal
_____ **9.**	disorder
	i. altered personality

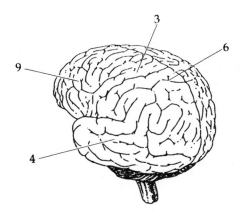

PSYCHOLOGY APPLIED

Answer these questions the day before an exam as a final check on your understanding of the chapter's terms and concepts.

Multiple-Choice Questions

1. A biological psychologist would be *more* likely to study:
   a. how you learn to express emotions.
   b. how to help people overcome emotional disorders.
   c. life-span changes in the expression of emotion.
   d. the chemical changes that accompany emotions.

2. The part of the human brain that is most like that of a fish is the:
   a. cortex.
   b. limbic system.
   c. brainstem.
   d. right hemisphere.

3. You are able to pull your hand quickly away from hot water before pain is felt because:
   a. movement of the hand is a reflex that involves intervention of the spinal cord only.
   b. movement of the hand does not require intervention by the central nervous system.
   c. the brain reacts quickly to prevent severe injury.
   d. the autonomic division of the peripheral nervous system intervenes to speed contraction of the muscles of the hand.

4. In order to pinpoint the location of a tumor, a neurosurgeon electrically stimulated parts of the patient's sensory cortex. If the patient was conscious during the procedure, which of the following was probably experienced?
   a. "hearing" faint sounds
   b. "seeing" random visual patterns
   c. movement of the arms or legs
   d. a sense of having the skin touched

5. If Dr. Rogers wishes to conduct an experiment on the effects of stimulating the reward centers of a rat's brain, he should insert an electrode into the:
   a. thalamus.
   b. sensory cortex.
   c. hypothalamus.
   d. corpus callosum.

6. A split-brain patient has a picture of a knife flashed to her left hemisphere and that of a fork to her right hemisphere. She will be able to:
   a. identify the fork using her left hand.
   b. identify a knife using her left hand.
   c. identify a knife using either hand.
   d. identify a fork using either hand.

7. Several shy neurons send an inhibitory message to neighboring neuron Joni. At the same time, a larger group of party-going neurons send Joni excitatory messages. What will Joni do?
   a. fire, assuming that her threshold has been reached
   b. not fire, even if her threshold has been reached
   c. enter a refractory period
   d. become hyperpolarized

8. Following Jayshree's near-fatal car accident, her physician noticed that the pupillary reflex of her eyes was abnormal. This *may* indicate that Jayshree's _____ was damaged in the accident.
   a. occipital cortex
   b. autonomic nervous system
   c. left temporal lobe
   d. cerebellum

9. Anton is applying for a technician's job with a neurosurgeon. In trying to impress his potential employer with his knowledge of the brain, he says, "After my father's stroke I knew immediately that the blood clot had affected his left cerebral hemisphere because he no longer recognized a picture of his friend." Should Anton be hired?
   a. Yes. Anton obviously understands brain structure and function.
   b. No. The right hemisphere, not the left, specializes in picture recognition.
   c. Yes. Although blood clots never form in the left hemisphere, Anton should be rewarded for recognizing the left hemisphere's role in picture recognition.
   d. No. Blood clots never form in the left hemisphere, and the right hemisphere is more involved than the left in recognizing pictures.

10. Which of the following is *not* true regarding brain organization and handedness?
    a. If a person has a left-handed identical twin, odds are that he or she will also be left-handed.
    b. Right-handedness is far more common than left-handedness throughout the world.
    c. On average, right-handers live longer than left-handers.
    d. Left-handers are more common than usual among people with reading disabilities.

11. Dr. Johnson briefly flashed a picture of a key in the right visual field of a split-brain patient. The patient could probably:
    a. verbally report that a key was seen.
    b. write the word *key* using the left hand.
    c. draw a picture of a key using the left hand.
    d. do none of the above.

12. In primitive vertebrate animals, the brain primarily regulates _____ ; in lower mammals, the brain enables _____ .
    a. emotion; memory
    b. memory; emotion
    c. survival functions; emotion
    d. reproduction; emotion

13. Since Malcolm has been taking a drug prescribed by his doctor, he no longer enjoys the little pleasures of life, such as eating and drinking. His doctor explains that this is because the drug:
    a. triggers release of dopamine.
    b. inhibits release of dopamine.
    c. triggers release of ACh.
    d. inhibits release of ACh.

14. A scientist from another planet wishes to study the simplest brain mechanisms underlying emotion and memory. You recommend that the scientist study the:
    a. brainstem of a frog.
    b. limbic system of a dog.
    c. cortex of a monkey.
    d. cortex of a human.

15. Which of the following was a major problem with phrenology?
    a. It was "ahead of its time" and no one believed it could be true.
    b. The brain is not neatly organized into structures that correspond to our categories of behavior.
    c. The brains of humans and animals are much less similar than the theory implied.
    d. All of the above were problems with phrenology.

16. I am a relatively slow-acting (but long-lasting) chemical messenger carried throughout the body by the bloodstream. What am I?
    a. a hormone
    b. a neurotransmitter
    c. acetylcholine
    d. dopamine

17. Your brother has been taking prescription medicine and experiencing a number of unpleasant side effects, including unusually rapid heartbeat and excessive perspiration. It is likely that the medicine is exaggerating activity in the:
    a. reticular formation.
    b. sympathetic nervous system.
    c. parasympathetic nervous system.
    d. amygdala.

18. Dr. Frankenstein made a mistake during neurosurgery on his monster. After the operation, the monster "saw" with his ears and "heard" with his eyes. It is likely that Dr. Frankenstein "rewired" neural connections in the monster's:
    a. hypothalamus.
    b. cerebellum.
    c. amygdala.
    d. thalamus.

19. A bodybuilder friend suddenly seems to have grown several inches in height. You suspect that your friend's growth spurt has occurred because he has been using drugs that affect the:
    a. pituitary gland.
    b. thalamus.
    c. adrenal glands.
    d. medulla.

20. Raccoons have much more precise control of their paws than dogs. You would expect that raccoons have more cortical space dedicated to "paw control" in the _____ of their brains.
    a. frontal lobes
    b. parietal lobes
    c. temporal lobes
    d. occipital lobes

Essay Question

Discuss how the endocrine and nervous systems become involved when a student feels stress—such as that associated with an upcoming final exam. (Use the space below to list the points you want to make, and organize them. Then write the essay on a separate sheet of paper.)

KEY TERMS

Writing Definitions

Using your own words, on a piece of paper write a brief definition or explanation of each of the following terms.

1. biological psychology
2. neuron
3. dendrites
4. axon
5. myelin sheath
6. action potential
7. threshold
8. synapse
9. neurotransmitters
10. acetylcholine (ACh)
11. endorphins
12. nervous system
13. central nervous system (CNS)
14. peripheral nervous system (PNS)
15. nerves
16. sensory neurons
17. interneurons
18. motor neurons
19. somatic nervous system
20. autonomic nervous system
21. sympathetic nervous system
22. parasympathetic nervous system
23. reflex

24. neural networks
25. endocrine system
26. hormones
27. adrenal glands
28. pituitary gland
29. lesion
30. electroencephalogram (EEG)
31. PET (positron emission tomography) scan
32. MRI (magnetic resonance imaging)
33. fMRI (functional MRI)
34. brainstem
35. medulla
36. reticular formation
37. thalamus
38. cerebellum
39. limbic system
40. amygdala

41. hypothalamus
42. cerebral cortex
43. glial cells
44. frontal lobes
45. parietal lobes
46. occipital lobes
47. temporal lobes
48. motor cortex
49. sensory cortex
50. association areas
51. aphasia
52. Broca's area
53. Wernicke's area
54. plasticity
55. corpus callosum
56. split brain

Cross-Check

As you learned in the Prologue, reviewing and overlearning of material are important to the learning process. After you have written the definitions of the key terms in this chapter, you should complete the crossword puzzle to ensure that you can reverse the process—recognize the term, given the definition.

ACROSS

3. The division of the nervous system that connects the brain and spinal cord to the body's sense receptors, muscles, and glands.

6. Located on the sides of the brain, these lobes contain the auditory areas, which receive information from the ears.

7. Located at the back of the frontal lobe, the part of the cortex that controls voluntary movement.

9. Located just behind the forehead, these lobes are involved in speaking and muscle movements and in making plans and judgments.

12. Glands that produce the hormones epinephrine and norepinephrine.

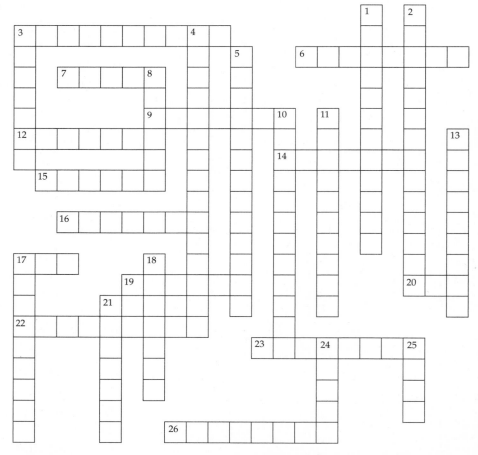

14. Located in the brainstem, this structure controls breathing and heartbeat.
15. The thin outer covering of the cerebral hemispheres.
16. Junction between the axon tip of the sending neuron and the dendrite or cell body of the receiving neuron.
17. Amplified recording of the waves of electrical activity of the brain.
19. Destruction of tissue.
20. Technique that uses magnetic fields and radio waves to produce computer-generated images of brain structures.
22. Located at the back and base of the brain, these lobes contain the visual cortex, which receives information from the eyes.
23. The part of the limbic system involved in regulation of the emotions of fear and rage.
26. Situated between the frontal and occipital lobes, these lobes contain the sensory cortex.

DOWN
1. Limbic system structure that regulates hunger, thirst, and body temperature and contains the so-called reward centers of the brain.
2. Large band of neural fibers that links the right and left hemispheres.
3. Technique that measures the levels of activity of different areas of the brain by tracing their consumption of a radioactive form of glucose.
4. Neural impulse generated by the movement of positively charged atoms in and out of channels in the axon's membrane.
5. Neurotransmitter that triggers muscle contractions.
8. Simple, automatic, inborn response to a sensory stimulus.
10. Doughnut-shaped neural system that plays an important role in the regulation of emotions and basic physiological drives.
11. Natural opiatelike neurotransmitters linked to pain control and to pleasure.
13. Division of the peripheral nervous system that controls the glands and the muscles of internal organs.
17. The body's slower chemical communication system, consisting of glands that secrete hormones into the bloodstream.
18. The brain and spinal cord, collectively, are the _____ nervous system.
21. An impairment of language as a result of damage to any of several cortical areas.
24. More numerous than cortical neurons, these cells of the brain guide neural connections and provide nutrients and insulating myelin.

25. Extension of a neuron that sends impulses to other nerve cells or to muscles or glands.

ANSWERS

Chapter Review

Introduction
1. biological
2. phrenology
3. biological psychologists

Neural Communication
1. biopsychosocial; subsystems; systems; system
2. biological; psychological; social-cultural
3. neurons
4. dendrites
5. axon; myelin sheath
6. a. dendrites
   b. cell body
   c. axon
   d. myelin sheath
7. action potential; axon
8. negatively; positively; resting potential; selectively permeable
9. positively; depolarized
10. refractory period; positively
11. excitatory; inhibitory; threshold; will not; all-or-none
12. does not
13. synapse; synaptic cleft (gap); Sir Charles Sherrington
14. neurotransmitters; ions
15. exciting; inhibiting; reuptake

A neural impulse is generated by excitatory signals minus inhibitory signals exceeding a certain threshold. The stimuli are received through the dendrites, combined in the cell body, and electrically transmitted in an all-or-none fashion down the length of the axon. When the combined signal reaches the end of the axon, chemical messengers called neurotransmitters are released into the synaptic cleft, or gap, between two neurons. Neurotransmitter molecules bind to receptor sites on the dendrites of neighboring neurons and have either an excitatory or inhibitory influence on that neuron's tendency to generate its own neural impulse.

16. dopamine; serotonin; norepinephrine; gamma-aminobutyric acid (GABA); glutamate
17. acetylcholine (ACh)

18. endorphins; heroin; morphine

19. agonists; receptor sites; antagonists; opiates; curare

20. blood-brain barrier

21. Parkinson's; dopamine; L-dopa

The Nervous System

1. nervous system

2. central; peripheral

3. nerves

4. sensory; interneurons

5. motor

6. somatic

7. autonomic

8. sympathetic

9. parasympathetic

The sympathetic division of the autonomic nervous system becomes aroused in response to an emergency. The physiological changes that occur include accelerated heartbeat, elevated blood sugar, dilation of arteries, slowing of digestion, and increased perspiration to cool the body. When the emergency is over, the parasympathetic nervous system produces the opposite physical reactions.

10. reflexes; spinal cord; knee-jerk; pain

From sensory receptors in the skin the message travels via sensory neurons to an interneuron in the spinal cord, which in turn activates a motor neuron. This motor neuron causes the muscles in the hand to contract, and the person jerks his or her hand away from the heat.

11. neural networks

The Endocrine System

1. endocrine system; hormones; slower; a longer time

2. adrenal; epinephrine; norepinephrine

3. pituitary; hypothalamus; growth

The hypothalamus in the brain influences secretions by the pituitary. The pituitary regulates other endocrine glands, which release hormones that influence behavior. The hypothalamus monitors these changes in blood chemistry and thereby adjusts its inputs to the pituitary.

The Brain

1. lesions; clinical observation

2. electroencephalogram (EEG)

3. PET scan

By depicting the brain's consumption of radioactively labeled glucose, the PET scan allows researchers to see which brain areas are most active as a person performs various tasks. This provides additional information on the specialized functions of various regions of the brain.

4. MRI (magnetic resonance imaging)

5. functional MRI; anterior cingulate cortex; urges

6. brainstem

7. medulla; breathing; heartbeat; pons

8. brainstem

9. reticular formation; arousal; alert (awake); coma

10. thalamus; smell; medulla; cerebellum

11. cerebellum; nonverbal learning; balance

12. conscious; outside

13. limbic; hippocampus

14. amygdala

15. psychosurgery; seldom

16. hypothalamus; hunger, thirst, body temperature (or sex); hormones; pituitary; reward

17. addictive; reward deficiency syndrome

18. cerebral cortex; information-processing

19. glial cells; learning; thinking

20. more wrinkled; increases

21. a. frontal lobe
    b. parietal lobe
    c. occipital lobe
    d. temporal lobe

22. motor; frontal; greater; neural prosthetics; paralyzed; thoughts (or brains)

23. sensory; touch

24. sensory cortex

25. occipital; temporal

26. association areas; three-fourths; frontal; parietal; temporal

27. aphasia; Broca's area; Wernicke's area; angular gyrus

28. unified whole

29. plasticity; young children

30. will not; reorganize; can; stem

31. left; dominant (major)

32. corpus callosum; split brain

33. right; name; right

The word *pencil* when flashed to a split-brain patient's right visual field would project only to the opposite, or left, hemisphere of the patient's brain.

Because the left hemisphere contains the language control centers of the brain, the patient would be able to read the word aloud. The left hand is controlled by the right hemisphere of the brain. Because the right hemisphere would not be aware of the word, it would not be able to guide the left hand in identifying a pencil by touch.

34. left; right; unconscious; can

35. have; lateralization; right; left

36. left

37. right; play; primate

38. decreases; left

Left-handers are more likely to have experienced premature or stressful births. They also have more headaches and accidents, use more tobacco and alcohol, and suffer more immune system problems.

Progress Test 1

Multiple-Choice Questions

1. **b.** is the answer. (p. 55)
   a. Glial cells support and nourish nerve cells.
   c. Acetylcholine is a neurotransmitter that triggers muscle contraction.
   d. Endorphins are opiatelike neurotransmitters linked to pain control and to pleasure.

2. **b.** is the answer. The autonomic nervous system controls internal functioning, including heartbeat, digestion, and glandular activity. (p. 62)
   a. The functions mentioned are all automatic, not voluntary, so this answer cannot be correct.
   c. This answer is incorrect because most organs are affected by both divisions of the autonomic nervous system.
   d. The somatic nervous system transmits sensory input to the central nervous system and enables voluntary control of skeletal muscles.

3. **c.** is the answer. Stimulus strength can affect only the number of times a neuron fires or the number of neurons that fire. (p. 56)
   a., b., & d. These answers are incorrect because firing is an all-or-none response, so intensity remains the same regardless of stimulus strength. Nor can stimulus strength change the neuronal threshold or the impulse speed.

4. **a.** is the answer. Endorphins are neurotransmitters that function as natural painkillers. When the body has a supply of artificial painkillers such as heroin, endorphin production stops. (p. 59)

   b. The production of neurotransmitters other than endorphins does not cease.
   c. Neurotransmitter production does not increase during withdrawal.
   d. Heroin makes use of the same receptor sites as endorphins.

5. **a.** is the answer. The PET scan measures glucose consumption in different areas of the brain to determine their levels of activity. (p. 69)
   b. The fMRI compares MRI scans taken less than a second apart to reveal brain anatomy and function.
   c. The EEG is a measure of electrical activity in the brain.
   d. MRI uses magnetic fields and radio waves to produce computer-generated images of soft tissues of the body.

6. **d.** is the answer. (pp. 55–56)

7. **a.** is the answer. (p. 72)
   b. The reticular formation is linked to arousal.
   c. The brainstem governs the mechanisms of basic survival—heartbeat and breathing, for example—and has many other roles.
   d. The cerebellum coordinates movement output and balance.

8. **c.** is the answer. In a simple reflex, a sensory neuron carries the message that a sensory receptor has been stimulated to an interneuron in the spinal cord. The interneuron responds by activating motor neurons that will enable the appropriate response. (p. 63)

9. **c.** is the answer. Wernicke's area is involved in comprehension, and people with aphasia who have damage to Wernicke's area are unable to understand what is said to them. (p. 81)
   a. The angular gyrus translates printed words into speech sounds; damage would result in the inability to read aloud.
   b. Broca's area is involved in the physical production of speech; damage would result in the inability to speak fluently.
   d. The cortex's association areas are involved in, among other things, processing language; damage to these areas wouldn't specifically affect comprehension.

10. **d.** is the answer. (p. 88)
    a. In most persons, language is primarily a left hemisphere function.
    b. Learned movements are unrelated to hemispheric specialization.
    c. Arithmetic reasoning is generally a left hemisphere function.

11. **d.** is the answer. Biological psychologists study the links between biology (in this case, neurotransmitters) and psychology (depression, in this example). (p. 54)

12. **d.** is the answer. As animals increase in complexity, there is an increase in the amount of association areas. (p. 79)
    a. The brainstem controls basic survival functions and is not related to the complexity of an animal's behavior.
    b. The ratio of body and brain weight is a poor predictor of behavior complexity.
    c. The frontal lobe is concerned with personality, planning, and other mental functions, but its size is unrelated to intelligence or the complexity of behavior.

13. **b.** is the answer. (p. 62)
    a., c., & d. The autonomic nervous system, which is divided into the sympathetic and parasympathetic divisions, is concerned with regulating basic bodily maintenance functions.

14. **c.** is the answer. (p. 56)
    a. An action potential will occur only when the neuron's threshold is *exceeded.*
    b. An excitatory input that does not reach the neuron's threshold will not trigger an action potential.
    d. This answer is incorrect because some neurotransmitters inhibit a neuron's readiness to fire.

15. **d.** is the answer. A neuron receives incoming stimuli on its dendrites and cell body. These electrochemical signals are combined in the cell body, generating an impulse that travels down the axon, causing the release of neurotransmitter substances into the synaptic cleft or gap. (pp. 55–57)

16. **c.** is the answer. (p. 65)
    a. Agonists are drugs that excite neural firing by mimicking a particular neurotransmitter.
    b. Neurotransmitters are the chemicals involved in synaptic transmission in the nervous system.
    d. Enzymes are chemicals that facilitate various chemical reactions throughout the body but are not involved in communication within the endocrine system.

17. **c.** is the answer. The reticular formation plays an important role in arousal. (p. 71)
    a. The thalamus relays sensory input.
    b. The corpus callosum links the two cerebral hemispheres.
    d. The cerebellum is involved in coordination of movement output and balance.

18. **d.** is the answer. (p. 87)

19. **b.** is the answer. Association areas interpret, inte-grate, and act on information from other areas of the cortex. (p. 79)

20. **b.** is the answer. (p. 64)
    a. Action potentials are neural impulses that occur in all forms of communication in the nervous system.
    c. The endocrine system is the body's glandular system of chemical communication.
    d. Dendrites are the branching extensions of neurons that receive messages from other nerve cells.

Matching Items

1. d (p. 73)	**5.** g (p. 71)	**9.** k (p. 72)
2. e (p. 68)	**6.** b (p. 69)	**10.** i (p. 72)
3. a (p. 68)	**7.** c (p. 72)	**11.** j (p. 71)
4. f (p. 69)	**8.** h (p. 84)	

Progress Test 2

Multiple-Choice Questions

1. **a.** is the answer. The visual cortex is located at the very back of the brain. (p. 76)

2. **b.** is the answer. (p. 88)
   a., c., & d. Spatial reasoning, perceptual skills, and the left side of the body are primarily influenced by the right hemisphere.

3. **a.** is the answer. Sensory neurons in the somatic nervous system relay such messages. (p. 62)
   b. & c. These divisions of the autonomic nervous system are concerned with the regulation of bodily maintenance functions such as heartbeat, digestion, and glandular activity.
   d. The spinal cord itself is part of the central nervous system, but the message is carried to the spinal cord by the somatic division of the peripheral nervous system.

4. **c.** is the answer. As automatic responses to stimuli, reflexes are the simplest complete units of behavior and require only simple neural pathways. (p. 63)
   a., b., & d. Emotions, drives, and voluntary movements are all behaviors that are much more complex than reflexes and therefore involve much more complicated neural pathways.

5. **b.** is the answer. Endorphins are neurotransmitters that function as natural painkillers and are evidently involved in the "runner's high" and other situations in which discomfort or fatigue is expected but not experienced. (p. 59)

a. ACh is a neurotransmitter involved in muscular control.

c. Dopamine is a neurotransmitter involved in, among other things, motor control.

d. Norepinephrine is an adrenal hormone released to help us respond in moments of danger.

6. **a.** is the answer. Parkinson's disease causes the death of brain tissue that produces dopamine. (p. 60)

   b. & c. This disease affects both hemispheres of the cortex.

   d. This disease causes insufficient production of the neurotransmitters.

7. **d.** is the answer. (p. 69)

   a. The EEG is an amplified recording of the brain's electrical activity.

   b. A lesion is destruction of tissue.

   c. The PET scan is a visual display of brain activity that detects the movement of a radioactive form of glucose as the brain performs a task.

8. **a.** is the answer. (p. 55)

   c. & d. Myelin sheaths are not involved in regulating the release of neurotransmitters.

9. **c.** is the answer. (pp. 55–56)

10. **b.** is the answer. ACh is a neurotransmitter that causes the contraction of muscle fibers when stimulated by motor neurons. This function explains its location. (p. 58)

    a. & c. Sensory neurons and interneurons do not directly stimulate muscle fibers.

11. **d.** is the answer. The pituitary regulates body growth, and some of its secretions regulate the release of hormones from other glands. (p. 66)

    a. The adrenal glands are stimulated by the autonomic nervous system to release epinephrine and norepinephrine.

    b. The thyroid gland produces a hormone that controls the rates of various chemical reactions in the body.

    c. The hypothalamus regulates the pituitary but does not itself directly regulate growth.

12. **d.** is the answer. Also known as adrenaline and noradrenaline, epinephrine and norepinephrine are hormones released by the adrenal glands. (p. 66)

13. **d.** is the answer. The cerebellum is involved in the coordination of voluntary muscular movements. (p. 72)

    a. The medulla regulates breathing and heartbeat.

b. The thalamus relays sensory inputs to the appropriate higher centers of the brain.

c. The hypothalamus is concerned with the regulation of basic drives and emotions.

14. **a.** is the answer. The reticular formation controls arousal via its connections to the cortex. Thus, separating the two produces a coma. (p. 71)

    b., c., & d. None of these structures controls arousal. The hypothalamus regulates hunger, thirst, sexual behavior, and other basic drives; the thalamus is a sensory relay station; and the cerebellum is involved in the coordination of voluntary movement.

15. **b.** is the answer. (pp. 77–78)

    c. & d. These refer to the sensory cortex.

16. **b.** is the answer. (pp. 59–60)

    a. Abuse of certain drugs, such as heroin, may have this effect.

    c. This describes the effect of an antagonist.

    d. Drugs do not have this effect on neurons.

17. **c.** is the answer. The corpus callosum is a large band of neural fibers linking the right and left cerebral hemispheres. To sever the corpus callosum is in effect to split the brain. (p. 84)

18. **d.** is the answer. The frontal lobe is in the front of the brain. Just behind is the parietal lobe. The occipital lobe is located at the very back of the head and just below the parietal lobe. Next to the occipital lobe and toward the front of the head is the temporal lobe. (p. 76)

19. **d.** is the answer. As demonstrated in the case of Phineas Gage, injury to the frontal lobe may produce such changes in personality. (p. 80)

    a. Damage to the parietal lobe might disrupt functions involving the sensory cortex.

    b. Damage to the temporal lobe might impair hearing.

    c. Occipital damage might impair vision.

20. **c.** is the answer. (p. 82)

Matching Items

1. d (p. 86)	**5.** i (p. 82)	**9.** k (p. 79)
2. g (p. 71)	**6.** a (p. 81)	**10.** b (p. 86)
3. e (p. 75)	**7.** j (p. 81)	**11.** c (p. 81)
4. f (p. 80)	**8.** h (p. 72)	

Brain Damage Diagram (pp. 67–82)

1. a	**4.** d	**7.** f
2. h	**5.** e	**8.** g
3. c	**6.** b	**9.** i

Psychology Applied

Multiple-Choice Questions

1. **d.** is the answer. Biological psychologists study the links between biology (chemical changes in this example) and behavior (emotions in this example). (p. 54)

   a., b., & c. Experimental, clinical, and developmental psychologists would be more concerned with the learning of emotional expressions, the treatment of emotional disorders, and life-span changes in emotions, respectively.

2. **c.** is the answer. The brainstem is the oldest and most primitive region of the brain. It is found in lower vertebrates, such as fish, as well as in humans and other mammals. The structures mentioned in the other choices are associated with stages of brain evolution beyond that seen in the fish. (p. 70)

3. **a.** is the answer. Since this reflex is an automatic response and involves only the spinal cord, the hand is jerked away before the brain has even received the information that causes the sensation of pain. (p. 63)

   b. The spinal cord, which organizes simple reflexes such as this one, is part of the central nervous system.

   c. The brain is not involved in directing spinal reflexes.

   d. The autonomic nervous system controls the glands and the muscles of the internal organs; it does not influence the skeletal muscles controlling the hand.

4. **d.** is the answer. Stimulation of the sensory cortex elicits a sense of touch, as the experiments of Penfield demonstrated. (p. 78)

   a., b., & c. Hearing, seeing, or movement might be expected if the temporal, occipital, and motor regions of the cortex, respectively, were stimulated.

5. **c.** is the answer. As Olds and Milner discovered, electrical stimulation of the hypothalamus is a highly reinforcing event because it is the location of the animal's reward centers. The other brain regions mentioned are not associated with reward centers. (p. 73)

6. **a.** is the answer. The left hand, controlled by the right hemisphere, would be able to identify the fork, the picture of which is flashed to the right hemisphere. (pp. 84–85)

7. **a.** is the answer.(p. 56)

   b. Because she has reached her threshold, she will probably fire.

   c. The refractory period is a resting period. Because Joni has received a large number of excitatory messages, she will not be at rest.

   d. *Hyperpolarization* is not a term.

8. **b.** is the answer. Simple reflexes, such as this one, are governed by activity in the autonomic nervous system. (p. 62)

   a. The occipital lobes process sensory messages from the eyes; they play no role in the reflexive response of the pupils to light.

   c. The left temporal lobe specializes in processing language.

   d. The cerebellum specializes in coordinating movement.

9. **b.** is the answer. (p. 88)

   a., c., & d. The left hemisphere does not specialize in picture recognition. And blood clots can form anywhere in the brain.

10. **a.** is the answer. In fact, handedness is one of only a few traits that identical twins are not especially likely to share. (pp. 89–90)

11. **a.** is the answer. The right visual field projects directly to the verbal left hemisphere. (p. 85)

    b. & c. The left hand is controlled by the right hemisphere, which, in this situation, would be unaware of the word since the picture has been flashed to the left hemisphere.

12. **c.** is the answer. (p. 70)

    d. Reproduction is only one of the basic survival functions the brain regulates.

13. **b.** is the answer. (pp. 58, 74)

    a. By triggering release of dopamine, such a drug would probably *enhance* Malcolm's enjoyment of the pleasures of life.

    c. & d. ACh is the neurotransmitter at synapses between motor neurons and muscle fibers.

14. **b.** is the answer. The hippocampus of the limbic system is involved in processing memory. The amygdala of the limbic system influences fear and anger. (p. 72)

    a. The brainstem controls vital functions such as breathing and heartbeat; it is not directly involved in either emotion or memory.

    c. & d. These answers are incorrect because the limbic system is an older brain structure than the cortex. Its involvement in emotions and memory is therefore more basic than that of the cortex.

15. b. is the answer. (p. 54)
a. "Ahead of its time" implies the theory had merit, which later research clearly showed it did not. Moreover, phrenology *was* accepted as an accurate theory of brain organization by many scientists.
c. Phrenology said nothing about the similarities of human and animal brains.

16. a. is the answer. (p. 65)
b., c., & d. Acetylcholine and dopamine are fast-acting neurotransmitters released at synapses, not in the bloodstream.

17. b. is the answer. Sympathetic arousal produces several effects, including accelerated heartbeat and excessive perspiration. (p. 62)
a. Stimulation of the reticular formation increases alertness, but would not necessarily accelerate heartbeat or cause excessive perspiration.
c. Arousal of the parasympathetic nervous system would have effects opposite to those stated.
d. If the medication were affecting his amygdala, your brother might experience emotions such as anger or fear at illogical times.

18. d. is the answer. The thalamus relays sensory messages from the eyes, ears, and other receptors to the appropriate projection areas of the cortex. "Rewiring" the thalamus, theoretically, could have the effects stated in this question. (p. 72)
a., b., & c. These brain structures are not directly involved in brain processes related to sensation or perception.

19. a. is the answer. Hormones of the pituitary gland regulate body growth. (p. 66)
b. & d. Because they are not endocrine glands, the thalamus and medulla are not influenced by hormones.
c. The adrenal glands produce hormones that provide energy during emergencies; they are not involved in regulating body growth.

20. a. is the answer. The motor cortex, which determines the precision with which various parts of the body can be moved, is located in the frontal lobes. (p. 77)
b. The parietal lobes contain the sensory cortex, which controls sensitivity to touch.
c. The temporal lobes contain the primary projection areas for hearing and, on the left side, are also involved in language use.
d. The occipital lobes contain the primary projection areas for vision.

Essay Question

The body's response to stress is regulated by the nervous system. As the date of the exam approaches, the stressed student's cerebral cortex activates the hypothalamus, triggering the release of hormones that in turn activate the sympathetic branch of the autonomic nervous system and the endocrine system. The autonomic nervous system controls involuntary bodily responses such as breathing, heartbeat, and digestion. The endocrine system contains glands that secrete hormones into the bloodstream that regulate the functions of body organs.

In response to activation by the hypothalamus, the student's pituitary gland would secrete a hormone which in turn triggers the release of epinephrine, norepinephrine, and other stress hormones from the adrenal glands. These hormones would help the student's body manage stress by making nutrients available to meet the increased demands for energy stores the body often faces in coping with stress. As these hormones activate the sympathetic division of the autonomic system, the body's fight-or-flight response occurs, including increased heart rate, breathing, and blood pressure and the suppression of digestion. After the exam date has passed, the student's body would attempt to restore its normal, pre-stress state. The parasympathetic branch of the autonomic system would slow the student's heartbeat and breathing and digestive processes would no longer be suppressed, perhaps causing the student to feel hungry.

Key Terms

Writing Definitions

1. **Biological psychology** is the study of the links between biology and behavior. (p. 54)

2. The **neuron**, or nerve cell, is the basic building block of the nervous system. (p. 55)

3. The **dendrites** of a neuron are the bushy, branching extensions that receive messages from other nerve cells and conduct impulses toward the cell body. (p. 55)

4. The **axon** of a neuron is the extension that sends impulses to other nerve cells or to muscles or glands. (p. 55)

5. The **myelin sheath** is a layer of fatty tissue that segmentally covers many axons and helps speed neural impulses. (p. 55)

6. An **action potential** is a neural impulse generated by the movement of positively charged atoms in and out of channels in the axon's membrane. (p. 55)

7. A neuron's **threshold** is the level of stimulation that must be exceeded in order for the neuron to fire, or generate an electrical impulse. (p. 56)

8. A **synapse** is the junction between the axon tip of the sending neuron and the dendrite or cell body of the receiving neuron. The tiny gap at this junction is called the synaptic gap or cleft. (p. 57)

9. **Neurotransmitters** are chemicals that are released into synaptic gaps and so *transmit neural messages* from neuron to neuron. (p. 57)

10. **Acetylcholine (ACh)** is a neurotransmitter that enables learning and memory and also triggers muscle contraction. (p. 58)

11. **Endorphins** are natural, opiatelike neurotransmitters linked to pain control and to pleasure. (p. 59)

    Memory aid: <u>End</u>orphins *end* pain.

12. The **nervous system** is the speedy, electrochemical communication system, consisting of all the nerve cells in the peripheral and central nervous systems. (p. 61)

13. The **central nervous system (CNS)** consists of the brain and spinal cord; it is located at the *center*, or internal core, of the body. (p. 61)

14. The **peripheral nervous system (PNS)** includes the sensory and motor neurons that connect the central nervous system to the body's sense receptors, muscles, and glands; it is at the *periphery* of the body relative to the brain and spinal cord. (p. 61)

15. **Nerves** are bundles of neural axons, which are part of the PNS, that connect the central nervous system with muscles, glands, and sense organs. (p. 62)

16. **Sensory neurons** carry information from the sense receptors to the central nervous system for processing. (p. 62)

17. **Interneurons** are the neurons of the central nervous system that link the sensory and motor neurons in the transmission of sensory inputs and motor outputs. (p. 62)

18. **Motor neurons** carry information and instructions for action from the central nervous system to muscles and glands. (p. 62)

19. The **somatic nervous system** is the division of the peripheral nervous system that enables voluntary control of the skeletal muscles; also called the skeletal nervous system. (p. 62)

20. The **autonomic nervous system** is the division of the peripheral nervous system that controls the glands and the muscles of internal organs and thereby controls internal functioning; it regulates the *automatic* behaviors necessary for survival. (p. 62)

21. The **sympathetic nervous system** is the division of the autonomic nervous system that arouses the body, mobilizing its energy in stressful situations. (p. 62)

22. The **parasympathetic nervous system** is the division of the autonomic nervous system that calms the body, conserving its energy. (p. 62)

23. A **reflex** is a simple, automatic, inborn response to a sensory stimulus; it is governed by a very simple neural pathway. (p. 63)

24. **Neural networks** are interconnected neural cells, the specific connections of which are strengthened as learning occurs. (p. 64)

25. The **endocrine system**, the body's "slower" chemical communication system, consists of glands that secrete hormones into the bloodstream. (p. 65)

26. **Hormones** are chemical messengers, mostly those manufactured by the endocrine glands, that are produced in one tissue and circulate through the bloodstream to their target tissues, on which they have specific effects. (p. 65)

27. The **adrenal glands** produce epinephrine and norepinephrine, hormones that prepare the body to deal with emergencies or stress. (p. 66)

28. The **pituitary gland**, under the influence of the hypothalamus, regulates growth and controls other endocrine glands; sometimes called the "master gland." (p. 66)

29. A **lesion** is destruction of tissue; studying the consequences of lesions in different regions of the brain—both surgically produced in animals and naturally occurring—helps researchers to determine the normal functions of these regions. (p. 68)

30. An **electroencephalogram (EEG)** is an amplified recording of the waves of electrical activity of the brain. *Encephalo* comes from a Greek word meaning "related to the brain." (p. 68)

31. The **PET (positron emission tomography) scan** measures the levels of activity of different areas of the brain by tracing their consumption of a radioactive form of glucose, the brain's fuel. (p. 69)

32. **MRI (magnetic resonance imaging)** uses magnetic fields and radio waves to produce computer-generated images that show brain structures more clearly. (p. 69)

33. In a **fMRI (functional magnetic resonance imaging)**, MRI scans taken less than a second apart are compared to reveal blood flow and, therefore, brain anatomy and function. (p. 69)

34. The **brainstem**, the oldest and innermost region of the brain, is an extension of the spinal cord and is the central core of the brain; its structures direct automatic survival functions. (p. 71)

35. Located in the brainstem, the **medulla** controls breathing and heartbeat. (p. 71)

36. Also part of the brainstem, the **reticular formation** is a nerve network that plays an important role in controlling arousal. (p. 71)

37. Located atop the brainstem, the **thalamus** routes incoming messages to the appropriate cortical centers and transmits replies to the medulla and cerebellum. (p. 72)

38. The **cerebellum** processes sensory input and coordinates movement output and balance. (p. 72)

39. A doughnut-shaped neural system, the **limbic system** is associated with emotions such as fear and aggression and basic physiological drives. (p. 72)

    Memory aid: Its name comes from the Latin word *limbus*, meaning "border"; the **limbic system** is at the border of the brainstem and cerebral hemispheres.

40. The **amygdala** is part of the limbic system and influences the emotions of fear and aggression. (p. 72)

41. Also part of the limbic system, the **hypothalamus** regulates hunger, thirst, body temperature, and sex; helps govern the endocrine system via the pituitary gland; and contains the so-called reward centers of the brain. (p. 73)

42. The **cerebral cortex** is a thin intricate covering of interconnected neural cells atop the cerebral hemispheres. The seat of information processing, the cortex is responsible for those complex functions that make us distinctively human. (p. 74)

    Memory aid: Cortex in Latin means "bark." As bark covers a tree, the **cerebral cortex** is the "bark of the brain."

43. More numerous than cortical neurons, the **glial cells** of the brain guide neural connections, provide nutrients and insulating myelin, and help remove excess ions and neurotransmitters. (p. 75)

44. Located at the front of the brain, just behind the forehead, the **frontal lobes** are involved in speaking and muscle movements and in making plans and judgments. (p. 76)

45. Situated between the frontal and occipital lobes, the **parietal lobes** contain the sensory cortex. (p. 76)

46. Located at the back and base of the brain, the **occipital lobes** contain the visual cortex, which receives information from the eyes. (p. 76)

47. Located on the sides of the brain, the **temporal lobes** contain the auditory areas, which receive information from the ears. (p. 76)

    Memory aid: The **temporal lobes** are located near the *temples*.

48. Located at the back of the frontal lobe, the **motor cortex** controls voluntary movement. (p. 77)

49. The **sensory cortex** is located at the front of the parietal lobes, just behind the motor cortex. It registers and processes body touch and movement sensations. (p. 78)

50. Located throughout the cortex, **association areas** of the brain are involved in higher mental functions, such as learning, remembering, and abstract thinking. (p. 79)

    Memory aid: Among their other functions, **association areas** of the cortex are involved in integrating, or *associating*, information from different areas of the brain.

51. **Aphasia** is an impairment of language as a result of damage to any of several cortical areas, including Broca's area and Wernicke's area. (p. 80)

52. **Broca's area**, located in the left frontal lobe, is involved in controlling the motor ability to produce speech. (p. 81)

53. **Wernicke's area**, located in the left temporal lobe, is involved in language comprehension and expression. (p. 81)

54. **Plasticity** is the brain's capacity for modification, as evidenced by brain reorganization following damage (especially in children). (p. 82)

55. The **corpus callosum** is the large band of neural fibers that links the right and left cerebral hemispheres. Without this band of nerve fibers, the two hemispheres could not interact. (p. 84)

56. **Split brain** is a condition in which the major connections between the two cerebral hemispheres (the corpus callosum) are severed, literally resulting in a split brain. (p. 84)

Cross-Check

ACROSS	DOWN
3. peripheral	**1.** hypothalamus
6. temporal	**2.** corpus callosum
7. motor	**3.** PET scan
9. frontal	**4.** action potential
12. adrenal	**5.** acetylcholine
14. medulla	**8.** reflex
15. cortex	**10.** limbic system
16. synapse	**11.** endorphins
17. EEG	**13.** autonomic
19. lesion	**17.** endocrine
20. MRI	**18.** central
22. occipital	**21.** aphasia
23. amygdala	**24.** glial
26. parietal	**25.** axon

FOCUS ON VOCABULARY AND LANGUAGE

Page 53: . . . to shoot a basketball. . . . This means to throw the ball, in the game of basketball, through the hoop. Science today is intensely focused on (*riveted on*) research involving the brain and how it accomplishes a wide variety of mental and physical tasks.

Page 53: . . . an ill-fated theory. . . . Myers is referring to the theory that bumps or lumps on the skull could reveal our personality (*phrenology*). It was a theory destined for failure (*ill-fated*), despite its popularity during the early 1800s.

Page 53 (caption): A *wrongheaded* theory. Even though phrenology was without any scientific merit (*wrongheaded*), it did suggest the idea that different parts of the brain influence a variety of functions and behaviors.

Neural Communication

Page 54: For scientists, it is a *happy fact of nature* that the information systems of humans and other animals operate similarly. . . . The structure and function of neurons are very similar in humans and other animals (e.g., squids and sea slugs) and this is a good thing (*a happy fact of nature*) for those researching the nervous system. Myers makes the important point about this similarity, noting that it would not be possible to tell the difference between a small piece of your brain tissue and that of a monkey.

Page 55: Its *building blocks* are **neurons,** or nerve cells.

Building blocks are the basic or fundamental parts (e.g., bricks) that make up a structure (e.g., a house). The structure of our nervous system, or neural information system, is made up of neurons (*its building blocks*).

Page 55: . . . the neural impulse travels at speeds ranging from a *sluggish* 2 miles per hour to a *breakneck* 200 or more miles per hour. The speed of the neural impulse ranges from extremely slow (*sluggish*) to very fast (a *breakneck* speed). Compared to the speed of electricity or sophisticated electronics systems your neural impulses travel at a relatively slow pace.

Page 56: . . . The first bit of the axon opens its gates, *rather like manhole covers flipping open,* and positively charged sodium ions flood through the membrane. The circular metal tops that cover entrances to sewer lines, water pipes, etc., are called *manhole covers.* When a neuron fires the resting axon no longer blocks access to positive sodium ions (*the security parameters change*) and consequently the axon begins to open its gates in sequence, much like a series of lids that open in succession (*like manhole covers flipping open*) allowing sodium ions in. The sequential opening of each channel is like a chain reaction with each event affecting the next, and so on (*like dominoes falling, each one tripping the next*).

Page 56: The mind *boggles . . . Boggle* means to startle, alarm, or surprise. Our minds are amazed (*boggled*) by the astounding complexity and intricate activity of the brain and nervous system.

Page 56: Most of these signals are *excitatory, somewhat like pushing a neuron's accelerator.* Other signals are *inhibitory, more like pushing its brake.* Myers is making a comparison between the effect of a neuron firing and the effect of speeding up a car when accelerating (*excitatory effect*) or slowing it down by applying the brake (*inhibitory effect*). He also likens excitatory signals to those who love social gatherings (*party animals*), and inhibitory signals to those who do not (*party poopers*); if those who want to have a party outvote those who don't, then the party (*action potential*) will happen (i.e., *the party's on*).

Page 56: How do we distinguish a gentle touch from a big hug? This question is concerned with how we become aware of the magnitude of a stimulus, from a soft stroke or pat (*gentle touch*) to a strong embrace (*big hug*). The answer is that the intensity of the stimulus is a function of the number and frequency of neurons firing. A strong stimulus (*big hug*) does not initiate (*trigger*) a more powerful or faster impulse than a weak stimulus (*gentle touch*); rather, it triggers more neurons to fire, and to fire more often.

Page 57: . . . these near-unions of neurons—"*protoplasmic kisses*". . . were another of nature's marvels. The reference here is to the fact that the axon terminal of one neuron is separated from the receiving neuron by a tiny space called the synaptic gap. Protoplasm is the material that constitutes all living cells, and the communication between cells is likened to a kiss between cells (*protoplasmic kisses*). The transmission between sender and receiver is via chemicals called neurotransmitters. The cells don't actually touch but send messages across the synaptic gap.

Page 59: . . . "*runner's high*" . . . This refers to the feeling of emotional well-being or euphoria (*high*) following vigorous exercise such as running or jogging and is the result of the release of opiatelike substances called endorphins.

Page 59: They *trigger* unpleasant, *lingering aftereffects.* For suppressing the body's own neurotransmitter production, *nature charges a price.* Mood-altering drugs, such as alcohol, nicotine, heroin, and morphine, all initiate (*trigger)* disagreeable changes that persist for a long period of time (*lingering aftereffects*). When flooded with these opiates, the brain stops producing its own endorphins (i.e., they suppress production), and for the addict who stops taking the drugs the cost may be a great deal of pain and agony (*nature charges a price*).

Page 59: **Agonists** excite. . . . **Antagonists** inhibit. An *agonist* drug molecule is enough like the neurotransmitter to imitate (*mimic*) its effects (for example, by

producing a temporary euphoric feeling—a "high") or it may prevent (*block*) the *reuptake* of the neurotransmitter (for example, too much ACh flooding the synapses causes muscle contractions, convulsions, or even death). An *antagonist* drug, on the other hand, can stop (*inhibit*) the release of a neurotransmitter (for example, preventing the release of ACh from the sending neuron can cause paralysis), or it may *occupy* the receptor sites on the receiving neuron so the neuron can't fire (for example, toxins such as curare fill the ACh receptor sites, and paralysis will result when the neurons can't fire).

Page 60: But some chemicals can *slither through* this [blood-brain] barrier. The *blood-brain barrier* is a system that blocks or obstructs unwanted chemicals circulating in the blood from getting into the brain (*the brain fences them out*). Some neurotransmitter substances (chemicals) such as L-dopa can slide or slip smoothly (*slither*) through the blood-brain barrier. The brain then transforms this raw material into dopamine (which cannot cross the blood-brain barrier), allowing many Parkinson's patients to obtain better muscle control.

The Nervous System

Page 62: Like an *automatic pilot,* this system may be consciously *overridden.* The autonomic nervous system automatically takes care of the operation of our internal organs much as a plane can be flown by the automatic (*or mechanical/computerized*) pilot. The system can, however, be consciously taken over (*overridden*) in the same way that the real pilot can take over flying the plane.

Page 63: Tens of billions of neurons, each communicating with thousands of other neurons, *yield an everchanging wiring diagram that dwarfs a powerful computer.* The complexity of the central nervous system, which allows or makes possible (*enables*) our thinking, feeling, and behavior, is similar to the electronic circuitry (*wiring diagrams)* of the best computer, except, by comparison, the computer would appear to be extremely tiny or small (*dwarfed by*) and the brain's wiring would seem to be constantly modifying or altering itself (*ever-changing*).

Page 63: . . . *information highway.* . . . The spinal cord is similar to the freeway (*highway*), but instead of cars moving up and down, sensory and motor messages (*information*) travel between the peripheral nervous system and the brain. This information moves either up (*ascending*) to the brain or down (*descending*) from the brain.

Page 63: The knee-jerk response, for example, involves one such simple pathway; *a headless warm body could do it.* When the patellar tendon of a bent knee is struck, the whole leg reflexively straightens out (*the knee-jerk response*). This automatic reaction is a function of a simple spinal reflex pathway so it does not require mediation by the brain (*a headless warm* [live] *body could do it*).

Page 64: Being human *takes a lot of nerve.* Myers is using humor to make a point here. The expression "it takes a lot of nerve" means to be very brave or courageous (another expression, "it takes a lot of guts," means the same thing!). Thus, when Myers states that being human takes a lot of nerve, the literal meaning in this context is that humans are made up of many, many nerves (the humor is derived from the double meaning).

Page 64: Neurons cluster into *work groups* called neural networks. Myers points out that the brain works much like a computer making many simultaneous computations. This is accomplished by neural networks which are clusters of interconnected neurons (*work groups*). Neurons work with nearby neurons for much the same reason people live in cities—it is easier for brief, quick interactions.

The Endocrine System

Page 65: The endocrine system and nervous system are therefore *kindred* systems. These two systems are very similar and have a close relationship (*kindred systems*). The hormones of the endocrine system are chemically equivalent to neurotransmitters, but operate at a much slower speed. Messages in the nervous system move very rapidly (they zip along as fast as e-mail) compared to endocrine system messages which move relatively slowly (they trudge along like regular or "snail" mail).

Page 67: Conducting and coordinating this whole *electrochemical orchestra* is that *maestro* we call the brain. Myers is comparing the functioning of the neurotransmitters and hormones to a large group of musicians (*electrochemical orchestra*) whose movements and actions are directed by the conductor or master (*maestro*), the brain.

The Brain

Page 67: . . . *we live in our heads.* What this means is that you subjectively feel that the essence of your being, your mind, resides in your brain, which is inside your head. The brain in our head allows us to function psychologically as well as physically: *the mind is what the brain does.*

Page 68: The known universe's most amazing organ is being probed and mapped by a new generation of neural cartographers. A cartographer is someone who prepares or makes maps. Myers is suggesting that the brain (*the known universe's most amazing organ*) is going to be graphically depicted (*mapped*) by a new younger group of neuroscientists (a new generation of neural *cartographers*).

Page 68: We can *snoop on* the messages of individual neurons and *eavesdrop on the chatter* of billions of neurons. With today's technological tools it is possible to unobtrusively view or spy on (*snoop on*) single nerve cells (neurons) as well as covertly listen to (*eavesdrop on*) the back-and-forth communication (*chatter*) of millions and millions of cells.

Page 68: . . . the right side of the body is *wired* to the brain's left side, and *vice versa.* This means that the functions of one side of the body are controlled by (*wired to*) the opposite side of the brain. The right side of the body is controlled by the left hemisphere, and the converse, or opposite, is also true (*vice versa*): the left side of the body is controlled by the brain's right hemisphere.

Page 69: Newer windows into the brain give us a *Supermanlike* ability to see inside the living brain. Modern technological means of viewing the brain (*new windows into the brain*), such as the PET scan, MRI, and fMRI, provide us with a greater than normal (*Supermanlike*) ability to look inside the cortex without destroying tissue. (*Note:* Superman is a comic-book, TV, and movie character with x-ray vision which allows him to see through solid matter.)

Page 69: Such *snapshots* of the brain's changing *activity* provide new insights into how the brain *divides its labor.* The MRI technique allows pictures (*snapshots*) to be taken of different brain areas at work (the brain *divides its labor*) while a person is carrying out various mental tasks.

Page 71: This peculiar cross-wiring is but one of many surprises the brain has to offer. In the brainstem most nerves from the left side of the body connect to the right side of the brain and those from the right connect to the left side of the brain. This strange (*peculiar*) traverse of nerves from one side to the other (*cross-wiring*), which occurs in the pons, is one of the many marvels or astonishing findings (*surprises*) about the brain.

Page 72: Think of the thalamus as being to sensory input what *London is to England's trains.* London is the relay center for trains going to all parts of the country just as Chicago is the hub or relay center for many airlines flying to different parts of the United States. Myers uses this as an analogy for the thalamus, which receives messages from sensory neurons and sends them on, or relays them to higher brain areas (it also receives some of the higher brain's responses and directs them to the medulla and the cerebellum).

Page 72: . . . the *doughnut-shaped* **limbic system**. This system is in the shape of a ring (*doughnut-shaped*) and has three components: the **hippocampus,** which is involved in forming (*laying down*) new memories; the **amygdala,** which influences aggression and fear; and the **hypothalamus,** which regulates hunger, thirst, body temperature, and sexuality.

Page 73: In a few cases involving patients who suffered brain abnormalities, it ["*psychosurgery*"] *reduced fits of rage,* though sometimes with devastating side effects on the patient's everyday functioning. *Psychosurgery* refers to destruction (lesioning) of healthy brain tissue to achieve some psychological change in a patient, such as making a violent patient calm and relaxed (*reducing fits of rage*). Because there were also other severe changes (*side effects*), this drastic procedure is almost never used today.

Page 74: . . . they made *a magnificent mistake.* Olds and Milner accidentally discovered (*stumbled upon*) a brain area that provides a pleasurable reward and then went on to find other similar areas which they called "*pleasure centers.*" Myers calls this a splendid and spectacular error (*a magnificent mistake*). When rats are allowed to stimulate these areas by pressing a bar or lever (*pedal*) they seem to prefer this to any other activity and will continue at a very rapid rate (*feverish pace*) until they are too tired to go on (*until they drop from exhaustion*).

Page 75: If you opened a human skull, exposing the brain, you would see a *wrinkled* organ, shaped somewhat like the *meat of an oversized walnut.* The human brain has a convoluted (*wrinkled*) surface, and the cerebral cortex is divided into two halves or hemispheres just like the two lobes of the edible portion (*the meat or seed*) in the shell of a very large (*oversized*) walnut.

Page 75: Glial cells are *neural nannies.* A *nanny* (or *nannie*) is a child's nursemaid and takes care of the relatively helpless child's needs. **Glial cells** perform in a similar way by looking after the needs of neurons which, like children, cannot feed or insulate themselves (they are *neural nannies*). Glial cells may also be involved (play a role) in learning and thinking.

Page 77: . . . *spine-tingling thrills* that music lovers enjoy . . . For some people, listening to music generates viscerally pleasurable sensations (*spine-tingling thrills*), which appear to involve the same reward systems that are stimulated by sex and pleasant-tasting foods. The point is that activities such as listening to music are relatively complex and engage multiple brain areas.

Page 79: In a sense, we *do* have *eyes in the back of our head!* The reference here is to the visual cortex (or occipital lobes) which processes visual information and is located at the rear of the brain. So, in a way seeing is not just done with the eyes but also involves specialized areas at the back of the brain.

Page 79: . . . one of pop psychology's most widespread *falsehoods:* that we ordinarily *use only 10 percent of our brains.* Research into the association areas of the brain showed that they don't have specific functions but rather are involved in many different operations such as interpreting, integrating, and acting on information processed by the sensory areas. The incorrect notion (*falsehood*) that *we use only 10 percent of our brains* may have arisen because early researchers were unsure about the function of the association areas. Remember, we use all of our brain, all the time. Damage to the association areas would result in very serious deficits.

Page 80: With his frontal lobes *ruptured,* Gage's *moral compass* became disconnected from his behavior. Phineas Gage's frontal lobes were severely damaged (*ruptured*) when the tamping iron shot through his head. As a result, he lost many of his normal inhibitions, which caused him to veer away from his previous honest ways (he lost his moral compass).

Page 82: What you experience as a continuous, indivisible stream of perception is actually but the visible tip of the information-processing iceberg, most of which lies beneath the surface of your conscious awareness. Myers is making an analogy here. Most of the important functions that allow you to see the world as a whole are not part of conscious experience, but, like most of the mass of an iceberg, are below the surface and out of awareness.

Page 84: Waking from the surgery, one patient even managed to *quip* that he had a "*splitting headache*" . . . . People have had their corpus callosum severed or cut in order to control epileptic seizures. Despite such a major operation this patient managed to joke (*quip*) that he had a very bad headache (*a splitting headache*). Personality and intellectual functioning were not affected by this procedure, and you would not be able to detect anything unusual if you were having a casual conversation with a split-brain patient.

Page 85: When the "two minds" are at odds, the left hemisphere does *mental gymnastics* to *rationalize* reactions it does not understand. In split-brain patients, if information or commands are delivered to the right hemisphere (which does not have language), then the left hemisphere, which can talk, would not be aware of what was requested. So if the patient carried out the command to do something (e.g., "walk" or "clap"), the left hemisphere will go through all kinds of contortions (*mental gymnastics*) to create some plausible story that accounts for the response (it rationalizes and constructs theories to explain our behavior).

Page 87: When at their worst, they distort a *pretzel-shaped finding* into a *breadstick-shaped story*: Some people are left-brained, others right-brained. . . . A *pretzel* is a snack food, a piece of thinly rolled bread dough shaped like an open knot. A unique and unusual set of findings (*pretzel-shaped*) gets transformed through the process of oversimplification and distortion into something totally different (*a breadstick-shaped* [very straight] *story*). Thus, public myths, such as "*some people are left-brained, others right brained,*" develop and get more attention than the scientific facts.

Page 88: From simply looking at the two hemispheres, which *appear alike* to the *naked eye*, who would suppose that they contribute so uniquely to *the harmony of the whole?* Myers points out that research with split-brain people and normal people shows that we have unified brains with different parts that have specialized functions. Thus, if we observe the two hemispheres without optical aids (*with the naked eye*), they may seem to be the same (*appear alike*); however, their differential functioning combines to produce an integrated unit (*the harmony of the whole*).

Page 89: . . . *southpaws* . . . Left-handed people, especially those involved in sports such as boxing or baseball, are called *southpaws*. Stanley Coren found that the percentage of left-handers (*southpaws*) in the population declines with age. This finding is still somewhat mysterious.

Page 91: Yet what is unknown still *dwarfs* what is known. This means that all that has been discovered so far is very, very small (*dwarfed*) compared to what yet remains to be discovered.

3 : Nature, Nurture, and Human Diversity

CHAPTER OVERVIEW

Chapter 3 is concerned with the ways in which our biological heritage, or nature, interacts with our individual experiences, or nurture, to shape who we are. After a brief explanation of basic terminology, the chapter explores the fields of behavior genetics, which studies twins and adopted children to weigh genetic and environmental influences on behaviors, and molecular genetics, which focuses on the specific genes that influence behavior. The next section discusses psychology's use of evolutionary principles to answer universal questions about human behavior.

The next two sections of the chapter shift the spotlight to focus on environmental influences on behavior. The impact of parents, the prenatal environment, early experience, peers, and culture on the development of the brain and behavior are each discussed in depth. The final section of the chapter explores how genes and environment interact to shape both the biological and social aspects of our gender. In the end, the message is clear: our genes and our experience together form who we are.

NOTE: Answer guidelines for all Chapter 3 questions begin on page 87.

CHAPTER REVIEW

First, skim each section, noting headings and boldface items. After you have read the section, review each objective by answering the fill-in and essay-type questions that follow it. As you proceed, evaluate your performance by consulting the answers beginning on page 87. Do not continue with the next section until you understand each answer. If you need to, review or reread the section in the textbook before continuing.

Introduction (pp. 95–96)

Objective 1: Give examples of differences and of similarities within the human family.

1. Our differences as humans include our
   _____ , _____ , and
   _____ and _____
   backgrounds.
2. Our similarities as human beings include our
   common _____ _____ ,
   our shared _____ architecture, our
   ability to use _____ , and our
   _____ behaviors.
3. A fundamental question in psychology deals with
   the extent to which we are shaped by our heredity, called our _____ , and by our
   life history, called our _____ .

Behavior Genetics: Predicting Individual Differences (pp. 96–107)

David Myers at times uses idioms that are unfamiliar to some readers. If you do not know the meaning of the following words, phrases, or expressions in the context in which they appear in the text, refer to pages 93–94 for an explanation: *To disentangle the threads of heredity and environment, behavior geneticists often use two sets of tweezers; blue-collar families; stories of startling twin similarity; "Mom may be holding a full house while Dad has a straight flush"; yen; the area of a field is more the result of its length or width; sleuth; Blueprints; two-edged sword.*

Objective 2: Describe the types of questions that interest behavior geneticists.

1. Researchers who specifically study the effects of genes on behavior are called _____ _____ .

2. The term *environment* refers to every _____ influence.

Objective 3: Define *chromosome, DNA, gene,* and *genome,* and describe their relationships.

3. The master plans for development are stored in the _____ . In number, each person inherits _____ of these structures, _____ from each parent. Each is composed of a coiled chain of the molecule _____ .

4. If chromosomes are the "books" of heredity, the "words" that make each of us a distinctive human being are called _____ .

5. The complete instructions for making an organism are referred to as the human _____ . Human traits are influenced by many genes acting together in _____ _____ .

Objective 4: Explain how identical and fraternal twins differ, and cite ways that behavior geneticists use twin studies to understand the effects of environment and heredity.

6. To study the power and limits of genetic influences on behavior, researchers use _____ and _____ studies.

7. Twins who developed from a single egg are genetically _____ . Twins who developed from different fertilized eggs are no more genetically alike than siblings and are called _____ twins. In terms of the personality traits of extraversion and neuroticism, identical twins are _____ (more/no more) alike than are fraternal twins.

8. Divorce rates are _____ (more/no more) similar among identical twins than among fraternal twins.

Identify other dimensions that show strong genetic influences.

9. Through research on identical twins raised apart, psychologists are able to study the influence of the _____ .

Objective 5: Cite ways that behavior geneticists use adoption studies to understand the effects of environment and heredity.

10. Studies tend to show that the personalities of adopted children _____ (do/do not) closely resemble those of their adoptive parents.

11. Adoption studies show that parenting _____ (does/does not) matter. For example, adopted children often score _____ (higher/lower) than their biological parents on intelligence tests.

Objective 6: Discuss how the relative stability of our temperament illustrates the influence of heredity on development

12. The term that refers to the inborn personality, especially the child's emotional excitability, is _____ , which _____ (does/does not) endure over time.

13. From the first weeks of life, _____ babies are more _____ , _____ , and _____ . In contrast, _____ babies are _____ , _____ , and _____ .

14. Faced with a new or strange situation, highstrung infants become _____ (more/less) physiologically aroused than less excitable infants.

Objective 7: Discuss heritability's application to individuals and groups, and explain what we mean when we say genes are self-regulating.

15. The proportion of variation in a trait within a group that is attributable to genes is called its _____ .

16. As environments become more similar, heredity as a source of differences becomes _____ (more/less) important.

17. Heritable individual differences _____ (imply/need not imply) heritable group differences.

18. For _____ phenomena, human differences are nearly always the result of both _____ and _____ influences.

Objective 8: Give an example of a genetically influenced trait that can evoke responses in others, and give another example of an environment that can trigger gene activity.

19. Throughout life, we are the product of the _____ of our _____ predispositions and our surrounding _____ .

20. Environments trigger activity in_____ , and our genetically influenced traits evoke _____ in other people. This may explain why _____ twins recall greater variations in their early family life than do _____ twins.

Objective 9: Identify the potential promise and perils of molecular genetics research.

21. The subfield of biology that investigates the specific genes that influence behavior is _____ _____ .

22. Genetic tests can reveal at-risk populations for specific _____ .

23. One result of research in this field, genetic screening, allows expectant parents to ascertain, and even choose, the _____ of their offspring. Prenatal screening, however, raises many _____ issues.

Evolutionary Psychology: Understanding Human Nature (pp. 107–113)

> If you do not know the meaning of the following words, phrases, or expressions in the context in which they appear in the text, refer to pages 94–95 for an explanation: *cash strapped; tight genetic leash; Casual, impulsive sex; sexual come-on; In our ancestral history, females most often sent their genes into the future by pairing wisely, men by pairing widely; stick-around dads over likely cads; mobile gene machines.*

Objective 10: Describe the area of psychology that interests evolutionary psychologists.

1. Researchers who study natural selection and the adaptive nature of human behavior are called _____ _____ .

2. Researchers in this field focus mostly on what makes people so _____ (much alike/different from one another).

Objective 11: State the principle of natural selection, and point out some possible effects of natural selection in the development of human characteristics.

3. According to the principle of _____ _____ , traits that contribute to reproduction and survival will be most likely to be passed on to succeeding generations.

4. Genetic _____ are random errors in genetic replication that are the source of all genetic _____ .

5. Genetic constraints on human behavior are generally _____ (tighter/looser) than those on animal behavior. The human species' ability to _____ and to _____ in responding to different _____ contributes to our _____ , defined as our ability to _____ and _____ . Because of our genetic legacy, we love the tastes of sweets and _____ , which we tend to _____ , even though famine is unlikely in industrialized societies.

Objective 12: Identify some gender differences in sexuality.

6. The characteristics by which people define *male* and *female* constitute _____ . These characteristics are subject to _____ and _____ influences.

7. Compared to females, males are _____ (equally/more/less) likely to engage in casual, impulsive sex, and they are _____ (equally/more/less) likely to initiate sexual activity. This is an example of a _____ difference.

8. Men have a _____ (higher/lower) threshold for perceiving a woman's friendliness as a sexual come-on. This helps explain men's greater sexual _____ .

Objective 13: Describe evolutionary explanations for gender differences in sexuality.

9. The _____ explanation of gender differences in attitudes toward sex is based on differences in the optimal strategy by which women and men pass on their _____ . According to this view, males and females _____ (are/are not) selected for different patterns of sexuality.

10. Cross-cultural research reveals that men judge women as more attractive if they have a _____ appearance, whereas women judge men who appear _____ , _____ , _____ , and _____ as more attractive.

Objective 14: Summarize the criticisms of evolutionary explanations of human behaviors, and describe the evolutionary psychologists' responses to these criticisms.

11. Critics of the evolutionary explanation of the gender sexuality difference argue that it often works _____ (forward/backward) to propose a _____ explanation.

12. Another critique is that gender differences in sexuality vary with _____ expectations and social and family structures.

13. Gender differences in mate preferences are largest in cultures characterized by greater gender _____ (equality/inequality).

14. Evolutionary psychologists counter the criticisms by noting that the sexes, having faced similar adaptive problems, are more _____ (alike/different) than they are _____ (alike/different). They also note that evolutionary principles offer testable _____ .

Parents and Peers (pp. 114–118)

> If you do not know the meaning of any of the following words, phrases, or expressions in the context in which they appear in the text, refer to page 95 for an explanation: *while the excess connections are still on call; pathways through a forest; shuffle their gene decks; as a potter molds clay; vapors of a toxic climate are seeping into a child's life.*

Objective 15: Describe some of the conditions that can affect development before birth.

1. Environmental influences begin during the period of _____ development.

2. Even identical twins may differ in this respect, because they may or may not share the same _____ .

3. Compared with same-placenta identical twins, twins who develop with different placentas are less similar in their _____ traits.

Objective 16: Describe how experience can modify the brain.

4. Rosenzweig and Krech discovered that rats raised from a young age in enriched environments had _____ (thicker/thinner) cortexes than animals raised in isolation.

Describe the effects of sensory stimulation on neural development.

5. Experience shapes the brain by preserving activated _____ connections and allowing unused connections to _____ . This process, called _____ , results in a massive loss of unused connections by _____ .

Objective 17: Explain why we should be careful about attributing children's successes and failures to their parents' influence.

6. The idea that parents shape their children's futures came from _____ _____ and _____ .

7. Parents do influence some areas of their children's lives, such as their _____ _____ , _____ _____ , and _____ _____ .

8. In areas such as _____ , the environment siblings share at home accounts for less than _____ percent of their differences.

Objective 18: Evaluate the importance of peer influence on development.

9. Experiences with _____ have a powerful effect on how children develop, partly as a result of a "_____ effect" by which kids seek out others with similar attitudes and interests.

10. A group of parents can influence the _____ that shapes the peer group through what Judith Harris calls _____ effects.

Cultural Influences (pp. 119–126)

> If you do not know the meaning of any of the following words, phrases, or expressions in the context in which they appear in the text, refer to pages 95–96 for an explanation: *cerebral hard drive . . . cultural software; norms grease the social machinery; cultures collide; standoffish.*

Objective 19: Discuss the survival benefits of culture.

1. The enduring behaviors, ideas, attitudes, and traditions of a group of people and transmitted from one generation to the next defines the group's _____ .

2. One landmark of human culture is the preservation of _____ , which is derived from our mastery of _____ , so that we can pass it on to future generations.

Objective 20: Describe some ways that cultures differ.

3. All cultural groups evolve their own rules for expected behavior, called _____ .

4. One such rule involves the buffer zone that people maintain around their bodies, called _____ _____ .

Identify several cultural differences in personal space, expressiveness, and pace of life.

Objective 21: Explain why changes in the human gene pool cannot account for culture change over time.

5. Cultures change _____ (slowly/rapidly).

6. Many changes in Western culture have been driven by the discovery of new forms of _____ .

7. The speed at which culture changes is much _____ (faster/slower) than the pace of evolutionary changes in the human _____ _____ .

Objective 22: Identify some ways a primarily individualist culture differs from a primarily collectivist culture, and compare their effects on personal identity.

8. Cultures based on _____ value personal _____ and individual _____ . Examples of such cultures occur in the _____ _____ ,

_____ , and _____

_____ .

9. In contrast, cultures based on _____
value _____ , _____ ,
and _____ . Examples of such cultures occur in parts of _____ and

_____ .

10. Whereas people in _____ cultures
value freedom, they suffer more

_____ , divorce, and

_____ -related disease.

Objective 23: Describe some ways that child-rearing
differs in individualist and collectivist cultures.

11. Whereas most Western parents place more

emphasis on _____ (emotional close-

ness/independence) in their children, many

Asian and African parents focus on cultivating

_____ (emotional closeness/indepen-

dence).

12. Children in collectivist cultures grow up with a

strong sense of _____ _____ .

Objective 24: Describe some ways that humans are
similar, despite their cultural differences.

13. In general, differences between groups are

_____ (smaller/larger) than person-

to-person differences within groups.

Gender Development (pp. 126–134)

> If you do not know the meaning of any of the
> following words, phrases, or expressions in the
> context in which they appear in the text, refer
> to page 96 for an explanation: *surface early;*
> *throws a master switch; "tomboyish"; initiate dates*
> *. . . pick up the check; With the flick of an apron.*

Objective 25: Identify some biological and psychological differences between males and females.

1. Among your _____ (how many?)
chromosomes, _____ (how many?)
are unisex.

2. Compared to the average man, an average
woman has more _____ , less
_____ , and is a few inches
_____ . Women are more likely
than men to suffer from _____ ,
_____ , and
_____ _____ .

3. Compared to women, men are more likely to
commit _____ and to suffer
_____ . They are also more likely to
be diagnosed with _____ ,
_____-_____ ,
_____ , and
_____ _____
_____ .

Objective 26: Summarize the gender gap in aggression.

4. Aggression is defined as _____ or
_____ behavior that is
_____ to hurt someone.

5. Throughout the world, men are more likely than
women to engage in _____ ,
_____ , and _____ .

6. The aggression gender gap pertains to
_____ rather than _____
aggression.

Objective 27: Describe some gender differences in
social power.

7. Compared to women, men are perceived as being
more _____ , _____ , and
_____ . As leaders, they tend to be
more _____ , while women are
more _____ .

8. Compared to men, women are perceived as being
more _____ , _____ , and

_____ .

9. These perceived differences occur
_____ (throughout the world/only in
certain cultures).

Objective 28: Discuss gender differences in connectedness, or the ability to "tend and befriend."

10. According to Carol Gilligan, women are more concerned than men in making _____ with others.

11. This difference is noticeable in how children _____ , and it continues throughout the teen and adult years. Girls play in groups that are _____ and less _____ than boys' groups.

12. Because they are more _____ , women are likely to use conversation to _____ _____ , while men are likely to use conversation to _____ _____ .

13. Women tend and befriend—for example, they turn to others for _____ , especially when coping with _____ .

Objective 29: Explain how biological sex is determined, and describe the role of sex hormones in biological development and gender differences.

14. The twenty-third pair of chromosomes determines the developing person's _____ . The mother always contributes a(n) _____ chromosome. When the father contributes a(n) _____ chromosome, the testes begin producing the hormone _____ . In about the _____ (what week?), this hormone initiates the development of external male sex organs.

15. Genetically female infants who were exposed to excess testosterone during prenatal development develop _____-appearing genitals. Behaviorally, until adolescence, they tend to act in more aggressive "_____ " ways than do most girls.

16. Sex chromosomes control _____ that influence the brain's wiring. In adulthood, part of the _____ lobe , an area involved in _____ fluency, is thicker in women. Part of the brain's _____ lobe, a key area for _____ perception, is thicker in men.

Objective 30: Discuss the relative importance of environment on the development of gender roles, and describe two theories of gender typing.

17. Our expectations about the way men and women behave define our culture's _____ _____ .

18. Gender roles _____ (are/are not) rigidly fixed by evolution, as evidenced by the fact that they vary across _____ and over _____ . For instance, in _____ societies there tends to be minimal division of labor by sex; by contrast, in _____ societies, women remain close to home while men roam freely, herding cattle or sheep.

19. Our individual sense of being male or female is called our _____ _____ . The degree to which we exhibit traditionally male or female traits and interests is called _____- _____ .

20. According to _____ _____ theory, children learn gender-linked behaviors by observing others and being rewarded or punished. When their families discourage traditional gender-typing, children _____ (do/do not) organize themselves into "boy worlds" and "girl worlds."

21. Another theory, called _____ _____ theory, combines _____ _____ theory with _____ . According to this theory, children learn from their _____ what it means to be male or female and adjust their behavior accordingly.

Reflections on Nature and Nurture (pp. 134–137)

> If you do not know the meaning of any of the following words, phrases, or expressions in the context in which they appear in the text, refer to page 105 for an explanation: *won the day; boggles the mind.*

Objective 31: Describe the biopsychosocial approach to development.

1. As _____ _____ becomes more and more irrelevant to power and status, gender roles are _____ (converging/diverging).

2. We are the product of both _____ and _____ , but we are also a system that is _____ .

3. The principle that we should prefer the simplest of competing explanations for a phenomenon is called _____ _____ .

PROGRESS TEST 1

Multiple-Choice Questions

Circle your answers to the following questions and check them with the answers beginning on page 89. If your answer is incorrect, read the explanation for why it is incorrect and then consult the appropriate pages of the text (in parentheses following the correct answer).

1. Dr. Ross believes that principles of natural selection help explain why infants come to fear strangers about the time they become mobile. Dr. Ross is most likely a(n):
   a. behavior geneticist.
   b. molecular geneticist.
   c. evolutionary psychologist.
   d. molecular biologist.

2. A pair of adopted children or identical twins reared in the same home are most likely to have similar:
   a. temperaments.
   b. personalities.
   c. religious beliefs.
   d. emotional reactivity.

3. Collectivist cultures:
   a. give priority to the goals of their groups.
   b. value the maintenance of social harmony.
   c. foster social interdependence.
   d. are characterized by all of the above.

4. If a fraternal twin becomes schizophrenic, the likelihood of the other twin developing serious mental illness is much lower than with identical twins. This suggests that:

a. schizophrenia is caused by genes.
b. schizophrenia is influenced by genes.
c. environment is unimportant in the development of schizophrenia.
d. identical twins are especially vulnerable to mental disorders.

5. Of the following, the best way to separate the effects of genes and environment in research is to study:
   a. fraternal twins.
   b. identical twins.
   c. adopted children and their adoptive parents.
   d. identical twins raised in different environments.

6. Through natural selection, the traits that are most likely to be passed on to succeeding generations are those that contribute to:
   a. reproduction.   c. aggressiveness.
   b. survival.   d. a. and b.

7. Which of the following is *not* true regarding gender and sexuality?
   a. Men more often than women attribute a woman's friendliness to sexual interest.
   b. Women are more likely than men to cite affection as a reason for first intercourse.
   c. Men are more likely than females to initiate sexual activity.
   d. Gender differences in sexuality are noticeably absent among gay men and lesbian women.

8. Evolutionary psychologists attribute gender differences in sexuality to the fact that women have:
   a. greater reproductive potential than do men.
   b. lower reproductive potential than do men.
   c. weaker sex drives than men.
   d. stronger sex drives than men.

9. According to evolutionary psychology, men are drawn sexually to women who seem _____ , while women are attracted to men who seem _____ .
   a. nurturing; youthful
   b. youthful and fertile; mature and affluent
   c. slender; muscular
   d. exciting; dominant

10. Unlike _____ twins, who develop from a single fertilized egg, _____ twins develop from separate fertilized eggs.
    a. fraternal; identical
    b. identical; fraternal
    c. placental; nonplacental
    d. nonplacental; placental

11. Temperament refers to a person's characteristic:
    a. emotional reactivity and intensity.
    b. attitudes.
    c. behaviors.
    d. role-related traits.

12. When evolutionary psychologists use the word "fitness," they are specifically referring to:
    a. an animal's ability to adapt to changing environments.
    b. the diversity of a species' gene pool.
    c. the total number of members of the species currently alive.
    d. our ability to survive and reproduce.

13. In a hypothetical world where all schools are of uniform quality, all families equally loving, and all neighborhoods equally healthy, the heritability of person-to-person differences would be:
    a. large.
    b. small.
    c. zero.
    d. unpredictable.

14. The subfield that studies the specific genes that influence behavior is:
    a. behavior genetics.
    b. molecular genetics.
    c. evolutionary psychology.
    d. biopsychosocial genetics.

15. Which of the following most accurately expresses the extent of parental influence on personality?
    a. It is more extensive than most people believe.
    b. It is weaker today than in the past.
    c. It is more limited than popular psychology supposes.
    d. It is almost completely unpredictable.

16. Gender refers to:
    a. the biological and social definition of male and female.
    b. the biological definition of male and female.
    c. one's sense of being male or female.
    d. the extent to which one exhibits traditionally male or female traits.

17. The fertilized egg will develop into a boy if, at conception:
    a. the sperm contributes an X chromosome.
    b. the sperm contributes a Y chromosome.
    c. the egg contributes an X chromosome.
    d. the egg contributes a Y chromosome.

18. Which theory states that gender becomes a lens through which children view their experiences?
    a. social learning theory
    b. sociocultural theory
    c. cognitive theory
    d. gender schema theory

19. The hormone testosterone:
    a. is found only in females.
    b. determines the sex of the developing person.
    c. stimulates growth of the female sex organs.
    d. stimulates growth of the male sex organs.

20. Research studies have found that when infant rats and premature human babies are regularly touched or massaged, they:
    a. gain weight more rapidly.
    b. develop faster neurologically.
    c. have more agreeable temperaments.
    d. do a. and b.

Matching Items

Match each term with its corresponding definition or description.

Terms

_____ 1. X chromosome
_____ 2. heritability
_____ 3. fraternal
_____ 4. genes
_____ 5. DNA
_____ 6. identical
_____ 7. Y chromosome
_____ 8. gender role
_____ 9. gender identity
_____ 10. gender-typing
_____ 11. environment

Functions or Descriptions

a. the biochemical units of heredity
b. twins that develop from a single egg
c. one's personal sense of being female or male
d. a set of expected behaviors for males and females
e. twins that develop from separate eggs
f. variation among individuals due to genes
g. nongenetic influences
h. the sex chromosome found in both women and men
i. the acquisition of a traditional gender role
j. a complex molecule containing the genetic information that makes up the chromosomes
k. the sex chromosome found only in men

PROGRESS TEST 2

Progress Test 2 should be completed during a final chapter review. Answer the following questions after you thoroughly understand the correct answers for the section reviews and Progress Test 1.

Multiple-Choice Questions

1. Each cell of the human body has a total of:
   a. 23 chromosomes.
   b. 23 genes.
   c. 46 chromosomes.
   d. 46 genes.

2. Genes direct our physical development by synthesizing:
   a. hormones.
   b. proteins.
   c. DNA.
   d. chromosomes.

3. The human genome is best defined as:
   a. a complex molecule containing genetic information that makes up the chromosomes.
   b. a segment of DNA.
   c. the complete instructions for making an organism.
   d. the code for synthesizing protein.

4. Most human traits are:
   a. learned.
   b. determined by a single gene.
   c. influenced by many genes acting together.
   d. unpredictable.

5. Mutations are random errors in _____ replication.
   a. gene
   b. chromosome
   c. DNA
   d. protein

6. Casual, impulsive sex is most frequent among:
   a. males with high circulating levels of testosterone.
   b. males with traditional masculine attitudes.
   c. females and males who are weakly gender-typed.
   d. females and males who are strongly gender-typed.

7. Evolutionary explanations of gender differences in sexuality have been criticized because:
   a. they offer "after-the-fact" explanations.
   b. standards of attractiveness vary with time and place.
   c. they underestimate cultural influences on sexuality.
   d. of all of the above reasons.

8. Several studies of long-separated identical twins have found that these twins:
   a. have little in common, due to the different environments in which they were raised.
   b. have many similarities, in everything from medical histories to personalities.
   c. have similar personalities, but very different likes, dislikes, and life-styles.
   d. are no more similar than are fraternal twins reared apart.

9. Adoption studies show that the personalities of adopted children:
   a. closely match those of their adoptive parents.
   b. bear more similarities to their biological parents than to their adoptive parents.
   c. closely match those of the biological children of their adoptive parents.
   d. closely match those of other children reared in the same home, whether or not they are biologically related.

10. Of the following, parents are most likely to influence their children's:
    a. temperament.
    b. personality.
    c. faith.
    d. emotional reactivity.

11. Chromosomes are composed of small segments of
    a. DNA called genes.
    b. DNA called neurotransmitters.
    c. genes called DNA.
    d. DNA called enzymes.

12. When the effect of one factor (such as environment) depends on another (such as heredity), we say there is a(n) _____ between the two factors.
    a. norm
    b. positive correlation
    c. negative correlation
    d. interaction

13. Compared to children raised in Western societies, those raised in communal societies, such as Japan or China:
    a. grow up with a stronger integration of the sense of family into their self-concepts.
    b. exhibit greater shyness toward strangers.
    c. exhibit greater concern for loyalty and social harmony.
    d. have all of the above characteristics.

14. The *selection effect* in peer influence refers to the tendency of children and youth to:
    a. naturally separate into same-sex playgroups.
    b. establish large, fluid circles of friends.
    c. seek out friends with similar interests and attitudes.
    d. choose friends their parents like.

15. Which of the following is *not* true regarding cultural diversity?
    a. Culture influences emotional expressiveness.
    b. Culture influences personal space.
    c. Culture does not have a strong influence on how strictly social roles are defined.
    d. All cultures evolve their own norms.

16. Women and men are most likely to be attracted to strongly gender-typed mates in cultures characterized by:
    a. gender inequality.
    b. gender equality.
    c. flexible gender roles.
    d. few norms.

17. An evolutionary psychologist would be most interested in studying:
    a. why most parents are so passionately devoted to their children.
    b. hereditary influences on skin color.
    c. why certain diseases are more common among certain age groups.
    d. genetic differences in personality.

18. Children who are raised by parents who discourage traditional gender-typing:
    a. are less likely to display gender-typed behaviors themselves.
    b. often become confused and develop an ambiguous gender identity.
    c. nevertheless organize themselves into "girl worlds" and "boy worlds."
    d. display excessively masculine and feminine traits as adults.

19. Genetically female children often play in "masculine" ways if they were exposed to excess _____ during prenatal development.
    a. estrogen
    b. DNA
    c. testosterone
    d. oxygen

20. Providing a child with a stimulating educational environment during early childhood is likely to:
    a. ensure the formation of a strong attachment with parents.
    b. foster the development of a calm, easygoing temperament.
    c. prevent neural connections from degenerating.
    d. do all of the above.

True–False Items

Indicate whether each statement is true or false by placing *T* or *F* in the blank next to the item.

_____ 1. Gender differences in mate preferences vary widely from one culture to another.

_____ 2. The most emotionally reactive newborns tend to be the most restrained 9-month-olds.

_____ 3. Research on twins shows a substantial genetic influence on attitudes toward organized religion and many other issues.

_____ 4. As environments become less similar, heredity as a source of differences becomes more important.

_____ 5. Compared to identical twins reared in different families, fraternal twins recall their early family life more differently.

_____ 6. Parents have a stronger influence than do peers on whether a youth starts smoking.

_____ 7. Nature selects behavior tendencies that increase the likelihood of sending one's genes into the future.

_____ 8. People from individualist cultures say what they feel and what they presume others feel.

_____ 9. Parental influence on personality is more limited than popular psychology supposes.

_____ 10. North Americans prefer more personal space than do Latin Americans.

_____ 11. Lacking any exposure to language before adolescence, a person will never master any language.

PSYCHOLOGY APPLIED

Answer these questions the day before an exam as a final check on your understanding of the chapter's terms and concepts.

Multiple-Choice Questions

1. If chromosomes are the "books" of heredity, the "words" are the _____ .

   a. genes
   b. molecules
   c. genomes
   d. DNA

2. To say that the heritability of a trait is approximately 50 percent means that:

   a. genes are responsible for 50 percent of the trait in an individual, and the environment is responsible for the rest.
   b. the trait's appearance in a person will reflect approximately equal genetic contributions from both parents.
   c. of the variation in the trait within a group of people, 50 percent can be attributed to genes.
   d. all of the above are correct.

3. After comparing divorce rates among identical and fraternal twins, Dr. Alexander has concluded that genes do play a role. Dr. Alexander is most likely a(n):

   a. evolutionary psychologist.
   b. behavior geneticist.
   c. molecular geneticist.
   d. divorcee.

4. Despite growing up in the same home environment, Karen and her brother John have personalities as different from each other as two people selected randomly from the population. Why is this so?

   a. Personality is inherited. Because Karen and John are not identical twins, it is not surprising they have very different personalities.
   b. Gender is the most important factor in personality. If Karen had a sister, the two of them would probably be much more alike.
   c. The interaction of their individual genes and nonshared experiences accounts for the common finding that children in the same family are usually very different.

   d. Their case is unusual; children in the same family usually have similar personalities.

5. I am a rat whose cortex is lighter and thinner than my litter mates. What happened to me?

   a. You were born prematurely.
   b. You suffer from fetal alcohol syndrome.
   c. You were raised in an enriched environment.
   d. You were raised in a deprived environment.

6. Chad, who grew up in the United States, is more likely to encourage _____ in his future children than Asian-born Hidiyaki, who is more likely to encourage _____ in his future children.

   a. obedience; independence
   b. independence; emotional closeness
   c. emotional closeness; obedience
   d. loyalty; emotional closeness

7. One of the best ways to distinguish how much genetic and environmental factors affect behavior is to compare children who have:

   a. the same genes and environments.
   b. different genes and environments.
   c. similar genes and environments.
   d. the same genes but different environments.

8. My sibling and I developed from a single fertilized egg. Who are we?

   a. opposite-sex identical twins.
   b. same-sex identical twins.
   c. opposite-sex fraternal twins.
   d. same-sex fraternal twins.

9. A psychologist working from the evolutionary perspective is likely to suggest that people are biologically predisposed to:

   a. protect their offspring.
   b. fear heights.
   c. be attracted to fertile-appearing members of the opposite sex.
   d. do all of the above.

10. The heritability of a trait will be largest among genetically _____ individuals who grew up in _____ environments.

    a. dissimilar; dissimilar
    b. dissimilar; similar
    c. similar; similar
    d. similar; dissimilar

11. Compared with men, women:
    a. use conversation to communicate solutions.
    b. emphasize freedom and self-reliance.
    c. talk more openly.
    d. do all of the above.

12. Of the relatively few genetic differences among humans _____ are differences among population groups.
    a. less than 1 percent
    b. less than 10 percent
    c. approximately 25 percent
    d. approximately 40 to 50 percent

13. Responding to the argument that gender differences are often by-products of a culture's social and family structures, an evolutionary psychologist is most likely to point to:
    a. our great human capacity for learning.
    b. the tendency of cultural arguments to reinforce traditional gender inequalities.
    c. the infallibility of "hindsight" explanations.
    d. all of the above.

14. A person whose twin has Alzheimer's disease has _____ risk of sharing the disease if they are identical twins than if they are fraternal twins.
    a. less
    b. about the same
    c. much greater
    d. It is unpredictable.

15. Which of the following is an example of an interaction?
    a. Swimmers swim fastest during competition against other swimmers.
    b. Swimmers with certain personality traits swim fastest during competition, while those with other personality traits swim fastest during solo time trials.
    c. As the average daily temperature increases, sales of ice cream decrease.
    d. As the average daily temperature increases, sales of lemonade increase.

16. Which of the following most accurately summarizes the findings of the 40-year fox-breeding study described in the text?
    a. Wild wolves cannot be domesticated.
    b. "Survival of the fittest" seems to operate only when animals live in their natural habitats.

    c. By mating aggressive and unaggressive foxes, the researchers created a mutant species.
    d. By selecting and mating the tamest males and females, the researchers have produced affectionate, unaggressive offspring.

17. Compared to men, women are more likely to:
    a. be concerned with their partner's physical attractiveness.
    b. initiate sexual activity.
    c. cite "liking one another" as a justification for having sex in a new relationship.
    d. be less accepting of casual sex.

18. When his son cries because another child has taken his favorite toy, Brandon admonishes him by saying, "Big boys don't cry." Evidently, Brandon is an advocate of _____ in accounting for the development of gender-linked behaviors.
    a. gender schema theory
    b. gender identity theory
    c. gender-typing theory
    d. social learning theory

19. The fact that after age 2, language forces children to begin organizing their worlds on the basis of gender is most consistent with which theory of how gender-linked behaviors develop?
    a. gender schema theory
    b. gender identity theory
    c. gender-typing theory
    d. social learning theory

20. Three-year-old Jack is inhibited and shy. As an adult, Jack is likely to be:
    a. cautious and unassertive.
    b. spontaneous and fearless.
    c. socially assertive.
    d. Who knows? This aspect of personality is not very stable over the life span.

Essay Question

Lakia's new boyfriend has been pressuring her to become more sexually intimate than she wants to at this early stage in their relationship. Strongly gender-typed and "macho" in attitude, Jerome is becoming increasingly frustrated with Lakia's hesitation, while Lakia is starting to wonder if a long-term relationship with this type of man is what she really wants. In light of your understanding of the evolutionary explanation of gender differences in sexuality, explain why the tension between Lakia and Jerome would be considered understandable.

KEY TERMS

Writing Definitions

Using your own words, on a piece of paper write a brief definition or explanation of each of the following terms.

1. environment
2. behavior genetics
3. chromosomes
4. DNA
5. genes
6. genome
7. identical twins
8. fraternal twins
9. temperament
10. heritability
11. interaction
12. molecular genetics
13. evolutionary psychology
14. natural selection
15. mutation
16. gender
17. culture
18. norm
19. personal space
20. individualism
21. collectivism
22. aggression
23. X chromosome
24. Y chromosome
25. testosterone
26. role
27. gender role
28. gender identity
29. gender-typing
30. social learning theory
31. gender schema theory

Cross-Check

As you learned in the Prologue, reviewing and overlearning of material are important to the learning process. After you have written the definitions of the key terms in this chapter, you should complete the crossword puzzle to ensure that you can reverse the process—recognize the term, given the definition.

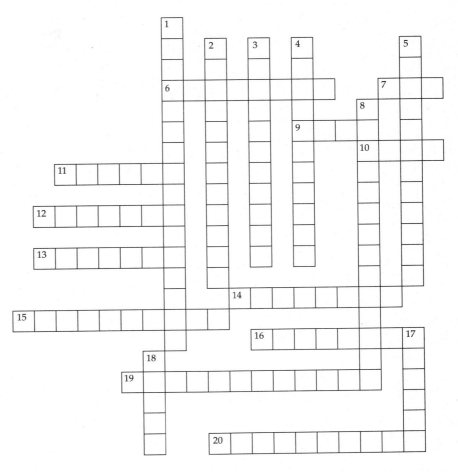

ACROSS

6. Parents whose personalities bear little relevance to their children's personalities.
7. Complex molecule containing the genetic information that makes up the chromosomes.
9. Set of expected behaviors for those who occupy a particular social position.
10. An understood rule for expected and accepted behavior.
11. The biological and social characteristics by which people define male and female.
12. The enduring behaviors, ideas, attitudes, and traditions shared by a large group of people.
13. Environmental influences on behavior.
14. According to the evolutionary perspective, women are drawn to healthy-looking men who are also _____ .
15. Behavior geneticists often compare the traits of adopted children to those of their _____ parents.
16. Source of all genetic diversity.
19. The proportion of variation among individuals that can be attributed to genes.
20. Threadlike structure made up largely of DNA molecules.

DOWN

1. The study of the relative power and limits of genetic and environmental influences on behavior.
2. Subfield of psychology that uses principles of natural selection to explore human traits and behaviors.
3. When the effect of one factor depends on another factor.
4. Any nongenetic influence.
5. A lens through which children organize their understanding of being male or female.

8. One's personal sense of being female or male.
17. Another word for heredity.
18. Segments of DNA capable of synthesizing proteins.

ANSWERS

Chapter Review

Introduction

1. personalities; interests; cultural; family
2. biological heritage; brain; language; social
3. nature; nurture

Behavior Genetics: Predicting Individual Differences

1. behavior geneticists
2. nongenetic
3. chromosomes; 46; 23; DNA
4. genes
5. genome; gene complexes
6. twin; adoption
7. identical; fraternal; more
8. more

Other dimensions that reflect genetic influences are abilities, personal traits, and interests.

9. environment
10. do not
11. does; higher
12. temperament; does
13. difficult; irritable; intense; unpredictable; easy; cheerful; relaxed; predictable in feeding and sleeping
14. more
15. heritability
16. more
17. need not imply
18. psychological; genetic; environmental
19. interaction; genetic; environment
20. genes; responses; fraternal; identical
21. molecular genetics
22. diseases
23. sex; ethical

Evolutionary Psychology: Understanding Human Nature

1. evolutionary psychologists
2. much alike
3. natural selection
4. mutations; diversity
5. looser; learn; adapt; environments; fitness; survive; reproduce; fat; store
6. gender; biological; social
7. more; more; gender
8. lower; assertiveness
9. evolutionary; genes; are
10. youthful; mature; dominant; bold; affluent
11. backward; hindsight
12. cultural
13. inequality
14. alike; different; predictions

Parents and Peers

1. prenatal
2. placenta
3. psychological
4. thicker

Research has shown that human and animal infants given extra sensory stimulation develop faster neuro-logically. Throughout life, sensory stimulation activates and strengthens particular neural connections, while other connections weaken with disuse. In this way, our experiences shape the very structure of the neural pathways that process those experiences.

5. neural; degenerate; pruning; puberty
6. Freudian psychiatry; psychology
7. political attitudes; personal manners; religious beliefs
8. personality; 10
9. peers; selection
10. culture; parents'-group-to-children's-group

Cultural Influences

1. culture
2. innovation; language
3. norms
4. personal space

Most North Americans, the British, and Scandinavians prefer more personal space than do Latin Americans, Arabs, and the French. Cultural differences in expressiveness and the pace of life often create misunderstandings. For example, people with northern European roots may perceive people from Mediterranean cultures as warm and charming but inefficient, while Mediterraneans may see the northern Europeans as efficient but emotionally cold.

5. rapidly
6. technology
7. faster; gene pool
8. individualism; independence (or control); achievement; United States; Canada; Western Europe
9. collectivism; interdependence; tradition; harmony; Africa; Asia
10. individualist; loneliness; stress
11. independence; emotional closeness
12. family self
13. smaller

Gender Development

1. 46; 45
2. fat; muscle; shorter; depression; anxiety; eating disorders
3. suicide; alcoholism; autism, color-blindness, hyperactivity, antisocial personality disorder
4. physical; verbal; intended
5. hunting; fighting; warring

6. physical; verbal

7. dominant; forceful; independent; directive (or autocratic); democratic

8. deferential; nurturant; affiliative

9. throughout the world

10. connections

11. play; smaller; competitive

12. interdependent; explore relationships; communicate solutions

13. support; stress

14. sex; X; Y; testosterone; seventh

15. male; tomboyish

16. hormones; frontal; verbal; parietal; space

17. gender roles

18. are not; cultures; time; nomadic; agricultural

19. gender identity; gender-typing

20. social learning; do

21. gender schema; social learning; cognition; schemas

Reflections on Nature and Nurture

1. brute strength; converging

2. nature; nurture; open

3. Occam's razor

Progress Test 1

Multiple-Choice Questions

1. **c.** is the answer. (p. 108)
   a., b., & d. Whereas evolutionary psychologists attempt to explain universal human tendencies, these researchers investigate genetic differences among individuals.

2. **c.** is the answer. Research has not shown a strong parental influence on personality, temperament, or emotional reactivity. (p. 101)

3. **d.** is the answer. (p. 122)

4. **b.** is the answer. (p. 98)
   a. & c. Although an identical twin is at increased risk, the relationship is far from perfect. Mental disorders, like all psychological traits, are influenced by *both* nature and nurture.
   d. This is not at all implied by the evidence from twin studies.

5. **d.** is the answer. (p. 99)
   a., b., & c. In order to pinpoint the influence of one of the two factors (genes and environment), it is necessary to hold one of the factors constant.

6. **d.** is the answer. (p. 108)
   c. Natural selection favors traits that send one's genes into the future, such as surviving longer and reproducing more often. Aggression does not necessarily promote either.

7. **d.** is the answer. Such gender differences characterize both heterosexual and homosexual people. (p. 110)

8. **b.** is the answer. Women can incubate only one infant at a time. (p. 111)
   c. & d. The text does not suggest that there is a gender difference in the strength of the sex drive.

9. **b.** is the answer. (p. 111)
   a. According to this perspective, women prefer mates with the potential for long-term nurturing investment in their joint offspring.
   c. While men are drawn to women whose waists are roughly a third narrower than their hips, the text does not suggest that women equate muscularity with fertility.
   d. Excitement was not mentioned as a criterion for mating.

10. **b.** is the answer. (pp. 97–98)
    c. & d. There are no such things as "placental" or "nonplacental" twins. All twins have a placenta during prenatal development.

11. **a.** is the answer. (p. 102)

12. **d.** is the answer. (p. 109)
    a. Survival ability is only one aspect of fitness.
    b. & c. Neither of these is related to fitness.

13. **a.** is the answer. (pp. 102–103)
    b., c., & d. This hypothetical world is one in which there is no environmental variation. Therefore, any individual differences are predictably due to genes.

14. **b.** is the answer. (p. 105)
    a. Behavior geneticists use twin and adoption studies to explore the relative power and limits of nature and nurture on behavior.
    c. Evolutionary psychologists study how natural selection favored behavioral tendencies that contributed to the survival and spread of our ancestors' genes.
    d. Although this sounds intriguing, there is no such field.

15. **c.** is the answer. (pp. 116–117)

16. **a.** is the answer. (p. 110)
    c. This defines gender identity.
    d. This defines gender-typing.

17. **b.** is the answer. (p. 129)
    a. In this case, a female would develop.

c. & d. The egg can contribute only an X chromosome. Thus, the sex of the child is determined by which chromosome the sperm contributes.

18. **d.** is the answer. (p. 132)
    a. According to social learning theory, gender-typing evolves through imitation and reinforcement.
    b. & c. Neither theory focuses on gender-typing.

19. **d.** is the answer. (p. 130)
    a. Although testosterone is the principal male hormone, it is present in both females and males.
    b. This is determined by the sex chromosomes.
    c. In the absence of testosterone, female sex organs will develop.

20. **d.** is the answer. (p. 115)

Matching Items

1. h (p. 129)   5. j (p. 96)   9. c (p. 132)
2. f (p. 102)   6. b (p. 97)   10. i (p. 132)
3. e (p. 98)   7. k (p. 129) 11. g (p. 96)
4. a (p. 96)   8. d (p. 131)

Progress Test 2

Multiple-Choice Questions

1. **c.** is the answer. (p. 96)
   b. & d. Each cell of the human body contains hundreds of genes.

2. **b.** is the answer. (p. 96)
   a. Hormones are chemical messengers produced by the endocrine glands.
   c. & d. Genes are segments of DNA, which are the make-up of chromosomes.

3. **c.** is the answer. (p. 96)
   a. This defines DNA.
   b. This defines a gene.
   d. The genes provide the code for synthesizing proteins.

4. **c.** is the answer. (p. 97)

5. **a.** is the answer. (p. 108)

6. **b.** is the answer. (p. 110)
   a. Testosterone levels have not been linked to the frequency of casual sex.
   c. & d. Males are far more accepting of casual sex than are females.

7. **d.** is the answer. (pp. 112–113)

8. **b.** is the answer. (pp. 99–100)
   a., c., & d. Despite being raised in different environments, long-separated identical twins often have much in common, including likes, dislikes,

and life-styles. This indicates the significant heritability of many traits.

9. **b.** is the answer. (pp. 100–101)
   a., c., & d. The personalities of adopted children do not much resemble those of their adoptive parents (therefore, not a.) or other children reared in the same home (therefore, not c. or d.).

10. **c.** is the answer. (pp. 101, 117)
    a. & d. Temperament, which refers to a person's emotional reactivity, is determined primarily by genes.
    b. Genes limit parents' influence on their children's personalities.

11. **a.** is the answer. (p. 96)
    b. Neurotransmitters are the chemicals involved in synaptic transmission in the nervous system.
    d. Enzymes are chemicals that facilitate various chemical reactions throughout the body but are not involved in heredity.

12. **d.** is the answer. (p. 105)
    a. A norm is a culturally determined set of expected behaviors for a particular role, such as a gender role.
    b. & c. When two factors are correlated, it means either that increases in one factor are accompanied by increases in the other (positive correlation) or that increases in one factor are accompanied by decreases in the other (negative correlation).

13. **d.** is the answer. (p. 122)

14. **c.** is the answer. (p. 118)

15. **c.** is the answer. (pp. 119–121)

16. **a.** is the answer. (p. 131)
    b. In such cultures gender differences in mate preferences tend to be much smaller.
    c. Although flexibility in gender roles was not discussed per se, it is likely that greater flexibility would equate with greater equality in gender roles.
    d. All cultures develop norms.

17. **a.** is the answer. This is an example of a trait that contributes to survival of the human species and the perpetuation of one's genes. (p. 109)
    b., c., & d. These traits and issues would likely be of greater interest to a behavior geneticist, since they concern the influence of specific genes on behavior.

18. **c.** is the answer. (p. 132)
    b. & d. There is no evidence that being raised in a "gender neutral" home confuses children or fosters a backlash of excessive gender-typing.

19. **c.** is the answer. (p. 130)

20. **c.** is the answer. (p. 115)

a. Although early experiences are a factor in the development of attachment (discussed in a later chapter), educational stimulation is probably less important than warmth and nurturance.

b. Because temperament appears to be a strongly genetic trait, it is unlikely that early educational experiences would affect its nature.

True–False Items

1. F (p. 111)	**5.** T (p. 105)	**9.** T (p. 116)
2. F (p. 102)	**6.** F (p. 118)	**10.** T (p. 120)
3. F (p. 101)	**7.** T (p. 108)	**11.** T (p. 115)
4. F (p. 103)	**8.** F (p. 122)	

Psychology Applied

Multiple-Choice Questions

1. **a.** is the answer. (p. 96)

   b. DNA is a molecule.

   c. & d. Genes are segments of DNA.

2. **c.** is the answer. Heritability is a measure of the extent to which a trait's variation within a group of people can be attributed to heredity. (p. 102)

   a. & b. Heritability is not a measure of how much of an individual's behavior is inherited, nor of the relative contribution of genes from that person's mother and father. Furthermore, the heritability of any trait depends on the context, or environment, in which that trait is being studied.

3. **b.** is the answer. (pp. 96, 97–98)

   a. Evolutionary psychologists study the evolution of behavior using the principles of natural selection.

   c. Molecular geneticists search for the specific genes that influence behaviors. In his example, the researcher is merely comparing twins.

   d. Who knows?

4. **c.** is the answer. (pp. 98, 103)

   a. Although heredity does influence certain traits, such as outgoingness and emotional instability, it is the interaction of heredity and experience that ultimately molds personality.

   b. There is no single "most important factor" in personality. Moreover, for the same reason two sisters or brothers often have dissimilar personalities, a sister and brother may be very much alike.

   d. Karen and John's case is not at all unusual.

5. **d.** is the answer. (pp. 114–115)

   a. & b. Premature birth and fetal alcohol syndrome (discussed in a later chapter) usually do not have this effect on the developing brain.

   c. If the question had stated "I have a heavier and thicker cortex," this answer would be correct.

6. **b.** is the answer. Although parental values differ from one time and place to another, studies reveal that Western parents today want their children to think for themselves, while Asian and African parents place greater value on emotional closeness. (p. 124)

   d. Both of these values are more typical of Asian than Western cultures.

7. **d.** is the answer. To separate the influences of heredity and experience on behavior, one of the two must be held constant. (pp. 99–100)

   a., b., & c. These situations would not allow one to separate the contributions of heredity and environment.

8. **b.** is the answer. (pp. 97–98)

   a. Because they are genetically the same, identical twins are always of the same sex.

   c. & d. Fraternal twins develop from two fertilized eggs.

9. **d.** is the answer. (pp. 108–109, 111)

10. **b.** is the answer. Because their environments are largely the same, differences in the traits of such individuals are likely to be due to genetic differences. (p. 103)

    c. & d. If two individuals are genetically similar, any differences in their behaviors and traits are likely to be due to environmental factors.

11. **c.** is the answer. (p. 129)

12. **b.** is the answer. Actually, only 5 percent are differences among population groups. (p. 108)

13. **a.** is the answer. (p. 113)

    b. & c. In fact, these are typical criticisms of evolutionary psychology.

14. **c.** is the answer. (p. 98)

15. **b.** is the answer. (p. 105)

    a. An interaction requires at least two variables; in this example there is only one (competition).

    c. This is an example of a negative correlation.

    d. This is an example of a positive correlation.

16. **d.** is the answer. (p. 108)

17. **d.** is the answer. (p. 110)

    a., b., & c. These are typical male attitudes and behaviors.

18. **d.** is the answer. Following social learning theory, Brandon is using verbal punishment to discourage what he believes to be an inappropriate gender-linked behavior in his son. (p. 132)

    a. Gender schema theory maintains that children adjust their behaviors to match their cultural concept of gender. In this example, we have only the father's behavior on which to base our answer. **b. & c.** No such theories were discussed.

19. **a.** is the answer. Many aspects of language, including masculine and feminine pronouns, provide children with schemas through which they begin organizing their worlds on the basis of gender. (p. 132)

20. **a.** is the answer. (p. 103)
    b., c., & d. Temperament is one of the most stable personality traits.

Essay Question

Evolutionary psychologists would not be surprised by the tension between Lakia and Jerome and would see it as a reflection of women's more relational and men's more recreational approach to sex. Since eggs are expensive, compared with sperm, women prefer mates with the potential for long-term investment in their joint offspring. According to this perspective, this may be why Lakia is not in a hurry to become sexually intimate with Jerome. Men, on the other hand, are selected for "pairing widely" but not necessarily wisely in order to maximize the spreading of their genes. This is especially true of men like Jerome, who have traditional masculine attitudes.

Key Terms

Writing Definitions

1. In behavior genetics, **environment** refers to every nongenetic, or external, influence on our traits and behaviors. (p. 96)

2. **Behavior genetics** is the study of genetic and environmental influences on behavior. (p. 96)

3. **Chromosomes** are threadlike structures made of DNA molecules, which contain the genes. In conception, the 23 chromosomes in the egg are paired with the 23 chromosomes in the sperm. (p. 96)

4. **DNA** (deoxyribonucleic acid) is a complex molecule containing the genetic information that makes up the chromosomes. (p. 96)

5. **Genes** are the biochemical units of heredity that make up the chromosomes; they are segments of the DNA molecules capable of synthesizing a protein. (p. 96)

6. A **genome** is the complete set of genetic instructions for making an organism. (p. 96)

7. **Identical twins** develop from a single fertilized egg that splits in two and therefore are genetically identical. (p. 97)

8. **Fraternal twins** develop from two separate eggs fertilized by different sperm and therefore are no more genetically similar than ordinary siblings. (p. 98)

9. **Temperament** refers to a person's characteristic emotional reactivity and intensity. (p. 102)

10. **Heritability** is the proportion of variation among individuals in a trait that is attributable to genetic factors. Current estimates place the heritability of intelligence at about 50 to 70 percent. (p. 102)

11. An **interaction** occurs when the effects of one factor (such as environment) depend on another factor (such as heredity). (p. 105)

    Example: Because the way people react to us (an environmental factor) depends on our genetically influenced temperament (a genetic factor), there is an **interaction** between environment and heredity.

12. **Molecular genetics** is the subfield of biology that seeks to identify the specific genes that influence specific human traits and behaviors. (p. 105)

13. **Evolutionary psychology** is the study of the evolution of behavior and the mind, using the principles of natural selection. (p. 107)

14. **Natural selection** is the evolutionary principle that traits that contribute to reproduction and survival are the most likely to be passed on to succeeding generations. (p. 108)

15. **Mutations** are random errors in gene replication that are the source of genetic diversity within a species. (p. 108)

16. **Gender** refers to the biological and social characteristics by which people define *male* and *female*. (p. 110)

17. A **culture** is the enduring behaviors, ideas, attitudes, and traditions shared by a large group of people and transmitted from one generation to the next. (p. 119)

18. **Norms** are understood social prescriptions, or rules, for accepted and expected behavior. (p. 120)

19. **Personal space** refers to the buffer zone, or mobile territory, that people like to maintain around their bodies. (p. 120)

20. **Individualism** is giving priority to personal goals over group goals and defining one's identity in terms of personal attributes rather than group identification. (p. 121)

21. **Collectivism** is giving priority to the goals of one's group, and defining one's identity accordingly. (p. 121)

22. **Aggression** is physical or verbal behavior intended to hurt someone. (p. 127)

23. The **X chromosome** is the sex chromosome found in both men and women. Females inherit an X chromosome from each parent. (p. 129)

24. The **Y chromosome** is the sex chromosome found only in men. Males inherit an X chromosome from their mothers and a Y chromosome from their fathers. (p. 129)

25. **Testosterone** is the principal male sex hormone. During prenatal development, testosterone stimulates the development of the external male sex organs. (p. 130)

26. A **role** is a cluster of prescribed behaviors expected of those who occupy a particular social position. (p. 131)

27. A **gender role** is a set of expected behaviors for males and females. (p. 131)

28. **Gender identity** is one's personal sense of being male or female. (p. 132)

29. **Gender-typing** is the acquisition of a traditional feminine or masculine gender role. (p. 132)

30. According to **social learning theory**, people learn social behavior (such as gender roles) by observing and imitating and by being rewarded or punished. (p. 132)

31. According to **gender schema theory**, children acquire a cultural concept of what it means to be female or male and adjust their behavior accordingly. (p. 132)

Cross-Check

ACROSS

6. adoptive
7. DNA
9. role
10. norm
11. gender
12. culture
13. nurture
14. affluent
15. biological
16. mutation
19. heritability
20. chromosome

DOWN

1. behavior genetics
2. evolutionary
3. interaction
4. environment
5. gender schema
8. gender identity
17. nature
18. genes

FOCUS ON VOCABULARY AND LANGUAGE

Behavior Genetics: Predicting Individual Differences

Page 97: To *disentangle the threads* of heredity and environment, behavior geneticists often use *two sets of tweezers*: twin studies and adoption studies. Myers is using an analogy here: to separate out (*disentangle*) two different strings (*threads*) that are tightly intertwined, you can use a small pincers (*tweezers*). Similarly, in an attempt to discover and separate out (*tease apart*) the differential effects of the environment and genes (*threads that are entangled*), behavior geneticists use two approaches (*two sets of tweezers*): twin studies and adoption studies.

Page 99: blue-collar families . . . This phrase refers to a social category based on the type of work people do. Traditionally, manual workers wore blue (denim) work shirts (*blue-collar workers*) in contrast to office workers, managers, etc., who wore white shirts (*white-collar workers*). The identical twins (both named Jim) were adopted by similar working-class (*blue-collar*) families.

Page 100: The stories of *startling twin similarity* do not impress Bouchard's critics, who remind us that "the plural of anecdote is not data." Bouchard's investigation into the similarities between separated twins suggests that genes influence many behaviors, such as career choices, TV-watching habits, and food likes and dislikes (*startling stories*). The critics point out that any two strangers of the same sex and age would probably have many coincidental things in common if they were to spend hours comparing their behaviors and life histories. Furthermore, stories by, or about, individuals (*single anecdotes*) do not constitute scientific data, even if there are many of them (*the plural of anecdote is not data*).

Page 101 (margin): "Mom may be *holding a full house* while Dad has a straight flush, yet when Junior gets a random half of each of their cards his *poker-hand may be a loser"* David Lykken (2001). To make sense of this quote you need to be familiar with card games such as poker. In this game, a "full house" and a "straight flush" are sequences of cards (*hands*) that usually are winners. Even if Mom and Dad have "winner" sets of genes, similar to the winning cards in poker, the random genes they pass on to their off-spring (*Junior*) will not necessarily be a "winning" set of genes too (*his poker-hand may be a loser*).

Page 103: We all are driven to eat, but depending on our culturally learned tastes, we may have a *yen* for fish eyes, black bean salad, or chicken legs. *Go barefoot* for a summer and you will develop toughened callused feet—a biological adaptation to friction. Meanwhile, your *shod neighbor will remain a tenderfoot.* The enormous adaptive capacity is a common, but extremely valuable, characteristic of human beings (*the behavioral hallmark of our species*). We share a need for food (*we all are driven to eat*); however, our particular food preferences tend to be learned, and our desire (*yen*) for various foods is typically culturally transmitted. If someone doesn't wear shoes (*he goes barefoot*), his feet will become tough, which is a biological adaptation. If a person wears shoes (*your shod neighbor*), his feet will be tender or soft (*he will be a tenderfoot*); this is also the product of a biological mechanism. However, it is the environment that causes the difference between the two people. (Note: the word *tenderfoot* traditionally referred to someone who was new to ranching in the western United States and is now used to describe any newcomer or novice.)

Page 104: Thus, asking whether your personality is more a product of your genes or environment is like asking . . . whether *the area of a field is more the result of its length or width.* The area of a space, such as a soccer field or a football field, is determined by multiplying the length by the width. Obviously, you cannot find the area of the field without both length and width. Likewise, we do not become who we are without both nature and nurture. As Myers notes, for psychological characteristics, human differences are almost always the result of both genetic (*nature*) and environmental (*nurture*) factors.

Page 105 . . . *sleuth* . . . A *sleuth* is a detective. Just like detectives trying to catch the criminal and solve the crime, researchers throughout the world are currently trying to locate (*sleuth*) the genes responsible for many disorders.

Page 106: Blueprints for "designer babies" . . . A *blueprint* is an architectural term for a copy of an original diagram or plan used as a working drawing for creating a building or structure. Myers notes that

genes and environment interact. Genes, rather than acting as master plans (*blueprints*) that always lead to the same result, instead react and respond to their environments.   Thus, people with identical genes (identical twins) but with different experiences end up with similar but not identical minds.

Page 106: But as always, progress is a *two-edged sword,* raising both hopeful possibilities and difficult problems. Myers is using the metaphor of a sword with two cutting edges (*two-edged sword*) to illustrate the fact that progress has two aspects to it, one positive (hopeful possibilities) and one negative (new ethical issues and difficult problems).

Evolutionary Psychology: Understanding Human Nature

Page 108: cash-strapped . . . This means to be in desperate need of money (*strapped for cash*). Russian researchers selectively bred only the tamest and friendliest foxes from each of 30 generations over a 40-year period. The present breed of foxes are affectionate, docile, and eager to please; in order to raise funds for the financially destitute (*cash-strapped*) institute, they are being marketed as house pets.

Page 108: But the tight genetic *leash* . . . is looser on humans. Just as a dog is restrained or held in check by a strap or cord (*leash*), genes generally determine the fairly rigid or fixed patterns of behaviors of many animals. In humans, however, genes are less influential; thus, the usually strong genetic constraints (*tight genetic leash*) operate in a less determined way (*are looser*).

Page 110: Casual, impulsive sex is most frequent among males with traditional masculine attitudes (Pleck & others, 1993). There are large gender differences in sexual values and attitudes, which are reflected in differences in male-female behaviors. Males (especially those with stereotyped views of females) tend to be lacking in restraint (*impulsive*) and nonchalant (*casual*) about having sex with someone they have just met and hardly know (*casual, impulsive sex*).

Page 110: Men also have a lower threshold for perceiving warm responses as a *sexual come-on.* Males will typically misinterpret an affable, affectionate, friendly female's behavior (*her warmth*) as an invitation to have sex (*a sexual come-on*). Numerous studies have shown that men are more likely than women to attribute a woman's friendliness to sexual interest.

Page 111: In our *ancestral history*, women most often sent their genes into the future by *pairing wisely*, men by *pairing widely*. Evolutionary psychologists note that our normal desires (*natural yearnings*) help perpetuate our genes. In our evolutionary past (*ancestral history*) females accomplished this best by being selective in their choice of mate (*pairing wisely*) and men by more promiscuous behavior (*pairing widely*). Myers points out, however, that environmental factors, such as cultural expectations, can alter or shape how sexual behavior is expressed by both males and females (*can bend the genders*).

Page 111: They (women) prefer *stick-around dads over likely cads.* Women tend to prefer males who are more likely to be supportive of their children (their *offspring*) and who are also more willing to make a lasting contribution to their protection (*stick-around dads*) rather than males who indicate little or no willingness to make such a co-parenting commitment (*likely cads*).

Page 111: As *mobile gene machines*, we are designed to prefer whatever worked for our ancestors in their environments. Evolutionary psychologists believe that behavioral tendencies that increase the probability of getting one's genes into the future have been selected for over the course of evolution. Humans who actively seek out mates and successfully procreate (*mobile gene machines*) are passing on inherited tendencies to behave in certain ways (*our natural yearnings*) because these behaviors were adaptive for our ancestors.

Parents and Peers

Page 115: During early childhood—while the excess connections are *still on call*— . . . . To *be on call* means to be ready and available for use. Thus, during the early childhood years while there are many neural connections ready for use (*still on call*), an enriched and stimulating environment is extremely important for intellectual, perceptual, and social development. As Myers puts it, "... use it or lose it."

Page 115: Similar to *pathways* through a forest, less traveled paths gradually disappear, and *popular paths* are broadened. This analogy suggests that brain development goes on throughout life. Neural connections (*pathways*) that are frequently used (*popular paths*) are widened and more clearly defined, while those connections that are seldom used (*in disuse*) become weakened and may eventually disappear.

Page 116: In procreation, a woman and a man *shuffle their gene decks and deal a life-forming hand* to their child-to-be . . . The idea here is that just as cards are randomly interspersed (*shuffled*) and then passed on (*dealt*) to the players, a man and a woman intermingle their genes (*shuffle their gene decks*) and conceive offspring (*deal a life-forming hand to their child-to-be*). The child is then exposed to numerous environmental factors beyond parental control that limit how much the parents influence the child's development (*children are not formless blobs sculpted by parental nurture*).

Page 116: And society reinforces such parent-blaming: Believing that parents shape their children as a *potter molds clay*, people readily praise parents for their children's virtues and blame them for their children's vices. Myers suggests that, because some factors that affect development are under the parent's control and others are not, it is not appropriate to be judgmental. We should be slower to praise parents for their children's achievements (children's virtues) and slower yet to be critical when the children do not perform up to our expectations (children's vices). Children are not simply formed by their parents' child-rearing abilities (*as a potter molds clay*) but rather are influenced by many factors beyond their control.

Page 118: If the vapors of a toxic climate are seeping into a child's life, that climate—not just the child—needs *reforming*. Myers is suggesting that when problem behaviors arise it is important to look at the whole context that is influencing the child rather than just focusing on the youngster. If the environment (*whole school or neighborhood*) is unhealthy and dangerous (*a toxic climate*) and is slowly leaking (*seeping*) into a child's life, then it is important to change (*reform*) these environmental influences instead of simply trying to change the child.

Cultural Influences

Page 119: We come equipped with a huge *cerebral hard drive ready to receive many gigabytes of cultural software.* Myers is comparing our capacity to learn and adapt through cultural transmission to that of a computer's operating system (*cerebral hard drive*) which, like a human, is capable of receiving very large amounts of information through programming (*gigabytes of cultural software*).

Page 120: Yet, norms *grease the social machinery.* Every society has its own rules and regulations about accepted and appropriate modes of conduct (social norms), and these standards differ from culture to culture. These proscriptions may sometimes seem unjust or senseless, but because they are known and practiced by most people, they serve the function of helping society run smoothly (*they grease the social machinery*).

Page 120:   When cultures collide, their differing norms often *befuddle*. When people from different cultures meet, the interaction can be confusing (*befuddling*). Personal space (the distance we like to have between us and others) varies; someone who prefers more space may end up constantly retreating (*backpedaling*) from someone who needs to be close in order to have a comfortable conversation.

Page 120: . . . *standoffish* . . . This means to be distant or unfriendly in social interactions. North Americans have a need for a bigger personal space than do people from some other cultures. So, when that space is infringed upon (*invaded*), the natural reaction is to back away, which may give the impression of being aloof and unfriendly (*standoffish*).

Gender Development

Page 128: These gender differences *surface early*, in children's play. Males and females differ in their feelings of belonging (*connectedness*), a disparity that is noticeable from a young age (*surfaces early*). When playing, boys tend to engage in competitive group activity without much close, confidential, or affectionate dialogue. Girls typically are more intimate with each other and play in smaller groups, frequently with one friend, and they are less competitive and more supportive and empathic.

Page 130: The Y chromosome includes a single gene that *throws a master switch* triggering the testes to develop and produce the principal male hormone, testosterone. . . . We all get an X chromosome from our mothers and either an X (you'll be a girl) or a Y (you'll be a boy) from our fathers. Thus, the Y chromosome is crucial to making males, and a single gene is responsible for initiating the process (*it throws the switch*) that activates (*triggers*) the production of testosterone by the testes.

Page 130: . . . "*tomboyish*" . . . A tomboy is a girl who likes to play boys' sports and games. When a female embryo is exposed to too much testosterone (the male sex hormone), the developing child will act

more aggressively and behave in ways more typical of boys (she will act in a *tomboyish* way).

Page 131: Thirty years ago, it was standard for men to *initiate dates*, drive the car, and *pick up the check*, and for women to decorate the home, buy and care for the children's clothes, and select the wedding gifts. Gender roles are a culture's expectations for male and female behaviors, but these behaviors change over time and across cultures, and vary from generation to generation. Traditionally (*as was common practice 30 years ago*), males asked females to go out (*initiated dates*) and paid for the meal and entertainment (*picked up the check*), and women looked after domestic concerns, including purchasing and looking after the children's clothes and choosing presents for those who were getting married (*wedding gifts*).

Page 131: With the *flick of an apron*, the number of U.S. college women hoping to be full-time homemakers *plunged* during the late 1960s and early 1970s. Over time, gender roles have changed. Within a relatively brief period of time (*with the flick of an apron*), the number of women engaged in the traditional female role (full-time homemaker) declined rapidly (*plunged*) and the number of women in the work force increased substantially, especially in traditional male fields such as medicine, law, and engineering.

Reflections on Nature and Nurture

Page 136: won the day . . . Galileo's theory that the Earth revolved around the Sun, and not the other way around (vice-versa), was eventually accepted (*it won the day*). His explanation was a coherent account (*it hung together*) of the way the solar system actually works.

Page 136: It *boggles* the mind—the entire universe *popping out of a single point* some 14 billion years ago. . . . When something is startling, unexpected, or hard to comprehend, we say that "it *boggles* the mind." The idea that the entire universe arose from a singularity (*popped out of a single point*) approximately 14 billion years ago is one such "mind-boggling" idea that leaves even scientists full of reverence and wonder (*they are awestruck*).

4 : Developing Through the Life Span

CHAPTER OVERVIEW

Developmental psychologists study the life cycle, from conception to death, examining how we develop physically, mentally, and socially. Chapter 4 covers physical, cognitive, and social development over the life span and introduces two major issues in developmental psychology: (1) whether development is best described as gradual and continuous or as a discontinuous sequence of stages and (2) whether the individual's personality remains stable or changes over the life span. The issue of the relative impact of genes and experience on behavior is the subject of Chapter 3.

Although there are not too many terms to learn in this chapter, there are a number of important research findings to remember. Pay particular attention to the stage theories of Piaget, Kohlberg, and Erikson, as well as to the discussion regarding intellectual stability during adulthood. Writing carefully prepared answers to the section preview items should be especially helpful in mastering the material in this chapter.

NOTE: Answer guidelines for all Chapter 4 questions begin on page 115.

CHAPTER REVIEW

First, skim this section, noting headings and boldface items. After you have read the section, review each objective by completing the sentences and answering the questions that follow it. As you proceed, evaluate your performance by consulting the answers beginning on page 115. Do not continue with the next section until you understand each answer. If you need to, review or reread the section in the textbook before continuing.

Introduction (p. 139)

> David Myers at times uses idioms that are unfamiliar to some readers. If you do not know the meaning of the following expression in the context in which it appears in the text, refer to page 124 for an explanation: . . . *journey through life—from womb to tomb.*

Objective 1: State the three areas of change that developmental psychologists study, and identify the three major issues in developmental psychology.

1. Scientists who study physical, cognitive, and social changes throughout the life cycle are called

   _____ _____ .

2. One of the major issues in developmental psychology concerns the relative importance of genes and experience in determining behavior; this is called the _____ /

   _____ issue.

3. A second developmental issue,

   _____ / _____ ,

   concerns whether developmental changes are gradual or abrupt.

4. A third controversial issue concerns the consistency of personality and whether development is characterized more by _____ over time or by change.

Prenatal Development and the Newborn
(pp. 139–144)

Objective 2: Describe the union of sperm and egg at conception.

1. Conception begins when a woman's _____ releases a mature _____ .

2. The few _____ from the man that reach the egg release digestive _____ that eat away the egg's protective covering. As soon as one sperm penetrates the egg, the egg's surface _____ all other sperm.

3. The egg and sperm _____ fuse and become one.

Objective 3: Define *zygote*, *embryo*, and *fetus*, and explain how teratogens can affect development.

4. Fertilized human eggs are called _____ . During the first week, the cells in this cluster begin to specialize in structure and function, that is, they begin to _____ . The outer part of the fertilized egg attaches to the _____ wall, forming the _____ .

5. From about 2 until 8 weeks of age the developing human, formed from the inner cells of the fertilized egg, is called a(n) _____ . During the final stage of prenatal development, the developing human is called a(n) _____ .

6. Along with nutrients, a range of harmful substances known as _____ can pass through the placenta.

7. Moderate consumption of alcohol during pregnancy _____ (usually does not affect/can affect) the fetal brain. If a mother drinks heavily, her baby is at risk for the birth defects and mental retardation that accompany _____ _____ .

Objective 4: Describe some abilities of the newborn, and explain how researchers use habituation to assess infant sensory and cognitive abilities.

8. When an infant's cheek is touched, it will vigorously search for a nipple, a response known as the _____ _____ .

9. American psychologist _____ believed that the newborn experiences a "blooming, buzzing confusion." This belief is _____ (correct/incorrect).

Give some evidence supporting the claim that a newborn's sensory equipment is biologically prewired to facilitate social responsiveness.

10. (Close-Up) To study infants' thinking, developmental researchers have focused on a simple form of learning called _____ , which involves a _____ in responding with repeated stimulation. Using this procedure, researchers have found that infants can discriminate _____ , _____ , and _____ ; they also understand some basic concepts of _____ and _____ .

Infancy and Childhood (pp. 144–164)

If you do not know the meaning of any of the following words, phrases, or expressions in the context in which they appear in the text, refer to pages 124–126 for an explanation: *toddler; wild growth spurt; formatted; fruitless; flop his beret; double take; realizes her "grandmother" is really a wolf; it gets high marks; cognitive milestones; concrete demonstrations . . . think for themselves; pit the drawing power; gosling; "Mere exposure"; mobile sperm banks; footprints on the brain; sneakily dabbed rouge; parenting styles . . . lax; heed this caution.*

Objective 5: Describe some developmental changes in a child's brain, and explain why maturation accounts for many of our similarities.

1. The developing brain _____ (over/under)produces neurons, with the number peaking at _____ (what age?). At birth the human nervous system _____ (is/is not) fully mature.

2. Between 3 and 6 years of age, the brain is developing most rapidly in the _____ lobes, which enable _____ _____ .

3. After puberty, a process of _____ shuts down some neural connections and strengthens others.

4. Biological growth processes that enable orderly changes in behavior are called _____ .

Objective 6: Outline four events in the motor development sequence from birth to toddlerhood, and evaluate the effects of maturation and experience on that sequence.

5. Infants pass the milestones of _____ development at different rates, but the basic _____ of stages is fixed. They sit before they _____ and walk before they _____ .

6. Genes play a _____ (major/minor) role in motor development.

7. Until the necessary muscular and neural maturation is complete, including the rapid development of the brain's _____ , experience has a _____ (large/small) effect on behavior.

Objective 7: Explain why we have few memories of experiences during our first three years of life.

8. Our earliest memories generally do not occur before age _____ .

9. This phenomenon has been called "_____ _____".

10. Memories of the preschool years are very few because infants' _____ memories do not easily translate into their later _____ .

Objective 8: State Piaget's understanding of how the mind develops, and discuss the importance of assimilation and accommodation in this process.

11. The first researcher to show that the thought processes of adults and children are very different was _____ .

12. To organize and interpret his or her experiences, the developing child constructs cognitive concepts called _____ .

13. The interpretation of new experiences in terms of existing ideas is called _____ . The adaptation of existing ideas to fit new experiences is called _____ .

Objective 9: Outline Piaget's four main stages of cognitive development, and comment on how children's thinking changes during these four stages.

14. The term for all the mental activities associated with thinking, remembering, communicating, and knowing is _____ .

15. In Piaget's first stage of development, the _____ stage, children experience the world through their motor and sensory interactions with objects. This stage occurs between infancy and nearly age _____ .

16. The awareness that things continue to exist even when they are removed from view is called _____ _____ . This awareness begins to develop at about _____ months of age.

17. Developmental researchers have found that Piaget and his followers _____ (overestimated/underestimated) young children's competence. For instance, babies have an understanding of _____ , as Karen Wynn demonstrated.

18. According to Piaget, during the preschool years and up to age _____ , children are in the _____ stage.

19. The principle that the quantity of a substance remains the same even when the shape of its container changes is called _____ . Piaget believed that preschoolers _____ (have/have not) developed this concept.

20. Preschoolers have difficulty perceiving things from another person's point of view. This inability is called _____ .

21. The child's growing ability to take another's perspective is evidence that the child is acquiring a _____ _____ . Between 3¹/₂ and 4, children come to realize that others may hold _____ _____ . Between 5 and 8, they learn that self-produced thoughts can create _____ .

22. (Close-Up) The disorder characterized by deficient _____ and _____ interaction and an impaired _____ _____ is _____ . This disorder is related to malfunctions of brain areas that enable _____ to others. The "high functioning" form of this disorder is called _____ _____ .

23. (Close-Up) A new theory proposes that autism represents an "extreme _____ brain." According to this theory, girls tend to be _____ , who are better than boys at reading facial expressions and gestures. Boys tend to be _____ , who understand things in terms of rules or laws.

24. In contrast to Piaget's findings, researchers have more recently discovered that the ability to perform mental _____ , to think _____ , and to take another's _____ develops _____ (abruptly/gradually) during the preschool years.

25. Russian psychologist _____ _____ noted that by age _____ children stop thinking aloud and instead rely on _____ . When parents give children words, they provide, according to this theorist, a _____ upon which the child can build higher-level thinking.

26. Piaget believed that children acquire the mental abilities needed to comprehend mathematical transformations and conservation by about _____ years of age. At this time, they enter the _____ _____ stage.

27. In Piaget's final stage, the _____ _____ stage, reasoning expands from the purely concrete to encompass _____ thinking. Piaget believed most children begin to enter this stage by age _____ .

Objective 10: Discuss psychologists' current views on Piaget's theory of cognitive development.

Explain briefly how contemporary researchers view Piaget's theory.

Objective 11: Define *stranger anxiety.*

28. Soon after _____ _____ emerges and children become mobile, a new fear, called _____ _____ , emerges.

29. This fear emerges at age _____ .

Objective 12: Discuss the effects of nourishment, body contact, and familiarity on infant social attachment.

30. The development of a strong emotional bond between infant and parent is called

_____ .

31. Harlow's studies of monkeys have shown that mother-infant attachment does not depend on the mother providing nourishment as much as it does on her providing the comfort of

_____ _____ . Another

key to attachment is _____ .

32. Human attachment involves one person providing another with a _____

_____ when distressed and a

_____ _____ from

which to explore.

33. In some animals, attachment will occur only during a restricted time called a

_____ _____ .

Konrad Lorenz discovered that young birds would follow almost any object if it were the first moving thing they observed. This phenomenon is called _____ .

34. Human infants _____ (do/do not) have a precise critical period for becoming attached.

Objective 13: Contrast secure and insecure attachment, and discuss the roles of parents and infants in the development of attachment and an infant's feelings of basic trust.

35. Placed in a research setting called the

_____ _____ , children

show one of two patterns of attachment:

_____ attachment or

_____ attachment.

Contrast the responses of securely and insecurely attached infants to strange situations.

Discuss the impact of responsive parenting on infant attachment.

36. A father's love and acceptance for his children are

_____ (comparable to/less important than) a mother's love in predicting their children's health and well-being.

37. Separation anxiety peaks in infants around

_____ months, then

_____ (gradually declines/remains constant for about a year). This is true of children

_____ (in North America/throughout the world).

38. According to Erikson, securely attached infants approach life with a sense of

_____ _____ .

Objective 14: Assess the impact of parental neglect, family disruption, and day care on attachment patterns and development.

39. Harlow found that when monkeys reared in social isolation are placed with other monkeys, they reacted with either fear or _____ .

40. Most abused children _____ (do/do not) later become abusive parents.

41. Although most children who grow up under adversity are _____ and become normal adults, early abuse and excessive exposure to _____ _____ may alter the development of the brain' chemical

_____ .

42. When placed in a more positive and stable environment, most infants _____ (recover/do not recover) from disruptions in attachment.

43. Experts agree that child care per se _____ (does/does not) constitute a risk factor in children's development. High-quality child care consists of warm, supportive interactions with adults in an environment that is _____ , _____ , and _____ . More important than time spent in day care in influencing a child's development are _____ _____ .

Objective 15: Trace the onset and development of children's self-concept.

44. The primary social achievement of childhood is the development of a _____ , which occurs in most children by age _____ .

45. A child's self-image generally becomes stable between the ages of _____ and _____ , when children begin to describe themselves in terms of gender, group memberships, and psychological _____ .

Identify several characteristics of children who have formed a positive self-image.

Objective 16: Describe three parenting styles, and offer three potential explanations for the link between authoritative parenting and social competence.

46. Parents who impose rules and expect obedience are exhibiting a(n) _____ style of parenting.

47. Parents who make few demands of their children and tend to submit to their children's desires are identified as _____ parents.

48. Setting and enforcing standards after discussion with their children is the approach taken by _____ parents.

49. Studies have shown that there tends to be a correlation between high self-esteem on the part of the child and the _____ style of parenting. This may be because this parenting style gives children the greatest sense of _____ over their lives.

Explain why the correlation between authoritative parenting and social competence does not necessarily reveal cause and effect.

Adolescence (pp. 164–175)

If you do not know the meaning of any of the following words, phrases, or expressions in the context in which they appear in the text, refer to pages 126–127 for an explanation: *pays dividends; out of sync; intellectual summit; character—the psychological muscles for controlling impulses; moral ladder; throw a switch; talk is cheap; slack; psychosocial task; forge their identity; emotional ties with parents loosen; gap . . . morphing.*

Objective 17: Define *adolescence*.

1. Adolescence is defined as the transition period between _____ and _____ .

2. The "storm and stress" view of adolescence is credited to _____ , one of the first American psychologists to describe adolescence.

Objective 18: Identify the major physical changes during adolescence.

3. Adolescence begins with the time of developing sexual maturity known as _____ . A two-year period of rapid physical development begins in girls at about the age of _____

and in boys at about the age of
_____ . This growth spurt is marked
by the development of the reproductive organs
and external genitalia, or _____
_____ characteristics, as well as by
the development of traits such as pubic hair and
enlarged breasts in females and facial hair in
males. These nonreproductive traits are known as

_____ _____
characteristics.

4. The first menstrual period is called
_____ . In boys, the first ejaculation
is called _____ .

5. The _____ (timing/sequence) of
pubertal changes is more predictable than their
_____ (timing/sequence).

6. Boys who mature _____
(early/late) tend to be more popular, self-
assured, and independent; they also are at
increased risk for _____

_____ .

For girls, _____ (early/late) matura-
tion can be stressful, especially when their bodies
are out of sync with their _____
_____ . This reminds us that
_____ and _____
interact.

7. The adolescent brain undergoes a selective
_____ of unused connections. Also,
teens' occasional impulsiveness and risky
behaviors may be due, in part, to the fact that
development in the brain's _____
_____ lags behind that of the

_____ _____ .

Objective 19: Describe the changes in reasoning abilities that Piaget called formal operations.

8. Adolescents' developing ability to reason gives
them a new level of _____ aware-
ness and _____ judgment.

9. During the early teen years, reasoning is often
_____ , as adolescents often feel
their experiences are unique.

10. Piaget's final stage of cognitive development is
the stage of _____
_____ . The adolescent in this stage
is capable of thinking logically about
_____ as well as concrete propositions. This enables them to detect
_____ in others' reasoning and to
spot hypocrisy.

Objective 20: Discuss moral development from the
perspectives of moral thinking, moral feeling, and
moral action.

11. The theorist who proposed that moral thought
progresses through stages is
_____ . These stages are divided
into three basic levels: _____ ,
_____ , and _____ .

12. In the preconventional stages of morality, characteristic of children, the emphasis is on obeying
rules in order to avoid _____ or gain
_____ .

13. Conventional morality usually emerges by early
_____ . The emphasis is on gaining
social _____ or upholding the social
_____ .

14. Individuals who base moral judgments on their
own perceptions of basic ethical principles are
said by Kohlberg to employ
_____ morality.

Summarize the criticisms of Kohlberg's theory of
moral development.

15. The idea that moral feelings precede moral reasoning is expressed in the _____
_____ explanation of morality.
Research studies using _____
_____ support the idea that moral

judgment involves more than merely thinking; it is also gut-level feeling.

16. Morality involves doing the right thing, and what we do depends on _____ influences. Today's _____

_____ _____ focus on moral issues and doing the right thing.

17. Children who learn to delay _____ become more socially responsible, often engaging in responsible action through _____ learning. They also become more _____ successful and productive.

18. Moral ideas grow _____ (stronger/ weaker) when acted on.

Objective 21: Identify Erikson's eight stages of psychosocial development and their accompanying issues.

Complete the missing information in the following table of Erikson's stages of psychosocial development.

Group Age	Psychosocial Stage
Infancy	_____
_____	Autonomy vs. shame and doubt
Preschooler	_____
_____	Competence vs. inferiority
Adolescence	_____
_____	Intimacy vs. isolation
Middle adulthood	_____
_____	Integrity vs. despair

Objective 22: Explain how the search for identity affects us during adolescence, and discuss how forming an identity prepares us for intimacy.

19. To refine their sense of identity, adolescents in Western cultures experiment with different _____ in different situations. The result may be role _____ , which is resolved by forming a self-definition, or _____ .

20. Cultures that place less value on _____ inform adolescents about who they are, rather than letting them decide on their own. Some adolescents may form a _____ identity in opposition to parents and society.

21. During the early to mid-teen years, self-esteem generally _____ (rises/falls/remains stable). During the late teens and twenties, self-esteem generally _____ (rises/falls/remains stable) and identity becomes more _____ .

22. Erikson saw the formation of identity as a prerequisite for the development of _____ in young adulthood.

Objective 23: Contrast parental and peer influences during adolescence.

23. Adolescence is typically a time of increasing influence from one's _____ and decreasing influence from _____ .

24. Most adolescents report that they _____ (do/do not) get along with their parents.

25. When rejected adolescents withdraw, they are vulnerable to _____ , low _____ , and _____ .

Objective 24: Discuss the characteristics of emerging adulthood.

26. As a result of increased _____ _____ and weakened _____-_____ bonds, sexual maturity is beginning _____ (earlier/later) than in the past.

27. Because the time from 18 to the mid-twenties is increasingly a not-yet-settled phase of life, some psychologists refer to this period as a time of _____ _____ .

Adulthood (pp. 175–192)

> If you do not know the meaning of any of the following words, phrases, or expressions in the context in which they appear in the text, refer to pages 127–128 for an explanation: *misconceptions about aging exploded by recent research; stairs get steeper, the print gets smaller, and people seem to mumble more; levies a tax; "Use it or lose it"; myth . . . laid to rest; hold their own; "Pair-bonding is a trademark of the human animal"; test-driving life together; shower one another with affection; Highs become less high.*

1. During adulthood, age _____ (is/is not) a very good predictor of people's traits.

2. The mid-twenties are the peak years for

   _____ _____ ,
   _____ _____ ,
   _____ _____ , and
   _____ _____ . Because
   they mature earlier, _____ (women/men) also peak earlier.

Objective 25: Identify the major physical changes that occur in middle adulthood.

3. During early and middle adulthood, physical vigor has less to do with _____ than with a person's _____ and _____ habits.

4. The cessation of the menstrual cycle, known as _____ , occurs within a few years of _____ . This biological change results from lowered levels of the hormone _____ . A woman's experience during this time depends largely on her _____ and _____ .

5. Although men experience no equivalent to menopause, they do experience a more gradual decline in _____ count, level of the hormone _____ , and speed of erection and ejaculation during later life.

Objective 26: Compare life expectancy in the mid-twentieth and early twenty-first centuries, and discuss changes in sensory abilities and health (including frequency of dementia) in older adults.

6. Worldwide, life expectancy at birth increased from 49 years in 1950 to _____ years and beyond in 2004 in some developed countries. Women outlive men by nearly _____ years worldwide and by _____ years in Canada, the United States, and Australia.

7. According to one evolutionary theory, our bodies age and wear out because once we've completed our _____-_____ task by raising our young, there are no _____ _____ pressures against genes that cause degeneration in later life.

8. With age, the eye's pupil _____ (shrinks/enlarges) and its lens becomes _____ (more/less) transparent. As a result, the amount of light that reaches the retina is _____ (increased/reduced).

9. Although older adults are _____ (more/less) susceptible to life-threatening ailments, they suffer from short-term ailments such as flu _____ (more/less) often than younger adults.

10. Aging _____ (slows/speeds/has no effect on) neural processing and causes a gradual loss of _____ _____ .

11. Physical exercise stimulates _____ _____ development, thanks to increased _____ and nutrient flow.

12. The mental erosion that results from progressive damage to the brain is called _____ .

13. The irreversible disorder that causes progressive brain deterioration is _____ disease. This disease has been linked to a deterioration of neurons that produce the neurotransmitter _____ .

Objective 27: Assess the impact of aging on recall and recognition in adulthood.

14. Studies of developmental changes in learning and memory show that during adulthood there is a decline in the ability to _____ (recall/recognize) new information but not in the ability to _____ (recall/recognize) such information. One factor that influences memory in the elderly is the _____ of material.

15. Adults' _____ memory remains strong when events help trigger recall.

16. Cognitive abilities among 70-year-olds are _____ (less/more) varied than among 20-year-olds.

Objective 28: Summarize the contributions of cross-sectional and longitudinal studies to our understanding of the normal effects of aging on adult intelligence.

17. A research study in which people of various ages are compared with one another is called a _____-_____ study. This kind of study found evidence of intellectual _____ during adulthood.

18. A research study in which the same people are retested over a period of years is called a _____ study. This kind of study found evidence of intellectual _____ during adulthood.

Explain why studies of intellectual decline and aging yielded conflicting results.

19. The accumulation of stored information that comes with education and experience is called _____ intelligence, which tends to _____ with age.

20. The ability to reason abstractly is referred to as _____ intelligence, which tends to _____ with age.

Objective 29: Explain why the path of adult development need not be tightly linked to one's chronological age.

21. Contrary to popular opinion, job and marital dissatisfaction do not surge during the forties, thus suggesting that a midlife _____ need not occur.

22. The term used to refer to the culturally preferred timing for leaving home, getting a job, marrying, and so on is the _____ _____ .

23. Today, the timing of such life events is becoming _____ (more/less) predictable. More important than age are _____ _____ and chance encounters.

Objective 30: Discuss the importance of love, marriage, and children in adulthood, and comment on the contribution of one's work to feelings of self-satisfaction.

24. According to Erikson, the two basic tasks of adulthood are achieving _____ and _____ . According to Freud, the healthy adult is one who can _____ and _____ .

25. Human societies have nearly always included a relatively _____ bond. Marriage bonds are usually lasting when couples marry after age _____ and are _____ _____ .

26. Marriages today are _____ (half/twice) as likely to end in divorce as they were in the 1960s. Couples who live together before marrying have a _____ (higher/ lower) divorce rate than those who do not.

27. Of those who divorce, _____ percent eventually remarry. Marriage is a predictor of _____ , _____ _____ , _____ , and _____ . Lesbian couples report _____ (greater/less) well-being than those who are alone.

28. As children begin to absorb time and energy, satisfaction with the marriage itself _____ (increases/decreases). This is particularly true among _____ women, who shoulder most of the burden.

29. For most couples, the children's leaving home produces a(n) _____ (increase/decrease) in marital satisfaction.

30. Research studies of women who are or are not employed have found that a woman's satisfaction in life depends on the _____ of her experience in her life's role.

Objective 31: Describe trends in people's life satisfaction across the life span.

31. From early adulthood to midlife, people typically experience a strengthening sense of _____ , _____ , and _____ .

32. According to studies, older people _____ (do/do not) report as much happiness and satisfaction with life as younger people do. In addition, their feelings _____ (do/do not) mellow.

33. As we age, the brain area called the _____ shows _____ (increased/decreased) activity in response to negative events.

Objective 32: Describe the range of reactions to the death of a loved one.

34. Grief over a loved one's death is especially severe when it comes _____ .

35. Reactions to a loved one's death _____ (do/do not) vary according to cultural norms. Those who express the strongest grief immediately _____ (do/do not) purge their grief more quickly.

36. Terminally ill and bereaved people _____ (do/do not) go through predictable stages.

37. According to Erikson, the final task of adulthood is to achieve a sense of _____ .

Reflections on Two Major Developmental Issues (pp. 193–194)

> If you do not know the meaning of any of the following words, phrases, or expressions in the context in which they appear in the text, refer to page 128 for an explanation: *as a giant redwood differs from its seedling; goof-off.*

Objective 33: Summarize current views on continuity versus stages and stability versus change in lifelong development.

1. Stage theories that have been considered include the theory of cognitive development proposed by _____ , the theory of moral development proposed by _____ , and the theory of psychosocial development proposed by _____ .

2. Although research casts doubt on the idea that life proceeds through age-linked _____ , there are spurts of _____ growth during childhood and puberty that correspond roughly to the stages proposed by _____ .

3. The first two years of life _____ (do/do not) provide a good basis for predicting a person's eventual traits.

4. Research on the consistency of personality shows that some traits, such as those related to _____ , are more stable than others, such as social attitudes.

PROGRESS TEST 1

Circle your answers to the following questions and check them with the answers beginning on page 118. If your answer is incorrect, read the explanation for why it is incorrect and then consult the appropriate pages of the text (in parentheses following the correct answer).

Multiple-Choice Questions

1. Dr. Joan Goodman is studying how memory changes as people get older. She is most likely a(n) _____ psychologist.
   a. social
   b. cognitive
   c. developmental
   d. experimental

2. In Piaget's stage of concrete operational intelligence, the child acquires an understanding of the principle of:
   a. conservation.
   b. deduction.
   c. attachment.
   d. object permanence.

3. Piaget held that egocentrism is characteristic of the:
   a. sensorimotor stage.
   b. preoperational stage.
   c. concrete operational stage.
   d. formal operational stage.

4. During which stage of cognitive development do children acquire object permanence?
   a. sensorimotor
   b. preoperational
   c. concrete operational
   d. formal operational

5. The rooting reflex occurs when a:
   a. newborn's foot is tickled.
   b. newborn's cheek is touched.
   c. newborn hears a loud noise.
   d. newborn makes eye contact with his or her caregiver.

6. Harlow's studies of attachment in monkeys showed that:
   a. provision of nourishment was the single most important factor motivating attachment.
   b. a cloth mother produced the greatest attachment response.
   c. whether a cloth or wire mother was present mattered less than the presence or absence of other infants.
   d. attachment in monkeys is based on imprinting.

7. When psychologists discuss maturation, they are referring to stages of growth that are *not* influenced by:
   a. conservation.
   b. nature.
   c. nurture.
   d. continuity.

8. The developmental theorist who suggested that securely attached children develop an attitude of basic trust is:
   a. Piaget.
   b. Harlow.
   c. Vygotsky.
   d. Erikson.

9. Research findings on infant motor development are consistent with the idea that:
   a. cognitive development lags significantly behind motor skills development.
   b. maturation of physical skills is relatively unaffected by experience.
   c. in the absence of relevant earlier learning experiences, the emergence of motor skills will be slowed.
   d. in humans, the process of maturation may be significantly altered by cultural factors.

10. According to Erikson, the central psychological challenges pertaining to adolescence, young adulthood, and middle age, respectively, are:
    a. identity formation; intimacy; generativity.
    b. intimacy; identity formation; generativity.
    c. generativity; intimacy; identity formation.
    d. intimacy; generativity; identity formation.

11. In preconventional morality, the person:
    a. obeys out of a sense of social duty.
    b. conforms to gain social approval.
    c. obeys to avoid punishment or to gain concrete rewards.
    d. follows the dictates of his or her conscience.

12. Which of the following is correct?
    a. Early maturation places both boys and girls at a distinct social advantage.
    b. Early maturing girls are more popular and self-assured than girls who mature late.
    c. Early maturation places both boys and girls at a distinct social disadvantage.
    d. Early maturing boys are more popular and self-assured than boys who mature late.

13. A person's general ability to think abstractly is called _____ intelligence. This ability generally _____ with age.
    a. fluid; increases
    b. fluid; decreases
    c. crystallized; decreases
    d. crystallized; increases

14. Among the hallmarks of growing up are a boy's first ejaculation and a girl's first menstrual period, which also is called:
    a. puberty.   c. menarche.
    b. menopause.   d. generativity.

15. An elderly person who can look back on life with satisfaction and reminisce with a sense of completion has attained Erikson's stage of:
    a. generativity.   c. isolation.
    b. intimacy.   d. integrity.

16. According to Piaget, the ability to think logically about abstract propositions is indicative of the stage of:
    a. preoperational thought.
    b. concrete operations.
    c. formal operations.
    d. fluid intelligence.

17. The cognitive ability that has been shown to decline during adulthood is the ability to:
    a. recall new information.
    b. recognize new information.
    c. learn meaningful new material.
    d. use judgment in dealing with daily life problems.

18. Which of the following statements concerning the effects of aging is true?
    a. Aging almost inevitably leads to dementia if the individual lives long enough.
    b. Aging increases susceptibility to short-term ailments such as the flu.
    c. Significant increases in life satisfaction are associated with aging.
    d. The aging process can be significantly affected by the individual's activity patterns.

19. Longitudinal tests:
    a. compare people of different ages.
    b. study the same people at different times.
    c. usually involve a larger sample than do cross-sectional tests.
    d. usually involve a smaller sample than do cross-sectional tests.

20. The average age at which puberty begins is _____ in boys; in girls, it is _____ .
    a. 14; 13   c. 11; 10
    b. 13; 11   d. 10; 9

21. After puberty, the self-concept usually becomes:
    a. more positive in boys.
    b. more positive in girls.
    c. more positive in both boys and girls.
    d. more negative in both boys and girls.

22. Adolescence is marked by the onset of:
    a. an identity crisis.
    b. parent-child conflict.
    c. the concrete operational stage.
    d. puberty.

23. Of the following, which is a possible cause of dementia?
    a. stroke
    b. brain tumor
    c. alcoholism
    d. All of the above are possible causes.

24. The end of menstruation is called:
    a. menarche.
    b. menopause.
    c. the midlife crisis.
    d. generativity.

25. The popular idea that terminally ill and bereaved people go through predictable stages, such as denial, anger, and so forth:
    a. is widely supported by research.
    b. more accurately describes grieving in some cultures than others.
    c. is true of women but not men.
    d. is not supported by research studies.

True–False Items

Indicate whether each statement is true or false by placing *T* or *F* in the blank next to the item.

_____   1. Most abused children later become abusive parents.
_____   2. At birth, the brain and nervous system of a healthy child are fully developed.
_____   3. The sequence in which children develop motor skills varies from one culture to another.
_____   4. Recent research shows that young children are more capable and development is more continuous than Piaget believed.

_____ 5. The process of grieving is much the same throughout the world.

_____ 6. The impact of day care on child development, even if it is high quality, remains controversial.

_____ 7. During adulthood, age only moderately correlates with people's traits.

_____ 8. Intelligence declines throughout adulthood.

_____ 9. By the age of 50, most adults have experienced a "midlife crisis."

_____ 10. Compared to those who are younger, elderly people are more susceptible to short-term ailments such as flu and cold viruses.

_____ 11. The symptoms of Alzheimer's disease are simply an intensified version of normal aging.

PROGRESS TEST 2

Progress Test 2 should be completed during a final chapter review. Answer the following questions after you thoroughly understand the correct answers for the section reviews and Progress Test 1.

1. Stranger anxiety develops soon after:
   a. the concept of conservation.
   b. egocentrism.
   c. a theory of mind.
   d. the concept of object permanence.

2. Before Piaget, people were more likely to believe that:
   a. the child's mind is a miniature model of the adult's.
   b. children think about the world in radically different ways from adults.
   c. the child's mind develops through a series of stages.
   d. children interpret their experiences in terms of their current understandings.

3. Which is the correct sequence of stages in Piaget's theory of cognitive development?
   a. sensorimotor, preoperational, concrete operational, formal operational
   b. sensorimotor, preoperational, formal operational, concrete operational
   c. preoperational, sensorimotor, concrete operational, formal operational
   d. preoperational, sensorimotor, formal operational, concrete operational

4. A child can be born a drug addict because:
   a. drugs used by the mother will pass into the child's bloodstream.
   b. addiction is an inherited personality trait.
   c. drugs used by the mother create genetic defects in her chromosomes.
   d. the fetus' blood has not yet developed a resistance to drugs.

5. A child whose mother drank heavily when she was pregnant is at heightened risk of:
   a. being emotionally excitable during childhood.
   b. becoming insecurely attached.
   c. being born with the physical and cognitive abnormalities of fetal alcohol syndrome.
   d. addiction to a range of drugs throughout life.

6. Which is the correct order of stages of prenatal development?
   a. zygote, fetus, embryo
   b. zygote, embryo, fetus
   c. embryo, zygote, fetus
   d. embryo, fetus, zygote

7. The term *critical period* refers to:
   a. prenatal development.
   b. the initial 2 hours after a child's birth.
   c. the preoperational stage.
   d. a restricted time for learning.

8. Which of the following was *not* found by Harlow in socially deprived monkeys?
   a. They had difficulty mating.
   b. They showed extreme fear or aggression when first seeing other monkeys.
   c. They showed abnormal physical development.
   d. The females were abusive mothers.

9. Most people's earliest memories do not predate _____ of age.
   a. 6 months   c. 2 years
   b. 1 year   d. 4 years

10. Insecurely attached infants who are left by their mothers in an unfamiliar setting often will:
    a. hold fast to their mothers on their return.
    b. explore the new surroundings confidently.
    c. be indifferent toward their mothers on their return.
    d. display little emotion at any time.

11. Whose stage theory of moral development was based on how people reasoned about ethical dilemmas?
    a. Erikson
    b. Piaget
    c. Harlow
    d. Kohlberg

12. The cross-sectional method:
    a. compares people of different ages with one another.
    b. studies the same group of people at different times.
    c. tends to paint too favorable a picture of the effects of aging on intelligence.
    d. is more appropriate than the longitudinal method for studying intellectual change over the life span.

13. The social clock refers to:
    a. an individual or society's distribution of work and leisure time.
    b. adulthood responsibilities.
    c. typical ages for starting a career, marrying, and so on.
    d. age-related changes in one's circle of friends.

14. To which of Kohlberg's levels would moral reasoning based on the existence of fundamental human rights pertain?
    a. preconventional morality
    b. conventional morality
    c. postconventional morality
    d. generative morality

15. In Erikson's theory, individuals generally focus on developing _____ during adolescence and then _____ during young adulthood.
    a. identity; intimacy
    b. intimacy; identity
    c. basic trust; identity
    d. identity; basic trust

16. After menopause, most women:
    a. experience anxiety and a sense of worthlessness.
    b. experience hot flashes.
    c. secrete unusually high levels of estrogen.
    d. feel a new sense of freedom.

17. Notable achievements in fields such as _____ are often made by younger adults in their late twenties or early thirties, when _____ intelligence is at its peak.
    a. mathematics; fluid
    b. philosophy; fluid
    c. science; crystallized
    d. literature; crystallized

18. After their grown children have left home, most couples experience:
    a. the distress of the "empty nest syndrome."
    b. increased strain in their marital relationship.
    c. both a. and b.
    d. greater happiness and enjoyment in their relationship.

19. Underlying Alzheimer's disease is a deterioration in neurons that produce:
    a. epinephrine.
    b. norepinephrine.
    c. serotonin.
    d. acetylcholine.

20. A person's accumulation of stored information, called _____ intelligence, generally _____ with age.
    a. fluid; decreases
    b. fluid; increases
    c. crystallized; decreases
    d. crystallized; increases

21. In terms of incidence, susceptibility to short-term illnesses _____ with age and susceptibility to long-term ailments _____ with age.
    a. decreases; increases
    b. increases; decreases
    c. increases; increases
    d. decreases; decreases

22. Stage theories have been criticized because they fail to consider that development may be significantly affected by:
    a. variations in the social clock.
    b. each individual's experiences.
    c. each individual's historical and cultural setting.
    d. all of the above.

23. Research on the American family indicates that:
    a. fewer than 23 percent of unmarried adults, but nearly 40 percent of married adults, report being "very happy" with life.
    b. the divorce rate is now one-half the marriage rate.
    c. of those who divorce, 75 percent remarry.
    d. all of the above are true.

PSYCHOLOGY APPLIED

Answer these questions the day before an exam as a final check on your understanding of the chapter's terms and concepts.

Multiple-Choice Questions

1. Compared to when he was younger, 4-year-old Antonio is better able to empathize with his friend's feelings. This growing ability to take another's perspective indicates that Antonio is acquiring a:
    a. self-concept.
    b. schema.
    c. temperament.
    d. theory of mind.

2. Calvin, who is trying to impress his psychology professor with his knowledge of infant motor development, asks why some infants learn to roll over before they lift their heads from a prone position, while others develop these skills in the opposite order. What should Calvin's professor conclude from this question?
    a. Calvin clearly understands that the sequence of motor development is not the same for all infants.
    b. Calvin doesn't know what he's talking about. Although some infants reach these developmental milestones ahead of others, the order is the same for all infants.
    c. Calvin needs to be reminded that rolling over is an inherited reflex, not a learned skill.
    d. Calvin understands an important principle: motor development is unpredictable.

3. Deborah is a mathematician and Willie is a philosopher. Considering their professions:
    a. Deborah will make her most significant career accomplishments at an earlier age than Willie will.
    b. Deborah will make her most significant career accomplishments at a later age than Willie will.
    c. Deborah will make her most significant career accomplishments at about the same time as Willie.
    d. there is still not enough information for predicting such accomplishments.

4. Based on the text discussion of maturation and popularity, who among the following is probably the most popular sixth grader?
    a. Jessica, the most physically mature girl in the class
    b. Roger, the most intellectually mature boy in the class
    c. Rob, the tallest, most physically mature boy in the class
    d. Cindy, who is average in physical development and is on the school debating team

5. As a child observes, liquid is transferred from a tall, thin tube into a short, wide jar. The child is asked if there is now less liquid in order to determine if she has mastered:
    a. the schema for liquids.
    b. the concept of object permanence.
    c. the concept of conservation.
    d. the ability to reason abstractly.

6. I am 14 months old and fearful of strangers. I am in Piaget's _____ stage of cognitive development.
    a. sensorimotor
    b. preoperational
    c. concrete operational
    d. formal operational

7. I am 3 years old, can use language, and have trouble taking another person's perspective. I am in Piaget's _____ stage of cognitive development.
    a. sensorimotor
    b. preoperational
    c. concrete operational
    d. formal operational

8. In Piaget's theory, conservation is to egocentrism as the _____ stage is to the _____ stage.
    a. sensorimotor; formal operational
    b. formal operational; sensorimotor
    c. preoperational; sensorimotor
    d. concrete operational; preoperational

9. Four-year-old Jamail has a younger sister. When asked if he has a sister, he is likely to answer _____ ; when asked if his sister has a brother, Jamail is likely to answer _____ .
    a. yes; yes
    b. no; no
    c. yes; no
    d. no; yes

10. In a 1998 movie, a young girl finds that a gaggle of geese follow her wherever she goes because she was the first "object" they saw after they were born. This is an example of:
    a. conservation.
    b. imprinting.
    c. egocentrism.
    d. basic trust.

11. Joshua and Ann Bishop have a 13-month-old boy. According to Erikson, the Bishops' sensitive, loving care of their child contributes to:
    a. the child's sense of basic trust.
    b. the child's secure attachment.
    c. the child's sense of control.
    d. a. and b. only.

12. Fourteen-year-old Cassandra feels freer and more open with her friends than with her family.

Knowing this is the case, Cassandra's parents should:

a. be concerned, because deteriorating parent-teen relationships, such as this one, are often followed by a range of problem behaviors.

b. encourage Cassandra to find new friends.

c. seek family counseling.

d. not worry, since adolescence is typically a time of growing peer influence and diminishing parental influence.

13. Thirteen-year-old Irene has no trouble defeating her 11-year-old brother at a detective game that requires following clues in order to deduce the perpetrator of a crime. How might Piaget explain Irene's superiority at the game?

a. Being older, Irene has had more years of schooling.

b. Girls develop intellectually at a faster rate than boys.

c. Being an adolescent, Irene is beginning to develop abstract reasoning skills.

d. Girls typically have more experience than boys at playing games.

14. Which of the following was *not* mentioned in the text as a criticism of Kohlberg's theory of moral development?

a. It does not account for the fact that the development of moral reasoning is culture-specific.

b. Postconventional morality appears mostly in educated, middle-class persons.

c. The theory is biased against the moral reasoning of people in communal societies such as China.

d. The theory is biased in favor of moral reasoning in men.

15. Sixty-five-year-old Calvin cannot reason as well as he could when he was younger. More than likely, Calvin's _____ intelligence has declined.

a. analytic   c. fluid
b. crystallized   d. both b. and c.

16. Cross-sectional studies of intelligence are potentially misleading because:

a. they are typically based on a very small and unrepresentative sample of people.

b. retesting the same people over a period of years allows test performance to be influenced by practice.

c. they compare people who are not only different in age, but of different eras, education levels, and affluence.

d. of all the above reasons.

17. Which statement illustrates cognitive development during the course of adult life?

a. Adults in their forties have better recognition memory than do adults in their seventies.

b. Recall and recognition memory both remain strong throughout life.

c. Recognition memory decreases sharply at midlife.

d. Adults in their forties have better recall memory than adults in their seventies.

18. Given the text discussion of life satisfaction patterns, which of the following people is likely to report the greatest life satisfaction?

a. Billy, a 7-year-old second-grader
b. Kathy, a 17-year-old high-school senior
c. Mildred, a 70-year-old retired teacher
d. too little information to tell

19. Which of the following statements is consistent with the current thinking of developmental psychologists?

a. Development occurs in a series of sharply defined stages.

b. The first two years are the most crucial in determining the individual's personality.

c. The consistency of personality in most people tends to increase over the life span.

d. Social and emotional style are among the characteristics that show the least stability over the life span.

20. Sam, a junior in high school, regularly attends church because his family and friends think he should. Which stage of moral reasoning is Sam in?

a. preconventional
b. conventional
c. postconventional
d. too little information to tell

21. Research on social relationships between parents and their adolescent children shows that:

a. parental influence on children increases during adolescence.

b. high school girls who have the most affectionate relationships with their mothers tend to enjoy the most intimate friendships with girlfriends.

c. high school boys who have the most affectionate relationships with their fathers tend to enjoy the most intimate friendships with friends.

d. most teens are strongly influenced by parents in matters of personal taste.

22. Most contemporary developmental psychologists believe that:

 a. personality is essentially formed by the end of infancy.

 b. personality continues to be formed until adolescence.

 c. the shaping of personality continues during adolescence and well beyond.

 d. adolescent development has very little impact on adult personality.

23. After a series of unfulfilling relationships, 30-year-old Carlos tells a friend that he doesn't want to marry because he is afraid of losing his freedom and independence. Erikson would say that Carlos is having difficulty with the psychosocial task of:

 a. trust versus mistrust.

 b. autonomy versus doubt.

 c. intimacy versus isolation.

 d. identity versus role confusion.

24. Research on the relationship between self-reported happiness and employment in American women has revealed that:

 a. women who work tend to be happier.

 b. women who do not work tend to be happier.

 c. women today are happier than in the past, whether they are working or not.

 d. the quality of a woman's experience in her various roles is more predictive of happiness than the presence or absence of a given role.

Essay Question

Sheryl is 12 years old and in the sixth grade. Describe the developmental changes she is likely to be experiencing according to Piaget, Kohlberg, and Erikson. (Use the space below to list the points you want to make, and organize them. Then write the essay on a separate sheet of paper.)

KEY TERMS

Using your own words, on a piece of paper write a brief definition or explanation of each of the following terms.

 1. developmental psychology

 2. zygote

 3. embryo

 4. fetus

 5. teratogens

 6. fetal alcohol syndrome (FAS)

 7. rooting reflex

 8. habituation

 9. maturation

10. schema

11. assimilation

12. accommodation

13. cognition

14. sensorimotor stage

15. object permanence

16. preoperational stage

17. conservation

18. egocentrism

19. theory of mind

20. autism

21. concrete operational stage

22. formal operational stage

23. stranger anxiety

24. attachment

25. critical period

26. imprinting

27. basic trust

28. self-concept

29. adolescence

30. puberty

31. primary sex characteristics

32. secondary sex characteristics

33. menarche

34. identity

35. intimacy

36. menopause

37. Alzheimer's disease

38. cross-sectional study

39. longitudinal study

40. crystallized intelligence

41. fluid intelligence

42. social clock

Cross-Check

As you learned in the Prologue, reviewing and overlearning of material are important to the learning process. After you have written the definitions of the key terms in this chapter, you should complete the crossword puzzle to ensure that you can reverse the process—recognize the term, given the definition.

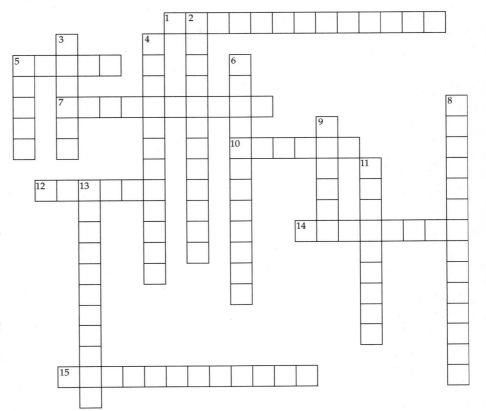

ACROSS

1. In Piaget's theory, changing an existing schema to incorporate new information.

5. Type of intelligence that relates to reasoning speedily and abstractly.

7. Process by which certain animals form attachments during a critical period.

10. The developing person from 2 weeks through 2 months after conception.

12. Mental concepts or frameworks that organize information.

14. The first menstrual period.

15. A study in which the same people are retested over a period of years.

Down

2. Type of intelligence that reflects accumulated learning.

3. A childhood disorder marked by deficiencies in communication and social interaction.

4. In Piaget's theory, interpreting a new experience in terms of an existing schema.

5. The developing person from 9 weeks after conception until birth.

6. Principle that properties such as number and volume remain constant despite changes in appearance.

8. A study in which people of different ages are compared with one another.

9. Fertilized human egg.

11. Any drug, virus, or other toxic substance that crosses the mother's placenta.

13. Decreasing responsiveness to a stimulus that is repeatedly presented

ANSWERS

Chapter Review

Introduction

1. developmental psychologists

2. nature/nurture

3. continuity/stages

4. stability

Prenatal Development and the Newborn

1. ovary; egg

2. sperm; enzymes; blocks

3. nuclei

4. zygotes; differentiate; uterine; placenta

5. embryo; fetus

6. teratogens

7. can affect; fetal alcohol syndrome

8. rooting reflex

9. William James; incorrect

Newborns reflexively turn their heads in the direction of human voices. They gaze longer at a drawing of a human face than at a bull's-eye pattern. They focus best on objects about 8 to 12 inches away, which is about the distance between a nursing infant's eyes and the mother's. Within days, they recognize their mother's smell and voice.

10. habituation; decrease; colors, shapes, sounds; numbers; physics

Infancy and Childhood

1. over; 28 weeks; is not
2. frontal; rational planning
3. pruning
4. maturation
5. motor; sequence; crawl; run
6. major
7. cerebellum; small
8. 3
9. infantile amnesia
10. preverbal; language
11. Piaget
12. schemas
13. assimilation; accommodation
14. cognition
15. sensorimotor; 2
16. object permanence; 8
17. underestimated; numbers
18. 6 or 7; preoperational
19. conservation; have not
20. egocentrism
21. theory of mind; false beliefs; feelings
22. communication; social; theory of mind; autism; attending; Asperger syndrome
23. male; empathizers; systemizers
24. operations; symbolically; perspective; gradually
25. Lev Vygotsky; 7; inner speech; scaffold
26. 6 or 7; concrete operational
27. formal operational; abstract; 12

Contemporary researchers see development as more continuous than did Piaget. By detecting the beginnings of each type of thinking at earlier ages, they have revealed conceptual abilities that Piaget missed. They also see formal logic as a smaller part of cognition than Piaget did. Despite these revisions to Piaget's theory, studies support the basic idea that cognitive development unfolds as a sequence of distinct stages.

28. object permanence; stranger anxiety
29. 8 months
30. attachment
31. body contact; familiarity
32. safe haven; secure base
33. critical period; imprinting
34. do not
35. strange situation; secure; insecure

Placed in a strange situation, securely attached infants play comfortably, happily exploring their new environment. In contrast, insecurely attached infants are less likely to explore their surroundings and may even cling to their mothers. When separated from their mothers, insecurely attached infants are much more distressed than securely attached infants. When reunited with their mothers, insecurely attached infants may be indifferent.

Research studies conducted by Mary Ainsworth have revealed that sensitive, responsive mothers tend to have securely attached infants, whereas insensitive, unresponsive mothers often have insecurely attached infants. Other studies have found that temperamentally difficult infants whose mothers receive training in responsive parenting are more likely to become securely attached than are control infants. This points to the importance of considering the infant's temperament in studying attachment.

36. comparable to
37. 13; gradually declines; throughout the world
38. basic trust
39. aggression
40. do not
41. resilient; stress hormones; serotonin
42. recover
43. does not; safe; healthy; stimulating; the mother's sensitivity, the child's temperament, and the family's economic and educational level
44. self-concept; 12
45. 8; 10; traits

Children who have formed a positive self-concept tend to be more confident, independent, optimistic, assertive, and sociable.

46. authoritarian
47. permissive
48. authoritative
49. authoritative; control

There are at least three possible explanations for the correlation between authoritative parenting and social competence in children. (1) Parenting may foster children's competence. (2) Children's competence may promote authoritative parenting. (3) A third factor, such as heredity or parental education or socioeconomic status, may foster both authoritative parenting and child competence.

Adolescence

1. childhood; adulthood
2. G. Stanley Hall
3. puberty; 11; 13; primary sex; secondary sex
4. menarche; spermarche
5. sequence; timing
6. early; alcohol use and premature sexual activity; early; emotional maturity; heredity; environment
7. pruning; frontal lobe; limbic system
8. social; moral
9. self-focused
10. formal operations; abstract; inconsistencies
11. Kohlberg; preconventional; conventional; postconventional
12. punishment; rewards
13. adolescence; approval; order
14. postconventional

Critics of Kohlberg's theory argue that the perception of postconventional moral reasoning as the highest level of moral development reflects a Western middle-class bias. Others have argued that for women, morality is less a matter of abstract, impersonal justice and more an ethic of caring relationships.

15. social intuitionist; moral paradoxes
16. social; character education programs
17. gratification; service; academically
18. stronger

Erikson's stages of psychosocial development

Group Age	Psychosocial Stage
Infancy	Trust vs. mistrust
Toddlerhood	Autonomy vs. shame and doubt
\Preschooler	Initiative vs. guilt
Elementary school	Competence vs. inferiority
Adolescence	Identity vs. role confusion
Young adulthood	Intimacy vs. isolation
Middle adulthood	Generativity vs. stagnation
Late adulthood	Integrity vs. despair

19. selves; confusion; identity
20. individualism; negative
21. falls; rises; personalized
22. intimacy
23. peers; parents
24. do
25. loneliness; self-esteem; depression
26. body fat; parent-child; earlier
27. emerging adulthood

Adulthood

1. is not
2. muscular strength, reaction time, sensory keenness, cardiac output; women
3. age; health; exercise
4. menopause; 50; estrogen; expectations; attitude
5. sperm; testosterone
6. 75; 4; 5 to 6
7. gene-reproducing; natural selection
8. shrinks; less; reduced
9. more; less
10. slows; brain cells
11. brain cell; oxygen
12. dementia
13. Alzheimer's; acetylcholine
14. recall; recognize; meaningfulness
15. prospective
16. more
17. cross-sectional; decline
18. longitudinal; stability

Because cross-sectional studies compare people not only of different ages but also of different eras, education levels, family size, and affluence, it is not surprising that such studies reveal cognitive decline with age. In contrast, longitudinal studies test one group over a span of years. However, because those who survive to the end of longitudinal studies may be the brightest and healthiest, these studies may underestimate the average decline in intelligence. Research is also complicated by the fact that certain tests measure only one type of intelligence. Tests that measure fluid intelligence reveal decline with age; tests that measure crystallized intelligence reveal just the opposite.

19. crystallized; increase
20. fluid; decrease
21. transition (crisis)
22. social clock

23. less; life events
24. intimacy; generativity; love; work
25. monogamous; 20; well educated
26. twice; higher
27. 75; happiness; sexual satisfaction; health; income; greater
28. decreases; employed
29. increase
30. quality
31. identity; confidence; self-esteem
32. do; do
33. amygdala; decreased
34. suddenly and before its expected time on the social clock
35. do; do not
36. do not
37. integrity

Reflections on the Two Major Developmental Issues

1. Piaget; Kohlberg; Erikson
2. stages; brain; Piaget
3. do not
4. temperament

Progress Test 1

Multiple-Choice Questions

1. **c.** is the answer. Developmental psychologists study physical, cognitive (memory, in this example), and social change throughout the life span. (p. 139)
   a. Social psychologists study how people influence and are influenced by others.
   b. Cognitive psychologists *do* study memory; because Dr. Goodman is interested in life-span *changes* in memory, she is more likely a developmental psychologist.
   d. Experimental psychologists study physiology, sensation, perception, learning, and other aspects of behavior. Only developmental psychologists focus on developmental changes in behavior and mental processes.

2. **a.** is the answer. (p. 153)
   b. Deduction, or deductive reasoning, is a formal operational ability.
   c. Piaget's theory is not concerned with attachment.
   d. Attaining object permanence is the hallmark of sensorimotor thought.

3. **b.** is the answer. The preoperational child sees the world from his or her own vantage point. (p. 150)
   a. As immature as egocentrism is, it represents a significant cognitive advance over the sensorimotor child, who knows the world only through senses and actions. Even simple self-awareness takes a while to develop.
   c. & d. As children attain the operational stages, they become more able to see the world through the eyes of others.

4. **a.** is the answer. Before object permanence is attained, "out of sight" is truly "out of mind." (p. 149)
   b., c., & d. Developments during the preoperational, concrete operational, and formal operational stages include the use of language, conservation, and abstract reasoning, respectively.

5. **b.** is the answer. The infant turns its head and begins sucking when its cheek is stroked. (p. 142)
   a., c., & d. These stimuli produce other reflexes in the newborn.

6. **b.** is the answer. (p. 155)
   a. When given the choice between a wire mother with a bottle and a cloth mother without, the monkeys preferred the cloth mother.
   c. The presence of other infants made no difference.
   d. Imprinting plays no role in the attachment of higher primates.

7. **c.** is the answer. Through maturation—an orderly sequence of biological growth processes that are relatively unaffected by experience—all humans develop. (p. 145)
   a. Conservation is the cognitive awareness that objects do not change with changes in shape.
   b. The forces of nature *are* those that direct maturation.
   d. The continuity/stages debate has to do with whether development is a gradual and continuous process or a discontinuous, stagelike process. Those who emphasize maturation see development as occurring in stages, not continuously.

8. **d.** is the answer. Erikson proposed that development occurs in a series of stages, in the first of which the child develops an attitude of either basic trust or mistrust. (p. 158)
   a. Piaget's theory is concerned with cognitive development.
   b. Harlow conducted research on attachment and deprivation.
   c. Vygotsky focused on the influence of social factors on cognitive development.

9. **b.** is the answer. (pp. 145–146)

10. a. is the answer. (p. 170)

11. c. is the answer. At the preconventional level, moral reasoning centers on self-interest, whether this means obtaining rewards or avoiding punishment. (p. 168)

a. & b. Moral reasoning based on a sense of social duty or a desire to gain social approval is associated with the conventional level of moral development.

d. Reasoning based on ethical principles is characteristic of the postconventional level of moral development.

12. d. is the answer. Boys who show early physical maturation are generally stronger and more athletic than boys who mature late; these qualities may lead to greater popularity and self-assurance. (p. 166)

a. & c. Early maturation tends to be socially advantageous for boys but not for girls.

b. Early-maturing girls often suffer embarrassment and are objects of teasing.

13. b. is the answer. (p. 184)

a. Fluid intelligence tends to decrease with age.

c. & d. Crystallized intelligence refers to the accumulation of facts and general knowledge that takes place during a person's life. Crystallized intelligence generally *increases* with age.

14. c. is the answer. (p. 166)

a. Puberty refers to the early adolescent period during which accelerated growth and sexual maturation occur, not to the first menstrual period.

b. Menopause is the cessation of menstruation, which typically occurs in the early fifties.

d. In Erikson's theory, generativity, or the sense of contributing and being productive, is the task of middle adulthood.

15. d. is the answer. (p. 191)

a. Generativity is associated with middle adulthood.

b. & c. Intimacy and isolation are associated with young adulthood.

16. c. is the answer. Once formal operational thought has been attained, thinking is no longer limited to concrete propositions. (p. 154)

a. & b. Preoperational thought and concrete operational thought emerge before, and do not include, the ability to think logically about abstract propositions.

d. Fluid intelligence refers to abstract reasoning abilities; however, it is unrelated to Piaget's theory and stages.

17. a. is the answer. (pp. 181–182)

b., c., & d. These cognitive abilities remain essentially unchanged as the person ages.

18. d. is the answer. "Use it or lose it" seems to be the rule: often, changes in activity patterns contribute significantly to problems regarded as being part of usual aging. (pp. 175–176)

a. Most elderly people do not develop dementia; even among the very old, the risk of dementia is only 40 percent.

b. Although the elderly are more subject to long-term ailments than younger adults, they actually suffer fewer short-term ailments.

c. People of all ages report equal happiness or satisfaction with life.

19. b. is the answer. (p. 183)

a. This answer describes cross-sectional research.

c. & d. Sample size does not distinguish cross-sectional from longitudinal research.

20. b. is the answer. (p. 165)

21. c. is the answer. Because the late teen years provide many new opportunities for trying out possible roles, adolescents' identities typically incorporate an increasingly positive self-concept. (p. 171)

22. d. is the answer. The physical changes of puberty mark the onset of adolescence. (p. 165)

a. & b. An identity crisis or parent-child conflict may or may not occur during adolescence; neither of these formally marks its onset.

c. Formal operational thought, rather than concrete reasoning, typically develops in adolescence.

23. d. is the answer. (p. 180)

24. b. is the answer. (p. 176)

a. Menarche refers to the onset of menstruation.

c. When it does occur, the midlife crisis is a psychological, rather than biological, phenomenon.

d. Generativity is Erikson's term for productivity during middle adulthood.

25. d. is the answer. (p. 191)

True–False Items

1. F (p. 158)	**5.** F (p. 191)	**9.** F (p. 186)
2. F (p. 144)	**6.** F (p. 160)	**10.** F (p. 179)
3. F (p. 145)	**7.** T (p. 186)	**11.** F (pp. 180)
4. T (p. 154)	**8.** F (p. 184)	

Progress Test 2

1. d. is the answer. With object permanence, a child develops schemas for familiar objects, including faces, and may become upset by a stranger who does not fit any of these schemas. (p. 155)

a. The concept of conservation develops during the concrete operational stage, whereas stranger anxiety develops during the sensorimotor stage.

b. & c. Egocentrism and a theory of mind both develop during the preoperational stage. This follows the sensorimotor stage, during which stranger anxiety develops.

2. **a.** is the answer. (p. 147)

   b., c., & d. Each of these is an understanding developed by Piaget.

3. **a.** is the answer. (p. 148)

4. **a.** is the answer. Any drug taken by the mother passes through the placenta and enters the child's bloodstream. (p. 141)

   b. Addiction cannot be inherited; it requires exposure to an addictive drug.

   c. Drugs may disrupt the mechanisms of heredity, but there is no evidence that such changes promote addiction.

   d. This answer is incorrect because at no age does the blood "resist" drugs.

5. **c.** is the answer. (p. 142)

   a., b., & d. A child's emotional temperament, attachment, and addiction have not been linked to the mother's drinking while pregnant.

6. **b.** is the answer. (pp. 140–141)

7. **d.** is the answer. A critical period is a restricted time during which an organism must be exposed to certain influences or experiences for a particular kind of learning to occur. (p. 156)

   a. Critical periods refer to developmental periods after birth.

   b. Critical periods vary from behavior to behavior, but they are not confined to the hours following birth.

   c. Critical periods are not specifically associated with the preoperational period.

8. **c.** is the answer. Deprived monkeys were impaired in their social behaviors but not in their physical development. (p. 158)

   a., b., & d. Each of these was found in socially deprived monkeys.

9. **d.** is the answer. This is because of a lack of neural connections before that age. (p. 146)

10. **c.** is the answer. (p. 156)

    a. Insecurely attached infants often cling to their mothers when placed in a new situation; yet, when the mother returns after an absence, the infant's reaction tends to be one of indifference.

    b. These behaviors are characteristic of securely attached infants.

    d. Insecurely attached infants in unfamiliar sur-

roundings will often exhibit a range of emotional behaviors.

11. **d.** is the answer. (p. 168)

    a. Erikson is known for his theory of psychosocial development.

    b. Piaget is known for his theory of cognitive development.

    c. Harlow is known for his studies of attachment in infant monkeys.

12. **a.** is the answer. (p. 183)

    b. This answer describes the longitudinal research method.

    c. & d. Cross-sectional studies have tended to exaggerate the negative effects of aging on intellectual functioning; for this reason they may not be the most appropriate method for studying life-span development.

13. **c.** is the answer. Different societies and eras have somewhat different ideas about the age at which major life events should ideally occur. (p. 187)

14. **c.** is the answer. (p. 168)

    a. Preconventional morality is based on avoiding punishment and obtaining rewards.

    b. Conventional morality is based on gaining the approval of others and/or on following the law and social convention.

    d. There is no such thing as generative morality.

15. **a.** is the answer. (p. 170)

    b. According to Erikson, identity develops before intimacy.

    c. & d. The formation of basic trust is the task of infancy.

16. **d.** is the answer. (p. 176)

    a. Most women do not experience anxiety and distress following menopause; moreover, the woman's experience will depend largely on her expectations and attitude.

    b. Only 4 or 5 in 10 postmenopausal Canadian and U.S. women and 1 in 7 postmenopausal Japanese women experience hot flashes.

    c. Menopause is caused by a *reduction* in estrogen.

17. **a.** is the answer. A mathematician's skills are likely to reflect abstract reasoning, or fluid intelligence, which declines with age. (p. 185)

    b. & d. Philosophy and literature are fields in which individuals often do their most notable work later in life, after more experiential knowledge (crystallized intelligence) has accumulated.

    c. Scientific achievements generally reflect fluid, rather than crystallized, intelligence.

18. **d.** is the answer. (p. 188)

    a., b., & c. Most couples do not feel a loss of purpose or marital strain following the departure of grown children.

19. **d.** is the answer. Significantly, drugs that block the activity of the neurotransmitter acetylcholine produce Alzheimer's-like symptoms. (p. 180)

    a. & b. Epinephrine and norepinephrine are hormones produced by glands of the endocrine system.

    c. Serotonin is a neurotransmitter and hence is produced by neurons, but it has not been implicated in Alzheimer's disease.

20. **d.** is the answer. (p. 184)

    a. & b. Fluid intelligence, which decreases with age, refers to the ability to reason abstractly.

    c. Crystallized intelligence increases with age.

21. **a.** is the answer. (p. 179)

22. **d.** is the answer. (pp. 185–186)

23. **d.** is the answer. (p. 187)

Psychology Applied

Multiple-Choice Questions

1. **d.** is the answer. (p. 151)

2. **b.** is the answer. (p. 145)

    a. & d. Although the rate of motor development varies from child to child, the basic sequence is universal and, therefore, predictable.

    c. Rolling over and head lifting are both learned.

3. **a.** is the answer. Mathematical and philosophical reasoning involve fluid and crystallized intelligence, respectively. Because fluid intelligence generally declines with age while crystallized intelligence increases, it is likely that significant mathematical accomplishments will occur at an earlier age than philosophical accomplishments. (p. 185)

4. **c.** is the answer. Early maturing boys tend to be more popular. (p. 166)

    a. Early maturing girls may temporarily suffer embarrassment and be the objects of teasing.

    b. & d. The social benefits of early or late maturation are based on physical development, not on cognitive skills.

5. **c.** is the answer. This test is designed to determine if the child understands that the quantity of liquid is conserved, despite the shift to a container that is different in shape. (p. 150)

    a. These are general processes related to concept building.

    b. Object permanence is the concept that an object continues to exist even when not perceived; in

this case, the water is perceived throughout the experiment.

    d. This experiment does not require abstract reasoning, only the ability to reason logically about the concrete.

6. **a.** is the answer. This child's age and stranger anxiety clearly place him within Piaget's sensorimotor stage. (pp. 149, 155)

7. **b.** is the answer. This child's age, ability to use language, and egocentrism clearly place her within Piaget's preoperational stage. (p. 150)

8. **d.** is the answer. Conservation is a hallmark of the concrete operational stage; egocentrism is a hallmark of the preoperational stage. (pp. 150, 153)

9. **c.** is the answer. Being 4 years old, Jamail would be in Piaget's preoperational stage. Preoperational thinking is egocentric, which means Jamail would find it difficult to "put himself in his sister's shoes" and perceive that she has a brother. (p. 150)

10. **b.** is the answer. (p. 156)

    a. Conservation is the ability to realize that the amount of an object does not change even if its shape changes.

    c. Egocentrism is having difficulty perceiving things from another's perspective.

    d. According to Erikson, basic trust is feeling that the world is safe as a result of sensitive, loving caregivers.

11. **a.** is the answer. Although loving parents will also produce securely attached children, Erikson's theory deals with trust or mistrust. (p. 158)

    c. Control is not a factor in this stage of Erikson's theory.

12. **d.** is the answer. (p. 172)

    a. This description of Cassandra's feelings does not suggest that her relationship with her parents is deteriorating. Cassandra's social development, like that of most adolescents, is coming under increasing peer influence and diminishing parental influence.

    b. & c. Because Cassandra's feelings are normal, there is no reason for her to change her circle of friends or for her parents to seek counseling.

13. **c.** is the answer. (p. 154)

    a., b., & d. Piaget did not link cognitive ability to amount of schooling, gender, or differences in how boys and girls are socialized.

14. **a.** is the answer. Children in various cultures do seem to progress through Kohlberg's preconventional and conventional levels, which indicates

that some aspects of the development of moral reasoning are universal. (p. 168)

15. **c.** is the answer. Reasoning is based on fluid intelligence. (p. 184)

   a. There is no "analytic" intelligence.

   b. Crystallized intelligence increases up to old age.

16. **c.** is the answer. Because several variables (education, affluence, etc.) generally distinguish the various groups in a cross-sectional study, it is impossible to rule out that one or more of these, rather than aging, is the cause of the measured intellectual decrease. (p. 183)

   a. Small sample size and unrepresentativeness generally are not limitations of cross-sectional research.

   b. This refers to longitudinal research.

17. **d.** is the answer. (pp. 181–182)

   a. & c. In tests of recognition memory, the performance of older persons shows little decline.

   b. The ability to recall material, especially meaningless material, declines with age.

18. **d.** is the answer. Research has not uncovered a tendency for people of any particular age group to report greater feelings of satisfaction or well-being. (p. 189)

19. **c.** is the answer. Although some researchers emphasize consistency and others emphasize potential for change, they all agree that consistency increases over the life span. (p. 194)

   a. One criticism of stage theories is that development does not occur in sharply defined stages.

   b. Research has shown that individuals' adult personalities cannot be predicted from their first two years.

   d. Social and emotional style are two of the most stable traits.

20. **b.** is the answer. Conventional morality is based in part on a desire to gain others' approval. (p. 168)

   a. Preconventional reasoning is based on external incentives such as gaining a reward or avoiding punishment.

   c. Postconventional morality reflects an affirmation of agreed-upon rights or universal ethical principles.

   d. Fear of others' disapproval is one of the bases of conventional moral reasoning.

21. **b.** is the answer. (p. 172)

   a. In fact, just the opposite is true: parental influence on children *decreases* during adolescence.

   d. Teens reflect their parents' social, political, and religious views, but rely on peers for matters of personal taste.

22. **c.** is the answer. (p. 194)

23. **c.** is the answer. Carlos' age and struggle to form a close relationship place him squarely in this stage. (p. 170)

   a. Trust versus mistrust is the psychosocial task of infancy.

   b. Autonomy versus doubt is the psychosocial task of toddlerhood.

   d. Identity versus role confusion is the psychosocial task of adolescence.

24. **d.** is the answer. (p. 189)

Essay Question

Sheryl's age would place her at the threshold of Piaget's stage of formal operations. Although her thinking is probably still somewhat self-focused, Sheryl is becoming capable of abstract, logical thought. This will increasingly allow her to reason hypothetically and deductively. Because her logical thinking also enables her to detect inconsistencies in others' reasoning and between their ideals and actions, Sheryl and her parents may be having some heated debates about now.

According to Kohlberg, Sheryl is probably at the threshold of postconventional morality. When she was younger, Sheryl probably abided by rules in order to gain social approval, or simply because "rules are rules" (conventional morality). Now that she is older, Sheryl's moral reasoning will increasingly be based on her own personal code of ethics and an affirmation of people's agreed-upon rights. Because she is a woman, her morality may be more concerned with caring about relationships.

According to Erikson, psychosocial development occurs in eight stages, each of which focuses on a particular task. As an adolescent, Sheryl's psychosocial task is to develop a sense of self by testing roles, then integrating them to form a single identity. Erikson called this stage "identity versus role confusion."

Key Terms

1. **Developmental psychology** is the branch of psychology concerned with physical, cognitive, and social change throughout the life span. (p. 139)

2. The **zygote** (a term derived from the Greek word for "joint") is the fertilized egg, that is, the cluster of cells formed during conception by the union of sperm and egg. (p. 140)

3. The **embryo** is the developing prenatal organism from about 2 weeks through 2 months after conception. (p. 141)

4. The **fetus** is the developing prenatal human from 9 weeks after conception to birth. (p. 141)

5. **Teratogens** (literally, poisons) are any drugs, viruses, or other substances that cross the mother's placenta and can harm the developing embryo or fetus. (p. 141)

6. **Fetal alcohol syndrome (FAS)** refers to the physical and cognitive abnormalities that heavy drinking by a pregnant woman may cause in the developing child. (p. 142)

7. The **rooting reflex** is the newborn's tendency, when his or her cheek is stroked, to orient toward the touch, open the mouth, and search for the nipple. (p. 142)

8. A simple form of learning used to study infant cognition, **habituation** is decreasing responsiveness to a stimulus that is repeatedly presented. (p. 143)

9. **Maturation** refers to the biological growth processes that enable orderly changes in behavior and are relatively uninfluenced by experience or other environmental factors. (p. 145)

   Example: The ability to walk depends on a certain level of neural and muscular **maturation**. For this reason, until the toddler's body is physically ready to walk, practice "walking" has little effect.

10. In Piaget's theory of cognitive development, **schemas** are mental concepts or frameworks that organize and interpret information. (p. 147)

11. In Piaget's theory, **assimilation** refers to interpreting a new experience in terms of an existing schema. (p. 148)

12. In Piaget's theory, **accommodation** refers to changing an existing schema to incorporate new information that cannot be assimilated. (p. 148)

13. **Cognition** refers to all the mental processes associated with thinking, knowing, remembering, and communicating. (p. 148)

14. In Piaget's theory of cognitive stages, the **sensorimotor stage** lasts from birth to about age 2. During this stage, infants gain knowledge of the world through their senses and their motor activities. (p. 149)

15. **Object permanence**, which develops during the sensorimotor stage, is the awareness that things do not cease to exist when not perceived. (p. 149)

16. In Piaget's theory, the **preoperational stage** lasts from about 2 to 6 or 7 years of age. During this stage, language development is rapid, but the child is unable to understand the mental operations of concrete logic. (p. 150)

17. **Conservation** is the principle that properties such as number, volume, and mass remain constant despite changes in the forms of objects; it is acquired during the concrete operational stage. (p. 150)

18. In Piaget's theory, **egocentrism** refers to the difficulty that preoperational children have in considering another's viewpoint. "Ego" means "self," and "centrism" indicates "in the center"; the preoperational child is "self-centered." (p. 150)

19. Our ideas about our own and others' thoughts, feelings, and perceptions and the behaviors these might predict constitute our **theory of mind**. (p. 151)

20. **Autism** is a disorder that appears in childhood and is marked by deficiencies in communication, social interaction, and theory of mind. (p. 152)

21. During the **concrete operational stage,** lasting from about ages 6 or 7 to 11, children can think logically about concrete events and objects. (p. 153)

22. In Piaget's theory, the **formal operational stage** normally begins about age 12. During this stage people begin to think logically about abstract concepts. (p. 154)

   Memory aid: To help differentiate Piaget's stages remember that "operations" are mental transformations. *Pre*operational children, who lack the ability to perform transformations, are "before" this developmental milestone. Concrete operational children can operate on real, or concrete, objects. Formal operational children can perform logical transformations on abstract concepts.

23. **Stranger anxiety** is the fear of strangers that infants begin to display at about 8 months of age. (p. 155)

24. **Attachment** is an emotional tie with another person, shown in young children by their seeking closeness to a caregiver and showing distress on separation. (p. 155)

25. A **critical period** is a limited time shortly after birth during which an organism must be exposed to certain experiences or influences if it is to develop properly. (p. 156)

26. **Imprinting** is the process by which certain animals form attachments during a limited critical period early in life. (p. 156)

27. According to Erikson, **basic trust** is a sense that the world is predictable and trustworthy—a concept that infants form if their needs are met by responsive caregiving. (p. 158)

28. **Self-concept** is a person's sense of identity and personal worth. (p. 161)

29. **Adolescence** refers to the life stage from puberty to independent adulthood, denoted physically by a growth spurt and maturation of primary and secondary sex characteristics, cognitively by the onset of formal operational thought, and socially by the formation of identity. (p. 164)

30. **Puberty** is the early adolescent period of sexual maturation, during which a person becomes capable of reproduction. (p. 165)

31. The **primary sex characteristics** are the body structures (ovaries, testes, and external genitalia) that enable reproduction. (p. 165)

32. The **secondary sex characteristics** are the nonreproductive sexual characteristics, for example, female breasts, male voice quality, and body hair. (p. 165)

33. **Menarche** is the first menstrual period. (p. 166)

34. In Erikson's theory, establishing an **identity**, or one's sense of self, is the primary task of adolescence. (p. 171)

35. In Erikson's theory, **intimacy**, or the ability to establish close, loving relationships, is the primary task of late adolescence and early adulthood. (p. 172)

36. **Menopause** is the cessation of menstruation and typically occurs in the early fifties. It also refers to the biological and psychological changes experienced during a woman's years of declining ability to reproduce. (p. 176)

37. **Alzheimer's disease** is a progressive and irreversible brain disorder caused by deterioration of neurons that produce acetylcholine. It is characterized by a gradual loss of memory, reasoning, language, and, finally, physical functioning. (p. 180)

38. In a **cross-sectional study**, people of different ages are compared with one another. (p. 183)

39. In a **longitudinal study**, the same people are tested and retested over a period of years. (p. 183)

40. **Crystallized intelligence** refers to those aspects of intellectual ability, such as vocabulary and general knowledge, that reflect accumulated learning. Crystallized intelligence tends to increase with age. (p. 184)

41. **Fluid intelligence** refers to a person's ability to reason speedily and abstractly. Fluid intelligence tends to decline with age. (p. 184)

42. The **social clock** refers to the culturally preferred timing of social events, such as leaving home, marrying, having children, and retiring. (p. 187)

Cross-Check

ACROSS	DOWN
1. accommodation	2. crystallized
5. fluid	3. autism
7. imprinting	4. assimilation
10. embryo	5. fetus
12. schema	6. conservation
14. menarche	8. cross-sectional
15. longitudinal	9. zygote
	11. teratogen
	13. habituation

FOCUS ON VOCABULARY AND LANGUAGE

Page 139: As we *journey* through life—from *womb to tomb*—when, how, and why do we develop? In the process of becoming who we are, and as we travel (*journey*) through life, from conception to death (*womb to tomb*) we change and mature physically, psychologically, and socially. (Another humorous expression describing the life span or life cycle is from "sperm to worm.")

Infancy and Childhood

Page 144: . . . toddler . . . This describes a child who is beginning to learn to walk and who walks with short, uneven steps.

Page 144: After birth, the neural networks that eventually enabled you to walk, talk, and remember had *a wild growth spurt.* Myers points out that when you were born, you had all the brain cells that you will ever have. But after birth there is a very rapid development (*a wild growth spurt*) in the number of connections between neurons.

Page 146: Trying to access memories of those first four years *is like trying to read a document formatted by an earlier version of a computer operating system.* This reference is to the similarity between the brain and a computer. If computer software used for creating a document was programmed (*formatted*) on an earlier version of a computer, then it will not be easy to read the document on a newer version. Early preschool memories may not have been erased, but because they were programmed on a different, or earlier, system (*the child*), they are hard to access or retrieve later on a newer system (*the adult*).

Page 147: . . . fruitless . . . This word means to be unproductive or useless (like a tree that does not produce fruit). It is pointless (*fruitless*), according to Piaget's theory, to try to teach a child who is in the preoperational stage of development how to use abstract logic to solve a complex problem (formal operational reasoning).

Page 149: In one of his tests, Piaget would show an infant an appealing toy and then *flop his beret over it* to see whether the infant searched for the toy. When Piaget tested object permanence, he showed the child an attractive toy and then covered it with his soft round hat (*he flopped his beret over it*). Very young babies do not search for the hidden toy—when they can't see it, they don't appear to think about it (*what is out of sight is out of mind*).

Page 149: When she lifted the screen, the infants sometimes *did a double take*, staring longer when shown a wrong number of objects. In this experiment with 5-month-old infants, Karen Wynn showed that these very young children were capable of conceptual thinking. She did this by measuring their reaction time to expected and unexpected outcomes. Shown an impossible outcome, infants stared longer (*they did a double take*) and they also demonstrated a mental capacity for detecting changes or differences in the frequency of events (*they have a head for numbers*).

Page 151: When Little Red Riding Hood realizes her *"grandmother" is really a wolf,* she swiftly revises her ideas about the creature's intentions and races away. Preschoolers gradually begin to understand that other people have mental capacities, intentions, motivations, feelings, etc. (*children form a theory of mind*). This is illustrated when the young girl in the children's story called *Little Red Riding Hood* recognizes that the big bad wolf (disguised as her grandmother) has very bad intentions toward her, and she quickly escapes (*races away*).

Page 154: Piaget's stage theory has been influential. In some respects, it gets high marks. Piaget's theory has been controversial, having both supporters and critics. Cross-cultural research supports the basic stages he proposed (*it gets high marks*), but most researchers believe that development is more continuous than Piaget thought. Children have more conceptual abilities at earlier periods than his theory suggested.

Page 154: . . . cognitive milestones . . . A milestone is an event of significance or importance. (Originally, a milestone was a large stone by the roadside inscribed with the distance in miles to nearby towns.) Myers notes that the age at which children usually succeed at important mental tasks (*cognitive milestones*) is of less relevance than the developmental order or sequence in which these abilities appear.

Page 154: Teachers would do better to *build on* what children already know, engaging them in *concrete demonstrations* and stimulating them to *think for themselves.* Preschool and elementary school children think differently from adults. In order for them to become independent thinkers (*think for themselves*), Piaget recommends that they be given specific, tangible examples (*concrete demonstrations*) that utilize (*build on*) their existing knowledge.

Page 155: To pit the drawing power of a food source against the contact comfort of the blanket, Harlow created two artificial mothers. Harlow's experiment was designed to test whether food or nourishment was more rewarding than the comfort of a soft terry cloth. Thus, when he tested the attraction (*pitted the drawing power*) of the artificial mother who supplied food against the soft comfort of the terry cloth mother (*contact comfort*), he was surprised that they preferred the cloth mother. They used "her" as a *secure base* from which to explore and a safe place (*safe haven*) to return to when frightened or anxious.

Page 156: The first moving object a *gosling, duckling, or chick* sees during the hours shortly after *hatching* is normally its mother. A *gosling* is a young goose, a *duckling* a young duck, and a *chick* a young chicken. What all these young fowl have in common is a tendency to follow, or trail after, the first larger moving object they see shortly after they emerge (*hatch*) from the eggshell. This attachment process is called **imprinting**.

Page 156: "*Mere exposure*" to people and things fosters *fondness.* Children do not imprint in the same way that ducklings and other animals do; nevertheless, repeated encounters with (or *exposure to*) other humans and objects encourage or promote liking and attachment (*fosters fondness*). As Myers puts it, "familiarity breeds content." This is a twist on the old saying "familiarity breeds contempt" and suggests that intimacy creates (*breeds*) satisfaction (*contentment*) rather than scorn (*contempt*).

Page 157: But evidence increasingly indicates that fathers are more than just *mobile sperm banks.* A *sperm bank* is where donated sperm is stored until it is used for artificial insemination. More and more research shows that fathers are not simply sperm producers who can move around (*mobile sperm banks*) and get mothers pregnant. Rather, evidence suggests they are capable caregivers who may interact with their babies much as mothers do.

Page 159: . . . can leave *footprints* on the brain. Traumatic experiences that occur early in development can have an effect on brain functioning; metaphorically, they can leave impressions (*footprints*) on the brain. The production of neurotransmitters such as serotonin, which calms aggressive impulses, is slower (*sluggish*) in abused children who become aggressive teens and adults.

Page 161: In a simple variation of the mirror procedure, researchers *sneakily dabbed rouge* on children's noses before placing them in front of the mirror. In order to find out at what point in development a child realizes that her mirror image is herself and not another child, researchers use a clever technique. Unobtrusively (*sneakily*) and without the child's awareness, they gently rubbed (*dabbed*) some red makeup (*rouge*) on the child's nose before allowing her to view herself in the mirror. If children have the concept of self, they will be surprised at the red spot and touch their noses. This actually happens around 15 to 18 months of age, and self-concept begins to grow from then on.

Page 161: Parenting styles vary. Some parents *spank*, some *reason*. Some are *strict*, some are *lax*. When it comes to child-rearing practices (*parenting styles*), there is much variability: (a) some parents use strict controls and physical punishment (*spanking*); (b) others talk and discuss problems and issues with their children (*reason with them*); and (c) still others allow the children to do what they want and make few demands of them (*they are lax*). Myers identifies these parenting styles as (a) *authoritarian*, (b) *authoritative*, and (c) *permissive*.

Page 162: Before jumping to conclusions about the results of different parenting styles, *heed this caution*. Myers is suggesting that we must be careful (*heed a caution*) before quickly deciding (*jumping to conclusions*) about the merits of various parenting styles. He points out that the evidence is correlational and does not imply cause and effect. Thus, there may be other factors that are causally involved (e.g., some children may, because of their temperament, engender [elicit] greater trust and warmth from their parents).

Adolescence

Page 166: Early maturation *pays dividends* for boys. If onset of puberty occurs before the expected or usual time (*early maturation*), it will be much less stressful for boys than for girls. In general, for boys in their early teen years, being stronger and more athletic leads to more self-assurance, greater popularity, and greater independence (*it pays dividends*).

Page 166: If a young girl's body is *out of sync* with her own emotional maturity and her friends' physical development and experiences, she may begin associating with older adolescents or may suffer teasing or sexual harassment. *Sync* is an abbreviation of *synchronize*, which means to occur at the same time. So, if a girl's biological development is not proceeding at the same rate (*out of sync*) with her emotional and social development, she may start fraternizing (*associating*) with and imitating the behavior of older girls. Thus, early maturation can be a problem for girls, especially if the people around them react in an inappropriate or suggestive manner to their physical development (*sexual harassment*) or make fun of them (*tease them*).

Page 167: Gradually, though, most achieve the *intellectual summit* that Piaget called *formal operations*. The *formal operational* stage is the highest level in Piaget's theory of cognitive development (*intellectual summit*). Most adolescents reach this stage and are capable of logical and abstract reasoning. For example, many think about (*ponder*) and discuss (*debate*) such issues as good and evil, truth and justice, and other abstract topics about human nature.

Page 168: A crucial task of childhood and adolescence is discerning right from wrong and developing *character—the psychological muscles for controlling impulses.* *Character* refers to the total qualities a person possesses, including attitudes, beliefs, interests, actions, and a philosophy of life. By developing *character*, adolescents learn to have the intellectual strength (*psychological muscles*) to refrain from acting immorally (*controlling impulses*). Kohlberg proposed a controversial stage theory of moral development which has three levels: preconventional, conventional, and postconventional.

Page 168: Kohlberg's claim was that these levels form a *moral ladder* (Figure 4.22). In Kohlberg's view children have to go through each of the three stages (preconventional, conventional, and postconventional) in succession much as a person climbs a ladder, one rung at a time, from bottom to top. The lowest rung on this *moral ladder* involves self-interest and avoidance of punishment; the highest rung, which often develops during and after adolescence, is concerned with personal ethical principles and universal justice. Critics contend that the theory has cultural and gender biases.

Page 169: . . . throw a switch . . . This means to pull a lever. People's moral reasoning and judgments are affected by basic emotional reactions (*gut-level feelings*). This phenomenon is evident in the situation requiring a choice between two unpleasant alternatives (*a dilemma*). Either pulling a lever (*throwing a switch*) or pushing a person onto the tracks results in five people being saved and one person dying, but the latter choice causes much more emotional conflict (*the brain's emotion areas light up*).

Page 170: Our moral thinking and feeling surely affect our moral talk. But sometimes *talk is cheap* and emotions are fleeting. The expression *talk is cheap* means that it is easy to say you believe something or to say that you are going to do something; it costs you nothing just to speak about it (*talk is cheap*). However, action, or actually carrying out the correct behavior, is also involved in morality.

Page 170: . . . psychosocial task . . . According to Erikson, each stage of life involves a dilemma (*crisis*) that has to be resolved before we can move on to the next stage. These tasks involve interactions between ourselves, our surroundings, and other people; thus, they are *social* in nature. The psychosocial assignment (*psychosocial task*) of adolescence involves *role confusion vs. forming an identity.* (This is sometimes called an **identity crisis**).

Page 171: Erikson noticed that some adolescents *forge* their identity early, simply by taking on their parents' values and expectations. *Forge* literally means to form or shape by heating and hammering metal. Erikson observed that some young people form (*forge*) their identities early, while others never quite appear to acquire a strong feeling of who they are (i.e., they don't *find themselves*).

Page 173: As people mature in young adulthood, *their emotional ties with parents loosen.* During their early twenties, many still *lean heavily on their parents.* The time period between 18 and the mid-twenties is sometimes called the emerging adulthood stage. During this period, young adults have less need for close emotional contact with parents (*emotional ties with parents loosen*); nevertheless, many still rely on their parents for financial and social support (*they still lean heavily on their parents*).

Page 173: That *gap*—the years spent *morphing* from child to adult—is adolescence. The time period (*gap*) between the end of childhood and the beginning of adulthood involves many social and biological changes; the person is transformed (*morphed*) from one type of entity (a child) to something quite different (an adult).

Adulthood

Page 177: The above statements—all false—are among the *misconceptions* about aging *exploded* by recent research on the world's most rapidly growing population group. To "explode misconceptions" means to dispel or get rid of erroneous beliefs that have no foundation in fact. The false statements (*misconceptions*) listed in the text have all been refuted by the results of new experiments and investigations.

Page 178: In later life, the stairs get steeper, the print gets smaller, and people seem to *mumble* more. This is not meant to be taken literally. Myers is pointing out that as we become older, our sensory and perceptual abilities change so that our reaction time and our ability to see and hear decline. Thus, the stairs *appear* steeper, the print *seems* smaller, and people do not appear to be speaking clearly (*they mumble*).

Page 179: Aging *levies a tax* on the brain by slowing our neural processing. Myers is pointing out that aging is accompanied by a decrease in some perceptual and cognitive abilities. Just as you have less money after taxes have been assessed (*levied*) on your income, there are some losses in the brain's ability to function optimally due to the aging process.

Page 180: We are more likely to *rust from disuse than to wear out from overuse.* "Use it or lose it" is sound advice. When adults remain active physically, sexually, and mentally (they *"use it"*), they are less likely to become inactive later in life (*"lose it"*). If we follow sedentary life-styles, we will be like unused pieces of metal machinery that suffer from rust; on the other hand, keeping active will not do us any harm (*we won't wear out from overuse*); instead, we may benefit both mentally and physically.

Page 183: According to this more optimistic view, the *myth* that intelligence sharply declines with age is *laid to rest.* The false idea (*myth*) that our intellectual abilities decrease as we get older has been destroyed or buried (*laid to rest*) by recent **longitudinal research**. This research tests the same group of people over many years and may give more accurate results than testing many groups of people (each group having a different age range) at one period in time (**cross-sectional research**). However, both research methods have their own problems (*pitfalls*).

Page 184: . . . hold their own . . . Older adults compare favorably with younger adults (*they hold their own*) on tests that assess such things as general vocabulary, knowledge, ability to integrate information, and good judgment. As Myers notes, **crystallized intelligence** (accumulated knowledge and verbal skills) tends to increase with age, whereas **fluid intelligence** (ability to reason rapidly and abstractly —*quick thinking smarts*) tends to decrease during late adulthood.

Page 187: "*Pair-bonding is a trademark of the human animal,*" notes anthropologist Helen Fisher (1993). *Pair-bonding* refers to the monogamous attachment formed between one person and another, such as with a marriage partner, and this affiliation is characteristic (*a trademark*) of human beings.

Page 187: Might *test-driving life together* in a "trial marriage" minimize divorce risk? Does premarital cohabitation or a "trial marriage" (*test-driving life together*) increase the probability of a successful later marriage and reduce the likelihood of divorce (*minimize divorce risk*)? The research suggests it does not. Those who live together before marriage are more likely to get divorced than those who don't. (These findings are correlational and can't be used to make causal inferences.)

Page 188: Some couples fight but also *shower* one another with affection. Other couples never raise their voices yet also seldom praise one another or *nuzzle*. Myers notes that some couples have many open conflicts but also treat each other with warmth and care (*shower one another with affection*), while others who seldom argue loudly (*never raise their voices*) may fail to be openly complimentary (*praise one another*) or to tenderly embrace or cuddle up together (*nuzzle*). Although both styles can work, the best predictor of marital success is a ratio of at least 5 to 1 of positive interactions (smiling, touching, complimenting, and laughing) to negative interactions (sarcasm, criticism, putdowns, and insults).

Page 190: As the years go by, *feelings mellow.* . . . *Highs become less high, lows less low.* Our feelings become less extreme (*they mellow*) as we age: the excitement and elation (*highs*) and the depression and gloom (*lows*) do not encompass such a broad range of feelings as they once did. Myers states it nicely when he says, "As we age, life becomes less an emotional roller coaster, more like paddling a canoe."

Reflections on Two Major Developmental Issues

Page 193: . . . *do they differ as a giant redwood differs from its seedling . . . or . . . as a butterfly differs from a caterpillar . . . ?* The giant redwood is a large coniferous tree that grows in a continuous, cumulative way from seedling to mature tree. On the other hand, the butterfly emerges as a different creature after passing through a stage as a caterpillar. The question developmental psychologists ask is: Are changes throughout the life span (from infant to adult) due to a slow, continuous shaping process (like the tree), or do we go through a series of genetically preprogrammed stages (like the butterfly)?

Page 194: Many a 20-year-old *goof-off* has matured into a 40-year-old business or cultural leader. To *goof off* means to avoid work and act in a lazy manner; a person who behaves this way is called a *goof-off*. Some traits, such as temperament, are relatively stable over time, but everyone changes in some way with age. Thus, a lazy youth (*20-year-old goof-off*) may develop (*mature*) into a more productive adult (*40-year-old leader*).

5: Sensation

CHAPTER OVERVIEW

Sensation refers to the process by which we detect physical energy from the environment and encode it as neural signals. This chapter describes the senses of vision, hearing, taste, touch, smell, kinesthesis, and the vestibular sense. It also presents research findings from studies of subliminal stimulation.

In this chapter there are many terms to learn and several theories you must understand. Many of the terms are related to the structure of the eye, ear, and other sensory receptors. Doing the chapter review several times, labeling the diagrams, and rehearsing the material frequently will help you to memorize these structures and their functions. The theories discussed include the signal detection, Young-Helmholtz three-color and opponent-process theories of color vision, and the frequency and place theories of pitch. As you study these theories, concentrate on understanding the strengths and weaknesses (if any) of each.

NOTE: Answer guidelines for all Chapter 5 questions begin on page 145.

CHAPTER REVIEW

First, skim each section, noting headings and boldface items. After you have read the section, review each objective by answering the fill-in and essay-type questions that follow it. As you proceed, evaluate your performance by consulting the answers beginning on page 145. Do not continue with the next section until you understand each answer. If you need to, review or reread the section in the textbook before continuing.

Introduction (pp. 197–198)

> David Myers at times uses idioms that are unfamiliar to some readers. If you do not know the meaning of the following expression in the context in which it appears in the text, refer to page 154 for an explanation: . . . *in a mirror she is again stumped.*

Objective 1: Contrast sensation and perception, and explain the difference between bottom-up and top-down processing.

1. The process by which we detect physical energy from the environment and encode it as neural signals is _____ . The process by which sensations are selected, organized, and interpreted is _____ .

2. Sensory analysis, which starts at the entry level and works up, is called _____-
_____ _____.

   Perceptual analysis, which works from our experience and expectations, is called

   _____-_____

   _____ .

3. The perceptual disorder in which a person has lost the ability to recognize familiar faces is

   _____ .

Sensing the World: Some Basic Principles
(pp. 198–203)

> If you do not know the meaning of any of the following words, phrases, or expressions in the context in which they appear in the text, refer to page 154 for an explanation: *A frog could starve to death knee-deep in motionless flies; The shades on our senses are open just a crack; the faintest whimper from the cradle; "satanic messages"; hucksters; price hike . . . to raise the eyebrows; So everywhere that Mary looks, the scene is sure to go.*

Objective 2: Distinguish between absolute and difference thresholds, and discuss whether we can sense stimuli below our absolute thresholds and be influenced by them.

1. The study of relationships between the physical characteristics of stimuli and our psychological experience of them is _____ .

2. The _____ _____ refers to the minimum stimulation necessary for a stimulus to be detected _____ percent of the time.

3. The theory of _____ _____ led to the concept that absolute thresholds depend not only on the strength of the signal but also on a person's _____ state.

4. Some entrepreneurs claim that exposure to "below threshold," or _____ , stimuli can be persuasive, but their claims are probably unwarranted.

5. Some weak stimuli may trigger in our sensory receptors a response that is processed by the brain, even though the response doesn't cross the threshold into _____ awareness.

6. Under certain conditions, an invisible image or word can _____ a person's response to a later question. The _____ _____ illustrates that much of our information processing occurs _____ .

7. The minimum difference required to distinguish two stimuli 50 percent of the time is called the

   _____ _____ .

   Another term for this value is the

   _____ _____

   _____ .

8. The principle that the difference threshold is not a constant amount, but a constant proportion, is known as _____

   _____ . The proportion depends on the _____ .

Objective 3: Describe sensory adaptation, and explain how we benefit from being unaware of changing stimuli.

9. After constant exposure to an unchanging stimulus, the receptor cells of our senses begin to fire less vigorously; this phenomenon is called

   _____ _____ .

10. This phenomenon illustrates that sensation is designed to focus on _____ changes in the environment.

Explain why sensory adaptation is beneficial.

Vision (pp. 204–215)

> If you do not know the meaning of any of the following words, phrases, or expressions in the context in which they appear in the text, refer to pages 154–155 for an explanation: *blind spot; Rods have no such hotline; Holy Grail; blindsight; Color, like all aspects of vision, . . . the theater of*

Objective 4: Define *transduction,* and specify the form of energy our visual system converts into the neural messages our brain can interpret.

1. Stimulus energy is converted into _____ messages through the process of sensory _____ .

2. The visible spectrum of light is a small portion of the larger spectrum of _____ radiation.

3. The distance from one light wave peak to the next is called _____ . This value

determines the wave's color, or
_____ .

4. The amount of energy in light waves, or
_____ , determined by a wave's
_____ , or height, influences the
_____ of a light.

Objective 5: Describe the major structures of the eye, and explain how they guide an incoming ray of light toward the eye's receptor cells.

5. Light enters the eye through the
_____ , then passes through a
small opening called the _____ ;
the size of this opening is controlled by the
colored _____ .

6. By changing its curvature, the
_____ can focus the image of an
object onto the _____ , the light-
sensitive inner surface of the eye.

7. The process by which the lens changes shape to
focus images is called _____ .
Clarity, or sharpness, of vision is called
_____ .

8. In nearsightedness, light rays from
_____ (nearby/distant) objects
converge _____ (in front of/in
back of) the retina, rather than on it, and
_____ (nearby/distant) objects
are seen more clearly than
_____ (nearby/distant) objects. In
farsightedness, light rays from _____
(nearby/distant) objects converge _____
(in front of/in back of) the retina, and
_____ (nearby/distant) objects are
seen more clearly than _____
(nearby/distant) objects.

Objective 6: Contrast the two types of receptor cells in the retina, and describe the retina's reaction to light.

9. The retina's receptor cells are the
_____ and _____ .

10. The neural signals produced in the rods and
cones activate the neighboring
_____ cells, which then activate a

network of _____ cells. The axons
of ganglion cells converge to form the
_____ _____ ,
which carries the visual information to the
_____ .

11. Where this nerve leaves the eye, there are no
receptors; thus the area is called the
_____ _____ .

12. Most cones are clustered around the retina's
point of central focus, called the
_____ , whereas the rods are concentrated in more _____
regions of the retina. Many cones have their own
_____ cells to communicate with
the visual cortex.

13. It is the _____ (rods/cones) of the
eye that permit the perception of color, whereas
_____ (rods/cones) enable black-
and-white vision.

14. Unlike cones, in dim light the rods are
_____ (sensitive/insensitive).
Adapting to a darkened room will take the retina
approximately _____ minutes.

Objective 7: Discuss the different levels of processing that occur as information travels from the retina to the brain's cortex.

15. Visual information percolates through progressively more _____ levels. In the
brain, it is routed by the _____ to
higher-level brain areas. Hubel and Wiesel discovered that certain neurons in the _____
_____ of the brain respond only to
specific features of what is viewed. They called
these neurons _____
_____ .

16. Feature detectors pass their information to
higher-level brain cells in the brain, including an
area in the _____ cortex, which
responds to specific visual scenes. Research has
shown that in monkey brains such cells specialize
in responding to a specific
_____ , _____
_____ , _____ , or
_____ _____ .

Researchers have also identified nerve cells that may respond or not, depending on how a monkey _____ a given image.

Objective 8: Define *parallel processing*, and discuss its role in visual information processing.

17. The brain achieves its remarkable speed in visual perception by processing several subdivisions of a stimulus _____ (simultaneously/sequentially). This procedure, called _____ _____ , may explain why people who have suffered a stroke may lose just one aspect of vision. Other brain-damaged people may demonstrate _____ by responding to a stimulus that is not consciously perceived.

18. Once the distributed parts of the brain have processed sensory stimuli, EEG recordings reveal a moment of neural _____ , lasting for about a fourth of a second and creating _____ waves. Other senses process information with _____ (similar/slower/faster) speed and intricacy.

Objective 9: Explain how the Young-Helmholtz and opponent-process theories help us understand color vision.

19. An object appears to be red in color because it _____ the long wavelengths of red and because of our mental _____ of the color.

20. One out of every 50 people is color deficient; this is usually a male because the defect is genetically _____ - _____ .

21. According to the _____ - _____ _____ theory, the eyes have three types of color receptors: one reacts most strongly to _____ , one to _____ , and one to _____ . Mixing lights, as Young and von Helmholtz did, is _____ color mixing, unlike mixing paints, which is _____ .

22. After staring at a green square for a while, you will see the color red, its _____ color, as an _____ .

23. Hering's theory of color vision is called the _____ - _____ theory. According to this theory, after visual information leaves the receptors it is analyzed in terms of pairs of opposing colors: _____ versus _____ , _____ versus _____ , and also _____ versus _____ .

Summarize the two stages of color processing.

Objective 10: Explain the importance of color constancy.

24. The experience of color depends on the _____ in which an object is seen.

25. In an unvarying context, a familiar object will be perceived as having consistent color, even as the light changes. This phenomenon is called _____ _____ .

26. We see color as a result of our brains' computations of the light _____ by any object relative to its _____ .

Hearing (pp. 215–224)

If you do not know the meaning of any of the following words, phrases, or expressions in the context in which they appear in the text, refer to page 155 for an explanation: *sensitive to faint sounds, an obvious boon; A piccolo produces much shorter, faster sound waves than does a tuba; earlids; If a car to the right honks; cock your head; the culprits are . . . ear-splitting noise or music.*

Objective 11: Describe the pressure waves we experience as sound.

1. The stimulus for hearing, or
_____ , is sound waves, created by
the compression and expansion of
_____ _____ .

2. The amplitude of a sound wave determines the
sound's _____ .

3. The pitch of a sound is derived from the
_____ of its wave.

4. Sound energy is measured in units called
_____ . The absolute threshold for
hearing is arbitrarily defined as
_____ such units.

Objective 12: Describe the three regions of the ear, and outline the series of events that triggers the electrical impulses sent to the brain.

5. The ear is divided into three main parts: the
_____ ear, the
_____ ear, and the
_____ ear.

6. The outer ear channels sound waves toward the
_____ , a tight membrane that then
vibrates.

7. The middle ear transmits the vibrations through a
piston made of three small bones: the
_____ , _____ , and
_____ .

8. In the inner ear, a coiled tube called the
_____ contains the receptor cells
for hearing. The incoming vibrations cause the
_____ _____ to
vibrate the fluid that fills the tube, which causes
ripples in the _____
_____ , which is lined with
_____ _____ . This
movement triggers impulses in adjacent nerve
fibers that converge to form the auditory nerve,
which carries the neural messages (via the
_____) to the _____
lobe's auditory cortex. The brain interprets loudness from the _____ of hair cells a
sound activates.

9. (Close-Up) On tasks requiring alert performance,
people in noisy environments work
_____ (more/less) efficiently.
People who live in noisy environments suffer elevated rates of _____ -related disorders such as _____
_____ _____ ,
_____ , and _____
_____ .
Noise is especially stressful when it is
_____ or _____ .

Objective 13: Contrast place and frequency theories, and explain how they help us to understand pitch perception.

10. One theory of pitch perception proposes that different pitches activate different places on the
cochlea's basilar membrane; this is the
_____ theory. This theory has difficulty accounting for how we hear
_____ -pitched sounds, which do
not have such localized effects.

11. A second theory proposes that neural impulses,
sent to the brain at the same frequency as the
sound wave, allow the perception of different
pitches. This is the _____ theory.
This theory fails to account for the perception of
_____ -pitched sounds, because
individual neurons cannot fire faster than
_____ times per second.

12. For the higher pitches, cells may alternate their
firing to match the sound's frequency, according
to the _____ principle.

Objective 14: Describe how we pinpoint sounds.

13. We locate a sound by sensing differences in the
_____ and _____
with which it reaches our ears.

14. A sound that comes from directly ahead will be
_____ (easier/harder) to locate
than a sound that comes from off to one side.

15. As with visual information, the brain uses
_____ _____ as
specialized neural teams work on different auditory tasks simultaneously.

Objective 15: Contrast the two types of hearing loss, and describe some of their causes.

16. Problems in the mechanical conduction of sound waves through the outer or middle ear may cause _____ _____ _____ .

17. Damage to the cochlea's hair cell receptors or their associated auditory nerves can cause _____ hearing loss. It may be caused by disease, but more often it results from the biological changes linked with _____ and prolonged exposure to ear-splitting noise or music.

18. Scientists have discovered ways to _____ hair cell regeneration.

Objective 16: Describe how cochlear implants function, and explain why Deaf culture advocates object to these devices.

19. An electronic device that restores hearing among nerve-deafened people is a _____ _____ .

20. Advocates of _____ _____ object to the use of these implants on _____ before they have learned to _____ . The basis for their argument is that deafness is not a _____ .

21. Sign language _____ (is/is not) a complete language, _____ (with/without) its own grammar, syntax, and semantics. Those who learn only sign language during childhood _____ (have/do not have) difficulty later learning to read and write. People who lose one channel of sensation (such as hearing) _____ (seem to/do not seem to) compensate with a slight enhancement in their other sensory abilities.

22. People who become deaf, or who lose another channel of sensation, often experience _____ _____ in another ability.

23. (Close-Up) Deaf children raised in a household where sign language is used express higher _____ and feel more _____ .

Other Important Senses (pp. 224–235)

> If you do not know the meaning of any of the following words, phrases, or expressions in the context in which they appear in the text, refer to pages 155–156 for an explanation: *we yearn to touch—to kiss, to stroke, to snuggle; Rubbing the area around your stubbed toe; Sometimes the pain in sprain is mainly in the brain; firewalking, . . . putting his feet where his mouth was; A well-trained nurse may distract needle-shy patients by chatting with them; there is more to taste than meets the tongue; bathing your nostrils in a stream of scent-laden molecules; Words more readily portray the sound of coffee brewing than its aroma; biological gyroscopes.*

Objective 17: Describe the sense of touch.

1. The sense of touch is a mixture of at least four senses: _____ , _____ , _____ , and _____ . Other skin sensations, such as tickle, itch, hot, and wetness, are _____ of the basic ones.

2. The _____-_____ influence on touch is illustrated by the fact that a self-produced tickle produces less activation in the _____ _____ than someone else's tickle.

Objective 18: State the purpose of pain, and describe the biopsychosocial approach to pain.

3. People born without the ability to feel pain may be unaware of experiencing severe _____ . People with illness-related _____ experience extreme sensitivity to things others find only mildly painful.

4. Pain is a property of the _____ as well as of the _____ and our _____ .

5. A sensation of pain in an amputated leg is referred to as a _____ _____ sensation. Another example is _____ , experienced by people who have a ringing-in-the-ears sensation.

6. Pain-producing brain activity may be triggered with or without _____ _____ .

7. The pain system _____ (is/is not) triggered by one specific type of physical energy. The body _____ (does/does not) have specialized receptor cells for pain.

8. Melzack and Wall have proposed a theory of pain called the _____-_____ theory, which proposes that there is a neurological _____ in the _____ _____ that blocks pain signals or lets them through. It may be opened by activation of _____ (small/large) nerve fibers and closed by activation of _____ (small/large) fibers or by information from the _____ .

9. Individual differences in perceiving pain are an example of _____ influences on pain. Such influences demonstrate that pain is not merely a _____ phenomenon, as proposed centuries ago by _____ . Rather, pain is created by the _____ .

List some pain control techniques used in the Lamaze method of prepared childbirth and in other health care situations.

Objective 19: Describe the sense of taste, and explain the principle of sensory interaction.

10. The basic taste sensations are _____ , _____ , _____ , and a meaty taste called _____ .

11. Taste, which is a _____ sense, is enabled by the 200 or more _____ _____ on the top and sides of the tongue. Each contains a _____ that catches food chemicals.

12. Taste receptors reproduce themselves every _____ . As we age, the number of taste buds _____ (increases/decreases/remains unchanged) and our taste sensitivity _____ (increases/decreases/remains unchanged). Taste is also affected by _____ and by _____ use.

13. When the sense of smell is blocked, as when we have a cold, foods do not taste the same; this illustrates the principle of _____ _____ . The _____ effect occurs when we _____ a speaker saying one syllable while _____ another.

Objective 20: Describe the sense of smell, and explain why specific odors so easily trigger memories.

14. Like taste, smell, or _____ , is a _____ sense. Unlike light, an odor _____ (can/cannot) be separated into more elemental odors.

15. The ability to identify scents peaks in _____ _____ and declines thereafter.

16. The attractiveness of smells depends on _____ associations.

17. Odors are able to evoke memories and feelings because there is a direct link between the brain area that gets information from the nose and the ancient _____ centers associated with memory and emotion.

Objective 21: Distinguish between kinesthesis and the vestibular sense.

18. The system for sensing the position and movement of body parts is called _____ . The receptors for this sense are located in the _____ , _____ , and _____ of the body.

19. The sense that monitors the position and movement of the head (and thus the body) is the _____ _____ .

The receptors for this sense are located in the
_____ _____ and
_____ _____ of the
inner ear.

PROGRESS TEST 1

Multiple-Choice Questions

Circle your answers to the following questions and check them with the answers beginning on page 146. If your answer is incorrect, read the explanation for why it is correct and then consult the appropriate pages of the text (in parentheses following the correct answer).

1. Which of the following is true?
    a. The absolute threshold for any stimulus is a constant.
    b. The absolute threshold for any stimulus varies somewhat.
    c. The absolute threshold is defined as the minimum amount of stimulation necessary for a stimulus to be detected 75 percent of the time.
    d. The absolute threshold is defined as the minimum amount of stimulation necessary for a stimulus to be detected 60 percent of the time.

2. Nearsightedness is a condition in which the:
    a. lens has become inflexible.
    b. lens is too thin.
    c. image falls behind the retina.
    d. image falls in front of the retina.

3. If you can just notice the difference between 10- and 11-pound weights, which of the following weights could you differentiate from a 100-pound weight?
    a. 101-pound weight
    b. 105-pound weight
    c. 110-pound weight
    d. There is no basis for prediction.

4. A decrease in sensory responsiveness accompanying an unchanging stimulus is called:
    a. sensory fatigue.
    b. accommodation.
    c. sensory adaptation.
    d. sensory interaction.

5. The size of the pupil is controlled by the:
    a. lens.   c. cornea.
    b. retina.   d. iris.

6. The process by which the lens changes its curvature is:
    a. accommodation.   c. feature detection.
    b. sensory adaptation. d. transduction.

7. The receptor of the eye that functions best in dim light is the:
    a. fovea.   c. bipolar cell.
    b. cone   d. rod.

8. The Young-Helmholtz theory proposes that:
    a. there are three different types of color-sensitive cones.
    b. retinal cells are excited by one color and inhibited by its complementary color.
    c. there are four different types of cones.
    d. rod, not cone, vision accounts for our ability to detect fine visual detail.

9. Frequency is to pitch as _____ is to _____ .
    a. wavelength; loudness
    b. amplitude; loudness
    c. wavelength; intensity
    d. amplitude; intensity

10. Our experience of pain when we are injured depends on:
    a. our biological make-up and the type of injury we have sustained.
    b. how well medical personnel deal with our injury.
    c. our physiology, experiences and attention, and surrounding culture.
    d. what our culture allows us to express in terms of feelings of pain.

11. The place theory of pitch perception cannot account for how we hear:
    a. low-pitched sounds.
    b. middle-pitched sounds.
    c. high-pitched sounds.
    d. chords (three or more pitches simultaneously).

12. The hearing losses that occur with age are especially pronounced for:
    a. low-pitched sounds.
    b. middle-pitched sounds.
    c. high-pitched sounds.
    d. chords.

13. According to the gate-control theory, a way to alleviate chronic pain would be to stimulate the _____ nerve fibers that _____ the spinal gate.
    a. small; open
    b. small; close
    c. large; open
    d. large; close

14. The transduction of light energy into nerve impulses takes place in the:
    a. iris.
    b. retina.
    c. lens.
    d. optic nerve.

15. The brain breaks vision into separate dimensions such as color, depth, movement, and form, and works on each aspect simultaneously. This is called:
    a. feature detection.
    b. parallel processing.
    c. accommodation.
    d. opponent processing.

16. Kinesthesis involves:
    a. the bones of the middle ear.
    b. information from the muscles, tendons, and joints.
    c. membranes within the cochlea.
    d. the body's sense of balance.

17. One light may appear reddish and another greenish if they differ in:
    a. wavelength.
    b. amplitude.
    c. opponent processes.
    d. brightness.

18. Which of the following explains why a rose appears equally red in bright and dim light?
    a. the Young-Helmholtz theory
    b. the opponent-process theory
    c. feature detection
    d. color constancy

19. Which of the following is an example of sensory adaptation?
    a. finding the cold water of a swimming pool warmer after you have been in it for a while
    b. developing an increased sensitivity to salt the more you use it in foods
    c. becoming very irritated at the continuing sound of a dripping faucet
    d. All of the above are examples.

20. Most color-deficient people will probably:
    a. lack functioning red- or green-sensitive cones.
    b. see the world in only black and white.
    c. also suffer from poor vision.
    d. have above-average vision to compensate for the deficit.

Matching Items

Match each of the structures with its function or description.

Structures or Conditions

_____ 1. lens
_____ 2. iris
_____ 3. pupil
_____ 4. rods
_____ 5. cones
_____ 6. middle ear
_____ 7. inner ear
_____ 8. large nerve fiber
_____ 9. small nerve fiber
_____ 10. semicircular canals
_____ 11. sensors in joints
_____ 12. acuity
_____ 13. farsightedness
_____ 14. nearsightedness

Functions or Descriptions

a. amplifies sounds
b. closes pain gate
c. vestibular sense
d. controls pupil
e. accommodation
f. eyeball is too short
g. opens pain gate
h. admits light
i. eyeball is too long
j. vision in dim light
k. transduction of sound
l. sharpness of vision
m. kinesthesis
n. color vision

PROGRESS TEST 2

Progress Test 2 should be completed during a final chapter review. Answer the following questions after you thoroughly understand the correct answers for the section reviews and Progress Test 1.

Multiple-Choice Questions

1. Which of the following is *not* one of the basic tastes?
   a. sweet
   b. salty
   c. umami
   d. bland

2. Of the four distinct skin senses, the only one that has definable receptors is:
   a. warmth.
   b. cold.
   c. pressure.
   d. pain.

3. The process by which sensory information is converted into neural energy is:
   a. sensory adaptation.
   b. feature detection.
   c. signal detection.
   d. transduction.

4. The receptors for taste are located in the:
   a. taste buds.
   b. cochlea.
   c. fovea.
   d. cortex.

5. The inner ear contains receptors for:
   a. audition and kinesthesis.
   b. kinesthesis and the vestibular sense.
   c. audition and the vestibular sense.
   d. audition, kinesthesis, and the vestibular sense.

6. According to the opponent-process theory:
   a. there are three types of color-sensitive cones.
   b. the process of color vision begins in the cortex.
   c. neurons involved in color vision are stimulated by one color's wavelength and inhibited by another's.
   d. all of the above are true.

7. Nerve deafness is caused by:
   a. wax buildup in the outer ear.
   b. damage to the eardrum.
   c. blockage in the middle ear because of infection.
   d. damage to the cochlea.

8. What enables you to feel yourself wiggling your toes even with your eyes closed?
   a. vestibular sense
   b. sense of kinesthesis
   c. the skin senses
   d. sensory interaction

9. The frequency theory of hearing is better than place theory at explaining our sensation of:
   a. the lowest pitches.
   b. pitches of intermediate range.
   c. the highest pitches.
   d. all of the above.

10. Hubel and Wiesel discovered feature detectors in the visual:
   a. fovea.
   b. optic nerve.
   c. iris.
   d. cortex.

11. Weber's law states that:
   a. the absolute threshold for any stimulus is a constant.
   b. the jnd for any stimulus is a constant.
   c. the absolute threshold for any stimulus is a constant proportion.
   d. the jnd for any stimulus is a constant proportion.

12. The principle that one sense may influence another is:
   a. transduction.
   b. sensory adaptation.
   c. Weber's law.
   d. sensory interaction.

13. Which of the following is the correct order of the structures through which light passes after entering the eye?
   a. lens, pupil, cornea, retina
   b. pupil, cornea, lens, retina
   c. pupil, lens, cornea, retina
   d. cornea, pupil, lens, retina

14. In the opponent-process theory, the three pairs of processes are:
   a. red-green, blue-yellow, black-white.
   b. red-blue, green-yellow, black-white.
   c. red-yellow, blue-green, black-white.
   d. dependent upon the individual's experience.

15. Wavelength is to _____ as_____ is to brightness.
   a. hue; intensity
   b. intensity; hue
   c. frequency; amplitude
   d. brightness; hue

16. Concerning the evidence for subliminal stimulation, which of the following is the best answer?
    a. The brain processes some information without our awareness.
    b. Stimuli too weak to cross our thresholds for awareness may trigger a response in our sense receptors.
    c. Because the "absolute" threshold is a statistical average, we are able to detect weaker stimuli some of the time.
    d. All of the above are true.

17. Which of the following is the most accurate description of how we process color?
    a. Throughout the visual system, color processing is divided into separate red, green, and blue systems.
    b. Red-green, blue-yellow, and black-white opponent processes operate throughout the visual system.
    c. Color processing occurs in two stages: (1) a three-color system in the retina and (2) opponent-process cells en route to the visual cortex.
    d. Color processing occurs in two stages: (1) an opponent-process system in the retina and (2) a three-color system en route to the visual cortex.

18. Which of the following is the most accurate explanation of how we discriminate pitch?
    a. For all audible frequencies, pitch is coded according to the place of maximum vibration on the cochlea's basilar membrane.
    b. For all audible frequencies, the rate of neural activity in the auditory nerve matches the frequency of the sound wave.
    c. For very high frequencies, pitch is coded according to place of vibration on the basilar membrane; for lower pitches, the rate of neural activity in the auditory nerve matches the sound's frequency.
    d. For very high frequencies, the rate of neural activity in the auditory nerve matches the frequency of the sound wave; for lower frequencies, pitch is coded according to the place of vibration on the basilar membrane.

19. One reason that your ability to detect fine visual details is greatest when scenes are focused on the fovea of your retina is that:
    a. there are more feature detectors in the fovea than in the peripheral regions of the retina.
    b. cones in the fovea are nearer to the optic nerve than those in peripheral regions of the retina.

    c. many rods, which are clustered in the fovea, have individual bipolar cells to relay their information to the cortex.
    d. many cones, which are clustered in the fovea, have individual bipolar cells to relay their information to the cortex.

20. Given normal sensory ability, a person standing atop a mountain on a dark, clear night can see a candle flame atop a mountain 30 miles away. This is a description of vision's:
    a. difference threshold.   c. absolute threshold.
    b. jnd.   d. signal detection.

PSYCHOLOGY APPLIED

Answer these questions the day before an exam as a final check on your understanding of the chapter's terms and concepts.

Multiple-Choice Questions

1. In shopping for a new stereo, you discover that you cannot differentiate between the sounds of models X and Y. The difference between X and Y is below your:
   a. absolute threshold.   c. receptor threshold.
   b. signal detection.   d. difference threshold.

2. In order to maximize your sensitivity to fine visual detail you should:
   a. stare off to one side of the object you are attempting to see.
   b. close one eye.
   c. decrease the intensity of the light falling upon the object.
   d. stare directly at the object.

3. The phantom limb sensation indicates that:
   a. pain is a purely sensory phenomenon.
   b. the central nervous system plays only a minor role in the experience of pain.
   c. pain involves the brain's interpretation of neural activity.
   d. all of the above are true.

4. While competing in the Olympic trials, marathoner Kirsten O'Brien suffered a stress fracture in her left leg. That she did not experience significant pain until the race was over is probably attributable to the fact that during the race:

   a. the pain gate in her spinal cord was closed by information coming from her brain.

   b. her body's production of endorphins decreased.

   c. an increase in the activity of small pain fibers closed the pain gate.

   d. a decrease in the activity of large pain fibers closed the pain gate.

5. Which of the following is an example of sensory interaction?

   a. finding that despite its delicious aroma, a weird-looking meal tastes awful

   b. finding that food tastes bland when you have a bad cold

   c. finding it difficult to maintain your balance when you have an ear infection

   d. All of the above are examples.

6. In comparing the human eye to a camera, the film would be located in the eye's:

   a. pupil.   **c.** cornea.

   b. lens.   **d.** retina.

7. Sensation is to _____ as perception is to _____ .

   a. recognizing a stimulus; interpreting a stimulus

   b. detecting a stimulus; recognizing a stimulus

   c. interpreting a stimulus; detecting a stimulus

   d. seeing; hearing

8. I am a cell in the thalamus that is excited by red and inhibited by green. I am a(n):

   a. feature detector.   **c.** bipolar cell.

   b. cone.   **d.** opponent-process cell.

9. Which of the following correctly lists the order of structures through which sound travels after entering the ear?

   a. auditory canal, eardrum, middle ear, cochlea

   b. eardrum, auditory canal, middle ear, cochlea

   c. eardrum, middle ear, cochlea, auditory canal

   d. cochlea, eardrum, middle ear, auditory canal

10. Dr. Frankenstein has forgotten to give his monster an important part; as a result, the monster cannot transduce sound. Dr. Frankenstein omitted the:

   a. eardrum.   **c.** semicircular canals.

   b. middle ear.   **d.** basilar membrane.

11. Seventy-five-year-old Claude has difficulty hearing high-pitched sounds. Most likely his hearing problem involves:

   a. his eardrum.

   b. his auditory canal.

   c. the bones of his middle ear.

   d. the hair cells of his inner ear.

12. Which of the following is true of cones?

   a. Cones enable color vision.

   b. Cones are highly concentrated in the foveal region of the retina.

   c. Cones have a higher absolute threshold for brightness than rods.

   d. All of the above are true.

13. Assuming that the visual systems of humans and other mammals function similarly, you would expect that the retina of a nocturnal mammal (one active only at night) would contain:

   a. mostly cones.

   b. mostly rods.

   c. an equal number of rods and cones.

   d. more bipolar cells than an animal active only during the day.

14. As the football game continued into the night, LeVar noticed that he was having difficulty distinguishing the colors of the players' uniforms. This is because the _____ , which enable color vision, have a _____ absolute threshold for brightness than the available light intensity.

   a. rods; higher   **c.** rods; lower

   b. cones; higher   **d.** cones; lower

15. After staring at a very intense red stimulus for a few minutes, Carrie shifted her gaze to a beige wall and "saw" the color _____ . Carrie's experience provides support for the _____ theory.

   a. green; trichromatic

   b. blue; opponent-process

   c. green; opponent-process

   d. blue; trichromatic

16. Elderly Mrs. Martinez finds that she must spice her food heavily or she cannot taste it. Unfortunately, her son often finds her cooking inedible because it is so spicy. What is the likely explanation for their taste differences?
    a. Women have higher taste thresholds than men.
    b. Men have higher taste thresholds than women.
    c. Being elderly, Mrs. Martinez probably has fewer taste buds than her son.
    d. All of the above are likely explanations.

17. When admiring the texture of a piece of fabric, Calvin usually runs his fingertips over the cloth's surface. He does this because:
    a. if the cloth were held motionless, sensory adaptation to its feel would quickly occur.
    b. the sense of touch does not adapt.
    c. a relatively small amount of brain tissue is devoted to processing touch from the fingertips.
    d. of all the above reasons.

18. Superman's eyes used _____ , while his brain used _____ .
    a. perception; sensation
    b. top-down processing; bottom-up processing
    c. bottom-up processing; top-down processing
    d. sensory adaptation; subliminal perception

19. How does pain differ from other senses?
    a. It has no special receptors.
    b. It has no single stimulus.
    c. It is influenced by both physical and psychological phenomena.
    d. All the above are true.

20. Tamiko hates the bitter taste of her cough syrup. Which of the following would she find most helpful in minimizing the syrup's bad taste?
    a. tasting something very sweet before taking the cough syrup
    b. keeping the syrup in her mouth for several seconds before swallowing it
    c. holding her nose while taking the cough syrup
    d. gulping the cough syrup so that it misses her tongue

Essay Question

A dancer in a chorus line uses many sensory cues when performing. Discuss three senses that dancers rely on and explain why each is important. (Use the space below to list the points you want to make, and organize them. Then write the essay on a separate sheet of paper.)

Summing Up

Use the diagrams to identify the parts of the eye and ear, then list them in the order in which they contribute to vision and hearing. Also, briefly explain the role of each structure.

The Eye

1. _____

   _____

2. _____

   _____

3. _____

   _____

4. _____

   _____

5. _____

   _____

6. _____

   _____

7. _____

   _____

The Ear

1. _____

   _____

2. _____

   _____

3. _____

   _____

4. _____

   _____

5. _____

   _____

6. _____

   _____

7. _____

   _____

8. _____

Key Terms

Writing Definitions

Using your own words, on a piece of paper write a brief definition or explanation of each of the following terms.

1. sensation
2. perception
3. bottom-up processing
4. top-down processing
5. psychophysics
6. absolute threshold
7. signal detection theory
8. subliminal
9. priming
10. difference threshold
11. Weber's law
12. sensory adaptation
13. transduction
14. wavelength and hue
15. intensity
16. pupil
17. iris
18. lens
19. accommodation
20. retina
21. acuity

22. nearsightedness
23. farsightedness
24. rods and cones
25. optic nerve
26. blind spot
27. fovea
28. feature detectors
29. parallel processing
30. Young-Helmholtz trichromatic (three-color) theory
31. opponent-process theory
32. color constancy
33. audition
34. pitch and frequency
35. middle ear
36. cochlea
37. inner ear
38. place theory
39. frequency theory
40. conduction hearing loss
41. sensorineural hearing loss
42. cochlear implant
43. gate-control theory
44. sensory interaction
45. kinesthesis
46. vestibular sense

Cross-Check

As you learned in the Prologue, reviewing and overlearning of material are important to the learning process. After you have written the definitions of the key terms in this chapter, you should complete the crossword puzzle to ensure that you can reverse the process—recognize the term, given the definition.

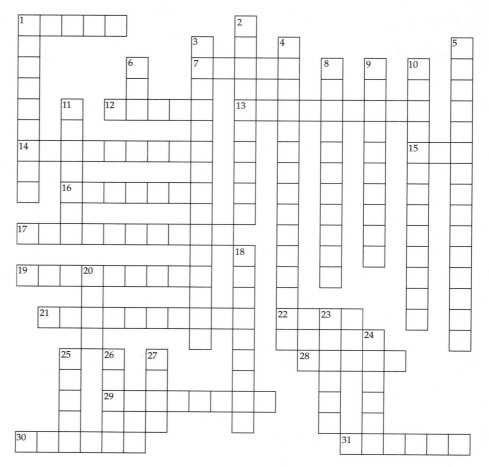

ACROSS

1. The retina's point of central focus.
7. Types of fibers that close the "pain gate."
12. Nerve that carries visual information to the brain.
13. Aspect of light and sound determined by the amplitude of energy waves.
14. Unit of measurement for electromagnetic energy.
15. The perceptual experience of color.
16. Membrane that lies at the end of the auditory canal.
17. Term for the color seen after staring at its opponent for a while.
19. Physical dimension of light and sound that determines brightness and loudness, respectively.
21. Type of deafness that results from damage in the mechanics of the outer or middle ear.
22. Membrane "window" at the entrance to the ear's cochlea.
28. Adjustable opening in the eye through which light enters.
29. Sense of hearing.
30. Transparent protective membrane through which light enters the eye.
31. Inner surface of the eye that contains the rods and cones.

DOWN

1. Theory of hearing that the rate of auditory nerve impulses matches the frequency of tones, enabling us to sense pitch.
2. Type of vision caused by a shorter-than-normal eyeball.
3. Energy spectrum that contains visible light.
4. Type of brain cell discovered by Hubel and Wiesel.
5. The basis of a "bionic ear."

6. _____-down processing is information processing guided by higher-level mental processes.
8. Sense of the position and movement of body parts.
9. Ability of some brain-damaged patients to respond to something that is not consciously perceived.
10. Study of the relationship between the physical characteristics of stimuli and our psychological experience of them.
11. Perception of color is strongly influenced by the object's _____ .
18. Region of the retina where the optic nerve leaves the eye.
20. Part of the eye that changes shape to focus images on the retina.
23. Sharpness of vision.
24. Region of the ear that contains the hammer, anvil, and stirrup.
25. Region of the ear that contains the cochlea.
26. Theory that the region of maximum vibration along the basilar membrane is the basis of pitch discrimination.
27. Visual receptors that are concentrated in the periphery of the retina.

ANSWERS

Chapter Review

Introduction

1. sensation; perception
2. bottom-up processing; top-down processing
3. prosopagnosia

Sensing the World: Some Basic Principles

1. psychophysics
2. absolute threshold; 50
3. signal detection; psychological
4. subliminal
5. conscious
6. prime; priming effect; automatically
7. difference threshold; just noticeable difference
8. Weber's law; stimulus
9. sensory adaptation
10. informative

Although sensory adaptation reduces our sensitivity, it enables us to focus our attention on informative changes in the environment without being distracted by the uninformative, constant stimulation that bombards our senses.

Vision

1. neural; transduction
2. electromagnetic
3. wavelength; hue
4. intensity; amplitude; brightness
5. cornea; pupil; iris
6. lens; retina
7. accommodation; acuity
8. distant; in front of; nearby; distant; nearby; in back of; distant; nearby
9. rods; cones
10. bipolar; ganglion; optic nerve; brain
11. blind spot
12. fovea; peripheral; bipolar
13. cones; rods
14. sensitive; 20
15. abstract; thalamus; visual cortex; feature detectors
16. temporal; gaze; head angle; posture; body movement; perceives
17. simultaneously; parallel processing; blindsight
18. integration; gamma; similar
19. reflects (rejects); construction
20. sex-linked
21. Young-Helmholtz trichromatic; red; green; blue; additive; subtractive
22. opponent; afterimage
23. opponent-process; red; green; yellow; blue; black; white

In the first stage of color processing, the retina's red, green, and blue cones respond in varying degrees to different color stimuli, as suggested by the three-color theory. The resulting signals are then processed in the thalamus by red-green, blue-yellow, and black-white opponent-process cells, which are stimulated by one wavelength and inhibited by its opponent.

24. context
25. color constancy
26. reflected; surrounding objects

Hearing

1. audition; air molecules
2. loudness
3. frequency
4. decibels; 0
5. outer; middle; inner
6. eardrum
7. hammer; anvil; stirrup
8. cochlea; oval window; basilar membrane; hair cells; thalamus; temporal; number
9. less; stress; high blood pressure; anxiety; feelings of helplessness; unanticipated; uncontrollable
10. place; low
11. frequency; high; 1000
12. volley
13. speed (timing); loudness
14. harder
15. parallel processing
16. conduction hearing loss
17. sensorineural; aging
18. stimulate
19. cochlear implant
20. Deaf culture; children; speak; disability
21. is; with; have; seem to
22. sensory compensation
23. self-esteem; accepted

Other Important Senses

1. pressure; warmth; cold; pain; variations

2. top-down; somatosensory cortex

3. injury; hyperalgesia

4. senses; brain; expectations

5. phantom limb; tinnitus

6. sensory input

7. is not; does not

8. gate-control; gate; spinal cord; small; large; brain

9. social; physical; René Descartes; brain

The Lamaze method of prepared childbirth combines several pain control techniques, including distraction, deep breathing and muscle relaxation, and counter-stimulation through gentle massage. Similarly, for burn victims, distraction during painful wound care can be created by immersion in a computer-generated 3-D world.

10. sweet; sour; salty; bitter; umami (meat)

11. chemical; taste buds; pore

12. week or two; decreases; decreases; smoking; alcohol

13. sensory interaction; McGurk; see; hearing

14. olfaction; chemical; cannot

15. early adulthood

16. learned

17. limbic

18. kinesthesis; muscles; tendons; joints

19. vestibular sense; semicircular canals; vestibular sacs

Progress Test 1

Multiple-Choice Questions

1. **b.** is the answer. Psychological factors can affect the absolute threshold for a stimulus. (pp. 199–200)
   a. The absolute threshold for detecting a stimulus depends not only on the strength of the stimulus but also on psychological factors such as experience, expectations, motivation, and fatigue. Thus, the threshold cannot be a constant.
   c. & d. The absolute threshold is defined as the minimum stimulus that is detected 50 percent of the time.

2. **d.** is the answer. In nearsightedness, objects converge in front of the retina; one cause of this is an eyeball longer than normal in relation to the lens. (p. 206)

   a. Inflexibility of the lens may cause the emergence of farsightedness as we get older.
   b. Thinness of the lens is unrelated to near- or far-sightedness.
   c. A shorter-than-normal eyeball is related to far-sightedness.

3. **c.** is the answer. According to Weber's law, the difference threshold is a constant proportion of the stimulus. There is a 10 percent difference between 10 and 11 pounds; since the difference threshold is a constant proportion, the weight closest to 100 pounds that can nonetheless be differentiated from it is 110 pounds (or 100 pounds plus 10 percent). (p. 201)

4. **c.** is the answer. (p. 202)
   a. "Sensory fatigue" is not a term in psychology.
   b. Accommodation refers to an adaptive change in shape by the lens of the eye.
   d. Sensory interaction is the principle that one sense may influence another.

5. **d.** is the answer. (p. 205)
   a. The lens lies behind the pupil and focuses light on the retina.
   b. The retina is the inner surface of the eyeball and contains the rods and cones.
   c. The cornea lies in front of the pupil and is the first structure that light passes through as it enters the eye.

6. **a.** is the answer. (p. 205)
   b. Sensory adaptation is our diminishing sensitivity to an unchanging stimulus.
   c. Feature detection is the process by which neural cells in the brain respond to specific visual features.
   d. Transduction refers to the conversion of an environmental stimulus, such as light, into a neural impulse by a receptor—a rod or a cone.

7. **d.** is the answer. (p. 208)
   a. The fovea is not a receptor; it is a region of the retina that contains only cones.
   b. Cones have a higher threshold for brightness than rods and therefore do not function as well in dim light.
   c. Bipolar cells are not receptors; they are neurons in the retina that link rods and cones with ganglion cells, which make up the optic nerve.

8. **a.** is the answer. The Young-Helmholtz theory proposes that there are red-, green-, and blue-sensitive cones. (p. 212)
   b. This answer describes Hering's opponent-process theory.
   c. The Young-Helmholtz theory proposes that there are three types of cones, not four.

d. The Young-Helmholtz theory concerns only color vision, not the detection of visual detail.

9. **b.** is the answer. Just as wave frequency determines pitch, so wave amplitude determines loudness. (p. 216)

   a. Amplitude is the physical basis of loudness; wavelength determines frequency and thereby pitch.

   c. & d. Wavelength, amplitude, and intensity are physical aspects of light and sound. Because the question is based on a relationship between a physical property (frequency) of a stimulus and its psychological attribute (pitch), these answers are incorrect.

10. **c.** is the answer. The biopsychosocial approach tells us that our experience of pain depends on biological, psychological, and social-cultural factors.. (p. 226)

11. **a.** is the answer. (p. 219)

   b. & c. Although the localization of low-pitched sounds along the basilar membrane is poor, that for sounds of middle and, especially, high pitch is good. Therefore, place theory accounts well for high-pitched sounds and, together with frequency theory, can account for middle-pitched sounds.

   d. As long as the notes of a chord are within the range of responsiveness of the basilar membrane, chord perception can be accounted for by place theory.

12. **c.** is the answer. (p. 220)

   d. Chord perception, except for chords comprised exclusively of high-frequency notes, shows no age-dependent decline.

13. **d.** is the answer. The small fibers conduct most pain signals; the large fibers conduct most other sensory signals from the skin. The gate either allows pain signals to pass on to the brain or blocks them from passing. When the large fibers are stimulated, the pain gate is closed and other sensations are felt in place of pain. (p. 227)

14. **b.** is the answer. (pp. 206–207)

   a. The iris controls the diameter of the pupil.

   c. The lens accommodates its shape to focus images on the retina.

   d. The optic nerve carries nerve impulses from the retina to the visual cortex.

15. **b.** is the answer. (p. 210)

   a. Feature detection is the process by which nerve cells in the brain respond to specific visual features of a stimulus, such as movement or shape.

   c. Accommodation is the process by which the lens changes its curvature to focus images on the retina.

d. The opponent-process theory suggests that color vision depends on the response of brain cells to red-green, yellow-blue, and black-white opposing colors.

16. **b.** is the answer. Kinesthesis, or the sense of the position and movement of body parts, is based on information from the muscles, tendons, and joints. (p. 233)

   a. & c. The ear plays no role in kinesthesis.

   d. Equilibrium, or the sense of balance, is not involved in kinesthesis but is, rather, a companion sense.

17. **a.** is the answer. Wavelength determines hue, or color. (pp. 204–205)

   b. & d. The amplitude of light determines its brightness.

   c. Opponent processes are neural systems involved in color vision, not properties of light.

18. **d.** is the answer. Color constancy is the perception that a familiar object has consistent color, even if changing illumination alters the wavelengths reflected by that object. (pp. 213–214)

   a. & b. These theories explain how the visual system detects color; they do not explain why colors do not seem to change when lighting does.

   c. Feature detection explains how the brain recognizes visual images by analyzing their distinctive features of shape, movement, and angle.

19. **a.** is the answer. Sensory adaptation means a diminishing sensitivity to an unchanging stimulus. Only the adjustment to cold water involves a decrease in sensitivity; the other examples involve an increase. (p. 202)

20. **a.** is the answer. Thus, they have difficulty discriminating these two colors. (p. 212)

   b. Those who are color deficient are usually not "color blind" in a literal sense. Instead, they are unable to distinguish certain hues, such as red from green.

   c. Failure to distinguish red and green is separate from, and does not usually affect, general visual ability.

   d. Color deficiency does not enhance vision. A deficit in one sense often is compensated for by overdevelopment of another sense—for example, hearing in blind people.

Matching Items

1. e (p. 205)	**6.** a (p. 217)	**11.** m (p. 233)
2. d (p. 205)	**7.** k (p. 217)	**12.** l (p. 206)
3. h (p. 205)	**8.** b (p. 227)	**13.** f (p. 206)
4. j (p. 206)	**9.** g (p. 227)	**14.** i (p. 206)
5. n (p. 206)	**10.** c (p. 234)	

Progress Test 2

Multiple-Choice Questions

1. **d.** is the answer. (p. 229)

2. **c.** is the answer. Researchers have identified receptors for pressure but have been unable to do so for the other skin senses. (p. 225)

3. **d.** is the answer. (p. 204)
   a. Sensory adaptation refers to the diminished sensitivity that occurs with unchanging stimulation.
   b. Feature detection refers to the process by which nerve cells in the brain respond to specific aspects of visual stimuli, such as movement or shape.
   c. Signal detection is a task in which the observer must judge whether a faint signal is present.

4. **a.** is the answer. (p. 230)
   b. The cochlea contains receptors for hearing.
   c. The fovea contains receptors for vision (the cones).
   d. The cortex is the outer layer of the brain, where information detected by the receptors is processed.

5. **c.** is the answer. The inner ear contains the receptors for audition (hearing) and the vestibular sense; those for kinesthesis are located in the muscles, tendons, and joints. (pp. 217, 234)

6. **c.** is the answer. After leaving the receptor cells, visual information is analyzed in terms of pairs of opponent colors; neurons stimulated by one member of a pair are inhibited by the other. (p. 213)
   a. The idea that there are three types of color-sensitive cones is the basis of the Young-Helmholtz three-color theory.
   b. According to the opponent-process theory, and all other theories of color vision, the process of color vision begins in the retina.

7. **d.** is the answer. Sensorineural hearing loss is caused by destruction of neural tissue as a result of problems with the cochlea's receptors or the auditory nerve. (p. 220)
   a. & c. Wax buildup and blockage because of infection are temporary states; sensorineural hearing loss is permanent. Moreover, sensorineural hearing loss involves the inner ear, rather than the outer or middle ear.
   b. Damage to the eardrum impairs the mechanical system that conducts sound waves; it could therefore cause conduction hearing loss, not sensorineural hearing loss.

8. **b.** is the answer. Kinesthesis, the sense of movement of body parts, would enable you to feel your toes wiggling. (p. 233)
   a. The vestibular sense is concerned with movement and position, or balance, of the whole body, not of its parts.
   c. The skin, or tactile, senses are pressure, pain, warmth, and cold; they have nothing to do with movement of body parts.
   d. Sensory interaction, the principle that the senses influence each other, does not play a role in this example, which involves only the sense of kinesthesis.

9. **a.** is the answer. Frequency theory best explains the lowest pitches. Place theory best explains the highest pitches, and some combination of the two theories probably accounts for our sensation of intermediate-range pitches. (p. 219)

10. **d.** is the answer. Feature detectors are cortical neurons and hence are located in the visual cortex. (p. 209)
    a. The fovea contains cones.
    b. The optic nerve contains neurons that relay nerve impulses from the retina to higher centers in the visual system.
    c. The iris is simply a ring of muscle tissue, which controls the diameter of the pupil.

11. **d.** is the answer. Weber's law concerns difference thresholds (jnd's), not absolute thresholds, and states that these are constant proportions of the stimuli, not that they remain constant. (p. 202)

12. **d.** is the answer. (p. 230)
    a. Transduction is the process by which stimulus energy is converted into nerve impulses.
    b. Sensory adaptation is diminished sensitivity to unchanging stimulation.
    c. Weber's law states that the jnd is a constant proportion of a stimulus.

13. **d.** is the answer. (p. 205)

14. **a.** is the answer. (p. 213)

15. **a.** is the answer. Wavelength determines hue, and intensity determines brightness. (pp. 204–205)

16. **d.** is the answer. (pp. 200–201)

17. **c.** is the answer. (p. 211)
    a. This answer is incorrect because separate red, green, and blue systems operate only in the retina.
    b. This answer is incorrect because opponent-process systems operate en route to the brain, after visual processing in the receptors is completed.
    d. This answer is incorrect because it reverses the correct order of the two stages of processing.

18. **c.** is the answer. (p. 219)
    a. This answer describes how pitch is sensed in the case of high-pitched, but not low-pitched, sounds.
    b. This answer describes how pitch is sensed in the case of low-pitched, but not high-pitched, sounds.
    d. This answer is incorrect because it reverses the range of frequencies.

19. **d.** is the answer. (p. 207)
    a. Feature detectors are nerve cells located in the visual cortex, not in the fovea of the retina.
    b. The proximity of rods and cones to the optic nerve does not influence their ability to resolve fine details.
    c. Rods are concentrated in the peripheral regions of the retina, not in the fovea; moreover, several rods share a single bipolar cell.

20. **c.** is the answer. The absolute threshold is the minimum stimulation needed to detect a stimulus. (p. 199)
    a. & b. The difference threshold, which is also known as the jnd, is the minimum difference between two stimuli that a person can detect. In this example, there is only one stimulus—the sight of the flame.
    d. Signal detection is a research task, not a sensory phenomenon.

Psychology Applied

Multiple-Choice Questions

1. **d.** is the answer. (p. 201)
   a. The absolute threshold refers to whether a single stimulus can be detected, not to whether two stimuli can be differentiated.
   b. Signal detection is a task in which one must determine whether or not a faint stimulus is present.
   c. A receptor threshold is a minimum amount of energy that will elicit a neural impulse in a receptor cell.

2. **d.** is the answer. Greater sensitivity to fine visual detail is associated with the cones, which have their own bipolar cells to relay information to the cortex. The cones are concentrated in the fovea, the retina's point of central focus. For this reason, staring directly at an object maximizes sensitivity to fine detail. (p. 207)
   a. If you stare off to one side, the image falls onto peripheral regions of the retina, where rods are concentrated and sensitivity to fine visual detail is poor.

   b. Sensitivity to detail is not directly influenced by whether one or both eyes are stimulated.
   c. Decreasing the intensity of light would only impair the functioning of the cones, which are sensitive to visual detail but have a high threshold for light intensity.

3. **c.** is the answer. Since pain is felt in the limb that does not exist, the pain is simply the brain's (mis)interpretation of neural activity. (p. 227)
   a. If pain were a purely sensory phenomenon, phantom limb pain would not occur, since the receptors are no longer present.
   b. That pain is experienced when a limb is missing indicates that the central nervous system, especially the brain, is where pain is sensed.

4. **a.** is the answer. (p. 227)
   b. Since endorphins relieve pain, a decrease in their production would have made Kirsten more likely to experience pain. Moreover, because endorphins are released in response to pain, their production probably would have increased.
   c. Neural activity in small fibers tends to open the pain gate.
   d. An *increase* in large-fiber activity would tend to *close* the pain gate.

5. **d.** is the answer. Each of these is an example of the interaction of two senses—vision and taste in the case of a., taste and smell in the case of b., and hearing and the vestibular sense in the case of c. (p. 230)

6. **d.** is the answer. Just as light strikes the film of a camera, visual images entering the eye are projected onto the retina. (p. 206)
   a. The pupil would be analogous to the aperture of a camera, since both control the amount of light permitted to enter.
   b. The lens of the eye performs a focusing function similar to the lens of the camera.
   c. The cornea would be analogous to a camera's lens cap in that both protect delicate inner structures.

7. **b.** is the answer. (p. 197)
   a. Both recognition and interpretation are examples of perception.
   c. This answer would have been correct if the question had read, "Perception is to sensation as _____ is to _____."
   d. Sensation and perception are important processes in both hearing and seeing.

8. **d.** is the answer. (p. 213)
   a. Feature detectors are located in the visual cortex and respond to features such as movement, shape, and angle.
   b. & c. Cones and bipolar cells are located in the

retina. Moreover, neither are excited by some colors and inhibited by others.

9. **a.** is the answer. (p. 217)

10. **d.** is the answer. The hair cells, which transduce sound energy, are located on the basilar membrane. (p. 217)
a. & b. The eardrum and bones of the middle ear merely conduct sound waves to the inner ear, where they are transduced.
c. The semicircular canals are involved in the vestibular sense, not hearing.

11. **d.** is the answer. Hearing losses that result from aging are greatest in the higher frequencies and involve damage to the hair cells on the basilar membrane of the cochlea. (p. 220)
a., b., & c. Damage to the eardrum, auditory canal, or bones of the middle ear would probably cause conduction hearing loss and reduced sensitivity to sounds of all frequencies.

12. **d.** is the answer. (p. 207)

13. **b.** is the answer. Rods and cones enable vision in dim and bright light, respectively. If an animal is active only at night, it is likely to have more rods than cones in its retinas. (p. 208)
d. Bipolar cells link both cones and rods to ganglion cells. There is no reason to expect that a nocturnal mammal would have more bipolar cells than a mammal active both during the day and at night. If anything, because several rods share a single bipolar cell, whereas many cones have their own, a nocturnal animal (with a visual system consisting mostly of rods) might be expected to have fewer bipolar cells than an animal active during the day (with a visual system consisting mostly of cones).

14. **b.** is the answer. (p. 208)
a. & c. It is the cones, rather than the rods, that enable color vision.
d. If the cones' threshold were lower than the available light intensity, they would be able to function and therefore detect the colors of the players' uniforms.

15. **c.** is the answer. (p. 213)
a. The trichromatic theory cannot account for the experience of afterimages.
b. & d. Afterimages are experienced as the complementary color of a stimulus. Green, not blue, is red's complement.

16. **c.** is the answer. As people age they lose taste

buds and their taste thresholds increase. For this reason, Mrs. Martinez needs more concentrated tastes than her son to find food palatable. (p. 230)
a. & b. There is no evidence that women and men differ in their absolute thresholds for taste.

17. **a.** is the answer. (pp. 202–203)
b. The sense of touch (pressure) adapts very quickly.
c. On the contrary, the extreme sensitivity of the fingertips is due to the relatively large amount of cortical tissue that processes neural impulses from the fingertips.

18. **c.** is the answer. (p. 197)

19. **d.** is the answer. (pp. 226–227)

20. **c.** is the answer. Because of the powerful sensory interaction between taste and smell, eliminating the odor of the cough syrup should make its taste more pleasant. (p. 230)
a. If anything, the contrasting tastes might make the bitter syrup even less palatable.
b. If Tamiko keeps the syrup in her mouth for several seconds, it will ensure that her taste pores fully "catch" the stimulus, thus intensifying the bitter taste.
d. It's probably impossible to miss the tongue completely.

Essay Question

The senses that are most important to dancers are vision, hearing, kinesthesis, and the vestibular sense. Your answer should refer to any three of these senses and include, at minimum, the following information.

Dancers rely on vision to gauge their body position relative to other dancers as they perform specific choreographed movements. Vision also helps dancers assess the audience's reaction to their performance. Whenever dance is set to music, hearing is necessary so that the dancers can detect musical cues for certain parts of their routines. Hearing also helps the dancers keep their movements in time with the music. Kinesthetic receptors in dancers' muscles, tendons, and joints provide their brains with information about the position and movement of body parts to determine if their hands, arms, legs, and heads are in the proper positions. Receptors for the vestibular sense located in the dancers' inner ears send messages to their brains that help them maintain their balance and determine the correctness of the position and movement of their bodies.

Summing Up

The Eye

1. **Cornea.** Light enters the eye through this transparent membrane, which protects the inner structures from the environment.
2. **Iris.** The colored part of the eye, the iris functions like the aperture of a camera, controlling the size of the pupil to optimize the amount of light that enters the eye.
3. **Pupil.** The adjustable opening in the iris, the pupil allows light to enter.
4. **Lens.** This transparent structure behind the pupil changes shape to focus images on the retina.
5. **Retina.** The light-sensitive inner surface of the eye, the retina contains the rods and cones, which transduce light energy into neural impulses.
6. **Blind spot.** The region of the retina where the optic nerve leaves the eye, the blind spot contains no rods or cones and so there is no vision here.
7. **Optic nerve.** This bundle of nerve fibers carries neural impulses from the retina to the brain.

The Ear

1. **Outer ear.** Hearing begins as sound waves enter the auditory canal of the outer ear.
2. **Auditory canal.** Sound waves passing through the auditory canal are brought to a point of focus at the eardrum.
3. **Eardrum.** Lying between the outer and middle ear, this membrane vibrates in response to sound waves.
4. **Middle ear.** Lying between the outer and inner ear, this air-filled chamber contains the hammer, anvil, and stirrup.
5. **Hammer, anvil, and stirrup.** These tiny bones of the middle ear concentrate the eardrum's vibrations on the cochlea's oval window.
6. **Inner ear.** This region of the ear contains the cochlea and the semicircular canals, which play an important role in balance.
7. **Cochlea.** This fluid-filled multichambered structure contains the hair cell receptors that transduce sound waves into neural impulses.
8. **Auditory nerve.** This bundle of fibers carries nerve impulses from the inner ear to the brain.

Key Terms

Writing Definitions

1. **Sensation** is the process by which we detect physical energy from the environment and encode it as neural signals. (p. 197)

2. **Perception** is the process by which we select, organize, and interpret sensory information. (p. 197)
3. **Bottom-up processing** is analysis that begins with the sensory receptors and works up to the brain's integration of sensory information. (p. 197)
4. **Top-down processing** is information processing guided by higher-level mental processes. (p. 197)
5. **Psychophysics** is the study of relationships between the physical characteristics of stimuli and our psychological experience of them. (p. 199)
6. The **absolute threshold** is the minimum stimulation needed to detect a stimulus 50 percent of the time. (p. 199)
7. **Signal detection theory** explains precisely how and when we detect the presence of a faint stimulus ("signal"). Detection depends partly on experience, expectations, motivation, and alertness. (p. 199)
8. A stimulus that is **subliminal** is one that is below the absolute threshold for conscious awareness. (p. 200)

   Memory aid: Limen is the Latin word for "threshold." A stimulus that is **subliminal** is one that is *sub-* ("below") the *limen*, or threshold.
9. **Priming** is the activation of an association by an imperceptible stimulus, the effect of which is to predispose a perception, memory, or response. (p. 200)
10. The **difference threshold** (also called the just noticeable difference, or jnd), is the minimum difference between two stimuli that a subject can detect 50 percent of the time. (p. 201)
11. **Weber's law** states that the just noticeable difference between two stimuli is a constant minimum proportion of the stimulus. (p. 202)

    Example: If a difference of 10 percent in weight is noticeable, **Weber's law** predicts that a person could discriminate 10- and 11-pound weights or 50- and 55-pound weights.
12. **Sensory adaptation** refers to the decreased sensitivity that occurs with continued exposure to an unchanging stimulus. (p. 202)
13. In sensation, **transduction** refers to the process by which receptor cells in the eye, ear, skin, and nose convert stimulus energies into neural impulses. (p. 204)

14. **Wavelength**, which refers to the distance from the peak of one light (or sound) wave to the next, gives rise to the perceptual experiences of **hue**, or color, in vision (and **pitch** in sound). (pp. 204–205)

15. The **intensity** of light and sound is determined by the amplitude of the waves and is experienced as brightness and loudness, respectively. (p. 205)

    Example: Sounds that exceed 85 decibels in amplitude, or **intensity**, will damage the auditory system.

16. The **pupil** is the adjustable opening in the eye through which light enters. (205)

17. The **iris** is a ring of muscle tissue that forms the colored part of the eye that controls the diameter of the pupil. (p. 205)

18. The **lens** is the transparent structure of the eye behind the pupil that changes shape to focus images on the retina. (p. 205)

19. **Accommodation** is the process by which the lens of the eye changes shape to focus near objects on the retina. (p. 205)

20. The **retina** is the light-sensitive, multilayered inner surface of the eye that contains the rods and cones as well as neurons that form the beginning of the optic nerve. (p. 205)

21. **Acuity** refers to the sharpness of vision. (p. 206)

    Example: If your **acuity** is 20/10, you are able to see clearly at a distance of 20 feet a visual detail that most people cannot see beyond a distance of 10 feet.

22. **Nearsightedness** is a condition in which nearby objects are seen clearly but distant objects are blurred because light rays reflecting from them converge in front of the retina. (p. 206)

23. **Farsightedness** is a condition in which distant objects are seen clearly but nearby objects are blurred because light rays reflecting from them strike the retina **before** converging. (p. 206)

    Memory aid: To help you remember that farsightedness is caused by a shorter-than-normal eyeball, think of something falling "far short of the mark."

24. The **rods** and **cones** are visual receptors that transduce light into neural impulses. The rods are concentrated in the periphery of the retina, the cones in the fovea. The rods have poor sensitivity; detect black, white, and gray; function well in dim light; and are needed for peripheral vision. The cones have excellent sensitivity, enable color vision, and function best in daylight or bright light. (p. 206)

25. Comprised of the axons of retinal ganglion cells, the **optic nerve** carries neural impulses from the eye to the brain. (pp. 206–207)

26. The **blind spot** is the region of the retina where the optic nerve leaves the eye. Because there are no rods or cones in this area, there is no vision here. (p. 207)

27. The **fovea** is the retina's point of central focus. It contains only cones; therefore, images focused on the fovea are the clearest. (p. 207)

28. **Feature detectors**, located in the visual cortex of the brain, are nerve cells that selectively respond to specific visual features, such as movement, shape, or angle. Feature detectors are evidently the basis of visual information processing. (p. 209)

29. **Parallel processing** is information processing in which several aspects of a stimulus, such as light or sound, are processed simultaneously. (p. 210)

30. The **Young-Helmholtz trichromatic (three-color) theory** maintains that the retina contains red-, green-, and blue-sensitive color receptors that in combination can produce the perception of any color. This theory explains the first stage of color processing. (p. 212)

31. The **opponent-process theory** maintains that color vision depends on pairs of opposing retinal processes (red-green, yellow-blue, and white-black). This theory explains the second stage of color processing. (p. 213)

32. **Color constancy** is the perception that familiar objects have consistent color despite changes in illumination that shift the wavelengths they reflect. (pp. 213–214)

33. **Audition** refers to the sense of hearing. (p. 215)

34. The **pitch** of a sound is determined by its **frequency**, that is, the number of complete wavelengths that can pass a point in a given time. Frequency, in turn, is directly related to wavelength: longer waves produce lower pitch; shorter waves produce higher pitch. (p. 216)

35. The **middle ear** is the chamber between the eardrum and cochlea containing the three bones (hammer, anvil, and stirrup) that concentrate the eardrum's vibrations on the cochlea's oval window. (p. 217)

36. The **cochlea** is the coiled, bony, fluid-filled tube of the inner ear where the transduction of sound waves into neural impulses occurs. (p. 217)

37. The **inner ear** contains the semicircular canals and the cochlea, which includes the receptors that transduce sound energy into neural impulses.

Because it also contains the vestibular sac, the inner ear plays an important role in balance, as well as in audition. (p. 217)

38. The **place theory** of hearing states that we hear different pitches because sound waves of various frequencies trigger activity at different places on the cochlea's basilar membrane. (p. 219)

   Memory aid: **Place theory** maintains that the *place* of maximum vibration along the cochlea's membrane is the basis of pitch discrimination.

39. The **frequency theory** of hearing presumes that the rate, or frequency, of nerve impulses in the auditory nerve matches the frequency of a tone, thus enabling us to sense its pitch. (p. 219)

40. **Conduction hearing loss** refers to the hearing loss that results from damage in the mechanics of the outer or middle ear, which impairs the conduction of sound waves to the cochlea. (p. 220)

41. **Sensorineural hearing loss** (*nerve deafness*) is hearing loss caused by damage to the auditory receptors of the cochlea or to the auditory nerve due to disease, aging, or prolonged exposure to ear-splitting noise. (p. 220)

42. A **cochlear implant** is an electronic device that converts sounds into electrical signals that stimulate the auditory nerve. (p. 221)

43. Melzack and Wall's **gate-control theory** maintains that a "gate" in the spinal cord determines whether pain signals are permitted to reach the brain. Neural activity in small nerve fibers opens the gates; activity in large fibers or information from the brain closes the gate. (p. 227)

   Example: The **gate-control theory** gained support with the discovery of endorphins. Production of these opiatelike chemicals may be the brain's mechanism for closing the spinal gate.

44. **Sensory interaction** is the principle that one sense may influence another. (p. 230)

45. **Kinesthesis** is the sense of the position and movement of the parts of the body. (p. 233)

46. The sense of body movement and position, including the sense of balance, is called the **vestibular sense.** (p. 234)

Cross-Check

ACROSS	DOWN
1. fovea	1. frequency
7. large	2. farsighted
12. optic	3. electromagnetic
13. intensity	4. feature detector
14. nanometer	5. cochlear implant
15. hue	6. top
16. eardrum	8. kinesthesis
17. afterimage	9. blindsight
19. amplitude	10. psychophysics
21. conduction	11. context
22. oval	18. blindspot
28. pupil	20. lens
29. audition	23. acuity
30. cornea	24. middle
31. retina	25. inner
	26. place
	27. rods

FOCUS ON VOCABULARY AND LANGUAGE

Page 198: Shown her own face in a mirror she is again *stumped.* This person (E. H.) is suffering from *prosopagnosia* and cannot recognize faces and even fails (*she is stumped*) to recognize her own face in the mirror. What is interesting in this case is that she can process incoming sensory information (*bottom up*) but is unable to make any sense of it (*top down*). As Myers notes earlier, she has sensation (*bottom-up processing*), but her perception (*top-down processing*) is not working properly.

Sensing the World: Some Basic Principles

Page 198: A frog could starve to death *knee-deep* in motionless flies. But let one *zoom by* and the frog's *"bug detector"* cells *snap awake.* The frog's eyes and brain are organized in such a way that only fast moving (*zooming*), small, dark objects will cause these specialized feature detector nerve cells (*"bug detectors"*) to become active (*snap awake*). If the frog is surrounded by flies that don't move (*knee-deep in motionless flies*), it will die of hunger, completely unaware of the food at its feet.

Page 199: The *shades* on our senses are open just a *crack,* allowing us only a restricted awareness of this *vast sea* of energy. Just as sunblinds or curtains (*shades*) let only a little light in through any small opening (*a crack*), our sensory system is only able to detect a very small part of the large amount (*vast sea*) of the physical energy that exists in the world.

Page 199: Exhausted parents of a newborn will notice *the faintest whimper* from the *cradle.* . . . In **signal detection theory** there is no single absolute threshold for detecting stimuli; it all depends on the situation. Thus, parents who are sleeping soundly are more likely to become aware of the quietest cry of distress (*the faintest whimper*) from the infant in its small bed (*cradle*) than much louder but irrelevant noise.

Page 200: . . . *"satanic messages"* . . . It has been suggested that some rock music recordings have hidden or subliminal messages and that behavior can be influenced or manipulated by them (i.e., *hidden persuasion*). Claims have been made that some of these messages are antireligious and promote devil worship (*diabolical* or *satanic*). As Myers makes clear, there is not a shred of evidence to support these ideas.

Page 201: . . . *hucksters* . . . A *huckster* is someone who sells merchandise that may be of dubious value. Those who promote and sell subliminal tapes (*hucksters*) make claims that are not supported by scientif-ic research. In fact, the available evidence suggests that subliminal tapes do not have the profound, enduring effects on behavior claimed by their marketers.

Page 202: . . . it might take a £4000 *price hike* in a £40,000 Mercedes to *raise the eyebrows* of its potential buyers. *Raised eyebrows* express surprise. So a £4000 increase in the cost (*price hike*) of a luxury car (Mercedes-Benz), which normally costs £40,000, would be noticed by interested buyers (*would raise their eyebrows*). **Weber's law** states that a constant proportion of the original stimulus is needed in order for the difference to be detected, and the precise proportion will change depending on the stimulus. Thus, a $5 increase in the price of the car would not be a **just noticeable difference**, or **jnd**, but a $5 dollar increase (*price hike*) in the cost of a hamburger and fries would exceed a **jnd.**

Page 202: So everywhere that Mary looks, the scene is sure to go. In order to understand this sentence you need to be familiar with the old nursery rhyme: Mary had a little lamb, its fleece was white as snow, and *everywhere that Mary went the lamb was sure to go.* When a volunteer (*Mary*) is fitted with a special contact lens and miniature projector she sees the same image no matter where her eyes "look" (*everywhere that Mary looks the scene is sure to go*). When an image is projected onto the retina in this manner the scene disappears bit by bit and then reappears and disappears again (in meaningful units). This happens because the image, which normally would be moving back and forth rapidly (*quivering*) as a result of tiny eye movements, is now stationary with respect to the retina and its receptors. As the receptors fatigue the image disappears.

Vision

Page 207: . . . **blind spot** . . . You can use the suggestion in Figure 5.10 of your text to demonstrate that there are two small parts of your visual field (one in the left and one in the right) where you have no sight. These tiny areas (*blind spots*) are where the optic nerve exits the eye.

Page 207: Rods have no such *hotline* [to the brain]. . . . Cones, which are mostly clustered in the **fovea** and detect color and fine detail, have many more individual connections to the brain than the rods. Rods, which give us our black-and-white vision, have to share bipolar cells and so do not have as many individual connections (*hotlines*) to the brain (in dim light, however, this can be an advantage as several rods can focus or funnel their individual faint energy output onto a single bipolar cell).

Page 210 (caption): The answer to this question is the *Holy Grail* of vision research. The reference here is to the medieval legend that the cup (*grail*) Jesus Christ drank from at the Last Supper, and which was later used to catch his blood when he was crucified, survived and may have been brought to England. The quest, or search, for this sacred cup (*Holy Grail*) symbolized spiritual regeneration and enlightenment. Similarly, attempting to answer the question about how the brain deals with multiple aspects of a visual scene at the same time, automatically, and without our awareness (*parallel processing*), is an important undertaking that, if successful, will enlighten us about brain functioning (*the Holy Grail of vision research*).

Page 211: . . . blindsight . . . Blindsight refers to the fact that some people with neurological damage have the ability to see, to some degree, without any conscious awareness of the visual experience. They are blind, yet they can see (*blindsight*). This suggests that there are two parallel processing systems operating, one that unconsciously guides our actions (the zombie within), and one that gives us our conscious perceptions.

Page 212: Color, like all aspects of vision, resides not in the object but in the *theater of our brains.* Myers notes that when we view a colored object (for example, a blue balloon), it absorbs all the wavelengths except its own (blue) and reflects the wavelengths of blue back to us. The color we perceive is a product of our brain and exists only in the perceiver's mind (*theater of the brain*).

Hearing

Page 215: We also are remarkably sensitive to *faint sounds,* an obvious *boon* for our ancestors' survival when *hunting* or being *hunted* or detecting a *child's whimper.* Humans are very good at detecting very quiet noises (*faint sounds*), which was clearly beneficial (*a boon*) to our predecessors' ability to survive when they were both predator (*hunter*) and prey (*being hunted*). Likewise, the ability to notice and respond to a youngster's quiet cry of distress (*a child's whimper*) would have had adaptive value. We are also very sensitive to changes in sounds and we have the ability to differentiate among thousands of human voices.

Page 216: A *piccolo* produces much shorter, faster sound waves than does a *tuba.* Musical instruments produce stimulus energy called sound waves—molecules of air that bump and push each other

along—and these may be long (low frequency) or short (high frequency). A *tuba* (a large, deep-toned, brass-wind instrument) produces low-frequency sound waves and thus has a lower pitch than a *piccolo* (a small flute), which produces high-frequency waves and has a higher pitch.

Page 218 (Close-Up): If only our ears had *earlids.* Myers makes it clear that prolonged exposure to loud and unpredictable noise can affect our well-being and seriously damage our hearing. So, in a noisy urban environment it would be nice if we could close our ears (*with earlids*) as we can our eyes (*with eyelids*).

Page 219: If a car to the right *honks,* your right ear receives a more *intense* sound, and it receives sound slightly *sooner* than your left ear. We locate sounds because our ears are about 6 inches apart and there is a time, as well as a loudness difference, between auditory reception in each ear. If we hear the sound of a car horn (*it honks*) to our right, the left ear receives a less intense sound somewhat later than the right ear, and thus we locate the direction of the sound to the right.

Page 220: That is why, when trying to *pinpoint* a sound, you *cock your head,* so that your two ears will receive slightly different messages. When a sound is equidistant from our two ears (directly ahead, behind, or above), and there is no visual clue, we have trouble locating (*pinpointing*) the source. In this situation it helps to tilt (*cock*) our heads so that each ear receives a slightly different message (the sound will be a little louder and sensed a little sooner by one ear, and the brain uses this information to detect where the sound is coming from).

Page 220: Occasionally, disease causes sensorineural hearing loss, but more often the culprits are biological changes linked with heredity, aging and prolonged exposure to *ear-splitting* noise or music (Figure 5.26). Sensorineural hearing loss, or nerve deafness (cochlear damage), can sometimes be caused by illness, but the agents responsible (*the culprits*) are more likely to be age-related biological factors and extended encounters with extremely loud (*ear-splitting*) music or noise. While digital hearing aids are a partial remedy, the latest cochlear implants can restore hearing for children and most adults.

Other Important Senses

Page 224: As lovers, we *yearn* to touch—to kiss, to stroke, *to snuggle.* Our sense of touch involves a mixture of at least four distinct senses: pressure, warmth, cold, and pain. Intimate relations often involve a desire or longing (*we yearn*) to caress, kiss, and closely embrace each other (*snuggle*).

Page 227: Rubbing the area around your *stubbed toe* will create competing stimulation that will *block* some of the pain messages. If you hit your toe against a solid object (*stub your toe*), it really hurts. If, however, you massage (*rub*) the part around the sore spot, it makes you feel better because stimulation interferes with (*blocks*) some of the pain messages. This supports the **gate-control** model, which suggests that this stimulation (*rubbing*) will activate "gate-closing" in large neural fibers and, thus, will reduce pain.

Page 228: Sometimes the *pain in sprain is mainly in the brain.* Myers is doing a parody of the lyrics from a song in the musical *My Fair Lady,* "The rain in Spain stays mainly in the plain." The main point: reports of repetitive strain injury (the *pain in sprain*) were, in the case of groups (*pockets*) of Australian keyboard operators, due to social and psychological influences (*mainly in the brain*) and were not the result of damaged ligaments or muscles in the hands or arms, as is usually the case.

Page 228 (caption): After explaining heat-diffusion principles that permit *firewalking,* he then joined several others in *putting his feet where his mouth was.* The expression *"put your money where your mouth is"* means that you should be willing to back or support your words or claims with appropriate behavior. So physicist David Willey was willing to support his explanation of firewalking, which was based on scientific facts, by taking the necessary action. By actually walking or stepping across the hot coals without burning his bare feet, he put his feet (*firewalking*) where his mouth was (his scientific explanation) and showed that the claims of the "mind over matter" promoters were wrong in this case.

Page 229: A well-trained nurse may distract *needle-shy* patients by chatting with them and asking them to look away when inserting the needle. One method of pain control is through distraction. If you are nervous or anxious about being injected with a hypodermic needle (*a needle-shy patient*), the nurse may talk to you about unimportant matters (*she chats with you*) and request that you do not watch the procedure. This type of distraction can reduce the intensity of the pain.

Page 230: Taste buds are certainly essential for taste, *but there is more to taste than meets the tongue.* The common expression *"there is more to this than meets the eye"* suggests that there is something extra going on over and above the obvious or apparent. Myers creates a variation of this expression using a different sense (taste). The flavors we experience are a function of more than just the taste buds in the tongue; they involve **sensory interaction** with the sense of smell (**olfaction**). Thus, the sense of taste involves more than simply responding to the chemicals that stimulate taste receptors in the tongue (there is more to taste than meets the tongue).

Page 231: Each day, you inhale and exhale nearly 20,000 breaths of life-sustaining air, *bathing* your nostrils in a *stream of scent-laden molecules.* Smell (**olfaction**) is a chemical sense and as substances (flowers, feet, fish, fertilizer, etc.) release molecules, they are carried by the air we breathe (*a stream of scent-laden molecules*) and wash over (*bathe*) receptors in our nasal cavities (nostrils).

Page 232: Words more readily *portray* the sound of coffee brewing than its *aroma.* It is easier to talk about and describe (*portray*) the subtle aspects of coffee brewing than to put into words the sensory qualities involved in the smell (*aroma*) of coffee. Olfaction seems to be a more primitive sense than vision or audition.

Page 234: The biological *gyroscopes* for this sense of *equilibrium* are in the inner ear. A *gyroscope* is a mechanical device used as a stabilizer in navigation and scientific instruments. Likewise, we have biological stabilizers that monitor the movement and position of our bodies and provide us with a sense of balance (*equilibrium*). They are called the *semicircular canals* and the *vestibular sacs* and are located in the inner ear.

6 : Perception

CHAPTER OVERVIEW

Chapter 6 explores how we select, organize, and interpret our sensations into meaningful perceptions. The chapter introduces a wide range of terminology, especially in the Perceptual Organization section. Each of the two sections that follow deals with an important issue. The first issue is the role of experience, as opposed to heredity, in perception. Make sure you understand the results of studies of recovery from blindness, sensory deprivation, adaptation to distorted environments, and perceptual set. Note also the role of psychologists in human factors design.

The second issue considered in the chapter is the possible existence of ESP, or perception without sensation. You should be able to discuss both the claims made for ESP and the criticisms of these claims.

NOTE: Answer guidelines for all Chapter 6 questions begin on page 168.

CHAPTER REVIEW

First, skim each section, noting headings and boldface items. After you have read the section, review each objective by answering the fill-in and essay-type questions that follow it. As you proceed, evaluate your performance by consulting the answers beginning on page 168. Do not continue with the next section until you understand each answer. If you need to, review or reread the section in the textbook before continuing.

1. The philosopher _____ first proposed that we perceive objects through the senses, with the mind.

Selective Attention (pp. 237–240)

> David Myers at times uses idioms that are unfamiliar to some readers. If you do not know the meaning of any of the following words, phrases, or expressions in the context in which they appear in the text, refer to page 175 for an explanation: *your attentional spotlight shifts; you may draw a blank; sauntered; pop-out.*

Objective 1: Describe the interplay between attention and perception.

1. Our tendency to focus at any moment on only a limited aspect of all that we are capable of experiencing is called _____ _____ . This is illustrated using a figure called a _____ cube.

2. An example of this limited focus is the _____ _____ _____ —the ability to attend selectively to only one voice among many.

3. One example of our lack of awareness of happenings around us is _____ _____ , in which—after a brief _____ interruption—we fail to notice a change in the environment. Two forms of this phenomenon that involve vision and hearing, respectively, are _____ _____ and _____ _____ . Another example is _____ _____ .

Perceptual Illusions (pp. 240–242)

> If you do not know the meaning of any of the following words, phrases, or expressions in the context in which they appear in the text, refer to page 175 for an explanation: *ventriloquist's dummy; more to touch than meets the skin.*

Objective 2: Explain how illusions help us to understand some of the ways we organize stimuli into meaningful perceptions.

1. Illusions reveal the ways we normally
   _____ and _____
   our sensations.

2. The tendency of vision to dominate the other
   senses is referred to as _____

   _____ .

3. In a contest between hearing and touch,
   _____ dominates.

Perceptual Organization (pp. 242–254)

> If you do not know the meaning of any of the following words, phrases, or expressions in the context in which they appear in the text, refer to pages 175–176 for an explanation: *yen; Sometimes, however, they lead us astray; mothers then coaxed them to crawl out onto the glass; The floating finger sausage; As we move, objects that are actually stable may appear to move; by flashing 24 still pictures; through a paper tube; carpentered.*

Objective 3: Describe Gestalt psychology's contribution to our understanding of perception.

1. According to the _____ school of
   psychology, we tend to organize a cluster of sensations into a _____ , or
   form.

2. Our tendency to perceive complete forms
   involves sensory analysis, or

   _____-_____

   processing of stimuli, as well as

   _____-_____ pro-
   cessing that uses our _____
   and _____ to interpret our sensa-

tions. The distinction between sensation and perception in terms of these two types of information processing is _____ (clear cut/fuzzy).

Objective 4: Explain the figure-ground relationship, and identify principles of perceptual grouping in form perception.

3. When we view a scene, we see the central object,
   or _____ , as distinct from surrounding stimuli, or the _____ .

Identify the major contributions of Gestalt psychology to our understanding of perception.

4. Proximity, similarity, closure, continuity, and
   connectedness are examples of Gestalt rules of

   _____ .

5. The principle that we organize stimuli into
   smooth, continuous patterns is called
   _____ . The principle that we fill in
   gaps to create a complete, whole object is
   _____ . The grouping of items that
   are close to each other is the principle of
   _____ ; the grouping of items that
   look alike is the principle of
   _____ . The tendency to perceive
   uniform or attached items as a single unit is the
   principle of _____ .

Objective 5: Explain the importance of depth perception, and discuss the contribution of visual cliff research to our understanding of this ability.

6. The ability to see objects in three dimensions
   despite their two-dimensional representations on
   our retinas is called _____
   _____ . It enables us to estimate
   _____ .

7. Gibson and Walk developed the _____ _____ to test depth perception in infants. By _____ (what age?) infants demonstrate they are using Gestalt perception principles.

Summarize the results of Gibson and Walk's studies of depth perception.

Objective 6: Describe two binocular cues for perceiving depth, and explain how they help the brain to compute distance.

For questions 8–19, identify the depth perception cue that is defined.

8. Any cue that requires both eyes: _____ .

9. The greater the difference between the images received by the two eyes, the nearer the object: _____ _____ . 3-D movies simulate this cue by photographing each scene with two cameras. This chapter's fundamental lesson is that our _____ are the constructions of our _____ .

10. The more our eyes focus inward when we view an object, the nearer the object: _____ .

Objective 7: Explain how monocular cues differ from binocular cues, and describe several monocular cues for perceiving depth.

11. Any cue that requires either eye alone: _____ .

12. If two objects are presumed to be the same size, the one that casts a smaller retinal image is perceived as farther away: _____ _____ .

13. An object partially covered by another is seen as farther away: _____ .

14. Objects that appear hazy are seen as farther away: _____ _____ .

15. As an object becomes increasingly distant, it appears progressively less distinct: _____ _____ .

16. Objects lower in the visual field are seen as nearer: _____ _____ .

17. As we move, objects at different distances appear to move at different rates: _____ _____ .

18. Parallel lines appear to converge in the distance: _____ _____ .

19. Dimmer, or shaded, objects seem farther away: _____ _____ _____ .

Objective 8: State the basic assumption we make in our perceptions of motion, and explain how these perceptions can be deceiving.

20. In general, we are _____ (very good/not very good) at quickly detecting the speed of moving objects. Sometimes, we are fooled because larger objects seem to move _____ (faster/more slowly) than smaller objects.

21. The brain interprets a rapid series of slightly varying images as _____ . This phenomenon is called _____ .

22. The illusion of movement that results when two adjacent stationary spots of light blink on and off in quick succession is called the _____ _____ .

Objective 9: Explain the importance of perceptual constancy.

23. Our tendency to see objects as unchanging while the stimuli from them change in size, shape, and lightness is called _____ .

24. This _____ (bottom-up/top-down) process enables us to identify things regardless of the _____ , _____ , or _____ by which we view them.

Objective 10: Describe the shape and size constancies, and explain how our expectations about perceived size and distance contribute to some visual illusions.

25. Due to shape and size constancy, familiar objects _____ (do/do not) appear to change shape or size despite changes in our _____ images of them.

26. Several illusions, including the _____ , _____ , and _____-_____ illusions, are explained by the interplay between perceived _____ and perceived _____ . When distance cues are removed, these illusions are _____ (diminished/strengthened).

Explain how the size-distance relationship accounts for the Moon illusion.

27. People who have lived their lives in uncarpentered rural environments are _____ (more/less) susceptible to the Müller-Lyer illusion.

Objective 11: Discuss lightness constancy and its similarity to color constancy.

28. The brain computes an object's brightness _____ (relative to/independent of) surrounding objects.

29. The amount of light an object reflects relative to its surroundings is called _____ _____ .

30. Thanks to _____ _____ we see objects as having a constant hue relative to surrounding objects.

Perceptual Interpretation (pp. 254–264)

> If you do not know the meaning of any of the following words, phrases, or expressions in the context in which they appear in the text, refer to page 176 for an explanation: *Ping-Pong ball; we may feel slightly disoriented, even dizzy; to see is to believe . . . to believe is to see; a "monster" in Scotland's Loch Ness; from what's behind our eyes and between our ears; in the eyes of their beholders.*

Objective 12: Describe the contribution of restored-vision and sensory deprivation research in our understanding of the nature-nurture interplay in our perceptions.

1. The idea that knowledge comes from inborn ways of organizing sensory experiences was proposed by the philosopher _____ .

2. On the other side were philosophers who maintained that we learn to perceive the world by experiencing it. One philosopher of this school was _____ .

3. Studies of cases in which vision has been restored to a person who was blind from birth show that, upon *seeing* tactilely familiar objects for the first time, the person _____ (can/cannot) recognize them.

4. Studies of sensory deprivation demonstrate that visual experiences during _____ are crucial for perceptual development. Such experiences suggest that there is a _____ _____ for normal sensory and perceptual development. For this reason, human infants born with an opaque lens, called a _____ , typically have corrective surgery right away.

Objective 13: Explain how the research on distorting goggles increases our understanding of the adaptability of perception.

5. Humans given glasses that shift or invert the visual field _____ (will/will not) adapt to the distorted perception. This is called _____ _____ .

6. Animals such as chicks _____ (adapt/do not adapt) to distorting lenses.

7. When distorting goggles are first removed, most people experience a brief perceptual _____ , as their perceptual systems continue to compensate for the shifted visual input.

Objective 14: Define perceptual set, and explain how it influences what we do or do not perceive.

8. A mental predisposition that influences perception is called a _____ _____ .

9. Through experience, people acquire perceptual _____ , as reflected in children's drawings at different ages. This explains why we more accurately recognize _____ of famous faces than these people's actual faces.

10. Our face recognition is especially attuned to the expressive areas of the _____ and _____ .

Objective 15: Explain why the same stimulus can evoke different perceptions in different contexts.

11. How a stimulus is perceived depends on our perceptual schemas and the _____ in which it is experienced.

12. The context of a stimulus creates a _____ (top-down/bottom-up) expectation that influences our perception as we match our _____ (top-down/bottom-up) signal against it.

13. Our perception is also influenced by _____ about gender and the _____ context of our experiences.

Objective 16: Describe the role human factors psychologists play in creating user-friendly machines and work settings.

14. Psychologists who study the importance of considering perceptual principles in the design of machines, appliances, and work settings are called _____ _____ psychologists.

15. Victims of the "curse of knowledge," technology developers who assume that others share their _____ , may create designs that are unclear to others.

16. Another example of failure to consider the human factor in design is the "_____ _____ " technology that provides embarrassing headsets that amplify sound for people with hearing loss.

Is There Extrasensory Perception? (pp. 264–268)

If you do not know the meaning of any of the following words, phrases, or expressions in the context in which they appear in the text, refer to page 176 for an explanation: *uncanny; mind-blowing performance; unsatisfied hunger . . . an itch.*

Objective 17: Identify the three most testable forms of ESP, and explain why most research psychologists remain skeptical of ESP claims.

1. Perception outside the range of normal sensation is called _____ _____ .

2. Psychologists who study ESP are called _____ .

3. The form of ESP in which people claim to be capable of reading others' minds is called _____ . A person who "senses" that a friend is in danger might claim to have the ESP ability of _____ . An ability to "see" into the future is called _____ . A person who claims to be able to levitate and move objects is claiming the power of _____ .

4. Analyses of psychic visions and premonitions reveal _____ (high/chance-level) accuracy. Nevertheless, some people continue to believe in their accuracy because vague predictions often are later_____ to match events that have already occurred. In addition, people are more likely to recall or _____ dreams that seem to have come true.

5. Critics point out that a major difficulty for parapsychology is that ESP phenomena are not consistently _____ .

6. Researchers who tried to reduce external distractions between a "sender" and a "receiver" in an ESP experiment. reported performance levels that _____ (beat/did not beat) chance levels. More recent studies _____ (failed to replicate the results/found equally high levels of performance).

PROGRESS TEST 1

Multiple-Choice Questions

Circle your answers to the following questions and check them with the answers beginning on page 169. If your answer is incorrect, read the explanation for why it is incorrect and then consult the appropriate pages of the text (in parentheses following the correct answer).

1. The historical movement associated with the statement "The whole may exceed the sum of its parts" is:
   a. parapsychology.
   b. behavioral psychology.
   c. functional psychology.
   d. Gestalt psychology.

2. Figures tend to be perceived as whole, complete objects, even if spaces or gaps exist in the representation, thus demonstrating the principle of:
   a. connectedness.   c. continuity.
   b. similarity.   d. closure.

3. The figure-ground relationship has demonstrated that:
   a. perception is largely innate.
   b. perception is simply a point-for-point representation of sensation.
   c. the same stimulus can trigger more than one perception.
   d. different people see different things when viewing a scene.

4. When we stare at an object, each eye receives a slightly different image, providing a depth cue known as:
   a. convergence.   c. relative motion.
   b. linear perspective. d. retinal disparity.

5. As we move, viewed objects cast changing shapes on our retinas, although we do not perceive the objects as changing. This is part of the phenomenon of:
   a. perceptual constancy.
   b. relative motion.
   c. linear perspective.
   d. continuity.

6. Which of the following illustrates the principle of visual capture?
   a. We tend to form first impressions of other people on the basis of appearance.
   b. Because visual processing is automatic, we can pay attention to a visual image and any other sensation at the same time.
   c. We cannot simultaneously attend to a visual image and another sensation.
   d. When there is a conflict between visual information and that from another sense, vision tends to dominate.

7. A person claiming to be able to read another's mind is claiming to have the ESP ability of:
   a. psychokinesis.   c. clairvoyance.
   b. precognition.   d. telepathy.

8. Which philosopher maintained that knowledge comes from inborn ways of organizing our sensory experiences?
   a. Locke   c. Gibson
   b. Kant   d. Walk

9. Dr. Martin is using natural mapping to redesign the instrument gauges of automobiles to be more "user friendly." Dr. Martin is evidently a(n):
   a. psychophysicist.
   b. cognitive psychologist.
   c. human factors psychologist.
   d. experimental psychologist.

10. The visual cliff tests an infant's perceptual sensitivity to which depth cue?
    a. interposition   c. linear perspective
    b. relative height   d. texture gradient

11. Kittens and monkeys reared seeing only diffuse, unpatterned light:
    a. later had difficulty distinguishing color and brightness.
    b. later had difficulty perceiving color and brightness, but eventually regained normal sensitivity.
    c. later had difficulty perceiving the shape of objects.
    d. showed no impairment in perception, indicating that neural feature detectors develop even in the absence of normal sensory experiences.

12. Adults who are born blind but later have their vision restored:

    a. are almost immediately able to recognize familiar objects.
    b. typically fail to recognize familiar objects.
    c. are unable to follow moving objects with their eyes.
    d. have excellent eye-hand coordination.

13. _____ processing refers to how the physical characteristics of stimuli influence their interpretation.

    a. Top-down
    b. Bottom-up
    c. Parapsychological
    d. Human factors

14. Which of the following is *not* a monocular depth cue?

    a. texture gradient
    b. relative height
    c. retinal disparity
    d. interposition

15. The Moon illusion occurs in part because distance cues at the horizon make the Moon seem:

    a. farther away and therefore larger.
    b. closer and therefore larger.
    c. farther away and therefore smaller.
    d. closer and therefore smaller.

16. Figure is to ground as _____ is to _____ .

    a. night; day
    b. top; bottom
    c. cloud; sky
    d. sensation; perception

17. The study of perception is primarily concerned with how we:

    a. detect sights, sounds, and other stimuli.
    b. sense environmental stimuli.
    c. develop sensitivity to illusions.
    d. interpret sensory stimuli.

18. Which of the following influences perception?

    a. biological maturation
    b. the context in which stimuli are perceived
    c. expectations
    d. all of the above

19. Jack claims that he often has dreams that predict future events. He claims to have the power of:

    a. telepathy.
    b. clairvoyance.
    c. precognition.
    d. psychokinesis.

20. Researchers who investigated telepathy found that:

    a. when external distractions are reduced, both the "sender" and the "receiver" become much more accurate in demonstrating ESP.
    b. only "senders" become much more accurate.
    c. only "receivers" become much more accurate.
    d. over many studies, none of the above occur.

True–False Items

Indicate whether each statement is true or false by placing *T* or *F* in the blank next to the item.

_____ 1. Once we perceive an item as a figure, it is impossible to see it as ground.

_____ 2. Laboratory experiments have laid to rest all criticisms of ESP.

_____ 3. Six-month-old infants will cross a visual cliff if their mother calls.

_____ 4. Unlike other animals, humans have no critical period for visual stimulation.

_____ 5. Immanuel Kant argued that experience determined how we perceive the world.

_____ 6. People who live in a carpentered world are more likely than others to experience the Müller-Lyer illusion.

_____ 7. After a period of time, humans are able to adjust to living in a world made upside down by distorting goggles.

_____ 8. As our distance from an object changes, the object's size seems to change.

_____ 9. Perception is influenced by psychological factors such as set and expectation as well as by physiological events.

_____ 10. John Locke argued that perception is inborn.

PROGRESS TEST 2

Progress Test 2 should be completed during a final chapter review. Answer the following questions after you thoroughly understand the correct answers for the section reviews and Progress Test 1.

1. The tendency to organize stimuli into smooth, uninterrupted patterns is called:

    a. closure.
    b. continuity.
    c. similarity.
    d. proximity.

2. Which of the following is a monocular depth cue?

    a. light and shadow
    b. convergence
    c. retinal disparity
    d. All of the above are monocular depth cues.

3. Which of the following statements is consistent with the Gestalt theory of perception?
   a. Perception develops largely through learning.
   b. Perception is the product of heredity.
   c. The mind organizes sensations into meaningful perceptions.
   d. Perception results directly from sensation.

4. Experiments with distorted visual environments demonstrate that:
   a. adaptation rarely takes place.
   b. animals adapt readily, but humans do not.
   c. humans adapt readily, while lower animals typically do not.
   d. adaptation is possible during a critical period in infancy but not thereafter.

5. The phenomenon that refers to the ways in which an individual's expectations influence perception is called:
   a. perceptual set.
   b. retinal disparity.
   c. convergence.
   d. visual capture.

6. Thanks to _____ , TiVo and DVR have solved the TV recording problem caused by the complexity of VCRs.
   a. parapsychologists
   b. human factors psychologists
   c. psychokineticists
   d. Gestalt psychologists

7. According to the philosopher _____ , we learn to perceive the world.
   a. Locke
   b. Kant
   c. Gibson
   d. Walk

8. The tendency to perceive hazy objects as being at a distance is known as _____ . This is a _____ depth cue.
   a. linear perspective; binocular
   b. linear perspective; monocular
   c. relative clarity; binocular
   d. relative clarity; monocular

9. The phenomenon of size constancy is based upon the close connection between an object's perceived _____ and its perceived _____ .
   a. size; shape
   b. size; distance
   c. size; brightness
   d. shape; distance

10. Which of the following statements best describes the effects of sensory restriction?
    a. It produces functional blindness when experienced for any length of time at any age.
    b. It has greater effects on humans than on animals.
    c. It has more damaging effects when experienced during infancy.
    d. It has greater effects on adults than on children.

11. Psychologists who study ESP are called:
    a. clairvoyants.
    b. telepaths.
    c. parapsychologists.
    d. levitators.

12. The depth cue that occurs when we watch stable objects at different distances as we are moving is:
    a. convergence.
    b. interposition.
    c. relative clarity.
    d. relative motion.

13. Which of the following statements concerning ESP is true?
    a. Most ESP researchers are quacks.
    b. There have been a large number of reliable demonstrations of ESP.
    c. Most research psychologists are skeptical of the claims of defenders of ESP.
    d. There have been reliable laboratory demonstrations of ESP, but the results are no different from those that would occur by chance.

14. Each time you see your car, it projects a different image on the retinas of your eyes, yet you do not perceive it as changing. This is because of:
    a. perceptual set.
    b. retinal disparity.
    c. perceptual constancy.
    d. convergence.

15. The term *gestalt* means:
    a. grouping.
    b. sensation.
    c. perception.
    d. whole.

16. The perceptual error in which we fail to see an object when our attention is directed elsewhere is:
    a. visual capture.
    b. inattentional blindness.
    c. perceptual adaptation.
    d. divergence.

17. Studies of the visual cliff have provided evidence that much of depth perception is:
    a. innate.
    b. learned.
    c. innate in lower animals, learned in humans.
    d. innate in humans, learned in lower animals.

18. All of the following are laws of perceptual organization *except*:
    a. proximity.
    b. closure.
    c. continuity.
    d. convergence.

● ● ● ● ●

19. You probably perceive the diagram above as three separate objects due to the principle of:
    a. proximity.
    b. continuity.
    c. closure.
    d. connectedness.

20. _____ processing refers to how our knowledge and expectations influence perception.
    a. Top-down
    b. Bottom-up
    c. Parapsychological
    d. Human factors

PSYCHOLOGY APPLIED

Answer these questions the day before an exam as a final check on your understanding of the chapter's terms and concepts.

Multiple-Choice Questions

1. Although carpenter Smith perceived a briefly viewed object as a screwdriver, police officer Wesson perceived the same object as a knife. This illustrates that perception is guided by:
   a. linear perspective.
   b. shape constancy.
   c. retinal disparity.
   d. perceptual set.

2. Because the flowers in the foreground appeared coarse and grainy, the photographer decided that the picture was taken too near the subject. This conclusion was based on which depth cue?
   a. relative size
   b. interposition
   c. retinal disparity
   d. texture gradient

3. The fact that a white object under dim illumination appears lighter than a gray object under bright illumination is called:
   a. relative luminance.
   b. perceptual adaptation.
   c. color contrast.
   d. lightness constancy.

4. When two familiar objects of equal size cast unequal retinal images, the object that casts the smaller retinal image will be perceived as being:
   a. closer than the other object.
   b. more distant than the other object.
   c. larger than the other object.
   d. smaller than the other object.

5. If you slowly bring your finger toward your face until it eventually touches your nose, eye-muscle cues called _____ convey depth information to your brain.
   a. retinal disparity
   c. continuity

   b. interposition
   d. convergence

6. Concluding her presentation on sensation and perception, Kelly notes that:
   a. sensation is bottom-up processing.
   b. perception is top-down processing.
   c. a. and b. are both true.
   d. sensation and perception blend into one continuous process.

7. As her friend Milo walks toward her, Noriko perceives his size as remaining constant because his perceived distance _____ at the same time that her retinal image of him _____ .
   a. increases; decreases
   b. increases; increases
   c. decreases; decreases
   d. decreases; increases

8. In the *absence* of perceptual constancy:
   a. objects would appear to change size as their distance from us changed.
   b. depth perception would be based exclusively on monocular cues.
   c. depth perception would be based exclusively on binocular cues.
   d. depth perception would be impossible.

9. The illusion that the St. Louis Gateway arch appears taller than it is wide (even though its height and width are equal) is based on our sensitivity to which monocular depth cue?
   a. relative size
   b. interposition
   c. relative height
   d. retinal disparity

10. How do we perceive a pole that partially covers a wall?
    a. as farther away
    b. as nearer
    c. as larger
    d. There is not enough information to determine the object's size or distance.

11. An artist paints a tree orchard so that the parallel rows of trees converge at the top of the canvas. Which cue has the artist used to convey distance?
    a. interposition
    b. relative clarity
    c. linear perspective
    d. texture gradient

12. Objects higher in our field of vision are perceived as _____ due to the principle of _____ .
    a. nearer; relative height
    b. nearer; linear perspective
    c. farther away; relative height
    d. farther away; linear perspective

13. According to the principle of light and shadow, if one of two identical objects reflects more light to your eyes it will be perceived as:
    a. larger.
    b. smaller.
    c. farther away.
    d. nearer.

14. Your friend tosses you a frisbee. You know that it is getting closer instead of larger because of:
    a. shape constancy.
    b. relative motion.
    c. size constancy.
    d. all of the above.

15. Which explanation of the Müller-Lyer illusion is offered by the text?
    a. The corners in our carpentered world teach us to interpret outward- or inward-pointing arrowheads at the end of a line as a cue to the line's distance from us and so to its length.
    b. The drawing's violation of linear perspective makes one line seem longer.
    c. Top-down processing of the illusion is prevented because of the stimuli's ambiguity.
    d. All of the above were offered as explanations.

16. When the traffic light changed from red to green, the drivers on both sides of Leon's vehicle pulled quickly forward, giving Leon the disorienting feeling that his car was rolling backward. Which principle explains Leon's misperception?
    a. relative motion
    b. continuity
    c. visual capture
    d. proximity

17. Regina claims that she can bend spoons, levitate furniture, and perform many other "mind over matter" feats. Regina apparently believes she has the power of:
    a. telepathy.
    b. clairvoyance.
    c. precognition.
    d. psychokinesis.

18. The predictions of leading psychics are:
    a. often ambiguous prophecies later interpreted to match actual events.
    b. no more accurate than guesses made by others.
    c. nearly always inaccurate.
    d. all of the above.

19. Studying the road map before her trip, Colleen had no trouble following the route of the highway she planned to travel. Colleen's ability illustrates the principle of:
    a. closure.
    b. similarity.
    c. continuity.
    d. proximity.

20. The insensitivity of many rural Africans to the Müller-Lyer illusion proves that perception:
    a. is largely a "bottom-up" phenomenon.
    b. is unpredictable.
    c. is influenced by cultural experience.
    d. is characterized by all of the above.

Essay Question

In many movies from the 1930s, dancers performed seemingly meaningless movements which, when viewed from above, were transformed into intricate patterns and designs. Similarly, the formations of marching bands often create pictures and spell words. Identify and describe at least four Gestalt principles of grouping that explain the audience's perception of the images created by these types of formations. (Use the space below to list the points you want to make, and organize them. Then write the essay on a separate piece of paper.)

KEY TERMS

Writing Definitions

Using your own words, on a separate piece of paper write a brief definition or explanation of each of the following terms.

1. selective attention
2. inattentional blindness
3. visual capture
4. gestalt
5. figure-ground
6. grouping
7. depth perception
8. visual cliff
9. binocular cue
10. retinal disparity
11. convergence
12. monocular cue

13. phi phenomenon
14. perceptual constancy
15. perceptual adaptation
16. perceptual set

17. human factors psychology
18. extrasensory perception (ESP)
19. parapsychology

Cross-Check

As you learned in the Prologue, reviewing and overlearning of material are important to the learning process. After you have written the definitions of the key terms in this chapter, you should complete the crossword puzzle to ensure that you can reverse the process—recognize the term, given the definition.

ACROSS

1. Part of the visual field that surrounds the figure.
8. The tendency to perceive the convergence of parallel lines as indicating decreasing distance is the _____ perspective.
13. Depth cues that depend on information from both eyes.
15. Principle that we tend to group stimuli that are near one another.
16. Part of the visual field that stands out from its surroundings.
17. Philosopher who believed that all knowledge arises from experience.
18. Perceptual tendency to fill in incomplete figures to create the perception of a whole object.
19. Process by which we tend to organize stimuli into coherent groups.
20. Means "organized whole."

DOWN

2. Figure-ground relationships are often _____ .
3. Creating three-dimensional perceptions from the two-dimensional images that strike the retina requires _____ perception.
4. The ability to attend to only one voice among many is the _____ effect.
5. Because of _____ attention, we focus our aware-

ness on only a limited aspect of all that we are capable of experiencing.
6. Illusion of movement created by adjacent lights that blink off and on in succession.
7. Classic visual illusion involving the perception of line length.
9. Depth cue in which nearby objects partially obscure more distant objects.
10. The amount of light an object reflects relative to its surroundings.
11. Tendency of distant objects to appear hazier than nearer objects.
12. Gestalt principle that we perceive uniform and linked spots, lines, or areas as a single unit.
14. The irreversible effects of sensory restriction during infancy suggest the existence of a _____ for normal sensory and perceptual development.

ANSWERS

Chapter Review

1. Plato

Selective Attention

1. selective attention; Necker
2. cocktail party effect
3. inattentional blindness; visual; change blindness; change deafness; choice blindness

Perceptual Illusions

1. organize; interpret
2. visual capture
3. hearing

Perceptual Organization

1. Gestalt; whole
2. bottom-up; top-down; experiences; expectations; fuzzy
3. figure; ground

The Gestalt psychologists described some key principles of perceptual organization and, in so doing, demonstrated that perception is far more than a simple sensory process. The reversible figure-ground relationship, for example, demonstrates that a single stimulus can trigger more than one perception. As Gestalt psychologists showed, we continually filter sensory information and construct our perceptions in ways that make sense to us.

4. grouping
5. continuity; closure; proximity; similarity; connectedness
6. depth perception; distance
7. visual cliff; 3 months

Research on the visual cliff suggests that in many species the ability to perceive depth is present at, or very shortly after, birth.

8. binocular
9. retinal disparity; perceptions; brains
10. convergence
11. monocular
12. relative size
13. interposition
14. relative clarity
15. texture gradient

16. relative height
17. relative motion (motion parallax)
18. linear perspective
19. light and shadow
20. very good; more slowly
21. movement; stroboscopic movement
22. phi phenomenon
23. perceptual constancy
24. top-down; angle; distance; illumination
25. do not; retinal
26. Moon; Ponzo; Müller-Lyer; size; distance; diminished

A partial reason for the illusion that the Moon at the horizon appears up to 50 percent larger than the Moon directly overhead is that cues to the distance of objects at the horizon make the Moon, behind them, seem farther away and therefore larger. When we see the Moon overhead in the sky, these misleading cues are lacking.

27. less
28. relative to
29. relative luminance
30. color constancy

Perceptual Interpretation

1. Kant
2. Locke
3. cannot
4. infancy; critical period; cataract
5. will; perceptual adaptation
6. do not adapt
7. aftereffect
8. perceptual set
9. schemas; caricatures
10. eyes; mouth
11. context
12. top-down; bottom-up
13. stereotypes; emotional
14. human factors
15. expertise
16. assistive listening

Is There Extrasensory Perception?

1. extrasensory perception
2. parapsychologists

3. telepathy; clairvoyance; precognition; psychokinesis

4. chance-level; interpreted (retrofitted); reconstruct

5. reproducible

6. beat; failed to replicate the results

Progress Test 1

Multiple-Choice Questions

1. **d.** is the answer. Gestalt psychology, which developed in Germany early in the twentieth century, was interested in how clusters of sensations are organized into "whole" perceptions. (pp. 242–243)
   a. Parapsychology is the study of ESP and other paranormal phenomena.
   b. & c. Behavioral and functional psychology developed later in the United States.

2. **d.** is the answer. (p. 244)
   a. Connectedness refers to the tendency to see uniform and linked items as a unit.
   b. Similarity refers to the tendency to group similar items.
   c. Continuity refers to the tendency to group stimuli into smooth, continuous patterns.

3. **c.** is the answer. Although we always differentiate a stimulus into figure and ground, those elements of the stimulus we perceive as figure and those as ground may change. In this way, the same stimulus can trigger more than one perception. (p. 243)
   a. The idea of a figure-ground relationship has no bearing on the issue of whether perception is innate.
   b. Perception cannot be simply a point-for-point representation of sensation, since in figure-ground relationships a single stimulus can trigger more than one perception.
   d. Figure-ground relationships demonstrate the existence of general, rather than individual, principles of perceptual organization. Significantly, even the same person can see different figure-ground relationships when viewing a scene.

4. **d.** is the answer. The greater the retinal disparity, or difference between the images, the less the distance. (p. 246)
   a. Convergence is the extent to which the eyes move inward when looking at an object.
   b. Linear perspective is the monocular distance cue in which parallel lines appear to converge in the distance.
   c. Relative motion is the monocular distance cue in which objects at different distances change their relative positions in our visual image, with those closest moving most.

5. **a.** is the answer. Perception of constant shape, like perception of constant size, is part of the phenomenon of perceptual constancy. (p. 250)
   b. Relative motion is a monocular distance cue in which objects at different distances appear to move at different rates.
   c. Linear perspective is a monocular distance cue in which lines we know to be parallel converge in the distance, thus indicating depth.
   d. Continuity is the perceptual tendency to group items into continuous patterns.

6. **d.** is the answer. (p. 242)
   a., b., & c. Visual capture has nothing to do with forming impressions of people or whether we can attend to more than one stimulus at a time.

7. **d.** is the answer. (p. 265)
   a. Psychokinesis refers to the claimed ability to perform acts of "mind over matter."
   b. Precognition refers to the claimed ability to perceive future events.
   c. Clairvoyance refers to the claimed ability to perceive remote events.

8. **b.** is the answer. (p. 254)
   a. Locke argued that knowledge is not inborn but comes through learning.
   c. & d. Gibson and Walk studied depth perception using the visual cliff; they made no claims about the source of knowledge.

9. **c.** is the answer. (p 261)

10. **d.** is the answer. There is, of course, no actual drop-off. The texture gradient of the checkerboard pattern beneath the glass table imparts the impression of depth. The other cues mentioned would not be relevant to the situation in this experiment. (pp. 245, 247)

11. **c.** is the answer. (p. 255)
    a. & b. The kittens had difficulty only with lines they had never experienced, and never regained normal sensitivity.
    d. Both perceptual and feature-detector impairment resulted from visual deprivation.

12. **b.** is the answer. Because they have not had early visual experiences, these adults typically have difficulty learning to perceive objects. (p. 255)
    a. Such patients typically could not visually recognize objects with which they were familiar by touch, and in some cases this inability persisted.
    c. Being able to perceive figure-ground relation-

ships, patients *are* able to follow moving objects with their eyes.

d. This answer is incorrect because eye-hand coordination is an acquired skill and requires much practice.

13. b. is the answer. (p. 237)

a. Top-down processing refers to how our knowledge and expectations influence perception.

c. Parapsychology is the study of perception outside normal sensory input.

d. Human factors psychology is concerned with how best to design machines and work settings to take into account human perception.

14. c. is the answer. Retinal disparity is a *binocular* cue; all the other cues mentioned are monocular. (p. 246)

15. a. is the answer. The Moon appears larger at the horizon than overhead in the sky because objects at the horizon provide distance cues that make the Moon seem farther away and therefore larger. In the open sky, of course, there are no such cues. (p. 251)

16. c. is the answer. We see a cloud as a figure against the background of sky. (p. 243)

a., b., & d. The figure-ground relationship refers to the organization of the visual field into objects (figures) that stand out from their surroundings (ground).

17. d. is the answer. (p. 237)

a. & b. The study of sensation is concerned with these processes.

c. Although studying illusions has helped psychologists understand ordinary perceptual mechanisms, it is not the primary focus of the field of perception.

18. d. is the answer. (pp. 254–261)

19. c. is the answer. (p. 265)

a. This answer would be correct had Jack claimed to be able to read someone else's mind.

b. This answer would be correct had Jack claimed to be able to sense remote events, such as a friend in distress.

d. This answer would be correct had Jack claimed to be able to levitate objects or bend spoons without applying any physical force.

20. d. is the answer. (p. 267)

True–False Items

1. F (p. 243)	**5.** F (p. 254)	**8.** F (p. 250)
2. F (p. 267)	**6.** T (p. 251)	**9.** T (pp. 257–259)
3. F (p. 245)	**7.** T (p. 256)	**10.** F (p. 254)
4. F (p. 256)		

Progress Test 2

1. b. is the answer. (p. 244)

a. Closure refers to the tendency to perceptually fill in gaps in recognizable objects in the visual field.

c. Similarity refers to the tendency to group items that are similar.

d. Proximity refers to the tendency to group items that are near one another.

2. a. is the answer. (p. 248)

b. & c. Convergence and retinal disparity are both binocular cues that depend on information from both eyes.

3. c. is the answer. (p. 243)

a. & b. The Gestalt psychologists did not deal with the origins of perception; they were more concerned with its form.

d. In fact, they argued just the opposite: Perception is more than mere sensory experience.

4. c. is the answer. Humans and certain animals, such as monkeys, are able to adjust to upside-down worlds and other visual distortions, figuring out the relationship between the perceived and the actual reality; lower animals, such as chickens and fish, are typically unable to adapt. (p. 256)

a. Humans and certain animals are able to adapt quite well to distorted visual environments (and then to readapt).

b. This answer is incorrect because humans are the most adaptable of creatures.

d. Humans are able to adapt at any age to distorted visual environments.

5. a. is the answer. (p. 257)

b. Retinal disparity is a binocular depth cue based on the fact that each eye receives a slightly different view of the world.

c. Convergence is a binocular depth cue based on the fact that the eyes swing inward to focus on near objects.

d. Visual capture refers to the tendency of vision to dominate the other senses.

6. b. is the answer. (p. 261)

a. Parapsychologists study claims of ESP.

c. Psychokineticists are people who claim ESP has the power of "mind over matter."

d. Gestalt psychologists emphasize the organization of sensations into meaningful perceptions.

7. a. is the answer. (p. 254)

b. Kant claimed that knowledge is inborn.

c. & d. Gibson and Walk make no claims about the origins of perception.

8. **d.** is the answer. (p. 247)
   a. & b. Linear perspective, which is a monocular cue, refers to the tendency of parallel lines to converge in the distance.
   c. Relative clarity requires only one eye and is therefore a monocular cue.

9. **b.** is the answer. (pp. 250–251)

10. **c.** is the answer. There appears to be a critical period for perceptual development, in that sensory restriction has severe, even permanently, disruptive effects when it occurs in infancy but not when it occurs later in life. (p. 256)
    a. & d. Sensory restriction does not have the same effects at all ages, and it is more damaging to children than to adults. This is because there is a critical period for perceptual development; whether functional blindness will result depends in part on the nature of the sensory restriction.
    b. Research studies have not indicated that sensory restriction is more damaging to humans than to animals.

11. **c.** is the answer. (p. 264)
    a., b., & d. These psychics claim to exhibit the phenomena studied by parapsychologists.

12. **d.** is the answer. When we move, stable objects we see also appear to move, and the distance and speed of the apparent motion cue us to the objects' relative distances. (p. 248)
    a., b., & c. These depth cues are unrelated to movement and thus work even when we are stationary.

13. **c.** is the answer. (p. 267)
    a. Many ESP researchers are sincere, reputable researchers.
    b. & d. There have been no reliable demonstrations of ESP.

14. **c.** is the answer. Because of perceptual constancy, we see the car's shape and size as always the same. (p. 250)
    a. Perceptual set is a mental predisposition to perceive one thing and not another.
    b. Retinal disparity means that our right and left eyes each receive slightly different images.
    d. Convergence is a form of neuromuscular feedback in which the eyes swing in, or out, as we view objects at different distances.

15. **d.** is the answer. Gestalt means a "form" or "organized whole." (p. 242)

16. **b.** is the answer. (pp. 238)
    a. Visual capture is the tendency for vision to dominate the other senses.
    c. Perceptual adaptation is the ability to adjust to an artificially displaced or even inverted visual field.

d. Divergence or divergent thinking is not discussed in this chapter.

17. **a.** is the answer. Most infants refused to crawl out over the "cliff" even when coaxed, suggesting that much of depth perception is innate. Studies with the young of "lower" animals show the same thing. (p. 245)

18. **d.** is the answer. (p. 244)

19. **d.** is the answer. (p. 244)
    a. Proximity is the tendency to group objects near to one another. The diagram is perceived as three distinct units, even though the points are evenly spaced.
    b. Continuity is the tendency to group stimuli into smooth, uninterrupted patterns. There is no such continuity in the diagram.
    c. Closure is the perceptual tendency to fill in gaps in a form. In the diagram, three disconnected units are perceived rather than a single whole.

20. **a.** is the answer. (p. 237)
    b. Bottom-up processing refers to the physical characteristics of stimuli rather than their perceptual interpretation.
    c. Parapsychology is the study of perception outside normal sensory input.
    d. Human factors psychology is concerned with how best to design machines and work settings to take into account human perception.

Psychology Applied

Multiple-Choice Questions

1. **d.** is the answer. The two people interpreted a briefly perceived object in terms of their perceptual sets, or mental predispositions, in this case conditioned by their work experiences. (p. 257)
   a. Both Smith and Wesson had the same sensory experience of the object, so linear perspective cues would not cause their differing perceptions.
   b. Shape constancy refers to the perception that objects remain constant in shape even when our retinal images of them change.
   c. Retinal disparity is a binocular depth cue; it has nothing to do with individual differences in perception.

2. **d.** is the answer. When the texture of an object is coarse and grainy, we perceive the object as nearer than when its texture is finer and less distinct. (p. 247)
   a. & b. Relative size and interposition are used to judge the relative distances of two or more objects; because only one photograph was involved, these cues are irrelevant.

c. Retinal disparity refers to the different images our eyes receive; whether the photograph's texture was coarse or fine, the retinal disparity would be the same.

3. **d.** is the answer. Although the amount of light reflected from a white object is less in dim light than in bright light—and may be less than the amount of light reflected from a brightly lit gray object—the brightness of the white object is perceived as remaining constant. Because a white object reflects a higher percentage of the light falling on it than does a gray object, and the brightness of objects is perceived as constant despite variations in illumination, white is perceived as brighter than gray even under dim illumination. (p. 253)

a. Relative luminance refers to the relative intensity of light falling on surfaces that are in proximity. Lightness constancy is perceived despite variations in illumination.

b. Perceptual adaptation refers to the ability to adjust to an artificially modified perceptual environment, such as an inverted visual field.

c. Color contrast is not discussed in this text.

4. **b.** is the answer. The phenomenon described is the basis for the monocular cue of relative size. (p. 246)

a. The object casting the *larger* retinal image would be perceived as closer.

c. & d. Because of size constancy, the perceived size of familiar objects remains constant, despite changes in their retinal image size.

5. **d.** is the answer. As an object comes closer in our field of vision, the eyes swing inward (converge) and provide muscular cues as to the object's distance. (p. 246)

a. Retinal disparity refers to the slightly different images of an object received by the two eyes due to their different angles of viewing.

b. Interposition is a monocular cue to distance in which an object that partially blocks another is seen as closer.

c. Continuity is a Gestalt grouping principle, rather than a distance cue.

6. **d.** is the answer. (p. 243)

7. **d.** is the answer. (p. 251)

8. **a.** is the answer. Because we perceive the size of a familiar object as constant even as its retinal image grows smaller, we perceive the object as being farther away. (pp. 250–251)

b. & c. Perceptual constancy is a cognitive, rather than sensory, phenomenon. Therefore, the absence of perceptual constancy would not alter sensitivity to monocular or binocular cues.

d. Although the absence of perceptual constancy would impair depth perception based on the size-distance relationship, other cues to depth, such as texture gradient, could still be used.

9. **c.** is the answer. We perceive objects higher in our field of vision as farther away. Thus, the brain perceives a vertical line the same length as a horizontal line to be more distant and mentally adjusts its apparent length to make it seem longer. (pp. 241, 247)

a. & b. These monocular cues are irrelevant in this particular illusion.

d. Retinal disparity is a *binocular* cue to depth.

10. **b.** is the answer. This is an example of the principle of interposition in depth perception. (p. 246)

a. The partially *obscured* object is perceived as farther away.

c. The perceived size of an object is not altered when that object overlaps another.

11. **c.** is the answer. (pp. 248, 249)

a. Interposition is a monocular depth cue in which an object that partially covers another is perceived as closer.

b. Had the artist painted the trees so that the images of some were sharp and others hazy, the artist would have been using relative clarity.

d. Had the artist painted the trees so that there was a gradual change from a coarse, distinct to a fine, indistinct texture, texture gradient would have been used to convey depth.

12. **c.** is the answer. (p. 247)

b. & d. Linear perspective is the apparent convergence of parallel lines as a cue to distance.

13. **d.** is the answer. Nearby objects reflect more light to the eyes. Thus, given two identical objects, the brighter one seems nearer. (p. 248)

a. & b. Because of the principle of size constancy, an object's perceived size is unaffected by its distance, angle of viewing, or illumination.

14. **c.** is the answer. This is an illustration of the size-distance relationship in depth perception. (pp. 250–251)

a. Although the frisbee's shape is perceived as constant (even as the shape of its retinal image changes), this is not a cue to its distance.

b. Relative motion is the perception that when we move, stationary objects at different distances change their relative positions in our visual image, with those closest moving most. In this example, only the frisbee is moving.

15. a. is the answer. (p. 251)

16. c. is the answer. Although Leon's other senses would have told him his car was not moving, the visual images of the other cars moving forward "captured" his awareness and created the perception that he was rolling backward. (p. 242)
a. Relative motion is a distance cue that occurs when stationary objects appear to move as we move. Just the opposite is happening to Leon.
b. & d. Continuity and proximity are Gestalt principles of grouping, rather than cues to distance.

17. d. is the answer. (p. 265)
a. Telepathy is the claimed ability to "read" minds.
b. Clairvoyance refers to the claimed ability to perceive remote events.
c. Precognition refers to the claimed ability to perceive future events.

18. d. is the answer. (pp. 265–266)

19. c. is the answer. She perceives the line for the road as continuous, even though it is interrupted by lines indicating other roads. (p. 244)
a. Closure refers to the perceptual filling in of gaps in a stimulus to create a complete, whole object.
b. Similarity is the tendency to perceive similar objects as belonging together. On a road map, all the lines representing roads appear similar. Thus, this cue could not be the basis for Colleen's ability to trace the route of a particular road.
d. Proximity is the tendency to group objects near to one another as a single unit.

20. c. is the answer. (p. 251)
a. If perception were entirely based on the physical characteristics of a stimulus ("bottom-up"), lack of experience with a carpentered environment would not reduce sensitivity to the illusion.
b. Principles of grouping, depth perception, and sensitivity to illusions all demonstrate that perception often *is* predictable.

Essay Question

1. *Proximity.* We tend to perceive items that are near each other as belonging together. Thus, a small section of dancers or members of a marching band may separate themselves from the larger group in order to form part of a particular image.

2. *Similarity.* Because we perceive similar figures as belonging together, choreographers and band directors often create distinct visual groupings within the larger band or dance troupe by having the members of each group wear a distinctive costume or uniform.

3. *Continuity.* Because we perceive smooth, continuous patterns rather than discontinuous ones, dancers or marching musicians moving together (as in a column, for example) are perceived as a separate unit.

4. *Closure.* If a figure has gaps, we complete it, filling in the gaps to create a whole image. Thus, we perceptually fill in the relatively wide spacing between dancers or marching musicians in order to perceive the complete words or forms they are creating.

Key Terms

Writing Definitions

1. Selective attention is the focusing of conscious awareness on a particular stimulus out of all of those that we are capable of experiencing. (p. 237)

2. Inattentional blindness is a perceptual error in which we fail to see a visible object when our attention is directed elsewhere. (p. 238)

3. Visual capture is the tendency for vision to dominate the other senses. (p. 242)

4. Gestalt means "organized whole." The Gestalt psychologists emphasized our tendency to integrate pieces of information into meaningful wholes. (p. 242)

5. Figure-ground refers to the organization of the visual field into two parts: the figure, which stands out from its surroundings, and the surroundings, or background. (p. 243)

6. Grouping is the perceptual tendency to organize stimuli into coherent groups. Gestalt psychologists identified various principles of grouping. (p. 243)

7. Depth perception is the ability to see objects in three dimensions although the images that strike the retina are two-dimensional; it allows us to judge distance. (p. 245)

8. The **visual cliff** is a laboratory device for testing depth perception, especially in infants and young animals. In their experiments with the visual cliff, Gibson and Walk found strong evidence that depth perception is at least in part innate. (p. 245)

9. Binocular cues are depth cues that depend on information from both eyes. (p. 245)
Memory aid: Bi- indicates "two"; *ocular* means something pertaining to the eye. **Binocular cues** are cues for the "two eyes."

10. **Retinal disparity** refers to the differences between the images received by the left eye and the right eye as a result of viewing the world from slightly different angles. It is a binocular depth cue, since the greater the difference between the two images, the nearer the object. (p. 246)

11. **Convergence** is a neuromuscular binocular depth cue based on the extent to which the eyes converge, or turn inward, when looking at near or distant objects. The more the eyes converge, the nearer the objects. (p. 246)

12. **Monocular cues** are depth cues that depend on information from either eye alone. (p. 246)

    Memory aid: *Mono-* means one; a monocle is an eyeglass for one eye. A **monocular cue** is one that is available to either the left or the right eye.

13. The **phi phenomenon** is an illusion of movement created when two or more adjacent lights blink on and off in succession. (p. 250)

14. **Perceptual constancy** is the perception that objects have consistent lightness, color, shape, and size, even as illumination and retinal images change. (p. 250)

15. **Perceptual adaptation** refers to our ability to adjust to an artificially displaced or even inverted visual field. Given distorting lenses, we perceive things accordingly but soon adjust by learning the relationship between our distorted perceptions and the reality. (p. 256)

16. **Perceptual set** is a mental predisposition to perceive one thing and not another. (p. 257)

17. **Human factors psychology** explores how people and machines interact and how machines and physical environments can be adapted to human behaviors and thus to increase safety and productivity. (p. 261)

18. **Extrasensory perception (ESP)** refers to the controversial claim that perception can occur without sensory input. Supposed ESP powers include telepathy, clairvoyance, and precognition. (p. 264)

    Memory aid: *Extra-* means "beyond" or "in addition to"; **extrasensory perception** is perception outside or beyond the normal senses.

19. **Parapsychology** is the study of ESP, psychokinesis, and other paranormal forms of interaction between the individual and the environment. (p. 264)

    Memory aid: *Para-*, like *extra-*, indicates "beyond"; thus, paranormal is beyond the normal and **parapsychology** is the study of phenomena beyond the realm of psychology and known natural laws.

Cross-Check

ACROSS
1. ground
8. linear
13. binocular
15. proximity
16. figure
17. Locke
18. closure
19. grouping
20. gestalt

DOWN
2. reversible
3. depth
4. cocktail party
5. selective
6. phi phenomenon
7. Müller-Lyer
9. interposition
10. relative luminance
11. relative clarity
12. connectedness
14. critical period

FOCUS ON VOCABULARY AND LANGUAGE

Selective Attention and Perceptual Illusions

Page 238: Now, suddenly, *your attentional spotlight shifts.* Your *feet feel encased, your nose stubbornly intrudes on the page* before you. **Selective attention** refers to our tendency to focus on only a small part of what is possible for us to experience. If you do attend to more aspects of your experience (*your attentional spotlight shifts*), you will be surprised at the amount of stimulation you process without awareness, such as the feel of the shoes on your feet (*your feet feel encased*) and the fact that your nose actually blocks your line of vision (*your nose stubbornly intrudes on the page*).

Page 238: . . . *you may draw a blank* . . . This means that you do not achieve the result you want; you don't succeed. When you attend to only one voice among many (*the cocktail party effect*), you may be unable to say what someone else, who was clearly within your hearing range, was saying (*you draw a blank*). Interestingly, you would very likely hear your own name if it were spoken by this person.

Page 238: . . . a young woman carrying an umbrella *sauntered* across the screen. In this experiment, subjects had to watch a video of basketball players and signal when the ball was passed. Because of their intense selective attention, they generally failed to notice a female walking slowly (*sauntering*) through the players.

Page 239: . . . we experience *pop-out,* when a strikingly distinct stimulus, such as the only smiling face in Figure 6.4, draws our eye. A very unique object or event (a *strikingly distinct stimulus*) will automatically attract our attention (*it draws our eye*). This experience is called the pop-out phenomenon.

Page 242: . . . (much as we perceive a voice from *the ventriloquist's dummy*). A ventriloquist is an entertainer who makes the audience believe his voice is coming from a silent doll (*dummy*). Due to the phenomenon of **visual capture** we assume that because the doll's mouth is moving and the ventriloquist's is not, the voice is coming from the dummy.

Page 242: There is more to touch than meets the skin. As noted earlier, "there is more to this than meets the eye" is a common expression meaning something is going on beyond the obvious or the apparent. In this variation of the expression, Myers is noting that there is a hearing phenomenon similar to visual capture (which is the tendency for vision to dominate the other senses). Experimental participants' sense of hearing tended to dominate their sense of touch, creating the illusion of receiving more than a single touch (thus, there is *more to touch than meets the skin*).

Perceptual Organization

Page 243: . . . *yen* . . . This means to have a desire or deep need (*yen*) to do something. Myers notes that our brain's desire (*yen*) to put together bits and pieces of sensory input into coherent units involves both "bottom-up" and "top-down" processing. We actively impose structure and infer meaning (top-down) and are not simply registering sensory stimulation (bottom-up) in a passive manner. Thus, there is no sharply defined line (the boundary is *fuzzy*) between sensory and perceptual processes.

Page 244: Usually, these grouping principles help us construct reality. Sometimes, however, they *lead us astray.* Although we put together elements of sensation through active organization (the Gestalt grouping principles) and end up with a unitary experience, we sometimes make mistakes in the process (*we are led astray*).

Page 245: Their mothers then *coaxed* them to *crawl* out onto the glass. In the experiment with the **visual cliff,** 6- to 14-month-old children were gently encouraged (*coaxed*) by their mothers to move, on their hands and knees (*crawl*), onto the invisible glass top on the "deep" side of the apparatus. Most could not be persuaded to do so, leading to the conclusion that depth perception may be innate (inborn). The idea for this famous experiment came to Gibson when she was at the Grand Canyon and wondered if a young child (toddler) looking (*peering*) over the edge of the canyon would recognize the steep, unsafe, incline (*dangerous drop-off*) and retreat (*draw back*).

Page 246: The floating *finger sausage* (Figure 6.9). Try the demonstration and you will experience the effect of **retinal disparity** and see a tubular shape (*finger sausage*) made by your brain from the two different images of your fingers.

Page 248: As we move, objects that are actually *stable* may appear to move. Things that are stationary and do not move (*stable objects*) seem to move relative to us when we move.

Page 250: A motion picture creates this illusion by flashing 24 still pictures each second. When we view a film, we do not experience a rapid series of nonmoving images (*still pictures*); rather, our brain constructs the perceived motion. This is called stroboscopic movement.

Page 251: Take away these distance cues—by looking at the horizon Moon (or each monster or each bar) through a *paper tube*—and the object immediately shrinks. Observers have argued for centuries about why the Moon near the horizon seems so much larger than the Moon overhead in the sky. One explanation involves the interaction of perceived size and perceived distance. Distance cues at the horizon make the Moon appear farther away than when it is overhead (where there are no distance cues). The Moon casts the *same retinal image* in both situations, so the image that appears to be more distant (i.e., near the horizon) will therefore seem larger. We can eliminate the distance cues by looking at the Moon through a rolled-up piece of paper (*paper tube*); the Moon will appear much smaller (*it shrinks*).

Page 251 (Figure 6.15): . . . carpentered . . . A carpenter is someone who constructs objects, houses, furniture, boats, etc., out of wood. In Western cultures many of these objects are angular, with 90° angles and corners, rather than circular or round. Our experiences with rectangular shapes (*carpentered context*) contributes to the Müller-Lyer illusion.

Perceptual Interpretation

Page 255: Most had been born with cataracts—clouded lenses that allowed them to see only diffused light, rather as you or I might see a diffuse fog through a *Ping-Pong* ball sliced in half. People born with cataracts cannot see clearly because the normally transparent lenses in their eyes are opaque. To understand what their vision is like, imagine what you would see if you had your eyes covered with half of a small, white, plastic ball that is used in table tennis (*Ping-Pong*). When cataract patients have their vision restored, after being blind since birth, they can sense colors and distinguish figure from ground (innate capacities), but they cannot visually recognize things that were familiar by touch.

Page 256: Given a new pair of glasses, we may feel slightly disoriented, even dizzy. When we start wearing ordinary eyeglasses or when we are fitted with a new pair, our initial reaction is a little confusion and vertigo (*dizziness*). However, we quickly adapt within a few days. We can also adapt to lenses that distort what we are looking at by 40° to one side, and even to distortion lenses that invert reality (turn the visual image upside down—a topsy-turvy world). Fish, frogs, salamanders, and young chickens cannot adapt in this way.

Page 257: As everyone knows, *to see is to believe.* As we also know, but less fully appreciate, *to believe is to see.* The expression *"seeing is believing"* means that we put much reliance on visual information when deciding (believing) what is true. Myers shows us that, on the contrary, what we believe may actually affect what we see. Our assumptions, expectations, and mental predispositions (**perceptual sets**) determine, to a large extent, our perceptions.

Page 257: In 1972, a British newspaper published genuine, unretouched photographs of *a "monster"* in Scotland's Loch Ness. . . . People who had heard about, or believed in, the Loch Ness Monster before seeing a very ambiguous picture of a log were more inclined to see what they expected to see (i.e., a monster) because of their **perceptual set**.

Page 258: Clearly, much of what we perceive comes not just from the world "out there" but also *from what's behind our eyes and between our ears.* Myers is reiterating the point that our mental predispositions, expectations, beliefs, etc. (*what's behind our eyes and between our ears*) influence much more of what we perceive than the sensory stimulation received from the outside world.

Page 261: Some differences, it seems, exist merely in the eyes of their beholders. The familiar saying *"beauty is in the eye of the beholder"* means that what is perceived as beautiful has more to do with what the perceiver subjectively believes than with the absolute qualities of the person or object being judged. Likewise, our stereotypes (rigid, conventional ideas or beliefs) about gender or culture can greatly influence (*color*) what is perceived.

Is There Extrasensory Perception?

Page 266: . . . uncanny . . . People who have dreams that coincide, by pure chance, with later events often have an eerie or strange (*uncanny*) feeling about the accuracy of their *apparent* precognitions.

Page 267: . . . mind-blowing performances. Some alleged (*so-called*) psychics, using magic tricks and not extrasensory ability, unethically manipulate and deceive (*exploit*) gullible (*unquestioning*) audiences with impressive and wondrous demonstrations (*mind-blowing performances*). As Myers points out, after many, many years of investigation and thousands of experiments there is no scientific evidence that extrasensory abilities exist (believers in the paranormal need only produce one person who can demonstrate a single, reproducible ESP phenomenon to refute the claim that there is no ESP—this has not happened).

Page 267: But some people also have an *unsatisfied hunger* for wonderment, *an itch* to experience the magical. Some people are predisposed to believe in ESP because they have a deeply felt need (*unsatisfied hunger*) for surprise and amazement and a strong ambition or desire (*an itch*) to explore the mysterious and unknown.

7 : States of Consciousness

CHAPTER OVERVIEW

Consciousness—our awareness of ourselves and our environment—can be experienced in various states. Chapter 7 examines not only normal consciousness, but also sleep and dreaming, hypnotic states, drug-altered states, and near-death experiences.

Most of the terminology in this chapter is introduced in the sections on Sleep and Dreams and on Drugs and Consciousness. Among the issues discussed are why we sleep and dream, whether hypnosis is a unique state of consciousness, and possible psychological and social-cultural roots of drug use.

NOTE: Answer guidelines for all Chapter 7 questions begin on page 192.

CHAPTER REVIEW

First, skim each section, noting headings and boldface items. After you have read the section, review each objective by answering the fill-in and essay-type questions that follow it. As you proceed, evaluate your performance by consulting the answers beginning on page 192. Do not continue with the next section until you understand each answer. If you need to, review or reread the section in the textbook before continuing.

Consciousness and Information Processing
(pp. 271–273)

> David Myers at times uses idioms that are unfamiliar to some readers. If you do not know the meaning of any of the following words, phrases, or expressions in the context in which they appear in the text, refer to page 200 for an explanation (note that one item appears in the chapter introduction): *a fundamental yet slippery concept; Psychology had nearly lost consciousness;*

> *consciousness is but the tip of the information-processing iceberg; to lag behind the brain events that evoke it; Running on automatic pilot.*

Objective 1: Discuss the history of psychology's study of consciousness, and contrast conscious and unconscious information processing.

1. The study of _____ was central in the early years of psychology and in recent decades, but for quite some time it was displaced by the study of observable

   _____ .

2. Advances in neuroscience made it possible to relate _____ _____

   to various mental states; as a result,

   _____ _____ began

   to reenter psychology.

Define consciousness in a sentence.

3. Asked to press a button when they feel a tap, people respond _____ (before/after) they become conscious they have responded. In comparison with unconscious processing, conscious processing has a(n) _____ (limited/unlimited) capacity, is relatively _____ (fast/slow), and processes pieces of information _____ (simultaneously/serially).

4. Novel tasks _____(require/do not require) conscious attention.

Sleep and Dreams (pp. 274–290)

> If you do not know the meaning of any of the following words, phrases, or expressions in the context in which they appear in the text, refer to pages 200–202 for an explanation: *move in concert; body depressed; we may fret over concerns: Does a lovers' spat signal a split?; Pulling an all-nighter; jet lag; the machine went wild . . . deep zigzags; in deep slumber; you ascend from your initial sleep dive; As the night wears on; drowsy; sleep patterns that thwart . . .; Many fill this need by using their first class for an early siesta and after-lunch study hall for a slumber party; "spring forward" . . . "fall backward"; riddle of sleep; next-day blahs; "snoozing is second only to boozing"; a dream provides a psychic safety valve; it is time to wake up; buzz.*

Objective 2: Distinguish four types of biological rhythms, and give an example of each.

1. Our bodies' internal "clocks" control several _____ _____ .
   Among these are _____
   _____ , which may give rise to seasonal variations in _____
   _____ .

2. Some people, especially those in far northern regions, may experience a depressed winter mood called a _____
   _____ _____
   _____ . We may also experience cycles lasting _____ days, such as the female _____ _____ ;
   _____-hour cycles of varying
   _____ ;
   and _____ -minute cycles, such as the various stages of sleep.

Objective 3: Describe the cycle of our circadian rhythm, and identify some events that can disrupt this biological clock.

3. The sleep-waking cycle follows a 24-hour clock called the _____
   _____ .

4. When people are at their daily peak in circadian arousal, _____ is sharpest and _____ is most accurate. In contrast to university students, who often are at their peak in the _____ (morning/evening), older adults tend to peak in the _____ .

5. We may experience _____
   _____ if our circadian rhythm is interrupted by travel across time zones. Our circadian rhythm also may be interrupted by _____ changes, such as the one that occurs in the spring in many areas, and by work _____ .

6. Resetting of a disrupted biological clock is facilitated by exposure to _____
   _____ , which triggers proteins in the _____ of the eyes to signal the brain's _____ gland to increase or decrease its production of _____ .
   The cluster of cells called the _____
   _____ controls the circadian clock.
   The longer we remain awake, the more our brains accumulate _____ , which tends to _____ certain neurons and make us sleepy. We can also reset our biological clocks by adjusting our _____
   _____ .

Objective 4: List the stages of the sleep cycle, and explain how they differ.

7. The sleep cycle consists of _____ distinct stages.

8. The rhythm of sleep cycles was discovered when Aserinsky noticed that, at periodic intervals during the night, the _____ of a sleeping child moved rapidly. This stage of sleep, during which _____ occur, is called _____ _____ .

9. The relatively slow brain waves of the awake but relaxed state are known as _____ waves.

10. During Stage 1 sleep, people often experience _____ sensations similar to _____ . These sensations may later be incorporated into _____ .

11. The bursts of brain-wave activity that occur during Stage 2 sleep are called _____ _____ .

12. Large, slow brain waves are called _____ waves. First in Stage _____ , and increasingly during Stage _____ sleep, which are therefore called _____-_____ sleep. A person in the latter stage of sleep generally will be _____ (easy/difficult) to awaken. It is during this stage that people may engage in sleep _____ .

Describe the bodily changes that accompany REM sleep.

13. During REM sleep, the motor cortex is _____ (active/relaxed), while the muscles are _____ (active/relaxed). For this reason, REM is often referred to as _____ sleep.

14. The rapid eye movements generally signal the beginning of a _____ . PET scans reveal heightened activity in the _____ and _____ areas of the brain during REM sleep.

15. The sleep cycle repeats itself about every _____ minutes. As the night progresses, Stage 4 sleep becomes _____ (longer/briefer) and REM periods become _____ (longer/briefer). Approximately _____ percent of a night's sleep is spent in REM sleep.

Objective 5: Explain why sleep patterns and duration vary from person to person.

16. Newborns spend nearly _____ (how much?) of their day asleep, while adults spend no more than _____ .

17. Sleep patterns are influenced by _____ , as indicated by the fact that sleep patterns among _____ (identical/fraternal) twins are very similar. Sleep is also influenced by _____ .

18. Allowed to sleep unhindered, most people will sleep 9 hours a night. People who sleep less than that for several nights in a row often show signs of _____ _____ .

Objective 6: Discuss several risks associated with sleep deprivation.

19. Teenagers typically need _____ hours of sleep but now average nearly _____ hours less sleep than teenagers of 80 years ago. To psychologist William _____ , this indicates that the vast majority of students are dangerously sleep-deprived. One indication of the hazards of this state is that the rate of _____ tends to increase immediately after the spring time change in Canada and the United States. Another is that sleep deprivation may suppress the functioning of the body's _____ system and alter metabolic and hormonal functioning in ways that mimic _____ and are conducive to _____ , _____ , and _____ .

Describe the effects of sleep deprivation.

Objective 7: Identify four theories of why we sleep.

20. Two possible reasons for sleep are to
_____ us and to help restore body
tissues, especially those of the
_____ . Animals with high waking
_____ produce an abundance of
chemical _____ _____
that are toxic to _____ . Sleep also
facilitates our _____ of the day's
experiences and stimulates _____
thinking.

21. During sleep a growth hormone is released by the
_____ gland. Adults spend
_____ (more/less) time in deep
sleep than children and so release
_____ (more/less) growth hormone.

Objective 8: Identify the major sleep disorders.

22. A persistent difficulty in falling or staying asleep
is characteristic of _____ . Sleeping
pills and alcohol may make the problem worse
since they tend to _____ (increase/
reduce) REM sleep.

23. The sleep disorder in which a person experiences
uncontrollable sleep attacks is _____ .
People with this disorder may collapse directly
into _____ sleep and experience a
loss of _____ _____ .
The brains of people with this disorder lack a
neural center in the _____ that produces the neurotransmitter _____ .

24. Individuals suffering from _____
_____ stop breathing while
sleeping. This disorder is especially prevalent
among _____ _____ .

25. The sleep disorder characterized by extreme
fright and rapid heartbeat and breathing is called
_____ _____ . Unlike
nightmares, these episodes usually happen early
in the night, during Stage _____
sleep. The same is true of episodes of
_____ and _____ ,

problems that _____ (run/do not
run) in families. These sleep episodes are most
likely to be experienced by _____
(young children/adolescents/older adults), in
whom this stage tends to be the
_____ and _____ .

Objective 9: Describe the most common content of
dreams.

26. Dreams experienced during _____
sleep are vivid, emotional, and bizarre. During
_____ dreams, the dreamer may be
sufficiently aware to wonder whether he or she
is, in fact, dreaming.

27. For both men and women, 8 in 10 dreams are
marked by _____ (positive/nega-
tive) emotions, such as fears of being
_____ .

28. Although females tend to dream equally often
about males and females, males tend to dream
more about _____ . This gender difference _____ (is/is not) found in
cultures worldwide.

Objective 10: Compare the major perspectives on
why we dream.

29. Freud referred to the actual content of a dream as
its _____ content. Freud believed
that this is a censored, symbolic version of the
true meaning, or _____
_____ , of the dream.

30. According to Freud, most of the dreams of adults
reflect _____ wishes and are the key
to understanding inner _____ .

31. Freud's theory has given way to the theory that
dreams serve an _____-processing
function. Support for this theory is provided by
the fact that REM sleep facilitates
_____ .

32. Other theories propose that dreaming serves
some _____ function, for example,
that REM sleep provides the brain with needed
_____ . Such an explanation is

supported by the fact that _____ (infants/adults) spend the most time in REM sleep.

33. Still other theories propose that dreams are elicited by random bursts of _____ activity originating in lower regions of the brain, such as the _____ . According to the _____-_____ theory, dreams are the brain's attempt to make sense of this activity. The bursts are believed to be given their emotional tone by the brain's _____ system. PET scans of sleeping people reveal increased activity in the brain's _____ system, especially the _____ . Other theorists see dreams as a natural part of brain _____ and _____ development.

34. Researchers agree that we _____ (need/do not need) REM sleep. After being deprived of REM sleep, a person spends more time in REM sleep; this is the _____ _____ effect.

35. REM sleep _____ (does/does not) occur in other mammals. Animals such as fish, whose behavior is less influenced by learning, _____ (do/do not) dream. This finding supports the _____-_____ theory of dreaming.

Hypnosis (pp. 290–296)

> If you do not know the meaning of any of the following words, phrases, or expressions in the context in which they appear in the text, refer to page 202 for an explanation: *or mesmerism, as it was then called; psychological truth serum . . . considerable mischief; might the two views . . . be bridged?*

Objective 11: Define *hypnosis,* and note some similarities between the behavior of hypnotized people and that of motivated unhypnotized people.

1. Hypnosis is a _____ _____ in which a hypnotist suggests that a subject will experience certain feelings or thoughts, for example. Its discovery is attributed to _____ , who claimed to have discovered an "_____ _____ ."

2. The weight of research evidence suggests that hypnosis _____ (does/does not) allow a person to perform feats that are impossible in the normal waking state. The strength, stamina, learning, and perceptual abilities of hypnotized people _____ (are/are not) like those of motivated unhypnotized people.

Objective 12: Discuss the characteristics of people who are susceptible to hypnosis, and evaluate claims that hypnosis can influence people's memory, will, health, and perception of pain.

3. Most people are _____ (somewhat/not at all) hypnotically suggestible.

Describe people who are the most susceptible to hypnosis.

4. If people are led to expect that they are hypnotizable, their responsiveness under hypnosis _____ (will/will not) increase.

5. The hypnotic demonstration in which a subject supposedly relives earlier experiences is referred to as _____ _____ . Research studies show that the subjects in such demonstrations have memories that are _____ (more/no more) accurate than the memories of fully conscious persons.

6. An _____ person in a legitimate _____ can induce people—hypnotized or not—to perform some unlikely acts.

7. Hypnotherapists have helped some people alleviate headaches, asthma, and stress-related skin disorders through the use of _____ suggestions.

8. For _____ such as smoking and drug use, a subject's hypnotic responsiveness

_____ (does/does not) make a difference in the effectiveness of hypnosis.

9. One statistical digest showed that hypnosis _____ (is/is not) especially helpful for the treatment of obesity.

10. Hypnosis _____ (can/cannot) relieve pain. One theory of hypnotic pain relief is that hypnosis separates, or _____ , the sensory and emotional aspects of pain. Another is that hypnotic pain relief is due to selective _____ , that is, to the person's focusing on stimuli other than pain.

11. PET scans show that hypnosis reduces brain activity in a region involved in _____ to painful stimuli, but not in the _____ cortex that receives the raw _____ input.

Objective 13: Give arguments for and against hypnosis as an altered state of consciousness.

12. Skeptics believe that hypnosis may reflect the workings of _____

_____ . These findings provide support for the _____ _____ theory of hypnosis.

Summarize the argument that hypnosis is not an altered state of consciousness.

13. Hilgard has advanced the idea that during hypnosis there is a _____ , or split, between different levels of consciousness.

14. The existence of a separate consciousness, which is aware of what takes place during hypnosis, is expressed in the concept of the

_____ _____ .

Although this theory has provoked controversy, there is little doubt that _____ influences do play an important role in hypnosis.

Discuss the current view of hypnosis as a blend of the two views.

Drugs and Consciousness (pp. 296–304)

> If you do not know the meaning of any of the following words, phrases, or expressions in the context in which they appear in the text, refer to pages 202–203 for an explanation: _tipsy on one can of beer; kicked the habit; tipsy restaurant patrons leave extravagant tips; a staggering problem; quicker pick-her-upper; one pays a long-term price . . . gnawing craving for another fix; crack; "acid trip"; marijuana may spell relief._

Objective 14: Define _psychoactive drug._

1. Drugs that alter moods and perceptions are called _____ drugs.

Objective 15: Discuss the nature of drug dependence, and identify three common misconceptions about addiction.

2. Drug users who require increasing doses to experience a drug's effects have developed _____ for the drug. The user's brain counteracts the disruption to its normal functioning; thus, the user experiences _____ .

3. After ceasing to use a drug, a person who experiences _____ symptoms has developed a physical _____ . Regular use of a drug to relieve stress is an example of a _____ dependence. A person who has a compulsive craving for a substance despite adverse consequences is _____ to that substance.

Briefly state three common misconceptions about addiction.

Objective 16: Name the main categories of psychoactive drugs, and list three ways these substances can interfere with neurotransmission in the brain.

4. The three broad categories of drugs discussed in the text include _____ , which tend to slow body functions; _____ , which speed body functions; and _____ , which alter perception. These drugs all work by mimicking, stimulating, or inhibiting the activity of the brain's _____ . Psychologically, our _____ also play a role.

Objective 17: Explain how depressants affect nervous system activity and behavior, and summarize the findings on alcohol use and abuse.

5. Depressants _____ nervous system activity and _____ body function. Low doses of alcohol, which is classified as a _____ , slow the activity of the _____ nervous system.

6. Alcohol may make a person more _____ , more _____ , or more _____ daring. Alcohol affects memory by interfering with the process of transferring experiences into _____-_____ memory. Also, blackouts after drinking result from alcohol's suppression of _____ _____ .

7. Excessive use of alcohol can also affect cognition by _____ the brain, especially in _____ (men/women). Alcohol also reduces _____ and focuses one's attention on the _____ _____ and away from _____ _____ .

Describe how a person's expectations can influence the behavioral effects of alcohol.

8. Tranquilizers, which are also known as _____ , have effects similar to those of alcohol.

9. Opium, morphine, and heroin all _____ (excite/depress) neural functioning. Together, these drugs are called the _____ . When they are present, the brain eventually stops producing _____ .

Objective 18: Identify the major stimulants, and explain how they affect neural activity and behavior.

10. The most widely used stimulants are _____ , _____ , the _____ , _____ , _____ , and _____ . Stimulants _____ (are/are not) addictive.

11. Cocaine and crack deplete the brain's supply of the neurotransmitters _____ , _____ , and _____ , and result in depression as the drugs' effects wear off. They do this by blocking the _____ of the neurotransmitters, which remain in the nerve cells' _____ .

12. Cocaine's psychological effects depend not only on dosage and form but also on _____ , _____ , and the _____ .

13. The drug _____ , or MDMA, is both a _____ and a _____ _____ . This drug triggers the release of the neurotransmitters _____ and _____ and blocks the reabsorption of _____ . Among the adverse effects of this drug are disruption of the body's _____ clock, suppression of the _____ _____ , and impaired _____ and other _____ functions.

Objective 19: Describe the physiological and psychological effects of hallucinogens, and summarize the effects of LSD and marijuana.

14. Hallucinogens are also referred to as

_____ . Two common synthetic hallucinogens are _____ and LSD, which is chemically similar to a subtype of the neurotransmitter _____ . LSD works by _____ the actions of this neurotransmitter.

15. The active ingredient in marijuana is abbreviated _____ . Marijuana is being used therapeutically with those who suffer from _____ . However, these medical uses are complicated by marijuana's toxicity, which can cause _____

_____ .

Describe some of the physical and psychological effects of marijuana.

16. The negative aftereffects of drug use may be explained in part by the principle that emotions trigger _____ _____ .

Objective 20: Discuss the biological, psychological, and social-cultural factors that contribute to drug use.

17. Drug use by North American youth _____ (increased/declined) during the 1970s, then declined until the early 1990s due to increased _____ _____ and efforts by the media to deglamorize drug use.

18. In the twenty-first century, attitudes toward alcohol _____ (have/have not) changed, with _____ (more/fewer) people abstaining from drinking.

19. Adopted individuals are more susceptible to

alcoholism if they had a(n) _____ (adoptive/biological) parent with a history of alcoholism. Boys who at age 6 are _____ (more/less) excitable are more likely as teens to smoke, drink, and use other drugs. Genes that are more common among people predisposed to alcoholism may cause deficiencies in the brain's _____ _____ system.

Identify some of the psychological and social-cultural roots of drug use.

20. Among teenagers, drug use _____ (varies/is about the same) across _____ and _____ groups.

21. African-American high school seniors report the _____ (highest/lowest) rates of drug use. A major social influence on drug use is the _____ culture.

22. State three possible channels of influence for drug prevention and treatment programs.

a. _____

b. _____

c. _____

Near-Death Experiences (pp. 309–310)

> If you do not know the meaning of any of the following words in the context in which they appear in the text, refer to page 203 for an explanation: *taking the bull by the horns; monists generally believe that death is real and that without bodies we truly are nobodies.*

Objective 21: Describe the near-death experience and the controversy over whether it provides evidence for a mind-body dualism.

1. The reports of people who have had near-death experiences are very similar to the _____ reported by drug users. These

experiences may be the result of a deficient supply of _____ or other insults to the brain.

2. That the mind and body are distinct entities is the position of the theorists known as _____ . In contrast, the _____ believe that the mind and body are one.

PROGRESS TEST 1

Multiple-Choice Questions

Circle your answers to the following questions and check them with the answers beginning on page 194. If your answer is incorrect, read the explanation for why it is incorrect and then consult the appropriate pages of the text (in parentheses following the correct answer).

1. As defined by the text, consciousness includes which of the following?
   a. focused attention
   b. sleeping
   c. hypnosis
   d. all of the above

2. The cluster of brain cells that control the circadian rhythm is the:
   a. amygdala.
   b. suprachiasmatic nucleus.
   c. adenosine.
   d. pineal.

3. When our _____ is disrupted, we experience jet lag.
   a. Stage 1 sleep
   b. REM sleep
   c. circadian rhythm
   d. Stage 4 sleep

4. Sleep spindles predominate during which stage of sleep?
   a. Stage 2
   b. Stage 3
   c. Stage 4
   d. REM sleep

5. During which stage of sleep does the body experience increased heart rate, rapid breathing, and genital arousal?
   a. Stage 2
   b. Stage 3
   c. Stage 4
   d. REM sleep

6. The sleep cycle is approximately _____ minutes.
   a. 30
   b. 50
   c. 75
   d. 90

7. The effects of chronic sleep deprivation include:
   a. suppression of the immune system.
   b. altered metabolic and hormonal functioning.
   c. impaired creativity.
   d. all of the above.

8. One effect of sleeping pills is to:
   a. decrease REM sleep.
   b. increase REM sleep.
   c. decrease Stage 2 sleep.
   d. increase Stage 2 sleep.

9. Cocaine and crack produce a euphoric rush by:
   a. blocking the actions of serotonin.
   b. depressing neural activity in the brain.
   c. blocking the reuptake of dopamine in brain cells.
   d. stimulating the brain's production of endorphins.

10. Which of the following is classified as a depressant?
    a. methamphetamine
    b. LSD
    c. marijuana
    d. alcohol

11. The modern discovery of hypnosis is generally attributed to:
    a. Freud.
    b. Mesmer.
    c. Spanos.
    d. Hilgard.

12. Which of the following statements concerning hypnosis is true?
    a. People will do anything under hypnosis.
    b. Hypnosis is the same as sleeping.
    c. Hypnosis is in part an extension of the division between conscious awareness and automatic behavior.
    d. Hypnosis improves memory recall.

13. People who heard unusual phrases prior to sleep were awakened each time they began REM sleep. The fact that they remembered less the next morning provides support for the _____ theory of dreaming.
    a. manifest content
    b. physiological
    c. information-processing
    d. activation-synthesis

14. According to Freud, dreams are:
    a. a symbolic fulfillment of erotic wishes.
    b. the result of random neural activity in the brainstem.
    c. the brain's mechanism for self-stimulation.
    d. the disguised expressions of inner conflicts.

15. Psychoactive drugs affect behavior and perception through:
    a. the power of suggestion.
    b. the placebo effect.
    c. alteration of neural activity in the brain.
    d. psychological, not physiological, influences.

16. All of the following are common misconceptions about addiction, *except* the statement that
    a. to overcome an addiction a person almost always needs professional therapy.
    b. psychoactive and medicinal drugs very quickly lead to addiction.
    c. biological factors place some individuals at increased risk for addiction.
    d. many other repetitive, pleasure-seeking behaviors fit the drug-addiction-as-disease-needing-treatment model.

17. At its beginning, psychology focused on the study of:
    a. observable behavior.
    b. consciousness.
    c. abnormal behavior.
    d. all of the above.

18. Which of the following is *not* a theory of dreaming mentioned in the text?
    a. Dreams facilitate information processing.
    b. Dreaming stimulates the developing brain.
    c. Dreams result from random neural activity originating in the brainstem.
    d. Dreaming is an attempt to escape from social stimulation.

19. The sleep-waking cycles of young people who stay up too late typically are _____ hours in duration.
    a. 23   c. 25
    b. 24   d. 26

20. The lowest rates of drug use among high school seniors is reported by:
    a. white males.
    b. white females.
    c. black males.
    d. Latinos.

Matching Items

Match each term with its appropriate definition or description.

Definitions or Descriptions

_____ 1. surface meaning of dreams
_____ 2. deeper meaning of dreams
_____ 3. stage(s) of sleep associated with delta waves
_____ 4. stage(s) of sleep associated with muscular relaxation
_____ 5. sleep disorder in which breathing stops
_____ 6. sleep disorder occurring in Stage 4 sleep
_____ 7. depressant
_____ 8. hallucinogen
_____ 9. stimulant
_____ 10. twilight stage of sleep associated with imagery resembling hallucinations
_____ 11. disorder in which sleep attacks occur

Terms

a. marijuana
b. alcohol
c. Stage 1 sleep
d. night terrors
e. manifest content
f. cocaine
g. narcolepsy
h. sleep apnea
i. Stages 3 and 4 sleep
j. REM sleep
k. latent content

PROGRESS TEST 2

Progress Test 2 should be completed during a final chapter review. Answer the following questions after you thoroughly understand the correct answers for the section reviews and Progress Test 1.

Multiple-Choice Questions

1. Which of the following statements regarding REM sleep is true?
    a. Adults spend more time than infants in REM sleep.
    b. REM sleep deprivation results in a REM rebound.
    c. People deprived of REM sleep adapt easily.
    d. Sleeping medications tend to increase REM sleep.

2. Which theorists believe that the mind and the body are separate entities?
    a. the behaviorists
    b. the monists
    c. the dualists
    d. the Freudians

3. Alcohol has the most profound effect on:
    a. the transfer of experiences to long-term memory.
    b. immediate memory.
    c. previously established long-term memories.
    d. all of the above.

4. A person whose EEG shows a high proportion of alpha waves is most likely:
    a. dreaming.
    b. in Stage 2 sleep.
    c. in Stage 3 or 4 sleep.
    d. awake and relaxed.

5. Circadian rhythms are the:
    a. brain waves that occur during Stage 4 sleep.
    b. muscular tremors that occur during opiate withdrawal.
    c. regular body cycles that occur on a 24-hour schedule.
    d. brain waves that are indicative of Stage 2 sleep.

6. A person who requires increasing amounts of a drug in order to feel its effect is said to have developed:
    a. tolerance.
    b. physical dependency.
    c. psychological dependency.
    d. resistance.

7. Which of the following is *not* an example of a biological rhythm?
    a. feeling depressed during the winter months
    b. the female menstrual cycle
    c. the five sleep stages
    d. sudden sleep attacks during the day

8. Which of the following is characteristic of REM sleep?
    a. genital arousal
    b. increased muscular tension
    c. night terrors
    d. alpha waves

9. Which of the following is *not* a stimulant?
    a. amphetamines
    b. caffeine
    c. nicotine
    d. alcohol

10. Hypnotic responsiveness is:
    a. the same in all people.
    b. generally greater in women than men.
    c. generally greater in men than women.
    d. greater when people are led to *expect* it.

11. According to Hilgard, hypnosis is:
    a. no different from a state of heightened motivation.
    b. the same as dreaming.
    c. a dissociation between different levels of consciousness.
    d. a type of "animal magnetism."

12. Which of the following was *not* cited in the text as evidence that heredity influences alcohol use?
    a. Children whose parents abuse alcohol have a lower tolerance for multiple alcoholic drinks taken over a short period of time.
    b. Boys who are impulsive and fearless at age 6 are more likely to drink as teenagers.
    c. Laboratory mice have been selectively bred to prefer alcohol to water.
    d. Adopted children are more susceptible if one or both of their biological parents has a history of alcoholism.

13. As a form of therapy for relieving problems such as warts, hypnosis is:
    a. ineffective.
    b. no more effective than positive suggestions given without hypnosis.
    c. highly effective.
    d. more effective with adults than children.

14. Which of the following is usually the most powerful determinant of whether teenagers begin using drugs?
    a. family strength
    b. religiosity
    c. school adjustment
    d. peer influence

15. THC is the major active ingredient in:
   a. nicotine.
   c. marijuana.
   b. MDMA.
   d. cocaine.

16. Those who believe that hypnosis is a social phenomenon argue that "hypnotized" individuals are:
   a. consciously faking their behavior.
   b. merely acting out a role.
   c. underachievers striving to please the hypnotist.
   d. all of the above.

17. *Consciousness* is defined in the text as:
   a. mental life.
   b. selective attention to ongoing perceptions, thoughts, and feelings.
   c. information processing.
   d. our awareness of ourselves and our environment.

18. I am a synthetic stimulant and mild hallucinogen that produces euphoria and social intimacy by triggering the release of dopamine and serotonin. What am I?
   a. LSD
   c. THC
   b. MDMA
   d. cocaine

19. According to the activation-synthesis theory, dreaming represents:
   a. the brain's efforts to integrate unrelated bursts of activity in visual brain areas with the emotional tone provided by limbic system activity.
   b. a mechanism for coping with the stresses of daily life.
   c. a symbolic depiction of a person's unfulfilled wishes.
   d. an information-processing mechanism for converting the day's experiences into long-term memory.

20. How a particular psychoactive drug affects a person depends on:
   a. the dosage and form in which the drug is taken.
   b. the user's expectations and personality.
   c. the situation in which the drug is taken.
   d. all of the above.

Matching Items

Match each term with its appropriate definition or description.

Definitions or Descriptions

_____ **1.** drug that is both a stimulant and mild hallucinogen
_____ **2.** drugs that increase energy and stimulate neural activity
_____ **3.** brain wave of awake, relaxed person
_____ **4.** brain-wave activity during Stage 2 sleep
_____ **5.** sleep stage associated with dreaming
_____ **6.** drugs that reduce anxiety and depress central nervous system activity
_____ **7.** natural painkillers produced by the brain
_____ **8.** neurotransmitter that LSD resembles
_____ **9.** our awareness of ourselves and our environment
_____ **10.** theory that dreaming reflects our erotic drives
_____ **11.** a split between different levels of consciousness

Terms

a. Freud's theory
b. serotonin
c. Ecstasy
d. alpha
e. dissociation
f. amphetamines
g. consciousness
h. sleep spindle
i. endorphins
j. REM
k. barbiturates

PSYCHOLOGY APPLIED

Answer these questions the day before an exam as a final check on your understanding of the chapter's terms and concepts.

Multiple-Choice Questions

1. A person who falls asleep in the midst of a heated argument probably suffers from:
   a. sleep apnea.
   b. narcolepsy.
   c. night terrors.
   d. insomnia.

2. Which of the following was *not* suggested by the text as an important aspect of drug prevention and treatment programs?
   a. education about the long-term costs of a drug's temporary pleasures
   b. efforts to boost people's self-esteem and purpose in life
   c. attempts to modify peer associations
   d. "scare tactics" that frighten prepubescent children into avoiding drug experimentation

3. REM sleep is referred to as *paradoxical sleep* because:
   a. studies of people deprived of REM sleep indicate that REM sleep is unnecessary.
   b. the body's muscles remain relaxed while the brain and eyes are active.
   c. it is very easy to awaken a person from REM sleep.
   d. the body's muscles are very tense while the brain is in a nearly meditative state.

4. An attorney wants to know if the details and accuracy of an eyewitness's memory for a crime would be improved under hypnosis. Given the results of relevant research, what should you tell the attorney?
   a. Most hypnotically retrieved memories are either false or contaminated.
   b. Hypnotically retrieved memories are usually more accurate than conscious memories.
   c. Hypnotically retrieved memories are purely the product of the subject's imagination.
   d. Hypnosis only improves memory of anxiety-provoking childhood events.

5. Dan has recently begun using an addictive, euphoria-producing drug. Which of the following will probably occur if he repeatedly uses this drug?
   a. As tolerance to the drug develops, Dan will experience increasingly pleasurable "highs."
   b. The dosage needed to produce the desired effect will increase.
   c. After each use, he will become more and more elated.
   d. Dependence will become less of a problem.

6. Although her eyes are closed, Adele's brain is generating bursts of electrical activity. It is likely that Adele is:
   a. under the influence of a depressant.
   b. under the influence of an opiate.
   c. in REM sleep.
   d. having a near-death experience.

7. Concluding his presentation on levels of information processing, Miguel states that:
   a. humans process both conscious and unconscious information in parallel.
   b. conscious processing occurs in parallel, while unconscious processing is serial.
   c. conscious processing is serial, while unconscious processing is parallel.
   d. all information processing is serial in nature.

8. Roberto is moderately intoxicated by alcohol. Which of the following changes in his behavior is likely to occur?
   a. If angered, he is more likely to become aggressive than when he is sober.
   b. He will be less self-conscious about his behavior.
   c. If sexually aroused, he will be less inhibited about engaging in sexual activity.
   d. All of the above are likely.

9. Jill dreams that she trips and falls as she walks up the steps to the stage to receive her college diploma. Her psychoanalyst suggests that the dream might symbolize her fear of moving on to the next stage of her life—a career. The analyst is evidently attempting to interpret the _____ content of Jill's dream.
   a. manifest
   b. latent
   c. dissociated
   d. overt

10. Barry has participated in a sleep study for the last four nights. He was awakened each time he entered REM sleep. Now that the experiment is over, which of the following can be expected to occur?

    a. Barry will be too tired to sleep, so he'll continue to stay awake.

    b. Barry will sleep so deeply for several nights that dreaming will be minimal.

    c. There will be an increase in sleep Stages 1–4.

    d. There will be an increase in Barry's REM sleep.

11. Of the following individuals, who is likely to be the most hypnotically suggestible?

    a. Bill, a reality-oriented stockbroker

    b. Janice, an actress with a rich imagination

    c. Megan, a sixth-grader who has trouble focusing her attention on a task

    d. Darren, who has never been able to really "get involved" in movies or novels

12. Which of the following statements concerning alcoholism is *not* true?

    a. Adopted individuals are more susceptible to alcoholism if they had an adoptive parent with alcoholism.

    b. Having an identical twin with alcoholism puts a person at increased risk for alcohol problems.

    c. Geneticists have identified genes that are more common among people predisposed to alcoholism.

    d. Researchers have bred rats that prefer alcohol to water.

13. Research studies of the effectiveness of hypnosis as a form of therapy have demonstrated that:

    a. for problems of self-control, such as smoking, hypnosis is equally effective with people who can be deeply hypnotized and those who cannot.

    b. posthypnotic suggestions have helped alleviate headaches, asthma, and stress-related skin disorders.

    c. as a form of therapy, hypnosis is no more effective than positive suggestions given without hypnosis.

    d. all of the above are true.

14. A PET scan of a sleeping person's brain reveals increased activity in the visual and auditory areas. This most likely indicates that the sleeper:

    a. has a neurological disorder.

    b. is not truly asleep.

    c. is in REM sleep.

    d. suffers from narcolepsy.

15. Levar believes that once the body has died, the mind also ceases to exist. Evidently, Levar is a(n):

    a. behaviorist.   c. dualist.

    b. monist.   d. atheist.

16. Which of the following statements concerning marijuana is true?

    a. The by-products of marijuana are cleared from the body more slowly than are the by-products of alcohol.

    b. Regular users may need a larger dose of the drug to achieve a high than occasional users would need to get the same effect.

    c. Marijuana is as addictive as nicotine or cocaine.

    d. Even small doses of marijuana hasten the loss of brain cells.

17. Which of the following statements concerning near-death experiences is true?

    a. Fewer than 1 percent of patients who come close to dying report having them.

    b. They typically consist of fantastic, mystical imagery.

    c. They are more commonly experienced by females than by males.

    d. They are more commonly experienced by males than by females.

18. Those who consider hypnosis a social phenomenon contend that:

    a. hypnosis is an altered state of consciousness.

    b. hypnotic phenomena are unique to hypnosis.

    c. hypnotized subjects become unresponsive when they are no longer motivated to act as instructed.

    d. all of the above are true.

19. Which of the following statements concerning the roots of drug use is true?

    a. Heavy users of alcohol, marijuana, and cocaine often are always on a high.

    b. If an adolescent's friends use drugs, odds are that he or she will, too.

    c. Teenagers who are academically average students seldom use drugs.

    d. It is nearly impossible to predict whether or not a particular adolescent will experiment with drugs.

20. Concluding her presentation on contemporary theories of why sleep is necessary, Marilynn makes all of the following points *except*:
    a. Sleep may have evolved because it kept our ancestors safe during potentially dangerous periods.
    b. Sleep gives the brain time to heal, as it restores and repairs damaged neurons.
    c. Sleep encourages growth through a hormone secreted during Stage 4.
    d. Slow-wave sleep provides a "psychic safety valve" for stressful waking experiences.

Essay Question

You have just been assigned the task of writing an article tentatively titled "Alcohol and Alcoholism: Roots, Effects, and Prevention." What information should you include in your article? (Use the space below to list the points you want to make, and organize them. Then write the essay on a separate piece of paper.)

KEY TERMS

Writing Definitions

Using your own words, on a separate piece of paper write a brief definition or explanation of each of the following terms.

1. consciousness
2. biological rhythm
3. circadian rhythm
4. REM sleep
5. alpha waves
6. sleep
7. hallucinations
8. delta waves
9. insomnia
10. narcolepsy
11. sleep apnea
12. night terrors
13. dream
14. manifest content
15. latent content
16. REM rebound
17. hypnosis
18. posthypnotic suggestion
19. dissociation
20. psychoactive drugs
21. tolerance
22. withdrawal
23. physical dependence
24. psychological dependence
25. addiction
26. depressants
27. barbiturates
28. opiates
29. stimulants
30. amphetamines
31. methamphetamines
32. Ecstasy (MDMA)
33. hallucinogens
34. LSD
35. THC
36. near-death experience
37. dualism
38. monism

Cross-Check

As you learned in the Prologue, reviewing and overlearning of material are important to the learning process. After you have written the definitions of the key terms in this chapter, you should complete the crossword puzzle to ensure that you can reverse the process—recognize the term, given the definition.

ACROSS

1. Term for REM sleep reflecting that the body is aroused but the muscles are relaxed.
7. Neurotransmitter whose reuptake is blocked by cocaine.
8. Widely used stimulant that is inhaled.
10. Dreams in which the dreamer is sufficiently aware to wonder if he or she is dreaming.
12. Powerful hallucinogen first used by Albert Hofmann.
13. Type of processing that describes how we deal with conscious information.
14. Type of brain wave that occurs during Stage 2 sleep.
17. Drug category that includes alcohol.
18. Stage 1 dream sensation similar to a hallucination.
19. Also known as tranquilizers.
21. Time of day at which the thinking and memory of older adults tend to be best.
22. Time of day at which the thinking and memory of college students tend to be best.

DOWN

2. In hypnosis, the supposed reliving of earlier experiences.
3. Drugs that "speed up" neural activity.
4. Drugs that depress neural activity, temporarily lessening pain.
5. Theory suggesting that dreams help fix daily experiences in our memories.
6. Drug that disrupts the processing of recent experiences into long-term memories.
9. Ernest Hilgard's term describing a hypnotized subject's awareness of unreported experiences.
11. Brain wave that predominates in Stage 4 sleep.
15. Divided consciousness (as during hypnosis).
16. Relatively slow brain waves of a relaxed, awake state.
18. Depressant that causes a rush of euphoria.
20. Active ingredient in marijuana.

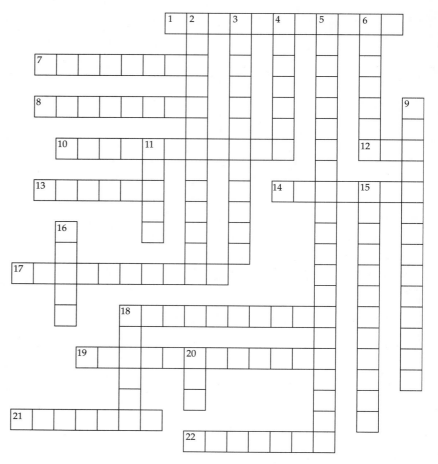

ANSWERS

Chapter Review

Consciousness and Information Processing

1. consciousness; behavior
2. brain activity; mental concepts

Consciousness is our awareness of ourselves and our environment.

3. before; limited; slow; successively
4. require

Sleep and Dreams

1. biological rhythms; annual cycles; appetite, sleep length, and moods
2. seasonal affective disorder; 28; menstrual cycle; 24; alertness, body temperature, and growth hormone secretion; 90
3. circadian rhythm

4. thinking; memory; evening; morning

5. jet lag; time; shifts

6. bright light; retinas; pineal; melatonin; suprachiasmatic nucleus; adenosine; inhibit; sleep schedules

7. 5

8. eyes; dreams; REM sleep

9. alpha

10. hypnagogic; hallucinations; memories

11. sleep spindles

12. delta; 3; 4; slow-wave; difficult; walking

During REM sleep, brain waves become as rapid as those of Stage 1 sleep, heart rate and breathing become more rapid and irregular, and genital arousal and rapid eye movements occur.

13. active; relaxed; paradoxical

14. dream; visual; auditory

15. 90; briefer; longer; 20 to 25

16. two-thirds; one-third

17. genes; identical; culture

18. sleep deprivation

19. 8 or 9; 2; Dement; accidents; immune; aging; obesity; hypertension; memory impairment

The major effect of sleep deprivation is sleepiness. Other effects include impaired creativity, concentration, and communication; slowed performance; and irritability.

20. protect; brain; metabolism; free radicals; neurons; memory; creative

21. pituitary; less; less

22. insomnia; reduce

23. narcolepsy; REM; muscular tension; hypothalamus; hypocretin

24. sleep apnea; overweight men

25. night terrors; 4; sleepwalking; sleeptalking; run; young children; lengthiest; deepest

26. REM; lucid

27. negative; attacked, pursued, or rejected

28. males; is

29. manifest; latent content

30. erotic; conflicts

31. information; memory

32. physiological; stimulation; infants

33. neural; brainstem; activation-synthesis; limbic; limbic; amygdala; maturation; cognitive

34. need; REM rebound

35. does; do not; information-processing

Hypnosis

1. social interaction; Mesmer; animal magnetism

2. does not; are

3. somewhat

Those who are most susceptible frequently become deeply absorbed in imaginative activities. They also tend to have rich fantasy lives.

4. will

5. age regression; no more

6. authoritative; context

7. posthypnotic

8. addictions; does not

9. is

10. can; dissociates; attention

11. attending; sensory; sensory

12. normal consciousness; social influence

The behavior of hypnotized subjects is not fundamentally different from that of other people. Therefore, hypnosis may be mainly a social phenomenon, with hypnotized subjects acting out the role of a "good hypnotic subject."

13. dissociation

14. hidden observer; social

The social influence and divided consciousness views work together to explain hypnosis as an extension both of normal principles of social influence and of everyday dissociations between our conscious awareness and our automatic behaviors.

Drugs and Consciousness

1. psychoactive

2. tolerance, neuroadaptation

3. withdrawal; dependence; psychological; addicted

The following myths about addiction are false:
   a. Taking a psychoactive drug automatically leads to addiction.
   b. One cannot overcome an addiction without professional help.
   c. The addiction-as-disease-needing-treatment model is applicable to a broad spectrum of pleasure-seeking behaviors.

4. depressants; stimulants; hallucinogens; neurotransmitters; expectations

5. calm; slow; depressant; sympathetic

6. aggressive; helpful; sexually; long-term; REM sleep

7. shrinking; women; self-awareness; immediate situation; future consequences

Studies have found that if people believe that alcohol affects social behavior in certain ways, then, when they drink alcohol (or even mistakenly think that they have been drinking alcohol), they will behave according to their expectations, which vary by culture. For example, if people believe alcohol promotes sexual feeling, on drinking they are likely to behave in a sexually aroused way.

8. barbiturates

9. depress; opiates; endorphins

10. caffeine; nicotine; amphetamines; cocaine; Ecstasy; methamphetamine; are

11. dopamine; norepinephrine; serotonin; reuptake; synapses

12. expectations; personality; situation

13. Ecstasy; stimulant; mild hallucinogen; dopamine; serotonin; serotonin; circadian; immune system; memory; cognitive

14. psychedelics; MDMA; serotonin; blocking

15. THC; AIDS; cancer, lung damage, and pregnancy complications

Like alcohol, marijuana relaxes, disinhibits, and may produce a euphoric feeling. Also like alcohol, marijuana impairs perceptual and motor skills. Marijuana is a mild hallucinogen; it can amplify sensitivity to colors, sounds, tastes, and smells. Marijuana also interrupts memory formation.

16. opposing emotions

17. increased; drug education

18. have; more

19. biological; more; dopamine reward

A psychological factor in drug use is the feeling that one's life is meaningless and lacks direction. Regular users of psychoactive drugs often have experienced stress or failure and are somewhat depressed. Drug use often begins as a temporary way to relieve depression, anger, anxiety, or insomnia. A powerful social factor in drug use, especially among adolescents, is peer influence. Peers shape attitudes about drugs, provide drugs, and establish the social context for their use.

20. varies; cultural; ethnic

21. lowest; peer

22. **a.** education about the long-term costs of a drug's temporary pleasures
b. efforts to boost people's self-esteem and purpose in life
c. attempts to "inoculate" youth against peer pressures

Near-Death Experiences

1. hallucinations; oxygen

2. dualists; monists

PROGRESS TEST 1

Multiple-Choice Questions

1. **d.** is the answer. (p. 271)

2. **b.** is the answer. (p. 275)
a. The amygdala is an emotion center in the limbic system.
c. Adenosine is a brain chemical that makes us sleepy.
d. The pineal is a gland that produces the sleep-inducing hormone melatonin.

3. **c.** is the answer. Jet lag is experienced because, having traveled across time zones, we are awake at a time when our biological clock says, "Sleep!" This biological clock is the circadian rhythm. (p. 275)

4. **a.** is the answer. (p. 277)
b. & c. Delta waves predominate during Stages 3 and 4. Stage 3 is the transition between Stages 2 and 4 and is associated with a pattern that has elements of both stages.
d. Faster, nearly waking brain waves occur during REM sleep.

5. **d.** is the answer. (p. 278)
a., b., & c. During non-REM Stages 1–4 heart rate and breathing are slow and regular and the genitals are not aroused.

6. **d.** is the answer. (p. 279)

7. **d.** is the answer. (pp. 280–281)

8. **a.** is the answer. Like alcohol, sleeping pills carry the undesirable consequence of reducing REM sleep and may make insomnia worse in the long run. (p. 283)
b., c., & d. Sleeping pills do not produce these effects.

9. **c.** is the answer. They also block the reuptake of serotonin and norepinephrine. (p. 301)
a. This answer describes the effect of LSD.
b. Depressants such as alcohol have this effect. Cocaine and crack are classified as stimulants.
d. None of the psychoactive drugs has this effect. Opiates, however, *suppress* the brain's production of endorphins.

10. **d.** is the answer. Alcohol, which slows body functions and neural activity, is a depressant. (p. 298)
    a. Methamphetamine is a stimulant.
    b. & c. LSD and marijuana are hallucinogens.

11. **b.** is the answer. Hypnosis was originally referred to as "mesmerism." (p. 291)
    a. In the area of consciousness, Freud is best known for his theory of dreaming.
    c. Spanos is best known for his contention that hypnosis is an extension of everyday social behavior.
    d. Hilgard is known for his theory of dissociation and the hidden observer in hypnosis.

12. **c.** is the answer. (p. 295)
    a. Hypnotized subjects usually perform only acts they might perform normally.
    b. The text does not suggest that sleeping and hypnosis are the same states. In fact, the brain waves of hypnotized subjects are not like those associated with sleeping.
    d. Hypnosis typically *disrupts*, or contaminates, memory.

13. **c.** is the answer. They remembered less than if they were awakened during other stages. (p. 287)

14. **a.** is the answer. Freud saw dreams as psychic safety valves that discharge unacceptable feelings that are often related to erotic wishes. (p. 287)
    b. & c. These physiological theories of dreaming are not associated with Freud.
    d. According to Freud, dreams represent the individual's conflicts and wishes but in disguised, rather than transparent, form.

15. **c.** is the answer. Such drugs work primarily at synapses, altering neural transmission. (p. 296)
    a. What people believe will happen after taking a drug will likely have some effect on their individual reactions, but psychoactive drugs actually work by altering neural transmission.
    b. Since a placebo is a substance without active properties, this answer is incorrect.
    d. This answer is incorrect because the effects of psychoactive drugs on behavior, perception, and so forth have a physiological basis.

16. **c.** is the answer. This is true. Heredity, for example, influences tendencies toward alcoholism. (pp. 297–298)

17. **b.** is the answer. (p. 271)
    a. The behaviorists' emphasis on observable behavior occurred much later in the history of psychology.
    c. Psychology has never been primarily concerned with abnormal behavior.

18. **d.** is the answer. (pp. 287–288)
    a., b., & c. Each of these describes a valid theory of dreaming that was mentioned in the text.

19. **c.** is the answer. We can reset our biological clocks by adjusting our sleep schedules. Thus, young adults adopt something closer to a 25-hour day by staying up too late to get 8 hours of sleep. (p. 276)

20. **c.** is the answer. (p. 307)

Matching Items

1. e (p. 286)   5. h (p. 284)   9. f (p. 301)
2. k (p. 287)   6. d (p. 284)   10. c (p. 277)
3. i (p. 277)   7. b (p. 298)   11. g (p. 284)
4. j (p. 276)   8. a (p. 303)

PROGRESS TEST 2

Multiple-Choice Questions

1. **b.** is the answer. Following REM deprivation, people temporarily increase their amount of REM sleep, in a phenomenon known as REM rebound. (p. 288)
   a. Just the opposite is true: The amount of REM sleep is greatest in infancy.
   c. Deprived of REM sleep by repeated awakenings, people return more and more quickly to the REM stages after falling back to sleep. They by no means adapt easily to the deprivations.
   d. Just the opposite occurs: they tend to suppress REM sleep.

2. **c.** is the answer. (p. 310)
   a. Behaviorists focus on observable behaviors and avoid concepts such as the mind.
   b. The monists believe that the mind and body are one.
   d. Freudians focus on unconscious and conscious aspects of the mind and have little to say regarding the mind-body relationship.

3. **a.** is the answer. Alcohol disrupts the processing of experiences into long-term memory but has little effect on either immediate or previously established memories. (p. 299)

4. **d.** is the answer. (p. 277)
   a. The brain waves of REM sleep (dream sleep) are more like those of Stage 1 sleepers.
   b. Stage 2 is characterized by sleep spindles.
   c. Stages 3 and 4 are characterized by slow, rolling delta waves.

5. **c.** is the answer. (p. 275)

6. **a.** is the answer. (p. 297)

b. Physical dependence may occur in the absence of tolerance. The hallmark of physical dependence is the presence of withdrawal symptoms when the person is off the drug.

c. Psychological dependence refers to a felt, or psychological, need to use a drug, for example, a drug that relieves stress.

d. There is no such thing as drug "resistance."

7. **d.** is the answer. (p. 274)

8. **a.** is the answer. (p. 278)
b. During REM sleep, muscular tension is low.
c. Night terrors are associated with Stage 4 sleep.
d. Alpha waves are characteristic of the relaxed, awake state.

9. **d.** is the answer. Alcohol is a depressant. (p. 298)

10. **d.** is the answer. (p. 291)
a. Hypnotic responsiveness varies greatly from person to person.
b. & c. There is no evidence of a gender difference in hypnotic responsiveness.

11. **c.** is the answer. Hilgard believes that hypnosis reflects a dissociation, or split, in consciousness, as occurs normally, only to a much greater extent. (p. 294)

12. **a.** is the answer. Compared with other children, children whose parents abuse alcohol have a *higher* tolerance for multiple drinks, making it more likely that they will, in fact, consume more alcohol. (p. 305)

13. **b.** is the answer. (p. 293)
a. & c. Hypnosis *can* be helpful in treating these problems, but it is no more effective than other forms of therapy.
d. Adults are not more responsive than children to hypnosis.

14. **d.** is the answer. If adolescents' friends use drugs, the odds are that they will, too. (p. 307)
a., b., & c. These are also predictors of drug use but seem to operate mainly through their effects on peer association.

15. **c.** is the answer. (p. 303)

16. **b.** is the answer. (p. 294)
a. & c. There is no evidence that hypnotically responsive individuals fake their behaviors or that they are underachievers.

17. **d.** is the answer. (p. 271)

18. **b.** is the answer. (p. 302)
a. & c. Unlike stimulants, LSD and THC do not speed up body functions.
d. Unlike hallucinogens, cocaine is a stimulant and does not generally distort perceptions.

19. **a.** is the answer. (p. 288)
b. & c. These essentially Freudian explanations of the purpose of dreaming are based on the idea that a dream is a psychic safety valve that harmlessly discharges otherwise inexpressible feelings.
d. This explanation of the function of dreaming is associated with the information-processing viewpoint.

20. **d.** is the answer. (pp. 300–302)

Matching Items

1. c (p. 302)
2. f (p. 300)
3. d (p. 277)
4. h (p. 277)
5. j (p. 276)
6. k (p. 300)
7. i (p. 300)
8. b (p. 302)
9. g (p. 271)
10. a (p. 287)
11. e (p. 293)

Psychology Applied

Multiple-Choice Questions

1. **b.** is the answer. Narcolepsy is characterized by uncontrollable sleep attacks. (p. 284)
a. Sleep apnea is characterized by the temporary cessation of breathing while asleep.
c. Night terrors are characterized by high arousal and terrified behavior, occurring during Stage 4 sleep.
d. Insomnia refers to chronic difficulty in falling or staying asleep.

2. **d.** is the answer. (p. 307)

3. **b.** is the answer. Although the body is aroused internally, the messages of the activated motor cortex do not reach the muscles. (p. 278)
a. Studies of REM-deprived people indicate just the opposite.
c. It is difficult to awaken a person from REM sleep.
d. Just the opposite occurs in REM sleep: the muscles are relaxed, yet the brain is aroused.

4. **a.** is the answer. Although people recall more under hypnosis, they "recall" a lot of fiction along with fact and appear unable to distinguish between the two. (p. 292)
b. Hypnotically refreshed memories are usually no more accurate than conscious memories.
c. Although the hypnotized subject's imagination may influence the memories retrieved, some actual memory retrieval also occurs.
d. Hypnotically retrieved memories don't normally focus on anxiety-provoking events.

5. **b.** is the answer. Continued use of a drug produces a tolerance; to experience the same "high,"

Dan will have to use larger and larger doses. (p. 297)

6. **c.** is the answer. The rapid eye movements of REM sleep coincide with bursts of activity in the visual cortex. (p. 278)

7. **c.** is the answer. (p. 272)

8. **d.** is the answer. Alcohol reduces self-consciousness and loosens inhibitions, making people more likely to act on their feelings of anger or sexual arousal. It also disrupts the processing of experience into long-term memory. (pp. 298–299)

9. **b.** is the answer. The analyst is evidently trying to go beyond the events in the dream and understand the dream's hidden meaning, or the dream's latent content. (p. 287)
   a. The manifest content of a dream is its actual story line.
   c. Dissociation refers to a split in levels of consciousness.
   d. There is no such term. In any case, "overt" would be the same as "manifest" content.

10. **d.** is the answer. Because of the phenomenon known as REM rebound, Barry, having been deprived of REM sleep, will now increase his REM sleep. (p. 288)
    a. Increased irritability is an effect of sleep deprivation in general, not of REM deprivation specifically.
    b. REM rebound will cause Barry to dream more than normal.
    c. The increase in REM sleep is necessarily accompanied by decreases in Stages 1–4 sleep.

11. **b.** is the answer. People with rich fantasy lives and the ability to become imaginatively absorbed have essentially the characteristics associated with hypnotic suggestibility. The fact that Janice is an actress also suggests she possesses such traits. (p. 291)
    a. Bill's reality orientation makes him an unlikely candidate for hypnosis.
    c. The hypnotically suggestible are generally able to focus on tasks or on imaginative activities.
    d. People who are hypnotically suggestible tend to become deeply engrossed in novels and movies.

12. **a.** is the answer. Adopted individuals are more susceptible to alcoholism if they had a *biological* parent with alcoholism. (p. 305)
    b., c., & d. Each of these is true, which indicates that susceptibility to alcoholism is at least partially determined by heredity.

13. **d.** is the answer. (pp. 292–293)

14. **c.** is the answer. (p. 278)

a. & d. Increased activity in the visual and auditory areas of the sleeping brain is perfectly normal during REM sleep.
b. In fact, people cannot easily be awakened from REM sleep.

15. **b.** is the answer. Monists such as Levar believe that the mind and body are inseparable. Thus, when the body dies, the mind ceases to exist. (p. 310)
    a. Behaviorists avoid references to the mind.
    c. Dualists believe that the mind can exist apart from the body.
    d. The text does not discuss the relationship between religious belief and near-death experiences.

16. **a.** is the answer. THC, the active ingredient in marijuana, and its by-products linger in the body for a month or more. (p. 303)

17. **b.** is the answer. (p. 309)
    a. Approximately 12 to 40 percent of people who have come close to death report some sort of near-death experience.
    c. & d. There is no gender difference in the prevalence of near-death experiences.

18. **c.** is the answer. (p. 294)

19. **d.** is the answer. (p. 307)

20. **d.** is the answer. Freud's theory proposed that dreams, which occur during fast-wave, REM sleep, serve as a psychic safety valve. (pp. 282–283)

Essay Question

As a depressant, alcohol slows neural activity and body functions. Although low doses of alcohol may produce relaxation, with larger doses reactions slow, speech slurs, skilled performance deteriorates, and the processing of recent experiences into long-term memories is disrupted. Alcohol also reduces self-awareness and may facilitate sexual and aggressive urges the individual might otherwise resist.

Some people may be biologically vulnerable to alcoholism. This is indicated by the fact that individuals who have a biological parent with alcoholism, or people who have an identical twin with alcoholism, are more susceptible to alcoholism.

Stress, depression, and the feeling that life is meaningless and without direction are common feelings among heavy users of alcohol and may create a psychological vulnerability to alcoholism.

Especially for teenagers, peer group influence is strong. If an adolescent's friends use alcohol, odds are that he or she will too.

Research suggests three important channels of

influence for drug prevention and treatment programs: (1) education about the long-term consequences of alcohol use; (2) efforts to boost people's self-esteem and purpose in life; and (3) attempts to counteract peer pressure that leads to experimentation with drugs.

KEY TERMS

Writing Definitions

1. For most psychologists, **consciousness** is our awareness of ourselves and our environment. (p. 271)

2. **Biological rhythms** are periodic fluctuations in our bodies' physiological states, including annual variations in appetite, 90-minute sleep cycles, the 28-day menstrual cycle, and circadian rhythms. (p. 274)

3. A **circadian rhythm** is any regular bodily rhythm, such as body temperature and sleep-wakefulness, that follows a 24-hour cycle. (p. 275)

   Memory aid: In Latin, *circa* means "about" and *dies* means "day." A **circadian rhythm** is one that is about a day, or 24 hours, in duration.

4. **REM sleep** is the sleep stage in which the brain and eyes are active, the muscles are relaxed, and vivid dreaming occurs; also known as *paradoxical sleep*. (p. 276)

   Memory aid: **REM** is an acronym for rapid eye movement, the distinguishing feature of this sleep stage that led to its discovery.

5. **Alpha waves** are the relatively slow brain waves characteristic of an awake, relaxed state. (p. 277)

6. **Sleep** is the natural, periodic, reversible loss of consciousness, on which the body and mind depend for healthy functioning. (p. 277)

7. **Hallucinations** are false sensory experiences that occur without any sensory stimulus. (p. 277)

8. **Delta waves** are the large, slow brain waves associated with deep sleep. (p. 277)

9. **Insomnia** is a sleep disorder in which the person regularly has difficulty in falling or staying asleep. (p. 283)

10. **Narcolepsy** is a sleep disorder in which the victim suffers sudden, uncontrollable sleep attacks, often characterized by entry directly into REM. (p. 284)

11. **Sleep apnea** is a sleep disorder in which the person ceases breathing while asleep, briefly arouses to gasp for air, falls back asleep, and repeats this cycle throughout the night. (p. 284)

    Example: One theory of the sudden infant death syndrome is that it is caused by **sleep apnea**.

12. A person suffering from **night terrors** experiences episodes of high arousal with apparent terror. Night terrors usually occur during Stage 4 sleep. (p. 284)

13. **Dreams** are vivid sequences of images, emotions, and thoughts, the most vivid of which occur during REM sleep. (p. 285)

14. In Freud's theory of dreaming, the **manifest content** is the remembered story line. (p. 286)

15. In Freud's theory of dreaming, the **latent content** is the underlying but censored meaning of a dream. (p. 287)

    Memory aids for 14 and 15: Manifest means "clearly apparent, obvious"; *latent* means "hidden, concealed." A dream's **manifest content** is that which is obvious; its **latent content** remains hidden until its symbolism is interpreted.

16. **REM rebound** is the tendency for REM sleep to increase following REM sleep deprivation. (p. 288)

17. **Hypnosis** is a social interaction in which one person (the hypnotist) suggests to another (the subject) that certain perceptions, feelings, thoughts, or behaviors will spontaneously occur. (p. 290)

18. A **posthypnotic suggestion** is a suggestion made during a hypnosis session that is to be carried out when the subject is no longer hypnotized. (p. 292)

19. **Dissociation** is a split between different levels of consciousness, allowing a person to divide attention between two or more thoughts. (p. 293)

20. **Psychoactive drugs**—which include stimulants, depressants, and hallucinogens—are chemical substances that alter mood and perception. They work by affecting or mimicking the activity of neurotransmitters. (p. 296)

21. **Tolerance** is the diminishing of a psychoactive drug's effect that occurs with repeated use, requiring progressively larger doses in order to produce the same effect. (p. 297)

22. **Withdrawal** refers to the discomfort and distress that follow the discontinued use of addictive drugs. (p. 297)

23. **Physical dependence** is a physiological need for a drug that is indicated by the presence of withdrawal symptoms when the drug is not taken. (p. 297)

24. The psychological need to use a drug is referred to as **psychological dependence**. (p. 297)

25. An **addiction** is a compulsive craving for a drug despite adverse consequences and withdrawal symptoms. (p. 297)

26. **Depressants** are psychoactive drugs, such as alcohol, opiates, and barbiturates, that reduce neural activity and slow body functions. (p. 298)

27. **Barbiturates** are depressants, sometimes used to induce sleep or reduce anxiety. (p. 300)

28. **Opiates** are depressants derived from the opium poppy, such as opium, morphine, and heroin; they reduce neural activity and temporarily lessen pain and anxiety. (p. 300)

29. **Stimulants** are psychoactive drugs, such as caffeine, nicotine, amphetamines, and cocaine, that excite neural activity and speed up body functions. (p. 300)

30. **Amphetamines** are a type of stimulant and, as such, speed up body functions and neural activity. (p. 300)

31. **Methamphetamine** is a powerfully addictive stimulant that speeds up body functions and is associated with energy and mood changes. (p. 300)

32. Classified as both a (synthetic) stimulant and a mild hallucinogen, **Ecstasy (MDMA)** produces short-term euphoria by increasing serotonin levels in the brain. Repeated use may permanently damage serotonin neurons, suppress immunity, and disrupt cognition. (p. 302)

33. **Hallucinogens** are psychoactive drugs, such as LSD and marijuana, that distort perception and evoke sensory images in the absence of sensory input. (p. 302)

34. **LSD** (lysergic acid diethylamide) is a powerful hallucinogen capable of producing vivid false perceptions and disorganization of thought pro-cesses. LSD produces its unpredictable effects partially because it blocks the action of the neurotransmitter serotonin. (p. 302)

35. The major active ingredient in marijuana, **THC** is classified as a mild hallucinogen. (p. 303)

36. The **near-death experience** is an altered state of consciousness that has been reported by some people who have had a close brush with death. (p. 309)

37. **Dualism** is the philosophical belief that the mind and body are distinct entities—the mind non-physical, the body physical. (p. 310)

Example: Those who believe that **near-death experiences** are proof of immortality are expressing the **dualist** position that mind and body are separate entities.

38. **Monism** is the philosophical belief that the mind and body are different aspects of the same thing. (p. 310)

Example: The belief that death is final and that no afterlife exists is a reflection of the **monist** position that mind and body are one.

Cross-Check

ACROSS
1. paradoxical
7. dopamine
8. nicotine
10. lucid dreams
12. LSD
13. serial
14. spindle
17. depressant
18. hypnagogic
19. barbiturates
21. morning
22. evening

DOWN
2. age regression
3. amphetamines
4. opiates
5. information processing
6. alcohol
9. hidden observer
11. delta
15. dissociation
16. alpha
18. heroin
20. THC

FOCUS ON VOCABULARY AND LANGUAGE

Page 271: To psychologists, consciousness is similarly a *fundamental* yet *slippery* concept. In science many fundamental concepts are difficult to define (e.g., life, matter, energy). Consciousness is one of the most basic (*fundamental*) ideas in psychology, yet it is an elusive and difficult concept to grasp (*a slippery concept*).

Consciousness and Information Processing

Page 271: Psychology had nearly *lost consciousness.* Myers is using a little humor here in order to illustrate the fact that changes (*swings*) have taken place during psychology's history. To *"lose consciousness"* can have two meanings in the above sentence: (1) to fall unconscious or pass out and (2) to fail to keep (lose) "consciousness" as the subject matter of psychology. Psychology started out as the study of conscious experience; then, because of problems in scientifically investigating the mind, overt behavior replaced consciousness in the 1920s. Finally, in the 1960s, psychology regained consciousness as a legitimate subject for psychologists to study.

Pages 271–272: . . . yet *consciousness* is but *the tip of the information-processing iceberg.* Just as most of the mass or volume of an iceberg is below the surface of the ocean and out of sight, most mental functioning goes on without conscious awareness. Consciousness is a small part (*the tip of the iceberg*) of total information processing.

Page 272: . . . so, consciousness is known to *lag* behind the brain events that *evoke* it. *To lag* means to be late or to follow. So our conscious awareness always follows after (*lags behind*) the neural activities in the brain that give rise to, or create (*evoke*), it.

Page 272: Running on automatic pilot allows consciousness—the mind's *CEO*—to monitor the whole system and deal with new challenges. Myers is pointing out that much of our information processing occurs outside of conscious awareness (*we run on automatic pilot*) and that conscious awareness is similar to the top manager of an organization (*CEO or chief executive officer*) whose many assistants take care of all the routine tasks, allowing him or her to pay attention to (*monitor*) the total system and tackle (*deal with*) new challenges.

Sleep and Dreams

Page 274: . . . limbs often *move in concert.* . . . To *"move in concert"* is to move simultaneously or in synchrony. When we dream of doing something, our arms and legs do *not* move in synchrony (*do not move in concert*) with the activity in the dream.

Page 275: Awake at 4:00 A.M., *body depressed,* we may *fret* over concerns: Does a *lovers' spat* signal a split? Our body temperature drops after we go to sleep and begins to rise again toward morning. So if we wake up in the middle of the night our temperature may be low (*the body is depressed*). We may start to worry (*fret*) over problems. For example, if we've had a minor disagreement or argument with a loved one (*lovers' spat*), we may think this means the relationship is going to end (*signals a split*).

Page 275: Pulling an all-nighter, we feel *groggiest* about 4:00 A.M., and then *we get a second wind* after our normal wake-up time arrives. If we decide to stay up all night (*pull an all-nighter*), say, to finish a term paper by the deadline, we feel most mentally confused and uncoordinated (*groggiest*) around the middle of the night, but as our usual time for getting up approaches, we begin to feel renewed energy (*we get a second wind*).

Page 275: . . . *jet lag* . . . When we travel by plane across several time zones we may experience mental and physical fatigue (*jet lag*). Because our biological clocks naturally tend toward a 25-hour day, we may find it easier to jet west, which gives us a longer day, than to travel east. Exposure to bright light helps reset the circadian clock and reduces jet lag because it prompts (*tweaks*) the *suprachiasmatic nucleus* to decrease production of chemicals such as the sleep-inducing hormone melatonin.

Page 276: Before long, the machine *went wild,* tracing *deep zigzags* on the graph paper. The discovery of REM (Rapid Eye Movement) occurred accidentally. To see if an EEG (electroencephalograph) was working properly Aserinsky placed the electrodes near his 8-year-old son's eyes. Periodically during the night the machine responded vigorously (*went wild*), producing a pattern of high-frequency waves (*deep zigzags*) on the printout. These patterns were produced by rapid, spasmodic (*jerky*) eye movements and accompanied by very frantic brain activity, and when awakened during one of these periods the boy said he was dreaming.

Page 278: Rather than continuing in deep *slumber,* you *ascend* from your initial *sleep dive.* During a typical night's sleep (*slumber*) you go through a number of distinct stages. If you are awake and relaxed, perhaps with your eyes closed, an EEG would show alpha waves. As you fall deeper and deeper into sleep (*sleep dive*), your brain waves continue to slow down. By Stage 4 your brain waves are long and slow (*delta waves*), but you don't stay here all night; instead, you go back up (*ascend*) through the stages into the most unique and interesting stage of all,

REM (Rapid Eye Movement) sleep, where most dreams occur. Here, the brain waves resemble the fast, uneven Stage 1 waves (*sawtoothed*), but there is much more internal physiological arousal now, and, paradoxically, your muscles are almost paralyzed.

Page 279: As the night *wears on*, deep Stage 4 sleep gets progressively briefer and then disappears. As the night progresses (*wears on*), the time spent in Stage 4 deep sleep gets shorter (and eventually ceases altogether) and time spent in REM sleep gets longer.

Page 280: . . . drowsy . . . If you were deprived of sleep for a few nights, you would feel very tired and sleepy (*drowsy*) and also unsteady and dazed (*groggy*).

Page 280: People today more than ever suffer from sleep patterns that *thwart* their having an energized feeling of well-being. Because of the pressures of work, school, social obligations, and so on, we often have sleep schedules that prevent (*thwart*) us from getting the amount of sleep we need. The consequence of this "sleep debt" (*accumulated insufficient sleep*) is a general lack of energy and discomfort (*malaise*) and a frequent feeling of sleepiness.

Page 280: Many fill this need [for sleep] by using their first class for an *early siesta* and after-lunch *study hall for a slumber party*. Today's young students often get much less sleep than they need and consequently many end up using the first class of the day for a short sleep or nap (*siesta*), and the quiet school period meant for study (*study hall*) may be occupied by whole groups of sleeping students (*slumber party*). Even so, 80 percent of students are still seriously sleep deprived (*they have a large sleep debt*), which results in diminished cognitive and intellectual functioning (*"a large sleep debt makes you stupid"*) and a tendency to fall asleep during routine lectures (*when the going gets boring, the students start snoring*).

Page 281: . . . "spring forward" to "daylight savings" time and *"fall backward"* to "standard" time. Many countries adopt daylight savings time, which means that in the spring people move their clocks ahead one hour (*spring forward*) and back one hour in the fall (*fall backward*). Consequently, people lose one hour of sleep in the spring, which results in more traffic accidents on the Monday following the Sunday time change; with the extra hour of sleep in the fall, traffic accidents decline on the Monday following the time change.

Page 283: These discoveries are beginning to solve the ongoing *riddle* of sleep. Recent research has shown that sleep helps us repair and restore body tissue (*recuperate*), promotes physical growth, increases memory and learning capacity, provides a protective mechanism (this was especially true in our evolutionary past), and enhances (*feeds*) creative thinking. These findings are starting to clear up the continuing puzzle (*riddle*) why we need to sleep.

Page 283: Alcohol and some sleep medications reduce REM sleep and can leave a person with *next-day blahs*. The most popular fast remedies (*quick fixes*) for insomnia are sleeping pills and alcohol. Unfortunately, they can make the problem worse (*aggravate it*) by suppressing REM sleep; the next day the person may have less energy and feel very tired (*next-day blahs*). When these "remedies" are discontinued, the insomnia may get worse.

Page 284: As a traffic menace, *"snoozing is second only to boozing,"* says the American Sleep Disorders Association, and those with narcolepsy are especially at risk (Aldrich, 1989). Falling asleep (*snoozing*) while driving is almost as serious a problem as drinking (*boozing*) and driving. People with **narcolepsy** suffer from occasional periods of uncontrollable sleepiness often associated with emotional arousal, and are thus in danger, and dangerous, while driving.

Page 287: . . . He [Freud] argued that by fulfilling wishes, a dream provides a *psychic safety valve* that discharges otherwise unacceptable feelings. The story line of the dream (**manifest content**) is a disguised version of the real, but hidden, meaning of the dream (**latent content**). According to Freud, by symbolically expressing our hidden desires and erotic wishes, dreams allow us to ventilate unconscious drives that might otherwise be harmful (*acts as a psychic safety valve*). (A *safety valve* allows a system to dissipate built-up pressure and thus may prevent an explosion.)

Page 287: However, his critics say *it is time to wake up* from Freud's dream theory, which is a scientific *nightmare*. Myers is having some fun with a play on words here. The expression "it is time to wake up from something" means one should start paying attention to reality and facts, rather than fantasy, and to say something is "a nightmare" means that it is unruly, difficult, or even frightening. Most contemporary psychologists believe that REM sleep and dreams are important aspects of our life but that Freud's theory of dream interpretation is erroneous, unscientific, and misguided (*a nightmare*); thus, we should not place much reliance on its explanations (*it is time to wake up from it*).

Page 287: . . . The brain regions that *buzz* as rats learn to navigate a maze, or as people learn to perform a visual-discrimination task, *buzz again* later during REM sleep. Studies demonstrate that sleeping helps memory and learning. The areas of the brain that are active (*that buzz*) when learning is taking place are also active once more (*they buzz again*) during REM sleep. This is important news for sleep-deprived students who tend to learn and remember less than their non-sleep-derived counterparts. Attempting to make up for the loss of sleep by sleeping longer and later on weekends (*a kind of sleep bulimia . . . binge sleeping*) will not compensate for the lower levels of learning and recall.

Hypnosis

Page 291: Thus, *hypnosis—or mesmerism,* as it was then called—became linked with *quackery.* Hypnosis—a social interaction in which a hypnotist suggests to a subject that certain perceptions, behaviors, and so on will spontaneously occur—was first referred to as *mesmerism* after the eighteenth-century physician Mesmer, who promoted its use. Because the Franklin commission found no scientific evidence for Mesmer's "cures," they concluded that hypnosis was fraudulent or bogus (*quackery*).

Page 292 (margin): "Hypnosis is not a psychological *truth serum,* and to regard it as such has been a source of considerable *mischief.*" Research shows that hypnotists can subtly influence what people recall and they may inadvertently create false memories by making suggestions and asking leading questions. Thus, hypnosis is not like a so-called *truth serum* (a drug alleged to make people tell the truth) but rather has caused a great deal of annoying—and possibly harmful—effects (*considerable mischief*).

Page 295: So, might the two views—social influence and divided consciousness—*be bridged?* Although there are a number of different explanations about what hypnosis really is, Myers suggests that it may be possible to bring together some of these theories (*bridge the differences*). Thus, hypnosis may be both a part of normal aspects of social influence and our ability to have a divided (*or split*) consciousness.

Drugs and Consciousness

Page 296: Why is it that a person who rarely drinks alcohol might get *tipsy* on one can of beer, but an experienced drinker may not get *tipsy* until the *second six-pack?* Prolonged use of a psychoactive drug produces the ability, through neuroadaptation, to take more and more of the substance (*tolerance*). Thus, an infrequent user of alcohol may get somewhat intoxicated (*tipsy*) from one beer, but for a reg-

ular drinker there might be little effect until six or more beers have been consumed (*until the second six-pack [of beer]*).

Page 298 . . . kicked the habit . . . This means that the person who has been using the substance on a regular basis (*habitual* or *addictive behavior*) has now stopped doing so (*has kicked the habit*). Myers notes that addiction is not a disease (such as diabetes) and many people voluntary stop using addictive drugs without treatment or therapy.

Pages 298–299: . . . as when *tipsy* restaurant patrons leave extravagant tips. Alcohol can increase both harmful and helpful inclinations. Thus, it often happens that restaurant clientele give a larger gratuity (extravagant *tips*) when they are more intoxicated (*tipsy*). Whatever tendencies you have when sober will be more obvious when you are drunk.

Page 299: . . . With larger doses, alcohol can become a *staggering problem.* Myers is using humor here to make an important point. To describe a problem as *staggering* means that the problem is enormous and has serious consequences (for example, a *staggering debt* is one that is overwhelming). One of the consequences of ingesting large amounts of alcohol is slowed reaction time, memory loss (*blackouts*), language disruptions (*slurred speech*), and uncoordinated physical movement (the person *staggers*). Thus, drinking too much alcohol has serious implications (it is a *staggering problem*).

Page 300: If, as commonly believed, liquor is the *quicker pick-her-upper,* the effect lies partly in that powerful sex organ, the mind. Alcohol (liquor) is thought by many to speed up the process of meeting members of the opposite sex and to lower sexual inhibitions. Thus, a male may believe that use of alcohol will facilitate his ability to initiate contact and get to know a female (a *quicker pick-her-upper*). Myers points out that not only alcohol is involved, but also our beliefs about its effects on sexual behavior (the effect lies partly in that *powerful sex organ, the mind*).

Page 300: But for short-term pleasure *one pays a long-term price,* which for the heroin user is the *gnawing craving* for another *fix . . . .* There is a cost (*one pays a long-term price*) for enjoying drug-induced pleasures, and for an addict this may be a persistent inner torment (*gnawing*) and an urgent, persistent desire (*craving*) for another dose of the drug (a *fix*).

Page 301: . . . crack . . . Crack is a very potent, synthetic form of cocaine which produces a feeling of euphoria (*a rush*) followed by deep depression, tiredness, and irritability (*a "crash"*).

Page 302: . . . *"acid trip"* . . . Taking any psychoactive drug is called a *trip* or *tripping out.* When LSD (acid) is used, it is called an *acid trip;* regular users are sometimes called *acid-heads.*

Page 303: . . . marijuana may *spell* relief. Although there are many reasons for not taking marijuana, it does have some therapeutic applications, such as alleviating the sick feelings that result from taking the drugs used to treat cancer (chemotherapy) and the pain, nausea, and weight loss associated with AIDS. Thus, it may provide (*spell*) relief for some patients.

Near-Death Experiences

Page 309: . . . And they tend to handle stress well, often *taking the bull by the horns* rather than becoming traumatized (Britton & Bootzin, 2004). The expression "taking the bull by the horns" means to confront a problem without fear or trepidation. For some people, a near-death experience may result in profound changes in their lives; they may become more generous, more spiritual, and more convinced about the possibility of life after death. In addition, they are better able to handle stress, often tackling problems assertively and fearlessly (they *take the bull by the horns*).

Page 310: Such monists generally believe that life is embodied, that death is real, and that without bodies we truly are *nobodies.* A *nobody* is someone of no importance. Myers is making a joke here: If mind and body are one (the **monist** position), then when we are dead and gone, there is nothing left, and we are *nobodies* (i.e., we have no bodies) and so have no afterlife existence.

8 : Learning

CHAPTER OVERVIEW

"No topic is closer to the heart of psychology than learning, a relatively permanent change in an organism's behavior due to experience." Chapter 8 covers the basic principles of three forms of learning: classical, or respondent, conditioning, in which we learn associations between events; operant conditioning, in which we learn to engage in behaviors that are rewarded and to avoid behaviors that are punished; and observational learning, in which we learn by observing and imitating others.

The chapter also covers several important issues, including the generality of principles of learning, the role of cognitive processes in learning, and the ways in which learning is constrained by the biological predispositions of different species.

NOTE: Answer guidelines for all Chapter 8 questions begin on page 219.

CHAPTER REVIEW

First, skim each section, noting headings and boldface items. After you have read the section, review each objective by answering the fill-in and essay-type questions that follow it. As you proceed, evaluate your performance by consulting the answers beginning on page 219. Do not continue with the next section until you understand each answer. If you need to, review or reread the section in the textbook before continuing.

How Do We Learn? (pp. 313–315)

> David Myers at times uses idioms that are unfamiliar to some readers. If you do not know the meaning of any of the following words, phrases, or expressions in the context in which they appear in the text, refer to page 227 for an explanation: . . . *breeds hope; mugged; Japanese rancher reportedly herds cattle.*

Objective 1: Define *learning*, and identify two forms of learning.

1. A relatively permanent change in an organism's behavior due to experience is called
   _____ .

2. More than 200 years ago, philosophers such as John Locke and David Hume argued that an important factor in learning is our tendency to _____ events that occur in sequence. Even simple animals, such as the sea snail *Aplysia*, can learn simple _____ between stimuli. This type of learning is called _____
   _____ .

3. The type of learning in which the organism learns to associate two stimuli is _____ conditioning.

4. The tendency of organisms to associate a response and its consequence forms the basis of _____ conditioning.

5. Complex animals often learn behaviors merely by _____ others perform them.

Classical Conditioning (pp. 315–326)

> If you do not know the meaning of any of the following words, phrases, or expressions in the context in which they appear in the text, refer to pages 227–229 for an explanation: *For many people, the name Ivan Pavlov . . . rings a bell; drooled; sets your mouth to watering; red-light district; breaking up . . . fire-breathing heartthrob; your heart may race; willy-nilly; the thought that counts; we stand on his shoulders; crack cocaine users often feel a craving; legendary significance.*

Objective 2: Define *classical conditioning* and *behaviorism,* and describe the basic components of classical conditioning.

1. Classical conditioning was first explored by the Russian physiologist _____ . Early in the twentieth century, psychologist _____ urged psychologists to discard references to mental concepts in favor of studying observable behavior. This view, called _____ , influenced American psychology during the first half of that century.

2. In Pavlov's classic experiment, a tone, or _____ _____ , is sounded just before food, the _____ _____ , is placed in the animal's mouth.

3. An animal will salivate when food is placed in its mouth. This salivation is called the _____ _____ .

4. Eventually, the dogs in Pavlov's experiment would salivate on hearing the tone. This salivation is called the _____ _____ .

Objective 3: Describe the timing requirements for the initial learning of a stimulus-response relationship.

5. The initial learning of a conditioned response is called _____ . For many conditioning situations, the optimal interval between a neutral stimulus and the US is _____ _____ .

6. When the US is presented prior to a neutral stimulus, conditioning _____ (does/does not) occur.

Explain why learning theorists consider classically conditioned behaviors to be biologically adaptive.

7. Michael Domjan's sexual conditioning studies with quail demonstrate that classical conditioning is highly adaptive because it helps animals _____ and _____ .

8. Associations that are not consciously noticed _____ (can/cannot) give rise to attitudes.

Objective 4: Summarize the processes of extinction, spontaneous recovery, generalization, and discrimination.

9. If a CS is repeatedly presented without the US, _____ soon occurs; that is, the CR diminishes.

10. Following a rest, however, the CR reappears in response to the CS; this phenomenon is called _____ _____ .

11. Subjects often respond to a similar stimulus as they would to the original CS. This phenomenon is called _____ .

Objective 5: Discuss the survival value of generalization and discrimination.

12. Subjects can also be trained not to respond to _____ stimuli. This learned ability is called _____ .

13. Being able to recognize differences among stimuli has _____ value because it lets us limit our learned responses to appropriate stimuli.

Objective 6: Discuss the importance of cognitive processes in classical conditioning.

14. The early behaviorists believed that to understand behavior in various organisms, any presumption of _____ was unnecessary.

15. Experiments by Rescorla and Wagner demonstrate that a CS must reliably _____ the US for an association to develop and, more generally, that _____ processes play a role in conditioning. It is as if the animal learns to _____ that the US will occur.

16. The importance of cognitive processes in human conditioning is demonstrated by the failure of classical conditioning as a treatment for

_____ .

Objective 7: Describe some of the ways that biological predispositions can affect learning by classical conditioning.

17. Some psychologists once believed that any natural _____ could be conditioned to any neutral _____ .

18. Garcia discovered that rats would associate _____ with taste but not with other stimuli. Garcia found that taste-aversion conditioning _____ (would/would not) occur when the delay between the CS and the US was more than an hour.

19. Results such as these demonstrate that the principles of learning are constrained by the _____ predispositions of each animal species and that they help each species _____ to its environment. They also demonstrate the importance of different _____ _____ _____ in understanding complex phenomena.

Objective 8: Summarize Pavlov's contribution to our understanding of learning.

20. Classical conditioning is one way that virtually all organisms learn to _____ to their environment.

21. Another aspect of Pavlov's legacy is that he showed how a process such as learning could be studied _____ .

Explain why the study of classical conditioning is important.

Objective 9: Describe some uses of classical conditioning to improve human health and well-being.

22. Through classical conditioning, drug users often develop a _____ when they encounter _____ associated with previous highs.

23. Research studies demonstrate that the body's immune system _____ (can/cannot) be classically conditioned.

Describe the Watson and Rayner experiment.

Operant Conditioning (pp. 326–340)

> If you do not know the meaning of any of the following words, phrases, or expressions in the context in which they appear in the text, refer to pages 229–231 for an explanation: *to pull habits out of a rat; . . . between Bach's music and Stravinsky's; pastes gold stars; snooze button; goofing off; the kick that often comes within seconds; a sale with every pitch; paid on a piecework basis; fly fishing; a choppy stop-start pattern; "You've got mail"; loses a treat; drawbacks; spanking is a hit; backfire; piggy bank; stirred a hornet's nest; rule of thumb.*

Objective 10: Identify the two major characteristics that distinguish classical conditioning from operant conditioning.

1. Classical conditioning associates _____ stimuli with stimuli that trigger responses that are _____ . Thus, in this form of conditioning, the organism _____ (does/does not) control the responses.

2. The reflexive responses of classical conditioning involve _____ behavior.

3. In contrast, behavior that is more spontaneous and that is influenced by its consequences is called _____ behavior.

Objective 11: State Thorndike's law of effect, and explain its connection to Skinner's research on operant conditioning.

4. B. F. Skinner used Thorndike's _____ _____ _____ as a starting point in developing a "behavioral technology." This principle states that _____ behavior is likely to _____ .

5. Skinner designed an apparatus, called the _____ _____ , to investigate learning in animals.

Objective 12: Describe the shaping procedure, and explain how it can increase our understanding of what animals and babies can discriminate.

6. The procedure in which a person teaches an animal to perform an intricate behavior by building up to it in small steps is called _____ . This method involves reinforcing successive _____ of the desired behavior.

7. In experiments to determine what an animal can perceive, researchers have found that animals are capable of forming _____ and _____ between stimuli. Similar experiments have been conducted with babies, who also can't verbalize their responses.

8. A situation, event, or signal that a certain response will be reinforced is a _____ _____ .

Objective 13: Compare positive and negative reinforcement, and give one example each of a primary reinforcer, a conditioned reinforcer, an immediate reinforcer, and a delayed reinforcer.

9. An event that increases the frequency of a preceding response is a _____ .

10. A stimulus that strengthens a response by presenting a typically pleasurable stimulus after a response is a _____ _____ .

11. A stimulus that strengthens a response by reducing or removing an aversive (unpleasant) stimulus is a _____ _____ .

12. Reinforcers, such as food and shock, that are related to basic needs and therefore do not rely on learning are called _____ _____ . Reinforcers that must be conditioned and therefore derive their power through association are called _____ _____ .

13. Children who are able to delay gratification tend to become _____ (more/less) socially competent and high achieving as they mature.

14. Immediate reinforcement _____ (is/is not) more effective than its alternative, _____ reinforcement. This explains in part the difficulty that _____ users have in quitting their habits, as well as the tendency of some teens to engage in risky, _____ _____ .

Objective 14: Discuss the strengths and weaknesses of continuous and partial (intermittent) reinforcement schedules, and identify four schedules of partial reinforcement.

15. The procedure involving reinforcement of each and every response is called _____ _____ . Under these conditions, learning is _____ (rapid/slow). When this

type of reinforcement is discontinued, extinction is _____ (rapid/slow).

16. The procedure in which responses are reinforced only part of the time is called _____ reinforcement. Under these conditions, learning is generally _____ (faster/slower) than it is with continuous reinforcement. Behavior reinforced in this manner is _____ (very/not very) resistant to extinction.

17. When behavior is reinforced after a set number of responses, a _____-_____ schedule is in effect.

18. Three-year-old Yusef knows that if he cries when he wants a treat, his mother will sometimes give in. When, as in this case, reinforcement occurs after an unpredictable number of responses, a _____-_____ schedule is being used.

19. Reinforcement of the first response after a set interval of time defines the _____-_____ schedule. An example of this schedule is _____ .

20. When the first response after varying amounts of time is reinforced, a _____-_____ schedule is in effect.

Describe the typical patterns of response under fixed-interval, fixed-ratio, variable-interval, and variable-ratio schedules of reinforcement.

Objective 15: Discuss the ways negative punishment, positive punishment, and negative reinforcement differ, and list some drawbacks of punishment as a behavior-control technique.

21. An aversive consequence that decreases the likelihood of the behavior that preceded it is called _____ . If an aversive stimulus is administered, it is called _____ _____ . If a desirable stimulus is withdrawn, it is called _____ _____ .

22. Because punished behavior is merely _____ , it may reappear.

23. Punishment can also lead to _____ and a sense of helplessness, as well as to the association of the aversive event with _____ .

24. Punishment also often increases _____ and does not guide the individual toward more desirable behavior.

Objective 16: Explain how latent learning and the effect of external rewards demonstrate that cognitive processing is an important part of learning.

25. Skinner and other behaviorists resisted the growing belief that expectations, perceptions, and other _____ processes have a valid place in the science of psychology.

26. When a well-learned route in a maze is blocked, rats sometimes choose an alternative route, acting as if they were consulting a _____ _____ .

27. Animals may learn from experience even when reinforcement is not available. When learning is not apparent until reinforcement has been provided, _____ _____ is said to have occurred.

28. Excessive rewards may undermine _____ _____ , which is the desire to perform a behavior for its own sake. The motivation to seek external rewards and avoid punishment is called _____ _____ .

Objective 17: Explain how biological predispositions place limits on what can be achieved through operant conditioning.

29. Operant conditioning _____
(is/is not) constrained by an animal's biological predispositions.

30. For instance, with animals it is difficult to use food as a _____ to _____ behaviors that are not naturally associated with _____ .

31. Biological constraints predispose organisms to learn associations that are naturally _____ . When animals revert to their biologically predisposed patterns, they are exhibiting what is called "_____ _____ ."

Objective 18: Describe the controversy over Skinner's views of human behavior.

32. Skinner's views were controversial because he insisted that _____ influences, rather than _____ _____ and _____ , shape behavior.

33. Skinner also advocated the use of _____ principles to influence people in ways that promote more desirable _____ .

34. Skinner's critics argued that he _____ people by neglecting their personal _____ and by seeking to _____ their actions.

Objective 19: Describe some ways to apply operant conditioning principles at school, in sports, at work, and at home.

35. The use of teaching machines and programmed textbooks was an early application of the operant conditioning procedure of _____ to education. On-line _____ systems , software that is _____ , and _____-based learning are newer examples of this application of operant principles. Reinforcement principles can also be

used to enhance _____ abilities by shaping successive approximations of new skills.

36. In boosting productivity in the workplace, positive reinforcement is _____ (more/less) effective when applied to specific behaviors than when given to reward general merit and when the desired performance is well defined and _____ . For such behaviors, immediate reinforcement is _____ (more/no more) effective than delayed reinforcement.

37. Many economists and psychologists believe that people's spending behavior is controlled by its consequences (its _____ and _____).

38. In using operant conditioning to change your own behavior, you would follow these four steps:
a. _____
b. _____
c. _____
d. _____

Objective 20: Identify the major similarities and differences between classical and operant conditioning.

39. Classical conditioning and operant conditioning are both forms of _____ _____ .

40. Both types of conditioning involve similar processes of _____ , _____ , _____ _____ , _____ , and _____ .

41. Classical and operant conditioning are both subject to the influences of _____ processes and _____ predispositions.

42. Through classical conditioning, an organism associates different _____ that it does not _____ and responds _____ .

43. Through operant conditioning, an organism associates its _____ _____ with their _____ .

Learning by Observation (pp. 341–346)

> If you do not know the meaning of the following phrases in the context in which they appear in the text, refer to page 231 for an explanation: *those who observed the model's aggressive outburst were much more likely to lash out at the doll; Does the reel world reflect the real world?*

Objective 21: Describe the process of observational learning, and explain the importance of the discovery of mirror neurons.

1. Learning by observing and imitating others is called _____ , or _____ _____ . This form of learning _____ (occurs/does not occur) in species other than our own.

2. Neuroscientists have found _____ neurons in the brain's _____ lobe that provide a neural basis for _____ learning. These neurons have been observed to fire when monkeys perform a simple task and when they _____ . This type of neuron _____ (has/has not) been found in human brains.

3. By age _____ , infants will imitate novel play behaviors. By age _____ , they will imitate acts modeled on television.

Objective 22: Describe Bandura's findings on what determines whether we will imitate a model.

4. The psychologist best known for research on observational learning is _____ .

5. In one experiment, the child who viewed an adult punch an inflatable doll played _____ (more/less) aggressively than the child who had not observed the adult.

6. Bandura believes people imitate a model because of _____ and _____ , those received by the model as well as by imitators.

7. These results may help explain why _____ parents might have _____ children. However, _____ factors may also be involved.

Objective 23: Discuss the impact of prosocial modeling.

8. Children will also model positive, or _____ , behaviors.

9. Models are most effective when they are perceived as _____ , _____ , or _____ . Models are also most effective when their words and actions are _____ .

Objective 24: Explain why correlations cannot prove that watching violent TV causes violent behavior, and cite some experimental evidence that helps demonstrate a cause-effect link.

10. Children in developed countries spend more time _____ _____ than they spend in school.

11. Compared to real-world crimes, television depicts a much higher percentage of crimes as being _____ in nature.

12. Correlational studies _____ (link/do not link) watching television violence with violent behavior.

13. The more hours children spend watching violent programs, the more at risk they are for _____ and _____ as teens and adults.

14. Correlation does not prove _____ . Most researchers believe that watching violence on television _____ (does/does not) lead to aggressive behavior.

15. The violence effect stems from several factors, including _____ of observed aggression and the tendency of prolonged exposure to violence to _____ viewers.

PROGRESS TEST 1

Multiple-Choice Questions

Circle your answers to the following questions and check them with the answers beginning on page 221. If your answer is incorrect, read the explanation for why it is incorrect and then consult the appropriate pages of the text (in parentheses following the correct answer).

1. Learning is best defined as:
   a. any behavior produced by an organism without being provoked.
   b. a change in the behavior of an organism.
   c. a relatively permanent change in the behavior of an organism due to experience.
   d. behavior based on operant rather than respondent conditioning.

2. The type of learning associated with Skinner is:
   a. classical conditioning.
   b. operant conditioning.
   c. respondent conditioning.
   d. observational learning.

3. In Pavlov's original experiment with dogs, the meat served as a(n):
   a. CS.   c. US.
   b. CR.   d. UR.

4. In Pavlov's original experiment with dogs, the tone was initially a(n) _____ stimulus; after it was paired with meat, it became a(n) _____ stimulus.
   a. conditioned; neutral
   b. neutral; conditioned
   c. conditioned; unconditioned
   d. unconditioned; conditioned

5. In order to obtain a reward a monkey learns to press a lever when a 1000-Hz tone is on but not when a 1200-Hz tone is on. What kind of training is this?
   a. extinction
   b. generalization
   c. classical conditioning
   d. discrimination

6. Which of the following statements concerning reinforcement is correct?
   a. Learning is most rapid with intermittent reinforcement, but continuous reinforcement produces the greatest resistance to extinction.
   b. Learning is most rapid with continuous reinforcement, but intermittent reinforcement produces the greatest resistance to extinction.
   c. Learning is fastest and resistance to extinction is greatest after continuous reinforcement.
   d. Learning is fastest and resistance to extinction is greatest following intermittent reinforcement.

7. Cognitive processes are:
   a. unimportant in classical and operant conditioning.
   b. important in both classical and operant conditioning.
   c. more important in classical than in operant conditioning.
   d. more important in operant than in classical conditioning.

8. The highest and most consistent rate of response is produced by a _____ schedule.
   a. fixed-ratio   c. fixed-interval
   b. variable-ratio   d. variable-interval

9. A response that leads to the removal of an unpleasant stimulus is one being:
   a. positively reinforced.
   b. negatively reinforced.
   c. punished.
   d. extinguished.

10. When a conditioned stimulus is presented without an accompanying unconditioned stimulus, _____ will soon take place.
    a. generalization   c. extinction
    b. discrimination   d. aversion

11. One difference between classical and operant conditioning is that:
    a. in classical conditioning the responses operate on the environment to produce rewarding or punishing stimuli.
    b. in operant conditioning the responses are triggered by preceding stimuli.
    c. in classical conditioning the responses are automatically triggered by stimuli.
    d. in operant conditioning the responses are reflexive.

12. In Garcia and Koelling's studies of taste-aversion learning, rats learned to associate:
    a. taste with electric shock.
    b. sights and sounds with sickness.
    c. taste with sickness.
    d. taste and sounds with electric shock.

13. In Pavlov's original experiment with dogs, salivation to meat was the:
    a. CS.   c. US.
    b. CR.   d. UR.

14. Learning by imitating others' behaviors is called _____ learning. The researcher best known for studying this type of learning is _____ .
    a. secondary; Skinner
    b. observational; Bandura
    c. secondary; Pavlov
    d. observational; Watson

15. Punishment is a controversial way of controlling behavior because:
    a. behavior is not forgotten and may return.
    b. punishing stimuli often create fear.
    c. punishment often increases aggressiveness.
    d. of all of the above reasons.

16. Classical conditioning experiments by Rescorla and Wagner demonstrate that an important factor in conditioning is:
    a. the subject's age.
    b. the strength of the stimuli.
    c. the predictability of an association.
    d. the similarity of stimuli.

17. Which of the following is an example of reinforcement?
    a. presenting a positive stimulus after a response
    b. removing an unpleasant stimulus after a response
    c. being told that you have done a good job
    d. All of the above are examples.

18. Which of the following is a form of associative learning?
    a. classical conditioning
    b. operant conditioning
    c. observational learning
    d. all of the above

19. For the most rapid conditioning, a CS should be presented:
    a. about 1 second after the US.
    b. about one-half second before the US.
    c. about 15 seconds before the US.
    d. at the same time as the US.

20. Mirror neurons are found in the brain's _____ and are believed to be the neural basis for _____ .
    a. frontal lobe; observational learning
    b. frontal lobe; classical conditioning
    c. temporal lobe; operant conditioning
    d. temporal lobe; observational learning

Matching Items

Match each definition or description with the appropriate term.

Definitions or Descriptions

_____ 1. presentation of a desired stimulus
_____ 2. tendency for similar stimuli to evoke a CR
_____ 3. removal of an aversive stimulus
_____ 4. an innately reinforcing stimulus
_____ 5. an acquired reinforcer
_____ 6. responses are reinforced after an unpredictable amount of time
_____ 7. the motivation to perform a behavior for its own sake
_____ 8. reinforcing closer and closer approximations of a behavior
_____ 9. the reappearance of a weakened CR
_____ 10. presentation of an aversive stimulus
_____ 11. learning that becomes apparent only after reinforcement is provided
_____ 12. each and every response is reinforced
_____ 13. a desire to perform a behavior due to promised rewards

Terms

a. shaping
b. punishment
c. spontaneous recovery
d. latent learning
e. positive reinforcement
f. negative reinforcement
g. primary reinforcer
h. generalization
i. conditioned reinforcer
j. continuous reinforcement
k. variable-interval schedule
l. extrinsic motivation
m. intrinsic motivation

PROGRESS TEST 2

Progress Test 2 should be completed during a final chapter review. Answer the following questions after you thoroughly understand the correct answers for the section reviews and Progress Test 1.

Multiple-Choice Questions

1. During extinction, the _____ is omitted; as a result, the _____ seems to disappear.
   a. US; UR
   b. CS; CR
   c. US; CR
   d. CS; UR

2. In Watson and Rayner's experiment, the loud noise was the _____ and the white rat was the _____.
   a. CS; CR
   b. US; CS
   c. CS; US
   d. US; CR

3. In which of the following may classical conditioning play a role?
   a. emotional problems
   b. the body's immune response
   c. helping drug addicts
   d. all of the above

4. Shaping is a(n) _____ technique for _____ a behavior.
   a. operant; establishing
   b. operant; suppressing
   c. respondent; establishing
   d. respondent; suppressing

5. In Pavlov's studies of classical conditioning of a dog's salivary responses, spontaneous recovery occurred:
   a. during acquisition, when the CS was first paired with the US.
   b. during extinction, when the CS was first presented by itself.
   c. when the CS was reintroduced following extinction of the CR and a rest period.
   d. during discrimination training, when several conditioned stimuli were introduced.

6. For operant conditioning to be most effective, when should the reinforcers be presented in relation to the desired response?
   a. immediately before
   b. immediately after
   c. at the same time as
   d. at least a half hour before

7. In distinguishing between negative reinforcers and punishment, we note that:
   a. punishment, but not negative reinforcement, involves use of an aversive stimulus.
   b. in contrast to punishment, negative reinforcement decreases the likelihood of a response by the presentation of an aversive stimulus.
   c. in contrast to punishment, negative reinforcement increases the likelihood of a response by the presentation of an aversive stimulus.
   d. in contrast to punishment, negative reinforcement increases the likelihood of a response by the termination of an aversive stimulus.

8. The "piecework," or commission, method of payment is an example of which reinforcement schedule?
   a. fixed-interval
   b. variable-interval
   c. fixed-ratio
   d. variable-ratio

9. Putting on your coat when it is cold outside is a behavior that is maintained by:
   a. discrimination learning.
   b. punishment.
   c. negative reinforcement.
   d. classical conditioning.

10. On an intermittent reinforcement schedule, reinforcement is given:
    a. in very small amounts.
    b. randomly.
    c. for successive approximations of a desired behavior.
    d. only some of the time.

11. You teach your dog to fetch the paper by giving him a cookie each time he does so. This is an example of:
    a. operant conditioning.
    b. classical conditioning.
    c. conditioned reinforcement.
    d. partial reinforcement.

12. In promoting observational learning, the most effective models are those that we perceive as:
    a. similar to ourselves.
    b. respected and admired.
    c. successful.
    d. any of the above.

13. A cognitive map is a(n):
    a. mental representation of one's environment.
    b. sequence of thought processes leading from one idea to another.
    c. set of instructions detailing the most effective means of teaching a particular concept.
    d. biological predisposition to learn a particular skill.

14. After exploring a complicated maze for several days, a rat subsequently ran the maze with very few errors when food was placed in the goal box for the first time. This performance illustrates:
    a. classical conditioning.
    b. discrimination learning.
    c. observational learning.
    d. latent learning.

15. Leon's psychology instructor has scheduled an exam every third week of the term. Leon will probably study the most just before an exam and the least just after an exam. This is because the schedule of exams is reinforcing studying according to which schedule?
    a. fixed-ratio   c. fixed-interval
    b. variable-ratio   d. variable-interval

16. Operant conditioning is to _____ as classical conditioning is to _____ .
    a. Pavlov; Watson   c. Pavlov; Skinner
    b. Skinner; Bandura   d. Skinner; Pavlov

17. On-line testing systems and interactive software are applications of the operant conditioning principles of:
    a. shaping and immediate reinforcement.
    b. immediate reinforcement and punishment.
    c. shaping and primary reinforcement.
    d. continuous reinforcement and punishment.

18. Which of the following is the best example of a conditioned reinforcer?
    a. putting on a coat on a cold day
    b. relief from pain after the dentist stops drilling your teeth
    c. receiving a cool drink after washing your mother's car on a hot day
    d. receiving an approving nod from the boss for a job well done

19. Experiments on taste-aversion learning demonstrate that:
    a. for the conditioning of certain stimuli, the US need not immediately follow the CS.
    b. any perceivable stimulus can become a CS.

    c. all animals are biologically primed to associate illness with the taste of a tainted food.
    d. all of the above are true.

20. Regarding the impact of watching television violence on children, most researchers believe that:
    a. aggressive children simply prefer violent programs.
    b. television simply reflects, rather than contributes to, violent social trends.
    c. watching violence on television leads to aggressive behavior.
    d. there is only a weak correlation between exposure to violence and aggressive behavior.

True–False Items

Indicate whether each statement is true or false by placing *T* or *F* in the blank next to the item.

_____ 1. Operant conditioning involves behavior that is primarily reflexive.

_____ 2. The optimal interval between CS and US is about 15 seconds.

_____ 3. Negative reinforcement decreases the likelihood that a response will recur.

_____ 4. The learning of a new behavior proceeds most rapidly with continuous reinforcement.

_____ 5. As a rule, variable schedules of reinforcement produce more consistent rates of responding than fixed schedules.

_____ 6. Cognitive processes are of relatively little importance in learning.

_____ 7. Although punishment may be effective in suppressing behavior, it can have several undesirable side effects.

_____ 8. All animals, including rats and birds, are biologically predisposed to associate taste cues with sickness.

_____ 9. Whether the CS or US is presented first seems not to matter in terms of the ease of classical conditioning.

_____ 10. Spontaneous recovery refers to the tendency of extinguished behaviors to reappear suddenly.

_____ 11. Researchers have discovered brain neurons that fire when a person performs a task *or* when another person is observed performing the same task.

PSYCHOLOGY APPLIED

Answer these questions the day before an exam as a final check on your understanding of the chapter's terms and concepts.

Multiple-Choice Questions

1. You always rattle the box of dog biscuits before giving your dog a treat. As you do so, your dog salivates. Rattling the box is a(n) _____ ; your dog's salivation is a(n) _____ .
   a. CS; CR   c. US; CR
   b. CS; UR   d. US; UR

2. You are expecting an important letter in the mail. As the regular delivery time approaches you glance more and more frequently out the window, searching for the letter carrier. Your behavior in this situation typifies that associated with which schedule of reinforcement?
   a. fixed-ratio   c. fixed-interval
   b. variable-ratio   d. variable-interval

3. Jack finally takes out the garbage in order to get his father to stop pestering him. Jack's behavior is being influenced by:
   a. positive reinforcement.
   b. negative reinforcement.
   c. a primary reinforcer.
   d. punishment.

4. Mrs. Ramirez often tells her children that it is important to buckle their seat belts while riding in the car, but she rarely does so herself. Her children will probably learn to:
   a. use their seat belts and tell others it is important to do so.
   b. use their seat belts but not tell others it is important to do so.
   c. tell others it is important to use seat belts but rarely use them themselves.
   d. neither tell others that seat belts are important nor use them.

5. A pigeon can easily be taught to flap its wings in order to avoid shock but not for food reinforcement. According to the text, this is most likely so because:
   a. pigeons are biologically predisposed to flap their wings in order to escape aversive events and to use their beaks to obtain food.
   b. shock is a more motivating stimulus for birds than food is.
   c. hungry animals have difficulty delaying their eating long enough to learn *any* new skill.
   d. of all of the above reasons.

6. From a casino owner's viewpoint, which of the following jackpot-payout schedules would be the most desirable for reinforcing customer use of a slot machine?
   a. variable-ratio   c. variable-interval
   b. fixed-ratio   d. fixed-interval

7. After discovering that her usual route home was closed due to road repairs, Sharetta used her knowledge of the city and sense of direction to find an alternate route. This is an example of:
   a. latent learning.
   b. observational learning.
   c. shaping.
   d. using a cognitive map.

For questions 8–11, use the following information.
As a child, you were playing in the yard one day when a neighbor's cat wandered over. Your mother (who has a terrible fear of animals) screamed and snatched you into her arms. Her behavior caused you to cry. You now have a fear of cats.

8. Identify the CS.
   a. your mother's behavior c. the cat
   b. your crying   d. your fear today

9. Identify the US.
   a. your mother's behavior c. the cat
   b. your crying   d. your fear today

10. Identify the CR.
    a. your mother's behavior c. the cat
    b. your crying   d. your fear today

11. Identify the UR.
    a. your mother's behavior c. the cat
    b. your crying   d. your fear today

12. The manager of a manufacturing plant wishes to use positive reinforcement to increase the productivity of workers. Which of the following procedures would probably be the most effective?
    a. Deserving employees are given a general merit bonus at the end of each fiscal year.
    b. A productivity goal that seems attainable, yet is unrealistic, is set for each employee.
    c. Employees are given immediate bonuses for specific behaviors related to productivity.
    d. Employees who fail to meet standards of productivity receive pay cuts.

13. Bill once had a blue car that was in the shop more than it was out. Since then he will not even consider owning blue- or green-colored cars. Bill's aversion to green cars is an example of:
    a. discrimination.
    b. generalization.
    c. latent learning.
    d. extinction.

14. After watching coverage of the Olympics on television recently, Lynn and Susan have been staging their own "summer games." Which of the following best accounts for their behavior?
    a. classical conditioning   c. latent learning
    b. observational learning   d. shaping

15. Two groups of rats receive classical conditioning trials in which a tone and electric shock are presented. For Group 1 the electric shock always follows the tone. For Group 2 the tone and shock occur randomly. Which of the following is likely to result?
    a. The tone will become a CS for Group 1 but not for Group 2.
    b. The tone will become a CS for Group 2 but not for Group 1.
    c. The tone will become a CS for both groups.
    d. The tone will not become a CS for either group.

16. Last evening May-ling ate her first cheeseburger and french fries at an American fast-food restaurant. A few hours later she became ill. It can be expected that:
    a. May-ling will develop an aversion to the sight of a cheeseburger and french fries.
    b. May-ling will develop an aversion to the taste of a cheeseburger and french fries.
    c. May-ling will not associate her illness with the food she ate.
    d. May-ling will associate her sickness with something she experienced immediately before she became ill.

17. Reggie's mother tells him that he can watch TV after he cleans his room. Evidently, Reggie's mother is attempting to use _____ to increase room cleaning.
    a. operant conditioning
    b. secondary reinforcement
    c. positive reinforcement
    d. all of the above

18. Which of the following is an example of shaping?
    a. A dog learns to salivate at the sight of a box of dog biscuits.
    b. A new driver learns to stop at an intersection when the light changes to red.
    c. A parrot is rewarded first for making any sound, then for making a sound similar to "Laura," and then for "speaking" its owner's name.
    d. A psychology student reinforces a laboratory rat only occasionally, to make its behavior more resistant to extinction.

19. Lars, a shoe salesman, is paid every two weeks, whereas Tom receives a commission for each pair of shoes he sells. Evidently, Lars is paid on a _____ schedule of reinforcement, and Tom on a _____ schedule of reinforcement.
    a. fixed-ratio; fixed-interval
    b. continuous; intermittent
    c. fixed-interval; fixed-ratio
    d. variable-interval; variable-ratio

20. Nancy decided to take introductory psychology because she has always been interested in human behavior. Jack enrolled in the same course because he thought it would be easy. Nancy's behavior was motivated by _____ , Jack's by _____ .
    a. extrinsic motivation; intrinsic motivation
    b. intrinsic motivation; extrinsic motivation
    c. drives; incentives
    d. incentives; drives

Essay Question

Describe the best way for a pet owner to condition her dog to roll over. (Use the space below to list the points you want to make, and organize them. Then write the essay on a separate piece of paper.)

KEY TERMS

Writing Definitions

Using your own words, on a piece of paper write a brief definition or explanation of each of the following terms.

1. learning
2. associative learning
3. classical conditioning
4. behaviorism
5. unconditioned response (UR)
6. unconditioned stimulus (US)
7. conditioned response (CR)
8. conditioned stimulus (CS)
9. acquisition
10. extinction
11. spontaneous recovery
12. generalization
13. discrimination
14. operant conditioning
15. respondent behavior
16. operant behavior
17. law of effect
18. operant chamber (Skinner box)
19. shaping
20. reinforcer
21. positive reinforcement
22. negative reinforcement
23. primary reinforcers
24. conditioned reinforcers
25. continuous reinforcement
26. partial (intermittent) reinforcement
27. fixed-ratio schedule
28. variable-ratio schedule
29. fixed-interval schedule
30. variable-interval schedule
31. punishment
32. cognitive map
33. latent learning
34. intrinsic motivation
35. extrinsic motivation
36. observational learning
37. modeling
38. mirror neurons
39. prosocial behavior

Cross-Check

As you learned in the Prologue, reviewing and overlearning of material are important to the learning process. After you have written the definitions of the key terms in this chapter, you should complete the crossword puzzle to ensure that you can reverse the process—recognize the term, given the definition.

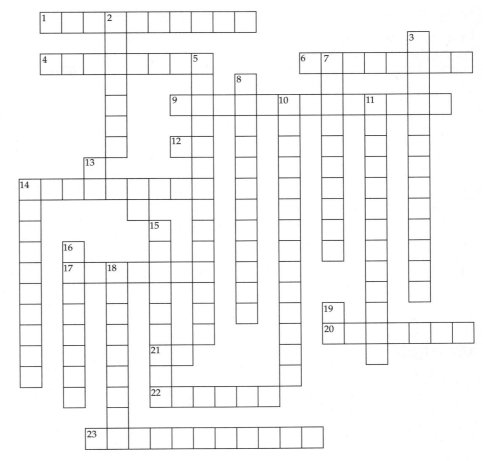

ACROSS

1. Behavior that occurs as an automatic response to a stimulus.
4. Relatively permanent change in behavior due to experience.
6. Reinforcer that, when removed after a response, strengthens the response.
9. Type of stimulus that naturally triggers an unconditioned response.
12. Unlearned, involuntary response.
14. Type of behavior that is positive and helpful.
17. Behavior that produces reinforcing or punishing stimuli.
20. Procedure that involves reinforcing successive approximations of a behavior.
21. Learned response to a previously neutral stimulus.
22. Learning that occurs in the absence of reinforcement but only becomes apparent when an incentive is introduced.
23. Initial stage of conditioning, in which a new response is established.

DOWN

2. Type of reinforcement in which responding is intermittently reinforced.
3. Schedule in which the first response following a set period of time is reinforced.
5. Tendency for stimuli similar to the original CS to evoke a CR.
7. This occurs when a response is no longer reinforced.
8. Mental picture of the environment
10. Responding differently to stimuli that signal whether a behavior will be reinforced.
11. Learning that involves watching and imitating others.

13. Stimulus that automatically triggers an unconditioned response.
14. The presentation of an aversive stimulus, which decreases the behavior it follows.
15. Type of learning also called Pavlovian conditioning.
16. The process of watching and then imitating a behavior.
18. Motivation to perform a behavior in order to obtain a reward or avoid a punishment.
19. Originally neutral stimulus that comes to trigger a conditioned response.

ANSWERS

Chapter Review

How Do We Learn?

1. learning
2. associate; associations; associative learning
3. classical
4. operant
5. observing

Classical Conditioning

1. Ivan Pavlov; John Watson; behaviorism
2. conditioned stimulus; unconditioned stimulus
3. unconditioned response
4. conditioned response
5. acquisition; one-half second
6. does not

Learning theorists consider classical conditioning to be adaptive because conditioned responses help organisms to prepare for good or bad events (unconditioned stimuli) that are about to occur.

7. survive; reproduce
8. can
9. extinction
10. spontaneous recovery
11. generalization
12. similar; discrimination
13. survival
14. cognition
15. predict; cognitive; expect
16. alcoholism
17. response; stimulus
18. sickness; would
19. biological; adapt; levels of analysis
20. adapt
21. objectively

Classical conditioning led to the discovery of general principles of learning that are the same for all species tested, including humans. Classical conditioning also provided an example to the young field of psychology of how complex, internal processes could be studied objectively. In addition, classical conditioning has proven to have many helpful applications to human health and well-being.

22. craving; cues
23. can

In Watson and Rayner's experiment, classical conditioning was used to condition fear of a rat in Albert, an 11-month-old infant. When Albert touched the white rat (neutral stimulus), a loud noise (unconditioned stimulus) was sounded. After several pairings of the rat with the noise, Albert began crying at the mere sight of the rat. The rat had become a conditioned stimulus, triggering a conditioned response of fear.

Operant Conditioning

1. neutral; automatic; does not
2. respondent
3. operant
4. law of effect; rewarded; recur
5. Skinner box (operant chamber)
6. shaping; approximations
7. concepts; discriminating
8. discriminative stimulus
9. reinforcer
10. positive reinforcer
11. negative reinforcer
12. primary reinforcers; conditioned reinforcers
13. more
14. is; delayed; drug; unprotected sex
15. continuous reinforcement; rapid; rapid
16. partial (intermittent); slower; very
17. fixed-ratio
18. variable-ratio
19. fixed-interval; checking the mail as delivery time approaches
20. variable-interval

Following reinforcement on a fixed-interval schedule, there is a pause in responding and then an increasing rate of response as time for the next reinforcement draws near. On a fixed-ratio schedule there also is a post-reinforcement pause, followed, however, by a return to a consistent, high rate of response. Both kinds of variable schedules produce steadier rates of response, without the pauses associated with fixed schedules. In general, schedules linked to responses produce higher response rates and variable schedules produce more consistent responding than the related fixed schedules.

21. punishment; positive punishment; negative punishment
22. suppressed
23. fear; the person who administered it
24. aggressiveness
25. cognitive
26. cognitive map
27. latent learning
28. intrinsic motivation; extrinsic motivation
29. is

30. reinforcer; shape; food
31. adaptive; instinctive drift
32. external; internal thoughts; feelings
33. operant; behavior
34. dehumanized; freedom; control
35. shaping; testing; interactive; Web; athletic
36. more; achievable; more
37. costs; benefits
38. **a.** State your goal.

    b. Monitor the behavior (when and where it occurs).

    c. Reinforce the desired behavior.

    d. Reduce the incentives to perform the undesirable behavior.
39. associative learning
40. acquisition; extinction; spontaneous recovery; generalization; discrimination
41. cognitive; biological
42. stimuli; control; automatically
43. operant behaviors; consequences

Learning by Observation

1. modeling; observational learning; occurs
2. mirror; frontal; observational; observe other monkeys performing the same task; has
3. 9 months; 14 months
4. Bandura
5. more
6. rewards; punishments
7. abusive; aggressive; genetic
8. prosocial
9. similar; successful; admirable; consistent
10. watching television
11. violent
12. link
13. aggression; crime
14. causation; does
15. imitation; desensitize

Progress Test 1

Multiple-Choice Questions

1. **c.** is the answer. (p. 313)
   a. This answer is incorrect because it simply de-

scribes any behavior that is automatic rather than being triggered by a specific stimulus.
   b. This answer is too general, since behaviors can change for reasons other than learning.
   d. Respondently conditioned behavior also satisfies the criteria of our definition of learning.

2. **b.** is the answer. (p. 327)
   a. & c. Classical conditioning is associated with Pavlov; respondent conditioning is another name for classical conditioning.
   d. Observational learning is most closely associated with Bandura.

3. **c.** is the answer. Meat automatically triggers the response of salivation and is therefore an unconditioned stimulus. (p. 317)
   a. A conditioned stimulus acquires its response-triggering powers through learning. A dog does not learn to salivate to meat.
   b. & d. Responses are behaviors triggered in the organism, in this case the dog's salivation. The meat is a stimulus.

4. **b.** is the answer. Prior to its pairing with meat (the US), the tone did not trigger salivation and was therefore a neutral stimulus. Afterward, the tone triggered salivation (the CR) and was therefore a conditioned stimulus (CS). (pp. 316–317)
   c. & d. Unconditioned stimuli, such as meat, innately trigger responding. Pavlov's dogs had to learn to associate the tone with the food.

5. **d.** is the answer. In learning to distinguish between the conditioned stimulus and another, similar stimulus, the monkey has received training in discrimination. (p. 320)
   a. In extinction training, a stimulus and/or response is allowed to go unreinforced.
   b. Generalization training involves responding to stimuli similar to the conditioned stimulus; here the monkey is being trained not to respond to a similar stimulus.
   c. This cannot be classical conditioning since the monkey is acting in order to obtain a reward. Thus, this is an example of operant conditioning.

6. **b.** is the answer. A continuous association will naturally be easier to learn than one that occurs on only some occasions, so learning is most rapid with continuous reinforcement. Yet, once the continuous association is no longer there, as in extinction training, extinction will occur more rapidly than it would have had the organism not always experienced reinforcement. (p. 331)

7. **b.** is the answer. (pp. 321, 334)
   c. & d. The text does not present evidence regarding the relative importance of cognitive processes in classical and operant conditioning.

8. **b.** is the answer. (p. 332)
   a. With fixed-ratio schedules, there is a pause following each reinforcement.
   c. & d. Because reinforcement is not contingent on the rate of response, interval schedules, especially fixed-interval schedules, produce lower response rates than ratio schedules.

9. **b.** is the answer. (p. 329)
   a. Positive reinforcement involves presenting a favorable stimulus following a response.
   c. Punishment involves presenting an unpleasant stimulus following a response.
   d. In extinction, a previously reinforced response is no longer followed by reinforcement. In this situation, a response causes a stimulus to be terminated or removed.

10. **c.** is the answer. In this situation, the CR will decline, a phenomenon known as extinction. (p. 319)
    a. Generalization occurs when the subject makes a CR to stimuli similar to the original CS.
    b. Discrimination is when the subject does not make a CR to stimuli other than the original CS.
    d. An aversion is a CR to a CS that has been associated with an unpleasant US, such as shock or a nausea-producing drug.

11. **c.** is the answer. (p. 326)
    a. In *operant* conditioning the responses operate on the environment.
    b. In *classical* conditioning responses are triggered by preceding stimuli.
    d. In *classical* conditioning responses are reflexive.

12. **c.** is the answer. (pp. 321–322)
    a. & d. These studies also indicated that rats are biologically predisposed to associate visual and auditory stimuli, but not taste, with shock.
    b. Rats are biologically predisposed to associate taste with sickness.

13. **d.** is the answer. A dog does not have to learn to salivate to food; therefore, this response is unconditioned. (p. 317)
    a. & c. Salivation is a response, not a stimulus.

14. **b.** is the answer. (pp. 341, 343)
    a. Skinner is best known for studies of *operant* learning. Moreover, there is no such thing as secondary learning.
    c. Pavlov is best known for classical conditioning.
    d. Watson is best known as an early proponent of behaviorism.

15. **d.** is the answer. (pp. 332–333)

16. **c.** is the answer. (p. 321)
    a., b., & d. Rescorla and Wagner's research did not address the importance of these factors in classical conditioning.

17. **d.** is the answer. a. is an example of positive reinforcement, b. is an example of negative reinforcement, and c. is an example of conditioned reinforcement. (p. 329)

18. **d.** is the answer. (p. 314)

19. **b.** is the answer. (p. 318)
    a. Backward conditioning, in which the US precedes the CS, is ineffective.
    c. This interval is longer than is optimum for the most rapid acquisition of a CS-US association.
    d. Simultaneous presentation of CS and US is ineffective because it does not permit the subject to anticipate the US.

20. **a.** is the answer. (p. 342)

Matching Items

1. e (p. 329)
2. h (p. 320)
3. f (p. 329)
4. g (p. 330)
5. i (p. 330)
6. k (p. 332)
7. m (p. 335)
8. a (p. 328)
9. c (p. 319)
10. b (p. 332)
11. d (p. 334)
12. j (p. 330)
13. l (p. 335)

Progress Test 2

Multiple-Choice Questions

1. **c.** is the answer. (p. 319)

2. **b.** is the answer. The loud noise automatically triggered Albert's fear and therefore functioned as a US. After being associated with the US, the white rat acquired the power to trigger fear and thus became a CS. (p. 324)

3. **d.** is the answer. (p. 324)

4. **a.** is the answer. Shaping works on operant behaviors by reinforcing successive approximations to a desired goal. (p. 328)

5. **c.** is the answer. (p. 319)
   a., b., & d. Spontaneous recovery occurs after a CR has been extinguished, and in the absence of the US. The situations described here all involve the continued presentation of the US and, therefore, the further strengthening of the CR.

6. **b.** is the answer. (p. 330)
   a., c., & d. Reinforcement that is delayed, presented before a response, or at the same time as a response does not always increase the response's frequency of occurrence.

7. **d.** is the answer. (pp. 329, 332)
   a. Both involve an aversive stimulus.
   b. All reinforcers, including negative reinforcers, increase the likelihood of a response.

c. In negative reinforcement, an aversive stimulus is withdrawn following a desirable response.

8. **c.** is the answer. Payment is given after a fixed number of pieces have been completed. (p. 331)
a. & b. Interval schedules reinforce according to the passage of time, not the amount of work accomplished.
d. Fortunately for those working on commission, the work ratio is fixed and therefore predictable.

9. **c.** is the answer. By learning to put on your coat before going outside, you have learned to reduce the aversive stimulus of the cold. (p. 329)
a. Discrimination learning involves learning to make a response in the presence of the appropriate stimulus and not other stimuli.
b. Punishment is the suppression of an undesirable response by the presentation of an aversive stimulus.
d. Putting on a coat is a response that operates on the environment. Therefore, this is an example of operant, not classical, conditioning.

10. **d.** is the answer. (p. 331)
a. Intermittent reinforcement refers to the ratio of responses to reinforcers, not the overall quantity of reinforcement delivered.
b. Unlike intermittent reinforcement, in which the delivery of reinforcement is contingent on responding, random reinforcement is delivered independently of the subject's behavior.
c. This defines the technique of shaping, not intermittent reinforcement.

11. **a.** is the answer. You are teaching your dog by rewarding him when he produces the desired behavior. (p. 326)
b. This is not classical conditioning because the cookie is a primary reinforcer presented after the operant behavior of the dog fetching the paper.
c. Food is a primary reinforcer; it satisfies an innate need.
d. Rewarding your dog each time he fetches the paper is continuous reinforcement.

12. **d.** is the answer. (p. 343)

13. **a.** is the answer. (p. 334)

14. **d.** is the answer. The rat had learned the maze but did not display this learning until reinforcement became available. (p. 334)
a. Negotiating a maze is clearly operant behavior.
b. This example does not involve learning to distinguish between stimuli.
c. This is not observational learning because the rat has no one to observe!

15. **c.** is the answer. Because reinforcement (earning a good grade on the exam) is available according to the passage of time, studying is reinforced on an interval schedule. Because the interval between exams is constant, this is an example of a fixed-interval schedule. (p. 332)

16. **d.** is the answer. (pp. 315, 327)
a. Pavlov and Watson are both associated with classical conditioning.
b. Skinner is associated with operant conditioning, and Bandura is associated with observational learning.

17. **a.** is the answer. On-line testing systems apply operant principles such as reinforcement, immediate feedback, and shaping to the teaching of new skills. (p. 337)
b. & d. On-line testing systems provide immediate, and continuous, reinforcement for correct responses, but do not use aversive control procedures such as punishment.
c. On-line testing systems are based on feedback for correct responses; this feedback constitutes conditioned, rather than primary, reinforcement.

18. **d.** is the answer. An approving nod from the boss is a conditioned reinforcer in that it doesn't satisfy an innate need but has become linked with desirable consequences. Cessation of cold, cessation of pain, and a drink are all primary reinforcers, which meet innate needs. (p. 330)

19. **a.** is the answer. Taste-aversion experiments demonstrate conditioning even with CS-US intervals as long as several hours. (pp. 321–322)
b. Despite being perceivable, a visual or auditory stimulus cannot become a CS for illness in some animals, such as rats.
c. Some animals, such as birds, are biologically primed to associate the *appearance* of food with illness.

20. **c.** is the answer. (p. 345)

True–False Items

1. F (p. 326)	**5.** T (pp. 331, 332)	**9.** F (p. 318)
2. F (p. 318)	**6.** F (pp. 321, 334)	**10.** T (p. 319)
3. F (p. 329)	**7.** T (pp. 332–333)	**11.** T (p. 341)
4. T (p. 330)	**8.** F (pp. 321–322)	

Psychology Applied

Multiple-Choice Questions

1. **a.** is the answer. Your dog had to learn to associate the rattling sound with the food. Rattling is therefore a conditioned, or learned, stimulus, and salivation in response to this rattling is a learned, or conditioned, response. (p. 317)

2. **c.** is the answer. Reinforcement (the letter) comes after a fixed interval, and as the likely end of the interval approaches, your behavior (glancing out the window) becomes more frequent. (p. 332)
   a. & b. These answers are incorrect because with ratio schedules, reinforcement is contingent upon the number of responses rather than on the passage of time.
   d. Assuming that the mail is delivered at about the same time each day, the interval is fixed rather than variable. Your behavior reflects this, since you glance out the window more often as the delivery time approaches.

3. **b.** is the answer. By taking out the garbage, Jack terminates an aversive stimulus—his father's nagging. (p. 329)
   a. Positive reinforcement would involve a desirable stimulus that increases the likelihood of the response that preceded it.
   c. This answer would have been correct if Jack's father had rewarded Jack for taking out the garbage by providing his favorite food.
   d. Punishment suppresses behavior; Jack is behaving in order to obtain reinforcement.

4. **c.** is the answer. Studies indicate that when a model says one thing but does another, subjects do the same and learn not to practice what they preach. (p. 344)

5. **a.** is the answer. As in this example, conditioning must be consistent with the particular organism's biological predispositions. (pp. 335–336)
   b. Some behaviors, but certainly not all, are acquired more rapidly than others when shock is used as negative reinforcement.
   c. Pigeons are able to acquire many new behaviors when food is used as reinforcement.

6. **a.** is the answer. Ratio schedules maintain higher rates of responding—gambling in this example—than do interval schedules. Furthermore, variable schedules are not associated with the pause in responding following reinforcement that is typical of fixed schedules. The slot machine would therefore be used more often, and more consistently, if jackpots were scheduled according to a variable-ratio schedule. (p. 332)

7. **d.** is the answer. Sharetta is guided by her mental representation of the city, or cognitive map. (p. 334)
   a. Latent learning, or learning in the absence of reinforcement that is demonstrated when reinforcement becomes available, has no direct relevance to the example.
   b. Observational learning refers to learning from watching others.
   c. Shaping is the technique of reinforcing successive approximations of a desired behavior.

8. **c.** is the answer. Because the cat was associated with your mother's scream, it triggered a fear response, and is thus the CS. (p. 317)

9. **a.** is the answer. Your mother's scream and evident fear, which naturally caused you to cry, was the US. (p. 317)

10. **d.** is the answer. Your fear of cats is the CR. An acquired fear is always a conditioned response. (p. 317)

11. **b.** is the answer. Your crying, automatically triggered by your mother's scream and fear, was the UR. (p. 317)

12. **c.** is the answer. (p. 337)
    a. Positive reinforcement is most effective in boosting productivity in the workplace when specific behavior, rather than vaguely defined general merit, is rewarded. Also, immediate reinforcement is much more effective than the delayed reinforcement described in a.
    b. Positive reinforcement is most effective in boosting productivity when performance goals are achievable, rather than unrealistic.
    d. The text does not specifically discuss the use of punishment in the workplace. However, it makes the general point that although punishment may temporarily suppress unwanted behavior, it does not guide one toward more desirable behavior. Therefore, workers who receive pay cuts for poor performance may learn nothing about how to improve their productivity.

13. **b.** is the answer. Not only is Bill extending a learned aversion to a specific blue car to all blue cars but also to cars that are green. (p. 320)
    a. Whereas discrimination involves responding only to a particular stimulus, Bill is extending his aversive response to other stimuli (green cars) as well.
    c. Latent learning is learning that becomes apparent only after reinforcement becomes available.
    d. Extinction is the weakening of the CR when the CS is no longer followed by the US.

14. **b.** is the answer. The girls are imitating behavior they have observed and admired. (p. 341)

 a. Because these behaviors are clearly willful rather than involuntary, classical conditioning plays no role.

 c. Latent learning plays no role in this example.

 d. Shaping is a procedure for teaching the acquisition of a new response by reinforcing successive approximations of the behavior.

15. **a.** is the answer. Classical conditioning proceeds most effectively when the CS and US are reliably paired and therefore appear predictably associated. Only for Group 1 is this likely to be true. (p. 318)

16. **b.** is the answer. (p. 322)

 a., c., & d. Taste-aversion research demonstrates that humans and some other animals, such as rats, are biologically primed to associate illness with the taste of tainted food, rather than with other cues, such as the food's appearance. Moreover, taste aversions can be acquired even when the interval between the CS and the illness is several hours.

17. **d.** is the answer. By making a more preferred activity (watching TV) contingent on a less preferred activity (room cleaning), Reggie's mother is employing the operant conditioning technique of positive reinforcement. (pp. 329, 330)

18. **c.** is the answer. The parrot is reinforced for making successive approximations of a goal behavior. This defines shaping. (p. 328)

 a. Shaping is an operant conditioning procedure; salivation at the sight of dog biscuits is a classically conditioned response.

 b. Shaping involves the systematic reinforcement of successive approximations of a more complex behavior. In this example there is no indication that the response of stopping at the intersection involved the gradual acquisition of simpler behaviors.

 d. This is an example of the partial reinforcement of an established response, rather than the shaping of a new response.

19. **c.** is the answer. Whereas Lars is paid (reinforced) after a fixed period of time (fixed-interval), Tom is reinforced for each sale (fixed-ratio) he makes. (pp. 331–332)

20. **b.** is the answer. Wanting to do something for its own sake is intrinsic motivation; wanting to do something for a reward (in this case, presumably, a high grade) is extrinsic motivation. (p. 335)

 a. The opposite is true. Nancy was motivated to take the course for its own sake, whereas Jack was evidently motivated by the likelihood of a reward in the form of a good grade.

 c. & d. A good grade, such as the one Jack is expecting, is an incentive. Drives, however, are aroused states that result from physical deprivation; they are not involved in this example.

Essay Question

The first step in shaping an operant response, such as rolling over, is to find an effective reinforcer. Some sort of biscuit or dog treat is favored by animal trainers. This primary reinforcement should be accompanied by effusive praise (secondary reinforcement) whenever the dog makes a successful response.

Rolling over (the goal response) should be divided into a series of simple approximations, the first of which is a response, such as lying down on command, that is already in the dog's repertoire. This response should be reinforced several times. The next step is to issue a command, such as "Roll over," and withhold reinforcement until the dog (usually out of frustration) makes a closer approximation (such as rotating slightly in one direction). Following this example, the trainer should gradually require closer and closer approximations until the goal response is attained. When the new response has been established, the trainer should switch from continuous to partial reinforcement, in order to strengthen the skill.

Key Terms

Writing Definitions

1. **Learning** is any relatively permanent change in an organism's behavior due to experience. (p. 313)

2. In **associative learning**, organisms learn that certain events occur together. Two variations of associative learning are classical conditioning and operant conditioning. (p. 314)

3. Also known as Pavlovian conditioning, **classical conditioning** is a type of learning in which a neutral stimulus becomes capable of triggering a conditioned response after having become associated with an unconditioned stimulus. (p. 315)

4. **Behaviorism** is the view that psychology should be an objective science that studies only observable behaviors without reference to mental processes. (p. 316)

 Example: Because he was an early advocate of the study of observable behavior, John Watson is often called the father of behaviorism.

5. In classical conditioning, the **unconditioned response (UR)** is the unlearned, involuntary response to the unconditioned stimulus. (p. 317)

6. In classical conditioning, the **unconditioned stimulus (US)** is the stimulus that naturally and automatically triggers the reflexive unconditioned response. (p. 317)

7. In classical conditioning, the **conditioned response (CR)** is the learned response to a previously neutral conditioned stimulus, which results from the acquired association between the CS and US. (p. 317)

8. In classical conditioning, the **conditioned stimulus (CS)** is an originally neutral stimulus that comes to trigger a CR after association with an unconditioned stimulus. (p. 317)

9. In a learning experiment, **acquisition** refers to the initial stage of conditioning in which the new response is established and gradually strengthened. In operant conditioning, it is the strengthening of a reinforced response. (p. 318)

10. **Extinction** refers to the weakening of a CR when the CS is no longer followed by the US; in operant conditioning extinction occurs when a response is no longer reinforced. (p. 319)

11. **Spontaneous recovery** is the reappearance of an extinguished CR after a rest period. (p. 319)

12. **Generalization** refers to the tendency, once a response has been conditioned, for stimuli similar to the original CS to evoke a CR. (p. 320)

13. **Discrimination** in classical conditioning refers to the ability to distinguish the CS from similar stimuli that do not signal a US. In operant conditioning, it refers to responding differently to stimuli that signal a behavior will be reinforced or will not be reinforced. (p. 320)

14. **Operant conditioning** is a type of learning in which behavior is strengthened if followed by a reinforcer or diminished if followed by a punisher. (p. 326)

    Example: Unlike classical conditioning, which works on automatic behaviors, **operant conditioning** works on behaviors that operate on the environment.

15. **Respondent behavior** is that which occurs as an automatic response to some stimulus. (p. 326)

    Example: In classical conditioning, conditioned and unconditioned responses are examples of **respondent behavior** in that they are automatic responses triggered by specific stimuli.

16. **Operant behavior** is behavior that operates on the environment, producing consequences. (p. 326)

17. E. L. Thorndike proposed the **law of effect**, which states that behaviors followed by favorable consequences are likely to recur, and that behaviors followed by unfavorable consequences become less likely. (p. 327)

18. An **operant chamber** (*Skinner box*) is an experimental chamber for the operant conditioning of an animal such as a pigeon or rat. The controlled environment enables the investigator to present visual or auditory stimuli, deliver reinforcement or punishment, and precisely measure simple responses such as bar presses or key pecking. (p. 327)

19. **Shaping** is the operant conditioning procedure for establishing a new response by reinforcing successive approximations of the desired behavior. (p. 328)

20. In operant conditioning, a **reinforcer** is any event that strengthens the behavior it follows. (p. 329)

21. In operant conditioning, **positive reinforcement** strengthens a response by *presenting* a typically pleasurable stimulus after that response. (p. 329)

22. In operant conditioning, **negative reinforcement** strengthens a response by *removing* an aversive stimulus after that response. (p. 329)

23. The powers of **primary reinforcers** are inborn and do not depend on learning. (p. 330)

24. **Conditioned reinforcers** are stimuli that acquire their reinforcing power through their association with primary reinforcers. (p. 330)

25. **Continuous reinforcement** is the operant procedure of reinforcing the desired response every time it occurs. In promoting the acquisition of a new response it is best to use continuous reinforcement. (p. 330)

26. **Partial (intermittent) reinforcement** is the operant procedure of reinforcing a response intermittently. A response that has been partially reinforced is much more resistant to extinction than one that has been continuously reinforced. (p. 331)

27. In operant conditioning, a **fixed-ratio schedule** is one in which reinforcement is presented after a set number of responses. (p. 331)

    Example: Continuous reinforcement is a special kind of **fixed-ratio schedule**: Reinforcement is presented after *each* response, so the ratio of reinforcements to responses is one to one.

28. In operant conditioning, a **variable-ratio schedule** is one in which reinforcement is presented after a varying number of responses. (p. 332)

29. In operant conditioning, a **fixed-interval schedule** is one in which a response is reinforced after a specified time has elapsed. (p. 332)

30. In operant conditioning, a **variable-interval schedule** is one in which responses are reinforced after varying intervals of time. (p. 332)

31. In operant conditioning, **punishment** is the presentation of an aversive stimulus, such as shock, which decreases the behavior it follows. (p. 332)

    Memory aid: People often confuse negative reinforcement and **punishment**. The former strengthens behavior, while the latter weakens it.

32. A **cognitive map** is a mental picture of one's environment. (p. 334)

33. **Latent learning** is learning that occurs in the absence of reinforcement but only becomes apparent when there is an incentive to demonstrate it. (p. 334)

34. **Intrinsic motivation** is the desire to perform a behavior for its own sake, rather than for some external reason, and to be effective. (p. 335)

    Memory aid: Intrinsic means "internal": A person who is **intrinsically motivated** is motivated from within.

35. **Extrinsic motivation** is the desire to perform a behavior in order to obtain a reward or avoid a punishment. (p. 335)

    Memory aid: Extrinsic means "external": A person who is extrinsically motivated is motivated by some outside factor.

36. **Observational learning** is learning by watching and imitating the behavior of others. (p. 341)

37. **Modeling** is the process of watching and then imitating a specific behavior and is thus an important means through which observational learning occurs. (p. 341)

38. Found in the brain's frontal lobe, **mirror neurons** may be the neural basis for observational learning. These neurons generate impulses when certain actions are performed or when another individual who performs those actions is observed. (p. 341)

39. The opposite of antisocial behavior, **prosocial behavior** is positive, helpful, and constructive and is subject to the same principles of observational learning as is undesirable behavior, such as aggression. (p. 343)

Cross-Check

ACROSS	DOWN
1. respondent	2. partial
4. learning	3. fixed interval
6. negative	5. generalization
9. unconditioned	7. extinction
12. UR	8. cognitive map
14. prosocial	10. discrimination
17. operant	11. observational
20. shaping	13. US
21. CR	14. punishment
22. latent	15. classical
23. acquisition	16. modeling
	18. extrinsic
	19. CS

FOCUS ON VOCABULARY AND LANGUAGE

How Do We Learn?

Page 313: Learning breeds hope. The fact that we can change and adapt as a result of experience (*learn*) in so many different areas gives rise to optimism (*breeds hope*) about our future prospects.

*Page 314: . . . watching a TV character get *mugged* . . .* To be mugged means to be attacked, (sometimes) beaten, and robbed. This example shows how associations are formed between events, such as between the sounds that precede an attack and the *mugging* itself. In movies and on TV, a certain type of music is often played before a frightening event or scene. After a few such associations, the music itself can elicit fear before you actually see the frightening or scary event. This is an example of classical conditioning.

Page 314: A clever Japanese *rancher* reportedly *herds* cattle by outfitting them with electronic *pagers*, which he calls from his cell phone. In this example of conditioning, the cattle farmer (*rancher*) has trained his animals (steers or cattle) to gather together and move (*he herds them*) to the feeding station (*food trough*). They have learned to associate the sound of the tone (*the beep*) made by the signaling device (*electronic pager*) with the delivery of food (classical conditioning), and they have also learned that moving fast (*hustling*) to the food container (*trough*) is followed by the good feeling of satiating their hunger (operant conditioning).

Classical Conditioning

Page 315: For many people, the name Ivan Pavlov (1849–1936) rings a bell. Myers is making a little joke here. A common expression when hearing something familiar but vague is to say, *"That rings a bell."* Pavlov's name is familiar to many people, who may also be vaguely aware that his research involved dogs and ringing bells (classical conditioning).

Page 316: . . . what the dog was thinking and feeling as it *drooled.* . . . To *drool* means to salivate or produce spit. When food (US) is placed in a dog's mouth, the dog will automatically salivate or *drool* (UR). If a tone (CS) is sounded before (or precedes) the US over a number of trials, then the CS alone (the tone) will be able to elicit salivation (CR). Pavlov decided that the dog's internal mental state (thinking and feeling) was not important in reaching an understanding of fundamental learning principles, and that focusing attention on cognitive processes only led to futile arguments (*fruitless debates*).

Page 318: (margin note): If the *aroma* of cake baking *sets your mouth to watering*, what is the US? The CS? The CR? When you bake a cake in the oven, there is a lovely smell (*aroma*) which makes you salivate or drool (*sets your mouth to watering*). This is an example of classical conditioning: the taste of the cake in your mouth is the US (this automatically produces saliva, the UR), the aroma is the CS, and, because of its past associations with the US, it can now, by itself, elicit saliva (the CR).

Page 314: Moreover, the male quail developed a preference for their cage's *red-light district.* Traditionally, a red lamp hung in the window identified the house as a brothel, and the area of town populated by many brothels became known as the *red-light district.* In Domjan's experiments with male quail a red light (CS) was used to signal the arrival of a receptive female quail (US), which elicited sexual arousal (UR). Eventually, the red light (CS) alone elicited sexual arousal (CR), and the male quail appeared to develop a general liking (*preference*) for the cage with the red light (*the red-light district*).

Page 319: After *breaking up* with his *fire-breathing heartthrob,* Tirrell also experienced extinction and spontaneous recovery. He recalls that "the smell of onion breath (CS), no longer paired with the kissing (US), lost its ability to *shiver my timbers.*" This paragraph describes the end of the relationship (*breaking up*) with his girlfriend (*heartthrob*) who loved to eat onions and thus had hot, smelly breath (*fire-breathing*). The repeated smell of onions or onion breath (CS) without the US (kissing) resulted in extinction of his conditioned aroused state (CR), and, consequently, the CS lost its ability to get him excited (*shiver his timbers*). He later experienced spontaneous recovery (the extinguished CR

returned briefly) when he smelled onion breath once more. [The idiom "shiver my timbers" has no simple explanation; it may be an old expression dating back to the days of wooden (*timbered*) sailing ships that would tremble or shiver in a storm, or alternatively, it may have been used in the game of cricket to describe what happens when the cricket ball shakes and scatters (*shivers*) the wooden wicket and stumps (*timbers*).]

Page 320: Confronted by a pit bull, *your heart may race;* confronted by a golden retriever, it probably will not. Pit bulls are dogs (*not cattle*) that are generally perceived as aggressive and potentially dangerous; golden retrievers are dogs that are usually gentle and friendly. Thus, when you encounter a pit bull, you may experience physiological arousal (*your heart may race*) and you may experience fear, but the sight of a golden retriever will not likely cause the same reaction. To be able to tell the difference (*discriminate*) between two stimuli (in this case, two types of dogs) is an adaptive ability that has obvious survival value

Page 321: . . . *willy-nilly* . . . This means without any forethought, intention, or purpose—at random. An organism does not randomly (*willy-nilly*) form associations. The associations have to be meaningful; the CS needs to have informational value and be able to reliably predict the occurrence of the US.

Page 321: So, even in classical conditioning, it is, especially with humans, not only the simple CS–US association but also *the thought that counts.* The expression "it's the thought that counts" recognizes that a person's intentions and motivations (*thoughts*) are just as important as the actual behavior. Myers is making the point that cognitions (*thoughts, perceptions, expectation*) are now viewed as being critically important in the process of learning through classical conditioning.

Page 323: But if we *see further* than Pavlov did, it is because we *stand on his shoulders.* This phrase is not to be taken literally; it simply means that we now know more than Pavlov did (*we see further*) because we can build and expand on his great work (*stand on his shoulders*).

Page 324: Former *crack* cocaine users often feel a *craving* when they again encounter cues (people, places) associated with previous *highs.* Crack cocaine users are drug addicts who use a drug that is a synthetic, but very potent, form of cocaine (*crack*). For those who are attempting abstinence, the strong desire (*craving*) for the drug may be a classically conditioned response (CR) to the sight or presence of people or places (CSs). These people or places (CSs) were associated with taking the drug (US) which produced the UR (euphoric feelings or *highs*). Drug addicts are therefore advised to avoid (steer clear of) settings, equipment (*paraphernalia*), or people related to previous drug-taking activity.

Page 324: . . . *legendary significance* . . . Watson and Rayner's work with Little Albert was the first investigation of how phobias or irrational fears might develop through the process of classical conditioning. Thus, the story was passed on to future generations of psychologists (it became a legend) and influenced their research.

Operant Conditioning

Page 327: . . . *to pull habits out of a rat.* David Myers is having fun playing with the English language here. The expression "to pull rabbits out of a hat" refers to stage magicians who are able to extract rabbits from a seemingly empty hat. Can you see the way Myers has twisted this expression? Both classical and operant conditioning involve teaching new habits to various organisms, including rats. Following classical conditioning the CS triggers a new response from the animal (i.e., the CS *"pulls a habit out of the rat"*), or the sight of the lever may elicit the habit of lever pressing (operant conditioning).

Page 328: With training, pigeons have even been taught to discriminate between *Bach's music and Stravinsky's.* Bach and Stravinsky were composers whose styles of musical composition were quite different. Through shaping (rewarding behaviors that are closer and closer to the target or desired response), psychologists have been able to train pigeons to discriminate (or choose) between the two musical sounds. For example, pigeons may be rewarded for pecking a disk when Bach is playing and for refraining from pecking when Stravinsky is playing. They can be trained to discriminate, or tell the difference, between the two.

Page 329: Or consider a teacher who pastes *gold stars on a wall chart* after the names of children scoring 100 percent on spelling tests. Teachers often use extrinsic rewards such as small, bright stickers (*gold stars*) and typically display them on a classroom bulletin board (*pastes them on a wall chart*) for, say, the very best spellers in the class. Unfortunately, if only the top few students (*academic all-stars*) are recognized in this way, the rest of the students may lose motivation because, even if they improve their spelling and work very hard (but still don't get 100%), they don't get any reinforcers. Myers recommends a shaping

procedure that rewards even small improvements and recognizes the child for making the effort to do better and better.

Page 329: Pushing the *snooze button* silences the annoying alarm. When your radio alarm goes off in the morning, you may press the switch (*snooze button*) which turns off the irritating tone for a brief period of time. The ensuing quiet period, which may allow you to go back to sleep for a while (*snooze*), and the absence of the buzzer are negative reinforcers for pushing the snooze button. (Your button-pushing behavior has been strengthened because it removed an aversive event, the alarm.) Likewise, a regular smoker (*nicotine addict*) may be negatively reinforced for inhaling tobacco smoke (*dragging on a cigarette*) because doing so diminishes the pain (*pangs*) associated with going without the drug.

Page 329 . . . *goofing off and getting a bad exam grade* . . . Students may score poorly on an exam because they were doing something unproductive, such as watching TV, instead of studying (they were *goofing off*). As a consequence, they may decide to change their behavior and work hard to avoid further exam anxiety and the unpleasant possibility of getting a low grade. The new behavior may be strengthened if it avoids the aversive consequences of anxiety (negative reinforcement); in addition, getting a good score on the exam can positively reinforce good study habits. Remember, reinforcers of either kind (positive or negative) always strengthen behavior.

Page 330: . . . the *kick* that often comes within seconds [after taking drugs] . . . The term *kick* as used here refers to a jolt of pleasure (not as in "to kick the ball"). Myers is making the point that behaviors such as smoking, drinking, and drug taking, in general, are followed by some immediate pleasurable consequence, which controls the behavior more than does the delayed consequence (e.g., lung cancer, memory loss, cognitive impairment, or even a headache the next day [*a hangover in the morning*], etc.).

Page 331: A salesperson does not make a sale with every *pitch*, nor does an *angler* get a bite with every *cast*. The *pitch* referred to here is the sales talk (*pitch*) that the salesperson uses to promote the product or service. The bite the angler (fisherman) does not get refers to the fact that throwing out the line (*casting*) does not always result in fish biting the bait. The idea is that much of our behavior is not continuously reinforced but persists, nevertheless, by being partially reinforced (you make a sale or catch a fish only once in a while despite many responses). Thus, intermittent rewards encourage the expectation of future reinforcement (*hope springs eternal*) and create greater resistance to extinction of the behavior compared to a continuous schedule.

Page 331: . . . paid on a piecework basis . . . This refers to situations in which someone is paid for the number of items produced (and not by the hour or the week). A worker gets paid only if he or she produces, so the number of responses (i.e., the number of items produced) is reinforced on a **fixed-ratio schedule.** An example would be factory worker sewing shirts who would be paid five dollars for each finished shirt (*piecework*). The more shirts she makes, the more money she earns, and thus the rate of responding is usually high.

Page 332: . . . fly fishing . . . This refers to a style of fishing in which artificial insects, such as flies, are used as bait to catch the fish. People who fly fish are reinforced only once in a while despite making many responses. This variable-ratio schedule of reinforcement makes the target behavior very persistent and hard to suppress (the behavior is very resistant to extinction) because ultimately the more responding, the more reinforcement.

Page 332: . . . a choppy stop-start pattern . . . When reinforcement is for the first response after a set time period (a **fixed-interval schedule**), responding is typically more frequent as the expected time for the reinforcer gets closer (*draws near*) and is much less frequent after the reward has been received. The pattern of responding is consequently uneven (*choppy*) because cycles of post-reinforcement pauses followed by higher levels of responding (a *stop-start pattern*) are characteristic of the fixed-interval schedule.

Page 332: . . . . "You've got mail" . . . E-mails can arrive at unpredictable times, so it is best to check on-line every once in a while if you are expecting an e-mail from someone. Slow, steady responding like this, typical of a **variable-interval schedule,** may be reinforced with the *"You've got mail"* announcement.

Page 332: . . . the child who *loses a treat* after running into the street . . . Here the phrase *"loses a treat"* refers to the withholding of some pleasant consequence such as a candy bar or piece of cake (appetitive stimulus) following some unwanted behavior. This is one type of punishment; it decreases the probability of the behavior being repeated. Another example is *time out*, in which the child is put in a situation (such as in the corner) in which no reinforcement is available.

Page 333: . . . drawbacks . . . This means problems or bad consequences. One problem (*drawback*) with using punishment is that the behavior may be temporarily suppressed in the presence of the punisher but may reappear in other, safer settings. In addition, punishment may elicit aggression, create fear and apprehension, and generate avoidance behavior in those being punished. As Myers notes, punishment teaches what not to do, whereas reinforcement teaches what to do.

Page 333: No wonder *spanking is a hit* with so many U.S. parents of 3- and 4-year-olds. . . . *Hit* has a number of meanings; it can mean to physically strike someone or something (*hit the ball*), but it can also mean to be popular (*to be a hit*). Parents who physically punish (*hit or swat*) their young children are negatively reinforced for doing so if the bad behavior is suppressed or eliminated. It is not surprising then that spanking (*hitting or swatting*) is popular (*it is a hit*) with so many parents.

Page 335: Actually, promising children a reward for a task they already enjoy can *backfire.* If children enjoy doing something because it is fun (intrinsic motivation), they may lose interest in the task if they are promised a reward for it (extrinsic motivation). Thus, in some circumstances offering material gains (a *payoff*) may have an effect opposite to the one expected (it can *backfire*). Applied properly, however, rewards can motivate high performance levels (*they fuel your efforts*), increase creativity, enhance enjoyment of tasks, and raise (*boost*) feelings of competence, especially if they suggest (*signal*) that a job was well done

Page 336: . . . piggy bank . . . This is a small container for saving money (usually coins) that is often in the shape of a pig. Children can learn to save their money by putting it in their *piggy bank*. However, as Myers points out, pigs who were trained to put big wooden coins in a large *piggy bank* soon reverted to their natural behavior of pushing the coins with their snouts (noses) despite the fact that they received no reward for doing this. This is an example of the biological constraints on learning. This example of *instinctive drift* illustrates the biological constraints on learning.

Page 336: . . . stirred a hornet's nest. . . . A hornet is a large yellow and black stinging insect belonging to the wasp family. Up to 200 hornets live together in a sheltered home (*nest*); if disturbed or agitated (*stirred*), they will attack in an angry and aggressive manner. B. F. Skinner aroused a great deal of anger and hostility and was vehemently attacked by many people (*he stirred a hornet's nest*) for insisting that mental events and free will (internal events) were of little relevance as determinants of behavior compared to environmental factors such as rewards and punishments (external influences).

Page 338: . . . *rule of thumb* . . . This is a simple guide or principle that is true in general. Applying the principles of operant conditioning to economics, Al Gore noted that, as a general principle (*rule of thumb*), whatever is taxed tends to decrease and whatever is subsidized tends to increase.

Learning by Observation

Page 343: Compared with children not exposed to the adult model, those who observed the model's *aggressive outburst* were much more likely to *lash out* at the doll. Bandura's experiments on observational learning demonstrated that children who saw an adult engage in (*model*) violent behavior (an *aggressive outburst*) were more inclined to attack and beat up (*lash out at*) a Bobo doll and copy (*imitate*) the words and gestures used by the role model.

Page 344: Does the *reel world reflect the real world?* Traditionally motion pictures (*movies*) were projected on the screen from a large reel (*spool*) of film. Thus, the "reel" world referred to here is the fantasy world created by movie companies, TV networks, cable companies, etc. (*the media*). Myers notes that the actual (*real*) world is not accurately reflected in movies, TV shows, video games, cable programming, and so on (*the reel world*). Watching the excessive aggression and violence depicted in the media tends to be **correlated** with increased acceptance of aggressive attitudes, indifference to violent acts, and higher levels of antisocial behavior.

9: Memory

CHAPTER OVERVIEW

Chapter 9 explores human memory as a system that processes information in three steps. Encoding refers to the process of putting information into the memory system. Storage is the purely passive mechanism by which information is maintained in memory. Retrieval is the process by which information is accessed from memory through recall or recognition.

Chapter 9 also discusses the important role of meaning, imagery, and organization in encoding new memories, how memory is represented physically in the brain, and how forgetting may result from failure to encode or store information or to find appropriate retrieval cues. The final section of the chapter discusses the issue of memory construction. How "true" are our memories of events? A particularly controversial issue in this area involves suspicious claims of long-repressed memories of sexual abuse and other traumas that are "recovered" with the aid of hypnosis and other techniques. As you study this chapter, try applying some of the memory and studying tips discussed in the text.

NOTE: Answer guidelines for all Chapter 9 questions begin on page 248.

CHAPTER REVIEW

First, skim this section, noting headings and boldface items. After you have read the section, review each objective by completing the sentences and answering the questions that follow it. As you proceed, evaluate your performance by consulting the answers beginning on page 248. Do not continue with the next section until you understand each answer. If you need to, review or reread the section in the textbook before continuing.

The Phenomenon of Memory (pp. 349–353)

> David Myers at times uses idioms that are unfamiliar to some readers. If you do not know the meaning of any of the following words, phrases, or expressions in the context in which they appear in the text, refer to pages 256–257 for an explanation: . . . *mind's storehouse, the reservoir; the roots and fruits; medal winners in a memory Olympics; memory feats; shine the flashlight beam of our attention on.*

Objective 1: Define *memory*, and explain how flashbulb memories differ from other memories.

1. Learning that persists over time indicates the existence of _____ for that learning.

2. Memories for surprising, significant moments that are especially clear are called _____ memories. Like other memories, these memories _____ (can/cannot) err.

Objective 2: Describe Atkinson-Shiffrin's classic three-stage processing model of memory, and explain how the contemporary model of working memory differs.

3. Both human memory and computer memory can be viewed as _____-_____ systems that perform three tasks: _____ , _____ , and _____ .

4. The classic model of memory has been Atkinson and Shiffrin's _____-_____ _____ model. According to this model, we first record information as a fleeting _____ . _____ , from which it is processed into _____-_____ memory, where the information is _____ through rehearsal into _____-_____ memory for later retrieval.

5. The phenomenon of short-term memory has been clarified by the concept of _____ memory, which focuses more on the processing of briefly stored information. This form of memory has both _____ and _____-_____ subsystems, which are coordinated by a _____ _____ processor that, with the help of the _____ buffer, allows us to process images and words _____ .

6. Brain scans show that the _____ _____ are active during complex thinking, whereas areas in the _____ and _____ _____ are active when auditory and visual information is in working memory.

Encoding: Getting Information In
(pp. 353–361)

> If you do not know the meaning of any of the following words, phrases, or expressions in the context in which they appear in the text, refer to pages 256–257 for an explanation: *boost; nonsense syllables; a raw script . . . finished stage production; mental snapshots; "talk until you are blue in the face"; "peg-word"; Motionless while learning the numbers.*

Objective 3: Describe the types of information we encode automatically.

1. Encoding that does not require conscious attention or effort is called _____ _____ . Some processing requires effort at first but with _____ and _____ it becomes effortless.

Give examples of material that is typically encoded with little or no effort.

Objective 4: Contrast effortful processing with automatic processing, and discuss the next-in-line effect, the spacing effect, and the serial position effect.

2. Encoding that requires attention and effort is called _____ _____ .

3. With novel information, conscious repetition, or _____ , boosts memory.

4. A pioneering researcher in verbal memory was _____ . In one experiment, he found that the longer he studied a list of nonsense syllables, the _____ (fewer/greater) the number of repetitions he required to relearn it later.

5. After material has been learned, additional repetition, or _____ , usually will increase retention.

6. When people go around a circle reading words, their poorest memories are for the _____ (least/most) recent information heard. This phenomenon is called the _____-_____-_____ effect.

7. Memory studies also reveal that distributed rehearsal is more effective for retention; this is called the _____ _____ .

8. The tendency to remember the first and last items in a list best is called the _____ _____ _____ . Following a delay, first items are remembered _____ (better/less well) than last items.

Objective 5: Compare the benefits of visual, acoustic, and semantic encoding in remembering verbal information, and describe a memory-enhancing strategy related to the self-reference effect.

9. Encoding the meaning of words is referred to as _____ encoding; encoding by

sound is called _____ encoding; encoding the image of words is _____ encoding.

10. Craik and Tulving's study comparing visual, acoustic, and semantic encoding showed that memory was best with _____ encoding.

11. Our excellent recall of information that relates to ourselves is called the _____– _____ effect.

Objective 6: Explain how encoding imagery aids effortful processing, and describe some memory-enhancing strategies that use visual encoding.

12. Memory that consists of mental pictures is based on the use of _____ . Because they tend to be highly memorable, they aid _____ _____ .

13. Concrete, high-imagery words tend to be remembered _____ (better/less well) than abstract, low-imagery words.

14. Memory for concrete nouns is facilitated when we encode them _____ and _____ .

15. Our tendency to recall the high points of pleasurable events such as family vacations illustrates the phenomenon of _____ _____ .

16. Memory aids are known as _____ devices. One such device involves forming associations between a familiar series of locations and to-be-remembered words; this technique is called the "_____-_____ ."

17. Using a jingle, such as the one that begins "one is a bun," is an example of the "_____-_____" system.

Objective 7: Discuss the use of chunking and hierarchies in effortful processing.

18. Memory may be aided by grouping information into meaningful units called _____ . An example of this technique involves forming words from the first letters of to-be-remembered words; the resulting word is called an _____ .

19. In addition, material may be processed into _____ , which are composed of a few broad concepts divided into lesser concepts, categories, and facts.

Storage: Retaining Information (pp. 361–370)

> If you do not know the meaning of any of the following words, phrases, or expressions in the context in which they appear in the text, refer to pages 257–258 for an explanation: *lightning flashes; Sherlock Holmes; champion memorist; with tongue only partly in cheek; Arousal can sear certain events into the brain; mirror-image writing . . . jigsaw puzzle; London cabbie; Savoring.*

Objective 8: Contrast two types of sensory memory.

1. Stimuli from the environment are first recorded in _____ memory.

2. George Sperling found that when people were briefly shown three rows of letters, they could recall _____ (virtually all/about half) of them. When Sperling sounded a tone immediately after a row of letters was flashed to indicate which letters were to be recalled, the subjects were much _____ (more/less) accurate. This suggests that people have a brief photographic, or _____ , memory lasting about a few tenths of a second.

3. Sensory memory for sounds is called _____ memory. This memory fades _____ (more/less) rapidly than photographic memory, lasting for as long as _____ .

Objective 9: Describe the duration and working capacity of short-term memory.

4. Peterson and Peterson found that when _____ was prevented by asking subjects to count backward, memory for letters was gone after 12 seconds. Without _____ processing, short-term memories have a limited life.

5. Our short-term memory capacity is about _____ chunks of information. This capacity was discovered by _____ .

6. Short-term memory for random _____ (digits/letters) is slightly better than for random _____ (digits/letters), and memory for information we hear is somewhat _____ (better/worse) than that for information we see.

7. Both children and adults have short-term recall for roughly as many words as they can speak in _____ (how many?) seconds.

Objective 10: Describe the capacity and duration of long-term memory.

8. In contrast to short-term memory—and contrary to popular belief—the capacity of permanent memory is essentially _____ .

9. Penfield's electrically stimulated patients _____ (do/do not) provide reliable evidence that our stored memories are precise and durable.

10. Psychologist _____ attempted to locate memory by cutting out pieces of rats' _____ after they had learned a maze. He found that no matter where he cut, the rats _____ (remembered/forgot) the maze.

11. It is likely that forgetting occurs because new experiences _____ with our retrieval of old information, and the physical memory trace _____ with the passage of time.

Objective 11: Discuss the synaptic changes that accompany memory formation and storage.

12. Researchers believe that memory involves a strengthening of certain neural connections, which occurs at the _____ between neurons.

13. Kandel and Schwartz have found that when learning occurs in the sea snail *Aplysia*, the neurotransmitter _____ is released in greater amounts, making synapses more efficient.

14. After learning has occurred, a sending neuron needs _____ (more/less) prompting to fire, and the number of _____ _____ it stimulates may increase. This phenomenon, called _____-_____ _____ , may be the neural basis for learning and memory. Blocking this process with a specific _____ , or by genetic engineering that causes the absence of an _____ , interferes with learning. Rats given a drug that enhances _____ will learn a maze _____ (faster/more slowly).

15. Drugs that boost production of the protein _____ , or the neurotransmitter _____ , may enhance memory.

16. After LTP has occurred, an electric current passed through the brain _____ (will/will not) disrupt old memories and _____ (will/will not) wipe out recent experiences.

Objective 12: Discuss some ways stress hormones can affect memory.

17. Hormones released when we are excited or under stress often _____ (facilitate/impair) learning and memory.

18. Two emotion-processing clusters, the _____ , in the brain's _____ system increase activity in the brain's memory-forming areas.

19. Drugs that block the effects of stress hormones _____ (facilitate/disrupt) memories of emotional events. Stress that is prolonged, however, may cause an area of the brain (the _____) that is vital for laying down memories to _____ .

Objective 13: Distinguish between implicit and explicit memory, and identify the main brain structure associated with each.

20. The loss of memory is called _____ . Studies of people who have lost their memory suggest that there _____ (is/is not) a single unified system of memory.

21. Although amnesia victims typically _____ (have/have not) lost their capacity for learning, which is called _____ memory, they _____ (are/are not) able to declare their memory, suggesting a deficit in their _____ memory systems.

22. Amnesia patients typically have suffered damage to the _____ of their limbic system. This brain structure is important in the processing and storage of _____ memories. Damage on the left side of this structure impairs _____ memory; damage on the right side impairs memory for _____ designs and locations. The rear part of this structure processes _____ memory.

23. The hippocampus seems to function as a zone where the brain _____ (temporarily/permanently) stores the elements of a memory. However, memories _____ (do/do not) migrate for storage elsewhere. The hippocampus is active during _____-_____ sleep, as memories are processed for later retrieval. Recalling past experiences activates various parts of the _____ and _____ lobes.

24. The cerebellum is important in the processing of _____ memories. Humans and lab-oratory animals with a damaged cerebellum are incapable of simple _____-_____ conditioning. Those with damage to the _____ are incapable of _____ conditioning, indicating that this brain region is important in the formation of _____ memories.

25. The dual explicit-implicit memory system helps explain _____ amnesia. We do not have explicit memories of our first three years because the _____ is one of the last brain structures to mature.

Retrieval: Getting Information Out (pp. 370–375)

> If you do not know the meaning of any of the following words, phrases, or expressions in the context in which they appear in the text, refer to page 258 for an explanation: *buoyant mood . . . rose-colored glasses; morph from devils into angels.*

Objective 14: Contrast the recall, recognition, and relearning measures of memory.

1. The ability to retrieve information not in conscious awareness is called _____ .

2. Bahrick found that 25 years after graduation, people were not able to _____ (recall/recognize) the names of their classmates but were able to _____ (recall/recognize) 90 percent of their names and their yearbook pictures.

3. If you have learned something and then forgotten it, you will probably be able to _____ it _____ (more/less) quickly than you did originally.

Objective 15: Explain how retrieval cues help us access stored memories, and describe the process of priming.

4. The process by which associations can lead to retrieval is called _____ .

5. The best retrieval cues come from the associations formed at the time we _____ a memory.

Objective 16: Cite some ways that context can affect retrieval.

6. Studies have shown that retention is best when learning and testing are done in _____ (the same/different) contexts.

Summarize the text explanation of the déjà vu experience.

Objective 17: Describe the effects of internal states on retrieval.

7. The type of memory in which emotions serve as retrieval cues is referred to as _____-_____ memory.

8. Our tendency to recall experiences that are consistent with our current emotional state is called _____-_____ memory.

Describe the effects of mood on memory.

9. People who are currently depressed may recall their parents as _____ .

People who have recovered from depression typically recall their parents about the same as do people who _____

_____ . Moods also influence how we _____ other people's behavior.

Forgetting (pp. 375–381)

> If you do not know the meaning of any of the following words, phrases, or expressions in the context in which they appear in the text, refer to pages 258–259 for an explanation: *applause for memory; may lie poised on the tip of the tongue; mental attic; sheepishly; The words relit a blown-out candle in the mind.*

Objective 18: Explain why we should value our ability to forget, and distinguish three general ways our memory fails us.

1. Without the ability to _____ , we would constantly be overwhelmed by information.

2. Memory researcher Daniel Schacter has identified the seven sins of memory, divided into three categories that identify the ways in which our memory can fail: the three sins of _____ , the three sins of _____ , and the one sin of _____ .

Objective 19: Discuss the role of encoding failure in forgetting.

3. The first type of forgetting is caused by _____ failure.

4. This type of forgetting occurs because some of the information that we sense never actually _____ .

5. One reason for age-related memory decline is that the brain areas responsible for _____ new information are _____ (more/less) responsive in older adults.

Objective 20: Discuss the concept of storage decay, and describe Ebbinghaus' forgetting curve.

6. Studies by Ebbinghaus and by Bahrick indicate that most forgetting occurs _____ (soon/a long time) after the material is learned.

7. This type of forgetting is known as _____ _____ , which may be caused by a gradual fading of the physical _____ _____ .

8. When information that is stored in memory temporarily cannot be found, _____ failure has occurred.

Objective 21: Contrast proactive and retroactive interference, and explain how they can cause retrieval failure.

9. Research suggests that memories are also lost as a result of _____ , which is especially possible if we simultaneously learn similar, new material.

10. The disruptive effect of previous learning on current learning is called _____ _____ . The disruptive effect of learning new material on efforts to recall material previously learned is called _____ _____ .

11. Jenkins and Dallenbach found that if subjects went to sleep after learning, their memory for a list of nonsense syllables was _____ (better/worse) than it was if they stayed awake.

12. In some cases, old information facilitates our learning of new information. This is called _____ _____ .

Objective 22: Summarize Freud's concept of repression, and state whether this view is reflected in current memory research.

13. Freud proposed that motivated forgetting, or _____ , may protect a person from painful memories.

14. Increasing numbers of memory researchers think that motivated forgetting is _____ (less/more) common than Freud believed.

15. Emotions and their associated _____ hormones generally _____ memories.

Memory Construction (pp. 382–390)

> If you do not know the meaning of any of the following words, phrases, or expressions in the context in which they appear in the text, refer to page 259 for an explanation: *reconstruction as well as reproduction; "hypnotically refreshed"; sincerely wrong.*

Objective 23: Explain how misinformation and imagination can distort our memory of an event.

1. Research has shown that recall of an event is often influenced by past experiences and present assumptions. The workings of these influences illustrate the process of memory _____ .

2. When witnesses to an event receive misleading information about it, they may experience a _____ _____ and misremember the event. A number of experiments have demonstrated that false memories _____ (can/cannot) be created when people are induced to imagine nonexistent events; that is, these people later experience "_____ _____ ." People who believe they have recovered memories of alien abduction and child sex abuse tend to have _____ _____ .

Describe what Loftus' studies have shown about the effects of misleading postevent information on eyewitness reports.

Objective 24: Describe source amnesia's contribution to false memories.

3. At the heart of many false memories is

_____ _____ , which

occurs when we _____ an event to the wrong source.

Objective 25: List some differences and similarities between true and false memories.

4. Researchers compare memories to

_____ , noting that people's initial

_____ of events influence their memories.

5. The persistence of a memory _____ (does/does not) reveal whether or not it derives from an actual experience. Whereas real memories have more _____ , gist memories are more _____ .

6. Eyewitnesses' confidence in their memories

_____ (is/is not) related to the accuracy of those memories.

7. Memory construction explains why memories "refreshed" under _____ are often inaccurate.

Objective 26: Give arguments supporting and rejecting the position that very young children's reports are reliable.

8. Research studies of children's eyewitness recall reveal that preschoolers _____ (are/are not) more suggestible than older children or adults. For this reason, whether a child produces an accurate eyewitness memory depends heavily on how he or she is

_____ .

9. Children are most accurate when it is a first interview with a _____ person who asks _____ questions.

Objective 27: Discuss the controversy over reports of repressed and recovered memories of childhood sexual abuse.

10. Researchers increasingly agree that memories obtained under the influence of hypnosis or drugs _____ (are/are not) reliable.

11. Memories of events that happened before age _____ are unreliable. This phenomenon is called _____

_____ .

12. Memory construction makes it clear that memory is best understood not only as a _____ and biological event, but also as a

_____-_____

phenomenon.

Improving Memory (pp. 391–392)

> If you do not know the meaning of the following word in the context in which it appears in the text, refer to page 259 for an explanation: *Sprinkled.*

Objective 28: Explain how an understanding of memory can contribute to effective study techniques.

1. The SQ3R study technique identifies five strategies for boosting memory: _____ ,

_____ , _____ ,

_____ , and _____ .

Discuss several specific strategies for improving memory.

PROGRESS TEST 1

Multiple-Choice Questions

Circle your answers to the following questions and check them with the answers beginning on page 250. If your answer is incorrect, read the explanation for why it is incorrect and then consult the appropriate pages of the text (in parentheses following the correct answer).

1. The three steps in memory information processing are:
   a. input, processing, output.
   b. input, storage, output.
   c. input, storage, retrieval.
   d. encoding, storage, retrieval.

2. Visual sensory memory is referred to as:
   a. iconic memory.
   b. echoic memory.
   c. photomemory.
   d. semantic memory.

3. Echoic memories fade after approximately:
   a. 1 hour.
   b. 1 minute.
   c. 1 second.
   d. 3 to 4 seconds.

4. Which of the following is *not* a measure of retention?
   a. recall
   b. recognition
   c. relearning
   d. retrieval

5. Our short-term memory span is approximately _____ items.
   a. 2
   b. 5
   c. 7
   d. 10

6. Memory techniques such as the method of loci, acronyms, and the peg-word system are called:
   a. consolidation devices.
   b. imagery techniques.
   c. encoding strategies.
   d. mnemonic devices.

7. One way to increase the amount of information in memory is to group it into larger, familiar units. This process is referred to as:
   a. consolidating.
   b. organization.
   c. encoding.
   d. chunking.

8. Kandel and Schwartz have found that when learning occurs, more of the neurotransmitter _____ is released into synapses.
   a. ACh
   b. dopamine
   c. serotonin
   d. noradrenaline

9. Research on memory construction reveals that memories:
   a. are stored as exact copies of experience.
   b. reflect a person's biases and assumptions.
   c. may be chemically transferred from one organism to another.
   d. even if long term, usually decay within about five years.

10. In a study on context cues, people learned words while on land or when they were underwater. In a later test of recall, those with the best retention had:
    a. learned the words on land, that is, in the more familiar context.
    b. learned the words underwater, that is, in the more exotic context.
    c. learned the words and been tested on them in different contexts.

d. learned the words and been tested on them in the same context.

11. The spacing effect means that:
    a. distributed study yields better retention than cramming.
    b. retention is improved when encoding and retrieval are separated by no more than 1 hour.
    c. learning causes a reduction in the size of the synaptic gap between certain neurons.
    d. delaying retrieval until memory has consolidated improves recall.

12. Studies demonstrate that learning causes permanent neural changes in the _____ of animals' neurons.
    a. myelin
    b. cell bodies
    c. synapses
    d. all the above

13. In Sperling's memory experiment, research participants were shown three rows of three letters, followed immediately by a low, medium, or high tone. The participants were able to report:
    a. all three rows with perfect accuracy.
    b. only the top row of letters.
    c. only the middle row of letters.
    d. any one of the three rows of letters.

14. Studies of amnesia victims suggest that:
    a. memory is a single, unified system.
    b. there are two distinct types of memory.
    c. there are three distinct types of memory.
    d. memory losses following brain trauma are unpredictable.

15. Memory for skills is called:
    a. explicit memory.
    b. declarative memory.
    c. prime memory.
    d. implicit memory.

16. The eerie feeling of having been somewhere before is an example of:
    a. state dependency.
    b. encoding failure.
    c. priming.
    d. déjà vu.

17. When Gordon Bower presented words grouped by category or in random order, recall was:
    a. the same for all words.
    b. better for the categorized words.
    c. better for the random words.
    d. improved when participants developed their own mnemonic devices.

18. The three-stage processing model of memory was proposed by:
    a. Atkinson and Shiffrin.
    b. Herman Ebbinghaus.
    c. Loftus and Palmer.
    d. George Sperling.

19. Hypnotically "refreshed" memories may prove inaccurate—especially if the hypnotist asks leading questions—because of:
    a. encoding failure.
    b. state-dependent memory.
    c. proactive interference.
    d. memory construction.

20. Which area of the brain is most important in the processing of implicit memories?
    a. hippocampus   c. hypothalamus
    b. cerebellum   d. amygdala

21. Which of the following terms does *not* belong with the others?
    a. misattribution   c. suggestibility
    b. blocking   d. bias

Matching Items

Match each definition or description with the appropriate term.

Definitions or Descriptions

_____ 1. sensory memory that decays more slowly than visual sensory memory

_____ 2. the process by which information gets into the memory system

_____ 3. mental pictures that aid memory

_____ 4. the blocking of painful memories

_____ 5. the phenomenon in which one's mood can influence retrieval

_____ 6. memory for a list of words is affected by word order

_____ 7. "one is a bun, two is a shoe" mnemonic device

_____ 8. matching each of a series of locations with a visual representation of to-be-remembered items

_____ 9. new learning interferes with previous knowledge

_____ 10. a measure of memory

_____ 11. old knowledge interferes with new learning

_____ 12. misattributing the origin of an event

_____ 13. the fading of unused information over time

_____ 14. the lingering effects of misinformation

_____ 15. a memory sin of intrusion

Terms

a. repression
b. relearning
c. serial position effect
d. persistence
e. peg-word system
f. method of loci
g. proactive interference
h. transience
i. retroactive interference
j. source amnesia
k. suggestibility
l. imagery
m. mood-congruent memory
n. echoic memory
o. encoding

PROGRESS TEST 2

Progress Test 2 should be completed during a final chapter review. Answer the following questions after you thoroughly understand the correct answers for the section reviews and Progress Test 1.

Multiple-Choice Questions

1. Which of the following best describes the typical forgetting curve?
   a. a steady, slow decline in retention over time
   b. a steady, rapid decline in retention over time
   c. a rapid initial decline in retention becoming stable thereafter
   d. a slow initial decline in retention becoming rapid thereafter

2. Jenkins and Dallenbach found that memory was better in subjects who were:
   a. awake during the retention interval, presumably because decay was reduced.
   b. asleep during the retention interval, presumably because decay was reduced.
   c. awake during the retention interval, presumably because interference was reduced.
   d. asleep during the retention interval, presumably because interference was reduced.

3. Which of the following measures of retention is the least sensitive in triggering retrieval?
   a. recall   c. relearning
   b. recognition   d. They are equally sensitive.

4. Amnesia victims typically have experienced damage to the _____ of the brain.
   a. frontal lobes   c. thalamus
   b. cerebellum   d. hippocampus

5. According to the serial position effect, when recalling a list of words you should have the greatest difficulty with those:
   a. at the beginning of the list.
   b. at the end of the list.
   c. at the end and in the middle of the list.
   d. in the middle of the list.

6. Experimenters gave people a list of words to be recalled. When the participants were tested after a delay, the items that were best recalled were those:
   a. at the beginning of the list.
   b. in the middle of the list.
   c. at the end of the list.
   d. at the beginning and the end of the list.

7. Craik and Tulving had research participants process words visually, acoustically, or semantically. In a subsequent recall test, which type of processing resulted in the greatest retention?
   a. visual
   b. acoustic
   c. semantic
   d. Acoustic and semantic processing were equally beneficial.

8. Lashley's studies, in which rats learned a maze and then had various parts of their brains surgically removed, showed that the memory:
   a. was lost when surgery took place within 1 hour of learning.
   b. was lost when surgery took place within 24 hours of learning.
   c. was lost when any region of the brain was removed.
   d. remained no matter which area of the brain was tampered with.

9. The disruption of memory that occurs when football players have been knocked out provides evidence for the importance of:
   a. consolidation in the formation of new memories.
   b. consolidation in the retrieval of long-term memories.
   c. nutrition in normal neural functioning.
   d. all of the above.

10. Long-term potentiation refers to:
    a. the disruptive influence of old memories on the formation of new memories.
    b. the disruptive influence of recent memories on the retrieval of old memories.
    c. our tendency to recall experiences that are consistent with our current mood.
    d. the increased efficiency of synaptic transmission between certain neurons following learning.

11. Repression is an example of:
    a. encoding failure.   c. motivated forgetting.
    b. memory decay.   d. all of the above.

12. Studies by Loftus and Palmer, in which people were quizzed about a film of an accident, indicate that:

   a. when quizzed immediately, people can recall very little, due to the stress of witnessing an accident.
   b. when questioned as little as one day later, their memory was very inaccurate.
   c. most people had very accurate memories as much as 6 months later.
   d. people's recall may easily be affected by misleading information.

13. Which of the following was *not* recommended as a strategy for improving memory?

   a. active rehearsal
   b. distributed study
   c. speed reading
   d. encoding meaningful associations

14. The process of getting information out of memory storage is called:

   a. encoding.   c. rehearsal.
   b. retrieval.   d. storage.

15. Amnesia patients typically experience disruption of:

   a. implicit memories.   c. iconic memories.
   b. explicit memories.   d. echoic memories.

16. Information is maintained in short-term memory only briefly unless it is:

   a. encoded.   c. iconic or echoic.
   b. rehearsed.   d. retrieved.

17. Textbook chapters are often organized into _____ in order to facilitate information processing.

   a. mnemonic devices   c. hierarchies
   b. chunks   d. recognizable units

18. Memory researchers are suspicious of long-repressed memories of traumatic events that are "recovered" with the aid of drugs or hypnosis because:

   a. such experiences usually are vividly remembered.
   b. such memories are unreliable and easily influenced by misinformation.
   c. memories of events happening before about age 3 are especially unreliable.
   d. of all of the above reasons.

19. It is easier to recall information that has just been presented when the information:

   a. consists of random letters rather than words.
   b. is seen rather than heard.
   c. is heard rather than seen.
   d. is experienced in an unusual context.

20. The misinformation effect provides evidence that memory:

   a. is constructed during encoding.
   b. is unchanging once established.
   c. may be reconstructed during recall according to how questions are framed.
   d. is highly resistant to misleading information.

21. According to memory researcher Daniel Schacter, blocking occurs when:

   a. our inattention to details produces encoding failure.
   b. we confuse the source of information.
   c. our beliefs influence our recollections.
   d. information is on the tip of our tongue, but we can't get it out.

True–False Items

Indicate whether each statement is true or false by placing *T* or *F* in the blank next to the item.

_____ 1. Studying that is distributed over time produces better retention than cramming.

_____ 2. Generally speaking, memory for pictures is better than memory for words.

_____ 3. Recall of childhood abuse through hypnosis indicates that memory is permanent, due to the reliability of such reports.

_____ 4. Most people do not have memories of events that occurred before the age of 3.

_____ 5. Studies by Ebbinghaus show that most forgetting takes place soon after learning.

_____ 6. The persistence of a memory is a good clue as to whether or not it derives from an actual experience.

_____ 7. Recall of newly acquired knowledge is no better after sleeping than after being awake for the same period of time.

_____ 8. Time spent in developing imagery, chunking, and associating material with what you already know is more effective than time spent repeating information again and again.

_____ 9. Although repression has not been confirmed experimentally, most psychologists believe it happens.

_____ 10. Overlearning material by continuing to restudy it beyond mastery often disrupts recall.

PSYCHOLOGY APPLIED

Answer these questions the day before an exam as a final check on your understanding of the chapter's terms and concepts.

Multiple-Choice Questions

1. Complete this analogy: Fill-in-the-blank test questions are to multiple-choice questions as:
   a. encoding is to storage.
   b. storage is to encoding.
   c. recognition is to recall.
   d. recall is to recognition.

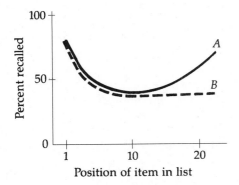

2. The above figure depicts the recall of a list of words under two conditions. Which of the following best describes the difference between the conditions?
   a. In *A*, the words were studied and retrieved in the same context; in *B*, the contexts were different.
   b. In *B*, the words were studied and retrieved in the same context; in *A*, the contexts were different.
   c. The delay between presentation of the last word and the test of recall was longer for *A* than for *B*.
   d. The delay between presentation of the last word and the test of recall was longer for *B* than for *A*.

3. Darren was asked to memorize a list of letters that included *v*, *q*, *y*, and *j*. He later recalled these letters as *e*, *u*, *i*, and *k*, suggesting that the original letters had been encoded:
   a. automatically.   c. semantically.
   b. visually.   d. acoustically.

4. After finding her old combination lock, Janice can't remember its combination because she keeps confusing it with the combination of her new lock. She is experiencing:
   a. proactive interference.
   b. retroactive interference.
   c. encoding failure.
   d. storage failure.

5. Which of the following sequences would be best to follow if you wanted to minimize interference-induced forgetting in order to improve your recall on the psychology midterm?
   a. study, eat, test
   b. study, sleep, test
   c. study, listen to music, test
   d. study, exercise, test

6. Being in a bad mood after a hard day of work, Susan could think of nothing positive in her life. This is best explained as an example of:
   a. priming.
   b. memory construction.
   c. mood-congruent memory.
   d. retrieval failure.

7. In an effort to remember the name of the classmate who sat behind her in fifth grade, Martina mentally recited the names of other classmates who sat near her. Martina's effort to refresh her memory by activating related associations is an example of:
   a. priming.   c. encoding.
   b. déjà vu.   d. relearning.

8. Walking through the halls of his high school 10 years after graduation, Tom experienced a flood of old memories. Tom's experience showed the role of:
   a. state-dependent memory.
   b. context effects.
   c. retroactive interference.
   d. echoic memory.

9. The first thing Karen did when she discovered that she had misplaced her keys was to re-create in her mind the day's events. That she had little difficulty in doing so illustrates:
   a. automatic processing.
   b. effortful processing.
   c. state-dependent memory.
   d. priming.

10. Which of the following is the best example of a flashbulb memory?
    a. suddenly remembering to buy bread while standing in the checkout line at the grocery store
    b. recalling the name of someone from high school while looking at his or her yearbook snapshot
    c. remembering to make an important phone call
    d. remembering what you were doing on September 11, 2001, when terrorists crashed planes into the World Trade Center towers.

11. When Carlos was promoted, he moved into a new office with a new phone extension. Every time he is asked for his phone number, Carlos first thinks of his old extension, illustrating the effects of:
    a. proactive interference.
    b. retroactive interference.
    c. encoding failure.
    d. storage failure.

12. Elderly Mr. Flanagan, a retired electrician, can easily remember how to wire a light switch, but he cannot remember the name of the president of the United States. Evidently, Mr. Flanagan's _____ memory is better than his _____ memory.
    a. implicit; explicit
    b. explicit; implicit
    c. declarative; procedural
    d. explicit; declarative

13. Although you can't recall the answer to a question on your psychology midterm, you have a clear mental image of the textbook page on which it appears. Evidently, your _____ encoding of the answer was _____ .
    a. semantic; automatic
    b. visual; automatic
    c. semantic; effortful
    d. visual; effortful

14. At your high school reunion you cannot remember the last name of your homeroom teacher. Your failure to remember is most likely the result of:
    a. encoding failure.
    b. storage failure.
    c. retrieval failure.
    d. state-dependent memory.

15. Brenda has trouble remembering her new five-digit ZIP plus four-digit address code. What is the most likely explanation for the difficulty Brenda is having?
    a. Nine digits are at or above the upper limit of most people's short-term memory capacity.
    b. Nine digits are at or above the upper limit of most people's iconic memory capacity.
    c. The extra four digits cannot be organized into easily remembered chunks.
    d. Brenda evidently has an impaired implicit memory.

16. Lewis cannot remember the details of the torture he experienced as a prisoner of war. According to Freud, Lewis's failure to remember these painful memories is an example of:
    a. repression.
    b. retrieval failure.
    c. state-dependent memory.
    d. flashbulb memory.

17. Which of the following illustrates the constructive nature of memory?
    a. Janice keeps calling her new boyfriend by her old boyfriend's name.
    b. After studying all afternoon and then getting drunk in the evening, Don can't remember the material he studied.
    c. After getting some good news, elated Kareem has a flood of good memories from his younger years.
    d. Although elderly Mrs. Harvey, who has Alzheimer's disease, has many gaps in her memory, she invents sensible accounts of her activities so that her family will not worry.

18. To help him remember the order of ingredients in difficult recipes, master chef Giulio often associates them with the route he walks to work each day. Giulio is using which mnemonic technique?
    a. peg-word system
    b. acronyms
    c. the method of loci
    d. chunking

19. During basketball practice Jan's head was painfully elbowed. If the trauma to her brain disrupts her memory, we would expect that Jan would be most likely to forget:
    a. the name of her teammates.
    b. her telephone number.
    c. the name of the play during which she was elbowed.
    d. the details of events that happened shortly after the incident.

20. After suffering damage to the hippocampus, a person would probably:
    a. lose memory for skills such as bicycle riding.
    b. be incapable of being classically conditioned.
    c. lose the ability to store new facts.
    d. experience all of the above changes.

21. When he was 8 years old, Frank was questioned by the police about a summer camp counselor suspected of molesting children. Even though he was not, in fact, molested by the counselor, today 19-year-old Frank "remembers" the counselor touching him inappropriately. Frank's false memory is an example of which "sin" of memory?
    a. blocking
    b. transience
    c. misattribution
    d. suggestibility

Essay Question

Discuss the points of agreement among experts regarding the validity of recovered memories of child abuse. (Use the space below to jot down notes for your essay; then write the essay on a separate piece of paper.)

KEY TERMS

Writing Definitions

Using your own words, on a separate piece of paper write a brief definition or explanation of each of the following terms.

1. memory
2. flashbulb memory
3. encoding
4. storage
5. retrieval
6. sensory memory
7. short-term memory
8. long-term memory
9. working memory
10. automatic processing
11. effortful processing
12. rehearsal
13. spacing effect
14. serial position effect
15. visual encoding
16. acoustic encoding
17. semantic encoding
18. imagery
19. mnemonics
20. chunking
21. iconic memory
22. echoic memory
23. long-term potentiation (LTP)
24. amnesia
25. implicit memory
26. explicit memory
27. hippocampus
28. recall
29. recognition
30. relearning
31. priming
32. déjà vu

33. mood-congruent memory

34. proactive interference

35. retroactive interference

36. repression

37. misinformation effect

38. source amnesia

Cross-Check

As you learned in the Prologue, reviewing and overlearning of material are important to the learning process. After you have written the definitions of the key terms in this chapter, you should complete the crossword puzzle to ensure that you can reverse the process—recognize the term, given the definition.

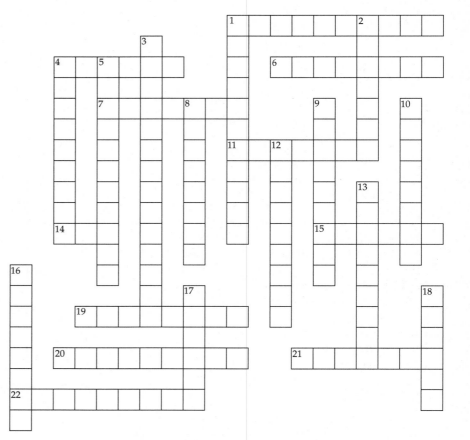

ACROSS

1. Example of motivated forgetting.
4. Sensory memories of auditory stimuli.
6. Encoding of information according to its meaning.
7. Activating associations in order to retrieve a specific memory.
11. Mental pictures.
14. Believed to be the neural basis for learning and memory.
15. Visual sensory memory.
19. Organizing material into familiar, meaningful units.
20. Unusually vivid memory of an emotionally important moment.
21. Loss of memory.
22. Effortful repetition of information.

DOWN

1. A measure of retention that requires identifying previously learned material.
2. The immediate, initial recording of information in memory.
3. An effect in which eyewitnesses to an event incorporate misleading information in their memories.
4. Type of processing that requires attention and some degree of work.
5. Brain area that processes explicit memories for storage.
8. Type of memory of skills, preferences, and dispositions.

9. Memory aids.
10. Encoding of information into memory according to its sound.
12. Unconscious encoding of incidental information into memory.
13. Type of interference in which old knowledge interferes with new learning.
16. Relatively permanent memory that is unlimited in capacity.
17. Encoding that uses imagery to process information into memory.
18. The false sense of having already experienced a situation.

ANSWERS

The Phenomenon of Memory

1. memory

2. flashbulb; can

3. information-processing; encoding; storage; retrieval

4. three-stage processing; sensory memory; short-term; encoded; long-term

5. working; auditory; visual-spatial; central executive; episodic; simultaneously

6. frontal lobes; parietal; temporal lobes

Encoding: Getting Information In

1. automatic processing; practice; experience

Automatic processing includes the encoding of information about space, time, and frequency. It also includes the encoding of word meaning, a type of encoding that appears to be learned.

2. effortful processing

3. rehearsal

4. Ebbinghaus; fewer

5. overlearning

6. most; next-in-line

7. spacing effect

8. serial position effect; better

9. semantic; acoustic; visual

10. semantic

11. self-reference

12. imagery; effortful processing

13. better

14. semantically; visually

15. rosy retrospection

16. mnemonic; method of loci

17. peg-word

18. chunks; acronym

19. hierarchies

Storage: Retaining Information

1. sensory

2. about half; more; iconic

3. echoic; less; 3 or 4 seconds

4. rehearsal; active

5. 7; George Miller

6. digits; letters; better

7. 2

8. unlimited (limitless)

9. do not

10. Karl Lashley; cortexes; remembered

11. interfere; decays

12. synapses

13. serotonin

14. less; receptor sites; long-term potentiation; drug; enzyme; LTP; faster

15. CREB; glutamate

16. will not; will

17. facilitate

18. amygdala; limbic

19. disrupt; hippocampus; shrink

20. amnesia; is not

21. have not; implicit; are not; explicit

22. hippocampus; explicit; verbal; visual; spatial

23. temporarily; do; slow-wave; frontal; temporal

24. implicit; eye-blink; amygdala; fear; implicit

25. infantile; hippocampus

Retrieval: Getting Information Out

1. recall

2. recall; recognize

3. relearn; more

4. priming

5. encode

6. the same

The déjà vu experience is most likely the result of being in a context similar to one that we have actually been in before. If we have previously been in a similar situation, though we cannot recall what it was, the current situation may present cues that unconsciously help us to retrieve the earlier experience.

7. state-dependent

8. mood-congruent

When happy, for example, we perceive things in a positive light and recall happy events; these perceptions and memories, in turn, prolong our good mood. Moods also influence how we interpret other people's behavior.

9. rejecting, punitive, and guilt-promoting; have never suffered depression; interpret

Forgetting

1. forget

2. forgetting; distortion; intrusion

3. encoding

4. enters the memory system

5. encoding; less

6. soon

7. storage decay; memory trace

8. retrieval

9. interference

10. proactive interference; retroactive interference

11. better

12. positive transfer

13. repression

14. less

15. stress; strengthen

Memory Construction

1. construction

2. misinformation effect; can; imagination inflation; vivid imaginations

When people viewed a film of a traffic accident and were quizzed a week later, phrasing of questions affected answers; the word "smashed," for instance, made viewers mistakenly think they had seen broken glass.

3. source amnesia; misattribute

4. perceptions; interpretations

5. does not; details; durable

6. is not

7. hypnosis

8. are; questioned

9. neutral; nonleading

10. are not

11. 3; infantile amnesia

12. cognitive; social-cultural

Improving Memory

1. Survey; Question; Read; Rehearse; Review

Suggestions for improving memory include rehearsing material over many separate and distributed study sessions with the objective of overlearning material. Studying should also involve active rehearsal, rather than mindless repetition of information. Organizing information, relating material to what is already known, developing numerous retrieval cues, and using mnemonic devices that incorporate vivid imagery are helpful too. Frequent activation of retrieval cues, such as the context and mood in which the original learning occurred, can also help strengthen memory, as can recalling events while they are fresh, before possible misinformation is encountered. Studying should also be arranged to minimize potential sources of interference. Finally, self-tests in the same format (recall or recognition) that will later be used on the actual test are useful.

Progress Test 1

Multiple-Choice Questions

1. **d.** is the answer. Information must be encoded, or put into appropriate form; stored, or retained over time; and retrieved, or located and gotten out when needed. (p. 351)

2. **a.** is the answer. Iconic memory is our fleeting memory of visual stimuli. (p. 362)
   b. Echoic memory is auditory sensory memory.
   c. There is no such thing as photomemory.
   d. Semantic memory is memory for meaning, not a form of sensory memory.

3. **d.** is the answer. Echoic memories last 3 to 4 seconds. (p. 362)

4. **d.** is the answer. Retrieval refers to the *process* of remembering. (p. 370)

5. **c.** is the answer. (p. 362)

6. **d.** is the answer. (pp. 358–359)
   a. There is no such term as "consolidation techniques."
   b. & c. Imagery and encoding strategies are important in storing new memories, but mnemonic device is the general designation of techniques that facilitate memory, such as acronyms and the peg-word system.

7. **d.** is the answer. (p. 359)
   a. There is no such process of "consolidating."
   b. Organization *does* enhance memory, but it does so through hierarchies, not grouping.
   c. Encoding refers to the processing of information into the memory system.

8. **c.** is the answer. Kandel and Schwartz found that when learning occurred in the sea snail *Aplysia*, serotonin was released at certain synapses, which then became more efficient at signal transmission. (p. 365)

9. **b.** is the answer. In essence, we construct our memories, bringing them into line with our biases and assumptions, as well as with our subsequent experiences. (pp. 382–383)

   a. If this were true, it would mean that memory construction does not occur. Through memory construction, memories may deviate significantly from the original experiences.

   c. There is no evidence that such chemical transfers occur.

   d. Many long-term memories are apparently unlimited in duration.

10. **d.** is the answer. In general, being in a context similar to that in which you experienced something will tend to help you recall the experience. (pp. 372–373)

    a. & b. The learning environment per se—and its familiarity or exoticness—did not affect retention.

11. **a.** is the answer. (p. 354)

    b. & d. The text does not suggest that there is an optimal interval between encoding and retrieval.

    c. Learning increases the efficiency of synaptic transmission in certain neurons, but not by altering the size of the synapse.

12. **c.** is the answer. (p. 365)

13. **d.** is the answer. When asked to recall all the letters, participants could recall only about half; however, if immediately after the presentation they were signaled to recall a particular row, their recall was near perfect. This showed that they had a brief photographic memory—so brief that it faded in less time than it would have taken to say all nine letters. (p. 362)

14. **b.** is the answer. Because amnesia victims lose their fact (explicit) memories but not their skill (implicit) memories or their capacity to learn, it appears that human memory can be divided into two distinct types. (p. 367)

    d. As studies of amnesia victims show, memory losses following damage to the hippocampus are quite predictable.

15. **d.** is the answer. (p. 367)

    a. & b. Explicit memory (also called declarative memory) is memory of facts and experiences that one can consciously know and declare.

    c. There is no such thing as prime memory.

16. **d.** is the answer. (p. 373)

a. State-dependent memory is the phenomenon in which information is best retrieved when the person is in the same emotional or physiological state he or she was in when the material was learned.

b. Encoding failure occurs when a person has not processed information sufficiently for it to enter the memory system.

c. Priming is the process by which a memory is activated through retrieval of an associated memory.

17. **b.** is the answer. When the words were organized into categories, recall was two to three times better, indicating the benefits of hierarchical organization in memory. (p. 360)

    d. This study did not examine the use of mnemonic devices.

18. **a.** is the answer. (p. 351)

    b. Herman Ebbinghaus conducted pioneering studies of verbal learning and memory.

    c. Loftus and Palmer conducted influential research studies of eyewitness memory.

    d. George Sperling is known for his research studies of iconic memory.

19. **d.** is the answer. It is in both encoding and retrieval that we construct our memories, and as Loftus' studies showed, leading questions affect people's memory construction. (p. 385)

    a. The memory encoding occurred at the time of the event in question, not during questioning by the hypnotist.

    b. State-dependent memory refers to the influence of one's own emotional or physiological state on encoding and retrieval, and would not apply here.

    c. Proactive interference is the interfering effect of prior learning on the recall of new information.

20. **b.** is the answer. (p. 369)

    a. The hippocampus is a temporary processing site for *explicit memories*.

    c. & d. These areas of the brain are not directly involved in the memory system.

21. **b.** is the answer. Blocking is an example of retrieval failure. Each of the others is an example of a "sin of distortion," in which memories, although inaccurate, are retrieved (p. 377)

Matching Items

1. n (p. 362)	**6.** c (p. 356)	**11.** g (p. 379)
2. o (p. 351)	**7.** e (p. 359)	**12.** j (p. 384)
3. l (p. 358)	**8.** f (p. 358)	**13.** h (p. 376)
4. a (p. 380)	**9.** i (p. 379)	**14.** k (p. 376)
5. m (p. 374)	**10.** b (p. 370)	**15.** d (p. 376)

Progress Test 2

Multiple-Choice Questions

1. **c.** is the answer. As Ebbinghaus and Bahrick both showed, most of the forgetting that is going to occur happens soon after learning. (p. 377)

2. **d.** is the answer. (pp. 379–380)
   a. & b. This study did not find evidence that memories fade (decay) with time.
   c. When one is awake, there are many *more* potential sources of memory interference than when one is asleep.

3. **a.** is the answer. A test of recall presents the fewest retrieval cues and usually produces the most limited retrieval. (p. 370)

4. **d.** is the answer. (p. 368)

5. **d.** is the answer. According to the serial position effect, items at the beginning and end of a list tend to be remembered best. (p. 356)

6. **a.** is the answer. (p. 356)
   b. In the serial position effect, the items in the middle of the list always show the *poorest* retention.
   c. & d. Delayed recall erases the memory facilitation for items at the end of the list.

7. **c.** is the answer. Processing a word in terms of its meaning (semantic encoding) produces much better retention than does visual or acoustic encoding. (p. 357)

8. **d.** is the answer. Surprisingly, Lashley found that no matter where he cut, the rats had at least a partial memory of how to solve the maze. (p. 364)
   a. & b. Lashley's studies did not investigate the significance of the interval between learning and cortical lesioning.

9. **a.** is the answer. A blow to the head wipes out recent experiences because information in STM did not have time to consolidate into LTM. (p. 366)
   b. Such injuries disrupt the formation, rather than the retrieval, of memories.
   c. Although nutrition plays an important role in neural functioning, the effects of such injuries are independent of nutrition.

10. **d.** is the answer. (p. 365)

11. **c.** is the answer. According to Freud, we repress painful memories to preserve our self-concepts. (p. 380)
    a. & b. The fact that repressed memories can sometimes be retrieved suggests that they were encoded and have not decayed with time.

12. **d.** is the answer. When misled by the phrasings of questions, subjects incorrectly recalled details of the film and even "remembered" objects that weren't there. (pp. 382–383)

13. **c.** is the answer. Speed reading, which entails little active rehearsal, yields poor retention. (pp. 391–392)

14. **b.** is the answer. (p. 351)
    a. Encoding is the process of getting information *into* memory.
    c. Rehearsal is the conscious repetition of information in order to maintain it in memory.
    d. Storage is the maintenance of encoded material over time.

15. **b.** is the answer. Amnesia patients typically have suffered damage to the hippocampus, a brain structure involved in processing explicit memories for facts. (pp. 367, 368)
    a. Amnesia patients do retain implicit memories for how to do things; these are processed in the more ancient parts of the brain.
    c. & d. Amnesia patients generally do not experience impairment in their iconic and echoic sensory memories.

16. **b.** is the answer. (p. 354)
    a. Information in short-term memory has *already* been encoded.
    c. Iconic and echoic are types of *sensory* memory.
    d. Retrieval is the process of getting material out of storage and into conscious, short-term memory. Thus, all material in short-term memory has either already been retrieved or is about to be placed in storage.

17. **c.** is the answer. By breaking concepts down into subconcepts and yet smaller divisions and showing the relationships among these, hierarchies facilitate information processing. Use of main heads and subheads is an example of the organization of textbook chapters into hierarchies. (p. 360)
    a. Mnemonic devices are the method of loci, acronyms, and other memory *techniques* that facilitate retention.
    b. Chunks are organizations of knowledge into familiar, manageable units.
    d. Recognition is a measure of retention.

18. **d.** is the answer. (pp. 387–388)

19. **c.** is the answer. Short-term recall is slightly better for information we hear rather than see, because echoic memory momentarily outlasts iconic memory. (p. 363)
    a. Meaningful stimuli, such as words, are usually remembered more easily than meaningless stimuli, such as random letters.

b. Iconic memory does not last as long as echoic memory in short-term recall.

d. Although context is a powerful retrieval cue, there is no general facilitation of memory in an unusual context.

20. **c.** is the answer. Loftus and Palmer found that eyewitness testimony could easily be altered when questions were phrased to imply misleading information. (pp. 382–383)

a. Although memories *are* constructed during encoding, the misinformation effect is a retrieval, rather than an encoding, phenomenon.

b. & d. In fact, just the opposite is true.

21. **d.** is the answer. (p. 376)

a. This defines absent-mindedness.

b. This is misattribution.

c. This is bias.

True–False Items

1. T (p. 355)	**6.** F (p. 385)
2. T (p. 363)	**7.** F (p. 380)
3. F (p. 385)	**8.** T (p. 392)
4. T (p. 388)	**9.** F (p. 381)
5. T (p. 377)	**10.** F (p. 354)

Psychology Applied

Multiple-Choice Questions

1. **d.** is the answer. (p. 370)

a. & b. In order to correctly answer either type of question, the knowledge must have been encoded and stored.

c. With fill-in-the-blank questions, the answer must be recalled with no retrieval cues other than the question. With multiple-choice questions, the correct answer merely has to be recognized from among several alternatives.

2. **d.** is the answer. (p. 356)

a. & b. A serial position effect would presumably occur whether the study and retrieval contexts were the same or different.

c. As researchers found, when recall is delayed, only the first items in a list are recalled more accurately than the others. With immediate recall, both the first and last items are recalled more accurately.

3. **d.** is the answer. That all four mistakes are based on a sound confusion suggests that the letters were encoded acoustically. (pp. 356–357)

a. Memorizing a list of letters would involve effortful, rather than automatic, processing.

b. The mistakes do not involve letters that are similar in appearance.

c. Semantic encoding would have been suggested by errors based on similarities in meaning.

4. **b.** is the answer. Retroactive interference is the disruption of something you once learned by new information. (p. 379)

a. Proactive interference occurs when old information makes it difficult to correctly remember new information.

c. & d. Interference produces forgetting even when the forgotten material was effectively encoded and stored. Janice's problem is at the level of retrieval.

5. **b.** is the answer. (pp. 379–380)

a., c., & d. Involvement in other activities, even just eating or listening to music, is more disruptive than sleeping.

6. **c.** is the answer. Susan's memories are affected by her bad mood. (p. 374)

a. Priming refers to the conscious or unconscious activation of particular associations in memory.

b. Memory construction refers to changes in memory as new experiences occur.

d. Although Susan's difficulty in recalling the good could be considered retrieval failure, it is caused by the mood-congruent effect, which is therefore the best explanation.

7. **a.** is the answer. Priming is the conscious or unconscious activation of particular associations in memory. (p. 372)

b. Déjà vu is the false impression of having previously experienced a current situation.

c. That Martina is able to retrieve her former classmates' names implies that they already have been encoded.

d. Relearning is a measure of retention based on how long it takes to relearn something already mastered. Martina is recalling her former classmates' names, not relearning them.

8. **b.** is the answer. Being back in the context in which the original experiences occurred triggered memories of these experiences. (p. 373)

a. The memories were triggered by similarity of place, not mood.

c. Retroactive interference would involve difficulties in retrieving old memories.

d. Echoic memory refers to momentary memory of auditory stimuli.

9. **a.** is the answer. Time and space—and therefore sequences of events—are often automatically processed. (p. 353)

b. That she had *little difficulty* indicates that the processing was automatic, rather than effortful.

c. & d. State-dependent memory and priming

have nothing to do with the automatic processing of space and time.

10. **d.** is the answer. Flashbulb memories are unusually clear memories of emotionally significant moments in life. (p. 351)

11. **a.** is the answer. Proactive interference occurs when old information makes it difficult to recall new information. (p. 379)

    b. If Carlos were having trouble remembering the old extension, this answer would be correct.

    c. & d. Carlos has successfully encoded and stored the extension; he's just having problems retrieving it.

12. **a.** is the answer. (p. 367)

    b., c., & d. Explicit memory, also called declarative memory, is the memory of facts that one can consciously "declare."

13. **b.** is the answer. (pp. 356, 357)

    a. & c. Your failure to recall the answer indicates that it was never encoded semantically.

    d. Spatial information, such as the location of an answer (but not the actual answer) on a textbook page, is often encoded automatically.

14. **c.** is the answer. (p. 378)

    a. & b. The name of your homeroom teacher, which you probably heard at least once each day of school, was surely processed into memory (encoded) and maintained there for some time (stored).

    d. State-dependent memory is the tendency to recall information best in the same emotional or physiological state as when it was learned. It is unlikely that a single state was associated with learning your homeroom teacher's name.

15. **a.** is the answer. Short-term memory capacity is approximately seven digits. (p. 362)

    b. Because iconic memory lasts no more than a tenth of a second, regardless of how much material is experienced, this cannot be the explanation for Brenda's difficulty.

    c. The final four digits should be no more difficult to organize into chunks than the first five digits of the address code.

    d. Memory for digits is an example of explicit, rather than implicit, memory.

16. **a.** is the answer. (p. 380)

    b. Although Lewis' difficulty in recalling these memories could be considered retrieval failure, it is caused by repression, which is therefore the *best* explanation.

    c. This answer is incorrect because it is clear that Lewis fails to remember these experiences

because they are painful memories and not because he is in a different emotional or physiological state.

    d. Flashbulb memories are especially *vivid* memories for emotionally significant events. Lewis has no memory at all.

17. **d.** is the answer. (p. 382)

    a. This is an example of proactive interference.

    b. This is an example of the disruptive effects of depressant drugs, such as alcohol, on the formation of new memories.

    c. This is mood-congruent memory.

18. **c.** is the answer. (p. 358)

    a. The peg-word system involves developing associations between rhyming words in a jingle and to-be-remembered items.

    b. Acronyms are words created from the first letters of to-be-remembered words.

    d. Chunking is the organization of information into meaningful units, such as acronyms.

19. **c.** is the answer. Blows to the head usually disrupt the most recent experiences, such as this one, rather than long-term memories like those in choices a. and b., or new learning such as that in choice d. (p. 366)

20. **c.** is the answer. The hippocampus is involved in processing new facts for storage. (p. 368)

    a., b., & d. Studies of amnesia victims with hippocampal damage show that neither classical conditioning nor skill memory are impaired, indicating that these aspects of memory are controlled by more primitive regions of the brain.

21. **d.** is the answer. In this example, the questions Frank was asked to answer created misinformation that later became part of his memory. (p. 376)

    a. This answer would have been correct if Frank had been molested by the counselor but had failed to encode it in his memory.

    b. This answer would have been correct if Frank had been molested but the memory trace had faded with time.

    c. Misattribution might have occurred if Frank had witnessed another camper being molested and later recalled himself as the actual victim.

Essay Question

Experts agree that child abuse is a real problem that can have long-term adverse effects on individuals. They also acknowledge that forgetting of isolated events, both good and bad, is an ordinary part of life. Although experts all accept the fact that recovered memories are commonplace, they warn that memories "recovered" under hypnosis or with the use of drugs are unreliable, as are memories of events before age 3. Finally, they agree that memories can be traumatic, whether real or false.

Key Terms

Writing Definitions

1. **Memory** is the persistence of learning over time via the storage and retrieval of information. (p. 349)

2. A **flashbulb memory** is an unusually vivid memory of an emotionally important moment in one's life. (p. 351)

3. **Encoding** is the first step in memory; information is translated into some form that enables it to enter our memory system. (p. 351)

4. **Storage** is the process by which encoded information is maintained over time. (p. 351)

5. **Retrieval** is the process of bringing to consciousness information from memory storage. (p. 351)

6. **Sensory memory** is the immediate, very brief recording of sensory information in the memory system. (p. 351)

7. **Short-term memory** is conscious memory, which can hold about seven items for a short time. (p. 351)

8. **Long-term memory** is the relatively permanent and unlimited capacity memory system into which information from short-term memory may pass. (p. 351)

9. **Working memory** is the newer way of conceptualizing short-term memory as a work site for the active processing of incoming auditory and visual-spatial information, and of information retrieved from long-term memory. (p. 352)

10. **Automatic processing** refers to our unconscious encoding of incidental information such as space, time, and frequency and of well-learned information. (p. 353)

11. **Effortful processing** is encoding that requires attention and conscious effort. (p. 354)

12. **Rehearsal** is the conscious, effortful repetition of information that you are trying either to maintain in consciousness or to encode for storage. (p. 354)

13. The **spacing effect** is the tendency for distributed study or practice to yield better long-term retention than massed study or practice. (p. 355)

14. The **serial position effect** is the tendency for items at the beginning and end of a list to be more easily retained than those in the middle. (p. 356)

15. **Visual encoding** is the use of imagery to process information into memory. (p. 356)

16. **Acoustic encoding** is the processing of information into memory according to its sound. (p. 356)

17. **Semantic encoding** is the processing of information into memory according to its meaning. (p. 356)

18. **Imagery** refers to mental pictures and can be an important aid to effortful processing. (p. 358)

19. **Mnemonics** are memory aids (the method of loci, acronyms, peg-words, etc.), which often use vivid imagery and organizational devices. (p. 358)

20. **Chunking** is the memory technique of organizing material into familiar, meaningful units. (p. 359)

21. **Iconic memory** is the visual sensory memory consisting of a perfect photographic memory, which lasts no more than a few tenths of a second. (p. 362)

    Memory aid: *Icon* means "image" or "representation." **Iconic memory** consists of brief visual images.

22. **Echoic memory** is the momentary sensory memory of auditory stimuli, lasting about 3 or 4 seconds. (p. 362)

23. **Long-term potentiation (LTP)** is an increase in a synapse's firing potential following brief, rapid stimulation. LTP is believed to be the neural basis for learning and memory. (p. 365)

24. **Amnesia** is the loss of memory. (p. 367)

25. **Implicit memories** are memories of skills, preferences, and dispositions. These memories are evidently processed, not by the hippocampus, but by a more primitive part of the brain, the cerebellum. They are also called *procedural* or *nondeclarative memories*. (p. 367)

26. **Explicit memories** are memories of facts, including names, images, and events. They are also called declarative memories. (p. 367)

27. The **hippocampus** is a neural center located in the limbic system that is important in the processing of explicit memories for storage. (p. 368)

28. **Recall** is a measure of retention in which the person must remember, with few retrieval cues, information learned earlier. (p. 370)

29. **Recognition** is a measure of retention in which one need only identify, rather than recall, previously learned information. (p. 370)

30. **Relearning** is also a measure of retention in that the less time it takes to relearn information, the more that information has been retained. (p. 370)

31. **Priming** is the activation, often unconscious, of a web of associations in memory in order to retrieve a specific memory. (p. 372)

32. **Déjà vu** is the false sense that you have already experienced a current situation. (p. 373)

33. **Mood-congruent memory** is the tendency to recall experiences that are consistent with our current mood. (p. 374)

34. **Proactive interference** is the disruptive effect of something you already have learned on your efforts to learn or recall new information. (p. 379)

35. **Retroactive interference** is the disruptive effect of something recently learned on old knowledge. (p. 379)

    Memory aid: *Retro* means "backward." **Retroactive interference** is "backward-acting" interference.

36. **Repression** is an example of motivated forgetting in that painful and unacceptable memories are prevented from entering consciousness. In psychoanalytic theory, it is the basic defense mechanism. (p. 381)

37. The **misinformation effect** is the tendency of eyewitnesses to an event to incorporate misleading information about the event into their memories. (p. 383)

38. At the heart of many false memories, **source amnesia** refers to misattributing an event to the wrong source. (p. 384)

Cross-Check

ACROSS	DOWN
1. repression	1. recognition
4. echoic	2. sensory
6. semantic	3. misinformation effect
7. priming	4. effortful
11. imagery	5. hippocampus
14. LTP	8. implicit
15. iconic	9. mnemonics
19. chunking	10. acoustic
20. flashbulb	12. automatic
21. amnesia	13. proactive
22. rehearsal	16. long term
	17. visual
	18. déjà vu

FOCUS ON VOCABULARY AND LANGUAGE

The Phenomenon of Memory

Page 349: Your memory is your mind's *storehouse*, the *reservoir* of your accumulated learning. Myers is using an analogy to help you understand the general concept of memory. Both *storehouses* and *reservoirs* are used to keep materials (water, food, etc.) until we need them. Likewise, your memory system retains most of the things you experienced (*accumulated learning*), and items can be recalled or retrieved as required.

Page 349: Some studies have explored *the roots and fruits* of memory loss. Some researchers have examined the origins and causes (*roots*) of memory loss, and others have noted the benefits (*fruits*) of not having a perfect memory for everything that happens.

Page 350: . . . *medal winners in a memory Olympics.* . . . People with exceptional memories are being likened or compared to the top athletes in the Olympic Games. S, for example, would clearly receive the top prize (*medal winner*) in any competition in which remembering vast amounts of information was being tested (*memory Olympics*).

Page 350: Do S's memory *feats* make your own memory seem *feeble*? Myers is pointing out that although S may have demonstrated spectacular abilities in remembering all sorts of things (*memory feats*), normal memory in the average person is no less astounding in many ways (*pretty staggering*). Despite our occasional failures, our ordinary memory accomplishments, which we tend to take for granted, are quite remarkable (*they are far from being feeble*).

Pages 351–352: Instead we *shine the flashlight beam of our attention on* certain incoming stimuli—often novel or important stimuli. One model of memory suggests that we only focus on (*shine the flashlight beam of our attention on*) and process one part or aspect of the total sensory input, particularly new (*novel*) or important stimuli. We can also locate and bring back stored information from long-term memory (**LTM**) into short-term memory (**STM**).

Encoding: Getting Information In

Page 354: . . . *boost* . . . One way to improve and increase the power of our memory is to use **rehearsal**. Thus, actively repeating some new information (such as a stranger's name or new terminology) will help strengthen (*boost*) our ability to remember this material. As Myers notes it is important for effective retention to space out or distribute rehearsals over time (*the spacing effect*) rather than doing the repetitions all at once (massed practice or cramming).

Page 354: His [Ebbinghaus'] solution was to form a list of all possible *nonsense syllables* created by *sandwiching* a vowel between two consonants. In order to avoid using meaningful words with prior associations, Hermann Ebbinghaus invented three-letter words that made no sense and had no meaning (*nonsense syllables*). He did this by putting a vowel (*sandwiching it*) between two consonants. His nonsense (*meaningless*) syllables were consonant (C), vowel (V), consonant (C), or CVCs.

Page 356: Gordon Bower and Daniel Morrow (1990) liken our minds to theater directors who, *given a raw script*, imagine a *finished stage production*. This suggests that what we remember is not an exact replica of reality. We construct some mental representation or model (*finished stage production*) from the basic sensory information (*raw script*) available to us, and so, when we recall something, it is our own version (*mental model*) that comes to mind and not the real thing.

Page 358: Thanks to the durability of our most vivid images, we sometimes recall our experiences with *mental snapshots* of their best or worst moments. The use of imagery or mental pictures (*snapshots*) is one way to enhance recall. We have exceptionally good memory for pictures and ideas that are encoded using visual imagery. As Myers notes, "imagery is at the heart of many memory aids" (e.g., method of loci, peg-word, etc.).

Page 358 (caption) . . . "*talk until you are blue in the face*". . . This refers to the situation in which someone says the same thing (e.g., a request, a plea, a warning) over and over, but saying it does not appear to have any effect on the listener. You can warn people repeatedly about the dangers (*health hazards*) of sun tanning and smoking (*you can talk until you are blue in the face*) with little or no change in the target audience's behavior. Visual images of the consequences of tanning and smoking have a greater impact.

Page 359: For example, the "*peg-word*" system requires that you first memorize a *jingle*. A *jingle* is an easily remembered succession of words that ring or resound against each other due to alliteration or rhyme and are often used in radio or TV commercials. The mnemonic (memory aid) called the "*peg-word*" method is based on memorizing a short 10-item poem (*jingle*) that can be associated with a new list of 10 items through visual imagery. The new items are hung on, or pegged to, the familiar items.

Page 360: *Motionless while learning the numbers*, Donatelli then *sprang alive*. He *whispered numbers, rubbed his chin, tapped his feet, counted on his fingers, and ran his hands through his hair*. By **chunking** (organizing material into meaningful units) we can increase the amount of information we can remember. Donatelli was able to recall up to 106 numbers read to him only once, one digit per second, by using chunking and hierarchies (clusters of chunks, organized from small to big). He was quiet while listening to the list but became very active and agitated (*he sprang alive*) as he used his mnemonic technique.

Storage: Retaining Information

Page 362: It was harder than reading by *lightning flashes*. In his investigation of sensory storage, George Sperling showed his subjects an array of nine letters for a very brief period (for about the length of a *flash of lightning*). He demonstrated that this was sufficient time for them to briefly view (*glimpse*) all nine letters and that an image remained for less than half a second before fading away; he called this brief (*fleeting*) memory of visual stimuli **iconic memory.**

Page 363: . . . *Sherlock Holmes* . . . Mystery writer Sir Arthur Conan Doyle's most popular character was a very intelligent and logical private detective named Sherlock Holmes. Holmes believed, as did many others, that our memory capacity was limited, much as a small empty room or attic can hold only so much furniture before it overflows. Contemporary psychologists now believe that our ability to store long-term memories is basically without any limit.

Page 363 (caption): Among animals, one contender for *champion memorist* would be a mere *birdbrain*—the Clark's nutcracker. . . . Clark's nutcracker is a small bird with a small brain (*birdbrain*) but a phenomenal memory (it is a *champion memorist*) of where it buries its food. It can recall, after a period of more than 6 months, 6000 different locations of hidden food (*caches*).

Pages 364–365: . . . *with tongue only partly in cheek*. When someone makes a statement that is not meant to be taken seriously, we note that it was said *with tongue in cheek*. When researchers stated that "memories are more of a spiritual than a physical reality," they were not totally serious (*tongue only partially in cheek*).

Page 366: Arousal *can sear* certain events into the brain. When arousal level rises because of stress, so too do the levels of certain hormones. These in turn signal the brain that something important has happened and the events that triggered the arousal make an indelible impression on the brain much as a hot grill burns (*sears*) its shape on the surface of the meat placed on it.

Page 367: They [people with amnesia] can be classically conditioned. . . . They can learn to read *mirror-image writing* or do a *jigsaw puzzle.* . . . They can be classically conditioned. People who have lost the ability to remember new information (*amnesics*) may nevertheless be capable of learning through association (classical conditioning) and of learning to solve problems (e.g., *jigsaw puzzles*) even if they are not aware of having done so. Myers notes that these findings suggest that memory is not a single, unified system. Amnesics can learn how to *do* something (**implicit memory**) without any knowledge of this learning (**explicit**, or **declarative**, **memory**).

Page 368: London cabbie . . . Taxi-cab drivers are often called *cabbies* and those who work in London, England (*London cabbies*), face an enormous challenge trying to memorize the complicated layout (*maze*) of city streets; the longer they work there the larger the rear area of the hippocampus (which specializes in spatial memory) becomes.

Page 369: Savoring that memory of a successful performance requires a *mental symphony conductor* that retrieves *snippets* from various cortical storage sites and integrates them with the emotional associations provided by your amygdala. Reliving and relishing (*savoring*) the memory of past accomplishments needs the mind's equivalent of an orchestra's director and organizer (*a mental symphony's conductor*) to locate pieces (*snippets*) from different brain areas (*various cortical storage sites*) and integrate them with emotional associations provided by the amygdala.

Retrieval: Getting Information Out

Page 374: If put in a *buoyant mood* . . . people recall the world through *rose-colored glasses.* . . . Our memories are affected by our emotional states (*moods*). Thus, if we are in a good or happy (*buoyant*) mood, we are more likely to view the total situation in a more optimistic and hopeful way (*through rose-colored glasses*). And if we are sad and unhappy, our memories are affected, or tainted, by our negative

mood (*being depressed sours memories*). Memory of events and people is influenced by the particular mood we are in, whether it is good or bad, and we tend to remember the events accordingly.

Page 374: When teenagers are *down*, their parents seem inhuman; as their mood *brightens*, their parents *morph from devils into angels.* Because our memories tend to be **mood-congruent**, we are likely to explain our present emotional state by remembering events and people as being consistent (*congruent*) with how we now feel. In one study when young adolescents were in a bad mood (*down*), they viewed their parents as cruel and uncaring (inhuman), but later when they were in a much better (*brighter*) mood their parents were described in much nicer terms. It seemed as though their parents had undergone an amazing change in character (*morphing from devils to angels*), but the change was simply in the teenagers' mood. As Myers notes, "*passions [or emotions] exaggerate.*"

Forgetting

Page 375: Amid all the *applause for memory* . . . have any voices been heard in praise of forgetting? We tend to focus on the importance of remembering and recalling information (*there is much applause for memory*). However, if we could not forget, we would be like the Russian memory expert (*memory whiz*) S who was overwhelmed by the amount of useless information he had stored (*haunted by his junk heap of memories*). Thus, many people, from William James to contemporary cognitive psychologists, acknowledge the importance of forgetting.

Page 378: A name *may lie poised on the tip of the tongue*, waiting to be retrieved. The expression *"it's on the tip of my tongue"* refers to the feeling you get when you are trying to remember something (a name, place, etc.) but can't, even though you feel you know it and can *almost* say it (*it's on the tip of your tongue*). Given an appropriate retrieval cue (such as the first letter of the name or something it rhymes with, etc.) we can often remember the item.

Page 379: As you collect more and more information, your *mental attic* never fills, but it certainly gets *cluttered.* We may have an unlimited amount of space in our memory system or *mental attic* (a room at the top of a house), but with a constant flow of new information coming in, the storage can become disorganized (*cluttered*). The new information may get in the way of recalling old material (**retroactive interference**), or old material may block or disrupt recall of new information (**proactive interference**).

Page 380: We *sheepishly* accepted responsibility for 89 cookies. Still, we had not come close; there had been 160. The Myers family obviously loves chocolate chip cookies, and the story of how all 160 were devoured (*scarfed, wolfed down, ate, consumed*) within 24 hours (*not a crumb was left*) is quite funny but makes an important point. Embarrassed, guilty, and feeling a little foolish (*sheepish*), they could only account for and remember eating 89. This illustrates the self-serving nature of memory and how, unknowingly, we change and revise our own histories.

Page 381: The words *relit a blown-out candle* in the mind . . . Just as an extinguished (*blown-out*) candle can be reignited (*relit*) with a match, the presentation of a retrieval cue may help someone recall or retrieve a long forgotten memory. Although Freud proposed that we repress memories of painful experiences in the unconscious mind in order to protect our self-concepts and minimize anxiety, Myers notes that most contemporary memory researchers believe repression rarely, if ever, happens.

Memory Construction

Page 384: Because memory is *reconstruction* as well as *reproduction*, we can't be sure whether a memory is real by how real it feels. It is difficult to determine if a memory is real simply by noting how real it feels or how confident we are about its accuracy. We not only recall and retrieve real memories (*reproduction*) but we also manufacture false memories (*reconstruction*).

Page 385: Memory construction helps explain why *"hypnotically refreshed"* memories of crimes so easily incorporate errors, some of which originate with the hypnotist's leading questions. Because of the tendency to manufacture events without being consciously aware of doing so (*memory construction*), people are likely to be influenced by suggestions and biased questions while under hypnosis. Their subsequent recollections (*"hypnotically refreshed"*) may therefore be a mixture of fact and fiction.

Page 386: If memories can be *sincere*, yet so *sincerely wrong*, might children's recollections of sexual abuse be prone to err? The evidence suggests that under appropriate conditions children's memories can be reliable and accurate (*sincere*), but that they are also prone to the misinformation effect and can be misled by biased questions and suggestions; later, the children are not able to reliably separate real from false (*sincerely wrong*) memories.

Improving Memory

Page 391: Sprinkled throughout this chapter and summarized here for easy reference are *concrete* suggestions for improving memory. This chapter on memory has many good ideas for memory improvement scattered or interspersed (*sprinkled*) throughout it, and Myers has pulled them together in an easy to understand format—the **SQ3R** (**S**urvey, **Q**uestion, **R**ead, **R**ehearse, **R**eview) method. These are real and tangible (*concrete*) ways that will help you improve your memory. Use them!!!

10: Thinking and Language

CHAPTER OVERVIEW

Most of Chapter 10 deals with thinking, with emphasis on how people logically—or at times illogically—use tools such as algorithms and heuristics when making decisions and solving problems. Also discussed are several common obstacles to problem solving, including fixations that prevent us from taking a fresh perspective on a problem and our bias to search for information that confirms rather than challenges existing hypotheses. The section concludes with a discussion of the power and perils of intuition.

The rest of the chapter is concerned with language, including its structure, development in children, relationship to thinking, and use by animals. Two theories of language acquisition are evaluated: Skinner's theory that language acquisition is based entirely on learning and Chomsky's theory that humans have a biological predisposition to acquire language.

NOTE: Answer guidelines for all Chapter 10 questions begin on page 274.

CHAPTER REVIEW

First, skim each section, noting headings and boldface items. After you have read the section, review each objective by answering the fill-in and essay-type questions that follow it. As you proceed, evaluate your performance by consulting the answers beginning on page 274. Do not continue with the next section until you understand each answer. If you need to, review or reread the section in the textbook before continuing.

Thinking (pp. 395–410)

> David Myers at times uses idioms that are unfamiliar to some readers. If you do not know the meaning of any of the following words, phrases, or expressions in the context in which they appear in the text, refer to pages 280–281 for an explanation: *kin to; birdier bird; stumbling upon one that worked; Try your hand . . . brain-teasers; shoot the basketball; seat-of-the-pants; snap judgment; "a broken promise"; plagues; road tested in the Stone Age; flip-flop; hunches; fuels social conflict; filled with straw; off-screen . . . displayed on-screen.*

Objective 1: Define *cognition.*

1. Cognition, or _____ , can be defined as _____ _____ .

2. Scientists who study these mental activities are called _____ _____ .

Objective 2: Describe the roles of categories, hierarchies, definitions, and prototypes in concept formation.

3. People tend to organize specific items into mental groupings called_____ , and many such groupings often are further organized into

   _____ .

4. Concepts are typically formed through the development of a best example, or _____ , of a category. People more easily detect _____ (male/female) prejudice against _____ (males/females) than vice versa.

Objective 3: Compare algorithms and heuristics as problem-solving strategies, and explain how insight differs from both of them.

5. Humans are especially capable of using their reasoning powers for coping with new situations, and thus for _____ _____ .

6. Finding a problem's solution by trying each possibility is called _____ _____ _____ .

7. Logical, methodical, step-by-step procedures for solving problems are called _____ .

8. Simple thinking strategies that provide us with problem-solving shortcuts are referred to as _____ .

9. When you suddenly realize a problem's solution, _____ has occurred. Research studies show that at such moments the brain displays a burst of activity in the _____ _____ _____ .

Objective 4: Contrast confirmation bias and fixation, and explain how they can interfere with effective problem solving.

10. The tendency of people to look for information that verifies their preconceptions is called the _____ _____ .

11. It is human nature to seek evidence that _____ our ideas more eagerly than to seek evidence that might _____ them.

12. Not being able to take a new perspective when attempting to solve a problem is referred to as _____ . One example of this obstacle to problem solving is the tendency to repeat solutions that have worked previously; this phenomenon is known as the development of a _____ _____ .

13. When a person is unable to envision using an object in an atypical way, _____ _____ is operating.

Objective 5: Contrast the representativeness and availability heuristics, and explain how they can cause us to underestimate or ignore important information.

14. People judge how well something matches a particular prototype; this is the _____ _____ .

15. When we judge the likelihood of something occurring in terms of how readily it comes to mind, we are using the _____ _____ .

Explain how these two heuristics may lead us to make judgmental errors.

16. (Thinking Critically) Many people fear _____ more than _____ , and _____ more than _____ , despite the fact that these fears are not supported by death and injury statistics. This type of faulty thinking occurs because we fear:
   a. _____
   b. _____
   c. _____
   d. _____

Objective 6: Describe the drawbacks and advantages of overconfidence in decision making.

17. The tendency of people to overestimate the accuracy of their knowledge results in _____ .

18. Overconfidence has _____ value because self-confident people tend to live _____ (more/less) happily and find it _____ (easier/harder) to make tough decisions.

19. When research participants are given feedback on the accuracy of their judgments, such feedback generally _____ (does/does not) help them become more realistic about how much they know.

Objective 7: Describe how others can use framing to elicit from us the answers they want.

20. The way an issue is posed is called _____ . This effect influences economic and business decisions, suggesting that our judgments _____ (may/may not) always be well reasoned.

Objective 8: Explain how our preexisting beliefs can distort our logic.

21. The tendency for our beliefs to distort logical reasoning is called _____ _____ .

22. This phenomenon makes it _____ (easier/more difficult) for us to see the illogic of conclusions that run counter to our beliefs.

Objective 9: Describe the remedy for the belief perseverance phenomenon.

23. Research has shown that once we form a belief or a concept, it may take more convincing evidence for us to change the concept than it did to create it; this is because of _____ _____ .

24. A cure for this is to _____ _____ _____ .

Objective 10: Describe the smart thinker's reaction to using intuition to solve problems.

25. Generally speaking, our cognition is _____ and _____ .

26. Intuitive reactions allow us to react _____ , and in ways that are usually _____ .

27. Smart thinkers check their intuitions against available _____ .

Language (pp. 410–418)

> If you do not know the meaning of any of the following words, phrases, or expressions in the context in which they appear in the text, refer to pages 281–282 for an explanation: *catapulting our species forward; They are hunting dogs; combine them on the fly; read lips; a Martian scientist; grammar switches are thrown.*

Objective 11: Describe the basic structural units of a language.

1. The basic sound units of language are its _____ . English has approximately _____ of these units. The basic units of sign language are defined by _____ _____ and _____ .

2. Phonemes are grouped into units of meaning called _____ .

3. The system of rules that enables us to use our language to speak to and understand others is called _____ .

4. The system by which meaning is derived from morphemes, words, and sentences is the _____ of a language.

5. The system of rules we use to combine words into grammatically sensible sentences is called _____ .

Objective 12: Trace the course of language acquisition from the babbling stage through the two-word stage.

6. By _____ months of age, babies can read lips and discriminate speech sounds. This marks the beginning of their _____ _____ , their ability to comprehend speech. This ability begins to mature before their _____ _____ , or ability to produce words.

7. The first stage of language development, in which children spontaneously utter different sounds, is the _____ stage. This stage typically begins at about _____ months of age. The sounds children make during this stage _____ (do/do not) include only the phonemes of the language that they hear.

8. Deaf infants _____ (do/do not) babble. Many natural babbling sounds are _____-_____ pairs formed by _____

_____ .

9. By about _____ months of age, infant babbling begins to resemble the household language. At about the same time, the ability to perceive phoneme differences is _____ (lost/acquired).

10. During the second stage, called the _____-_____ stage, children convey complete thoughts using single words. This stage begins at about _____ year(s) of age.

11. During the _____-_____ stage children speak in sentences containing mostly nouns and verbs. This type of speech is called _____ speech.

12. After this stage, children quickly begin to utter longer phrases that _____ (do/do not) follow the rules of syntax.

Objective 13: Discuss Skinner's and Chomsky's contributions to the nature-nurture debate over how children acquire language, and explain why statistical learning and critical periods are important concepts in children's language learning.

13. Skinner believed that language development follows the general principles of learning, including _____ , _____ , and _____ . When there is minimal reinforcement for speaking, as is the case for hearing children whose parents are _____ , the learning of spoken language proceeds _____ (more slowly/at a normal pace).

14. Other theorists believe that humans are biologically predisposed to learn language. One such theorist is _____ , who believes that we all are born with a _____ _____ _____ in which _____ switches are thrown as children experience their language. This theorist contends that all human languages have the same grammatical building blocks, which suggests that there is a _____ _____ .

15. Specific phonemes, morphemes, words, and sentences make up what Chomsky calls the _____ _____ of a language. The underlying meaning of these components of a language make up its _____ _____ . Thus, using multiple levels of understanding language development, _____ design the mechanisms and _____ modifies the brain.

Give several examples of linguistic behavior in children that support the argument that humans are biologically predisposed to acquire language.

16. Research by Jenny Saffran has demonstrated that even before _____ year(s) of age, infants are able to discern _____ _____ by analyzing which syllables most often go together.

17. Research studies of infants' knack for soaking up language suggest that babies come with a built-in readiness to learn _____ _____ .

18. This ability for _____ _____ is not lifelong. Childhood seems to represent a _____ _____ for mastering certain aspects

of language. Those who learn a second language as adults usually speak it with the _____ of their first language. Moreover, they typically show _____ (poorer/better) mastery of the _____ of the second language.

19. The window for learning language gradually begins to close after age _____ . When a young brain doesn't learn any language, its language-learning capacity _____ (never/may still) fully develops.

20. Considering the two theories together, we can say that although we are born with a readiness to learn language, _____ is also important, as shown in linguistically stunted children who have been isolated from language during the _____ _____ for its acquisition.

Thinking and Language (pp. 418–422)

> If you do not know the meaning of the following phrase in the context in which it appears in the text, refer to page 282 for an explanation: *chicken-and-egg questions.*

Objective 14: Summarize Whorf's linguistic determinism hypothesis, and comment on its standing in contemporary psychology.

1. According to the _____ _____ hypothesis, language shapes our thinking. The linguist who proposed this hypothesis is _____ .

2. Many people who are bilingual report feeling a different sense of _____, depending on which language they are using. There are an estimated _____ languages in the world today.

3. In several studies, researchers have found that using the pronoun "he" (instead of "he or she") _____ (does/does not) influence people's thoughts concerning gender.

4. Bilingual children, who learn to inhibit one language while using their other language, are better able to inhibit their _____ to irrele-

vant information. This has been called the _____ _____ .

5. One study of Canadian children found that English-speaking children who were _____ in French had higher _____ scores and math scores than control children.

Objective 15: Discuss the value of thinking in images.

6. It appears that thinking _____ (can/cannot) occur without the use of language. Athletes often supplement physical with _____ practice.

7. In one study of psychology students preparing for a midterm exam, the greatest benefits were achieved by those who visualized themselves _____ (receiving a high grade/studying effectively).

Summarize the probable relationship between thinking and language.

Animal Thinking and Language
(pp. 423–428)

> If you do not know the meaning of the following phrase in the context in which it appears in the text, refer to page 282 for an explanation: *rhapsodized; Spying the short stick; Were the chimps language champs or were the researchers chumps?*

Objective 16: List five cognitive skills shared by the great apes and humans.

1. Animals are capable of forming simple _____ . Wolfgang Köhler demonstrated that chimpanzees also exhibit the "Aha!" reaction that characterizes reasoning by _____ .

2. Forest-dwelling chimpanzees learn to use branches, stones, and other objects as _____ . These behaviors, along with behaviors related to

grooming and courtship, _____ (vary/ do not vary) from one group to another, suggesting the transmission of _____ customs.

3. Deception and mirror usage by chimpanzees and other apes suggests to some researchers that these animals may possess a rudimentary understanding of mental states called a _____

_____ _____ .

Researchers estimate apes' capacity for reasoning as similar to that of children at age

_____ .

Objective 17: Outline the arguments for and against the idea that animals and humans share the capacity for language.

4. Animals definitely _____ . For example, honeybees do so by means of a

_____ .

5. The Gardners attempted to communicate with the chimpanzee Washoe by teaching her

_____ _____ .

6. Human language may have evolved from _____ communications.

Summarize some of the arguments of skeptics of the "talking apes" research and some responses of believers.

PROGRESS TEST 1

Multiple-Choice Questions

Circle your answers to the following questions and check them with the answers beginning on page 275. If your answer is incorrect, read the explanation for why it is incorrect and then consult the appropriate pages of the text (in parentheses following the correct answer).

1. The text defines cognition as:
   a. silent speech.
   b. all mental activity.
   c. mental activity associated with processing, understanding, remembering, and communicating information.
   d. logical reasoning.

2. A mental grouping of similar things, events, or people is called a(n):
   a. prototype.   c. algorithm.
   b. concept.   d. heuristic.

3. When forming a concept, people often develop a best example, or _____ , of a category.
   a. denoter   c. prototype
   b. heuristic   d. algorithm

4. Confirmation bias refers to the tendency to:
   a. allow preexisting beliefs to distort logical reasoning.
   b. cling to one's initial conceptions after the basis on which they were formed has been discredited.
   c. search randomly through alternative solutions when problem solving.
   d. look for information that is consistent with one's beliefs.

5. The English language has approximately _____ phonemes.
   a. 25   c. 40
   b. 30   d. 45

6. Which of the following is *not* true of babbling?
   a. It is imitation of adult speech.
   b. It is the same in all cultures.
   c. It typically occurs from about age 4 months to 1 year.
   d. Babbling increasingly comes to resemble a particular language.

7. Mental set and functional fixedness are two types of:
   a. algorithms.   c. fixation.
   b. heuristics.   d. insight.

8. Which of the following has been argued by critics of ape language research?
   a. Ape language is merely imitation of the trainer's behavior.
   b. There is little evidence that apes can equal even a 3-year-old's ability to order words with proper syntax.
   c. By seeing what they wish to see, trainers attribute greater linguistic ability to apes than actually exists.
   d. All of the above have been argued.

9. Whorf's linguistic determinism hypothesis states that:
   a. language is primarily a learned ability.
   b. language is partially an innate ability.
   c. the size of a person's vocabulary reflects his or her intelligence.
   d. our language shapes our thinking.

10. Which of the following *best* describes Chomsky's view of language development?
    a. Language is an entirely learned ability.
    b. Language is an innate ability.
    c. Humans have a biological predisposition to acquire language.
    d. There are no cultural influences on the development of language.

11. Failing to solve a problem that requires using an object in an unusual way illustrates the phenomenon of:
    a. mental set.
    b. functional fixedness.
    c. framing.
    d. belief perseverance.

12. Which of the following is an example of the use of heuristics?
    a. trying every possible letter ordering when unscrambling a word
    b. considering each possible move when playing chess
    c. using the formula "area = length × width" to find the area of a rectangle
    d. playing chess using a defensive strategy that has often been successful for you

13. The chimpanzee Sultan used a short stick to pull a longer stick that was out of reach into his cage. He then used the longer stick to reach a piece of fruit. Researchers hypothesized that Sultan's discovery of the solution to his problem was the result of:
    a. trial and error.
    b. heuristics.
    c. functional fixedness.
    d. insight.

14. You hear that one of the Smith children is an outstanding Little League player and immediately conclude it's their one son rather than any of their four daughters. You reached your quite possibly erroneous conclusion as the result of:
    a. the confirmation bias.
    b. the availability heuristic.
    c. the representativeness heuristic.
    d. belief perseverance.

15. Researchers who are convinced that animals can think point to evidence that:
    a. monkeys demonstrate the ability to "count" by learning to touch pictures of objects in ascending numerical order.
    b. chimpanzees regularly use branches, stones, and other objects as tools in their natural habitats.
    c. chimps invent grooming and courtship customs and pass them on to their peers.
    d. all of the above occur.

16. Deaf children who are not exposed to sign language until they are teenagers:
    a. are unable to master the basic words of sign language.
    b. learn the basic words but not how to order them.
    c. are unable to master either the basic words or syntax of sign language.
    d. never become as fluent as those who learned to sign at a younger age.

17. According to the text, language acquisition is best described as:
    a. the result of conditioning and reinforcement.
    b. a biological process of maturation.
    c. an interaction between biology and experience.
    d. a mystery of which researchers have no real understanding.

18. Infants as young as 6 months old display a remarkable ability to learn statistical aspects of speech. Specifically, research studies have shown that they:
    a. are quickly able to recognize syllable sequences that appear repeatedly.
    b. respond to changes in the pitch of a speaker's voice.
    c. pay less attention to a same-gender voice.
    d. do all of the above.

19. The linguistic determinism hypothesis is challenged by the finding that:
    a. chimps can learn to communicate spontaneously by using sign language.
    b. people with no word for a certain color can still perceive that color accurately.
    c. the Eskimo language contains a number of words for snow, whereas English has only one.
    d. infants' babbling contains many phonemes that do not occur in their own language and that they therefore cannot have heard.

20. Several studies have indicated that the generic pronoun "he":
    a. tends for children and adults alike to trigger images of both males and females.
    b. tends for adults to trigger images of both males and females, but for children to trigger images of males.
    c. tends for both children and adults to trigger images of males but not females.
    d. for both children and adults triggers images of females about one-fourth of the time it is used.

Matching Items

Match each definition or description with the appropriate term.

Definitions or Descriptions

_____ 1. the basic units of sound in a language
_____ 2. the way an issue or question is posed
_____ 3. rules for combining words into sentences
_____ 4. the rules by which meaning is derived from sentences
_____ 5. presuming that something is likely if it comes readily to mind
_____ 6. the tendency to overestimate the accuracy of one's judgments
_____ 7. being unable to see a problem from a different angle
_____ 8. haphazard problem solving by trying one solution after another
_____ 9. the sudden realization of the solution to a problem
_____ 10. the tendency to repeat problem-solving techniques that worked in the past even though a fresh approach may be more appropriate.
_____ 11. the basic units of meaning in a language

Terms

a. syntax
b. morphemes
c. mental set
d. trial and error
e. availability heuristic
f. phonemes
g. semantics
h. insight
i. framing
j. overconfidence
k. fixation

PROGRESS TEST 2

Progress Test 2 should be completed during a final chapter review. Answer the following questions after you thoroughly understand the correct answers for the section reviews and Progress Test 1.

Multiple-Choice Questions

1. A common problem in everyday reasoning is our tendency to:
   a. accept as logical those conclusions that agree with our own opinions.
   b. accept as logical those conclusions that disagree with our own opinions.
   c. underestimate the accuracy of our knowledge.
   d. accept as logical conclusions that involve unfamiliar concepts.

2. Phonemes are the basic units of _____ in language.
   a. sound
   b. meaning
   c. grammar
   d. semantics

3. Syntax refers to the:
   a. sounds in a word.
   b. rules for grouping words into sentences.
   c. rules by which meaning is derived from sentences.
   d. overall rules of a language.

4. Skinner and other behaviorists have argued that language development is the result of:
   a. imitation.
   b. reinforcement.
   c. association.
   d. all of the above.

5. Many psychologists are skeptical of claims that chimpanzees can acquire language because the chimps have not shown the ability to:
   a. use symbols meaningfully.
   b. acquire speech.
   c. acquire even a limited vocabulary.
   d. use syntax in communicating.

6. Representativeness and availability are examples of:
   a. mental sets.
   b. belief bias.
   c. algorithms.
   d. heuristics.

7. The basic units of cognition are:
   a. phonemes.
   b. concepts.
   c. prototypes.
   d. morphemes.

8. Researchers who believe that some primates possess a rudimentary theory of mind point to evidence that:
   a. chimpanzees have been observed using mirrors to inspect themselves.
   b. vervet monkeys have different alarm calls for different predators.
   c. orangutans in the wild frequently use stones as tools.
   d. honeybees communicate the direction and distance of a food source by performing an intricate dance.

9. Assume that Congress is considering revising its approach to welfare and to this end is hearing a range of testimony. A member of Congress who uses the availability heuristic would be most likely to:
   a. want to experiment with numerous possible approaches to see which of these seems to work best.
   b. want to cling to approaches to welfare that seem to have had some success in the past.
   c. refuse to be budged from his or her beliefs despite persuasive testimony to the contrary.
   d. base his or her ideas on the most vivid, memorable testimony given, even though many of the statistics presented run counter to this testimony.

10. If you want to be absolutely certain that you will find the solution to a problem you know *is* solvable, you should use:
    a. a heuristic.
    b. an algorithm.
    c. insight.
    d. trial and error.

11. Complete the following: *-ed* is to *sh* as _____ is to _____.
    a. phoneme; morpheme
    b. morpheme; phoneme
    c. grammar; syntax
    d. syntax; grammar

12. Which of the following is *not* cited by Chomsky as evidence that language acquisition cannot be explained by learning alone?
    a. Children master the complicated rules of grammar with ease.
    b. Children create sentences they have never heard.
    c. Children make the kinds of mistakes that suggest they are attempting to apply rules of grammar.
    d. Children raised in isolation from language spontaneously begin speaking words.

13. Telegraphic speech is typical of the _____ stage.
    a. babbling
    b. one-word
    c. two-word
    d. three-word

14. Children first demonstrate a rudimentary understanding of syntax during the _____ stage.
    a. babbling
    b. one-word
    c. two-word
    d. three-word

15. The study in which people who immigrated to the United States at various ages were compared in terms of their ability to understand English grammar found that:
    a. age of arrival had no effect on mastery of grammar.
    b. those who immigrated as children understood grammar as well as native speakers.
    c. those who immigrated as adults understood grammar as well as native speakers.
    d. whether or not English was spoken in the home was the most important factor in mastering the rules of grammar.

16. Researchers taught the chimpanzee Washoe and the gorilla Koko to communicate by using:
    a. various sounds.
    b. plastic symbols of various shapes and colors.
    c. sign language.
    d. all of the above.

17. Regarding the relationship between thinking and language, which of the following most accurately reflects the position taken in the text?

    a. Language determines everything about our thinking.
    b. Language determines the way we think.
    c. Thinking without language is not possible.
    d. Thinking affects our language, which then affects our thought.

18. The rules most directly involved in permitting a person to derive meaning from words and sentences are rules of:

    a. syntax.   c. phonemic structure.
    b. grammar.   d. semantics.

19. Which of the following is true regarding the relationship between thinking and language?

    a. "Real" thinking requires the use of language.
    b. People sometimes think in images rather than in words.
    c. A thought that cannot be expressed in a particular language cannot occur to speakers of that language.
    d. All of the above are true.

20. One reason an English-speaking adult may have difficulty pronouncing Russian words is that:

    a. the vocal tracts of English- and Russian-speaking people develop differently in response to the demands of the two languages.
    b. although English and Russian have very similar morphemes, their phonemic inventories are very different.
    c. although English and Russian have very similar phonemes, their morphemic inventories are very different.
    d. after the babbling stage, a child who hears only English stops uttering other phonemes.

True–False Items

Indicate whether each statement is true or false by placing *T* or *F* in the blank next to the item.

_____ 1. The order in which children acquire an understanding of various morphemes is unpredictable.

_____ 2. According to the confirmation bias, people often interpret ambiguous evidence as support for their beliefs.

_____ 3. Most human problem solving involves the use of heuristics rather than reasoning that systematically considers every possible solution.

_____ 4. When asked, most people underestimate the accuracy of their judgments.

_____ 5. Studies have shown that even animals may sometimes have insight reactions.

_____ 6. Mental set is the tendency to repeat problem-solving solutions that have worked in the past.

_____ 7. Although the morphemes differ from language to language, the phonemes for all languages are the same.

_____ 8. Children of all cultures babble using the same phonemes.

_____ 9. Thinking without using language is not possible.

_____ 10. Most researchers believe that we can perform statistical analyses of language throughout our lives.

PSYCHOLOGY APPLIED

Answer these questions the day before an exam as a final check on your understanding of the chapter's terms and concepts.

Multiple-Choice Questions

1. The word "predates" contains _____ phonemes and _____ morphemes.

    a. 7; 3   c. 7; 2
    b. 3; 7   d. 3; 2

2. Which of the following utterances is an example of overgeneralization of a grammatical rule?

    a. "We goed to the store."
    b. "Ball pretty."
    c. "The sky is crying."
    d. "We eat 'paghetti."

3. A listener hearing a recording of Japanese, Spanish, and North American children babbling would:

    a. not be able to tell them apart.
    b. be able to tell them apart if they were older than 6 months.
    c. be able to tell them apart if they were older than 8 to 10 months.
    d. be able to tell them apart at any age.

4. Which of the following illustrates belief perseverance?

    a. Your belief remains intact even in the face of evidence to the contrary.
    b. You refuse to listen to arguments counter to your beliefs.

c. You tend to become flustered and angered when your beliefs are refuted.

d. You tend to search for information that supports your beliefs.

5. Complete the following analogy: Rose is to flower as:

 a. concept is to prototype.
 b. prototype is to concept.
 c. concept is to hierarchy.
 d. hierarchy is to concept.

6. Your stand on an issue such as the use of nuclear power for electricity involves personal judgment. In such a case, one memorable occurrence can weigh more heavily than a bookful of data, thus illustrating:

 a. belief perseverance.
 b. confirmation bias.
 c. the representativeness heuristic.
 d. the availability heuristic.

7. A dessert recipe that gives you the ingredients, their amounts, and the steps to follow is an example of a(n):

 a. prototype.   **c.** heuristic.
 b. algorithm.   **d.** mental set.

8. Marilyn was asked to solve a series of five math problems. The first four problems could only be solved by a particular sequence of operations. The fifth problem could also be solved following this sequence; however, a much simpler solution was possible. Marilyn did not realize this simpler solution and solved the problem in the way she had solved the first four. Her problem-solving strategy was hampered by:

 a. functional fixedness.
 b. the overconfidence phenomenon.
 c. mental set.
 d. her lack of a prototype for the solution.

9. Dr. Mendoza is studying the mental strategies people use when solving problems. Dr. Mendoza is clearly a(n):

 a. cognitive psychologist.
 b. experimental psychologist.
 c. organizational psychologist.
 d. developmental psychologist.

10. Boris the chess master selects his next move by considering moves that would threaten his opponent's queen. His opponent, a chess-playing computer, selects its next move by considering *all* possible moves. Boris is using a(n) _____ and the computer is using a(n) _____ .

 a. algorithm; heuristic
 b. prototype; mental set
 c. mental set; prototype
 d. heuristic; algorithm

11. During a televised political debate, the Republican and Democratic candidates each argued that the results of a recent public opinion poll supported their party's platform regarding sexual harassment. Because both candidates saw the information as supporting their belief, it is clear that both were victims of:

 a. functional fixedness.   **c.** belief bias.
 b. mental set.   **d.** confirmation bias.

12. The child who says "Milk gone" is engaging in _____ . This type of utterance demonstrates that children are actively experimenting with the rules of _____ .

 a. babbling; syntax
 b. telegraphic speech; syntax
 c. babbling; semantics
 d. telegraphic speech; semantics

13. Experts in a field prefer heuristics to algorithms because heuristics:

 a. guarantee solutions to problems.
 b. prevent mental sets.
 c. often save time.
 d. prevent fixation.

14. Rudy is 6 feet 6 inches tall, weighs 210 pounds, and is very muscular. If you think that Rudy is more likely to be a basketball player than a computer programmer, you are a victim of:

 a. belief bias.
 b. mental set.
 c. functional fixedness.
 d. the representativeness heuristic.

15. Failing to see that an article of clothing can be inflated as a life preserver is an example of:

 a. belief bias.
 b. the availability heuristic.
 c. the representativeness heuristic.
 d. functional fixedness.

16. Airline reservations typically decline after a highly publicized airplane crash because people overestimate the incidence of such disasters. In such instances, their decisions are being influenced by:
    a. belief bias.
    b. the availability heuristic.
    c. the representativeness heuristic.
    d. functional fixedness.

17. Most people tend to:
    a. accurately estimate the accuracy of their knowledge and judgments.
    b. underestimate the accuracy of their knowledge and judgments.
    c. overestimate the accuracy of their knowledge and judgments.
    d. lack confidence in their decision-making strategies.

18. In relation to ground beef, consumers respond more positively to an ad describing it as "75 percent lean" than to one referring to its "25 percent fat" content. This is an example of:
    a. the framing effect.   c. mental set.
    b. confirmation bias.   d. overconfidence.

19. The sentence "Blue jeans wear false smiles" has correct _____ but incorrect _____ .
    a. morphemes; phonemes
    b. phonemes; morphemes
    c. semantics; syntax
    d. syntax; semantics

20. In preparing her class presentation, "Updating Chomsky's Understanding of Language Development," Britney's outline includes all of the following evidence *except* that:
    a. computers programmed to learn to form the past tense of irregular verbs can learn to do so, even without "inborn" linguistic rules.
    b. infants rapidly learn to detect subtle differences between simple sequences of syllables.
    c. infants can recognize color differences even before they can name different colors.
    d. children isolated from language during the first seven years of life never fully develop language.

Essay Question

The lectures of your linguistics professor, who happens to be a staunch behaviorist, clearly imply that she believes language development can be explained according to principles of conditioning. What evidence should you present to convince her that she is wrong? (Use the space below to list the points you want to make, and organize them. Then write the essay on a separate piece of paper.)

KEY TERMS

Writing Definitions

Using your own words, on a piece of paper write a brief definition or explanation of each of the following terms.

1. cognition

2. concept

3. prototype

4. algorithm

5. heuristic

6. insight

7. confirmation bias

8. fixation

9. mental set

10. functional fixedness

11. representativeness heuristic

12. availability heuristic

13. overconfidence

14. framing

15. belief bias

16. belief perseverance

17. language

18. phonemes

19. morphemes

20. grammar

21. semantics

22. syntax

23. babbling stage

24. one-word stage

25. two-word stage

26. telegraphic speech

27. linguistic determinism

Cross-Check

As you learned in the Prologue, reviewing and overlearning of material are important to the learning process. After you have written the definitions of the key terms in this chapter, you should complete the crossword puzzle to ensure that you can reverse the process—recognize the term, given the definition.

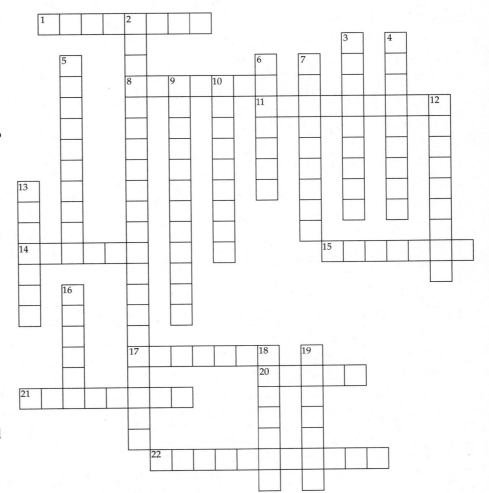

ACROSS

1. Stage of speech development characterized by the spontaneous utterance of speech sounds.
8. System of rules that enables us to communicate with and understand others.
11. Methodical problem-solving strategy that guarantees success.
14. Chimp that was taught sign language by the Gardners.
15. Theorist who believed that language development could be explained by principles of learning.
17. Sudden and often creative solution to a problem.
20. Theorist who formulated the linguistic determinism hypothesis.
21. Inability to approach a problem in a new way.
22. The economical speech of children in the two-word stage.

DOWN

2. The idea that language determines the way we think.
3. Simple thinking strategy for solving problems.
4. The best example of a particular category.
5. Tendency for preexisting beliefs to distort reasoning.
6. How an issue or question is posed.
7. Mental activity associated with processing, understanding, and communicating information.
9. Heuristic based on estimating the probability of events in terms of how readily they come to mind.
10. Tendency to continue applying a particular problem-solving strategy even when it is no longer helpful.
12. Smallest units of language that convey meaning.
13. Stage of language development that occurs between 1 and 2 years of age.

16. Aspect of grammar specifying the rules for combining words into grammatical sentences.
18. Stage of language development that begins about age 2.
19. Mental grouping of similar objects, events, or people.

ANSWERS

Thinking

1. thinking; the mental activity associated with processing, knowing, remembering, and communicating
2. cognitive psychologists
3. concepts; hierarchies
4. prototype; male; females
5. problem solving
6. trial and error
7. algorithms
8. heuristics
9. insight; right temporal lobe
10. confirmation bias
11. verifies; refute
12. fixation; mental set
13. functional fixedness
14. representativeness heuristic
15. availability heuristic

Using these heuristics often prevents us from processing other relevant information; because we overlook this information, we make judgmental errors. Thus, in the text example, the representativeness heuristic leads people to overlook the fact that there are many more truck drivers than Ivy League classics professors and, as a result, to wrongly conclude that the poetry reader is more likely to be an Ivy League classics professor. Also as noted in the text, the availability heuristic leads us to incorrectly think that words beginning with *k* are more common than words having *k* as their third letter.

16. flying; driving; terrorism; accidents
    a. what our ancestral history has prepared us to fear.
    b. what we cannot control.
    c. what is immediate.
    b. what is most readily available in memory.
17. overconfidence
18. adaptive; more; easier

19. does
20. framing; may not
21. belief bias
22. easier
23. belief perseverance
24. consider the opposite
25. effective; efficient
26. quickly; adaptive
27. evidence

Language

1. phonemes; 40; hand shapes; movements
2. morphemes
3. grammar
4. semantics
5. syntax
6. 4; receptive language; productive language
7. babbling; 4; do not
8. do; consonant-vowel; bunching the tongue in front of the mouth
9. 10; lost
10. one-word; 1
11. two-word; telegraphic
12. do
13. association; imitation; reinforcement; deaf; more slowly
14. Chomsky; language acquisition device; grammar; universal grammar
15. surface structure; deep structure; genes; experience

The rate at which children acquire vocabulary and grammar is too rapid to be explained solely by learning. Children create sentences that they have never heard and, therefore, could not be imitating. Children learn grammatical rules in a predictable order. Children's linguistic errors are often logical overextensions of grammatical rules.

16. 1; word breaks
17. grammatical rules
18. statistical analysis; critical period; accent; poorer; grammar
19. 7; never
20. experience; critical period

Thinking and Language

1. linguistic determinism; Whorf
2. self; 6000
3. does
4. attention; bilingual advantage
5. immersed; aptitude
6. can; mental
7. studying effectively

The relationship is probably a two-way one: the linguistic determinism hypothesis suggests that language helps shape thought; that words come into the language to express new ideas indicates that thought also shapes language.

Animal Thinking and Language

1. concepts; insight
2. tools; vary; cultural
3. theory of mind; 2
4. communicate; dance
5. sign language
6. gestural

Chimps have acquired only limited vocabularies and—in contrast to children—have acquired these vocabularies only with great difficulty. Also in contrast to children, it's unclear that chimps can use syntax to express meaning. Even simpler animals, such as birds, are capable of learning behavioral sequences that some chimp researchers consider language. The signing of chimps is often nothing more than imitation of the trainer's actions. People tend to interpret such ambiguous behavior in terms of what they want to see. Believers contend that although animals do not have our facility for language, they have the abilities to communicate. For example, Washoe and Loulis sign spontaneously. Also, pygmy chimps can learn to comprehend the spoken nuances of spoken English.

Progress Test 1

Multiple-Choice Questions

1. c. is the answer. (p. 395)
2. b. is the answer. (p. 396)
   a. A prototype is the best example of a particular category, or concept.
   c. & d. Algorithms and heuristics are problem-solving strategies.
3. c. is the answer. (p. 396)
   a. There is no such thing as a "denoter."
   b. & d. Heuristics and algorithms are problem-solving strategies.

4. d. is the answer. It is a major obstacle to problem solving. (p. 399)
   a. & b. These refer to belief bias and belief perseverance, respectively.
   c. This is trial-and-error problem solving.
5. c. is the answer. (p. 411)
6. a. is the answer. Babbling is not the imitation of adult speech since babbling infants produce phonemes from languages they have not heard and could not be imitating. (p. 412)
7. c. is the answer. Both involve failing to see a problem from a new perspective. (p. 400)
   a. & b. Algorithms and heuristics are problem-solving strategies.
   d. Insight is the sudden realization of a problem's solution.
8. d. is the answer. (pp. 426–427)
9. d. is the answer. (p. 418)
   a. This is Skinner's position regarding language development.
   b. This is Chomsky's position regarding language development.
   c. The linguistic determinism hypothesis is concerned with the content of thought, not intelligence.
10. c. is the answer. (p. 414)
    a. This is Skinner's position.
    b. According to Chomsky, although the *ability* to acquire language is innate, the child can only acquire language in association with others.
    d. Cultural influences are an important example of the influence of learning on language development, an influence Chomsky fully accepts.
11. b. is the answer. Functional fixedness is the tendency to think of things only in terms of their usual functions. (p. 400)
    a. Mental set is the tendency to approach a problem in a particular way that worked previously.
    c. Framing refers to the way an issue is posed; this often influences our judgment.
    d. Belief perseverance is the tendency to cling to one's beliefs even after they have been refuted.
12. d. is the answer. Heuristics are simple thinking strategies—such as playing chess defensively—that are based on past successes in similar situations. (p. 398)
    a., b., & c. These are all algorithms.
13. d. is the answer. Sultan suddenly arrived at a novel solution to his problem, thus displaying apparent insight. (p. 423)
    a. Sultan did not randomly try various strategies of reaching the fruit; he demonstrated the "light bulb" reaction that is the hallmark of insight.
    b. Heuristics are simple thinking strategies.

c. Functional fixedness is an impediment to problem solving. Sultan obviously solved his problem.

14. **c.** is the answer. Your conclusion is based on sex stereotypes, that is, athletic ability and participation are for you more *representative* of boys. Your conclusion is by no means necessarily right, however, especially since the Smiths have four daughters and only one son. (p. 401)

a. The confirmation bias is the tendency to look for information that confirms one's preconceptions.

b. The availability heuristic involves judging the probability of an event in terms of how readily it comes to mind.

d. Belief perseverance is the tendency to cling to beliefs, even when the evidence has shown that they are wrong.

15. **d.** is the answer. (pp. 423–424)

16. **d.** is the answer. Compared with deaf children exposed to sign language from birth, those who learn to sign as teens have the same grammatical difficulties as do hearing adults trying to learn a second spoken language. (p. 417)

17. **c.** is the answer. Children are biologically prepared to learn language as they and their caregivers interact. (p. 417)

a. This is Skinner's position.

b. No psychologist, including Chomsky, believes that language is entirely a product of biological maturation.

d. Although language acquisition is not completely understood, research has shed sufficient light on it to render it less than a complete mystery.

18. **a.** is the answer. (pp. 415–416)

b. & c. This research is unrelated to infants' ability to detect different pitches of voices or distinguish between male and female voices.

19. **b.** is the answer. The evidence that absence of a term for a color does not affect ability to perceive the color challenges the idea that language always shapes thought. (p. 419)

a. & d. These findings are not relevant to the linguistic determinism hypothesis, which addresses the relationship between language and thought.

c. This finding is in keeping with the linguistic determinism hypothesis.

20. **c.** is the answer. The generic pronoun *he* evidently tends, for both adults and children, to conjure up images of males. (p. 419)

Matching Items

1. f (p. 410)
2. i (p. 406)
3. a (p. 411)
4. g (p. 411)
5. e (p. 402)
6. j (p. 403)
7. k (p. 400)
8. d (p. 397)
9. h (p. 398)
10. c (p. 400)
11. b (p. 411)

Progress Test 2

Multiple-Choice Questions

1. **a.** is the answer. Reasoning in daily life is often distorted by our beliefs, which may lead us, for example, to accept conclusions that haven't been arrived at logically. (p. 407)

b., c., & d. These are just the opposite of what we tend to do.

2. **a.** is the answer. (p. 410)

b. Morphemes are the basic units of meaning.

c. & d. The text does not refer to basic units of grammar or semantics.

3. **b.** is the answer. (p. 411)

a. Phonemes are the sounds in a word.

c. Such rules are known as semantics.

d. Such rules are the language's grammar, which would include its syntax as well as its semantics.

4. **d.** is the answer. These are all basic principles of learning and, according to Skinner, explain language development. (p. 413)

5. **d.** is the answer. Syntax is one of the fundamental aspects of language, and chimps seem unable, for example, to use word order to convey differences in meaning. (p. 426)

a. & c. Chimps' use of sign language demonstrates both the use of symbols and the acquisition of fairly sizable vocabularies.

b. No psychologist would require the use of speech as evidence of language; significantly, all the research and arguments focus on what chimps are and are not able to do in acquiring other facets of language.

6. **d.** is the answer. Both are simple thinking strategies that allow us to make quick judgments. (pp. 401–402)

a. Mental sets are obstacles to problem solving, in which the person tends to repeat solutions that have worked in the past and is unable to conceive of other possible solutions.

b. Belief bias is the tendency for preexisting beliefs to distort logical reasoning.

c. Algorithms are methodical strategies that guarantee a solution to a particular problem.

7. **b.** is the answer. (p. 396)
   a. & d. Phonemes and morphemes are units of sound and meaning in language, respectively.
   c. Prototypes are the best examples of specific categories.

8. **a.** is the answer. (p. 424)
   b. & c. Alarm-calling and tool use are clear indicators of animal communication and thinking, respectively. However, they reveal nothing about the ability to infer mental states in oneself or another.
   d. Honeybees are insects, not primates!

9. **d.** is the answer. If we use the availability heuristic, we base judgments on the availability of information in our memories, and more vivid information is often the most readily available. (p. 402)
   a. This would exemplify use of the trial-and-error approach to problem solving.
   b. This would exemplify a mental set.
   c. This would exemplify belief perseverance.

10. **b.** is the answer. Because they involve the systematic examination of all possible solutions to a problem, algorithms guarantee that a solution will be found. (p. 397)
    a., c., & d. None of these methods guarantees that a problem's solution will be found.

11. **b.** is the answer. The morpheme *-ed* changes the *meaning* of a regular verb to form its past tense; the phoneme *sh* is a unique *sound* in the English language. (pp. 410, 411)
    c. & d. Syntax, which specifies rules for combining words into grammatical sentences, is one aspect of the grammar of a language.

12. **d.** is the answer. Chomsky believes that the inborn capacity for language acquisition must be activated by exposure to language. And, in fact, children raised in isolation will *not* begin to speak spontaneously. (p. 414)

13. **c.** is the answer. (p. 413)

14. **c.** is the answer. Although the child's utterances are only two words long, the words are placed in a sensible order. In English, for example, adjectives are placed before nouns. (p. 413)
    a. & b. Syntax specifies rules for *combining* two or more units in speech.
    d. There is no three-word stage.

15. **b.** is the answer. (p. 416)

16. **c.** is the answer. (pp. 425, 426)

17. **d.** is the answer. (p. 422)

18. **d.** is the answer. Semantic rules are directly concerned with the derivation of meaning from morphemes, words, and sentences. (p. 411)
    a. Syntax is the set of rules for a language that permits the combination of words into sentences.
    b. Grammar is the overall system of rules for using a language and, as such, includes syntax as well as semantics.
    c. Phonemic structure concerns the basic sounds, or phonemes, of a language.

19. **b.** is the answer. (pp. 420–421)
    a. Researchers do not make a distinction between "real" and other thinking, nor do they consider nonlinguistic thinking less valid than linguistic thinking.
    c. As indicated by several studies cited in the text, this is not true.

20. **d.** is the answer. Following the babbling stage, the child's ability to produce all phonemes becomes in a sense shaped and limited to the ability to produce those phonemes he or she hears. (p. 412)
    a. The vocal tract of *Homo sapiens* does not develop in specialized ways for different languages.
    b. & c. English and Russian differ significantly in both their phonemes and their morphemes. Nor is there any reason why differences in morphemes would in and of themselves cause pronunciation difficulties.

True–False Items

1. F (p. 412)	**6.** T (p. 400)
2. T (p. 399)	**7.** F (pp. 410–411)
3. T (p. 398)	**8.** T (p. 412)
4. F (p. 403)	**9.** F (pp. 420–421)
5. T (p. 423)	**10.** F (p. 416)

Psychology Applied

Multiple-Choice Questions

1. **a.** is the answer. Each sound of the word is a phoneme (note that the second letter "e" does not itself represent a sound); the morphemes are "pre," which means before; "date"; and "s," which indicates the plural. (p. 411)

2. **a.** is the answer. Adding *-ed* to the irregular verb *go* results in the ungrammatical *goed*—an overgeneralization of the rule by which the past tense of regular verbs is formed. (p. 414)
   b. This is an example of telegraphic speech.

c. This is a grammatical statement.

d. "'paghetti" is simply an immature pronunciation of "spaghetti"; young children often have difficulty with consonant clusters like "sp."

3. **a.** is the answer. (p. 412)

4. **a.** is the answer. (p. 407)

b. & c. These may very well occur, but they do not define belief perseverance.

d. This is the confirmation bias.

5. **b.** is the answer. A rose is a prototypical example of the concept *flower*. (p. 396)

c. & d. Hierarchies are organized clusters of concepts. In this example, there is only the single concept *flower*.

6. **d.** is the answer. The availability heuristic is the judgmental strategy that estimates the likelihood of events in terms of how readily they come to mind, and the most vivid information is often the most readily available. (p. 402)

7. **b.** is the answer. Follow the directions precisely and you can't miss! (p. 397)

a. A prototype is the best example of a concept.

c. Heuristics are simple thinking strategies that help solve problems but, in contrast to a recipe that is followed precisely, do not guarantee success.

d. A mental set is a tendency to approach a problem in a way that has been successful in the past.

8. **c.** is the answer. By simply following a strategy that has worked well in the past, Marilyn is hampered by the type of fixation called mental set. (p. 400)

a. Functional fixedness is being unable to conceive of an unusual function for an object.

b. Overconfidence is exhibited by the person who overestimates the accuracy of his or her judgments.

d. Prototypes are best examples of categories, not strategies for solving problems.

9. **a.** is the answer. Cognitive psychologists study how we process, understand, and communicate knowledge. Problem solving involves processing information and is therefore a topic explored by cognitive psychologists. (p. 395)

b. Cognitive psychologists often use experimentation to study phenomena but, because not all experimental psychologists study cognition, a. is the best answer.

c. Organizational psychologists study behavior in the workplace.

d. Developmental psychologists study the ways in which behavior changes over the life span.

10. **d.** is the answer. (pp. 397, 398)

b. & c. If Boris always attacks his opponent's queen when playing chess, he is a victim of mental set; prototypes, however, have nothing to do with chess playing.

11. **d.** is the answer. The confirmation bias is the tendency to search for information that confirms one's preconceptions. In this example, the politicians' preconceptions are biasing their interpretation of the survey results. (p. 399)

a. Functional fixedness is the inability to perceive an unusual use for a familiar object.

b. Mental set is the tendency to approach a problem in a particular way. There is no problem per se in this example.

c. Belief bias is the tendency for one's preexisting beliefs to distort logical reasoning. This answer is incorrect because it is not clear, in this example, whether either politician is reasoning illogically.

12. **b.** is the answer. Such utterances, characteristic of a child of about 2 years, are like telegrams, in that they consist mainly of nouns and verbs and show use of syntax. (p. 413)

a. & c. Babbling consists of phonemes, not words.

d. Semantics refers to the rules by which meaning is derived from sentences; this speech example indicates nothing in particular about the child's understanding of semantics.

13. **c.** is the answer. (p. 398)

a., b., & d. Heuristics do not guarantee solutions or prevent mental sets.

14. **d.** is the answer. Your conclusion is based on the stereotype that muscular build is more *representative* of athletes than computer programmers. (p. 401)

a. Belief bias is the tendency for one's preexisting beliefs to distort logical reasoning.

b. Mental set is the tendency to repeat solutions that have worked in the past.

c. Functional fixedness is the tendency to think of things only in terms of their usual functions.

15. **d.** is the answer. (p. 400)

16. **b.** is the answer. The publicity surrounding disasters makes such events vivid and seemingly more probable than they actually are. (p. 402)

a. The belief bias is the tendency for preexisting beliefs to distort logical thinking.

c. The representativeness heuristic operates when we judge the likelihood of things in terms of how well they represent particular prototypes. This example does not involve such a situation.

d. Functional fixedness operates in situations in which effective problem solving requires using an object in an unfamiliar manner.

17. **c.** is the answer. This is referred to as overconfidence. (p. 403)

18. **a.** is the answer. In this example, the way the issue is posed, or framed, has evidently influenced consumers' judgments. (p. 406)
    b. Confirmation bias is the tendency to search for information that confirms one's preconceptions.
    c. Mental set is the tendency to approach a problem in a particular way.
    d. Overconfidence is the tendency to be more confident than correct.

19. **d.** is the answer. This sentence, although semantically meaningless, nevertheless follows the grammatical rules of English syntax for combining words into sentences. (p. 411)
    a. & b. The phonemes (smallest units of sound) and morphemes (smallest units of meaning) of this sentence are equally correct.

20. **c.** is the answer. This fact challenges the linguistic determinism hypothesis; it neither supports nor refutes Chomsky's concept of an inborn universal grammar. (p. 418)

Essay Question

You should point out that the rate at which children acquire words and grammar is too extraordinary to be explained solely according to principles of learning. Children also utter all sorts of word forms they have never heard and could not, therefore, be imitating. Furthermore, children begin using morphemes in a predictable order, which learning theorists would not expect since each child experiences a unique linguistic environment. Children also make predictable errors that result from overuse of grammatical rules, rather than from imitation. It therefore seems clear that children are biologically prepared to acquire language and that the behaviorist position is incorrect.

Key Terms

1. **Cognition** refers to the mental activity associated with thinking, knowing, remembering, and communicating information. (p. 395)

2. A **concept** is a mental grouping of similar objects, events, and people. (p. 396)

3. A **prototype** is the best example of a particular category. (p. 396)

4. An **algorithm** is a methodical, logical procedure that, while sometimes slow, guarantees success. (p. 397)

5. A **heuristic** is a simple thinking strategy that often allows us to make judgments and solve problems efficiently. Although heuristics are more efficient than algorithms, they do not guarantee success and sometimes even impede problem solving. (p. 398)

6. **Insight** is a sudden and often novel realization of the solution to a problem. Insight contrasts with trial and error and, indeed, may often follow an unsuccessful episode of trial and error. (p. 398)

7. The **confirmation bias** is an obstacle to problem solving in which people tend to search for information that validates their preconceptions. (p. 399)

8. **Fixation** is an inability to approach a problem in a new way. (p. 400)

9. **Mental set** refers to the tendency to continue applying a particular problem-solving strategy even when it is no longer helpful. (p. 400)

10. **Functional fixedness** is a type of fixation in which a person can think of things only in terms of their usual functions. (p. 400)

11. The **representativeness heuristic** is the tendency to judge the likelihood of things in terms of how well they conform to one's prototypes. (p. 401)

12. The **availability heuristic** is based on estimating the probability of certain events in terms of how readily they come to mind. (p. 402)

13. Another obstacle to problem solving, **overconfidence** refers to the tendency to overestimate the accuracy of one's beliefs and judgments. (p. 403)

14. **Framing** refers to the way an issue or question is posed. It can affect people's perception of the issue or answer to the question. (p. 406)

15. **Belief bias** is the tendency for a person's preexisting beliefs to distort his or her logical reasoning. (p. 407)

16. **Belief perseverance** is the tendency for people to cling to a particular belief even after the information that led to the formation of the belief is discredited. (p. 407)

17. **Language** refers to spoken, written, or gestured words and how we combine them to communicate meaning. (p. 410)

18. **Phonemes** are the smallest units of sound in a language that are distinctive for speakers of the language. (p. 410)

19. **Morphemes** are the smallest units of language that convey meaning. (p. 411)
    Example: The word "dogs," which contains four phonemes, contains only two **morphemes**—"dog" and "-s." Although most morphemes are combinations of two or more phonemes, the plural "-s" conveys a distinctive meaning of "more than one."

20. **Grammar** is a system of rules that enables us to communicate with and understand others. (p. 411)

21. **Semantics** is the aspect of grammar that specifies the rules used to derive meaning from morphemes, words, and sentences in a given language. (p. 411)

    Example: One **semantic** rule of English is that adding *-ed* to a verb gives the verb a past-tense meaning.

22. **Syntax** is the aspect of grammar specifying the rules for combining words into grammatically sensible sentences in a given language. (p. 411)

    Example: One **syntactic** rule of English is that adjectives are positioned before nouns.

23. The **babbling stage** of speech development, which begins around 4 months, is characterized by the spontaneous utterance of speech sounds. During the babbling stage, children the world over sound alike. (p. 412)

24. Between 1 and 2 years of age children speak mostly in single words; they are therefore in the **one-word stage** of linguistic development. (p. 413)

25. Beginning about age 2, children are in the **two-word stage** and speak mostly in two-word sentences. (p. 413)

26. **Telegraphic speech** is the economical, telegram-like speech of children in the two-word stage. Utterances consist mostly of nouns and verbs; however, words occur in the correct order, showing that the child has learned some of the language's syntactic rules. (p. 413)

27. **Linguistic determinism** is Benjamin Whorf's hypothesis that language determines the way we think. (p. 418)

Cross-Check

ACROSS
1. babbling
8. grammar
11. algorithm
14. Washoe
15. Skinner
17. insight
20. Whorf
21. fixation
22. telegraphic

DOWN
2. linguistic determinism
3. heuristic
4. prototype
5. belief bias
6. framing
7. cognition
9. availability
10. mental set
12. morphemes
13. one-word
16. syntax
18. two-word
19. concept

FOCUS ON VOCABULARY AND LANGUAGE

Page 395: . . . our species is *kin to* . . . Myers notes that we are biological creatures related to (*kin to*) other species of animals. We have exceptional abilities for innovation, learning, memory, and rational thinking; yet, at the same time we are prone to making mistakes and thinking and acting irrationally.

Thinking

Page 397: For most of us, the robin with its smaller beak, and overall size, and its easier flight, is the *birdier bird* . . . We develop our ideas of how things go together (*concepts*) from definitions or by using **prototypes**. The best example (*prototype*) of a bird is a robin (*the birdier bird*) rather than a penguin, a kiwi, or an ostrich.

Page 397: Thomas Edison tried thousands of light bulb filaments before *stumbling upon one that worked*. Edison was a famous inventor and he used a trial-and-error method in developing the metal filament that makes the light bulb glow brightly. Using trial and error, he came upon the solution by chance (*stumbled upon one that worked*). Myers contrasts this method with following an **algorithm** (a step-by-step method that always ends with the answer and is typical of computer programs).

Page 399: Try your hand at these two classic *brain-teasers*. Myers offers you a chance to attempt (*try your hand at*) some intriguing mental puzzles (*brain-teasers*) taken from (*drawn from*) well-known experiments. If you encounter problems in solving these puzzles, it may be due to **fixation** (our inability to see things from a new or different perspective), **mental set** (repeating old solutions that worked before), or **functional fixedness** (our tendency to see things as having only one function or use).

Page 401: Should I *shoot* the basketball or pass to the player who's *hot?*—we seldom take the time and effort to reason systematically. (Don't take this sentence literally.) For example, in a game of basketball, the player holding the ball has to decide to throw it through the hoop (*shoot the basketball*) or pass it to a player who has scored frequently (*who's hot*). We usually follow our subjective feelings (*intuitions*) rather than taking the time to use logic and reason.

Page 401: . . . *seat-of-the-pants* decisions. When we make decisions based on subjective or intuitive reasons, rather than using logical, reflective problem-solving strategies, we are using *seat-of-the-pants* judgments. Thus, when we employ **heuristics** (simple thinking strategies), we may make decisions that are incorrect and not very smart (*dumb decisions*).

Page 401: The **representativeness heuristic** enabled you to make a *snap* judgment. We can make quick (*snap*) judgments using a strategy that allows us to determine the probability of things by how well they appear to be typical of some prototype (*representativeness heuristic*). For example, is person A, who is intelligent, unimaginative, compulsive, and generally lifeless, more likely to (a) play jazz for a hobby or (b) play jazz for a hobby and work as an accountant? The representativeness heuristic leads most people to incorrectly pick (b) as the answer.

Page 402: The faster people can remember an instance of some event (*"a broken promise"*), the more they expect it to recur. We tend to use whatever information is accessible in our memories when making decisions and judgments; similarly, events or mistakes that are easiest to access (i.e., those that most readily come to mind) will most likely be used. This is called the **availability heuristic.** So, if on one occasion, someone did not keep his or her word (*broke a promise*) about doing something, we tend to remember that event and use it in predicting future behavior. Sometimes the availability heuristic can cause errors in judgment.

Page 403: Overconfidence *plagues* decisions outside the laboratory, too. Many factors combine to produce the tendency to overestimate the accuracy of our decisions, judgments, and knowledge (**overconfidence**). In everyday life, as well as in lab experiments, our judgments are greatly afflicted (*plagued*) by overconfidence.

Page 405: Human emotions were *road tested in the Stone Age*. During our evolutionary past, certain traits or characteristics were selected for because they helped our ancestors survive, and those that survived because of these attributes passed them on to their descendants. Fearful reactions to snakes, lizards, spiders, confinement, and heights were selected for (*they were road tested*) during earlier times (*in the Stone Age*) and are part of human nature today.

Page 406: That our judgments *flip-flop* so dramatically is startling. Presenting the same information in two different ways can cause people to react more negatively or positively depending on how the (logically equivalent) information was **framed**. The framing effect can cause alarming and dramatic reversals (*flip-flops*) in people's decisions and judgments. For example, a very fatty food product made by grinding meat (*ground beef*) will be seen more positively if described as "75% lean" as opposed to "25% fat," despite the fact that exactly the same information is conveyed in each case.

Page 406: . . . hunches . . . We have a propensity to make mistakes because we seek information that will confirm our intuitive feelings (*hunches*) about situations, people, or future events. We rely on heuristics, we are overconfident in our estimates, and we are unduly influenced by (*fall prey to*) the effects of framing. Myers notes that it is difficult to escape bias even by use of forceful logic.

Page 407: Belief perseverance often *fuels social conflict.* Our irrationality also shows when we persist (*persevere*) in our views despite evidence to the contrary (**belief perseverance**). This can lead to an increase in strong feelings or passions over controversial issues (*fuels social conflict*). Myers suggests one solution for those who wish to restrain (*rein in*) the effect of belief perseverance, and that is to give serious consideration to beliefs *opposite* to your own.

Page 408: From this we might conclude that our heads are indeed *filled with straw*. The discussion about human irrationality might lead to the conclusion that we have ineffective and inefficient cognitions (*heads filled with straw*). Myers, however, is optimistic and suggests that we can learn about our irrational propensities (tendencies) and be alert to the dangers that can result in poor or foolish (*dumb*) decisions.

Page 409: More than we realize, *thinking occurs off-screen*, with the results occasionally *displayed on-screen*. Humans process a great deal of information without any conscious awareness of doing so. This is similar to a computer's hidden processing, which is not displayed on the monitor (*it occurs off-screen*). Once in a while the results of our unconscious processing enter consciousness (the results are occasionally *displayed on-screen*).

Language

Page 410: When the human vocal tract evolved the ability to utter vowels, *our capacity for language exploded, catapulting our species forward.* When the physiological ability for complex vocalization evolved, the ability to communicate orally expanded exponentially (*exploded*). This new linguistic capacity propelled (*catapulted*) our species to new levels of accomplishments, enabling us to communicate from person to person and to transmit civilization's accumulated knowledge from generation to generation.

Page 411: They are hunting dogs. The sentence *"They are hunting dogs"* is syntactically correct, but its meaning (semantics) is derived from the context. In one context it could mean that people (*they*) are out looking (*hunting*) for dogs, and in another it could refer to dogs that are used to track or seek (*hunt*) animals.

Page 412: With remarkably efficiency, you can selectively sample the tens of thousands of words in your memory, effortlessly *combine them on the fly* with near-perfect syntax, and *spew them out three words a second.* Humans have an amazing facility for language. With little or no effort, we can select the appropriate words from the tens of thousands in memory, put them together hurriedly (*combine them on the fly*), and verbally produce them in rapid succession (*spew them out three words a second*).

Page 412: Yet by 4 months of age, babies can *read lips* and *discriminate* speech sounds. When people speak, their lips move in ways that correspond to the sounds they utter. Many deaf people can understand what is being said by watching how the lips move (*lip reading*). Very young children can not only tell the difference (*discriminate*) between sounds, but can also recognize lip movements that correspond with certain sounds (*read lips*).

Page 414: Surely, Chomsky has said, *a Martian scientist* observing children in a single-language community would conclude that language is almost entirely inborn. The famous linguist Chomsky believes that the behaviorist's views (as exemplified by Skinner) are simplistic (*naive*). He argues that language acquisition could not be simply a function of experience or learning. Instead, he contends that any unbiased observer (e.g., *an imaginary scientist from the planet Mars*) would have to arrive at the inescapable fact that our capacity for language is almost totally biologically inherited (*inborn*). The specific language you speak is a product of your environment, which builds on your innate capacity for language. As Myers puts it, *"we are born with the hardware and an operating system for language, and our linguistic experiences write the software."*

Page 416: Chomsky would say that once the *grammar switches are thrown* during a child's developing years, mastering another grammar becomes more difficult. Chomsky likens learning a particular grammar during early childhood to turning on (*throwing*) switches that influence language acquisition. When they have been turned on for one grammar, it becomes much harder to master a second grammar. During the early years of language development, we easily and accurately acquire (*master*) grammar and

accent, but after that critical period the language acquisition system tends to work less hard (*it is inclined to rest on its laurels*), and mastering another grammar becomes more difficult (*the window for learning language gradually closes*).

Thinking and Language

Page 418: Thinking and language intricately intertwine. Asking which comes first is one of psychology's *chicken-and-egg* questions. "Which came first: the chicken or the egg?" Clearly, you need an egg to produce a chicken, but you also need a chicken to lay the egg. So, like this age-old conundrum (riddle), psychologists have argued over which comes first, our ideas and thoughts or the words we use to name and verbalize them. Myers concludes that language influences (but does not determine) thought, and our thinking affects our language, which in turn affects thought.

Animal Thinking and Language

Page 423: If in our use of language we humans are, as the psalmist long ago *rhapsodized*, "little lower than God," where do other animals fit in the scheme of things? The psalmist (an author of religious or sacred songs) spoke in an extravagantly enthusiastic manner (*rhapsodized*) about human nature, and Myers notes that it is our use of human language that elevates us above nonhumans. Nevertheless, we do share a capacity for language with other animals.

Page 423: Spying the short stick, Sultan (the chimp) grabbed it and tried to reach the fruit. Kohler's experiment with the chimpanzee Sultan showed that our closest relatives are capable of cognition. When the fruit was out of reach, Sultan noticed (*spied*) the short stick and used it to pull a longer stick into the cage, which he then used to get the fruit.

Page 426: Were the chimps *language champs* or were the researchers *chumps*? Critics of "ape language" argue that for animals, language acquisition is painfully slow, resembles conditioned responses, does not follow syntax, and is little more than imitation. In addition, demonstrations of animal language are always subjectively interpreted by their trainers. Myers asks: Were the chimps exceptionally talented (*language champs*) or were the researchers just easily fooled or duped (*were they chumps*) and were they acting foolishly (*making monkeys out of themselves*)? The answer is that the controversy has led to further research and progress, and a renewed appreciation of our own, as well as our closest relatives', capacity for communication and language.

11: Intelligence

CHAPTER OVERVIEW

An enduring controversy in psychology involves attempts to define and measure intelligence. Chapter 11 discusses whether intelligence is a single general ability or several specific ones as well as research that attempts to assess the neurological basis of intelligence. It also describes the historical origins of intelligence tests and discusses several important issues concerning their use. These include the methods by which intelligence tests are constructed and whether such tests are valid, reliable, and free of bias. The chapter also explores the stability of intelligence and the extent of genetic and environmental influences on intelligence.

NOTE: Answer guidelines for all Chapter 11 questions begin on page 298.

CHAPTER REVIEW

First, skim each section, noting headings and boldface items. After you have read the section, review each objective by answering the fill-in and essay-type questions that follow it. As you proceed, evaluate your performance by consulting the answers beginning on page 298. Do not continue with the next section until you understand each answer. If you need to, review or reread the section in the textbook before continuing.

What Is Intelligence? (pp. 431–442)

> David Myers at times uses idioms that are unfamiliar to some readers. If you do not know the meaning of any of the following words, phrases, or expressions in the context in which they appear in the text, refer to pages 304–305 for an explanation: *sparked debate; dumbfounded; island of brilliance; street-smart adolescent; how to read people; add spice to life; out of the blue; on the shoulders of others; quick-witted; in its heyday.*

Objective 1: Discuss the difficulty of defining intelligence, and explain what it means to "reify intelligence."

1. Psychologists _____ (do/do not) agree on a definition of intelligence.

2. To regard an abstract concept as a concrete entity is to commit the error known as

   _____ .

3. Intelligence is a _____ constructed concept.

4. In any context, intelligence can be defined as ____

   _____ .

5. One controversy regarding the nature of intelligence centers on whether intelligence is one _____ ability or several _____ abilities.

Objective 2: Present arguments for and against considering intelligence as one general mental ability.

6. The statistical procedure used to identify groups of items that appear to measure a common ability is called _____ _____ .

7. Charles Spearman, one of the developers of this technique, believed that a factor called *g*, or _____ _____ , runs through the more specific aspects of intelligence.

8. Opposing Spearman, _____ identified seven clusters of _____ _____ _____ .

9. Some psychologists believe that general intelligence evolved as a means of helping people solve _____ _____ .

Objective 3: Compare Gardner's and Sternberg's theories of intelligence.

10. People with _____ _____ score at the low end of intelligence tests but possess extraordinary specific skills.

11. Howard Gardner proposes that there are _____ _____ , each independent of the others. However, critics point out that the world is not so just: People with mental disadvantages often have lesser _____ abilities as well, and that some abilities, such as _____ and _____ skills, are more crucial than others. General intelligence scores _____ (do/do not) predict performance on complex tasks and in various jobs.

12. Sternberg's _____ theory distinguishes three types of intelligence: _____ intelligence, _____ intelligence, and _____ intelligence.

Objective 4: Describe the three aspects of emotional intelligence, and discuss criticisms of this concept.

13. Cantor and Kihlstrom distinguish between _____ intelligence and _____ intelligence. Support for this distinction comes from evidence that college grades _____ (accurately/ only modestly/do not) predict later work achievement.

14. A critical part of social intelligence is _____ _____ —the ability to _____ , _____ , _____ , and _____ emotions.

15. One research study found that 5-year-olds who could most accurately recognize and label _____ _____ later more easily made friends and effectively managed their emotions.

Briefly describe emotionally intelligent people.

16. A test that measures overall emotional intelligence also measures its components: the ability to _____ emotions in faces, the ability to _____ them and how they change and blend, the ability to _____ them correctly in varied situations, and the ability to use them to enable _____ or creative thinking.

17. Some scholars believe that the concept of _____ intelligence stretches the idea of multiple intelligences too far.

18. Although general intelligence is most important in occupations that are mentally demanding, successful people usually have other traits as well, such as _____ and being well connected and extremely energetic.

Objective 5: Identify the factors associated with creativity, and describe the relationship between creativity and intelligence.

19. The ability to produce ideas that are both novel and valuable is called _____ . The relationship between intelligence and creativity holds only up to a certain point—an intelligence score of about _____ .

20. Standard intelligence tests, which demand single correct answers to questions, measure _____ thinking. Tests that allow multiple possible answers to problems measure _____ thinking.

Describe five components of creativity other than intelligence.

21. Teresa Amabile's research demonstrates that people are more creative when they are unconcerned about _____ _____ .

Objective 6: Describe the relationship between intelligence and brain anatomy.

22. Earlier studies _____ (did/did not) reveal a clear-cut correlation between head size (relative to body size) and intelligence score.

23. Newer studies that measure brain _____ using _____ scans reveal a _____ (more/less) significant correlation between brain size (adjusted for body size) and intelligence score.

24. Autopsies reveal that the brains of highly educated people have more _____ than do those of people with less education. Other evidence suggests that highly intelligent people differ in their neural _____ . Higher intelligence scores have also been linked with more _____ _____ in brain areas known to be involved in _____ , _____ , and _____ .

25. A study of Einstein's brain revealed that it was 15 percent larger in the the lower _____ lobe—known to be an important neural center for processing _____ and _____ information.

Objective 7: Discuss findings on the correlations between perceptual speed, neural processing speed, and intelligence.

26. When people ponder intelligence test questions, an area in the brain's _____ _____ becomes especially active in the _____ (left/right) brain for verbal questions and _____ (in the right brain/in the left brain/on both sides of the brain) for spatial questions.

27. Studies looking at a range of tasks have found that people with high intelligence scores tend to process and retrieve information _____ (faster/more slowly) than people with low intelligence scores.

28. Other studies have found that the brain waves of highly intelligent people register stimuli more _____ and with greater _____ .

Assessing Intelligence (pp. 442–450)

> If you do not know the meaning of any of the following words, phrases, or expressions in the context in which they appear in the text, refer to pages 305–306 for an explanation: *heirs . . . pondered; "dull" child; "mental orthopedics"; feeble-mindedness; clear-cut; clustered; tape measure.*

Objective 8: Define *intelligence test*, and discuss the history of intelligence testing.

1. The early Greek philosopher _____ concluded that individuals differed in their natural endowments.

2. Tests that assess a person's mental capacities and compare them to those of others, using numerical scores, are called _____ tests.

3. The French psychologist who devised a test to predict the success of children in school was _____ . Predictions were made by comparing children's chronological ages with their _____ ages, which were determined by the test. This test _____ (was/was not) designed to measure inborn intelligence.

4. Lewis Terman's revision of Binet's test is referred to as the _____ - _____ . This test enables one to derive a(n) _____ _____ for an individual.

Give the original formula for computing IQ, and explain any items used in the formula.

5. Today's tests compute _____ (IQ/ a mental ability score) by comparing the individual's performance to the average performance of people of _____ (the same/different) age(s). These tests are designed so that a score of _____ is considered average.

6. When given intelligence tests in the early 1900s, immigrants arriving in the United States often scored _____ (above/below) average. This is because the tests were based on a particular _____ background.

Objective 9: Distinguish between aptitude and achievement tests, and describe modern tests of mental abilities such as the WAIS.

7. Tests designed to predict your ability to learn something new are called _____ tests. Tests designed to measure what you already have learned are called _____ tests.

8. The most widely used intelligence test is the

_____ _____

_____ _____ .

Consisting of 11 subtests, it provides not only a general intelligence score but also separate scores for _____ _____ ,

_____ _____ ,

_____ _____ , and

_____ _____ .

Objective 10: Discuss the importance of standardizing psychological tests, and describe the distribution of scores in a normal curve.

9. One requirement of a good test is the process of defining meaningful scores relative to a pretested comparison group, which is called _____ .

10. When scores on a test are compiled, they generally result in a bell-shaped pattern, or _____ distribution.

Describe the normal curve, and explain its significance in the standardization process.

11. The Stanford-Binet and the Wechsler Scales _____ (are/are not) periodically restandardized, thereby keeping the average score near _____ .

12. During the 1960s and 1970s, college entrance aptitude scores showed a steady _____ (increase/decline). At the same time, intelligence test performance _____ (improved/decreased). This phenomenon is called the

_____ _____ .

13. Although the actual cause of this effect is unknown, one explanation is that is due to improved _____ . The recent performance gains on the WAIS are greatest among people at the lowest _____ levels.

Objective 11: Explain what it means to say a test is reliable.

14. If a test yields consistent results, it is said to be

    _____ .

15. When a test is administered more than once to the same people, the psychologist is determining its _____-_____ reliability.

16. When a person's scores for the odd- and even-numbered questions on a test are compared,

    _____ -_____

    reliability is being assessed.

17. The Stanford-Binet, WAIS, and WISC have relia-bilities of about _____ .

Objective 12: Explain what it means to say a test is valid, and describe two types of validity.

18. The degree to which a test measures or predicts what it is supposed to is referred to as the test's

    _____ .

19. The degree to which a test measures the behavior it was designed to measure is referred to as the test's _____ _____ .

20. The degree to which a test predicts future perfor-mance of a particular behavior, called the test's

    _____ , is referred to as the test's

    _____ _____ .

Choose a specific example and use it to illustrate and explain the concept of criterion and its relationship to predictive validity.

21. Generally speaking, the predictive validity of general aptitude tests _____ (is/is not) as high as their reliability. The predictive validity of these tests _____ (increases/diminishes) as individuals move up the educational ladder.

The Dynamics of Intelligence (pp. 450–454)

> If you do not know the meaning of any of the following words, phrases, or expressions in the context in which they appear in the text, refer to page 306 for an explanation: *have left few stones unturned; the pendulum of opinion . . . complete swing.*

Objective 13: Describe the stability of intelligence scores over the life span.

1. Some studies have found that 2- to 7-month-old infants who quickly become bored when looking at a picture score _____ (higher/lower) on tests of brain speed and intelligence up to 11 years later.

2. Traditional intelligence tests before age _____ generally do not predict future scores.

3. During childhood, the stability of intelligence scores _____ (increases/decreases) with age. After about age_____ , intelligence scores stabilize. A long-term study of mental ability in Scottish children revealed that this _____ (holds/does not hold) through late adulthood.

Objective 14: Discuss the two extremes of the normal distribution of intelligence.

4. Individuals whose intelligence scores fall below 70 and who have difficulty adapting to life may be labeled _____

    _____ . This label applies to approximately _____ percent of the population.

5. Mental retardation sometimes has a physical basis, such as _____

    _____ , a genetic disorder caused by an extra chromosome.

6. The current view is that children with mild retardation should be integrated, or _____ , into regular classrooms.

7. At the high extreme, Lewis Terman's "gifted children" turned out to be _____ , well-_____ , and unusually successful _____ .

Discuss criticisms of programs that sort children into gifted and nongifted tracks.

Genetic and Environmental Influences on Intelligence (pp. 454–466)

> If you do not know the meaning of any of the following words, phrases, or expressions in the context in which they appear in the text, refer to page 306 for an explanation: *bludgeoning native intelligence; more newsworthy; sharpest at the extremes; computer camps.*

Objective 15: Discuss the evidence for the genetic contribution to individual intelligence, and explain what psychologists mean by the heritability of intelligence.

1. The position that both heredity and environment exert some influence on intelligence is _____ (controversial/generally accepted) among psychologists.

2. The intelligence scores of identical twins reared together are _____ (more/no more) similar than those of fraternal twins. Brain scans also reveal that identical twins have similar volume to their brain's _____ _____ , and those areas associated with _____ and _____ intelligence.

3. By inserting an extra gene that engineers a neural receptor involved in _____ into fertilized mouse eggs, researchers have created smarter mice.

4. The intelligence test scores of fraternal twins are _____ (more alike/no more alike) than the intelligence test scores of other siblings. This provides evidence of a(n) _____ (genetic/environmental) effect because fraternal twins, being the same _____ , are treated more alike.

5. Studies of adopted children and their adoptive and biological families demonstrate that with age, genetic influences on intelligence become _____ (more/less) apparent. Thus, children's intelligence scores are more like those of their _____ (biological/adoptive) parents than their _____ (biological/adoptive) parents.

6. The amount of variation in a trait within a group that is attributed to genetic factors is called its _____ . For intelligence, this has been estimated at _____ percent.

7. If we know a trait has perfect heritability, this knowledge _____ (does/does not) enable us to rule out environmental factors in explaining differences between groups.

Objective 16: Discuss the evidence for environmental influences on individual intelligence.

8. Studies indicate that neglected children _____ (do/do not) show signs of recovery in intelligence and behavior when placed in more nurturing environments. Although normal brain development can be retarded by _____ , _____ deprivation, and _____ _____ , there is no sure environment that will produce a "superbaby."

9. High-quality programs for disadvantaged children, such as the government-funded _____ _____ program, increase children's school readiness; that is, they increase their _____

_____ , creating better attitudes toward learning.

10. Intelligence scores _____ (rise/fall/remain stable) during the school year and _____ (rise/fall/remain stable) over the summer. The Flynn effect of rising IQ scores is partly due to the increasing years of _____ over the last 50 years.

Objective 17: Describe ethnic similarities and differences in intelligence test scores, and discuss some genetic and environmental factors that might explain them.

11. Research evidence suggests that group differences in intelligence may be entirely _____ (genetic/environmental).

Explain why heredity may contribute to individual differences in intelligence but not necessarily contribute to group differences.

12. Group differences in intelligence scores _____ (do/do not) provide an accurate basis for judging individuals. Individual differences within a race are _____ (greater than/less than) between-race differences. Furthermore, race _____ (is/is not) a neatly defined biological category.

13. Although Asian students on the average score _____ (higher/lower) than North American students on math tests, this difference may be due to the fact that _____

_____

_____ .

14. On an infant intelligence measure (preference for looking at novel stimuli), black infants score _____ (lower than/higher than/as well as) white infants.

Objective 18: Describe gender differences in abilities.

15. Girls tend to outscore boys on _____ tests and are more _____ fluent.

16. Although girls have an edge in math _____ , boys score higher in math _____ _____ . Boys tend to outscore girls on tests of _____

_____ .

17. Working from an _____ perspective, some theorists speculate that these gender differences in spatial manipulation helped our ancestors survive.

18. There is evidence that spatial abilities are enhanced by high levels of_____

_____ _____ during prenatal development.

19. According to many, boys' and girls' interests and abilities are shaped in large part by

_____ _____ and divergent opportunities.

Objective 19: Discuss whether intelligence tests are biased, and describe the stereotype threat phenomenon.

20. In the sense that they detect differences caused by cultural experiences, intelligence tests probably _____ (are/are not) biased.

21. Most psychologists agree that, in terms of predictive validity, the major aptitude tests _____ (are/are not) racially biased.

22. When women and members of ethnic minorities are led to expect that they won't do well on a test, a _____ _____ may result, and their scores may actually be lower.

PROGRESS TEST 1

Multiple-Choice Questions

Circle your answers to the following questions and check them with the answers beginning on page 299. If your answer is incorrect, read the explanation for why it is incorrect and then consult the appropriate pages of the text (in parentheses following the correct answer).

1. Studies of adopted children and their biological and adoptive families demonstrate that with age, genetic influences on intelligence:
   a. become more apparent.
   b. become less apparent.
   c. become more difficult to disentangle from environmental influences.
   d. become easier to disentangle from environmental influences.

2. A 6-year-old child has a mental age of 9. The child's IQ is:
   a. 96.   c. 125.
   b. 100.   d. 150.

3. Which of the following is *not* true?
   a. In math grades, the average girl typically equals or surpasses the average boy.
   b. The gender gap in math and science scores is increasing.
   c. Women are better than men at detecting emotions.
   d. Males score higher than females on tests of spatial abilities.

4. Most psychologists believe that racial gaps in test scores:
   a. have been exaggerated when they are, in fact, insignificant.
   b. indicate that intelligence is in large measure inherited.
   c. are in large measure caused by environmental factors.
   d. are increasing.

5. Standardization refers to the process of:
   a. determining the accuracy with which a test measures what it is supposed to.
   b. defining meaningful scores relative to a representative pretested group.
   c. determining the consistency of test scores obtained by retesting people.
   d. measuring the success with which a test predicts the behavior it is designed to predict.

6. Down syndrome is normally caused by:
   a. an extra chromosome in the person's genetic makeup.
   b. a missing chromosome in the person's genetic makeup.
   c. malnutrition during the first few months of life.
   d. prenatal exposure to an addictive drug.

7. Which of the following is *not* a requirement of a good test?
   a. reliability   c. reification
   b. standardization   d. validity

8. First-time parents Geena and Brad want to give their baby's intellectual abilities a jump-start by providing a super enriched learning environment. Experts would suggest that the new parents should:
   a. pipe stimulating classical music into the baby's room.
   b. hang colorful mobiles and artwork over the baby's crib.
   c. take the child to one of the new "superbaby" preschools that specialize in infant enrichment.
   d. relax, since there is no surefire environmental recipe for giving a child a superior intellect.

9. Which of the following statements is true?
   a. The predictive validity of intelligence tests is not as high as their reliability.
   b. The reliability of intelligence tests is not as high as their predictive validity.
   c. Modern intelligence tests have extremely high predictive validity and reliability.
   d. The predictive validity and reliability of most intelligence tests is very low.

10. Before about age _____ , intelligence tests generally do not predict future scores.
    a. 1   c. 5
    b. 3   d. 10

11. Sorting children into gifted and nongifted educational groups:
    a. creates a self-fulfilling prophecy.
    b. increases social isolation between the groups.
    c. promotes racial segregation and prejudice.
    d. has all of the above effects.

12. Which of the following best describes the relationship between creativity and intelligence?
   a. Creativity appears to depend on the ability to think imaginatively and has little if any relationship to intelligence.
   b. Creativity is best understood as a certain kind of intelligence.
   c. The more intelligent a person is, the greater his or her creativity.
   d. A certain level of intelligence is necessary but not sufficient for creativity.

13. Studies of 2- to 7-month-old babies show that babies who quickly become bored with a picture:
   a. often develop learning disabilities later on.
   b. score lower on infant intelligence tests.
   c. score higher on intelligence tests several years later.
   d. score very low on intelligence tests several years later.

14. The existence of _____ reinforces the generally accepted notion that intelligence is a multidimensional quality.
   a. adaptive skills
   b. mental retardation
   c. general intelligence
   d. savant syndrome

15. Which of the following provides the strongest evidence of the role of heredity in determining intelligence?
   a. The IQ scores of identical twins raised separately are more similar than those of fraternal twins raised together.
   b. The intelligence scores of fraternal twins are more similar than those of ordinary siblings.
   c. The intelligence scores of identical twins raised together are more similar than those of identical twins raised apart.
   d. The intelligence scores of adopted children show relatively weak correlations with scores of adoptive as well as biological parents.

16. Current estimates are that _____ percent of the total variation among intelligence scores can be attributed to genetic factors.
   a. less than 10
   b. approximately 25
   c. between 50 and 75
   d. over 75

17. Over the past 80 years, college aptitude test scores have _____ and WAIS scores have _____ .
   a. declined; remained stable
   b. remained stable; declined
   c. risen; declined
   d. declined; risen

18. Reported racial gaps in average intelligence scores are most likely attributable to:
   a. the use of biased tests of intelligence.
   b. the use of unreliable tests of intelligence.
   c. genetic factors.
   d. environmental factors.

19. The bell-shaped distribution of intelligence scores in the general population is called a:
   a. *g* distribution.
   b. standardization curve.
   c. bimodal distribution.
   d. normal distribution.

20. Research on the effectiveness of Head Start suggests that enrichment programs:
   a. produce permanent gains in intelligence scores.
   b. improve school readiness and may provide a small boost to emotional intelligence.
   c. improve intelligence scores but not school readiness.
   d. produce temporary gains in intelligence scores.

Matching Items

Match each term with its definition or description.

Terms

_____ **1.** mental ability score
_____ **2.** *g*
_____ **3.** eugenics
_____ **4.** savant syndrome
_____ **5.** factor analysis
_____ **6.** aptitude test
_____ **7.** achievement test
_____ **8.** Stanford-Binet
_____ **9.** criterion
_____ **10.** content validity
_____ **11.** reliability

Definitions or Descriptions

a. a test designed to predict a person's ability to learn something new
b. a test designed to measure current knowledge
c. the consistency with which a test measures performance
d. the degree to which a test measures what it is designed to measure
e. Terman's revision of Binet's original intelligence test
f. the behavior that a test is designed to predict
g. an underlying, general intelligence factor
h. a person's score on an intelligence test based on performance relative to the average performance of people the same age
i. a very low intelligence score accompanied by one extraordinary skill
j. a program for the selective breeding of the most intelligent individuals
k. a statistical technique that identifies related items on a test

PROGRESS TEST 2

Progress Test 2 should be completed during a final chapter review. Answer the following questions after you thoroughly understand the correct answers for the section reviews and Progress Test 1.

Multiple-Choice Questions

1. The test created by Alfred Binet was designed specifically to:
   a. measure inborn intelligence in adults.
   b. measure inborn intelligence in children.
   c. predict school performance in children.
   d. identify mentally retarded children so that they could be institutionalized.

2. Which of the following provides the strongest evidence of environment's role in intelligence?
   a. Adopted children's intelligence scores are more like their adoptive parents' scores than their biological parents'.
   b. Children's intelligence scores are more strongly related to their mothers' scores than to their fathers'.
   c. Children moved from a deprived environment into an intellectually enriched one show gains in intellectual development.

   d. The intelligence scores of identical twins raised separately are no more alike than those of siblings.

3. If a test designed to indicate which applicants are likely to perform the best on the job fails to do so, the test has:
   a. low reliability.
   b. low content validity.
   c. low predictive validity.
   d. not been standardized.

4. By creating a label such as "gifted," we begin to act as if all children are naturally divided into two categories, gifted and nongifted. This logical error is referred to as:
   a. rationalization.
   b. nominalizing.
   c. factor analysis.
   d. reification.

5. The formula for the intelligence quotient was devised by:
   a. Sternberg.   **c.** Terman.
   b. Binet.   **d.** Stern.

6. Current intelligence tests compute an individual's intelligence score as:
   a. the ratio of mental age to chronological age multiplied by 100.
   b. the ratio of chronological age to mental age multiplied by 100.
   c. the amount by which the test-taker's performance deviates from the average performance of others the same age.
   d. the ratio of the test-taker's verbal intelligence score to his or her nonverbal intelligence score.

7. J. McVicker Hunt found that institutionalized children given "tutored human enrichment":
   a. showed no change in intelligence test performance compared with institutionalized children who did not receive such enrichment.
   b. responded so negatively as a result of their impoverished early experiences that he felt it necessary to disband the program.
   c. thrived intellectually and socially on the benefits of positive caregiving.
   d. actually developed greater intelligence than control subjects who had lived in foster homes since birth.

8. The concept of a *g* factor implies that intelligence:
   a. is a single overall ability.
   b. is several specific abilities.
   c. cannot be defined or measured.
   d. is both a. and c.

9. Gerardeen has superb social skills, manages conflicts well, and has great empathy for her friends and co-workers. Peter Salovey and John Mayer would probably say that Gerardeen possesses a high degree of:
   a. *g*.
   b. social intelligence.
   c. practical intelligence.
   d. emotional intelligence.

10. By what age does a child's performance on an intelligence test stabilize?
    a. 2   c. 6
    b. 3   d. 7

11. The Flynn effect refers to the fact that:
    a. white and black infants score equally well on measures of infant intelligence.
    b. Asian students outperform North American students on math achievement tests.
    c. The IQ scores of today's better fed and educated population exceed that of the 1930s population.
    d. Individual differences within a race are much greater than between-race differences.

12. In his study of children with high intelligence scores, Terman found that:
    a. the children were more emotional and less healthy than a control group.
    b. the children were ostracized by classmates.
    c. the children were healthy and well-adjusted, and did well academically.
    d. later, as adults, they nearly all achieved great vocational success.

13. When highly skilled people are performing a task, their brains:
    a. retrieve information from memory more quickly.
    b. register simple stimuli more quickly.
    c. demonstrate a more complex brain-wave response to stimuli.
    d. do all of the above.

14. Most experts view intelligence as a person's:
    a. ability to perform well on intelligence tests.
    b. innate mental capacity.
    c. ability to learn from experience, solve problems, and adapt to new situations.
    d. diverse skills acquired throughout life.

15. Which of the following statements is true?
    a. About 1 percent of the population is mentally retarded.
    b. More males than females are mentally retarded.
    c. A majority of the mentally retarded can learn academic skills.
    d. All of the above are true.

16. High levels of male hormones during prenatal development may enhance:
    a. verbal reasoning.
    b. spatial abilities.
    c. overall intelligence.
    d. all of the above.

17. Which of the following is *not* cited as evidence of the reciprocal relationship between schooling and intelligence?
    a. Neither education level nor intelligence scores accurately predict income.
    b. Intelligence scores tend to rise during the school year.
    c. High school graduates have higher intelligence scores than do those who drop out early.
    d. High intelligence scores correlate with prolonged schooling.

18. Originally, IQ was defined as:
    a. mental age divided by chronological age and multiplied by 100.
    b. chronological age divided by mental age and multiplied by 100.
    c. mental age subtracted from chronological age and multiplied by 100.
    d. chronological age subtracted from mental age and multiplied by 100.

19. Tests of _____ measure what an individual can do now, whereas tests of _____ predict what an individual will be able to do later.
    a. aptitude; achievement
    b. achievement; aptitude
    c. reliability; validity
    d. validity; reliability

20. Which of the following statements most accurately reflects the text's position regarding the relative contribution of genes and environment in determining intelligence?
    a. Except in cases of a neglectful early environment, each individual's basic intelligence is largely the product of heredity.
    b. With the exception of those with genetic disorders such as Down syndrome, intelligence is primarily the product of environmental experiences.
    c. Both genes and life experiences significantly influence performance on intelligence tests.
    d. Because intelligence tests have such low predictive validity, the question cannot be addressed until psychologists agree on a more valid test of intelligence.

True–False Items

Indicate whether each statement is true or false by placing *T* or *F* in the blank next to the item.

_____ 1. In the current version of the Stanford-Binet intelligence test, one's performance is compared only with the performance of others the same age.

_____ 2. Intelligence scores in the United States have been dropping over the past 50 years.

_____ 3. Most of the major aptitude tests have higher validity than reliability.

_____ 4. People with high intelligence scores tend to process sensory information more quickly.

_____ 5. The gap in intelligence scores between black and white children is increasing.

_____ 6. The intelligence scores of adopted children are more similar to those of their adoptive parents than their biological parents.

_____ 7. The consensus among psychologists is that most intelligence tests are extremely biased.

_____ 8. Most psychologists agree that intelligence is mainly determined by heredity.

_____ 9. The Stanford-Binet test and the Wechsler scales are periodically restandardized.

_____ 10. The variation in intelligence scores within a racial group is much larger than that between racial groups.

_____ 11. Telling students they are unlikely to succeed often erodes their performance on aptitude tests.

PSYCHOLOGY APPLIED

Answer these questions the day before an exam as a final check on your understanding of the chapter's terms and concepts.

Multiple-Choice Questions

1. Vanessa is a very creative sculptress. We would expect that Vanessa also:
    a. has an exceptionally high intelligence score.
    b. is quite introverted.
    c. has a venturesome personality and is intrinsically motivated.
    d. lacks expertise in most other skills.

2. To say that the heritability of a trait is approximately 50 percent means:
    a. that genes are responsible for 50 percent of the trait in an individual, and the environment is responsible for the rest.
    b. that the trait's appearance in a person will reflect approximately equal genetic contributions from both parents.

c. that of the variation in the trait within a group of people, 50 percent can be attributed to heredity.

d. all of the above.

3. Twenty-two-year-old Dan has an intelligence score of 63 and the academic skills of a fourth-grader, and is unable to live independently. Dan *probably*:

a. has Down syndrome.

b. has savant syndrome.

c. is mentally retarded.

d. will eventually achieve self-supporting social and vocational skills.

4. At age 16, Angel's intelligence score was 110. What will her score probably be at age 32?

a. 125

b. 110

c. 115

d. There is no basis for predicting an individual's future IQ.

5. A school psychologist found that 85 percent of those who scored above 115 on an aptitude test were "A" students and 75 percent of those who scored below 85 on the test were "D" students. The psychologist concluded that the test had high:

a. content validity because scores on it correlated highly with the criterion behavior.

b. predictive validity because scores on it correlated highly with the criterion behavior.

c. content validity because scores on it correlated highly with the target behavior.

d. predictive validity because scores on it correlated highly with the target behavior.

6. Amelia recently took a test that assessed her ability to perform at the college level. The test she took was the:

a. WAIS.

b. WISC.

c. SAT.

d. None of the above, because they are all achievement tests.

7. Benito was born in 1937. In 1947, he scored 130 on an intelligence test. What was Benito's mental age when he took the test?

a. 9

b. 10

c. 11

d. 13

8. Melvin has been diagnosed as having savant syndrome, which means that he:

a. has an IQ of 120 or higher.

b. would score high on a test of analytical intelligence.

c. is limited in mental ability but has one exceptional ability.

d. was exposed to high levels of testosterone during prenatal development.

9. The contribution of environmental factors to racial gaps in intelligence scores is indicated by:

a. evidence that individual differences within a race are much greater than differences between races.

b. evidence that white and black infants score equally well on certain measures of infant intelligence.

c. the fact that Asian students outperform North American students on math achievement and aptitude tests.

d. all of the above.

10. Hiroko's math achievement score is considerably higher than that of most American students her age. Which of the following is true regarding this difference between Asian and North American students:

a. It is a recent phenomenon.

b. It may be due to the fact that Asian students have a longer school year.

c. It holds only for girls.

d. Both a. and b. are true.

11. Jack takes the same test of mechanical reasoning on several different days and gets virtually identical scores. This suggests that the test has:

a. high content validity.

b. high reliability.

c. high predictive validity.

d. been standardized.

12. You would not use a test of hearing acuity as an intelligence test because it would lack:

a. content reliability.

b. predictive reliability.

c. predictive validity.

d. content validity.

13. Before becoming attorneys, law students must pass a special licensing exam, which is an _____ test. Before entering college, high school students must take the SAT, which is an _____ test.
    a. achievement; aptitude
    b. aptitude; achievement
    c. achievement; achievement
    d. aptitude; aptitude

14. If you compare the same trait in people of similar heredity who live in very different environments, heritability for that trait will be _____ ; heritability for the trait is most likely to be _____ among people of very different heredities who live in similar environments.
    a. low; high
    b. high; low
    c. environmental; genetic
    d. genetic; environmental

15. A high-school psychologist who is looking at a student's intelligence score finds a jump of 30 points between the earliest score at age 2 and the most recent at age 17. The psychologist's knowledge of testing would probably lead her to conclude that such a jump:
    a. indicates that different tests were used, creating an apparent change in intelligence level, although it actually remained stable.
    b. signals a significant improvement in the child's environment over this period.
    c. is unsurprising, since intelligence scores do not become stable until late adolescence.
    d. is mainly the result of the age at which the first test was taken.

16. If you wanted to develop a test of musical aptitude in North American children, which would be the appropriate standardization group?
    a. children all over the world
    b. North American children
    c. children of musical parents
    d. children with known musical ability

17. Don's intelligence scores were only average, but he has been enormously successful as a corporate manager. Psychologists Sternberg and Wagner would probably suggest that:
    a. Don's verbal intelligence exceeds his performance intelligence.
    b. Don's performance intelligence exceeds his verbal intelligence.
    c. Don's academic intelligence exceeds his practical intelligence.
    d. Don's practical intelligence exceeds his academic intelligence.

18. According to the text, what can be concluded from early intelligence testing in the United States?
    a. Most European immigrants were "feeble-minded."
    b. Army recruits of other than West European heritage were intellectually deficient.
    c. The tests were biased against people who did not share the culture assumed by the test.
    d. Both a. and b. could be concluded.

19. If asked to guess the intelligence score of a stranger, your best guess would be:
    a. 75.
    b. 100.
    c. 125.
    d. "I don't know, intelligence scores vary too widely."

20. Which of the following is true of people who score high on aptitude tests?
    a. They achieve greater career success.
    b. They are likely to be happier.
    c. They always do well in college.
    d. None of the above is true.

Essay Question

You have been asked to devise a Psychology Achievement Test (PAT) that will be administered to freshmen who declare psychology as their major. What steps will you take to ensure that the PAT is a good intelligence test? (Use the space below to list the points you want to make, and organize them. Then write the essay on a separate sheet of paper.)

KEY TERMS

Writing Definitions

Using your own words, write on a separate piece of paper a brief definition or explanation of each of the following terms.

1. intelligence
2. factor analysis
3. general intelligence (*g*)
4. savant syndrome
5. emotional intelligence
6. creativity
7. intelligence test
8. mental age
9. Stanford-Binet
10. intelligence quotient (IQ)
11. aptitude tests
12. achievement tests
13. Wechsler Adult Intelligence Scale (WAIS)
14. standardization
15. normal curve (normal distribution)
16. reliability
17. validity
18. content validity
19. criterion
20. predictive validity
21. mental retardation
22. Down syndrome
23. stereotype threat

Cross-Check

As you learned in the Prologue, reviewing and overlearning of material are important to the learning process. After you have written the definitions of the key terms in this chapter, you should complete the crossword puzzle to ensure that you can reverse the process—recognize the term, given the definition.

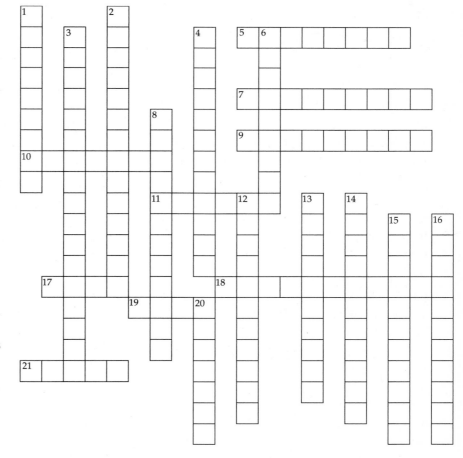

ACROSS

5. Type of intelligence assessed by standard intelligence tests.
7. Theorist who distinguished among three intelligences.
9. Type of intelligence often required for everyday tasks.
10. Theorist who proposed a large number of distinct types of intelligence.
11. Psychologist who revised Binet's original intelligence test.
17. The most widely used adult intelligence test.
18. Term that refers to viewing an abstract concept as if it were a real, concrete thing.
19. Most widely used intelligence test for children.
21. French psychologist who initiated the modern intelligence-testing movement.

DOWN

1. The age that typically corresponds to a given level of performance.

2. Statistical procedure that identifies clusters of related items on a test.

3. A condition of limited mental ability, as indicated by an IQ score below 70.

4. A condition of limited mental ability caused by an extra chromosome.

6. The behavior that a test is designed to predict.

8. The proportion of variation among individuals that is attributed to genes.

12. Type of test that is designed to measure what a person has already learned.

13. The success with which a test predicts the behavior it is designed to predict is its _____ validity.

14. Bell-shaped distribution that describes many physical and psychological traits.

15. The extent to which a test yields consistent results.

16. The phenomenon of rising intelligence-test performance.

20. The extent to which a test samples the behavior that is of interest is its _____ validity.

ANSWERS

Chapter Review

What Is Intelligence?

1. do not

2. reification

3. socially

4. the ability to learn from experience, solve problems, and use knowledge to adapt to new situations

5. overall (general); specific

6. factor analysis

7. general intelligence

8. Thurstone; primary mental abilities

9. novel problems

10. savant syndrome

11. multiple intelligences; physical; verbal; reasoning; do

12. triarchic; academic; practical; creative; academic

13. academic; social; only modestly

14. emotional intelligence; perceive; understand; manage; use

15. facial emotions

Emotionally intelligent people are self-aware. They can manage their emotions and they can delay gratification. They handle others' emotions skillfully. They also exhibit modestly better job performance.

16. recognize; predict; express; adaptive

17. emotional

18. conscientiousness

19. creativity; 120

20. convergent; divergent

Creative people tend to have expertise, or a solid base of knowledge; imaginative thinking skills, which allow them to see things in new ways, to recognize patterns, and to make connections; intrinsic motivation, or the tendency to focus on the pleasure and challenge of their work; and a venturesome personality that tolerates ambiguity and risk and seeks new experiences. Creative people also have generally benefited from living in creative environments.

21. social approval (or evaluation)

22. did not

23. volume; MRI; more

24. synapses; plasticity; gray matter; memory; attention; language

25. parietal; mathematical; spatial

26. frontal lobe; left; on both sides of the brain

27. faster

28. quickly; complexity

Assessing Intelligence

1. Plato

2. intelligence

3. Binet; mental; was not

4. Stanford-Binet; intelligence quotient

In the original formula for IQ, measured mental age is divided by chronological age and multiplied by 100. "Mental age" refers to the chronological age that most typically corresponds to a given level of performance.

5. a mental ability score; the same; 100

6. below; cultural

7. aptitude; achievement

8. Wechsler Adult Intelligence Scale; verbal comprehension; perceptual organization; working memory; processing speed

9. standardization

10. normal

The normal curve describes the distribution of many physical phenomena and psychological attributes (including IQ scores), with most scores falling near the average and fewer near the extremes. When a test is standardized on a normal curve, individual scores are assigned according to how much they deviate above or below the distribution's average.

11. are; 100
12. decline; improved; Flynn effect
13. nutrition; economic
14. reliable
15. test-retest
16. split-half
17. +.9
18. validity
19. content validity
20. criterion; predictive validity

The criterion is the particular behavior a predictive test, such as an aptitude test, is intended to predict. For example, performance in a relevant job situation would be the criterion for a test measuring managerial aptitude. The criterion determines whether a test has predictive validity. For example, the on-the-job success of those who do well on a job aptitude test would indicate the test has predictive validity.

21. is not; diminishes

The Dynamics of Intelligence

1. higher
2. 3
3. increases; 7; holds
4. mentally retarded; 1
5. Down syndrome
6. mainstreamed
7. healthy; adjusted; academically

Critics of ability tracking contend that it lowers students' self-esteem and sometimes creates self-fulfilling prophecies and that it promotes racial segregation and prejudice.

Genetic and Environmental Influences on Intelligence

1. generally accepted
2. more; gray matter; verbal; spatial
3. memory
4. more alike; environmental; age
5. more; biological; adoptive
6. heritability; 50 to 75
7. does not
8. do; malnutrition; sensory; social isolation
9. Head Start; emotional intelligence
10. rise; fall; schooling
11. environmental

Because of the impact of environmental factors such as education and nutrition on intelligence test perfor-

mance, even if the heritability of intelligence is high within a particular group, differences in intelligence among groups may be environmentally caused. One group may, for example, thrive in an enriched environment while another of the same genetic predisposition may falter in an impoverished one.

12. do not; greater than; is not
13. higher; Asian students have a longer school year and spend more time studying math
14. as well as
15. spelling; verbally
16. computation; problem solving; mental rotation
17. evolutionary
18. male sex hormones
19. social expectations
20. are
21. are not
22. stereotype threat

Progress Test 1

Multiple-Choice Questions

1. **a.** is the answer. (p. 456)
   c. & d. Separating genetic from environmental influences is difficult *at any age.*

2. **d.** is the answer. If we divide 9, the measured mental age, by 6, the chronological age, and multiply the result by 100, we obtain 150. (p. 444)

3. **b.** is the answer. As social expectations have changed, the gender gap in math and science scores is narrowing. (p. 464)

4. **c.** is the answer. (pp. 459–460)
   a. On the contrary, many *group* differences are highly significant, even though they tell us nothing about specific *individuals.*
   b. Although heredity contributes to individual differences in intelligence, it does not necessarily contribute to group differences.
   d. In fact, the difference has diminished somewhat in recent years.

5. **b.** is the answer. (p. 446)
   a. This answer refers to a test's content validity.
   c. This answer refers to test-retest reliability.
   d. This answer refers to predictive validity.

6. **a.** is the answer. (p. 452)
   b. Down syndrome is normally caused by an extra, rather than a missing, chromosome.
   c. & d. Down syndrome is a genetic disorder that is manifest during the earliest stages of prenatal

development, well before malnutrition and exposure to drugs would produce their harmful effects on the developing fetus.

7. **c.** is the answer. Reification is a reasoning error, in which an abstract concept such as IQ is regarded as though it were real. (p. 431)

8. **d.** is the answer. (p. 458)

9. **a.** is the answer. (p. 449)

c. & d. Most modern tests have high reliabilities of about +.9; their validity scores are much lower.

10. **b.** is the answer. (p. 451)

11. **d.** is the answer. (p. 453)

12. **d.** is the answer. Up to an intelligence score of about 120, there is a positive correlation between intelligence and creativity. But beyond this point the correlation disappears, indicating that factors other than intelligence are also involved. (p. 438)

a. The ability to think imaginatively and intelligence are *both* components of creativity.

b. Creativity, the capacity to produce ideas that are novel and valuable, is related to and depends in part on intelligence but cannot be considered simply a kind of intelligence.

c. Beyond an intelligence score of about 120 there is no correlation between intelligence scores and creativity.

13. **c.** is the answer. (p. 450)

14. **d.** is the answer. That people with savant syndrome excel in one area but are intellectually retarded in others suggests that there are multiple intelligences. (p. 433)

a. The ability to adapt defines the capacity we call intelligence.

b. Mental retardation is at the lower end of the range of human intelligence.

c. A general intelligence factor was hypothesized by Spearman to underlie each specific factor of intelligent behavior, but its existence is controversial and remains to be proved.

15. **a.** is the answer. Identical twins who live apart have the same genetic makeup but different environments; if their scores are similar, this is evidence for the role of heredity. (p. 455)

b. Because fraternal twins are no more genetically alike than ordinary siblings, this could not provide evidence for the role of heredity.

c. That twins raised together have more similar scores than twins raised apart provides evidence for the role of the environment.

d. As both sets of correlations are weak, little evidence is provided either for or against the role of heredity.

16. **c.** is the answer. Recent estimates are generally in the range of 50 to 75 percent. (p. 455)

17. **d.** is the answer. College aptitude tests are complex tests that are not periodically restandardized. The WAIS, a more basic test that is periodically restandardized so that the average is always 100, also reflects the performance of a more diverse group. (p. 447)

18. **d.** is the answer. Findings from a range of studies—including studies related to the Flynn effect and adoption studies—have led experts to focus on the influence of environmental factors. (pp. 460–461)

a. Most experts believe that in terms of predictive validity, the major tests are not racially biased.

b. The reliability of the major tests is actually very high.

c. The bulk of the evidence on which experts base their findings points to the influence of environmental factors.

19. **d.** is the answer. (p. 447)

a. *g* is Spearman's term for "general intelligence"; there is no such thing as a "*g* distribution."

b. There is no such thing.

c. A bimodal distribution is one having two (bi-) modes, or averages. The normal distribution has only one mode.

20. **b.** is the answer. Enrichment programs do improve school readiness, create better attitudes toward learning, and reduce school dropouts and criminality. (p. 458)

Matching Items

1. h (p. 444)
2. g (p. 432)
3. j (p. 444)
4. i (p. 433)

5. k (p. 432)
6. a (p. 444)
7. b (p. 444)
8. e (p. 443)

9. f (p. 448)
10. d (p. 448)
11. c (p. 448)

Progress Test 2

Multiple-Choice Questions

1. **c.** is the answer. French compulsory education laws brought more children into the school system, and the government didn't want to rely on teachers' subjective judgments to determine which children would require special help. (p. 443)

a. & b. Binet's test was intended for children, and Binet specifically rejected the idea that his test measured inborn intelligence, which is an abstract capacity that cannot be quantified.

d. This was not a purpose of the test, which dealt with children in the school system.

2. c. is the answer. (p. 457)
a., b., & d. None of these is true.

3. c. is the answer. Predictive validity is the extent to which tests predict what they are intended to predict. (p. 448)
a. Reliability is the consistency with which a test samples the particular behavior of interest.
b. Content validity is the degree to which a test measures what it is designed to measure.
d. Standardization is the process of defining meaningful test scores based on the performance of a representative group.

4. d. is the answer. Reification is the error of creating a concept and then assuming the created concept has a concrete reality. (p. 431)
a. To rationalize is to develop self-satisfying explanations of one's behavior.
b. The term "nominalizing" has no relevance to psychology.
c. Factor analysis is a statistical procedure that identifies clusters of related items, or factors, on a test.

5. d. is the answer. (p. 444)

6. c. is the answer. (p. 444)
a. This is William Stern's original formula for the intelligence quotient.
b. & d. Neither of these formulas is used to compute the score on current intelligence tests.

7. c. is the answer. Enrichment led to dramatic results and thereby testified to the importance of environmental factors. (p. 457)
a. & d. The study involved neither intelligence tests nor comparisons with control groups.
b. The children showed a dramatic positive response.

8. a. is the answer. (p. 432)

9. d. is the answer. (p. 436)
a. The concept of general intelligence pertains more to academic skills.
b. Although emotional intelligence *is* a key component of social intelligence, Salovey and Mayer coined the newer term "emotional intelligence" to refer to skills such as Gerardeen's.
c. Practical intelligence is that which is required for everyday tasks, not all of which involve emotions.

10. d. is the answer. Intelligence test performances begin to become predictive at about age 4 and become stable by about age 7. (p. 451)

11. c. is the answer. (p. 457)

12. c. is the answer. (p. 453)

a. & b. There was no evidence of either in the individuals studied by Terman.
d. Vocational success in adulthood varied.

13. d. is the answer. (pp. 440–441)

14. c. is the answer. (p. 431)
a. Performance ability and intellectual ability are separate traits.
b. This has been argued by some, but certainly not most, experts.
d. Although many experts believe that there are multiple intelligences, this would not be the same thing as diverse acquired skills.

15. d. is the answer. (pp. 452–453)

16. b. is the answer. (p. 463)

17. a. is the answer. Both schooling and intelligence enhance later income. (p. 458)

18. a. is the answer. (p. 443)

19. b. is the answer. (p. 444)
c. & d. Reliability and validity are characteristics of good tests.

20. c. is the answer. (p. 457)
a. & b. Studies of twins, family members, and adopted children point to a significant hereditary contribution to intelligence scores. These same studies, plus others comparing children reared in neglectful or enriched environments, indicate that life experiences also significantly influence test performance.
d. Although the issue of how intelligence should be defined is controversial, intelligence tests generally have predictive validity, especially in the early years.

True–False Items

1. T (p. 444)	6. F (p. 456)	11. T (p. 453)
2. F (p. 447)	7. F (p. 465)	
3. F (p. 449)	8. F (p. 455)	
4. T (p. 441)	9. T (p. 447)	
5. F (p. 459)	10. T (p. 460)	

Psychology Applied

Multiple-Choice Questions

1. c. is the answer. (p. 439)
a. Beyond an intelligence score of about 120, creativity and intelligence scores are not correlated.
b. & d. There is no evidence that creative people are more likely to be introverted.

2. **c.** is the answer. Heritability is a measure of the extent to which a trait's variation within a group of people can be attributed to heredity. (p. 456)

   a. & b. Heritability is *not* a measure of how much of an *individual's* behavior is inherited, nor of the relative contribution of genes from that person's mother and father. Further, the heritability of any trait depends on the context, or environment, in which that trait is being studied.

3. **c.** is the answer. To be labeled mentally retarded a person must have a test score below 70 and experience difficulty adapting to the normal demands of living independently. (p. 452)

   a. Down syndrome is a common cause of *severe* mental retardation; Dan's test score places him in the range of mild retardation.

   b. There is no indication that Dan possesses one extraordinary skill, as do people with savant syndrome.

   d. The text does not suggest that mentally retarded people eventually become self-supporting.

4. **b.** is the answer. Intelligence scores become quite stable during adolescence. (p. 451)

5. **b.** is the answer. (p. 448)

   a., c., & d. Content validity is the degree to which a test measures what it claims to measure. Furthermore, "target behavior" is not a term used by intelligence researchers.

6. **c.** is the answer. (p. 449)

   a. & b. The WAIS is a general aptitude test, and the WISC is for children.

   d. None of these tests are achievement tests; they are all aptitude tests.

7. **d.** is the answer. At the time he took the test, Benito's chronological age (CA) was 10. Knowing that IQ = 130 and CA = 10, solving the equation for mental age yields a value of 13. (p. 443)

8. **c.** is the answer. People with savant syndrome tend to score low on intelligence tests but have one exceptional ability. (p. 433)

9. **d.** is the answer. These reasons, along with other historical and cross-cultural reasons, all argue for the role of environment in creating and perpetuating the gap. (pp. 460–461)

10. **d.** is the answer. (p. 460)

    c. The racial gap is found in both girls and boys.

11. **b.** is the answer. (p. 448)

12. **d.** is the answer. Because the hearing acuity test would in no way sample behaviors relevant to intelligence, it would not have content validity as a test of intelligence. (p. 448)

    a. & b. There is no such thing as content reliability or predictive reliability.

c. There is nothing to indicate that, used to test hearing, this test would lack predictive validity.

13. **a.** is the answer. An exam for a professional license is intended to measure whether you have gained the overall knowledge and skill to practice the profession. The SAT is designed to predict ability, or aptitude, for learning a new skill. (p. 444)

14. **a.** is the answer. If everyone has nearly the same heredity, then heritability—the variation in a trait attributed to heredity—must be low. If individuals within a group come from very similar environments, environmental differences cannot account for variation in a trait; heritability, therefore, must be high. (p. 456)

15. **d.** is the answer. It is not until after age 4 that intelligence-test performance begins to predict adult scores. (p. 451)

    a. Such a conclusion is unlikely, given the high validity of the commonly used intelligence tests.

    b. No such conclusion is possible, because intelligence-test performance before age 4 does not predict later aptitude.

    c. Stability in intelligence scores is generally established by age 7—long before adulthood.

16. **b.** is the answer. A standardization group provides a representative comparison for the trait being measured by a test. Because this test will measure musical aptitude in North American children, the standardization group should be limited to North American children but should include children of all degrees of musical aptitude. (p. 446)

17. **d.** is the answer. Sternberg and Wagner distinguish among *academic* intelligence, as measured by intelligence tests; *practical* intelligence, which is involved in everyday life and tasks, such as managerial work; and *creative* intelligence. (p. 435)

    a. & b. Verbal and performance intelligence are both measured by standard intelligence tests such as the WAIS and would be included in Sternberg and Wagner's academic intelligence.

    c. Academic intelligence refers to skills assessed by intelligence tests; practical intelligence applies to skills required for everyday tasks and, often, for occupational success.

18. **c.** is the answer. (p. 444)

    a. & b. Although at the time the tests were administered some individuals reached these conclusions, they were, of course, misled.

19. **b.** is the answer. Modern intelligence tests are periodically restandardized so that the average remains near 100. (p. 444)

20. **d.** is the answer. As we move up the educational ladder, the predictive validity of aptitude tests diminishes. The narrower the range, the less predictive the test. Also, intelligence tests have nothing to do with happiness. (p. 449)

Essay Question

The first step in constructing the test is to create a valid set of questions that measure psychological knowledge and therefore give the test content validity. If your objective is to predict students' future achievement in psychology courses, the test questions should be selected to measure a criterion, such as information faculty members expect all psychology majors to master before they graduate.

To enable meaningful comparisons, the test must be standardized. That is, the test should be administered to a representative sample of incoming freshmen at the time they declare psychology to be their major. From the scores of your pretested sample you will then be able to assign an average score and evaluate any individual score according to how much it deviates above or below the average.

To check your test's reliability you might retest a sample of people using the same test or another version of it. If the two scores are correlated, your test is reliable. Alternatively, you might split the test in half and determine whether scores on the two halves are correlated.

Key Terms

Writing Definitions

1. Most experts define **intelligence** as the ability to learn from experience, solve problems, and use knowledge to adapt to new situations. (p. 431)

2. **Factor analysis** is a statistical procedure that identifies factors, or clusters of related items, that seem to define a common ability. Using this procedure, psychologists have identified several clusters, including verbal intelligence, spatial ability, and reasoning ability factors. (p. 432)

3. **General intelligence (*g*)**, according to Spearman and others, is a general factor that underlies each of the more specific mental abilities identified through factor analysis. (p. 432)

4. A person with **savant syndrome** has a very low intelligence score, yet possesses one exceptional ability, for example, in music or drawing. (p. 433)

5. **Emotional intelligence** is the ability to perceive, manage, understand, and use emotions. (p. 436)

6. Most experts agree that **creativity** refers to an ability to produce novel and valuable ideas. People with high IQs may or may not be creative, which indicates that intelligence is only one component of creativity. (p. 438)

7. **Intelligence tests** measure people's mental aptitudes and compare them to others' through numerical scores. (p. 442)

8. A concept introduced by Binet, **mental age** is the chronological age that most typically corresponds to a given level of performance. (p. 443)

9. The **Stanford-Binet** is Lewis Terman's widely used revision of Binet's original intelligence test. (p. 443)

10. The **intelligence quotient (IQ)** was defined originally as the ratio of mental age to chronological age multiplied by 100. Contemporary tests of intelligence assign a score of 100 to the average performance for a given age and define other scores as deviations from this average. (p. 444)

11. **Aptitude tests** are designed to predict future performance. They measure your capacity to learn new information, rather than measuring what you already know. (p. 444)

12. **Achievement tests** measure a person's current knowledge. (p. 444)

13. The **Wechsler Adult Intelligence Scale (WAIS)** is the most widely used intelligence test. It is individually administered, contains 11 subtests, and yields separate verbal and performance intelligence scores, as well as an overall intelligence score. (p. 445)

14. **Standardization** is the process of defining meaningful scores by comparison with a pretested standardization group. (p. 446)

15. The **normal curve** is a bell-shaped curve that represents the distribution (frequency of occurrence) of many physical and psychological attributes. The curve is symmetrical, with most scores near the average and fewer near the extremes. (p. 447)

16. **Reliability** is the extent to which a test produces consistent results. (p. 448)

17. **Validity** is the degree to which a test measures or predicts what it is supposed to. (p. 448)

18. The **content validity** of a test is the extent to which it samples the behavior that is of interest. (p. 448)

19. A test's **criterion** is the behavior the test is designed to predict. (p. 448)

20. **Predictive validity** is the extent to which a test predicts the behavior it is designed to predict; also called *criterion-related validity*. (p. 448)

21. The two criteria that designate **mental retardation** are an IQ below 70 and difficulty adapting to the normal demands of independent living. (p. 452)

22. A common cause of severe retardation and associated physical disorders, **Down syndrome** is usually the result of an extra chromosome in the person's genetic makeup. (p. 452)

23. **Stereotype threat** is the phenomenon in which a person's concern that he or she will be evaluated based on a negative stereotype (as on an aptitude test, for example) is actually followed by lower performance. (p. 465)

Cross-Check

ACROSS
5. academic
7. Sternberg
9. practical
10. Gardner
11. Terman
17. WAIS
18. reification
19. WISC
21. Binet

DOWN
1. mental age
2. factor analysis
3. mental retardation
4. Down syndrome
6. criterion
8. heritability
12. achievement
13. predictive
14. normal curve
15. reliability
16. Flynn effect
20. content

FOCUS ON VOCABULARY AND LANGUAGE

Page 419: Three huge controversies have *sparked debate* in and beyond psychology. The topic of intelligence (along with gender differences and the nature of repressed, recovered, and false memories) has provoked emotionally charged discussions (*sparked debate*) not only within psychology but in the larger community as well.

What Is Intelligence?

Page 432: You may also know a talented artist who is *dumbfounded by* the simplest mathematical problems . . . . Researchers have used a statistical approach (factor analysis) to identify groups of test items that measure a common ability. So, someone who has a group, or cluster, of abilities in one area may be very puzzled by and completely unable to solve (*dumbfounded by*) a relatively simple problem in a different area. Spearman argued that there was a common factor (*general intelligence, or g*) underlying particular abilities.

Page 433: People with **savant syndrome**, for example, often score low on intelligence tests but have an *island of brilliance*—some incredible ability, as in computation, drawing, or musical memory. Some people are functionally retarded in almost every aspect except for one very specific ability (*island of brilliance*) in which they are exceptionally gifted **(savant syndrome)**. Despite having very poor language skills and other cognitive dysfunctions, they may be capable of outstanding performance in computation, memory for music heard only once, draw-

ing, etc. Some psychologists argue that this is evidence for the notion of multiple intelligences.

Page 434: . . . *the street-smart* adolescent who becomes a *crafty* executive. Myers is attempting to simplify Howard Gardner's eight intelligences. As an example of one of these intelligences, he uses the adolescent who has the ability to survive in urban environments (he is *street smart*) becoming a clever (*crafty*) executive.

Page 435: . . . *how to read people* . . . People who have good practical managerial intelligence may not score high on academic ability but will be good at motivating people; assigning work to others appropriately; and knowing and understanding peoples' needs, desires, and ambitions (*knowing how to read people*). Other people may demonstrate different types of intelligences (for example, academic, creative, or emotional intelligence).

Page 435: They also agree that the differing *varieties of giftedness add spice to life* and challenges to education. The expression "variety adds spice to life" suggests that having many different experiences tends to make life more interesting (*adds spice to life*). The fact that people differ in their talents and gifts not only makes life more interesting but also poses opportunities for teachers to capitalize on the variety of abilities that students possess and to apply multiple intelligence in the classroom.

Page 438: . . . *out of the blue* . . . The solution to a very complex problem can occur unexpectedly and suddenly (*out of the blue*). This happened to Andrew

Wiles when he eventually solved Fermat's last theorem after thinking hard and long (*pondering*) about the problem for over 30 years. This example illustrates the creative process, the ability to produce novel and valuable ideas.

Page 439: Even Wiles *stood on the shoulders of others* and *wrestled* his problem with the collaboration of a former student. Don't take this literally. Wiles made use of the knowledge and wisdom of colleagues and a former student (*he stood on the shoulders of others*) when he was working hard and struggling to find the solution to Fermat's theorem (*he wrestled with the problem*).

Page 441 . . . quick-witted? This means being able to rapidly assess a situation or problem and respond appropriately without delay. (*Dim-witted* means to be slow and unintelligent.) Research shows that there is a positive correlation between intelligence-test scores and the speed demonstrated on a number of perceptual and neurological tests.

Page 441: The neurological approach to understanding intelligence (and so many other things in psychology) is currently *in its heyday*. Today, neurological psychology is enjoying unprecedented prosperity and growth (is *in its heyday*) and is vigorously researching many areas in psychology, including intelligence. Myers wonders if we will ultimately be able to describe and explain general intelligence (*g* factor) in pure biological terms, or if we are simply clinging obstinately to mistaken or inaccurate notions (are we *wrongheaded*). Perhaps intelligence is not a single trait but a combination of multiple abilities. The intense debate about what intelligence really is still continues.

Assessing Intelligence

Page 442: As *heirs* to Plato's individualism, people in Western societies have *pondered* how and why individuals differ. Western culture has inherited Plato's individualism. Thus, we are the recipients (*heirs*) of his ideas regarding the origins of individual differences and we think carefully and deeply (*ponder*) about how and why these differences occur. The scientific attempt to investigate this phenomenon began seriously (*in earnest*) about a century ago.

Page 443: On tests, therefore, a *"dull"* child should perform as does a typical younger child, and a *"bright"* child as does a typical older child. Children develop intellectually at different rates and so Binet and Simon developed the concept of **mental age**. Children who performed below the average level of

other children the same age (e.g., a 10-year-old who performed as the average 8-year-old did) would be considered retarded or slow in development (*"dull"*). Those who performed above the average (e.g., a 10-year-old who scored as the average 12-year-old did) would be considered developmentally advanced or precocious (*"bright"*).

Page 443: To raise the capacities of low-scoring children, he recommended *"mental orthopedics"* that would train them to develop their attention span and self-discipline. Binet did not believe that intellectual capacity was wholly genetic. Rather, he believed that intellectual capacity could be improved with remedial work. Once children who were likely to have problems in school were identified, he suggested the use of *"mental orthopedics."* (*Orthopedics* is concerned with the prevention and cure of physical deformities of bones, joints, and muscles, especially in children; *"mental orthopedics"* would apply the same principles to the mind.)

Page 444: In sympathy with *eugenics,* . . . Terman (1916, pp. 91–92) envisioned that the use of intelligence tests would "ultimately result in *curtailing the reproduction of feeble-mindedness* and in the elimination of an enormous amount of crime, *pauperism,* and *industrial inefficiency*" (p. 7). Terman's belief that mental capacity was inherited and that only the smartest should be allowed to procreate (*eugenics*) led him to speculate that the use of intelligence tests could result in reducing the number of children who are born with low intelligence (*curtailing the reproduction of feeble-mindedness*). He also believed that the widespread use of intelligence tests would get rid of, or reduce, crime, poverty (*pauperism*), and low worker productivity (*industrial inefficiency*).

Page 445: Actually, the differences between *aptitude* tests and *achievement* tests are not so *clear-cut.* Some tests measure your present ability and knowledge (*achievement*), as well as predict your future capacity to learn and develop (*aptitude*). Because what you know influences what you can learn in the future and what you are capable of learning is related to what you already know, there is no definite (*clear-cut*) distinction between aptitude and achievement tests. It is a practical matter; a test can be used either to predict future progress or to measure your present ability and skill.

Page 447: . . . scores often form a roughly symmetrical, bell-shaped distribution *clustered* around the average. Many variables that we measure (weight, height, intelligence, etc.) follow a bell-shaped curve when plotted on a frequency distribution. On intelligence tests, the average is 100; most scores (68%) are between 85 and 115, so they are gathered close together (*clustered*) near the mean (*average*).

Page 448: If you use an inaccurate *tape measure* to measure people's heights, your height report would have high *reliability* (consistency) but low *validity*. In order for a test to be *reliable*, the instrument should have consistent results over numerous tests. So, if you use a ruler (*tape measure*) that is not precise (*inaccurate*), it will meet the *reliability* criterion because it will always give you the same result; it will not, however, be valid. To be valid it should *accurately* measure what it is supposed to measure.

The Dynamics of Intelligence

Page 450: Developmental researchers have left few stones unturned in their search for indicators of infants' later intelligence. Can we predict later level of intelligence from observing the behavior of infants and very young children? Researchers have examined every possible variable (*they have left few stones unturned*) for accurate predictors. One test, which provides a rough (*crude*) indicator of later intelligence, involves observing how quickly children habituate to (*get bored* with) looking at a previously seen picture compared to a new one.

Page 452: During the last two centuries, *the pendulum of opinion* about how best to care for people with mental retardation has made a *complete swing.* Over time and in different ways we have taken care of the mentally retarded—first at home, then in small residential schools, then in massive institutions (*warehouses* for keeping people), and now back to a more normal situation in which they are integrated (*mainstreamed*) into regular classrooms. Our views about how people with mental retardation should be looked after have moved from one extreme to the other (*the pendulum of opinion . . . has made a complete swing*).

Genetic and Environmental Influences on Intelligence

Page 457: Extreme deprivation was *bludgeoning native intelligence.* In this investigation of a destitute

orphanage, Hunt (1982) found that the effect of extreme neglect was severe depression and a general mental and physical passivity (the children became "*glum lumps*"). Their inborn (*native*) intellectual capacity was taking a severe beating (*bludgeoning*) due to the *physical and emotional neglect.* As Myers notes, severe life experiences do leave footprints on the brain; that is, they can affect brain development and subsequent cognitive ability. Hunt's intervention program had dramatic results. This points to the strong influence of environment.

Page 461: Similarly, in the psychological domain, gender similarities vastly outnumber gender differences, but most people find the differences *more newsworthy.* Males and females are alike in many more ways than they are different. Although the similarities overwhelm (*vastly outnumber*) the dissimilarities, we are more intrigued by the dissimilarities, and gender differences are more likely to be reported by the media (*we find them more newsworthy*).

Page 463: The score differences are *sharpest* at the *extremes.* Although the variability in ability is greater within the two groups, people tend to focus on the between-group male-female differences. The differences in scores between males and females on the SAT test are more noticeable (*sharpest*) at the high and low ends of the distribution (*extremes*) than in the middle. Thus, among the very highest scorers in math, the majority are likely to be male.

Page 464: . . . *computer camps* . . . Because math and science have historically been viewed as male subjects, boys have been encouraged to become involved in special science activities and computer workshops (*computer camps*), whereas girls have been urged to take an interest in English. Today, a greater and greater number of females are involved in math and science, and the male-female difference in scores in these subjects is becoming smaller and smaller (*the gender gap is narrowing*).

12 : Motivation and Work

CHAPTER OVERVIEW

Motivation is the study of forces that energize and direct our behavior. Chapter 12 discusses various motivational concepts and looks closely at four motives: hunger, sex, the need to belong, and motivation at work. Research on hunger points to the fact that our biological drive to eat is strongly influenced by psychological and social-cultural factors. Sexual motivation in men and women is triggered less by physiological factors and more by external incentives. Even so, research studies demonstrate that sexual orientation is neither willfully chosen, nor easily changed. Research on worker motivation reveals that workers who view their careers as a meaningful calling, those working in jobs that optimize their skills, and those who become absorbed in activities that result in "flow" find work satisfying and enriching. Effective leaders recognize this and develop management styles that focus on workers' strengths and adapt their leadership style to the situation.

NOTE: Answer guidelines for all Chapter 12 questions begin on page 323.

CHAPTER REVIEW

First, skim each section, noting headings and boldface items. After you have read the section, review each objective by answering the fill-in and essay-type questions that follow it. As you proceed, evaluate your performance by consulting the answers beginning on page 323. Do not continue with the next section until you understand each answer. If you need to, review or reread the section in the textbook before continuing.

Perspectives on Motivation (p. 470–473)

> David Myers at times uses idioms that are unfamiliar to some readers. If you do not know the meaning of any of the following words, phrases, or expressions in the context in which they appear in the text, refer to page 330 for an explanation: *this fad for naming instincts collapsed under its own weight; feedback loops; monkey around.*

Objective 1: Define *motivation* as psychologists use the term today, and name four perspectives useful for studying motivated behaviors.

1. Motivation is defined as

   _____

   _____ .

2. Four perspectives on motivation are

   _____ theory (now replaced

   by the _____ perspective),

   _____-_____

   theory, _____ theory, and

   the _____ of needs proposed

   by _____ .

Objective 2: Discuss the similarities and differences between instinct theory and the evolutionary perspective.

3. As a result of Darwin's influence, many complex behaviors were classified as rigid, unlearned behavior patterns that are characteristic of a species, called _____ .

Discuss why early instinct theory failed as an explanation of human behavior.

4. The idea underlying the theory that _____ predispose species-typical behavior remains popular.

Objective 3: Explain how drive-reduction theory views human motivation.

5. According to another view of motivation, organisms may experience a physiological _____ , which creates a state of arousal that _____ the organism to reduce the need.

6. The aim of drive reduction is to maintain a constant internal state, called _____ .

7. Behavior is often not so much pushed by our drives as it is pulled by _____ in the environment.

Objective 4: Discuss the contribution of arousal theory to the study of motivation.

8. Rather than reduce a physiological need, some motivated behaviors actually _____ arousal. This demonstrates that human motives _____ (do/do not) always satisfy some biological need.

9. Human motivation aims not to eliminate _____ but to seek _____ _____ of arousal.

Objective 5: Describe Maslow's hierarchy of needs.

10. Starting from the idea that some needs take precedence over others, Maslow constructed a _____ of needs.

11. According to Maslow, the _____ needs are the most pressing, whereas the highest-order needs relate to _____ .

12. A criticism of Maslow's theory is that the sequence is _____ and not _____ experienced.

13. Surveys of life satisfaction reveal that _____ satisfaction is strongly predictive of subjective well-being in poorer nations, whereas _____-_____ satisfaction matters more in wealthy nations and _____ in individualist nations.

Hunger (pp. 473–480)

> If you do not know the meaning of any of the following words, phrases, or expressions in the context in which they appear in the text, refer to pages 330–331 for an explanation: *feasted their eyes on delectable forbidden foods; keeping tabs; miser; binge-purge.*

1. Ancel Keys observed that men became preoccupied with thoughts of food when they underwent _____ .

Objective 6: Describe the physiological determinants of hunger.

2. Cannon and Washburn's experiment using a balloon indicated that there is an association between hunger and _____ _____ .

3. When an animal has had its stomach removed, hunger _____ (does/does not) continue.

4. Increases in the hormone _____ diminish blood _____ , partly by converting it to stored fat, which causes hunger to _____ .

5. The brain area that plays a role in hunger and other bodily maintenance functions is the _____ . Animals will begin eating when the _____ _____ is electrically stimulated. When this region is destroyed, hunger _____ (increases/decreases). Animals will stop eating when the

_____ _____
is stimulated. When this area is destroyed,
animals _____ (overeat/
undereat).

6. When a rat is deprived of food and blood sugar
   levels wane, the _____
   _____ churns out the hunger-
   triggering hormone _____ .

7. When a portion of an obese person's stomach is
   surgically sealed off, the remaining stomach produces _____ (more/less) of
   the hunger-arousing hormone
   _____ .

For questions 8–12, identify the appetite hormone
that is described.

8. Hunger-triggering hormone: _____ .

9. Hormone secreted by empty stomach: _____ .

10. Hormone secreted by pancreas: _____ .

11. Chemical secreted by bloated fat cells:
    _____ .

12. Digestive tract hormone that signals fullness:
    _____ .

13. The weight level at which an individual's body is
    programmed to stay is referred to as the body's

    _____ _____ .

    A person whose weight goes beyond this level
    will tend to feel _____
    (more/less) hungry than usual and expend
    _____ (more/less) energy.

14. The rate of energy expenditure in maintaining
    basic functions when the body is at rest is the

    _____ _____

    rate. When food intake is reduced, the body com-
    pensates by _____ (raising/
    lowering) this rate.

15. The concept of a precise body set point that
    drives hunger _____ (is accept-
    ed/is not accepted) by all researchers. Some
    researchers believe that set point can be altered
    by _____

    _____ .

    In support of this idea is evidence that when

people and other animals are given unlimited
access to tasty foods, they tend to_____
and _____ _____ .
For these reasons, some researchers prefer to use
the term _____ _____
as an alternative to the idea that there is a fixed
set point.

Objective 7: Discuss psychological and cultural influences on hunger.

16. Research with amnesia patients indicates that
    part of knowing when to eat is our
    _____ of our last meal.

17. Carbohydrates boost levels of the neuro-
    transmitter _____ , which
    _____ (calms/arouses) the
    body.

18. Taste preferences for sweet and salty are
    _____ (genetic/learned). Other
    influences on taste include _____
    and _____ . We have a natural
    dislike of many foods that are
    _____ ; this _____
    was probably adaptive for our ancestors, and
    protected them from toxic substances.

Objective 8: Explain how the eating disorders
anorexia nervosa and bulimia nervosa demonstrate
the influence of psychological forces on physiologically motivated behaviors.

19. The disorder in which a person becomes signifi-
    cantly underweight and yet feels fat is known as
    _____ _____ .

20. A more common disorder is
    _____ _____ ,
    which is characterized by repeated
    _____-_____
    episodes and by feelings of depression or anxiety.

21. The families of bulimia patients have a high inci-
    dence of _____ ,
    _____ , and _____ .

The families of anorexia patients tend to be

_____ , _____- _____ , and _____ . Eating disorders _____ (provide/do not provide) a telltale sign of childhood sexual abuse.

22. Genetic factors _____ (may/do not) influence susceptibility to eating disorders. The genes for these disorders may be predisposed by _____ .

23. Vulnerability to eating disorders _____ (increases/does not increase) with greater body dissatisfaction.

24. Women students in _____ rate their actual shape as closer to the cultural ideal. In _____ cultures, however, the rise in eating disorders has coincided with an increasing number of women having a poor _____ _____ .

25. Stice and Shaw found that when young women were shown pictures of unnaturally thin models, they felt more _____ , _____ , and _____ with their own bodies.

26. In studying our motivation to eat, we must consider not only biological influences but also psychological influences such as the _____ and _____ of tasty foods and our mood and _____ - _____ influences such as the thinness ideal.

Sexual Motivation (pp. 481–494)

> If you do not know the meaning of any of the following words, phrases, or expressions in the context in which they appear in the text, refer to page 331 for an explanation: *shift it into high gear; X-rated; the pendulum of sexual values has swung; fired; neither willfully chosen nor willfully changed; swung the pendulum toward; double-edged sword.*

1. In the 1940s and 1950s, a biologist named _____ surveyed the sexual

practices of thousands of men and women. One of his major findings was that there _____ (was/was not) great diversity in "normal" sexual behavior.

Objective 9: Describe the human sexual response cycle, and discuss some causes of sexual disorders.

2. The two researchers who identified a four-stage sexual response cycle are _____ and _____ . In order, the stages of the cycle are the _____ phase, the _____ phase, _____ , and the _____ phase.

3. During resolution, males experience a _____ _____ , during which they are incapable of another orgasm.

4. Problems that consistently impair sexual functioning are called _____ _____ . Examples of such problems include _____ _____ , _____ _____ , and _____ _____ .

5. Personality disorders _____ (have/have not) been linked with most of the problems impairing sexual functioning. The most effective therapies for sexual problems are _____ oriented.

Objective 10: Discuss the impact of hormones on sexual motivation and behavior.

6. In most mammals, females are sexually receptive only during ovulation, when the hormone _____ has peaked.

7. The importance of the hormone _____ to male sexual arousal is confirmed by the fact that sexual interest declines in animals if their _____ are removed. In women, low levels of the hormone _____ may cause a waning of sexual interest.

8. Normal hormonal fluctuations in humans have
_____ (little/significant) effect
on sexual motivation. In later life, frequency of
intercourse _____ (increases/
decreases) as sex hormone levels
_____ (increase/decline).

Objective 11: Describe the role of external stimuli and
fantasies on sexual motivation and behavior.

9. Research has shown that erotic stimuli
_____ (are/are not) nearly as
arousing for women as for men.

10. Brain scans reveal more activity in the
_____ among
_____ (women/men) who are
viewing erotica.

11. With repeated exposure, the emotional response
to an erotic stimulus often _____ .

Explain some of the possible harmful consequences of
sexually explicit material.

12. Most women and men _____
(have/ do not have) sexual fantasies. Compared
to women's fantasies, men' sexual fantasies are
more _____
_____ .
Sexual fantasies do not indicate sexual
_____ or _____ .

Objective 12: Discuss some of the forces that influence teen pregnancy and teen attitudes toward con-
traception.

13. Attitudes toward premarital sex vary widely
from one _____ to another and
with the passage of _____ .

Rates of teen intercourse in the United States and

_____ _____
are much higher than those in _____
and _____ countries.
Compared with European teens, American teens
have _____ (higher/lower) rates
of intercourse, _____
(higher/lower) rates of contraceptive use, and
thus _____ (higher/lower) rates
of teen pregnancy and abortion.

State five factors that contribute to the high rate of
unprotected sex among teenagers.

Objective 13: Describe trends in the spread of sexually transmitted infections.

14. Unprotected sex has led to an increase in
adolescent rates of _____

_____ _____ .

Teenage girls, because of their lower levels of
protective _____ , may be espe-
cially vulnerable to STIs.

State several predictors of sexual restraint (reduced
teen sexuality and pregnancy).

Objective 14: Summarize current views on the number of people whose sexual orientation is homosexual, and discuss the research on environmental and
biological influences on sexual orientation.

15. A person's sexual attraction toward members of a
particular gender is referred to as

_____ _____ .

16. Historically, _____ (all/a slight
majority) of the world's cultures have been predominantly heterosexual. Most homosexuals

begin thinking of themselves as gay or lesbian around age _____ .

17. Studies in Europe and the United States indicate that approximately _____ percent of men and _____ percent of women are exclusively homosexual. This finding suggests that popular estimates of the rate of homosexuality are _____ (high/low/accurate).

18. A person's sexual orientation _____ (does/does not) appear to be voluntarily chosen. Several research studies reveal that sexual orientation among _____ (women/men) tends to be less strongly felt and potentially more changeable than among the other gender. This phenomenon has been called

_____ _____ .

19. Gays and lesbians suffer elevated rates of _____ and risk of _____ attempts.

20. Most gays and lesbians _____ (accept/do not accept) their orientation.

21. Childhood events and family relationships _____ (are/are not) important factors in determining a person's sexual orientation.

22. Homosexuality _____ (does/does not) involve a fear of the other gender that leads people to direct their sexual desires toward members of their own gender.

23. Sex hormone levels _____ (do/do not) predict sexual orientation.

24. As children, most homosexuals _____ (were/were not) sexually victimized.

25. Homosexual people appear more often in certain populations, including _____ , _____ _____ , _____ , and _____ .

26. Men who have older brothers are somewhat _____ (more/less) likely to be

gay. This phenomenon, which has been called the

_____ _____-_____ _____ ,

may represent a defensive maternal _____ response to substances produced by _____ (male/female) fetuses.

27. One theory proposes that people develop a homosexual orientation if they are segregated with _____ (their own/the other) gender at the time their sex drive matures. The fact that early homosexual behavior _____ (does/does not) make people homosexual _____ (supports/conflicts with) this theory.

28. Same-sex attraction _____ (does/does not) occur among animals.

29. Researcher Simon LeVay discovered a cluster of cells in the _____ that is larger in _____ men than in all others. Gays and lesbians differ from their straight counterparts in their preference for sex-related _____ . Other studies have found a section of the brain's

_____ _____

that is one-third larger in homosexual men than in heterosexual men.

30. Studies of twins suggest that genes probably _____ (do/do not) play a role in homosexuality.

31. In animals and some rare human cases, sexual orientation has been altered by abnormal _____ conditions during prenatal development. In humans, prenatal exposure to hormone levels typical of _____ , particularly between _____ and _____ months after conception, may predispose an attraction to males.

32. Gay males and lesbians may have certain physical traits more typical of those of the other gender, including _____ patterns, greater odds of being _____ (right/left)-handed, and anatomical traits of the _____ within the hearing system.

33. Most psychiatrists now believe that _____ (nature/nurture) plays the larger role in predisposing sexual orientation. Those who believe that sexual orientation is determined by _____ express more accepting attitudes toward homosexual persons.

34. Recent public opinion surveys reveal a _____ (more/less) accepting attitude toward homosexuality among Americans _____ (and/but not a liberalization of) all sex-related attitudes.

Objective 15: Discuss the place of values in sex research.

35. The study of sexual behavior and what motivates it _____ (can/cannot) be free of values.

36. Researchers' values _____ (should/should not) be openly stated.

The Need to Belong (pp. 495–498)

> If you do not know the meaning of any of the following words, phrases, or expressions in the context in which they appear in the text, refer to pages 331–332 for an explanation: *colors our thoughts and emotions; Even to be shunned—given the cold shoulder.*

Objective 16: Describe the adaptive value of social attachments, and identify both healthy and unhealthy consequences of our need to belong.

1. The philosopher _____ referred to humans as the _____ animal. From an evolutionary standpoint, social bonds in humans boosted our ancestors' _____ rates. If those who felt this need to _____ survived and reproduced more successfully, their _____ would in time predominate.

2. When asked what makes life meaningful, most people mention _____.

3. Feeling accepted and loved by others boosts our _____ .

4. Much of our _____ behavior aims to increase our belonging. For most people, familiarity leads to _____ (liking/disliking).

5. After years of placing individual refugee and immigrant families in _____ communities, U.S. policies today encourage _____ _____ .

6. _____ (Throughout the world/Only in certain cultures do) people use social exclusion, or _____ , to control social behavior.

7. Researchers have found that ostracism increased activity in the brain's _____ _____ , which is also activated in response to _____ _____ .

8. Researchers have found that people who are rejected are more likely to engage in _____ behaviors and may exhibit more _____ behavior, such as _____ .

9. People who perceive strong social support from others live with better _____ than those who lack social support. They also have a lower risk of _____ disorder and premature _____ .

Motivation at Work (pp. 498–510)

> If you do not know the meaning of any of the following words, phrases, or expressions in the context in which they appear in the text, refer to page 332 for an explanation: *beeped; what our gut tells us; superstar achievers; exude a self-confident charisma.*

Objective 17: Discuss the importance of flow, and identify the three subfields of industrial-organizational psychology.

1. According to Freud, the healthy life is filled with _____ and _____ .

2. Most people _____ (have/do not have) a predictable career path, which is one reason that many colleges focus less on _____ and more on _____ .

3. People who are unemployed _____ (report/do not report) lower well-being. People who view their work as a _____ report the greatest satisfaction.

4. Psychologist Mihaly Csikszentmihalyi formulated the concept of _____ , which is defined as a state of focused _____ and diminished awareness of _____ . People who experience this state also experience increased feelings of _____ , _____ , and _____ .

5. The nature of work has changed, from _____ to _____ to "_____ _____ ." In addition, work is increasingly being _____ to temporary employees.

6. The subjective sense of mutual obligations between workers and employers has been called the _____ _____ .

7. The field of _____-_____ psychology applies psychology's principles to the workplace. The subfield of _____ _____ focuses on employee recruitment, training, and development. Another subfield, _____ _____ , examines how work environments and _____ styles influence worker motivation. A third subfield, _____ _____ _____ , focuses on the design of appliances, machines, and work environments.

Objective 18: Describe how personnel psychologists help organizations with employee selection, work placement, and performance appraisal.

8. Personnel psychologists have found that the corporate world is generally quite _____ (good/bad) at capitalizing on the strengths of workers. One remedy to this is instituting a _____-_____ selection system which matches strengths to work.

9. (Close-Up) Satisfied and successful people devote less time to _____ _____ than to _____ _____ .

10. Interviewers' impressions of applicants tend to be highly _____ (accurate/error-prone).

11. Interviewers tend to _____ (over/under)estimate their interviewing skills and intuition—a phenomenon labeled the _____ _____ .

State four effects that fuel this phenomenon.

12. A more disciplined method of collecting information from job applicants is the _____ _____ , which asks the same questions of all applicants. This method enhances the _____ and _____ accuracy of the interview process.

13. Performance appraisal has several purposes, including helping organizations decide _____ , how to appropriately _____ _____ , and how to better harness employees' _____ . Performance appraisal methods include _____ , _____ _____ scales, and _____ _____ scales.

14. One form of bias in performance appraisal is the _____ _____ , which occurs when one _____ biases ratings of other work-related behaviors. Another is

the _____ error, which occurs when raters focus on easily remembered behavior. Two others are the _____ and _____ errors, in which an evaluator tends to be either too easy or too harsh on everyone.

Objective 19: Define *achievement motivation*, and explain why organizations would employ an I/O psychologist to help motivate employees and foster employee satisfaction.

15. Psychologists refer to the desire for significant accomplishments, mastering skills or ideas, and attaining a high standard as _____ _____ . People with high levels of this form of motivation _____ (do/do not) achieve more. What is most important in their achievement is not so much their creativity or intelligence as their _____ and their passionate dedication to an ambitious, long-term goal, or their _____ .

16. Positive moods at work contribute to worker _____ , _____ , and _____ . Researchers have also found a positive correlation between measures of organizational success and employee _____ , or the extent of workers' involvement, satisfaction, and enthusiasm.

Objective 20: Describe some effective management techniques.

17. Good managers help people _____ and measure their talents, match _____ to talents, care how people feel about their work, and _____ positive behaviors.

18. When people state not only goals but also their _____ _____ , they become more focused in their work and timely completion becomes more likely.

19. Managers who are directive, set clear standards, organize work, and focus attention on specific goals are said to employ _____ _____ . More democratic

managers who aim to build teamwork and mediate conflicts in the work force employ _____ _____ .

20. An outdated leadership theory, called the _____ _____ theory of leadership, assumes that all great leaders share certain _____ .

21. Effective leaders often possess a self-confident _____ that is a mixture of their _____ of some goal, coupled with an ability to _____ clearly and to _____ others. Similarly, _____ leaders articulate high standards, inspire others, and offer personal attention.

22. People respond more positively when they are given the opportunity to _____ their opinions during the decision-making process. This has been called the _____ _____ .

PROGRESS TEST 1

Multiple-Choice Questions

Circle your answers to the following questions and check them with the answers beginning on page 325. If your answer is incorrect, read the explanation for why it is incorrect and then consult the appropriate pages of the text (in parentheses following the correct answer).

1. Motivation is best understood as a state that:
   a. reduces a drive.
   b. aims at satisfying a biological need.
   c. energizes an organism to act.
   d. energizes and directs behavior.

2. Which of the following is a difference between a drive and a need?
   a. Needs are learned; drives are inherited.
   b. Needs are physiological states; drives are psychological states.
   c. Drives are generally stronger than needs.
   d. Needs are generally stronger than drives.

3. One problem with the idea of motivation as drive reduction is that:
   a. because some motivated behaviors do not seem to be based on physiological needs, they cannot be explained in terms of drive reduction.
   b. it fails to explain any human motivation.
   c. it cannot account for homeostasis.
   d. it does not explain the hunger drive.

4. Some scientific evidence makes a preliminary link between homosexuality and:
   a. late sexual maturation.
   b. the age of an individual's first erotic experience.
   c. atypical prenatal hormones.
   d. early problems in relationships with parents.

5. Increases in insulin will:
   a. lower blood sugar and trigger hunger.
   b. raise blood sugar and trigger hunger.
   c. lower blood sugar and trigger satiety.
   d. raise blood sugar and trigger satiety.

6. Electrical stimulation of the lateral hypothalamus will cause an animal to:
   a. begin eating.
   b. stop eating.
   c. become obese.
   d. begin copulating.

7. The text suggests that a *neophobia* for unfamiliar tastes:
   a. is more common in children than in adults.
   b. protected our ancestors from potentially toxic substances.
   c. may be an early warning sign of an eating disorder.
   d. only grows stronger with repeated exposure to those tastes.

8. I am a protein produced by fat cells and monitored by the hypothalamus. When in abundance, I cause the brain to increase metabolism. What am I?
   a. PYY   c. orexin
   b. ghrelin   d. leptin

9. Instinct theory and drive-reduction theory both emphasize _____ factors in motivation.
   a. environmental   c. psychological
   b. cognitive   d. biological

10. The correct order of the stages of Masters and Johnson's sexual response cycle is:
    a. plateau; excitement; orgasm; resolution.
    b. excitement; plateau; orgasm; resolution.
    c. excitement; orgasm; resolution; refractory.
    d. plateau; excitement; orgasm; refractory.

11. Few human behaviors are rigidly patterned enough to qualify as:
    a. needs.   c. instincts.
    b. drives.   d. incentives.

12. Which of the following is *not* true regarding sexual orientation?
    a. Sexual orientation is neither willfully chosen nor willfully changed.
    b. Most people accept their orientation.
    c. Men's sexual orientation is potentially more fluid and changeable than women's.
    d. Women, regardless of sexual orientation, respond to both female and male erotic stimuli.

13. In his study of men on a semistarvation diet, Keys found that:
    a. the metabolic rate of the subjects increased.
    b. the subjects eventually lost interest in food.
    c. the subjects became obsessed with food.
    d. the subjects' behavior directly contradicted predictions made by Maslow's hierarchy of needs.

14. When asked what makes life meaningful, most people first mention:
    a. good health.
    b. challenging work.
    c. satisfying relationships.
    d. serving others.

15. Bulimia nervosa involves:
    a. binging.
    b. purging.
    c. dramatic weight loss.
    d. a. and b.

16. Castration of male rats results in:
    a. reduced testosterone and sexual interest.
    b. reduced testosterone, but no change in sexual interest.
    c. reduced estrogen and sexual interest.
    d. reduced estrogen, but no change in sexual interest.

17. Which of the following has been found to be most effective in treating sexual disorders?
    a. psychoanalysis
    b. cognitive therapy
    c. drug therapy
    d. behavior therapy

18. It has been said that the body's major sex organ is the brain. With regard to sex education:
    a. transmission of value-free information about the wide range of sexual behaviors should be the primary focus of the educator.
    b. transmission of technical knowledge about the biological act should be the classroom focus, free from the personal values and attitudes of researchers, teachers, and students.
    c. the home, not the school, should be the focus of all instruction about reproductive behavior.
    d. people's attitudes, values, and morals cannot be separated from the biological aspects of sexuality.

19. Kinsey's studies of sexual behavior showed that:
    a. males enjoy sex more than females.
    b. females enjoy sex more than males.
    c. premarital sex is less common than is popularly believed.
    d. sexual behavior is enormously varied.

20. To increase employee productivity, industrial-organizational psychologists advise managers to:
    a. adopt a directive leadership style.
    b. adopt a democratic leadership style.
    c. instill competitiveness in each employee.
    d. deal with employees according to their individual motives.

Matching Items

Match each term with its definition or description.

Terms

_____ 1. organizational psychology
_____ 2. set point
_____ 3. drive
_____ 4. orexin
_____ 5. estrogen
_____ 6. homeostasis
_____ 7. sexual orientation
_____ 8. need
_____ 9. incentive
_____ 10. personnel psychology
_____ 11. ghrelin

Definitions or Descriptions

a. hormone secreted more by females than by males
b. the body's tendency to maintain a balanced internal state
c. environmental stimulus that motivates behavior
d. a person's attraction to members of a particular sex
e. examines organizational influences on worker satisfaction and productivity
f. focuses on employee selection and replacement
g. an aroused state arising from some physiological need
h. a state of deprivation
i. the body's weight-maintenance setting
j. hormone secreted by an empty stomach
k hunger-triggering hormone secreted by the hypothalamus

PROGRESS TEST 2

Progress Test 2 should be completed during a final chapter review. Answer the following questions after you thoroughly understand the correct answers for the section reviews and Progress Test 1.

Multiple-Choice Questions

1. One research study found that having an e-mail go unanswered, and other forms of ostracism, elicit increased activity in the brain's:
   a. amygdala.
   b. frontal lobe.
   c. cerebellum.
   d. anterior cingulate cortex.

2. Homeostasis refers to:
   a. the tendency to maintain a steady internal state.
   b. the tendency to seek external incentives for behavior.
   c. the setting of the body's "weight thermostat."
   d. a theory of the development of sexual orientation.

3. Which of the following was *not* identified as a contributing factor in the interviewer illusion?
   a. The fact that interviews reveal applicants' intentions but not necessarily their habitual behaviors.
   b. The tendency of interviewers to think that interview behavior only reflects applicants' enduring traits.
   c. The tendency of interviewers to more often follow the successful careers of applicants they hired rather than those who were not hired.
   d. The tendency of most interviewers to rely on unstructured rather than structured interviews.

4. Of the following parts of the world, teen intercourse rates are highest in:
   a. Western Europe.   c. The United States.
   b. Canada.   d. Asia.

5. Although the cause of eating disorders is still unknown, proposed explanations focus on all the following *except*:
   a. metabolic factors.
   b. genetic factors.
   c. family background factors.
   d. cultural factors.

6. The brain area that when stimulated suppresses eating is the:
   a. lateral hypothalamus.
   b. ventromedial hypothalamus.
   c. lateral thalamus.
   d. ventromedial thalamus.

7. Exposure of a fetus to the hormones typical of females between _____ and _____ months after conception may predispose the developing human to become attracted to males.
   a. 1; 3   c. 4; 7
   b. 2; 5   d. 6; 9

8. Which of the following statements concerning homosexuality is true?
   a. Homosexuals have abnormal hormone levels.
   b. As children, most homosexuals were molested by an adult homosexual.
   c. Homosexuals had a domineering opposite-sex parent.
   d. Research indicates that sexual orientation may be at least partly physiological.

9. Women in _____ rate their body ideals closest to their actual shape.
   a. Western cultures
   b. countries such as Africa, where thinness can signal poverty,
   c. countries such as India, where thinness is not idealized,
   d. Australia, New Zealand, and England

10. According to Maslow's theory:
    a. the most basic motives are based on physiological needs.
    b. needs are satisfied in a specified order.
    c. the highest motives relate to self-actualization.
    d. all of the above are true.

11. Which of the following is *inconsistent* with the drive-reduction theory of motivation?
    a. When body temperature drops below 98.6° Fahrenheit, blood vessels constrict to conserve warmth.
    b. A person is driven to seek a drink when his or her cellular water level drops below its optimum point.
    c. Monkeys will work puzzles even if not given a food reward.
    d. A person becomes hungry when body weight falls below its biological set point.

12. Which of the following is true concerning eating disorders?
    a. Genetic factors may influence susceptibility.
    b. Cultural pressures for thinness strongly influence teenage girls.
    c. Family background is a significant factor.
    d. All of the above are true.

13. Sexual orientation refers to:
    a. a person's tendency to display behaviors typical of males or females.
    b. a person's sense of identity as a male or female.
    c. a person's enduring sexual attraction toward members of a particular gender.
    d. all of the above.

14. Which of the following is *not* an aspect of Murray's definition of achievement motivation?
    a. the desire to master skills
    b. the desire for control
    c. the desire to gain approval
    d. the desire to attain a high standard

15. Hunger and sexual motivation are alike in that both are influenced by:
    a. internal physiological factors.
    b. external and imagined stimuli.
    c. cultural expectations.
    d. all of the above.

16. According to Masters and Johnson, the sexual response of males is most likely to differ from that of females during:
    a. the excitement phase.
    b. the plateau phase.
    c. orgasm.
    d. the resolution phase.

17. In animals, destruction of the lateral hypothalamus results in _____ , whereas destruction of the ventromedial hypothalamus results in _____ .
    a. overeating; loss of hunger
    b. loss of hunger; overeating
    c. an elevated set point; a lowered set point
    d. increased thirst; loss of thirst

18. Because Alethea is very friendly and likable, her supervisor gives her a positive rating on her overall job performance. By generalizing from these specific traits to a biased overall evaluation, Alethea's supervisor has committed a:
    a. leniency error.   c. halo error.
    b. severity error.   d. recency error.

19. Beginning with the most basic needs, which of the following represents the correct sequence of needs in the hierarchy described by Maslow?
    a. safety; physiological; esteem; belongingness and love; self-fulfillment
    b. safety; physiological; belongingness and love; esteem; self-fulfillment
    c. physiological; safety; esteem; belongingness and love; self-fulfillment
    d. physiological; safety; belongingness and love; esteem; self-fulfillment

20. While viewing erotica, men and women differ in the activity levels of which brain area?
    a. anterior cingulate cortex
    b. amygdala
    c. occipital lobe
    d. temporal lobe

True–False Items

Indicate whether each statement is true or false by placing *T* or *F* in the blank next to the item.

_____ 1. When body weight rises above set point, hunger increases.

_____ 2. According to Masters and Johnson, only males experience a plateau period in the cycle of sexual arousal.

_____ 3. Testosterone affects the sexual arousal of the male only.

_____ 4. Unlike men, women tend not to be aroused by sexually explicit material.

_____ 5. All taste preferences are conditioned.

_____ 6. Married people are less at risk for depression than are unattached people.

_____ 7. An increase in insulin increases blood glucose levels and triggers hunger.

_____ 8. Most types of sexual disorder are associated with personality disorders.

_____ 9. Interviewers' gut feelings derived from unstructured interviews are highly accurate in predicting worker performance.

_____ 10. One's sexual orientation is not voluntarily chosen.

_____ 11. People who view their work as a career, rather than a job or a calling, report the highest satisfaction with their work and their lives.

_____ 12. Public opinion surveys reveal that Americans today have more liberal attitudes related to homosexuality and all sex-related issues.

_____ 13. Effective managers focus their training on workers' weaknesses.

PSYCHOLOGY APPLIED

Answer these questions the day before an exam as a final check on your understanding of the chapter's terms and concepts.

Multiple-Choice Questions

1. Dr. Iverson conducts research on how management styles influence worker motivation. He would most accurately be described as a(n):
   a. motivation psychologist.
   b. personnel psychologist.
   c. organizational psychologist.
   d. human factors psychologist.

2. Rosa has been described as a "leader with a lot of charisma." An organizational psychologist would say that this means she:
   a. has a clear vision of her leadership goals.
   b. is able to communicate her goals clearly and simply.
   c. is able to inspire others.
   d. possesses all of the above characteristics.

3. Mary loves hang-gliding. It would be most difficult to explain Mary's behavior according to:
   a. incentives.
   b. achievement motivation.
   c. drive-reduction theory.
   d. Maslow's hierarchy of needs.

4. For two weeks, Orlando has been on a hunger strike in order to protest his country's involvement in what he perceives as an immoral war. Orlando's willingness to starve himself in order to make a political statement conflicts with the theory of motivation advanced by:
   a. Kinsey.   c. Keys.
   b. Murray.   d. Maslow.

5. Kathy has been undergoing treatment for bulimia. There is an above-average probability that one or more members of Kathy's family:
   a. are high achievers.
   b. are overprotective.
   c. have a history of childhood obesity.
   d. are or have all of the above.

6. Which of the following was *not* identified as a contributing factor in the high rate of unprotected sex among adolescents?
   a. alcohol use
   b. thrill-seeking
   c. mass media sexual norms
   d. ignorance

7. One shortcoming of the instinct theory of motivation is that it:
   a. places too much emphasis on environmental factors.
   b. focuses on cognitive aspects of motivation.
   c. applies only to animal behavior.
   d. does not explain human behaviors; it simply names them.

8. Which of the following is *not* typical of both anorexia and bulimia?
   a. far more frequent occurrence in women than in men
   b. preoccupation with food and fear of being overweight
   c. weight significantly and noticeably outside normal ranges
   d. low self-esteem and feelings of depression

9. Which of the following is *not* an example of homeostasis?
   a. perspiring in order to restore normal body temperature
   b. feeling hungry and eating to restore the level of blood glucose to normal
   c. feeling hungry at the sight of an appetizing food
   d. All of the above are examples of homeostasis.

10. Two rats have escaped from their cages in the neurophysiology lab. The technician needs your help in returning them to their proper cages. One rat is grossly overweight; the other is severely underweight. You confidently state that the overweight rat goes in the "_____-destruction" cage, while the underweight rat goes in the "_____-destruction" cage.
    a. hippocampus; amygdala
    b. amygdala; hippocampus
    c. lateral hypothalamus; ventromedial hypothalamus
    d. ventromedial hypothalamus; lateral hypothalamus

11. Which of the following individuals would be characterized as experiencing *flow*?
    a. Sheila, who, despite viewing her work as merely a job, performs her work conscientiously
    b. Larry, who sees his work as an artist as a calling
    c. Darren, who views his present job as merely a stepping stone in his career
    d. Montel, who often becomes so immersed in his writing that he loses all sense of self and time

12. Ali's parents have tried hard to minimize their son's exposure to sweet, fattening foods. If Ali has the occasion to taste sweet foods in the future, which of the following is likely?
   a. He will have a strong aversion to such foods.
   b. He will have a neutral reaction to sweet foods.
   c. He will display a preference for sweet tastes.
   d. It is impossible to predict Ali's reaction.

13. Summarizing his presentation on the origins of homosexuality, Dennis explains that the "fraternal birth-order effect" refers to the fact that:
   a. men who have younger brothers are somewhat more likely to be gay.
   b. men who have older brothers are somewhat more likely to be gay.
   c. women with older sisters are somewhat more likely to be gay.
   d. women with younger sisters are somewhat more likely to be gay.

14. Summarizing her report on the need to belong, Rolanda states that:
   a. "Cooperation amongst our ancestors was uncommon."
   b. "Social bonding is not in our nature; it is a learned human trait."
   c. "Because bonding with others increased our ancestors' success at reproduction and survival, it became part of our biological nature."
   d. both a. and b. are true.

15. Of the following individuals, who might be most prone to developing an eating disorder?
   a. Jason, an adolescent boy who is somewhat overweight and is unpopular with his peers
   b. Jennifer, a teenage girl who has a poor self-image and a fear of not being able to live up to her parents' high standards
   c. Susan, a 35-year-old woman who is a "workaholic" and devotes most of her energies to her high-pressured career
   d. Bill, a 40-year-old man who has had problems with alcoholism and is seriously depressed after losing his job of 20 years

16. Lucille has been sticking to a strict diet but can't seem to lose weight. What is the most likely explanation for her difficulty?
   a. Her body has a very low set point.
   b. Her prediet weight was near her body's set point.
   c. Her weight problem is actually caused by an underlying eating disorder.
   d. Lucille is an "external."

17. Randy, who has been under a lot of stress lately, has intense cravings for sugary junk foods, which tend to make him feel more relaxed. Which of the following is the most likely explanation for his craving?
   a. Randy feels that he deserves to pamper himself with sweets because of the stress he is under.
   b. The extra sugar gives Randy the energy he needs to cope with the demands of daily life.
   c. Carbohydrates boost levels of serotonin, which has a calming effect.
   d. The extra sugar tends to lower blood insulin level, which promotes relaxation.

18. Which of the following teens is most likely to delay the initiation of sex?
   a. Jack, who has below-average intelligence
   b. Jason, who is not religiously active
   c. Ron, who regularly volunteers his time in community service
   d. It is impossible to predict

19. In order to predict future excellence in a young scholar, athlete, or artist, one would best examine the individual's:
   a. preparation and daily discipline.
   b. natural talent.
   c. peer group.
   d. home environment.

20. For as long as she has been the plant manager, Juanita has welcomed input from employees and has delegated authority. Bill manages his department, with a more authoritarian, iron-fisted approach. Juanita's style is one of _____ leadership, whereas Bill's is one of _____ leadership.
   a. task; social
   b. social; task
   c. directive; democratic
   d. democratic; participative

Essay Question

Differentiate the three major theories of motivation, discuss their origins, and explain why they cannot fully account for human behavior. (Use the space below to list the points you want to make, and organize them. Then write the essay on a separate sheet of paper.)

KEY TERMS

Writing Definitions

Using your own words, write on a separate piece of paper a brief definition or explanation of each of the following terms.

1. motivation
2. instinct
3. drive-reduction theory
4. homeostasis
5. incentives
6. hierarchy of needs
7. glucose
8. set point
9. basal metabolic rate
10. anorexia nervosa
11. bulimia nervosa
12. sexual response cycle
13. refractory period
14. sexual disorder
15. estrogen
16. testosterone
17. sexual orientation
18. flow
19. industrial-organizational psychology
20. personnel psychology
21. organizational psychology
22. structured interview
23. achievement motivation
24. task leadership
25. social leadership

Cross-Check

As you learned in the Prologue, reviewing and overlearning of material are important to the learning process. After you have written the definitions of the key terms in this chapter, you should complete the cross-word puzzle to ensure that you can reverse the process—recognize the term, given the definition.

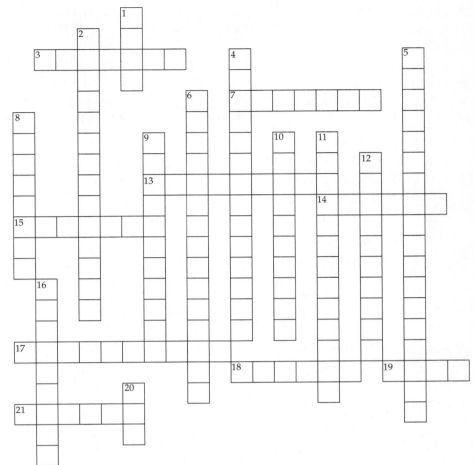

ACROSS

3. Hormone secreted by an empty stomach.
7. Region of the hypothalamus that, when electrically stimulated, causes an animal to eat.
13. In Maslow's theory, human needs are organized into a _____ .
14. In Maslow's theory, the needs that follow physiological needs in order of priority.
15. Major energy source for the body.
17. Final stage of the sexual response cycle.
18. Group-oriented leadership.
19. Goal-oriented leadership.
21. Early researcher on sexual behavior patterns.

DOWN

1. Type of error that occurs when an employer's overall work evaluation of an employee is biased by a single trait.
2. Theory that explains behavior as arising from physiological needs and the states of tension they create.
4. Eating disorder characterized by repeated "binge-purge" episodes.
5. The body's rate of energy expenditure at rest.
6. Eating disorder in which a person restricts food intake to become significantly underweight and yet still feels fat.
8. Sex hormone secreted in greater amount by females than by males.
9. Type of motivation that reflects the degree to which a person is motivated by a desire for significant accomplishment.
10. Initial stage of the sexual response cycle.

11. In Maslow's theory, the most basic types of needs.
12. The resting period after orgasm, during which a male cannot be aroused to another orgasm.
16. A positive or negative stimulus that motivates behavior.
20. Digestive tract hormone.

ANSWERS

Chapter Review

Perspectives on Motivation

1. a need or desire that energizes behavior and directs it toward a goal

2. instinct; evolutionary; drive-reduction; arousal; hierarchy; Abraham Maslow

3. instincts

According to instinct theory, any human behavior could be regarded as an instinct. The only evidence for each such "instinct" was the behavior used to identify it. Thus, instinct theory offered only circular explanations; it labeled behaviors but did not explain them.

4. genes
5. need; drives
6. homeostasis
7. incentives
8. increase; do not
9. arousal; optimum levels
10. hierarchy
11. physiological; self-actualization
12. arbitrary; universally
13. financial; home-life; self-esteem

Hunger

1. semistarvation
2. stomach contractions
3. does
4. insulin; glucose; increase
5. hypothalamus; lateral hypothalamus; decreases; ventromedial hypothalamus; overeat
6. lateral hypothalamus; orexin
7. less; ghrelin
8. orexin
9. ghrelin
10. insulin
11. leptin
12. PYY
13. set point; less; more
14. basal metabolic; lowering
15. is not accepted; slow, sustained changes in body weight; overeat; gain weight; settling point
16. memory
17. serotonin; calms
18. genetic; conditioning; culture; unfamiliar; neophobia
19. anorexia nervosa
20. bulimia nervosa; binge-purge
21. alcoholism; obesity; depression; competitive; high-achieving; protective; do not provide
22. may; evolution
23. increases
24. India; Western; body image
25. ashamed; depressed; dissatisfied
26. sight; smell; social-cultural

Sexual Motivation

1. Kinsey; was
2. Masters; Johnson; excitement; plateau; orgasm; resolution
3. refractory period
4. sexual disorders; premature ejaculation; erectile dysfunction; orgasmic disorder
5. have not; behaviorally
6. estrogen
7. testosterone; testes; testosterone
8. little; decreases; decline
9. are
10. amygdala
11. habituates

Erotic material may increase the viewer's acceptance of the false idea that women enjoy rape, may increase men's willingness to hurt women, may lead people to devalue their partners and relationships, and may diminish people's satisfaction with their own sexual partners.

12. have; frequent, physical, and less romantic; problems; dissatisfaction
13. culture; time; Western Europe; Asian; Arab; lower; lower; higher

Among the factors that contribute to unprotected sex among adolescents are (1) ignorance about the safe and risky times of the menstrual cycle, (2) guilt related to sexual activity, (3) minimal communication about birth control, (4) alcohol use that influences judgment, and (5) mass media norms of unprotected promiscuity.

14. sexually transmitted infection (STI); antibodies

Teens with high intelligence test scores, those who are actively religious, those whose father is present, and those who participate in service learning programs more often delay sex. Trends toward commitment show declining teen birth rates and sexual activity.

15. sexual orientation
16. all; 20
17. 3 or 4; 1 or 2; high
18. does not; women; erotic plasticity
19. depression; suicide
20. accept
21. are not
22. does not
23. do not
24. were not
25. poets; fiction writers; artists; musicians
26. more; fraternal birth-order effect; immune; male

27. their own; does not; conflicts with

28. does

29. hypothalamus; heterosexual; odors; anterior commissure

30. do

31. hormone; females; 2; 5

32. fingerprint; left; cochlea

33. nature; nature

34. more; but not a liberalization of

35. cannot

36. should

The Need to Belong

1. Aristotle; social; survival; belong; genes

2. close, satisfying relationships with family, friends, or romantic partners

3. self-esteem

4. social; liking

5. isolated; chain migration

6. Throughout the world; ostracism

7. anterior cingulate cortex; physical pain

8. self-defeating; antisocial; aggression

9. health; psychological; death

Motivation at Work

1. work; love

2. do not have; training job skills; enlarging capacities for understanding, thinking, and communicating in any work setting

3. report; calling

4. flow; consciousness; self; self-esteem, competence, well-being

5. farming; manufacturing; knowledge work; outsourced

6. psychological contract

7. industrial-organizational; personnel psychology; organizational psychology; management; human factors psychology

8. bad; strengths-based

9. correcting deficiencies; accentuating strengths

10. error-prone

11. over; interviewer illusion

    a. Interviews disclose the interviewee's good intentions, which are less revealing than their typical behaviors.

    b. Interviewers tend to follow the successful careers of people they hired and lose track of those they did not hire.

    c. Interviewers mistakenly presume that how interviewees present themselves reflects only their enduring traits.

    d. Interviewers' preconceptions and moods influence their perceptions of job applicants.

12. structured interview; reliability; predictive

13. who to retain; reward and pay workers; strengths; checklists; graphic rating; behavior rating

14. halo error; trait; recency; leniency; severity

15. achievement motivation; do; self-discipline; grit

16. creativity; persistence; helpfulness; engagement

17. identify; tasks; reinforce

18. implementation intentions

19. task leadership; social leadership

20. great person; traits

21. charisma; vision; communicate; inspire; transformational

22. voice; voice effect

Progress Test 1

Multiple-Choice Questions

1. **d.** is the answer. (p. 470)
   a. & b. Although motivation is often aimed at reducing drives and satisfying biological needs, this is by no means always the case, as achievement motivation illustrates.
   c. Motivated behavior not only is energized but also is directed at a goal.

2. **b.** is the answer. A drive is the psychological consequence of a physiological need. (p. 471)
   a. Needs are unlearned states of deprivation.
   c. & d. Since needs are physical and drives psychological, their strengths cannot be compared directly.

3. **a.** is the answer. The curiosity of a child or a scientist is an example of behavior apparently motivated by something other than a physiological need. (p. 471)
   b. & d. Some behaviors, such as thirst and hunger, are partially explained by drive reduction.
   c. Drive reduction is directly based on the principle of homeostasis.

4. c. is the answer. (p. 491)

a., b., & d. None of these is linked to homosexuality.

5. a. is the answer. Increases in insulin increase hunger indirectly by lowering blood sugar, or glucose. (p. 475)

6. a. is the answer. This area of the hypothalamus seems to elevate hunger. (p. 475)

b. Stimulating the ventromedial hypothalamus has this effect.

c. Lesioning the ventromedial hypothalamus has this effect.

d. The hypothalamus is involved in sexual motivation, but not in this way.

7. b. is the answer. (p. 477)

a. Neophobia for taste is typical of all age groups.

c. Neophobia for taste is *not* an indicator of an eating disorder.

d. With repeated exposure, our appreciation for a new taste typically *increases*.

8. d. is the answer. (p. 476)

a. PYY signals fullness, which is associated with decreased metabolism.

b. Ghrelin is a hormone secreted by the empty stomach that sends hunger signals.

c. Orexin is a hormone secreted by the hypothalamus.

9. d. is the answer. (pp. 470–471)

10. b. is the answer. (p. 481)

11. c. is the answer. (p. 470)

a. & b. Needs and drives are biologically based states that stimulate behaviors but are not themselves behaviors.

d. Incentives are the external stimuli that motivate behavior.

12. c. is the answer. Research studies suggest that women's sexual orientation is potentially more fluid and changeable than men's. (p. 488)

13. c. is the answer. The deprived subjects focused on food almost to the exclusion of anything else. (p. 474)

a. In order to conserve energy, the men's metabolic rate actually *decreased*.

b. & d. Far from losing interest in food, the subjects came to care only about food—a finding consistent with Maslow's hierarchy, in which physiological needs are at the base.

14. c. is the answer. (p. 495)

15. d. is the answer. (p. 478)

16. a. is the answer. (p. 482)

c. & d. Castration of the testes, which produce testosterone, does not alter estrogen levels.

17. d. is the answer. (p. 482)

a. Treating sexual disorder as though it were a personality disorder has not been successful.

b. & c. Neither type of therapy is discussed in the text. However, it seems likely that they would be as unsuccessful as more traditional methods.

18. d. is the answer. Sex is much more than just a biological act, and its study therefore inherently involves values, attitudes, and morals, which should thus be discussed openly. (p. 493)

19. d. is the answer. (p. 481)

a., b., & c. Kinsey's data do not support any of these statements.

20. d. is the answer. As different people are motivated by different things, in order to increase motivation and thus productivity, managers are advised to learn what motivates individual employees and to challenge and reward them accordingly. (p. 507)

a. & b. The most effective management style will depend on the situation.

c. This might be an effective strategy with some, but not all, employees.

Matching Items

1. e (p. 499)	**6.** b (p. 471)	**11.** j (p. 476)
2. i (p. 476)	**7.** d (p. 487)	
3. g (p. 471)	**8.** h (p. 471)	
4. k (p. 475)	**9.** c (p. 471)	
5. a (p. 482)	**10.** f (p. 499)	

Progress Test 2

Multiple-Choice Questions

1. d. is the answer. (p. 497)

a. The amygdala is involved in sexual arousal.

b. The frontal lobe is more involved in decision making and judgments.

c. The cerebellum is responsible for coordinating voluntary movement.

2. a. is the answer. (p. 471)

b. This describes extrinsic motivation.

c. This describes set point.

d. Homeostasis has nothing to do with sexual orientation.

3. d. is the answer. Although unstructured interviews *are* more prone to bias than structured interviews, the text does not suggest that they are used more often. (p. 502)

4. **a.** is the answer. (p. 485)

5. **a.** is the answer. The text does not indicate whether their metabolism is higher or lower than most. (pp. 479–480)
b., c., & d. Genes, family background, and cultural influence have all been proposed as factors in eating disorders.

6. **b.** is the answer. (p. 475)
a. Stimulation of the lateral hypothalamus triggers eating.
c. & d. The thalamus is a sensory relay station; stimulation of it has no effect on eating.

7. **b.** is the answer. The time between the middle of the second and fifth months after conception may be a critical period for the brain's neuro-hormonal control system. Exposure to abnormal hormonal conditions at other times has no effect on sexual orientation. (p. 491)

8. **d.** is the answer. Researchers have not been able to find any clear differences, psychological or otherwise, between homosexuals and heterosexuals. Thus, the basis for sexual orientation remains unknown, although recent evidence points more to a physiological basis. (pp. 489–491)

9. **c.** is the answer. (p. 479)

10. **d.** is the answer. (p. 472)

11. **c.** is the answer. Such behavior, presumably motivated by curiosity rather than any biological need, is inconsistent with a drive-reduction theory of motivation. (p. 471)
a., b., & d. Each of these examples is consistent with a drive-reduction theory of motivation.

12. **d.** is the answer. (p. 479)

13. **c.** is the answer. (p. 487)

14. **c.** is the answer. (p. 504)

15. **d.** is the answer. (p. 483)

16. **d.** is the answer. During the resolution phase males experience a refractory period. (p. 482)
a., b., & c. The male and female responses are very similar in each of these phases.

17. **b.** is the answer. (p. 475)
a. These effects are the reverse of what takes place.
c. If anything, set point is lowered by destruction of the lateral hypothalamus and elevated by destruction of the ventromedial hypothalamus.
d. These effects do not occur.

18. **c.** is the answer. (p. 504)
a. & b. These errors occur when an evaluator tends to be too easy (leniency error) or too harsh on all job applicants (severity error).

d. This error occurs when an evaluator focuses only on easily remembered recent behaviors.

19. **d.** is the answer. (p. 472)

20. **b.** is the answer. (p. 484)
a. The anterior cingulate cortex has been found to be implicated in feelings of ostracism.
c. & d. The occipital and temporal lobes do not play a major role in motivation.

True–False Items

1. F (p. 476)	**6.** T (p. 496)	**11.** F (p. 499)
2. F (p. 481)	**7.** F (p. 475)	**12.** F (p. 492)
3. F (p. 483)	**8.** F (p. 482)	**13.** F (p. 507)
4. F (p. 484)	**9.** F (p. 501)	
5. F (p. 477)	**10.** T (p. 488)	

Psychology Applied

Multiple-Choice Questions

1. **c.** is the answer. (p. 499)

2. **d.** is the answer. (p. 509)

3. **c.** is the answer. Drive-reduction theory maintains that behavior is motivated when a biological need creates an aroused state, driving the individual to satisfy the need. It is difficult to believe that Mary's hang-gliding is satisfying a biological need. (p. 471)
a., b., & d. Mary may enjoy hang-gliding because it is a challenge that "is there" (incentive), because it satisfies a need to accomplish something challenging (achievement), or because it increases her self-esteem and sense of fulfillment in life (Maslow's hierarchy of needs).

4. **d.** is the answer. According to Maslow's theory, physiological needs, such as the need to satisfy hunger, must be satisfied before a person pursues loftier needs, such as making political statements. (p. 472)
a. Kinsey was concerned with sexual behavior.
b. Murray was concerned with achievement motivation.
c. Keys was concerned with hunger.

5. **c.** is the answer. (p. 479)
a. & b. These are more typical of the families of anorexia patients.

6. **b.** is the answer. (pp. 485–486)

7. **d.** is the answer. (p. 470)
a. & b. Instinct theory emphasizes biological factors rather than environmental or cognitive factors.

c. Instinct theory applies to both humans and other animals.

8. **c.** is the answer. Although people with anorexia are significantly underweight, those with bulimia often are not unusually thin or overweight. (p. 478)

a., b., & d. Both anorexia and bulimia victims are more likely to be women than men, preoccupied with food, fearful of becoming overweight, and suffer from depression or low self-esteem.

9. **c.** is the answer. This is an example of salivating in response to an incentive rather than to maintain a balanced internal state. (p. 471)

a. & b. Both of these are examples of behavior that maintains a balanced internal state (homeostasis).

10. **d.** is the answer. Destruction of the ventromedial hypothalamus produces overeating and rapid weight gains. Destruction of the lateral hypothalamus suppresses hunger and produces weight loss. (p. 475)

a. & b. The hippocampus and amygdala are not involved in regulating eating behavior.

11. **d.** is the answer. (p. 498)

12. **c.** is the answer. Our preferences for sweet and salty tastes are genetic and universal. (p. 477)

13. **b.** is the answer. (p. 489)

14. **c.** is the answer. (p. 495)

15. **b.** is the answer. Adolescent females with low self-esteem and high-achieving families seem especially prone to eating disorders such as anorexia nervosa. (pp. 478–479)

a. & d. Eating disorders occur much more frequently in women than in men.

c. Eating disorders usually develop during adolescence, rather than during adulthood.

16. **b.** is the answer. The body acts to defend its set point, or the weight to which it is predisposed. If Lucille was already near her set point, weight loss would prove difficult. (p. 476)

a. If the weight level to which her body is predisposed is low, weight loss upon dieting should not be difficult.

c. The eating disorders relate to eating behaviors and psychological factors and would not explain a difficulty with weight loss.

d. Externals might have greater problems losing weight, since they tend to respond to food stimuli, but this can't be the explanation in Lucille's case, since she has been sticking to her diet.

17. **c.** is the answer. Serotonin is a neurotransmitter that is elevated by the consumption of carbohy-

drates and has a calming effect. (p. 477)

a. & b. These answers do not explain the feelings of relaxation that Randy associates with eating junk food.

d. The consumption of sugar tends to elevate insulin level rather than lower it.

18. **c.** is the answer. (p. 486)

a., b., & d. Teens with high rather than average intelligence (therefore, not a.), and those who are religiously active (therefore, not b.) are most likely to delay sex.

19. **a.** is the answer. (p. 504)

b. Natural talent is, of course, important, but preparation and daily discipline are generally more significant.

c. & d. These were not identified as factors in outstanding achievement.

20. **b.** is the answer. (p. 508)

a. Bill's style is one of task leadership, whereas Juanita's is one of social leadership.

c. Juanita's style is democratic/participative, whereas Bill's is directive.

d. The terms democratic and participative refer to the same style of leadership.

Essay Question

Under the influence of Darwin's evolutionary theory, it became fashionable to classify all sorts of behaviors as instincts. Instinct theory fell into disfavor for several reasons. First, instincts do not explain behaviors, they merely name them. Second, to qualify as an instinct, a behavior must have a fixed and automatic pattern and occur in all people, regardless of differing cultures and experiences. Apart from a few simple reflexes, however, human behavior is not sufficiently automatic and universal to meet these criteria. Although instinct theory failed to explain human motives, the underlying assumption that genes predispose many behaviors is as strongly believed as ever.

Instinct theory was replaced by drive-reduction theory and the idea that biological needs create aroused drive states that motivate the individual to satisfy these needs and preserve homeostasis. Drive-reduction theory failed as a complete account of human motivation because many human motives do not satisfy any obvious biological need. Instead, such behaviors are motivated by environmental incentives.

Arousal theory emerged in response to evidence that some motivated behaviors *increase*, rather than decrease, arousal.

KEY TERMS

Writing Definitions

1. **Motivation** is a need or desire that energizes and directs behavior. (p. 470)

2. An **instinct** is a complex behavior that is rigidly patterned throughout a species and is unlearned. (p. 470)

3. **Drive-reduction theory** attempts to explain behavior as arising from a physiological need that creates an aroused tension state (drive) that motivates an organism to satisfy the need. (p. 471)

4. **Homeostasis** refers to the body's tendency to maintain a balanced or constant internal state. (p. 471)

5. **Incentives** are positive or negative environmental stimuli that motivate behavior. (p. 471)

6. Maslow's **hierarchy of needs** proposes that human motives may be ranked from the basic, physiological level through higher-level needs for safety, love, esteem, and self-actualization; until they are satisfied, the more basic needs are more compelling than the higher-level ones. (p. 472)

7. **Glucose**, or blood sugar, is the major source of energy for the body's tissues. Elevating the level of glucose in the body will reduce hunger. (p. 475)

8. **Set point** is an individual's regulated weight level, which is maintained by adjusting food intake and energy output. (p. 476)

9. **Basal metabolic rate** is the body's base rate of energy expenditure when resting. (p. 476)

10. **Anorexia nervosa** is an eating disorder, most common in adolescent females, in which a person restricts food intake to become significantly underweight and yet still feels fat. (p. 478)

11. **Bulimia nervosa** is an eating disorder characterized by episodes of overeating followed by vomiting, laxative use, fasting, or excessive exercise. (p. 478)

12. The **sexual response cycle** described by Masters and Johnson consists of four stages of bodily reaction: excitement, plateau, orgasm, and resolution. (p. 481)

13. The **refractory period** is a resting period after orgasm, during which a male cannot be aroused to another orgasm. (p. 482)

14. A **sexual disorder** is a problem—such as erectile disorder, premature ejaculation, and orgasmic disorder—that consistently impairs sexual arousal or functioning. (p. 482)

15. **Estrogen** is a sex hormone secreted in greater amounts by females than by males. In mammals other than humans, estrogen levels peak during ovulation and trigger sexual receptivity. (p. 482)

16. **Testosterone** is a sex hormone secreted in greater amounts by males than by females. In males, higher testosterone levels stimulate the prenatal growth of the male sex organs and the development of the male sex characteristics during puberty. (p. 482)

17. **Sexual orientation** refers to a person's enduring attraction to members of either the same or the opposite gender. (p. 487)

18. **Flow** is a state of focused consciousness on a task that optimally engages a person's skills, often accompanied by a diminished awareness of self and time. (p. 498)

19. **Industrial-organizational (I/O) psychology** is a subfield of psychology that studies and advises on issues related to optimizing behavior in workplaces. (p. 499)

20. **Personnel psychology** is a subfield of industrial-organizational psychology that applies psychological methods and principles to the selection and evaluation of workers. (p. 499)

21. **Organizational psychology** is a subfield of industrial-organizational psychology that explores how work environments and management styles affect worker motivation, satisfaction, and productivity. (p. 499)

22. A **structured interview** is one in which an interviewer asks the same job-relevant questions of all interviewees, who are then rated on established evaluation scales. (p. 502)

23. **Achievement motivation** is a desire for significant accomplishment; for mastery of things, people, or ideas; and for attaining a high standard. (p. 504)

24. **Task leadership** is goal-oriented leadership that sets standards, organizes work, and focuses attention on goals. (p. 508)

25. **Social leadership** is group-oriented leadership that builds teamwork, mediates conflict, and offers support. (p. 508)

Cross-Check

ACROSS	DOWN
3. ghrelin	**1.** halo
7. lateral	**2.** drive-reduction
13. hierarchy	**4.** bulimia nervosa
14. safety	**5.** basal metabolic rate
15. glucose	**6.** anorexia nervosa
17. resolution	**8.** estrogen
18. social	**9.** achievement
19. task	**10.** excitement
21. Kinsey	**11.** physiological
	12. refractory
	16. incentive
	20. PYY

FOCUS ON VOCABULARY AND LANGUAGE

Perspectives on Motivation

Page 470: Before long, *this fad for naming instincts collapsed under its own weight.* A good example of the misuse of a theory was when it became very popular (fashionable) to categorize a very broad range of behaviors as innately determined (a fad for naming instincts). In Darwinian theory, an instinct is an unlearned behavior that follows a fixed pattern in all members of the species. This fashion (fad) of naming thousands of behaviors as instincts, rather than explaining them, grew so large and cumbersome that it was finally abandoned as a useful explanatory system (it collapsed under its own weight).

Page 471: Both systems operate through *feedback loops.* . . . A thermostat in a house and the body's temperature-regulation system are both examples of **homeostasis.** If temperature drops, the change is detected and the information is directed (*fed*) to the system so that necessary steps are taken to bring the temperature back up to its original position. This information is then transmitted back to the system, so that there is a continuous cycle of cooling down and heating up (*feedback loop*) in an attempt to maintain a steady state. This is the basis of **drive-reduction theory.**

Page 471: Curiosity drives monkeys to *monkey around* trying to figure out how to unlock a latch that opens nothing or how to open a window that allows them to see outside their room (Butler, 1954). The expression *"monkey around"* means to play or fool around (meddle) with something. Monkeys and young children have a very great need to explore and find out about their surroundings. Arousal theory suggests that we are driven to seek stimulation and increase our level of arousal to some comfortable state which is neither too high nor too low (*optimum level*).

Hunger

Page 474: They talked food. They daydreamed food. They collected recipes, read cookbooks, and *feasted their eyes on delectable forbidden foods.* In this experiment, subjects were given only half their normal intake of food, and the men became lethargic (*listless*), focused all their thoughts on the topic of food, and looked longingly at (*feasted their eyes on*) pictures of delicious, but unobtainable, foods (*delectable forbidden foods*). This behavior is consistent with Maslow's theory that there is a hierarchy of needs.

Page 475: This suggests that the body is somehow, somewhere, *keeping tabs on* its available resources. People and other animals naturally and automatically tend to control food intake in order to keep a relatively constant body weight. This indicates that there is a mechanism, or mechanisms, which monitor (*keep tabs on*) energy fluctuations. Levels of the blood sugar glucose and certain brain chemicals may play a role in this process.

Page 475: . . . rather like a *miser* who runs every bit of extra money to the bank and resists taking any out. One theory suggests that two parts of the hypothalamus, the lateral hypothalamus (LH) and ventromedial hypothalamus (VMH), regulate hunger. Stimulation of the LH increases hunger, while activity in the VMH depresses hunger. If the VMH is destroyed (*lesioned*), rats tend to create and store more fat, just as a person who loves money more than anything else (*a miser*) will keep banking money and use as little of it as possible.

Page 478: . . . *binge-purge* . . . People who have an eating disorder called **bulimia nervosa** may have episodes of overeating (*binging*) similar to those who engage in drinking bouts (*spurts of drinking*). The bulimic person (typically females in their teens or twenties) usually follows the overeating episode (*gorging*) with self-induced vomiting and excessive laxative use (*purging*).

Sexual Motivation

Page 483: The hormonal fuel is essential, but so are the psychological stimuli that *turn on the engine*, keep it running, and *shift it into high gear*. Myers makes an analogy between sex hormones and the fuel that propels a car. We need the hormones to be sexually motivated just as a car needs fuel to operate. In humans, however, there is a two-way interaction between the chemicals and sexuality. In addition to hormones, psychological factors are needed to initiate sexual desire (*turn on the engine*) and produce the associated behaviors (*shift it into high gear*).

Page 484: Viewing *X-rated sex films* similarly tends to diminish people's satisfaction with their own sexual partners (Zillmann, 1989). All films are rated by a censor, and those with an *X-rating* because of their sexually explicit content are restricted to adults only. There is much debate over the influence of such films on people, and some research suggests that there may be adverse effects. For example, they may create the false impression that females enjoy rape; they may increase men's willingness to hurt women; they tend to lead both males and females to devalue their partners and their relationships; and they may reduce people's feeling of fulfillment with their lovers.

Page 486: In recent history, the *pendulum* of sexual values has swung from the European eroticism of the early 1800s to the *conservative Victorian era* of the late 1800s, from the *libertine flapper era* of the 1920s to the family values period of the 1950s. The *pendulum* of a mechanical clock swings back and forth from one side, or extreme, to the other. Myers is pointing out that our views of sexuality tend to move from restrictive (*conservative Victorian*) at one extreme to those with fewer restraints (*libertine flapper*) at the other, during different periods of time (*eras*). Today's generation may be moving toward an era in which commitment and restraint are more important than sexual expression. (Note: A *flapper* was an emancipated young woman in the 1920s.)

Page 487: . . . *fired* . . . To be *fired* means to lose your job (*to be laid off, let go, or sacked*). Myers suggests that one way for heterosexual people to understand how a homosexual feels in a predominantly heterosexual society is to imagine what it would be like if the situation were reversed and homosexuality was the norm. How would it feel as a heterosexual to be ostracized (*ignored*), to lose one's job (*be fired*), or to be confronted by media that showed or indicated homosexuality as the societal norm?

Page 488: Most of today's psychologists therefore view sexual orientation as neither *willfully chosen* nor *willfully changed*. Myers compares sexual orientation to handedness. You don't deliberately decide (*willfully choose*) to be right-handed or left-handed and you can't intentionally alter (*willfully change*) your inherent inclination to use one hand over the other. Like handedness, sexual orientation is not linked to criminality nor is it associated with personality or psychological disorder.

Page 492: Regardless of the process, the consistency of the genetic, prenatal, and brain findings has *swung the pendulum toward* a biological explanation of sexual orientation (Rahman & Wilson, 2003). The debate over what causes different sexual orientations has continued for many years. Recent evidence from the research seems to favor (*has swung the pendulum toward*) a biologically based account.

Page 493: To gay and lesbian activists, the new biological research is a *double-edged sword* (Diamond, 1993). The research supporting a physiological explanation of sexual orientation has both positive and negative aspects (*a double-edged sword*). On the one hand, if sexual orientation is genetically influenced, there is a basis for claiming equal civil rights and there is no need to attribute blame. On the other hand, these findings create a nagging anxiety (*troubling possibility*) that sexual orientation may be controlled through genetic engineering or fetal abortions.

The Need to Belong

Page 495: The need to belong *colors our thoughts and emotions*. As humans, we have a desire to be connected to others and to develop close, long-lasting relationships, and this need to belong affects the way we think and feel (*colors our thoughts and emotions*).

Page 497: Even to be *shunned—given the cold shoulder or the silent treatment*, with others' eyes avoiding yours—is to have one's *need to belong threatened*. . . . For both adults and children, to be ignored (*shunned*), treated with disdain (*given the cold shoulder*), or deprived of verbal interactions with others (*given the silent treatment*) is very distressing and hurtful; this type of social ostracism makes us feel isolated and abandoned (*threatens our need to belong*) and can lead to depression and withdrawal.

Motivation at Work

Page 499: When the researchers *beeped* people at random intervals . . . When researchers used pagers to randomly signal people (*they were beeped*) and report what they were doing and how they were feeling, those engaged in purposeful activities reported more positive emotions and flow than those who were idle and doing nothing much (*vegetating*).

Page 502: If there is a contest between *what our gut tells us* about someone and what test scores, work samples, and past performance tells, we should distrust *our gut*. Subjective judgments (*gut feelings*) based on informal face-to-face meetings (*unstructured seat-of-the-pants interviews*) are very weak predictors of later behavior compared to what test scores, work samples, and previous performance reveal. Thus, we should not rely too much on subjective evaluations obtained (*gleaned*) from unstructured interviews (*we should distrust our gut*).

Page 504: These *superstar achievers* were distinguished not so much by their extraordinary *natural talent* as by their extraordinary daily discipline. Studies of people who were outstanding artists, scientists, athletes, etc. (*superstar achievers*) found that they were not different because of intelligence or innate skills (*natural talent*) but because of exceptional motivation and very high levels of self-discipline in relation to the daily pursuit of their goals.

Page 507: Effective leaders of laboratory groups, work teams, and large corporations also tend to *exude a self-confident charisma.* . . . Competent managers who lead groups of people in an effective and productive manner typically exhibit an ability to rely on their own capacities (*exude self-confidence*), project their vision of what needs to be done, and inspire others to follow them (*"charisma"*). This type of transformational leadership motivates others to want to belong to the group and to feel a strong commitment to its goal.

13 : Emotion

CHAPTER OVERVIEW

Emotions are responses of the whole individual, involving physiological arousal, expressive behaviors, and conscious experience. Chapter 13 first discusses several theoretical controversies concerning the relationship and sequence of the components of emotion, primarily regarding whether the body's response to a stimulus causes the emotion that is felt and whether thinking is necessary to and must precede the experience of emotion. After describing the physiology of emotion and emotional expressiveness, it examines the components of emotion in detail, particularly as they relate to the emotions of fear, anger, and happiness.

NOTE: Answer guidelines for all Chapter 13 questions begin on page 347.

CHAPTER REVIEW

First, skim each section, noting headings and boldface items. After you have read the section, review each objective by answering the fill-in and essay-type questions that follow it. As you proceed, evaluate your performance by consulting the answers beginning on page 347. Do not continue with the next section until you understand each answer. If you need to, review or reread the section in the textbook before continuing.

Theories of Emotion (pp. 513–515)

> David Myers at times uses idioms that are unfamiliar to some readers. If you do not know the meaning of any of the following expressions from the introduction and this section in the context in which they appear in the text, refer to page 354 for an explanation: *add color to your life; arousal of dread . . . elation of ecstasy; lash out.*

Objective 1: Identify the three components of emotions, and contrast the James-Lange, Cannon-Bard, and two-factor theories of emotion.

1. Emotions have three components: _____
   _____ , _____
   _____ , and _____
   _____ .

2. According to the James-Lange theory, emotional
   states _____ (precede/follow)
   body arousal.

Describe two problems that Walter Cannon identified with the James-Lange theory.

3. Cannon proposed that emotional stimuli in the
   environment are routed simultaneously to the
   _____ , which results in awareness of the emotion, and to the
   _____ nervous system, which
   causes the body's reaction. Because another scientist concurrently proposed similar ideas, this theory has come to be known as the
   _____-_____
   theory.

4. The two-factor theory of emotion proposes that
   emotion has two components:
   _____ arousal and a
   _____ label. This theory was proposed by _____ .

Embodied Emotion (pp. 516–523)

> If you do not know the meaning of any of the following words, phrases, or expressions in the context in which they appear in the text, refer to pages 354–355 for an explanation: *your stomach develops butterflies; shooting free throws; clutching, sinking sensation; peppy left hemisphere . . . perky disposition; Pinocchio . . . telltale sign; weeping, lumps in the throat . . .; Which is the chicken and which the egg?; white lie; testy; hijack; The heart is not always subject to the mind.*

Objective 2: Describe the role of the autonomic nervous system during emotional arousal.

1. Describe the major physiological changes that each of the following undergoes during emotional arousal:
   a. heart: _____
   b. muscles: _____
   c. liver: _____
   d. breathing: _____
   e. digestion: _____
   f. pupils: _____
   g. blood: _____
   h. skin: _____

2. The responses of arousal are activated by the _____ nervous system. In response to its signal, the _____ glands release the hormones _____ and _____ , which increase heart rate, blood pressure, and blood sugar.

3. When the need for arousal has passed, the body is calmed through activation of the _____ nervous system.

Objective 3: Discuss the relationship between arousal and performance.

4. People usually perform best when they feel _____ aroused.

5. The level of arousal for optimal performance _____ (varies/is the same) for different tasks.

6. For tasks that are _____ , peak performance comes with relatively _____ (high/low) arousal. For tasks that are _____ , optimal arousal is _____ (higher/lower).

Objective 4: Name three emotions that involve similar physiological arousal.

7. The various emotions are associated with _____ (similar/different) forms of physiological arousal. In particular, the emotions of _____ , _____ , and _____ are difficult to distinguish physiologically.

Objective 5: Describe some physiological and brain pattern indicators of specific emotions.

8. The emotions _____ and _____ are accompanied by differing _____ temperatures and _____ secretions.

9. The emotions _____ and _____ stimulate different facial muscles.

10. The brain circuits underlying different emotions _____ (are/are not) different. For example, seeing a fearful face elicits greater activity in the _____ than seeing a(n) _____ face. People who have generally negative personalities, and those who are prone to _____ , show more activity in the _____ _____ of the brain.

11. When people experience positive moods, brain scans reveal more activity in the _____ _____ _____ .

12. Individuals with more active _____ (right/left) _____ lobes tend to be more cheerful than those in whom this pattern of brain activity is reversed. This may be due to the rich supply of _____ receptors in this area of the brain.

13. Electrical areas of the brain's _____ _____ can trigger smiling and laughter.

14. (Thinking Critically) The technical name for the "lie detector" is the _____ .

(Thinking Critically) Explain how lie detectors supposedly indicate whether a person is lying.

15. (Thinking Critically) How well the lie detector works depends on whether a person exhibits _____ while lying.

16. (Thinking Critically) Those who criticize lie detectors feel that the tests are particularly likely to err in the case of the _____ (innocent/guilty), because different _____ all register as _____ .

17. (Thinking Critically) By and large, experts _____ (agree/do not agree) that lie detector tests are highly accurate.

18. (Thinking Critically) A test that assesses a suspect's knowledge of details of a crime that only the guilty person should know is the

_____ _____

_____ .

19. For victims with severed spinal cords who have lost all feeling below the neck, the intensity of emotions tends to _____ . This result supports the _____-_____ theory of emotion.

20. Most researchers _____ (agree/disagree) with Cannon and Bard's position that emotions involve _____ as well as arousal.

Objective 6: Explain how the spillover effect influences our experience of emotions.

21. The *spillover effect* refers to occasions when our _____ response to one event carries over into our response to another event.

22. Schachter and Singer found that physically aroused college men told that an injection would cause arousal _____ (did/did not) become emotional in response to an accomplice's aroused behavior. Physically aroused volunteers not expecting arousal _____ (did/did not) become emotional in response to an accomplice's behavior.

23. Arousal _____ emotion; cognition _____ emotion.

Objective 7: Distinguish the two alternative pathways that sensory stimuli may travel when triggering an emotional response.

24. Robert Zajonc believes that the feeling of emotion _____ (can/cannot) precede our cognitive labeling of that emotion.

Cite two pieces of evidence that support Zajonc's position.

25. A pathway from the _____ via the _____ to the _____ enables us to experience emotion before _____ . For more complex emotions, sensory input is routed through the _____ for interpretation.

26. The researcher who disagrees with Zajonc and argues that most emotions require cognitive processing is _____ . According to this view, emotions arise when we _____ an event as beneficial or harmful to our well-being.

27. Complex emotions arise from our _____ and _____ . Highly emotional people tend to _____ events as being directed at them. They also tend to _____ their experiences by blowing them out of proportion.

Express some general conclusions that can be drawn about cognition and emotion.

Expressed Emotion (pp. 524–532)

> If you do not know the meaning of any of the following words, phrases, or expressions in the context in which they appear in the text, refer to page 355 for an explanation: *good enough at reading; Fidgeting; Ditto; sneer; Fake a big grin.*

Objective 8: Describe some of the factors that affect our ability to decipher nonverbal cues.

1. Researchers have found that people who _____ (suppress/express) their emotions while watching a distressing film showed impaired _____ for details in the film. Emotions may be communicated in words and/or through body expressions, referred to as _____ communication.

2. Most people are especially good at interpreting nonverbal _____ . We read fear and _____ mostly from the

_____ , and happiness from the _____ .

3. Introverts are _____ (better/worse) at reading others' emotions, whereas extraverts are themselves _____ (easier/harder) to read.

4. Experience can _____ people to particular emotions, as revealed by the fact that children who have been physically abused are quicker than others at perceiving _____ .

Objective 9: Describe some gender differences in perceiving and communicating emotions.

5. Women are generally _____ (better/worse) than men at detecting nonverbal signs of emotion and in spotting _____ . Women possess greater emotional _____ than men, as revealed by the tendency of men to describe their emotions in _____ terms. This gender difference may be a by-product of traditional _____ _____ and may contribute to women's greater emotional _____ .

6. Although women are _____ (more/less) likely than men to describe themselves as empathic, physiological measures reveal a much _____ (smaller/larger) gender difference. Women are _____ (more/less) likely than men to express empathy.

7. Women are also better at conveying _____ (which emotion?), whereas men surpass women in conveying their _____ .

Objective 10: Discuss the research on reading and misreading facial and behavioral indicators of emotion.

8. Various emotions may be linked with hard-to-control _____ _____ . Most people _____ (are/are not) very accurate at detecting lying. Accuracy varies, however, with a person's _____ and training. For example, _____

(people in which professions?) seem to be especially good at detecting lying.

9. The absence of nonverbal cues to emotion is one reason that communications sent as _____ are easy to misread.

Objective 11: Discuss the culture-specific and culturally universal aspects of emotional expression, and explain how emotional expressions could enhance survival.

10. Gestures have _____ (the same/different) meanings in different cultures.

11. Studies of adults indicate that in different cultures facial expressions have _____ (the same/different) meanings. Studies of children indicate that the meaning of their facial expressions _____ (varies/does not vary) across cultures. The emotional facial expressions of blind children _____ (are/are not) the same as those of sighted children.

12. According to _____ , human emotional expressions evolved because they helped our ancestors communicate before language developed. It has also been adaptive for us to _____ faces in particular _____ .

13. In cultures that encourage _____ , emotional expressions are often intense and prolonged. Cultures such as that of Japan _____ (also show intense emotion/hide their emotions). This points to the importance of realizing that emotions are not only biological and psychological but also _____-_____ .

Objective 12: Discuss the facial feedback and behavior feedback phenomena, and give an example of each.

14. Darwin believed that when an emotion is accompanied by an outward facial expression, the emotion is _____ (intensified/diminished).

15. In one study, students who were induced to smile _____ (found/did not find) cartoons more humorous.

16. The _____ _____ effect occurs when expressions amplify our emotions by activating muscles associated with specific states.

17. Studies have found that imitating another person's facial expressions _____ (leads/does not lead) to greater empathy with that person's feelings.

18. Similarly, moving our body as we would when experiencing a particular emotion causes us to feel that emotion. This is the _____ _____ effect.

Experienced Emotion (pp. 532–544)

> If you do not know the meaning of any of the following words, phrases, or expressions in the context in which they appear in the text, refer to pages 355–356 for an explanation: *poisonous; Stone Age fears; hostile outbursts; drain off some of their tension; contradictory maxims; rush of euphoria; lob a bombshell; run amuck; Off your duffs, couch potatoes.*

Objective 13: Name several basic emotions, and describe two dimensions psychologists use to differentiate emotions.

1. Izard believes that there are _____ basic emotions, most of which _____ (are/are not) present in infancy. Although others claim that emotions such as pride and love should be added to the list, Izard contends that they are _____ of the basic emotions.

2. Throughout the world, people place emotions along two dimensions: _____ , which refers to whether a feeling is _____ or _____ , and high versus low _____ .

Objective 14: State two ways we learn our fears.

3. Fear can by and large be seen as a(n) _____ (adaptive/maladaptive) response.

4. Most human fears are acquired through
_____ .

5. In addition, some fears are acquired by
_____ parents and friends.

Objective 15: Discuss some of the biological components of fear.

Explain why researchers think that some fears are biologically predisposed.

6. A key to fear learning lies in the
_____ , a neural center in the
_____ system. Following damage to this area, humans who have been conditioned to fear a loud noise will _____ the conditioning but show no _____ effect of it.

7. The amygdala receives input from the
_____ _____
_____ , a higher-level center for processing emotion.

8. People who have suffered damage to the
_____ will show the
_____ _____ but _____ (will/will not) be able to remember why.

9. Patients who have lost use of the
_____ are unusually trusting of scary-looking people.

10. Fears that fall outside the average range are called _____ . Fearfulness is shaped by both our _____ and our _____ .

Objective 16: Identify some common triggers and consequences of anger, and assess the catharsis hypothesis.

11. In studying why we become angry, Averill has found that most people become angry several times per week and especially when another person's act seemed _____ ,
_____ , and _____ .

12. The belief that expressing pent-up emotion is adaptive is most commonly found in cultures that emphasize _____ . This is the _____ hypothesis. In cultures that emphasize _____ , such as those of _____ or _____ , expressions of anger are less common.

13. Psychologists have found that when anger has been provoked, retaliation may have a calming effect under certain circumstances. List the circumstances.
   a. _____
   b. _____
   c. _____

Identify some potential problems with expressing anger.

14. List two suggestions offered by experts for handling anger.
   a. _____
   b. _____

15. Researchers have found that students who mentally rehearsed times they _____ someone who had hurt them had lower bodily arousal than when they thought of times when they did not.

Objective 17: Describe how the feel-good, do-good phenomenon works, and discuss the importance of research on subjective well-being.

16. Happy people tend to perceive the world as
_____ .

17. Happy people are also _____ (more/less) willing to help others. This is called the _____-_____, _____-_____ phenomenon.

18. An individual's self-perceived happiness or satisfaction with life is called his or her _____ _____ . Research on this subject helps us sift reality from all the contradictory beliefs.

Objective 18: Discuss some of the daily and longer-term variations in the duration of emotions.

19. Positive emotions _____ (rise/fall) early in the day and _____ (rise/fall) during the later hours.

20. Most people tend to _____ (underestimate/overestimate) the long-term emotional consequences of very bad news.

21. After experiencing tragedy or dramatically positive events, people generally _____ (regain/do not regain) their previous degree of happiness.

Objective 19: Summarize the findings on the relationship between affluence and happiness.

22. Researchers have found that levels of happiness _____ (do/do not) mirror differences in standards of living.

23. Generally speaking, losses have a _____ (stronger/weaker) emotional impact than gains.

24. During the last four decades, spendable income in the United States has more than doubled; personal happiness has _____ (increased/decreased/remained almost unchanged).

25. Research has demonstrated that people generally experience a higher quality of life and greater well-being when they strive for _____ _____

_____ than when they strive for _____ .

Objective 20: Describe how adaptation and relative deprivation affect our appraisals of our achievements.

26. The idea that happiness is relative to one's recent experience is stated by the _____-_____ phenomenon.

Explain how this principle accounts for the fact that, for some people, material desires can never be satisfied.

27. The principle that one feels worse off than others is known as _____ _____ . This helps to explain why the middle- and upper-income people who compare themselves with the relatively poor are _____ (slightly more/slightly less/equally) satisfied with life.

Objective 21: Summarize the ways that we can influence our own levels of happiness.

28. List six factors that have been shown to be positively correlated with feelings of happiness.

_____

_____

_____

_____

_____

_____

29. List five factors that are evidently unrelated to happiness.

_____

_____

_____

_____

_____

30. Research studies of identical and fraternal twins have led to the estimate that _____ percent of the variation in people's happiness ratings is heritable.

31. (Close-Up) State several research-based suggestions for increasing your satisfaction with life.

PROGRESS TEST 1

Multiple-Choice Questions

Circle your answers to the following questions and check them with the answers beginning on page 349. If your answer is incorrect, read the explanation for why it is incorrect and then consult the appropriate pages of the text (in parentheses following the correct answer).

1. Which of the following is correct regarding the relationship between arousal and performance?
   a. Generally, performance is optimal when arousal is low.
   b. Generally, performance is optimal when arousal is high.
   c. On easy tasks, performance is optimal when arousal is low.
   d. On easy tasks, performance is optimal when arousal is high.

2. Which division of the nervous system is especially involved in bringing about emotional arousal?
   a. somatic nervous system
   b. peripheral nervous system
   c. sympathetic nervous system
   d. parasympathetic nervous system

3. Concerning emotions and their accompanying body responses, which of the following appears to be true?
   a. Each emotion has its own body response and underlying brain circuit.
   b. All emotions involve the same body response as a result of the same underlying brain circuit.
   c. Many emotions involve similar body responses but have different underlying brain circuits.

   d. All emotions have the same underlying brain circuits but different body responses.

4. The Cannon-Bard theory of emotion states that:
   a. emotions have two ingredients: physical arousal and a cognitive label.
   b. the conscious experience of an emotion occurs at the same time as the body's physical reaction.
   c. emotional experiences are based on an awareness of the body's responses to an emotion-arousing stimulus.
   d. emotional ups and downs tend to balance in the long run.

5. Electrical stimulation of which brain region can produce terror or rage in cats?
   a. limbic system   c. cortex
   b. hypothalamus   d. cerebellum

6. The body's response to danger is triggered by the release of _____ by the _____ gland(s).
   a. acetylcholine; adrenal
   b. epinephrine and norepinephrine; adrenal
   c. acetylcholine; pituitary
   d. epinephrine and norepinephrine; pituitary

7. Which of the following was *not* raised as a criticism of the James-Lange theory of emotion?
   a. The body's responses are too similar to trigger the various emotions.
   b. Emotional reactions occur before the body's responses can take place.
   c. The cognitive activity of the cortex plays a role in the emotions we experience.
   d. People with spinal cord injuries at the neck typically experience less emotion.

8. (Thinking Critically) Current estimates are that the polygraph is inaccurate approximately _____ of the time.
   a. three-fourths   c. one-third
   b. one-half   d. one-fourth

9. In the Schachter-Singer experiment, which college men reported feeling an emotional change in the presence of the experimenter's highly emotional confederate?
   a. those receiving epinephrine and expecting to feel physical arousal
   b. those receiving a placebo and expecting to feel physical arousal
   c. those receiving epinephrine but not expecting to feel physical arousal
   d. those receiving a placebo and not expecting to feel physical arousal

10. Which of the following is true regarding happiness?
    a. People with more education tend to be happier.
    b. Beautiful people tend to be happier than plain people.
    c. Women tend to be happier than men.
    d. People who are socially outgoing or who exercise regularly tend to be happier.

11. Catharsis will be most effective in reducing anger toward another person if:
    a. you wait until you are no longer angry before confronting the person.
    b. the target of your anger is someone you feel has power over you.
    c. your anger is directed specifically toward the person who angered you.
    d. the other person is able to retaliate by also expressing anger.

12. Emotions consist of which of the following components?
    a. physiological reactions
    b. behavioral expressions
    c. conscious feelings
    d. all of the above

13. Law enforcement officials sometimes use a lie detector to assess a suspect's responses to details of the crime believed to be known only to the perpetrator. This is known as the:
    a. inductive approach.
    b. deductive approach.
    c. guilty knowledge test.
    d. screening examination.

14. Research on nonverbal communication has revealed that:
    a. it is easy to hide your emotions by controlling your facial expressions.
    b. facial expressions tend to be the same the world over, while gestures vary from culture to culture.
    c. most authentic expressions last between 7 and 10 seconds.
    d. most gestures have universal meanings; facial expressions vary from culture to culture.

15. In laboratory experiments, fear and joy:
    a. result in an increase in heart rate.
    b. stimulate different facial muscles.
    c. increase heart rate and stimulate different facial muscles.
    d. result in a decrease in heart rate.

16. Research suggests that people generally experience the greatest well-being when they strive for:
    a. wealth.
    b. modest income increases from year to year.
    c. slightly higher status than their friends, neighbors, and co-workers.
    d. intimacy and personal growth.

17. Research indicates that a person is most likely to be helpful to others if he or she:
    a. is feeling guilty about something.
    b. is happy.
    c. recently received help from another person.
    d. recently offered help to another person.

18. With regard to emotions, Darwin believed that:
    a. the expression of emotions helped our ancestors to survive.
    b. all humans express basic emotions using similar facial expressions.
    c. human facial expressions of emotion retain elements of animals' emotional displays.
    d. all of the above are true.

19. A graph depicting the course of positive emotions over the hours of the day since waking would:
    a. start low and rise steadily until bedtime.
    b. start high and decrease steadily until bedtime.
    c. remain at a stable, moderate level throughout the day.
    d. rise over the early hours and dissipate during the day's last several hours.

20. Evidence that changes in facial expression can directly affect people's feelings and body states has convinced Robert Zajonc that:
    a. the heart is always subject to the mind.
    b. emotional reactions involve deliberate rational thinking.
    c. cognition is not necessary for emotion.
    d. the interpretation of facial expressions is a learned skill.

Matching Items

Match each definition or description with the appropriate term.

Definitions or Descriptions

_____ **1.** the tendency to react to changes on the basis of recent experience

_____ **2.** an individual's self-perceived happiness

_____ **3.** emotional release

_____ **4.** the tendency to evaluate our situation negatively against that of other people

_____ **5.** emotions consist of physical arousal *and* a cognitive label

_____ **6.** an emotion-arousing stimulus triggers cognitive and body responses simultaneously

_____ **7.** the division of the nervous system that calms the body following arousal

_____ **8.** the division of the nervous system that activates arousal

_____ **9.** a device that measures the physiological correlates of emotion

_____ **10.** the tendency of people to be helpful when they are in a good mood

_____ **11.** we are sad because we cry

Terms

a. adaptation-level phenomenon
b. two-factor theory
c. catharsis
d. sympathetic nervous system
e. James-Lange theory
f. polygraph
g. Cannon-Bard theory
h. parasympathetic nervous system
i. relative deprivation principle
j. feel-good, do-good phenomenon
k. subjective well-being

PROGRESS TEST 2

Progress Test 2 should be completed during a final chapter review. Answer the following questions after you thoroughly understand the correct answers for the section reviews and Progress Test 1.

Multiple-Choice Questions

1. Which of the following most accurately describes emotional arousal?
   a. Emotions prepare the body to fight or flee.
   b. Emotions are voluntary reactions to emotion-arousing stimuli.
   c. Because all emotions have the same physiological basis, emotions are primarily psychological events.
   d. Emotional arousal is always accompanied by cognition.

2. Schachter's two-factor theory emphasizes that emotion involves both:
   a. the sympathetic and parasympathetic divisions of the nervous system.
   b. verbal and nonverbal expression.
   c. physical arousal and a cognitive label.
   d. universal and culture-specific aspects.

3. When students studied others who were worse off than themselves, they felt greater satisfaction with their own lives. This is an example of the principle of:
   a. relative deprivation.
   b. adaptation level.
   c. behavioral contrast.
   d. opponent processes.

4. Which theory of emotion emphasizes the simultaneous experience of body response and emotional feeling?
   a. James-Lange theory
   b. Cannon-Bard theory
   c. two-factor theory
   d. valence theory

5. Izard believes that there are _____ basic emotions.
   a. 3   **c.** 7
   b. 5   **d.** 10

6. (Thinking Critically) The polygraph measures:
   a. lying.
   b. brain rhythms.
   c. chemical changes in the body.
   d. physiological indexes of arousal.

7. People who are exuberant and persistently cheerful show increased activity in the brain's _____ , which is rich in receptors for the neurotransmitter _____ .
   a. right frontal lobe; dopamine
   b. left frontal lobe; dopamine
   c. amygdala; serotonin
   d. thalamus; serotonin

8. Which of the following is true regarding gestures and facial expressions?
   a. Gestures are universal; facial expressions, culture-specific.
   b. Facial expressions are universal; gestures, culture-specific.
   c. Both gestures and facial expressions are universal.
   d. Both gestures and facial expressions are culture-specific.

9. Which theory of emotion implies that every emotion is associated with a unique physiological reaction?
   a. James-Lange theory
   b. Cannon-Bard theory
   c. two-factor theory
   d. valence theory

10. For which of the following fears do humans appear to be biologically prepared?
    a. fear of electricity   c. fear of flowers
    b. fear of cliffs   d. fear of flying

11. Which of the following was *not* presented in the text as evidence that some emotional reactions involve no deliberate, rational thinking?
    a. Some of the neural pathways involved in emotion are separate from those involved in thinking and memory.
    b. Emotional reactions are sometimes quicker than our interpretations of a situation.
    c. People can develop an emotional preference for visual stimuli to which they have been unknowingly exposed.
    d. Arousal of the sympathetic nervous system will trigger an emotional reaction even when artificially induced by an injection of epinephrine.

12. Concerning the catharsis hypothesis, which of the following is true?
    a. Expressing anger can be temporarily calming if it does not leave one feeling guilty or anxious.
    b. The arousal that accompanies unexpressed anger never dissipates.
    c. Expressing one's anger always calms one down.
    d. Psychologists agree that under no circumstances is catharsis beneficial.

13. In an emergency situation, emotional arousal will result in:
    a. increased rate of respiration.
    b. increased blood sugar.
    c. a slowing of digestion.
    d. all of the above.

14. A relatively high level of arousal would be most likely to facilitate:
    a. remembering the lines of a play.
    b. shooting free throws in basketball.
    c. sprinting 100 meters.
    d. taking a final exam in introductory psychology.

15. Several studies have shown that physical arousal can intensify just about any emotion. For example, when people who have been physically aroused by exercise are insulted, they often misattribute their arousal to the insult. This finding illustrates the importance of:
    a. cognitive labels of arousal in the conscious experience of emotions.
    b. a minimum level of arousal in triggering emotional experiences.
    c. the simultaneous occurrence of physical arousal and cognitive labeling in emotional experience.
    d. all of the above.

16. (Thinking Critically) Many psychologists are opposed to the use of lie detectors because:
    a. they represent an invasion of a person's privacy and could easily be used for unethical purposes.
    b. there are often serious discrepancies among the various indicators such as perspiration and heart rate.
    c. polygraphs cannot distinguish the various possible causes of arousal.
    d. they are accurate only about 50 percent of the time.

17. Most human fears are:

    a. universal.   **c.** present at birth.

    b. biologically determined. **d.** learned.

18. In studying what makes people angry, James Averill found that most people become angry:

    a. once a day.

    b. once a week.

    c. several times a week.

    d. several times a month.

19. Which of these factors have researchers *not* found to correlate with happiness?

    a. a satisfying marriage or close friendship

    b. high self-esteem

    c. religious faith

    d. education

20. In cultures that emphasize social interdependence:

    a. emotional displays are typically intense.

    b. emotional displays are typically prolonged.

    c. negative emotions are rarely displayed.

    d. all of the above are true.

True–False Items

Indicate whether each statement is true or false by placing *T* or *F* in the blank next to the item.

_____ **1.** For easy tasks, the optimal level of arousal is higher than for difficult tasks.

_____ **2.** Men are generally better than women at detecting nonverbal emotional expression.

_____ **3.** The sympathetic nervous system triggers physiological arousal during an emotion.

_____ **4.** The adrenal glands produce the hormones epinephrine and norepinephrine.

_____ **5.** When one imitates an emotional facial expression, the body may experience physiological changes characteristic of that emotion.

_____ **6.** People who have lost sensation only in their lower bodies experience a considerable decrease in the intensity of their emotions.

_____ **7.** Wealthy people tend to be much happier than middle-income people.

_____ **8.** Physical arousal can intensify emotion.

_____ **9.** All emotions involve conscious thought.

_____ **10.** The two-factor theory states that emotions are given a cognitive label before physical arousal occurs.

PSYCHOLOGY APPLIED

Answer these questions the day before an exam as a final check on your understanding of the chapter's terms and concepts.

Multiple-Choice Questions

1. You are on your way to school to take a big exam. Suddenly, on noticing that your pulse is racing and that you are sweating, you feel nervous. With which theory of emotion is this experience most consistent?

    a. Cannon-Bard theory

    b. James-Lange theory

    c. relative deprivation theory

    d. adaptation-level theory

2. When Professor Simon acquired a spacious new office, he was overjoyed. Six months later, however, he was taking the office for granted. His behavior illustrates the:

    a. relative deprivation principle.

    b. adaptation-level phenomenon.

    c. valence theory.

    d. optimum arousal principle.

3. After Brenda scolded her brother for forgetting to pick her up from school, the physical arousal that had accompanied her anger diminished. Which division of her nervous system mediated her physical *relaxation*?

    a. sympathetic division

    b. parasympathetic division

    c. somatic division

    d. peripheral nervous system

4. Two years ago Maria was in an automobile accident in which her spinal cord was severed, leaving her paralyzed from her neck down. Today, Maria finds that she experiences emotions less intensely than she did before her accident. This tends to support which theory of emotion?

    a. James-Lange theory

    b. Cannon-Bard theory

    c. adaptation-level theory

    d. relative deprivation theory

5. The candidate stepped before the hostile audience, panic written all over his face. It is likely that the candidate's facial expression caused him to experience:

    a. a lessening of his fear.

    b. an intensification of his fear.

    c. a surge of digestive enzymes in his body.

    d. increased body temperature.

6. Jane was so mad at her brother that she exploded at him when he entered her room. That she felt less angry afterward is best explained by the principle of:
   a. adaptation level.
   b. physiological arousal.
   c. relative deprivation.
   d. catharsis.

7. After hitting a grand-slam home run, Mike noticed that his heart was pounding. Later that evening, after nearly having a collision while driving on the freeway, Mike again noticed that his heart was pounding. That he interpreted this reaction as fear, rather than as ecstasy, can best be explained by the:
   a. James-Lange theory.
   b. Cannon-Bard theory.
   c. two-factor theory.
   d. adaptation-level theory.

8. As part of her job interview, Jan is asked to take a lie-detector test. Jan politely refuses and points out that:
   a. a guilty person can be found innocent by the polygraph.
   b. an innocent person can be found guilty.
   c. these tests err one-third of the time.
   d. all of the above are true.

9. A student participating in an experiment concerned with physical responses that accompany emotions reports that her mouth is dry, her heart is racing, and she feels flushed. Can the emotion she is experiencing be determined?
   a. Yes, it is anger.
   b. Yes, it is fear.
   c. Yes, it is ecstasy.
   d. No, it cannot be determined from the information given.

10. Who will probably be angrier after getting a parking ticket?
    a. Bob, who has just awakened from a nap
    b. Veronica, who has just finished eating a big lunch
    c. Dan, who has just completed a tennis match
    d. Alicia, who has been reading a romantic novel

11. Children in New York, Nigeria, and New Zealand smile when they are happy and frown when they are sad. This suggests that:
    a. the Cannon-Bard theory is correct.
    b. some emotional expressions are learned at a very early age.

    c. the two-factor theory is correct.
    d. facial expressions of emotion are universal and biologically determined.

12. Who is the *least* likely to display negative emotions openly?
    a. Paul, a game warden in Australia
    b. Niles, a stockbroker in Belgium
    c. Deborah, a physicist in Toronto
    d. Yoko, a dentist in Japan

13. Nine-month-old Nicole's left frontal lobe is more active than her right frontal lobe. We can expect that, all other things being equal, Nicole:
    a. may suffer from mild depression for most of her life.
    b. may have trouble "turning off" upsetting feelings later in her life.
    c. may be more cheerful than those with more active right frontal lobes.
    d. may have trouble expressing feelings later in her life.

14. Julio was extremely angry when he came in for a routine EEG of his brain activity. When he later told this to the doctor, she was no longer concerned about the:
    a. increased electrical activity in Julio's right hemisphere.
    b. increased electrical activity in Julio's left hemisphere.
    c. decreased electrical activity in Julio's amygdala.
    d. increased electrical activity in Julio's amygdala.

15. When the scientist electrically stimulated one area of a monkey's brain, the monkey became enraged. When another electrode was activated, the monkey cowered in fear. The electrodes were most likely implanted in the:
    a. pituitary gland.
    b. adrenal glands.
    c. limbic system.
    d. right hemisphere.

16. As elderly Mr. Hooper crosses the busy intersection, he stumbles and drops the packages he is carrying. Which passerby is most likely to help Mr. Hooper?
    a. Drew, who has been laid off from work for three months
    b. Leon, who is on his way to work
    c. Bonnie, who graduated from college the day before

d. Nancy, whose father recently passed away

17. Expressing anger can be adaptive when you:
    a. retaliate immediately.
    b. have mentally rehearsed all the reasons for your anger.
    c. count to ten, then blow off steam.
    d. first wait until the anger subsides, then deal with the situation in a civil manner.

18. Cindy was happy with her promotion until she found out that Janice, who has the same amount of experience, receives a higher salary. Cindy's feelings are *best* explained according to the:
    a. adaptation-level phenomenon.
    b. valence theory.
    c. catharsis hypothesis.
    d. principle of relative deprivation.

19. I am an emotionally literate person who is very accurate at reading others' nonverbal behavior, detecting lies, and describing my feelings. Who am I?
    a. an introvert
    b. an extravert
    c. a woman
    d. a man

20. Margaret is a finalist in the U.S. Ice Skating Championship. She is very excited about the competition and is feeling energized. More than likely, the two dimensions of her current emotion would be a _____ and _____ .
    a. positive valence; low arousal
    b. negative valence; low arousal
    c. positive valence; high arousal
    d. negative valence; high arousal

Essay Question

Discuss biological and cultural influences on emotions. (Use the space below to list the points you want to make, and organize them. Then write the essay on a separate sheet of paper.)

KEY TERMS

Writing Definitions

Using your own words, on a separate piece of paper write a brief definition or explanation of each of the following terms.

1. emotion
2. James-Lange theory
3. Cannon-Bard theory
4. two-factor theory
5. polygraph
6. catharsis
7. feel-good, do-good phenomenon
8. subjective well-being
9. adaptation-level phenomenon
10. relative deprivation

Cross-Check

As you learned in the Prologue, reviewing and overlearning of material are important to the learning process. After you have written the definitions of the key terms in this chapter, you should complete the crossword puzzle to ensure that you can reverse the process—recognize the term, given the definition.

ACROSS

1. Device that measures several of the physiological responses accompanying emotion.
6. Phenomenon in which people tend to be helpful when they are in a good mood.
8. Theory that the subjective experience of an emotion occurs at the same time as the body's physical reaction.

DOWN

2. Principle that we are worse off relative to those with whom we compare ourselves.
3. Theory that emotions have two ingredients: physical arousal and a cognitive label.
4. A response of the whole organism involving physical arousal, expressive behaviors, and conscious experience.
5. Phenomenon referring to our tendency to judge things relative to our prior experience.
7. Theory that emotional experiences are based on an awareness of the body's responses to emotion-arousing stimuli.
8. Emotional release.

ANSWERS

Chapter Review

Theories of Emotion

1. physiological arousal; expressive behaviors; conscious experience

2. follow

Cannon argued that the body's responses were not sufficiently distinct to trigger the different emotions and, furthermore, that physiological changes occur too slowly to trigger sudden emotion.

3. cortex; sympathetic; Cannon-Bard

4. physiological; cognitive; Schachter

Embodied Emotion

1. **a.** Heart rate increases.
   b. Muscles become tense.

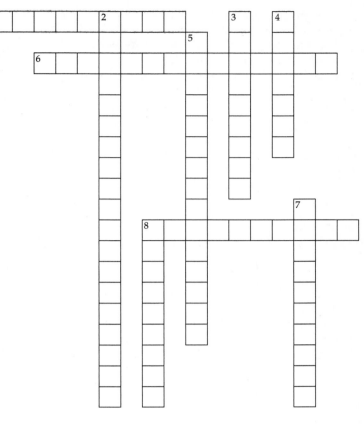

c. The liver pours extra sugar into the bloodstream.

d. Breathing rate increases.

e. Digestion slows.

f. Pupils dilate.

g. Blood tends to clot more rapidly.

h. Skin perspires.

2. sympathetic; adrenal; epinephrine (adrenaline); norepinephrine (noradrenaline)

3. parasympathetic

4. moderately

5. varies

6. easy; high; difficult; lower

7. similar; fear; anger; sexual arousal

8. fear; rage; finger; hormone

9. fear; joy

10. are; amygdala; angry; depression; right prefrontal cortex

11. left frontal lobe

12. left; frontal; dopamine

13. nucleus accumbens

14. polygraph

The polygraph measures several of the physiological responses that accompany emotion, such as changes in breathing, pulse rate, blood pressure, and perspiration. The assumption is that lying is stressful, so a person who is lying will become physiologically aroused.

15. anxiety

16. innocent; emotions; arousal

17. do not agree

18. guilty knowledge test

19. decrease; James-Lange

20. agree; cognition

21. arousal

22. did not; did

23. fuels; channels

24. can

First, experiments on subliminal perception indicate that although stimuli are not consciously perceived, people later prefer these stimuli to others they have never been exposed to. Second, there is some separation of the neural pathways involved in emotion and cognition.

25. eye or ear; thalamus; amygdala; cognition; cortex

26. Lazarus; appraise

27. interpretations; expectations; personalize; generalize

It seems that some emotional responses—especially simple likes, dislikes, and fears—involve no conscious thinking. Other emotions are greatly affected by our interpretations and expectations.

Expressed Emotion

1. suppress; memory; nonverbal

2. threats; anger; eyes; mouth

3. better; easier

4. sensitize; anger

5. better; lies; literacy; simpler; gender roles; responsiveness

6. more; smaller; more

7. happiness; anger

8. facial muscles; are not; experience; law enforcement (U.S. Secret Service agents and federal law officers, mostly CIA agents)

9. e-mail

10. different

11. the same; does not vary; are

12. Darwin; interpret; contexts

13. individuality; hide their emotions; social-cultural

14. intensified

15. found

16. facial feedback

17. leads

18. behavior feedback

Experienced Emotion

1. 10; are; combinations

2. valence; pleasant (positive valence); unpleasant (negative valence); arousal

3. adaptive

4. learning (conditioning)

5. observing

The fact that humans quickly learn and slowly unlearn to fear snakes, spiders, and cliffs—fears that were presumably very useful to our ancestors—suggests that these are biologically predisposed fears that develop with little or no learning.

6. amygdala; limbic; remember; emotional

7. anterior cingulate cortex

8. hippocampus; emotional reaction; will not

9. amygdala

10. phobias; experience; genes

11. willful; unjustified; avoidable

12. individuality; catharsis; interdependence; Tahiti; Japan

13. a. Retaliation must be directed against the person who provoked the anger.

   b. Retaliation must be justifiable.

   c. The target of the retaliation must not be someone who is intimidating.

One problem with expressing anger is that it breeds more anger, in part because it may trigger retaliation. Expressing anger can also magnify anger and reinforce its occurrence.

14. a. Wait to calm down.

   b. Deal with anger in a way that involves neither chronic anger nor passive sulking.

15. forgave

16. safer

17. more; feel-good, do-good

18. subjective well-being

19. rise; fall

20. overestimate

21. regain

22. do not

23. stronger

24. remained almost unchanged

25. intimacy, personal growth, and contribution to the community; wealth

26. adaptation-level

If we acquire new possessions, we feel an initial surge of pleasure. But we then adapt to having these new possessions, come to see them as normal, and require other things to give us another surge of happiness.

27. relative deprivation; slightly more

28. high self-esteem; satisfying marriage or close friendships; meaningful religious faith; optimistic outgoing personality; good sleeping habits and regular exercise; having work and leisure that engage our skills

29. age; gender; education; parenthood; physical attractiveness

30. 50

31. Realize that happiness doesn't come from financial success. Take control of your time. Act happy. Seek work and leisure that engages your skills. Engage in regular aerobic exercise. Get plenty of sleep. Give priority to close relationships. Focus beyond self. Be grateful. Nurture your spiritual self.

Progress Test 1

Multiple-Choice Questions

1. **d.** is the answer. Generally speaking, performance is optimal when arousal is moderate; for easy tasks, however, performance is optimal when arousal is high. For difficult tasks, performance is optimal when arousal is low. (p. 517)

2. **c.** is the answer. (p. 516)
   a. The somatic division of the peripheral nervous system carries sensory and motor signals to and from the central nervous system.
   b. The peripheral nervous system is too general an answer, since it includes the sympathetic and parasympathetic divisions, as well as the somatic division.
   d. The parasympathetic nervous system restores the body to its unaroused state.

3. **c.** is the answer. Although many emotions have the same general body arousal, resulting from activation of the sympathetic nervous system, they appear to be associated with different brain circuits. (p. 518)

4. **b.** is the answer. (p. 514)
   a. This expresses the two-factor theory.
   c. This expresses the James-Lange theory.
   d. This theory was not discussed.

5. **a.** is the answer. (p. 518)
   b. The hypothalamus is involved in eating, thirst, and sexual motivation.

   c. The cortex is the center of higher cognitive functions, such as memory and thinking.
   d. The cerebellum is involved in motor coordination.

6. **b.** is the answer. (p. 516)
   a. & c. Acetylcholine, a neurotransmitter involved in motor responses, is not a hormone and therefore is not secreted by a gland.

7. **d.** is the answer. The finding that people whose brains can't sense the body's responses experience considerably less emotion in fact supports the James-Lange theory, which claims that experienced emotion follows from body responses. (pp. 518–519)
   a., b., & c. All these statements go counter to the theory's claim that experienced emotion is essentially just an awareness of the body's response.

8. **c.** is the answer. (p. 520)

9. **c.** is the answer. The men who received epinephrine without an explanation felt arousal and experienced this arousal as whatever emotion the experimental confederate in the room with them was displaying. (pp. 519–520)
   a. Epinephrine recipients who expected arousal attributed their arousal to the drug and reported no emotional change in reaction to the confederate's behavior.
   b. & d. In addition to the two groups discussed in the text, the experiment involved placebo recipients; these subjects were not physically aroused and did not experience an emotional change.

10. **d.** is the answer. Education level, parenthood, gender, and physical attractiveness seem unrelated to happiness. (p. 544)

11. **c.** is the answer. (p. 536)
    a. This would not be an example of catharsis, since catharsis involves releasing, rather than suppressing, aggressive energy.
    b. Expressions of anger in such a situation tend to cause the person anxiety and thus tend not to be effective.
    d. One danger of expressing anger is that it will lead to retaliation and an escalation of anger.

12. **d.** is the answer. These are the three components of emotions identified in the text. (p. 513)

13. **c.** is the answer. If the suspect becomes physically aroused while answering questions about details only the perpetrator of the crime could know, it is presumed that he or she committed the crime. (p. 521)

14. **b.** is the answer. (p. 524)
    a. The opposite is true; relevant facial muscles are hard to control voluntarily.

c. Authentic facial expressions tend to fade within 4 or 5 seconds.

d. Facial expressions are generally universal; many gestures vary from culture to culture.

15. **c.** is the answer. Both fear and joy increase heart rate but stimulate different facial muscles. (p. 518)

16. **d.** is the answer. (p. 541)

17. **b.** is the answer. (p. 537)

  a., c., & d. Research studies have not found these factors to be related to altruistic behavior.

18. **d.** is the answer. (pp. 528, 529)

19. **d.** is the answer. (p. 538)

20. **c.** is the answer. (p. 521)

  a. & b. These answers imply that cognition *always* precedes emotion.

  d.   That changes in facial expression can directly affect people's feelings and body states does not imply a learned ability to interpret facial expressions. In fact, facial expressions apparently speak a universal language, which implies that the ability to interpret them is inborn.

Matching Items

1. a (p. 542)	**5.** b (p. 514)	**9.** f (p. 520)
2. k (p. 538)	**6.** g (p. 514)	**10.** j (p. 537)
3. c (p. 536)	**7.** h (p. 516)	**11.** e (p. 514)
4. i (p. 543)	**8.** d (p. 516)	

Progress Test 2

Multiple-Choice Questions

1. **a.** is the answer. Emotional arousal activates the sympathetic nervous system, causing the release of sugar into the blood for energy, pupil dilation, and the diverting of blood from the internal organs to the muscles, all of which help prepare the body to meet an emergency. (p. 516)

  b. Being autonomic responses, most emotions are *involuntary* reactions.

  c. All emotions do *not* have the same physiological basis.

  d. Some emotions occur without cognitive awareness.

2. **c.** is the answer. According to Schachter, the two factors in emotion are (1) physical arousal and (2) conscious interpretation of the arousal. (p. 514)

3. **a.** is the answer. The principle of relative deprivation states that happiness is relative to others' attainments. This helps explain why those who are relatively well off tend to be slightly more satisfied than the relatively poor, with whom the better-off can compare themselves. (p. 543)

b. Adaptation level is the tendency for our judgments to be relative to our prior experience.

  c. This phenomenon has nothing to do with the interpretation of emotion.

  d. Opponent processes are not discussed in the text in relation to emotion.

4. **b.** is the answer. (p. 514)

  a. The James-Lange theory states that the experience of an emotion is an awareness of one's physical response to an emotion-arousing stimulus.

  c. The two-factor theory states that to experience emotion one must be physically aroused and attribute the arousal to an emotional cause.

  d. There is no such theory, although valence is one dimension of emotion.

5. **d.** is the answer. (p. 532)

6. **d.** is the answer. No device can literally measure lying. The polygraph measures breathing, pulse rate, blood pressure, and perspiration for changes indicative of physiological arousal. (p. 520)

7. **b.** is the answer. (p. 518)

8. **b.** is the answer. Whereas the meanings of gestures vary from culture to culture, facial expressions seem to have the same meanings around the world. (pp. 524–525)

9. **a.** is the answer. If, as the theory claims, emotions are triggered by physiological reactions, then each emotion must be associated with a unique physiological reaction. (p. 514)

  b. According to the Cannon-Bard theory, the same general body response accompanies many emotions.

  c. The two-factor theory states that the cognitive interpretation of a general state of physical arousal determines different emotions.

  d. There is no such theory, although valence is one dimension of emotion.

10. **b.** is the answer. The fears for which humans seem biologically prepared are fears that probably were useful to our ancestors. (p. 534)

11. **d.** is the answer. As the Schachter-Singer study indicated, physical arousal is not always accompanied by an emotional reaction. Only when arousal was attributed to an emotion was it experienced as such. The results of this experiment, therefore, support the viewpoint that conscious interpretation of arousal must precede emotion. (pp. 519–520)

  a., b., & c. Each of these was presented as a supporting argument in the text.

12. **a.** is the answer. (p. 536)

  b. The opposite is true. Any emotional arousal will simmer down if you wait long enough.

c. Catharsis often magnifies anger, escalates arguments, and leads to retaliation.

d. When counterattack is justified and can be directed at the offender, catharsis may be helpful.

13. **d.** is the answer. (p. 516)

14. **c.** is the answer. Easy or well-rehearsed tasks, such as sprinting, are best performed when arousal is high; more difficult tasks are best performed when arousal is lower. (p. 517)

15. **a.** is the answer. That physical arousal can be misattributed demonstrates that it is the cognitive interpretation of arousal, rather than the intensity or specific nature of the body's arousal, that determines the conscious experience of emotions. (p. 520)

b. & c. The findings of these studies do not indicate that a minimum level of arousal is necessary for an emotional experience nor that applying a cognitive label must be simultaneous with the arousal.

16. **c.** is the answer. As heightened arousal may reflect feelings of anxiety or irritation rather than of guilt, the polygraph, which simply measures arousal, may easily err. (p. 520)

a. Misuse and invasion of privacy are valid issues, but Lykken primarily objects to the use of lie detectors because of their inaccuracy.

b. Although there are discrepancies among the various measures of arousal, this was not what Lykken objected to.

d. The lie detector errs about one-third of the time.

17. **d.** is the answer. (p. 533)

a. Because most fears are acquired through learning, people acquire highly individual fears.

b. & c. Only a few basic fears are biologically determined and present at birth.

18. **c.** is the answer. (p. 535)

19. **d.** is the answer. (p. 544)

20. **c.** is the answer. (p. 529)

a. & b. These are true of cultures that emphasize individuality rather than interdependence.

True–False Items

1. T (p. 517)	**6.** F (p. 519)
2. F (p. 525)	**7.** F (pp. 539–540)
3. T (p. 516)	**8.** T (pp. 519–520)
4. T (p. 516)	**9.** F (p. 521)
5. T (p. 530)	**10.** F (p. 514)

Psychology Applied

Multiple-Choice Questions

1. **b.** is the answer. The James-Lange theory proposes that the experienced emotion is an awareness of a prior body response: Your pulse races, and so you feel nervous. (p. 514)

a. According to the Cannon-Bard theory, your body's reaction would occur simultaneously with, rather than before, your experience of the emotion.

c. Relative deprivation refers to our sense that we are worse off than others with whom we compare ourselves.

d. The adaptation-level phenomenon concerns our tendency to judge stimuli on the basis of recent experience.

2. **b.** is the answer. Professor Simon's judgment of his office is affected by his recent experience: When that experience was of a smaller office, his new office seemed terrific; now, however, it is commonplace. (p. 542)

a. Relative deprivation is the sense that one is worse off than those with whom one compares oneself.

c. There is no such theory, although valence is one dimension of emotion.

d. This is the principle that there is an inverse relationship between the difficulty of a task and the optimum level of arousal.

3. **b.** is the answer. The parasympathetic division is involved in calming arousal. (p. 516)

a. The sympathetic division is active during states of arousal and hence would not be active in the situation described.

c. The somatic division is involved in transmitting sensory information and controlling skeletal muscles; it is not involved in arousing and calming the body.

d. This answer is too general, since the peripheral nervous system includes not only the parasympathetic division but also the sympathetic division and the somatic division.

4. **a.** is the answer. According to the James-Lange theory, Maria's emotions should be greatly diminished since her brain is unable to sense physical arousal. (p. 519)

b. Cannon and Bard would have expected Maria to experience emotions normally because they believed that the experiencing of emotions occurs separately from the body's responses.

c. & d. These theories and principles make no particular prediction regarding the importance of physical arousal in the conscious experience of emotion.

5. **b.** is the answer. Expressions may amplify the associated emotions. (pp. 530–531)

a. Laboratory studies have shown that facial expressions *intensify* emotions.

c. Arousal of the sympathetic nervous system, such as occurs when one is afraid, slows digestive function.

d. Increased body temperature accompanies anger but not fear.

6. **d.** is the answer. In keeping with the catharsis hypothesis, Jane feels less angry after releasing her aggression. (p. 536)

a. Adaptation level is our tendency to judge things relative to our experiences.

b. This is not a specific theory.

c. Relative deprivation is the sense that one is worse off relative to those with whom one compares oneself.

7. **c.** is the answer. According to the two-factor theory, it is cognitive interpretation of the same general physiological arousal that distinguishes the two emotions. (p. 514)

a. According to the James-Lange theory, if the same physical arousal occurred in the two instances, the same emotions should result.

b. The Cannon-Bard theory argues that conscious awareness of an emotion and body reaction occur at the same time.

d. Adaptation level concerns our tendency to judge things relative to our experiences.

8. **d.** is the answer. (pp. 520–521)

9. **d.** is the answer. (p. 517)

10. **c.** is the answer. Because physical arousal tends to intensify emotions, Dan (who is likely to be physically aroused after playing tennis) will probably be angrier than Bob or Veronica, who are in more relaxed states. (p. 520)

11. **d.** is the answer. (p. 528)

a. & c. The Cannon-Bard and two-factor theories of emotion do not address the universality of emotional expressions.

b. Even if it is true that emotional expressions are acquired at an early age, this would not necessarily account for the common facial expressions of children from around the world. If anything, the different cultural experiences of the children

might lead them to express their feelings in very *different* ways.

12. **d.** is the answer. In Japan and other Asian cultures that emphasize human connections and interdependence, negative emotional displays are rare and typically brief. (p. 529)

a., b., & c. In cultures that encourage individuality, as in Western Europe, Australia, and North America, emotional displays often are intense and prolonged.

13. **c.** is the answer. (p. 518)

a. Individuals with more active right frontal lobes tend to be less cheerful and are more likely to be depressed.

b. In fact, just the opposite is true: people with greater left frontal activity tend to be better able to turn off upsetting feelings.

d. The text does not suggest that greater left or right frontal activity influences a person's ability to express his or her feelings.

14. **a.** is the answer. As people experience negative emotions, such as anger, the right hemisphere becomes more electrically active. (p. 518)

c. & d. The EEG measures electrical activity on the surface of the cortex, not at the level of structures deep within the brain, such as the amygdala.

15. **c.** is the answer. (p. 518)

a., b., & d. Direct stimulation of these brain areas will not trigger fear or rage.

16. **c.** is the answer. People who are in a good mood are more likely to help others. Bonnie, who is probably pleased with herself following her graduation from college, is likely to be in a better mood than Drew, Leon, or Nancy. (p. 537)

17. **d.** is the answer. (p. 536)

a. Venting anger immediately may lead you to say things you later regret and/or may lead to retaliation by the other person.

b. Going over the reasons for your anger merely prolongs the emotion.

c. Counting to ten may give you a chance to calm down, but "blowing off steam" may rekindle your anger.

18. **d.** is the answer. Cindy is unhappy with her promotion because she feels deprived relative to Janice. (p. 543)

a. The adaptation-level phenomenon would predict that Cindy's raise would cause an increase in her happiness, since her most recent experience was to earn a lower salary.

b. There is no such theory, although valence is one dimension of emotion.

c. The catharsis hypothesis maintains that venting one's anger may relieve aggressive urges.

19. **c.** is the answer. (p. 525)

20. **c.** is the answer. (p. 533)

Essay Question

All emotions involve some degree of physiological arousal of the sympathetic nervous system. Although the arousal that occurs with different emotions is in most ways undifferentiated, there may be subtle differences in the brain pathways and hormones associated with different emotions.

Other examples of the influence of biological factors on emotion are the universality of facial expressions of emotion and the fact that humans seem biologically predisposed to learn some fears more quickly than others.

Unlike facial expressions of emotion, the meaning of many gestures is culturally determined. Culture also influences how people express their feelings. In cultures that encourage individuality, for example, emotional displays often are intense and prolonged. In cultures that emphasize human interdependence, negative emotions that might disrupt group harmony are rarely expressed, while displays of "other-sensitive" emotions such as sympathy, respect, and shame are more common than in the West.

KEY TERMS

Writing Definitions

1. **Emotion** is a response of the whole organism involving three components: (1) physical arousal, (2) expressive behaviors, and (3) conscious experience. (p. 513)

2. The **James-Lange theory** states that emotional experiences are based on an awareness of the body's responses to emotion-arousing stimuli: a stimulus triggers the body's responses that in turn trigger the experienced emotion. (p. 514)

3. The **Cannon-Bard theory** states that the subjective experience of an emotion occurs at the same time as the body's physical reaction. (p. 514)

4. The **two-factor theory** of emotion proposes that emotions have two ingredients: physical arousal and a cognitive label. Thus, physical arousal is a necessary, but not a sufficient, component of emotional change. For an emotion to be experienced, arousal must be attributed to an emotional cause. (p. 514)

5. The **polygraph**, or lie detector, is a device that measures several of the physiological responses accompanying emotion. (p. 520)

6. **Catharsis** is emotional release; according to the catharsis hypothesis, by expressing our anger, we can reduce it. (p. 536)

7. The **feel-good, do-good phenomenon** is the tendency of people to be helpful when they are in a good mood. (p. 537)

8. **Subjective well-being** refers to a person's sense of satisfaction with his or her life. (p. 538)

9. The **adaptation-level phenomenon** refers to our tendency to judge things relative to our prior experience. (p. 542)

10. The principle of **relative deprivation** is the perception that we are worse off relative to those with whom we compare ourselves. (p. 543)

Cross-Check

ACROSS	DOWN
1. polygraph	**2.** relative deprivation
6. feel-good-do-good	**3.** two-factor
8. Cannon-Bard	**4.** emotion
	5. adaptation level
	7. James-Lange
	8. catharsis

FOCUS ON VOCABULARY AND LANGUAGE

Page 513: No one needs to tell you that feelings add *color* to your life. . . . Without emotions we would experience a very dull and uninteresting existence; we would have no feelings of intense happiness or excitement nor would we experience depression and sadness. Thus, emotions add a variety of interesting qualities (*color*) to our lives.

Page 513: In an instant, the *arousal of dread* spilled into the *elation of ecstasy.* When Dr. Myers finally located his lost child (*toddler*) in the store, his apprehension and fear (*the arousal of dread*) transformed into a heightened and intense feeling of happiness (*the elation of ecstasy*) and he was overcome with positive emotions (*awash with joy*). This story illustrates the various components of emotion—physiological arousal, expressive behavior, and conscious experience.

Theories of Emotion

Page 514: Common sense tells most of us that we cry because we are sad, *lash out* because we are angry, *tremble* because we are afraid. The James-Lange theory states that physiological arousal precedes the experience of emotion. Thus, we cry first, then feel sad; we strike someone (*lash out*), then experience the anger; we shiver and shake (*tremble*), then feel fear. The Cannon-Bard theory proposes that physiological arousal and the experience of emotion occur at the same time but separately. One does not cause the other.

Embodied Emotion

Page 516: . . . *your stomach develops butterflies* . . . When you are apprehensive, fearful, and nervous, you have visceral (internal) sensations that may feel as though small flying insects (*butterflies*) are fluttering around in your stomach (*it develops butterflies*).

Page 517: Basketball players *shooting free throws*—a less automatic skill—may not perform quite as well if a *packed fieldhouse* makes them *hyperaroused* (Sokoll & Mynatt, 1984). When a basketball player is allowed (without interference) to throw the ball through the hoop (*shooting free throws*), it requires a lot of concentration because it is not a usual part of the game. If the player gets anxious and is overaroused (*hyperaroused*) because of the attention of a large crowd (*packed fieldhouse*), he is more likely to make a mistake. A high level of arousal is beneficial for the performance of easy, routine tasks.

Page 517: If afraid, you may feel a *clutching, sinking sensation* in your chest and a *knot in your stomach.* Different emotions (anger, fear, sadness) feel and look different. Someone who is extremely afraid may have certain visceral (internal) reactions such as tightness in the upper abdomen (*a clutching, sinking sensation*) and a feeling of a lump (*knot*) in the stomach. An angry person may experience an increase in temperature and sweating (may feel *"hot under the collar"*). There is some evidence of different physiological or brain patterns corresponding to each emotion.

Page 518: The left frontal lobe's rich supply of dopamine receptors may help explain why a *peppy left hemisphere* predicts a *perky* disposition. For some people, the left frontal lobe has more lively electrical activity (*it is peppy*), compared to the right, and these particular individuals tend to have more cheerful and happier personalities (*perky dispositions*).

Page 518 (Margin quote): Given the physical indicators of emotion, might we, like *Pinocchio*, give some *telltale sign* whenever we lie? Pinocchio is a fictional character in a children's story whose nose grows longer every time he tells a lie. The polygraph, or lie detector, does not detect lies; rather, it measures a number of physiological reactions (heart rate, blood pressure, and perspiration) (*telltale signs*) which indicate a change in emotional state. Unlike Pinocchio, people display no reliable or valid indicators of whether they are lying or telling the truth.

Page 519: Virtually all the men Hohmann interviewed reported increases in *weeping, lumps in the throat,* and getting *choked up* when saying *good-bye, worshipping,* or *watching a touching movie.* For emotions expressed mostly in body areas above the neck, people with high spinal cord injuries reported more intense reactions, such as crying (*weeping*), becoming inarticulate (*lumps in the throat*), and being overcome emotionally (*choked up*) when parting company (*saying good-bye*), participating in religious ceremonies (*worshipping*), or viewing a sentimental film (*watching a touching movie*). On the other hand, emotional intensity for most other feelings decreased substantially, especially if they involved body areas below the neck. This provides partial support for the James-Lange theory (*breathed new life into it*), which proposes that physical reactions are important in the experience of emotions.

Page 519: Which is the chicken and which the egg? The old riddle asks, "Which came first, the chicken or the egg?" Myers asks which comes first, our cognitions or our emotions? The two-factor theory suggests that physiological arousal has to be cognitively interpreted in order for one to experience different emotions. Stanley Schachter's research showed that the same arousal (*stirred-up state*) can be experienced as two very different emotional states (e.g., euphoria or irritation) depending on how we interpret and label it. Thus, thinking comes before feeling.

Page 520 (Box) . . . a white lie . . . When we tell a rather harmless or benign falsehood (*a white lie*), we are failing to reveal the truth about something relatively trivial. The polygraph can detect the physiological arousal that results from falsely answering control questions; this level of arousal is compared to reactions to the critical questions. Myers makes it clear that inferring guilt or innocence on the basis of these comparisons is fraught with problems. The innocent are more often labeled guilty than the guilty innocent; as Myers suggests, you should "never take a lie detector test if you are innocent."

Page 520: . . . testy . . . This means to be ill-tempered or irritable. Those subjects who were physiologically aroused but did not know why were affected by ("*caught*") the apparent emotional state of the person they were with. They made different attributions about their aroused (*stirred-up*) state ("I'm happy" or "I'm feeling testy") on the basis of whether the accomplice acted in a euphoric or irritated way.

Page 522: This makes it easier for our feelings to *hijack* our thinking than for our thinking to *rule* our feelings . . . Some neural pathways go from the ear or eye via the thalamus to the amygdala, an emotional control center, and detour around (*bypass*) the cortical areas involved in thinking. This makes it possible to have extremely rapid (*greased-lightning*) emotional responses before cognitive factors become involved. Thus, our feelings can take over (*hijack*) our thinking, instead of our thinking controlling (*ruling*) our emotions.

Page 522: The *heart* is not always subject to the *mind*. Robert Zajonc proposed that some emotional states are not preceded by cognitions. The emotions (*heart*) are not determined by our thoughts (*mind*). We can have *some* feelings, at least, without thinking first.

Expressed Emotion

Page 524: Most of us are good enough at *reading* nonverbal cues to decipher the emotions in an old *silent film*. We communicate our feelings with words (verbally) and through body language (nonverbally). Without hearing a single word, as in a movie with no soundtrack (*silent film*), we can discern much about someone's emotional state by observing (*reading*) his or her bodily actions and facial expressions. As Myers notes, when we look at a large group of faces, a single angry one will be extremely notice-

able (*it will "pop out"*) and will be detected more quickly than a single happy one.

Page 527: Fidgeting, for example, may reveal *anxiety* or *boredom.* Many popular books and articles suggest what to look for in body language during interviews, business meetings, and so on. However, specific interpretations of gestures or posture cannot be made accurately or reliably. For example, restlessness, accompanied by frequent small movements (*fidgeting*), may be indicative of either disinterest (*boredom*) or extreme nervousness (*anxiety*).

Page 528: Ditto for anger, and to a lesser extent the other basic expressions. There is a great deal of consistency across cultures in the interpretation of different emotional expressions. In tests, people the world over could reliably tell which face expressed happiness; this result was found over and over again (*ditto*), and similar results were found for other fundamental expressions (e.g., anger and fear).

Page 529: A *sneer,* for example, retains elements of an animal's baring its teeth in *a snarl.* Darwin believed that all humans have inherited the ability to express emotions through very similar facial expressions. Thus, a person's scornful or contemptuous grimace (*sneer*) has many aspects of the fierce growl with teeth showing (*a snarl*) typical of dogs and other animals. Emotional expressions are one form of social communication.

Page 530: Fake a big grin. Now scowl. Can you feel the smile therapy difference? Clearly, our moods affect how we look, but Myers is inviting you to test the idea that your facial expression can affect your mood. Make a large, false smile (*fake a grin*). Next, wrinkle or furrow your brow, frown and look sullen (*scowl*). Subjects in numerous experiments felt different emotions under these conditions. Smile and inside you feel happy, scowl and you may see the world as more miserable than it is.

Experienced Emotion

Page 533: Fear can be *poisonous.* To be very afraid is an adaptive emotion (it prepares our bodies for fight or flight, it creates cohesion in groups, it can protect us from harm, and it can constrain us from behaving badly). On the other hand, fear can obsess us, keep us awake at night, and keep us constantly worried. It can be a destructive and toxic reaction (*a poisonous emotion*).

Page 534: But our Stone Age fears leave us unprepared for high-tech dangers. Because of our evolutionary past we seem to be biologically inclined to learn some fears much more easily and quickly than others. Fear of heights, snakes, spiders, and so forth is easier to condition than fear of furniture, appliances, cars, electricity, and so on. Fears that were adaptive in the past (*Stone Age fears*) are not necessarily beneficial in today's technological era.

Page 536: Popular books and articles on aggression at times advise that even releasing angry feelings as *hostile outbursts* can be better than internalizing them. The idea is that expressing your anger openly (*hostile outbursts or "venting your anger"*) provides some form of emotional release (*catharsis*) and that this is better than not expressing your feelings and holding your anger inside (*internalizing it*). Under certain circumstances, this may provide temporary relief, but the evidence also suggests that expressing anger can increase or magnify (*breed more*) anger.

Page 536: If stressed managers find they can *drain off* some of their tension by *berating* an employee . . . Myers notes that if a supervisor severely and angrily scolds (*berates*) a worker this can increase or amplify the supervisor's hostile emotions, but, in addition, it may also be reinforcing because it releases some of the frustration (*it drains off some of the tension*). Consequently, the next time these feelings arise, the more likely it is that the hostile behavior will be repeated (*he or she will be more likely to explode*) .

Page 538: We have inherited many *contradictory maxims* concerning happiness. . . . Over the centuries, wise people have passed on to us a variety of principles (*maxims*) on the topic of happiness. Most of these are inconsistent and often in opposition to each other (*contradictory*). As Myers points out, to sort out (*sift*) the real predictors of happiness from the seemingly believable guesses (*plausible hunches*) requires research.

Page 539: Once their *rush of euphoria* wears off, state lottery winners typically find their overall happiness unchanged. . . . We probably all dream of winning large amounts of money through gambling (*state lottery winners*) and then living happily ever after. However, once the initial feelings of excitement (*rush of euphoria*) diminish, most winners discover that they are no happier. Myers puts it succinctly: "Wealth is like health. Its utter absence breeds misery, yet having it is no guarantee of happiness."

Page 541: Such findings *lob a bombshell* at modern materialism. . . . The contemporary tendency to accumulate wealth and possessions (*modern materialism*) in industrialized and affluent countries has not resulted in greater happiness. This finding challenges and destroys (*lobs a bombshell at*) the myth that riches (*affluence*) bring happiness and social well-being.

Page 542: When the victor belongs to the spoils and the possessor is possessed by possessions, adaptation level has *run amuck*. An old adage states that "to the victor belongs the spoils of the enemy." Myers has humorously and alliteratively rephrased this piece of wisdom. He points out that when we no longer own our belongings (*possessions*) but are owned (*possessed*) by them, then adaptation level is totally out of control (*has run amuck*). The **adaptation-level principle** states that happiness is relative to our prior experience.

Page 545 (Close-Up): *Off your duffs, couch potatoes.* This Close-Up, How to be Happier, lists a number of research-based suggestions for elevating our moods and for creating more contentment and fulfillment with life. One recommendation is to become more physically active (*join the "movement" movement*). A vast amount (*an avalanche*) of research shows very clearly the benefits of regular aerobic exercise in terms of better overall health, higher levels of energy, and lower levels of anxiety and depression. Myers advises sedentary people (*couch potatoes*) to get out of the sitting position (*get off your duffs*) and start exercising regularly.

14 : Stress and Health

CHAPTER OVERVIEW

Behavioral factors play a major role in maintaining health and causing illness. The effort to understand this role more fully has led to the emergence of the interdisciplinary field of behavioral medicine. The subfield of health psychology focuses on questions such as: How do our perceptions of a situation determine the stress we feel? How do our emotions and personality influence our risk of disease? How can psychology contribute to the prevention of illness?

Chapter 14 addresses key topics in health psychology. First and foremost is stress—its nature, its effects on the body, psychological factors that determine how it affects us, and how stress contributes to heart disease, infectious diseases, and cancer. The chapter concludes by looking at physical and psychological factors that promote good health, including exercise and social support, and examining two illness-related behaviors: smoking and obesity

NOTE: Answer guidelines for all Chapter 14 questions begin on page 372.

CHAPTER REVIEW

First, skim each section, noting headings and boldface items. After you have read the section, review each objective by answering the fill-in and essay-type questions that follow it. As you proceed, evaluate your performance by consulting the answers beginning on page 372. Do not continue with the next section until you understand each answer. If you need to, review or reread the section in the textbook before continuing.

Introducing Stress and Health (p. 549)

Objective 1: Identify some behavior-related causes of illness and death, and describe health psychology's contribution to the field of behavioral medicine.

1. The four leading causes of serious illness and death in the United States are _____ _____ , _____ , _____ , and _____ _____ .

2. Today, half the mortality from the 10 leading causes of death can be traced to people's _____ .

3. List several of the behaviors that have been linked to the leading causes of death:

   _____

   _____

4. The field that integrates behavioral and medical knowledge relevant to health and disease is

   _____ _____ .

5. The subfield of psychology that contributes to behavioral medicine is called _____ psychology.

Stress and Illness (pp. 549–561)

> David Myers at times uses idioms that are un-familiar to some readers. If you do not know the meaning of any of the following words, phrases, or expressions in the context in which they appear in the text, refer to pages 378–379 for an explanation: *tense . . . clenched teeth . . . churning stomach; slippery concept; heart rate zooms; uprooting; a cluster of crises; Daily Hassles; mellow and laid-back; after the honeymoon period; "combat ready"; headless horseman; hyping.*

Objective 2: Discuss the role of appraisal in the way we respond to stressful events.

1. Out of every ten people, _____ (how many?) report experiencing frequent stress.

2. Stress is not merely a _____ or a _____ . Rather, it is the _____ by which we perceive and respond to environmental threats and challenges.

3. This definition highlights the fact that stressors can have _____ (only negative/both positive and negative) effects, depending on how they are perceived.

Objective 3: Describe the dual-track system by which our body responds to stress, and identify the three phases of the general adaptation syndrome.

4. In the 1920s, physiologist Walter _____ began studying the effect of stress on the body. He discovered that the hormones _____ and _____ are released into the bloodstream in response to stress. This and other bodily changes due to stress are mediated by the _____ nervous system, thus preparing the body for _____ _____ .

5. Physiologists have discovered that in response to stress the cerebral cortex, via the _____ and the _____ gland, triggers the outer part of the _____ to release

_____ stress hormones such as _____ .

6. Another common response to stress among women has been called "_____ _____ _____ ," which refers to the increased tendency to _____ .

7. In studying animals' reactions to stressors, Selye repeatedly found three physiological effects: enlargement of the _____ cortex, shrinkage of the _____ gland, and bleeding _____ . He referred to this bodily response to stress as the _____ _____ _____ .

8. During the first phase of the GAS—the _____ reaction—the person is in a state of shock due to the sudden arousal of the _____ nervous system.

9. This is followed by the stage of _____ , in which the body's resources are mobilized to cope with the stressor.

10. If stress continues, the person enters the stage of _____ . During this stage, a person is _____ (more/less) vulnerable to disease.

11. One recent study found that women who suffered enduring caregiver stress had especially short _____ , which are pieces of _____ at the end of _____ that are important in allowing cells to _____ . In another study, people who suffered a prolonged flood of stress had a shrunken _____ , the brain structure responsible for explicit memories.

Objective 4: Discuss the health consequences of catastrophes, significant life changes, and daily hassles.

12. In the wake of catastrophic events, such as floods, hurricanes, and fires, there often is an increase in the number of _____ _____ .

13. Research studies have found that people who have recently been widowed, fired, or divorced are _____ (more/no more) vulnerable to illness than other people.

14. For most people, the most significant sources of stress are _____ _____ . The stresses that accompany poverty and unemployment, for example, often compounded by _____ , may account for the higher rates of _____ among residents of urban ghettos.

Objective 5: Discuss the role of stress in causing coronary heart disease, and contrast Type A and Type B personalities.

15. The leading cause of death in North America is _____ _____ _____ . List several risk factors for developing this condition: _____ _____ _____ .

16. Friedman and Rosenman discovered that tax accountants experience an increase in blood _____ level and blood- _____ speed during tax season. This showed there was a link between coronary warning indicators and _____ .

Friedman and Rosenman, in a subsequent study, grouped people into Type A and Type B personalities. Characterize these types, and indicate the difference that emerged between them over the course of this nine-year study.

17. In relaxed situations, Type A persons _____ (differ/do not differ) from Type B persons in measures of physiological reactivity.

18. An experiment by Williams showed that when Type A students were challenged, their output of stress hormones was _____ (greater than/the same as) that of their Type B classmates. These hormones may increase the buildup of _____ in the artery walls. The hardening of the arteries that may result is called _____ .

19. When a _____ (Type A/Type B) person is angered, blood flow is diverted away from the internal organs, including the liver, which is responsible for removing _____ and fat from the blood. Thus, such people have elevated levels of these substances in the blood.

20. The Type A characteristic that is most strongly linked with coronary heart disease is _____ _____ , especially _____ .

21. Another toxic emotion is _____ ; researchers have found that _____ are more than twice as likely to develop heart disease as _____ .

22. Depression _____ (increases/ has no effect on) one's risk of having a heart attack or developing other heart problems.

Objective 6: Distinguish between a psychophysiological illness and hypochondriasis.

23. In _____ illnesses, physical symptoms are produced by psychological causes. This is distinct from the misinterpretation of normal physical sensations as symptoms of a disease, called _____ .

24. Examples of such illnesses are certain types of _____ and _____ . Such illnesses appear to be linked to _____ .

25. The term _____ was once used to describe such illness. However, this term implied that symptoms were _____ .

Objective 7: Describe the effect of stress on immune system functioning.

26. The body's system of fighting disease is the _____ system. This system includes two types of white blood cells, called _____ : the _____ _____ , which fight bacterial infections, and the _____ _____ , which form in the _____ and attack viruses, cancer cells, and foreign substances. Another immune agent, called the _____ , pursues and ingests foreign substances.

27. Responding too strongly, the immune system may attack the body's tissues and cause _____ or an _____ reaction. Or it may _____ , allowing a dormant herpes virus to erupt or _____ cells to multiply.

28. _____ (Women/Men) are the immunologically stronger gender. This makes them less susceptible to _____ , but more susceptible to _____ diseases such as _____ and _____ _____ .

29. Stress can suppress the lymphocyte cells, resulting in a(n)_____ (increase/decrease) in disease resistance. Stress diverts energy from the _____ _____ to the _____ and _____ , mobilizing the body for action.

Objective 8: Discuss the findings on the link between stress and AIDS.

30. Worldwide, the fourth leading cause of death is _____ , caused by the _____ _____ _____ , which is spread primarily through the exchange of _____ and _____ .

31. Stressful life circumstances _____ (have/have not) been shown to accelerate the progression of this chronic disease.

32. Educational initiatives, support groups, and other efforts to control stress _____

(have/have not) been shown to have positive consequences on HIV-positive individuals.

Objective 9: Discuss the findings on the link between stress and cancer.

33. Stress and _____ emotions _____ (have/have not) been linked to cancer's rate of progression.

34. When rodents were inoculated with _____ cells or given _____ , tumors developed sooner in those that were also exposed to _____ stress.

35. Stress _____ (does/does not) create cancer cells.

Objective 10: Describe the impact of learning on immune system functioning.

36. Experiments by Ader and Cohen demonstrate that the functioning of the body's immune system _____ (can/cannot) be affected by conditioning.

37. In Ader and Cohen's classic experiment, the unconditioned stimulus was the _____ , and the unconditioned response was _____ _____ .

38. When stress is momentary, the health costs are _____ (still heavy/negligible).

39. It is important to remember that psychological states are _____ events that influence other parts of our _____ system.

Promoting Health (pp. 562–592)

If you do not know the meaning of any of the following words, phrases, or expressions in the context in which they appear in the text, refer to pages 379–380 for an explanation: *laughter is the best medicine; heartaches; cold fact . . . nothing to sneeze at; "open heart therapy"; run away from their troubles; boosts our mood; overblown and oversold; Is there fire underneath all this smoke?; cool models; slow-motion suicide; gauche rather than cool; win the battle of the bulge; apple-shaped; scarfing too many hot fudge sundaes; the specifics of our genes predispose the size of our jeans; thinner wallet; couch potatoes.*

Objective 11: Contrast problem-focused coping and emotion-focused coping.

1. People learn to _____ with stress by finding _____ , _____ , or _____ ways to alleviate it.

2. When we cope directly with a stressor, we are using _____-_____ coping.

3. When we attempt to alleviate stress by avoiding it and attending to emotional needs, we are using _____-_____ coping.

4. People tend to use _____-_____ coping when they feel a sense of _____ over a situation. They turn to _____-_____ coping when they cannot or believe they cannot _____ a situation.

Objective 12: Describe how a perceived lack of control can affect health.

5. Negative situations are especially stressful when they are appraised as _____ . Control may explain why poorer people are more at risk for premature _____ than those who are more affluent.

6. With higher economic status comes lower risks of infant _____ , a low _____ _____ , smoking, and _____ .

7. In animals and humans, sudden lack of control is followed by a drop in immune responses, a(n) _____ (increase/decrease) in blood pressure, and a rise in the levels of _____ _____ .

Objective 13: Discuss the links among explanatory style, stress, and health.

8. People who have an _____ explanatory style are less likely than others to suffer ill health.

9. Researchers have found that life events may be less stressful for people who have a good sense of _____ .

10. One study found that laughter caused improved _____ and increased _____ _____ .

Objective 14: Describe some of the ways that social support acts as a stress buffer.

11. Another buffer against the effects of stress is _____ support.

12. Longitudinal research reveals that a _____ _____ at age 50 predicts healthy aging better than _____ _____ at the same age.

State several possible reasons for the link between health and social support.

13. James Pennebaker has found that emotional _____ can adversely affect our physical health, while _____ suppressed thoughts may promote well-being.

14. Health can also be improved by _____ about personal traumas in a diary.

15. Another way to reduce stress is to talk about it. In another study by Pennebaker, Holocaust survivors who were the most _____ had the most improved health.

Objective 15: Discuss the advantages of aerobic exercise as a technique for managing stress and fostering well-being.

16. Sustained exercise that increases heart and lung fitness is known as _____ exercise.

17. Experiments _____
    (have/have not) been able to demonstrate conclu-
    sively that such exercise reduces anxiety, depres-
    sion, and stress.

18. Exercise increases the body's production of
    mood-boosting neurotransmitters such as

    _____ , _____ ,

    and the _____ . It also modestly
    enhances cognitive abilities, such as

    _____ .

19. By one estimate, moderate exercise adds
    _____ (how many?) years to
    one's life expectancy.

Objective 16: Compare the benefits of biofeedback
and relaxation training as stress-management techniques, and discuss meditation as a relaxation technique.

20. A system for recording a physiological response
    and providing information concerning it is called
    _____ . The instruments used in
    this system _____ (provide/do
    not provide) the individual with a means of con-
    trolling physiological responses.

21. Lowered blood pressure, heart rate, and oxygen
    consumption have been found to be characteristic
    of people who regularly practice
    _____ . The _____
    response accompanies sitting quietly, with closed
    eyes, while breathing deeply.

22. Brain scans of experienced meditators reveal
    decreased activity in the _____
    lobe and increased activity in the
    _____ lobe.

23. (Thinking Critically) Acupuncture, massage
    therapy, homeopathy, and similar treatments
    comprise the growing health care market called

    _____ _____

    _____ _____ . In
    China, _____ therapies have
    flourished for centuries, as have acupuncture and
    acupressure therapies that claim to correct imbal-
    ances in the flow of the energy called

    _____ .

24. (Thinking Critically) Critics of alternative medi-
    cine point out that such treatments seem especial-
    ly effective with _____ diseases
    such as arthritis and _____ , as
    well as with diseases that disappear naturally—a
    phenomenon called _____

    _____ . Critics also argue that
    the seeming effectiveness of alternative medicine
    is due to a _____ effect.

Objective 17: Discuss the correlation between reli-
giosity and longevity, and offer some possible explanations for this link.

25. Until fairly recently in history, the healing tradi-
    tions of _____ and
    _____ have worked
    _____ (together/separately).

26. Surveys reveal that most family physicians
    _____ (believe/do not believe)
    that religion and spirituality are related to health
    and healing.

27. Several recent studies demonstrate that religious
    involvement _____ (predicts/
    does not predict) health and longevity.

State two possible intervening variables that might
account for the "faith factor" in health.

Objective 18: Explain why people smoke.

28. Fewer than _____ percent of vis-
    its to primary care physicians are for problems
    that are clearly _____ . Most vis-
    its are presumed to be for problems that involve
    _____ factors.

State several of the physical and psychological problems that are correlated with smoking.

29. Smoking usually begins during _____
_____ and is especially common
among those who _____
_____ .

Those who start smoking have friends who serve
as _____ and whose behavior
they _____ .

30. As with other addictions, smokers become
_____ on nicotine, develop
_____ to its effects, and experience _____ symptoms when
attempting to quit.

31. By terminating an aversive state, smoking provides a person with a powerful
_____ . In addition, nicotine triggers the release of epinephrine and norepinephrine, which increase _____ and
mental _____ , and of neurotransmitters that calm _____ and
reduce _____ _____ .

32. Consistent with the _____
approach, twin studies indicate a _____
percent heritability of smoking addiction.
Smokers and nonsmokers also may differ in a
_____ that influences responses
to the neurotransmitter _____ .

Objective 19: Discuss ways of helping smokers to
quit smoking—or preventing young people from ever
starting.

33. Most programs to help people quit smoking
_____ (are/are not) very effec-
tive in the long run. The decline in the smoking
rate among Americans is most pronounced

among _____ (males/females)
and those at _____ (higher/
lower) socioeconomic levels.

34. Worldwide, per-person cigarette consumption is
near an all-time _____
(low/high). Rates of smoking are increasing most
dramatically in _____ countries
where many people are unaware of the dangers
of smoking.

35. Successful educational programs to prevent adolescents from ever starting smoking include three
key ingredients:

a. _____

b. _____

c. _____

36. Another effective technique for discouraging
smoking is to make it more immediately
_____ .

Objective 20: Discuss the adaptive advantages and
modern-day disadvantages of a body that stores fat.

37. In developing societies where people face
_____ , obesity is considered a
sign of _____ and
_____ _____ .

Cite some of the ways in which obesity is a threat to
health.

38. The risks of obesity are greater for people who
carry their weight at their _____ . It
also has been linked in women to their risk of
late-life _____ disease and brain
tissue loss.

39. People who are overweight at age 40 die
_____ years (how many?) earlier
than those who are not.

Objective 21: Describe some of the social effects of obesity.

40. Obese people are often stereotyped as

    _____ , _____ ,

    and _____ .

41. One study found that obese women earned

    _____ than a control group of

    nonobese women and were less likely to be

    _____ .

42. In one experiment, job applicants were rated as

    less worthy of hiring when they were made to

    appear _____ .

Objective 22: Discuss some research findings on the role of heredity and environment in determining body weight.

43. The energy equivalent of a pound of fat is

    approximately _____ calories.

    The immediate determinant of body fat is the size

    and number of _____

    _____ one has. This number is,

    in turn, determined by several factors, including

    _____

    _____ .

44. The size of fat cells _____

    (can/cannot) be decreased by dieting; the num-

    ber of fat cells _____ (can/can-

    not) be decreased by dieting.

45. Fat tissue has a _____

    (higher/lower) metabolic rate than lean tissue.

    The result is that fat tissue requires

    _____ (more/less) food energy

    to be maintained.

46. The body weight "thermostat" of obese people

    _____ (is/is not) set to maintain

    a higher-than-average weight. When weight

    drops below this setting, _____

    increases and _____ decreases.

Explain why, metabolically, many obese people find it so difficult to become and stay thin.

47. Studies of adoptees and twins _____

    (do/do not) provide evidence of a genetic influ-

    ence on obesity.

48. Recent experiments reveal that obese mice have a

    defective _____ for producing

    the protein_____ . Increased lev-

    els of this protein signal the _____

    to curb _____ and increase

    _____ . When obese mice are

    given injections of this protein, they become

    _____ (more/less) active and

    _____ (gain/lose) weight.

49. Obesity is _____ (more/less)

    common among lower-class than upper-class

    women and _____ (does/does

    not) vary from culture to culture.

Objective 23: Discuss the chances of success for an overweight person who wants to lose weight.

50. Most obese persons who lose weight

    _____ (gain/do not gain) it back.

51. People who try repeatedly to lose weight are

    _____ (more/no more) likely to

    succeed.

52. (Close-Up) State several pieces of advice for those

    who want to lose weight.

PROGRESS TEST 1

Circle your answers to the following questions and check them with the answers beginning on page 373. If your answer is incorrect, read the explanation for why it is incorrect and then consult the appropriate pages of the text (in parentheses following the correct answer).

1. Behavioral and medical knowledge about factors influencing health form the basis of the field of:
   a. health psychology.
   b. holistic medicine.
   c. behavioral medicine.
   d. osteopathic medicine.

2. The stress hormones epinephrine and norepinephrine are released by the _____ gland in response to stimulation by the _____ branch of the nervous system.

   a. pituitary; sympathetic
   b. pituitary; parasympathetic
   c. adrenal; sympathetic
   d. adrenal; parasympathetic

3. During which stage of the general adaptation syndrome is a person especially vulnerable to disease?

   a. alarm reaction
   b. stage of resistance
   c. stage of exhaustion
   d. stage of adaptation

4. The leading cause of death in North America is:

   a. lung cancer.
   b. AIDS.
   c. coronary heart disease.
   d. alcohol-related accidents.

5. Researchers Friedman and Rosenman refer to individuals who are very time-conscious, super-motivated, verbally aggressive, and easily angered as:

   a. ulcer-prone personalities.
   b. cancer-prone personalities.
   c. Type A.
   d. Type B.

6. One effect of stress hormones is to:

   a. lower the level of cholesterol in the blood.
   b. promote the buildup of plaques on the artery walls.
   c. divert blood away from the muscles of the body.
   d. reduce stress.

7. Genuine illnesses that are caused by stress are called _____ illnesses.

   a. psychophysiological
   b. hypochondriacal
   c. psychogenic
   d. psychotropic

8. Stress has been demonstrated to place a person at increased risk of:

   a. cancer.
   b. progressing from HIV infection to AIDS.
   c. bacterial infections.
   d. all of the above.

9. *Stress* is defined as:

   a. unpleasant or aversive events that cannot be controlled.
   b. situations that threaten health.
   c. the process by which we perceive and respond to challenging or threatening events.
   d. anything that decreases immune responses.

10. In one experiment, both "executive" rats and "subordinate" rats received identical electric shocks, the only difference being whether the shocks could be:

    a. predicted.   c. shortened.
    b. weakened.   d. controlled.

11. In studies of obese mice, researchers have found that some mice:

    a. had a defective gene for producing leptin, a fat-detecting hormone.
    b. had abnormally high levels of insulin, a hunger-triggering hormone.
    c. could be conditioned to avoid fatty foods.
    d. had fewer-than-normal receptor sites for a fat-detecting hormone.

12. Attempting to alleviate stress directly by changing a stressor or how we interact with it is an example of:

    a. problem-focused coping.
    b. emotion-focused coping.
    c. managing rather than coping with stress.
    d. hypochondriasis.

13. A study in which people were asked to confide troubling feelings to an experimenter found that participants typically:

    a. did not truthfully report feelings and events.
    b. experienced a sustained increase in blood pressure until the experiment was finished.
    c. became physiologically more relaxed after confiding their problem.
    d. denied having any problems.

14. Research suggests that _____ influences often lead a person to start smoking, whereas _____ influences become important in explaining why people continue to smoke.

    a. biological; social   c. biological; cognitive
    b. social; biological   d. cognitive; biological

15. Research on genetic influences on obesity reveals that:

    a. the body weight of adoptees correlates with that of their biological parents.
    b. the body weight of adoptees correlates with that of their adoptive parents.
    c. identical twins usually have very different body weights.
    d. the body weights of identical twin women are more similar than those of identical twin men.

16. Which of the following was *not* mentioned in the text as a potential health benefit of exercise?

    a. Exercise can increase ability to cope with stress.

    b. Exercise can lower blood pressure.

    c. Exercise can reduce stress, depression, and anxiety.

    d. Exercise improves functioning of the immune system.

17. Research studies demonstrate that after a catastrophe rates of _____ often increase.

    a. depression

    b. anxiety

    c. sleeplessness

    d. all of the above

18. In one study, laboratory rats drank sweetened water with a drug that causes immune suppression. After repeated pairings of the taste with the drug:

    a. the animals developed tolerance for the drug and immune responses returned to normal.

    b. sweet water alone triggered immune suppression.

    c. dependency on the drug developed and withdrawal symptoms appeared when the drug was withheld.

    d. many of the animals died.

19. Social support _____ our ability to cope with stressful events.

    a. has no effect on

    b. usually increases

    c. usually decreases

    d. has an unpredictable effect on

20. The AIDS virus is transmitted primarily by:

    a. airborne transmission of HIV.

    b. physical touching.

    c. an exchange of blood or semen.

    d. insect bites.

21. Research has demonstrated that as a predictor of health and longevity, religious involvement:

    a. has a small, insignificant effect.

    b. is more accurate for women than men.

    c. is more accurate for men than women.

    d. rivals nonsmoking and exercise.

PROGRESS TEST 2

Progress Test 2 should be completed during a final chapter review. Answer the following questions after you thoroughly understand the correct answers for the section reviews and Progress Test 1.

Multiple-Choice Questions

1. The field of health psychology is concerned with:

    a. the prevention of illness.

    b. the promotion of health.

    c. the treatment of illness.

    d. all of the above.

2. In order, the sequence of stages in the general adaptation syndrome is:

    a. alarm reaction, stage of resistance, stage of exhaustion.

    b. stage of resistance, alarm reaction, stage of exhaustion.

    c. stage of exhaustion, stage of resistance, alarm reaction.

    d. alarm reaction, stage of exhaustion, stage of resistance.

3. AIDS is a disorder that causes a breakdown in the body's:

    a. endocrine system.

    b. circulatory system.

    c. immune system.

    d. respiratory system.

4. "Tend and befriend" refers to:

    a. the final stage of the general adaptation syndrome.

    b. the health-promoting impact of having a strong system of social support.

    c. an alternative to the "fight-or-flight" response that may be more common in women.

    d. the fact that spiritual people typically are not socially isolated.

5. Which of the following statements concerning Type A and B persons is true?

    a. Even when relaxed, Type A persons have higher blood pressure than Type B persons.

    b. When stressed, Type A persons show greater output of stress hormones than Type B persons.

    c. Type B persons tend to suppress anger more than Type A persons.

    d. Type A persons tend to be more outgoing than Type B persons.

6. According to the text, one-half of all deaths from the 10 leading causes of death in the United States can be attributed to:
   a. stress.   c. nutrition.
   b. obesity.   d. behavior.

7. The disease- and infection-fighting cells of the immune system are:
   a. B lymphocytes.   c. both a. and b.
   b. T lymphocytes.   d. antigens.

8. One effect of stress on the body is to:
   a. suppress the immune system.
   b. facilitate the immune system response.
   c. increase disease resistance.
   d. increase the growth of B and T lymphocytes.

9. Compared to men, women:
   a. have stronger immune systems.
   b. are less susceptible to infections.
   c. are more susceptible to self-attacking diseases such as multiple sclerosis.
   d. have all the above characteristics.

10. In response to uncontrollable shock, levels of stress hormones _____ and immune responses are _____ .
    a. decrease; suppressed   c. decrease; increased
    b. increase; suppressed   d. increase; increased

11. Allergic reactions and arthritis are caused by:
    a. an overreactive immune system.
    b. an underreactive immune system.
    c. the presence of B lymphocytes.
    d. the presence of T lymphocytes.

12. Research on cancer patients reveals that:
    a. stress affects the growth of cancer cells by weakening the body's natural resources.
    b. patients' attitudes can influence their rate of recovery.
    c. cancer occurs slightly more often than usual among those widowed, divorced, or separated.
    d. all of the above are true.

13. The component of Type A behavior that is the most predictive of coronary disease is:
    a. time urgency.   c. high motivation.
    b. competitiveness.   d. anger.

14. Which of the following is true concerning smoking treatment programs?
    a. Most are effective in the long run.
    b. Hypnosis is more effective than behavior modification.
    c. Treatment programs are more effective with women than with men.
    d. Most participants eventually resume smoking.

15. During biofeedback training:
    a. a person is given sensory feedback for a subtle body response.
    b. biological functions controlled by the autonomic nervous system may come under conscious control.
    c. the accompanying relaxation is much the same as that produced by other, simpler methods of relaxation.
    d. all of the above occur.

16. Research on obesity indicates that:
    a. pound for pound, fat tissue requires more calories to maintain than lean tissue.
    b. once fat cells are acquired they are never lost, no matter how rigorously one diets.
    c. one pound of weight is lost for every 3500-calorie reduction in diet.
    d. when weight drops below the set point, hunger and metabolism also decrease.

17. The number of fat cells a person has is influenced by:
    a. genetic predisposition.
    b. childhood eating patterns.
    c. adulthood eating patterns.
    d. all of the above.

18. Which of the following was offered in the text as a reason people continue to smoke?
    a. Social pressure from peers is strong.
    b. Cigarettes serve as powerful reinforcers.
    c. Regular use of nicotine impairs the brain's ability to produce neurotransmitters such as serotonin.
    d. Most adults who smoke don't really want to quit.

19. The tendency to overeat when food is plentiful:
    a. is a recent phenomenon that is associated with the luxury of having ample food.
    b. emerged in our prehistoric ancestors as an adaptive response to alternating periods of feast and famine.
    c. is greater in developed, than in developing, societies.
    d. is stronger in women than in men.

20. Which of the following was *not* suggested as a possible explanation of the "faith factor" in health?
    a. Having a coherent worldview is a buffer against stress.
    b. Religious people tend to have healthier life-styles.
    c. Those who are religious have stronger networks of social support.
    d. Because they are more affluent, religiously active people receive better health care.

21. (Thinking Critically) Acupuncture, aromatherapy, and homeopathy are forms of:
    a. psychophysiological medicine.
    b. complementary and alternative medicine.
    c. Chi therapy.
    d. psychosomatic medicine.

True–False Items

Indicate whether each statement is true or false by placing *T* or *F* in the blank next to the item.

_____ 1. Most obese people who lose weight eventually gain it back.
_____ 2. Stressors tend to increase activity in the immune system and in this way make people more vulnerable to illness.
_____ 3. Events are most stressful when perceived as both negative and controllable.
_____ 4. Worldwide, per-person cigarette consumption is at an all-time low.
_____ 5. The single most important factor in causing obesity is heredity.
_____ 6. Obesity is often a sign of social status and affluence in developing countries.
_____ 7. Optimists cope more successfully with stressful events than do pessimists.
_____ 8. Type A persons are more physiologically reactive to stress than are Type B persons.

_____ 9. Chronic stress can lead to headaches and hypertension.
_____ 10. People with few social and community ties are more likely to die prematurely than are those who have many social ties.
_____ 11. The immune system can be classically conditioned.

PSYCHOLOGY APPLIED

Answer these questions the day before an exam as a final check on your understanding of the chapter's terms and concepts.

Multiple-Choice Questions

1. Which of the following is *not* necessarily a reason that obese people have trouble losing weight?
    a. Fat tissue has a lower metabolic rate than lean tissue.
    b. Once a person has lost weight, it takes fewer calories to maintain his or her current weight.
    c. The tendency toward obesity may be genetically based.
    d. Obese people tend to lack willpower.

2. After an initial rapid weight loss, a person on a diet loses weight much more slowly. This slow-down occurs because:
    a. most of the initial weight loss is simply water.
    b. when a person diets, metabolism decreases.
    c. people begin to "cheat" on their diets.
    d. insulin levels tend to increase with reduced food intake.

3. Concluding her presentation on spirituality and health, Maja notes that:
    a. historically, religion and medicine joined hands in caring for the sick.
    b. most Americans believe that spirituality and religion are related to health.
    c. people who attend religious services weekly have healthier life-styles.
    d. all of the above are true.

4. Malcolm's report on the effects of nicotine mentions each of the following *except*:
   a. increased heart rate.
   b. appetite suppression.
   c. increased circulation to extremities.
   d. release of endorphins triggered by nicotine.

5. Ricardo has been unable to resolve a stressful relationship with a family member. To cope, he turns to a close friend for social support. Ricardo's coping strategy is an example of:
   a. problem-focused coping.
   b. emotion-focused coping.
   c. managing rather than coping.
   d. hypochondriasis.

6. (Close-Up) Which of the following would be the *worst* piece of advice to offer to someone trying to lose weight?
   a. "In order to treat yourself to one 'normal' meal each day, eat very little until the evening meal."
   b. "Reduce your consumption of saturated fats."
   c. "Boost your metabolism by exercising regularly."
   d. "Without increasing total caloric intake, increase the relative proportion of carbohydrates in your diet."

7. Each semester, Bob does not start studying until just before midterms. Then he is forced to work around the clock until after final exams, which makes him sick, probably because he is in the _____ phase of the _____ .
   a. alarm; post-traumatic stress syndrome
   b. resistance; general adaptation syndrome
   c. exhaustion; general adaptation syndrome
   d. depletion; post-traumatic stress syndrome

8. Connie complains to the campus psychologist that she has too much stress in her life. The psychologist tells her that the level of stress people experience depends primarily on:
   a. how many activities they are trying to do at the same time.
   b. how they appraise the events of life.
   c. their physical hardiness.
   d. how predictable stressful events are.

9. To help him deal with a stressful schedule of classes, work, and studying Randy turns to a regular program of exercise and relaxation training. Randy's strategy is an example of:
   a. problem-focused coping.
   b. emotion-focused coping.
   c. managing rather than coping.
   d. hypochondriasis.

10. Karen and Kyumi are taking the same course with different instructors. Karen's instructor schedules quizzes every Friday, while Kyumi's instructor gives the same number of quizzes on an unpredictable schedule. Assuming that their instructors are equally difficult, and that the two students tend to perceive exam stress in the same way, which student is probably under more stress?
    a. Karen
    b. Kyumi
    c. There should be no difference in their levels of stress.
    d. It is impossible to predict stress levels in this situation.

11. Jill is an easygoing, noncompetitive person who is happy in her job and enjoys her leisure time. She would *probably* be classified as:
    a. Type A.
    b. Type B.
    c. Type C.
    d. There is too little information to tell.

12. A white blood cell that is formed in the thymus and that attacks cancer cells is:
    a. a macrophage.   c. a T lymphocyte.
    b. a B lymphocyte.   d. any of the above.

13. When would you expect that your immune responses would be *weakest*?
    a. during summer vacation
    b. during exam weeks
    c. just after receiving good news
    d. Immune activity would probably remain constant during these times.

14. Which of the following would be the *best* piece of advice to offer a person who is trying to minimize the adverse effects of stress on his or her health?

   a. "Avoid challenging situations that may prove stressful."
   b. "Learn to play as hard as you work."
   c. "Maintain a sense of control and a positive approach to life."
   d. "Keep your emotional responses in check by keeping your feelings to yourself."

15. I am a widely abused drug that has a calming effect by stimulating the release of dopamine in the central nervous system. What am I?

   a. caffeine
   b. alcohol
   c. nicotine
   d. cocaine

16. Kenny and his brother have nearly identical eating and exercise habits, yet Kenny is obese and his brother is very thin. The most likely explanation for the difference in their body weights is that they differ in:

   a. their set points.
   b. their metabolic rates.
   c. both a. and b.
   d. none of the above.

17. Dr. Williams, who conducts smoking cessation clinics, explains to his clients that smoking is best understood as an interaction of psychological, biological, and social influences. Dr. Williams is working within the _____ perspective.

   a. behavioral medicine
   b. behavioral
   c. general adaptation syndrome
   d. psychophysiological

18. Philip's physician prescribes a stress management program to help Philip control his headaches. The physician has apparently diagnosed Philip's condition as a _____ illness.

   a. psychogenic
   b. hypochondriac
   c. psychophysiological
   d. biofeedback

19. Camelia is worried that her 12-year-old son might begin smoking because many of his classmates do. According to the text, Camelia can most effectively help her son not begin smoking by:

   a. telling him about the dangers of smoking.
   b. telling him that if he begins smoking she will withhold his allowance.
   c. using role-playing to teach him refusal techniques to counteract peer pressure to smoke.
   d. insisting that he not associate with anyone who smokes.

20. You have just transferred to a new campus and find yourself in a potentially stressful environment. According to the text, which of the following would help you cope with the stress?

   a. believing that you have some control over your environment
   b. being able to predict when stressful events will occur
   c. feeling optimistic that you will eventually adjust to your new surroundings
   d. All of the above would help.

21. (Thinking Critically) Andrew, who is convinced that an expensive herbal remedy "cured" his arthritis, has decided to turn to homeopathy and herbal medicine for all of his health care. You caution him by pointing out that:

   a. arthritis is a cyclical disease that often improves on its own.
   b. botanical herbs have never been proven effective in controlled experiments.
   c. alternative medicine is a recent fad in this country that has few proponents in other parts of the world.
   d. all of the above are true.

Essay Question

Discuss several factors that enhance a person's ability to cope with stress. (Use the space below to list the points you want to make, and organize them. Then write the essay on a separate sheet of paper.)

KEY TERMS

Writing Definitions

Using your own words, on a separate piece of paper write a brief definition or explanation of each of the following terms.

1. behavioral medicine
2. health psychology
3. stress
4. general adaptation syndrome (GAS)
5. coronary heart disease
6. Type A
7. Type B
8. psychophysiological illness
9. lymphocytes
10. coping
11. problem-focused coping
12. emotion-focused coping
13. aerobic exercise
14. biofeedback
15. complementary and alternative medicine

Cross-Check

As you learned in the Prologue, reviewing and overlearning of material are important to the learning process. After you have written the definitions of the key terms in this chapter, you should complete the crossword puzzle to ensure that you can reverse the process—recognize the term, given the definition.

ACROSS

2. "Hardening" of the arteries that leads to heart disease.
7. Fat-detecting hormone.
12. Coronary-prone behavior pattern.
13. The three-stage bodily reaction to stress.
15. Type of exercise that may help alleviate anxiety.
17. During the _____ stage of the stress reaction, the body's sympathetic nervous system is suddenly activated.
18. Psychologist who first described the general adaptation syndrome.
19. During the _____ stage of the stress reaction, the body's reserves are depleted.
20. The "big eater" of the immune system.

DOWN

1. Friedman and Rosenman's term for easygoing, relaxed people.
3. Subfield of psychology that contributes to behavioral medicine.
4. The body's weight thermostat.
5. The processes by which people appraise and react to events they perceive as threatening.
6. Phrase coined by Cannon to describe the response of the sympathetic nervous system to a stressor.

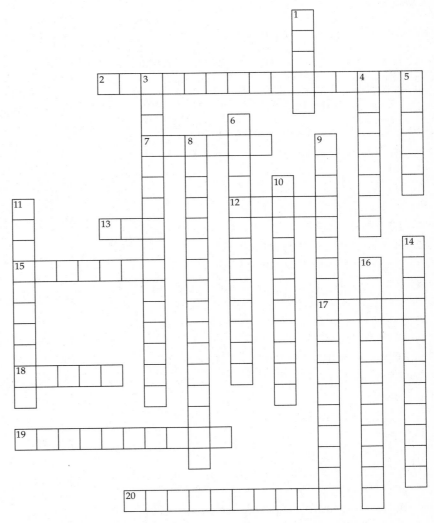

8. Our reaction to a potential stressor is determined in part by whether we feel we have _____ _____ over an event.

9. Interdisciplinary health field that treats disease and promotes health.

10. Another name for the stress hormone adrenaline.

11. When our body weight drops below its set point, _____ decreases.

14. White blood cells that form in the bone marrow and release antibodies that fight bacterial infections.

16. The leading cause of death in the United States.

ANSWERS

Chapter Review

Introducing Stress and Health

1. heart disease; cancer; stroke; chronic lung disease

2. behavior

3. cigarette smoking, alcohol abuse, unprotected sex, ignoring doctors' orders, insufficient exercise, use of illicit drugs, poor nutrition

4. behavioral medicine

5. health

Stress and Illness

1. 4

2. stimulus; response; process

3. both positive and negative

4. Cannon; epinephrine (adrenaline); norepinephrine (noradrenaline); sympathetic; fight or flight

5. hypothalamus; pituitary; adrenal glands; glucocorticoid; cortisol

6. tend and befriend; seek and give support

7. adrenal; thymus; ulcers; general adaptation syndrome

8. alarm; sympathetic

9. resistance

10. exhaustion; more

11. telomeres; DNA; chromosomes; divide; hippocampus

12. depression and other psychological disorders

13. more

14. daily hassles; racism; hypertension

15. coronary heart disease; smoking, obesity, high-fat diet, physical inactivity, elevated cholesterol level

16. cholesterol; clotting; stress

Type A people were competitive, hard-driving, supermotivated, impatient, time-conscious, verbally aggressive, and easily angered. Type B people were more relaxed and easygoing. Heart attack victims over the course of the study came overwhelmingly from the Type A group.

17. do not differ

18. greater than; plaque; atherosclerosis

19. Type A; cholesterol

20. negative emotions; the anger associated with an aggressively reactive temperament

21. pessimism; pessimists; optimists

22. increases

23. psychophysiological; hypochondriasis

24. hypertension; headaches; stress

25. psychosomatic; unreal

26. immune; lymphocytes; B lymphocytes; T lymphocytes; thymus; macrophage

27. arthritis; allergic; underreact; cancer

28. Women; infections; self-attacking; lupus; multiple sclerosis

29. decrease; immune system; brain; muscles

30. AIDS; human immunodeficiency virus (HIV); blood; semen

31. have

32. have

33. negative; have

34. tumor; carcinogens; uncontrollable

35. does not

36. can

37. drug; immune suppression

38. negligible (small)

39. physiological; physiological

Promoting Health

1. cope; emotional; cognitive; behavioral

2. problem-focused

3. emotion-focused

4. problem-focused; control; emotion-focused; change

5. uncontrollable; death

6. mortality; birth weight; violence

7. increase; stress hormones

8. optimistic

9. humor

10. tone; blood flow

11. social

12. good marriage; low cholesterol

People with strong social ties may be healthier because they eat better, exercise more, smoke and drink less, and are helped to receive medical treatment quicker. Close relationships also provide the opportunity to bolster self-esteem and to confide painful feelings, which may mitigate physical reactions to stressful events. Environments that foster our need to belong also foster stronger immune functioning.

13. suppression; disclosing

14. writing

15. self-disclosing

16. aerobic

17. have

18. norepinephrine; serotonin; endorphins; memory

19. two

20. biofeedback; do not provide

21. meditation (relaxation); relaxation

22. parietal; frontal

23. complementary and alternative medicine; herbal; Qi or Chi

24. cyclical; allergies; spontaneous remission; placebo

25. religion; medicine; together

26. believe

27. predicts

Religiously active people have healthier life-styles. They also tend to have stronger networks of social support and are more likely to be married.

28. 20; organic; psychosocial

Smoking is associated with lung cancer, respiratory ailments, and heart disease.

29. early adolescence; earn low grades, drop out of school, feel less competent and in control of their future, and whose friends, parents, and siblings smoke; models; imitate

30. dependent; tolerance; withdrawal

31. reinforcer; alertness; efficiency; anxiety; pain sensitivity

32. biopsychosocial; 60; gene; dopamine

33. are not; males; higher

34. high; developing

35. a. information about the effects of smoking

b. information about peer, parent, and media influences

c. training in refusal skills, through modeling and role playing

36. costly

37. famine; affluence; social status

Obesity increases one's risk of diabetes, high blood pressure and heart disease, gallstones, arthritis, and certain types of cancer.

38. abdomens (stomachs); Alzheimer's

39. 3

40. slow; lazy; sloppy

41. less; married

42. obese

43. 3500; fat cells; genetic predisposition, early childhood eating patterns, adult overeating

44. can; cannot

45. lower; less

46. is; hunger; metabolism

Obese persons have higher set-point weights than nonobese persons. During a diet, metabolic rate drops to defend the set-point weight. The dieter therefore finds it hard to progress beyond an initial weight loss. When the diet is concluded, the lowered metabolic rate continues, so that relatively small amounts of food may prove fattening. Also, some people have lower metabolic rates than others.

47. do

48. gene; leptin; brain; eating; activity; more; lose

49. more; does

50. gain

51. more

52. Begin only if you are motivated and self-disciplined. Minimize exposure to tempting food cues. Eat healthy foods. Don't starve all day and eat one big meal at night. Beware of binge eating. Be realistic and moderate. Boost your metabolism through exercise.

Progress Test 1

1. **c.** is the answer. (p. 549)

   a. Health psychology is a subfield within behavioral medicine.

   b. Holistic medicine is an older term that refers to medical practitioners who take more of an interdisciplinary approach to treating disorders.

   d. Osteopathy is a medical therapy that emphasizes manipulative techniques for correcting physical problems.

2. **c.** is the answer. (p. 551)
a., b., & d. The pituitary does not produce stress hormones nor is the parasympathetic division involved in arousal.

3. **c.** is the answer. (p. 553)
a. & b. During these stages the body's defensive mechanisms are at peak function.
d. This is not a stage of the GAS.

4. **c.** is the answer. Coronary heart disease is followed by cancer, stroke, and chronic lung disease. AIDS has not yet become one of the four leading causes of death in North America among the general population. (p. 555)

5. **c.** is the answer. (p. 555)
a. & b. Researchers have not identified such personality types.
d. Individuals who are more easygoing are labeled Type B.

6. **b.** is the answer. Stress hormones accelerate the buildup of plaques, or masses formed by cholesterol deposits, on the artery walls. This likely occurs because during arousal, blood is diverted from internal organs such as the liver, which removes cholesterol from the blood, to the muscles of the body. These hormones are released in response to stress; they do not reduce stress. (pp. 555–556)

7. **a.** is the answer. (p. 556)
b. Hypochondriacs think something is wrong with them, but nothing physical can be detected.
c. *Psychogenic* means "originating in the mind." One's reaction to stress is partially psychological, but this term is not used to refer to stress-related illness.
d. There is no such term in psychology.

8. **d.** is the answer. Because stress depresses the immune system, stressed individuals are prone to all of these conditions. (p. 557)

9. **c.** is the answer. (p. 550)
a., b., & d. Whether an event is stressful or not depends on how it is appraised.

10. **d.** is the answer. (p. 562–563)

11. **a.** is the answer. (p. 584)

12. **a.** is the answer. (p. 562)
b. In emotion-focused coping, we attempt to alleviate stress by avoiding or ignoring it.
c. This is an example of coping rather than managing stress because it involves an attempt to actually alleviate a stressor.
d. Hypochondriasis involves misinterpreting normal physical sensations as symptoms of a disease.

13. **c.** is the answer. The finding that talking about grief leads to better health makes a lot of sense in light of this physiological finding. (p. 566)
a., b., & d. The study by Pennebaker did not find these to be true.

14. **b.** is the answer. People generally *start* smoking in adolescence in order to gain peer acceptance; they continue smoking primarily because they have become addicted to nicotine. Thus, the factors that motivate people to start smoking are best described as social, whereas the factors that explain continued smoking are mainly biological. (pp. 577–578)

15. **a.** is the answer. (p. 585)

16. **d.** is the answer. Regular aerobic exercise has been shown to increase ability to cope with stress, lower blood pressure, and reduce depression and anxiety. The text does not cite evidence that exercise enhances immune function. (pp. 567–569)

17. **d.** is the answer. (p. 553)

18. **b.** is the answer. (pp. 559–560)

19. **b.** is the answer. (p. 565)

20. **c.** is the answer. (p. 558)

21. **d.** is the answer. (p. 573)
b. & c. The text does not indicate that a gender difference exists in the "faith factor" in health.

Progress Test 2

Multiple-Choice Questions

1. **d.** is the answer. This chapter deals with the topics of health psychology, namely, preventing illness, by developing better ways to cope with stress; treating illness, by improving the ways in which people notice and explain symptoms; and promoting health, for example, through nutrition and weight control. (p. 549)

2. **a.** is the answer. (p. 552)

3. **c.** is the answer. (p. 558)

4. **c.** is the answer. (p. 551)
a. The final stage of the general adaptation syndrome is exhaustion.
b. & d. Although both of these are true, neither has anything to do with "tend and befriend."

5. **b.** is the answer. The greater reactivity of Type A people includes much higher levels of stress hormones in stressful situations. (p. 556)
a. Under relaxed situations, there is no difference in blood pressure.

c. Anger, both expressed and suppressed, is more characteristic of Type A people.

d. The text doesn't indicate that Type A persons are more outgoing than Type B persons.

6. **d.** is the answer. Behaviors that contribute to the leading causes of mortality include smoking, excessive alcohol consumption, maladaptive responses to stress, insufficient exercise, use of illicit drugs, and poor nutrition. (p. 549)

7. **c.** is the answer. B lymphocytes fight bacterial infections; T lymphocytes attack cancer cells, viruses, and foreign substances. (p. 557)

d. Antigens cause the production of antibodies when they are introduced into the body.

8. **a.** is the answer. A variety of studies have shown that stress depresses the immune system, increasing the risk and potential severity of many diseases. (p. 557)

9. **d.** is the answer. (p. 557)

10. **b.** is the answer. Both human and animal studies indicate that uncontrollable negative events trigger an outpouring of stress hormones and a drop in immune responses. (pp. 562–563)

11. **a.** is the answer. (p. 557)

b. An *under*reactive immune system would make an individual more susceptible to infectious diseases or the proliferation of cancer cells.

c. & d. Lymphocytes are disease- and infection-fighting white blood cells in the immune system.

12. **d.** is the answer. (p. 559)

13. **d.** is the answer. The crucial characteristic of Type A behavior seems to be a tendency to react with negative emotions, especially anger; other aspects of Type A behavior appear not to predict heart disease, and some appear to be helpful to the individual. (p. 556)

14. **d.** is the answer. No particular treatment seemed to stand out in terms of effectiveness. All but one-fifth of the people who quit smoking in such programs eventually return to the habit. (p. 579)

15. **d.** is the answer. In biofeedback training, people are given sensory feedback about autonomic responses. Although biofeedback may promote relaxation, its benefits may be no greater than those produced by simpler, and less expensive, methods. (p. 569)

16. **b.** is the answer. Fat cells may change in size as a person gains or loses weight, but their number never decreases. (p. 584)

a. In fact, because of its lower metabolic rate, fat tissue can be maintained on *fewer* calories.

c. Because metabolism slows as food intake is restricted, a 3500-calorie reduction may not reduce weight by one pound.

d. In fact, just the opposite is true.

17. **d.** is the answer. (p. 584)

18. **b.** is the answer. By alleviating the aversive physiological state of nicotine withdrawal, cigarettes act as negative reinforcers. (p. 578)

a. This is one explanation of why adolescents *start* smoking.

c. There is no evidence that this occurs.

d. Most smokers would like to quit smoking.

19. **b.** is the answer. (p. 581)

c. If anything, just the opposite is true.

d. Men and women do not differ in the tendency to overeat.

20. **d.** is the answer. As a group, religiously active people are no more affluent than other people. (pp. 573–574)

21. **b.** is the answer. (p. 570)

a. There is no such subfield of medicine.

c. Chi is an alleged form of energy, imbalances of which Chinese herbal therapies and acupuncture are intended to treat.

d. The term psychosomatic was once used to describe psychologically caused symptoms. Many forms of alternative medicine, including acupuncture, are intended to treat a full range of symptoms and diseases.

True–False Items

1. T (p. 587)	**6.** T (p. 581)	**11.** T (p. 560)
2. F (p. 557)	**7.** T (p. 563)	
3. F (p. 563)	**8.** T (p. 555)	
4. F (p. 580)	**9.** T (p. 556)	
5. F (p. 585)	**10.** T (p. 566)	

Psychology Applied

Multiple-Choice Questions

1. **d.** is the answer. Most researchers today discount the idea that people are obese because they lack willpower. (pp. 584–586)

2. **b.** is the answer. Following the initial weight loss, metabolism drops as the body attempts to defend its set-point weight. This drop in metabolism means that eating an amount that once produced a loss in weight may now actually result in weight gain. (p. 584)

3. **d.** is the answer. (pp. 573–574)

4. **c.** is the answer. Nicotine *reduces* circulation to the extremities of the body. (p. 578)

5. **b.** is the answer. Ricardo is attempting to address his emotional needs, since he has been unable to alleviate stress directly. (p. 562)

6. **a.** is the answer. Dieting, including fasting, lowers the body's metabolic rate and reduces the amount of food energy needed to maintain body weight. (p. 589)
b., c., & d. Each of these strategies would be a good piece of advice to a dieter.

7. **c.** is the answer. According to Selye's general adaptation syndrome, diseases are most likely to occur in this final stage. (p. 553)
a. & b. Resistance to disease is greater during the alarm and resistance phases because the body's mobilized resources are not yet depleted.
d. There is no such thing as the "depletion phase." Moreover, the post-traumatic stress syndrome refers to the haunting nightmares and anxiety of those who have suffered extreme stress, such as that associated with combat.

8. **b.** is the answer. (p. 550)
a., c., & d. Each of these is a factor in coping with stress, but it is how an event is *perceived* that determines whether it is stressful or not.

9. **c.** is the answer. (p. 567)

10. **b.** is the answer. Unpredictable events are more stressful than predictable events. (p. 553)

11. **b.** is the answer. (p. 555)
a. Type A persons are hard-driving and competitive.
c. There is no such thing as a "Type C" person.

12. **c.** is the answer. (p. 557)
a. Macrophages are immune agents that search for and ingest harmful invaders.
b. B lymphocytes form in the bone marrow and release antibodies that fight bacterial infections.

13. **b.** is the answer. Stressful situations, such as exam weeks, decrease immune responses. (p. 552)

14. **c.** is the answer. (pp. 562–564)
a. This is not realistic.
b. & d. These might actually *increase* the health consequences of potential stressors.

15. **c.** is the answer. (p. 578)
a. Caffeine has a stimulating rather than a calming effect.
b. Alcohol *depresses* activity in the central nervous system.
d. Cocaine increases dopamine by blocking its reuptake from synapses.

16. **c.** is the answer. Individual differences in metabolism and set point explain why it is possible for two people to have very different weights despite similar patterns of eating and exercise. (pp. 584–585)

17. **a.** is the answer. (p. 549)
b. The behavioral perspective would emphasize only learned factors in smoking.
c. The general adaptation syndrome is a sequence of bodily responses to stress.
d. Psychophysiological illnesses are illnesses not caused by any known physical disorder.

18. **c.** is the answer. (p. 556)
a. The text does not discuss any such thing as a "psychogenic" illness.
b. Hypochondriasis is the misinterpreting of normal physical sensations as symptoms of a disease.
d. Biofeedback is a system for recording information regarding a subtle physiological state, such as blood pressure.

19. **c.** is the answer. (p. 581)

20. **d.** is the answer. (pp. 562–564)

21. **a.** is the answer. (p. 570)
b. In fact, botanical herbs have given us many widely used drugs, including morphine and penicillin, each of which was proven to be useful in controlled research studies.
c. Herbal remedies and acupuncture—to name two forms of complementary and alternative medicine—have a long tradition in other parts of the world, and remain enormously popular today.

Essay Question

When potentially stressful events occur, a person's appraisal is a major determinant of their impact. Catastrophes, significant life events, and daily hassles are especially stressful when appraised as negative, unpredictable, and uncontrollable, and when the person has a pessimistic outlook on life. Under these circumstances, stressful events may suppress immune responses and make the person more vulnerable to disease. If stressors cannot be eliminated, aerobic exercise, biofeedback, relaxation, and social support can help the person cope. Aerobic exercise can reduce stress, depression, and anxiety, perhaps by increasing production of mood-boosting neurotransmitters. During biofeedback training, people enjoy a calm, relaxing experience that can be helpful in reducing stress. Research demonstrates that people who regularly practice relaxation techniques enjoy a greater sense of tranquility and have lower blood pressure and stronger immune responses. People with strong social ties eat better, exercise more, and smoke and drink less. Social support may also help people evaluate and overcome stressful events. In addition, confiding painful feelings to others has been demonstrated to reduce the physiological responses linked to stress.

Key Terms

1. **Behavioral medicine** is the interdisciplinary field that applies behavioral and medical knowledge to the treatment of disease and the promotion of health. (p. 549)

2. **Health psychology** is a subfield of psychology that studies how health and illness are influenced by emotions, stress, personality, life-style, and other psychological factors. (p. 549)

3. **Stress** refers to the process by which people perceive and react to stressors, or to events they perceive as threatening or challenging. (p. 550)

4. The **general adaptation syndrome (GAS)** is the three-stage sequence of bodily reaction to stress outlined by Hans Selye. (p. 552)

5. The leading cause of death in North America today, **coronary heart disease** results from the clogging of the vessels that nourish the heart muscle. (p. 555)

6. **Type A** personality is Friedman and Rosenman's term for the coronary-prone behavior pattern of competitive, hard-driving, impatient, verbally aggressive, and anger-prone people. (p. 555)

7. **Type B** personality is Friedman and Rosenman's term for the coronary-resistant behavior pattern of easygoing, relaxed people. (p. 555)

8. A **psychophysiological illness** is any genuine illness such as hypertension and some headaches that is apparently linked to stress rather than caused by a physical disorder. (p. 556)

   Memory aid: *Psycho-* refers to mind; *physio-* refers to body; a **psychophysiological illness** is a mind-body disorder.

9. **Lymphocytes** are the two types of white blood cells of the immune system that fight bacterial infections (B lymphocytes) and viruses, cancer cells, and foreign substances in the body (T lymphocytes). (p. 557)

10. **Coping** refers to any effort to alleviate stress using emotional, cognitive, or behavioral methods. (p. 562)

11. **Problem-focused coping** involves reducing stress by directly changing a stressor or how we interact with it. (p. 562)

12. **Emotion-focused coping** involves reducing stress by avoiding or ignoring a stressor and attending to the emotional reactions it triggers. (p. 562)

13. **Aerobic exercise** is any sustained activity such as running, swimming, or cycling that promotes heart and lung fitness and may help alleviate depression and anxiety. (p. 567)

14. **Biofeedback** refers to a system for electronically recording, amplifying, and feeding back information regarding a subtle physiological state. (p. 569)

    Memory aid: A **biofeedback** device, such as a brain-wave trainer, provides auditory or visual feedback about biological responses.

15. **Complementary and alternative medicine** is a collection of health care remedies and treatments that have not been accepted by medical science or verified by controlled research trials. (p. 570)

Cross-Check

ACROSS

2. atherosclerosis	
7. leptin	
12. Type A	
13. GAS	
15. aerobic	
17. alarm	
18. Selye	
19. exhaustion	
20. macrophage	

1. Type B	
3. health psychology	
4. set point	
5. stress	
6. fight or flight	
8. perceived control	
9. behavioral medicine	
10. epinephrine	
11. metabolism	
14. B lymphocytes	
16. heart disease	

FOCUS ON VOCABULARY AND LANGUAGE

Stress and Illness

Page 550: Afterward, she notices her *tense* muscles, *clenched teeth*, and *churning stomach*. Our response to stress can be beneficial (e.g., Karl's escape from the snake) or destructive (e.g., Karen's reaction to relatively minor routine problems or *daily hassles*). Following a number of stressful events (missing her train, rush-hour pedestrian traffic, late for an appointment, etc.), she becomes aware of her physiological reaction. Her muscles feel strained and taut (*tense*), her jaws are clamped shut (*clenched teeth*), and her stomach feels upset (*churning stomach*).

Page 550: Stress is a *slippery concept*. The term *stress* is often used to describe a stimulus (a threatening or challenging event) or a response (fear or anxiety). Most psychologists refer to the former as a *stressor*, the latter as a *stress reaction*, and use the word *stress* to refer to the entire process of evaluating and dealing with threatening events. Thus, stress is not a simple or easily grasped (understood) construct (*it is a slippery concept*).

Page 552: Your heart rate *zooms*. According to Selye's general adaptation syndrome (GAS), there are three phases in our response to stress: *alarm reaction, resistance,* and *exhaustion*. During the first phase, the sympathetic nervous system responds rapidly; your heart rate quickly increases (*zooms*), blood is directed to the muscles, and you experience the weakness associated with being startled. You are now ready to fight or cope with the stressor (*resistance phase*); if the situation is not resolved soon, you will experience *exhaustion* (the third phase).

Page 553: . . . *uprooting* . . . Refugees and others who are forcibly made to leave their homes (*they are uprooted*) have increased rates of depression, anxiety, psychological disorders, and other stress symptoms. In most instances, the health impairments come from long-term exposure to stress.

Page 554: Experiencing *a cluster of crises* puts one even more at risk. Important and significant changes in our lives are other types of life-event stressors that increase the probability of health problems. If a number of these events occur close together (*a cluster of crises*), people become more vulnerable to disease.

Page 554: Daily Hassles Small, routine, annoying events and the little things that go wrong day by day (*daily hassles*) can have an accumulative effect on health and well-being. Some people can handle these daily hassles (*they shrug them off*) while others

are severely distressed (*"driven up the wall"*) by these inconveniences. Continual work-related hassles can lead to mental, physical, and emotional exhaustion.

Page 555: Moreover, not one of the *"pure"* Type Bs —the most *mellow* and *laid-back* of their group—had suffered a *heart attack*. Researchers have identified two personality types: Type As are reactive (*easily angered*), competitive, verbally aggressive, highly motivated, always rushed, and lacking in patience; Type Bs are less easily angered (*mellow*), are easygoing (*laid-back*), patient, understanding, and noncompetitive. The most prototypical (*"pure"*) Type Bs were the least likely to be afflicted by coronary heart disease (*heart attacks*).

Page 555: But *after the honeymoon period,* in which the finding seemed definitive and revolutionary, other researchers began asking, Is the finding reliable? The discovery of the relationship between personality type (A or B) and health and well-being aroused much interest. However, once the initial excitement abated (*after the honeymoon period*), other investigators started more detailed research and asked questions about the specific mechanisms involved in personality type and risk of disease.

Page 556: These findings suggest that reactive Type A individuals are more often *"combat ready."* Research has shown that Type As are physiologically more reactive and ready to fight (*combat ready*) than Type Bs. When stressed, their sympathetic nervous systems operate to increase the levels of cholesterol and fat in the blood; in addition, their negative (*toxic*) emotions, especially anger and depression, make them more coronary-prone.

Page 557: Your immune system is not *a headless horseman*. The immune system does not operate as an autonomous system independent of other systems (*a headless horseman*). Instead, it works in close harmony with various brain systems and with the endocrine system, which secretes hormones. All these interact and affect each other in a very complex way.

Page 559: One danger in *hyping* reports on attitudes and cancer is that some patients may be led to blame themselves for their illness. One problem with overstating (*hyping*) the relationship between attitudes and cancer is that some cancer victims may feel that they have somehow caused their sickness. The biological factors involved in the disease cannot easily be mitigated (*derailed*) by believing good health is due to a healthy character (the *wellness macho*). Nor is it appropriate to blame (*lay a guilt trip on*) those who develop the illness. As Myers notes, we should be aware of the fine distinction (*thin line*) that separates science from desperately hopeful beliefs (*wishful thinking*).

Promoting Health

Page 564: . . . *laughter is the best medicine.* This old saying proposes that mirthful humor may be good for our health. Some research has shown the beneficial effects of laughter, which appears to act as a block or buffer against stress-induced problems. Those who have a good sense of humor and can find something funny in stressful life events tend to be healthier and may live longer (*those who laugh, last*). (This final phrase is a twist on the saying *"Those who laugh last, laugh longest"* or *"Getting the last laugh."*)

Page 565: . . . *heartaches* . . . *Heartaches* is a term that refers to persistent mental anguish or suffering, usually resulting from the loss of a loved one or from disappointment in love. Myers points out that while close relationships and family tend to contribute to our well-being and contentment, they also can be the cause of much misery, strain, and strife (*heartaches*).

Page 566: The *cold fact* is that the effect of social ties is *nothing to sneeze at.* Myers is being humorous here. The expression "that is nothing to sneeze at" indicates that something (the object, event, accomplishment, etc.) is not minor or insignificant, and, of course, people with colds tend to sneeze a lot. In research on resistance to cold viruses, the finding that healthy volunteers who had the most social ties were less likely to catch a cold and produced less mucus (the *cold fact*) is not an insignificant result (*nothing to sneeze at*). In addition, research shows that social support calms the cardiovascular system, lowering blood pressure and stress hormones.

Page 566: Talking about our troubles can be *"open heart therapy."* Research has shown that those with close, supportive friends and family tend to have fewer health problems and live longer. One reason for this may be that trusting relationships provide the opportunity to talk about our problems and feelings and, just as "open-heart surgery" can save lives, having someone to talk to can be a form of *"open-heart therapy."*

Page 568: Many of them had, quite literally, *run away from their troubles.* Many research studies have shown the beneficial effect of aerobic exercise on depression and anxiety. In one study, women who took up jogging (*running*) showed a substantial reduction in depression. As Myers humorously puts it, they had, in reality, *run away from their problems.*

Page 568 (caption): The mood boost. Regular exercise increases longevity and cardiovascular fitness, reduces anxiety and depression, and enhances positive emotional states (*boosts our moods*). So the popular trend toward being more physically active has many benefits.

Page 569: After a decade of study, however, researchers decided the initial claims for biofeedback were *overblown and oversold* (Miller, 1985). Biofeedback became very popular in the 1970s, and the reports of its effectiveness for all kinds of problems led to much excitement. By the mid-1980s, however, when researchers took the time to evaluate the research findings objectively, it became clear that these assertions were exaggerated (*overblown*) and falsely promoted (*oversold*). Simple relaxation without the use of costly equipment is just as beneficial.

Page 573: Is there fire underneath all this smoke? The expression "there's no smoke without fire" indicates that there is usually a cause for an event, that there is something hidden that accounts for the phenomenon. Recently, there have been many claims for a positive correlation between spiritual or religious belief and health and healing. Myers questions whether in fact there is any real evidence (*the fire*) for the reported correlations (*the smoke*) and notes that correlations cannot be used to imply causation. He points to three possible intervening variables: (1) Religiously active people tend to have healthy life-styles. (2) Faith communities offer social support and encourage marriage. (3) Religious attendance may enhance positive emotions and decrease stress and anxiety.

Page 577: . . . *cool models* . . . People usually begin to smoke during early adolescence; those who don't start during the teen years are much less likely to become habitual smokers as adults. Smoking starts much like many other behaviors, through imitating others (*through modeling*); teenage smokers are often viewed by their peers as self-possessed, mature, strong, outgoing, and friendly (*cool models*).

Page 579: . . . *slow-motion suicide.* Smoking is continued because, among other reasons, it offers a pleasant feeling (*pleasurable lift*) and it escapes or avoids the unpleasant persistent desire (*craving*) of deprivation or withdrawal. The negative aspect of smoking, however, is the increased health risk which over time may result in the death of the smoker (*slow-motion suicide*).

Page 579: It's among college students and graduates that smoking has become *gauche* rather than *cool.* High school dropouts and those of lower socioeconomic status are more likely to smoke than college or university students and graduates. For this population, smoking is seen as undesirable, unpopular, and socially unacceptable (*gauche*) instead of being fashionably trendy (*cool*).

Page 581: And why do so few overweight people *win the battle of the bulge?* Most overweight people who diet do not manage to permanently lose the many pounds of fat they want to (*they do not win the battle of the bulge*). Myers discusses a number of factors: (a) the number of fat cells in the body does not decrease when you diet; (b) the tissue in fat is easier to maintain and uses less energy than other tissue; and (c) when body weight drops below the set point, your overall metabolic rate slows down. For those wanting to diet, Myers lists some useful tips.

Page 582: The risks are greater for *apple-shaped* people who carry their weight *in pot bellies* than for *pear-shaped* people with ample hips and thighs. Significant obesity increases the risk of many diseases and thus shortens life expectancy. People who have a more regularly proportioned physical build (*apple-shaped*) but whose excess weight tends to accumulate and protrude around the abdomen (*they carry their weight in pot bellies*) are more at risk than those people with a body shape that has proportionally more mass in the thighs and hips and less in the upper body (*they are pear-shaped*).

Page 585: Being overweight is therefore *not* simply a matter of *scarfing too many hot fudge sundaes*. And losing weight is not simply a matter of *mind over platter*. Research has shown that being obese (*overweight*) is not a function of hungrily devouring (*scarfing*) an excessive number of desserts made from ice cream covered with chocolate sauce, fruit, whipped cream, etc. (*hot fudge sundaes*), nor is it a matter of willpower (*mind over matter*) or the ability to be able to resist the food on your plate (*mind over platter*).

Page 585: So, the specifics of our genes predispose the size of our jeans. Myers is using a play on words here, suggesting that the complex interaction involved in our genetic make-up (*the specifics of our genes*) may influence the amount of excess weight we gain and correspondingly the size of the denim pants we wear (*the size of our jeans*).

Page 587: But for most people, the only long-term result of this losing battle is a *thinner wallet*. Most commercial weight-loss programs cost a great deal of money but, at best, only help people lose weight temporarily. For those who lose and then regain weight over and over again (*yo-yo dieting*), the end result is usually a greater weight gain each time and ultimately having less money (*thinner wallets*).

Page 589 (Close-Up): Couch potatoes beware . . . Myers admonishes those of us who sit around, watch TV, and eat junk food (*couch potatoes*) to get active.

15 : Personality

CHAPTER OVERVIEW

Personality refers to each individual's characteristic pattern of thinking, feeling, and acting. Chapter 15 examines four perspectives on personality. Psychoanalytic theory emphasizes the unconscious and irrational aspects of personality. The discussion concludes with an examination of the concept of self, which is the focus of many of today's researchers. Humanistic theory draws attention to the concept of self and to the human potential for healthy growth. Trait theory led to advances in techniques for evaluating and describing personality. The social-cognitive perspective emphasizes the effects of our interactions with the environment. Note that the text first describes and then evaluates the contributions, shortcomings, and historical significance of the psychoanalytic and humanistic perspectives. Next, the text turns to contemporary research on personality, focusing on how the trait and social-cognitive perspectives explore and assess traits.

NOTE: Answer guidelines for all Chapter 15 questions begin on page 399.

CHAPTER REVIEW

First, skim each section, noting headings and boldface items. After you have read the section, review each objective by answering the fill-in and essay-type questions that follow it. As you proceed, evaluate your performance by consulting the answers beginning on page 399. Do not continue with the next section until you understand each answer. If you need to, review or reread the section in the textbook before continuing.

Introducing Personality (pp. 595–596)

Objective 1: Define *personality*.

1. Personality is defined as an individual's characteristic pattern of _____ , _____ , and _____ .

2. The psychoanalytic perspective on personality was proposed by _____ _____ . A second, historically significant perspective was the _____ approach, which focused on people's capacities for _____ and _____-_____ .

3. Today's theories are more _____ and down-to-earth than these grand theories.

The Psychoanalytic Perspective (pp. 596–609)

> David Myers at times uses idioms that are unfamiliar to some readers. If you do not know the meaning of any of the following words, phrases, or expressions in the context in which they appear in the text, refer to pages 407–408 for an explanation: *ran up a bookstore debt; mind running; glimpse; virtuous . . . wantonly; utter biting sarcasm; twig of personality is bent; icebreaker; linguistic flip-flops; seared; scientific shortcomings; bumbling.*

Objective 2: Explain how Freud's experiences in private practice led to his theory of psychoanalysis.

1. Sigmund Freud was a medical doctor who specialized in _____ disorders.

2. Freud developed his theory in response to his observation that many patients had disorders that did not make _____ sense.

Objective 3: Discuss Freud's view of the mind as an iceberg, and explain how he used this image to represent conscious and unconscious regions of the mind.

3. At first, Freud thought _____ would unlock the door to the unconscious.

4. The technique later used by Freud, in which the patient relaxes and says whatever comes to mind, is called _____ _____ .

5. Freud called his theory and associated techniques, whereby painful unconscious memories are exposed, _____ .

6. According to this theory, the mind is like an iceberg in that many of a person's thoughts, wishes, and feelings are hidden in a large _____ region. Some of the thoughts in this region can be retrieved at will into consciousness; these thoughts are said to be _____ . Many of the memories of this region, however, are blocked, or _____ , from consciousness.

7. Freud believed that a person's _____ wishes are often reflected in his or her beliefs, habits, symptoms, and _____ of the tongue or pen. Freud called the remembered content of dreams the _____ _____ , which he believed to be a censored version of the dream's true _____ _____ .

Objective 4: Describe Freud's view of personality structure, and discuss the interactions of the id, ego, and superego.

8. Freud believed that all facets of personality arise from conflict between our _____ impulses and the _____ restraints against them.

9. According to Freud, personality consists of three interacting structures: the _____ , the _____ , and the _____ .

10. The id is a reservoir of energy that is primarily _____ (conscious/unconscious) and operates according to the _____ principle.

11. The ego develops _____ (before/after) the id and consists of perceptions, thoughts, and memories that are mostly _____ (conscious/unconscious). The ego operates according to the _____ principle.

Explain why the ego is considered the "executive" of personality.

12. The personality structure that reflects moral values is the _____ , which Freud believed began emerging at about age _____ .

13. A person with a _____ (strong/weak) superego may be self-indulgent; one with an unusually _____ (strong/weak) superego may be continually guilt-ridden.

Objective 5: Identify Freud's psychosexual stages of development, and describe the effects of fixation on behavior.

14. According to Freud, personality is formed as the child passes through a series of _____ stages, each of which is focused on a distinct body area called an _____ _____ .

15. The first stage is the _____ stage, which takes place during the first 18 months of life. During this stage, the id's energies are focused on behaviors such as _____ .

16. The second stage is the _____ stage, which lasts from about age _____ months to _____ months.

17. The third stage is the _____ stage, which lasts roughly from ages _____ to _____ . During this stage the id's energies are focused on the _____ . Freud also believed that during this stage children develop sexual desires for the_____ (same/opposite)-sex parent. Freud referred to these feelings as the _____ _____ in boys. Some psychoanalysts in Freud's era believed that girls experience a parallel _____ _____ .

18. Freud believed that _____ with the same-sex parent is the basis for

_____ _____ .

Explain how this complex of feelings is resolved through the process of identification.

19. During the next stage, sexual feelings are repressed: this phase is called the _____ stage and lasts until adolescence.

20. The final stage of development is called the _____ stage.

21. According to Freud, it is possible for a person's development to become blocked in any of the

stages; in such an instance, the person is said to be _____ . People who are messy and disorganized, or highly controlled and compulsively neat, were said to be anal _____ and anal _____ , respectively.

Objective 6: Describe the function of defense mechanisms, and identify six of them.

22. The ego attempts to protect itself against anxiety through the use of _____ _____ . The process underlying each of these mechanisms is

_____ .

23. Dealing with anxiety by returning to an earlier stage of development is called

_____ .

24. When a person reacts in a manner opposite that of his or her true feelings, _____ _____ is said to have occurred.

25. When a person attributes his or her own feelings to another person, _____ has occurred.

26. When a person offers a false, self-justifying explanation for his or her actions, _____ has occurred.

27. When impulses are directed toward an object other than the one that caused arousal, _____ has occurred.

Matching Items

Match each defense mechanism in the following list with the proper example of its manifestation.

Defense Mechanisms

_____ **1.** displacement
_____ **2.** projection
_____ **3.** reaction formation
_____ **4.** rationalization
_____ **5.** regression

Manifestations

a. nail biting or thumb sucking in an anxiety-producing situation
b. overzealous crusaders against "immoral behaviors," who don't want to acknowledge their own sexual desires
c. saying you drink "just to be sociable" when in reality you have a drinking problem
d. thinking someone hates you when in reality you hate that person
e. a child who is angry at his parents and vents this anger on the family pet, a less threatening target

28. Defense mechanisms are _____ (conscious/unconscious) processes.

Objective 7: Contrast the views of the neo-Freudians and psychodynamic theorists with Freud's original theory.

29. The theorists who established their own, modified versions of psychoanalytic theory are called

_____-_____ .

These theorists typically place _____ (more/less) emphasis on the conscious mind than Freud did and _____ (more/less) emphasis on sex and aggression.

Briefly summarize how each of the following theorists departed from Freud.

a. Adler _____

_____

b. Horney _____

_____

_____

c. Jung _____

_____

30. Today's psychologists _____ (accept/reject) the idea that people inherit a common reservoir of experiences, which _____ (which theorist?) called a _____

_____ .

31. More recently, some of Freud's ideas have been incorporated into _____ theory. Unlike Freud, the theorists advocating this perspective do not believe that _____ is the basis of personality. They do agree, however, that much of mental life is _____ , that _____ shapes personality, and that we often struggle with _____ _____ .

Objective 8: Describe two projective tests used to assess personality, and discuss some criticisms of them.

32. Tests that provide subjects with ambiguous stimuli for interpretation are called _____ tests.

33. Henry Murray introduced the personality assessment technique called the

_____

_____ Test.

34. The most widely used projective test is the _____ , in which subjects are shown a series of _____ . Generally, these tests appear to have _____ (little/significant) validity and reliability. This is because there

_____ (is/is not) a universal system for scoring these tests, and they _____ (are/are not) successful at predicting behaviors.

Objective 9: Summarize psychology's current assessment of Freud's theory of psychoanalysis.

35. Contrary to Freud's theory, research indicates that human development is _____ (fixed in childhood/lifelong), children gain their gender identity at a(n) _____ (earlier/later) age, and the presence of a same-sex parent _____ (is/is not) necessary for the child to become strongly masculine or feminine.

36. Recent research also disputes Freud's belief that dreams disguise _____ and that defense mechanisms disguise _____ and _____ impulses. Another Freudian idea that is no longer widely accepted is that psychological disorders are caused by _____ .

37. Psychoanalytic theory rests on the assumption that the human mind often _____ painful experiences. Many of today's researchers think that this process is much _____ (more common/rarer) than Freud believed. They also believe that when it does occur, it is a reaction to terrible _____ .

38. Today's psychologists agree with Freud that much of the mind's information processing is _____ . Research studies demonstrate that our capacity for _____ learning, sometimes called _____ _____ , is quite sophisticated.

39. Another Freudian idea that has received support is that people defend themselves against _____ . According to _____-_____

theory, when people are faced with a threatening world, they act to enhance their _____ , and may adhere more strongly to the _____ that create meaning in their lives.

40. An example of the defense mechanism that Freud called _____ is what researchers today call the _____ _____ effect. This refers to our tendency to _____ the extent to which others share our beliefs and behaviors.

41. Criticism of psychoanalysis as a scientific theory centers on the fact that it provides _____-_____-_____ explanations and does not offer _____ _____ .

State several of Freud's ideas that have endured.

The Humanistic Perspective (pp. 609–612)

> If you do not know the meaning of any of the following words, phrases, or expressions in the context in which they appear in the text, refer to page 408 for an explanation: *crippled spirits; thwarted . . . acorn, primed for growth; rugged individual; playing possum.*

Objective 10: Summarize Abraham Maslow's concept of self-actualization, and explain how his ideas illustrate the humanistic perspective.

1. Two influential theories of humanistic psychology were proposed by _____ and _____ .

2. According to Maslow, humans are motivated by needs that are organized into a _____ . Maslow refers to the process of fulfilling one's potential as

_____ . As a pioneer in the movement for a more humanistic psychology, Maslow emphasized the ways that healthy people strive for _____ and self-realization.

List some of the characteristics Maslow associated with those who fulfilled their potential.

Objective 11: Discuss Carl Rogers' person-centered perspective, and explain the importance of unconditional positive regard.

3. According to Rogers, a person nurtures growth in a relationship by being _____ , _____ , and _____ .

4. People who are accepting of others offer them _____ _____ _____ . By so doing, they enable others to be _____ without fearing the loss of their esteem.

5. For both Maslow and Rogers, an important feature of personality is how an individual perceives himself or herself; this is the person's _____ .

Objective 12: Explain how humanistic psychologists assessed personality.

6. Humanistic psychologists sometimes use _____ to assess personality, that is, to evaluate the _____ .

7. Carl Rogers developed a questionnaire that asked people to describe themselves both as they would _____ like to be and as they _____ are.

8. Some humanistic psychologists feel that questionnaires are _____ and prefer to use _____ to assess personality.

Objective 13: State the major criticisms of the humanistic perspective on personality.

9. Humanistic psychologists have influenced such diverse areas as _____ , _____ , _____ , and _____ . They have also had a major impact on today's _____ psychology, perhaps because the emphasis on the individual self strongly reflects _____ cultural values.

10. Research has shown that most people tend to have _____ (low/high) self-esteem.

State three criticisms of humanistic psychology.

The Trait Perspective (pp. 613–623)

> If you do not know the meaning of any of the following words, phrases, or expressions in the context in which they appear in the text, refer to pages 408–409 for an explanation: *Flabbergasted; scoff; suckering methods; "stock spiel"; spoofing; dubbed the Big Five; labeling and pigeon-holing.*

Objective 14: Cite the main difference between the trait and psychoanalytic perspectives on personality.

1. Gordon Allport developed trait theory, which defines personality in terms of people's characteristic _____ and conscious _____ . Unlike Freud, he was generally less interested in _____ individual traits than in _____ them.

2. The ancient Greeks classified people according to four types: _____ , or depressed; _____ , or cheerful;

_____ , or unemotional; and
_____ , or irritable.

3. The _____-_____
_____ _____
classifies people according to Carl Jung's
personality types. Although recently criticized for
its lack of predictive value, this test has been
widely used in _____
and _____ counseling.

Objective 15: Describe some of the ways psychologists have attempted to compile a list of basic personality traits.

4. To reduce the number of traits to a few basic
ones, psychologists use the statistical procedure
of _____ _____ .
The Eysencks think that two or three genetically
influenced personality dimensions are sufficient;
these include _____–
_____ and emotional
_____–_____ .

5. Some researchers believe that extraverts seek
stimulation because their level of
_____ _____ is
relatively low. PET scans reveal an area of the
brain's _____ lobe that is less
active in _____ (extraverts/introverts) than in _____ (extraverts/introverts).

6. Research increasingly reveals that our
_____ play an important role in
defining our _____ and
_____ style.

7. Jerome Kagan attributes differences in children's
_____ and _____
to autonomic nervous system reactivity.

8. Personality differences among dogs, birds, and
other animals _____ (are/are
not) stable.

Objective 16: Explain how psychologists use personality inventories to assess traits, and discuss the most widely used inventory.

9. Questionnaires that categorize personality traits
are called _____
_____ .

10. The most widely used of all such personality tests
is the _____ _____
_____ _____ ;
its questions are grouped into _____
(how many?) clinical scales.

11. This test was developed by testing a large pool of
items and selecting those that differentiated particular individuals; in other words, the test was
_____ derived.

(Thinking Critically) Explain several techniques used
by astrologers to persuade people to accept their
advice.

Objective 17: Identify the Big Five personality factors, and discuss some of the strengths of this approach to studying personality.

12. Researchers have arrived at a cluster of five factors that seem to describe the major features of
personality. List and briefly describe the Big Five.
a. _____
b. _____
c. _____
d. _____
e. _____

13. While some traits wane a bit after college, others
increase. For example, as young adults mature
and learn to manage their commitments,
_____ increases. From the thirties through the sixties, _____
increases.

14. In adulthood, the Big Five are quite
_____ (stable/variable), with
heritability estimated at _____
percent or more for each dimension. Moreover,
these traits _____ (describe/do
not describe) personality in other cultures and
_____ (predict/do not predict)
other personal attributes.

Objective 18: Summarize the person-situation controversy, and explain its importance as a commentary on the trait perspective.

15.   Human behavior is influenced both by our inner _____ and by the external _____ . The issue of which of these is the more important influence on personality is called the _____-_____ controversy.

16.   To be considered a personality trait, a characteristic must persist over _____ and across _____ . Research studies reveal that personality trait scores _____ (correlate/do not correlate) with scores obtained seven years later. The consistency of specific behaviors from one situation to the next is _____ (predictably consistent/not predictably consistent).

17.   An individual's score on a personality test _____ (is/is not) very predictive of his or her behavior in any given situation.

Objective 19: Explain why psychologists are interested in the consistency of the trait of expressiveness.

18.   People's expressive styles, which include their _____ , manner of _____ , and _____ , are quite _____ (consistent/inconsistent), which _____ (does/does not) reveal distinct personality traits.

Defend trait theory against the criticism that people seem not to have clear, consistent personalities.

The Social-Cognitive Perspective (pp. 623–631)

> If you do not know the meaning of any of the following words, phrases, or expressions in the context in which they appear in the text, refer to page 409 for an explanation: *cold shoulder; leaping a hurdle; put an optimistic spin on their setbacks; bombing the upcoming exam; dumbfounded.*

Objective 20: Describe the social-cognitive perspective, and explain how reciprocal determinism illustrates that perspective.

1.   Social-cognitive theory, which focuses on how the individual and the _____ interact, was proposed by _____ .

2.   Social-cognitive theorists propose that personality is shaped by the mutual influence of our _____ , _____ factors, and _____ factors. This is the principle of _____ _____ .

Describe three different ways in which the environment and personality interact.

Objective 21: Discuss the effects of a perception of internal or external control, and describe the concept of learned helplessness.

3.   In studying how we interact with our environment, social-cognitive theorists point to the importance of our sense of _____ _____ . Individuals who believe that they control their own destinies are said to perceive an _____ _____ _____ . Individuals who believe that their fate is determined by outside forces are said to perceive an _____ . _____ _____ _____ . Self-control, which is the ability to control _____ and _____ gratification, predicts good _____ , better _____ , and _____ success.

4.   Seligman found that exposure to inescapable punishment produced a passive resignation in behavior, which he called _____ _____ .

5. People become happier when they are given
_____ (more/less) control over
what happens to them.

Objective 22: Discuss the link between performance and optimistic or pessimistic attributional style, and contrast positive psychology with humanistic psychology.

6. One measure of a person's feelings of effectiveness is his or her degree of _____ .
Our characteristic manner of explaining negative and positive events is called our

_____ _____ .

7. Our natural positive-thinking bias can sometimes promote an _____
_____ about future life events that can be unhealthy.

8. (Close-Up) During its first century, psychology focused primarily on understanding and alleviating _____ _____ .
Today, however, thriving Western cultures have an opportunity to create a more _____ psychology, focused on three pillars:

   a. _____

   b. _____

   c. _____

9. Our natural positive thinking tends to vanish when we are about to face
_____ . People tend to be most overconfident of their abilities in areas where they are, in fact, most _____
(competent/incompetent).

Objective 23: Explain why social-cognitive researchers assess behavior in realistic situations.

10. It follows from the social-cognitive perspective that the best means of predicting people's future behavior is their _____

_____ .

Objective 24: State the major criticism of the social-cognitive perspective.

11. The major criticism of the social-cognitive perspective is that it fails to appreciate a person's

_____ _____ .

Exploring the Self (pp. 631–636)

If you do not know the meaning of any of the following words, phrases, or expressions in the context in which they appear in the text, refer to pages 409–410 for an explanation: *even after a blunder; negative about themselves; prowess; Lake Wobegon; flies in the face of pop psychology; pride does often go before a fall; swelled head; from fantasy to hogwash; put-downs.*

Objective 25: Explain why psychology has generated so much research on the self, and give three examples of current research on the self.

1. One of Western psychology's most vigorously researched topics today is the _____ .

2. Hazel Markus and colleagues introduced the concept of an individual's _____

_____ to emphasize how our aspirations motivate us through specific goals.

3. Our tendency to overestimate the extent to which others are noticing and evaluating us is called the

_____ _____ .

4. A third example of research on the self involves our ability to better recall information if we relate it to our own person or life, which is called the
_____ effect.

Objective 26: Give two alternative explanations for the positive correlation between low self-esteem and personal problems.

5. According to self theorists, personality development hinges on our feelings of self-worth, or
_____ . People who feel good about themselves are relatively
_____ (dependent on/independent of) outside pressures, while people who fall short of their ideals are more prone to
_____ and _____ .

6. People who are vulnerable to depression often feel they are falling short of their
_____ . Those vulnerable to anxiety often feel they are falling short of what they

_____ .

7. In a series of experiments, researchers found that people who were made to feel insecure were _____ (more/less) critical of other persons or tended to express heightened _____ _____ .

Objective 27: Discuss some ways that people maintain their self-esteem under conditions of discrimination or low status.

8. Research studies demonstrate that ethnic minorities, people with disabilities, and women generally _____ (have/do not have) lower self-esteem.

9. Members of stigmatized groups maintain self-esteem in three ways:

    a. _____

    b. _____

    c. _____

Objective 28: Discuss some evidence for self-serving bias, and contrast defensive and secure self-esteem.

10. Research has shown that most people tend to have _____ (low/high) self-esteem.

11. The tendency of people to judge themselves favorably is called the _____ bias.

12. Responsibility for success is generally accepted _____ (more/less) readily than responsibility for failure.

13. Most people perceive their own behavior and traits as being _____ (above/below) average.

14. Bushman and Baumeister found that students with unrealistically _____ (low/high) self-esteem were most likely to become exceptionally aggressive after criticism.

15. Some researchers distinguish _____ self-esteem, which is fragile and sensitive to _____ , from _____ self-esteem, which is less focused on _____ evaluations.

16. A number of psychologists have suggested that humans function best with modest self-enhancing _____ .

PROGRESS TEST 1

Multiple-Choice Questions

Circle your answers to the following questions and check them with the answers beginning on page 401. If your answer is incorrect, read the explanation for why it is incorrect and then consult the appropriate pages of the text (in parentheses following the correct answer).

1. The text defines *personality* as:
    a. the set of personal attitudes that characterizes a person.
    b. an individual's characteristic pattern of thinking, feeling, and acting.
    c. a predictable set of responses to environmental stimuli.
    d. an unpredictable set of responses to environmental stimuli.

2. Which of the following places the greatest emphasis on the unconscious mind?
    a. the humanistic perspective
    b. the social-cognitive perspective
    c. the trait perspective
    d. the psychoanalytic perspective

3. Which of the following is the correct order of psychosexual stages proposed by Freud?
    a. oral; anal; phallic; latency; genital
    b. anal; oral; phallic; latency; genital
    c. oral; anal; genital; latency; phallic
    d. anal; oral; genital; latency; phallic

4. According to Freud, defense mechanisms are methods of reducing:
    a. anger.   c. anxiety.
    b. fear.   d. lust.

5. Neo-Freudians such as Adler and Horney believed that:
    a. Freud placed too great an emphasis on the conscious mind.
    b. Freud placed too great an emphasis on sexual and aggressive instincts.
    c. the years of childhood were more important in the formation of personality than Freud had indicated.
    d. Freud's ideas about the id, ego, and superego as personality structures were incorrect.

6. Research on locus of control indicates that internals are _____ than externals.
   a. more dependent
   b. more intelligent
   c. better able to cope with stress
   d. more sociable

7. Which two dimensions of personality have the Eysencks emphasized?
   a. extraversion–introversion and emotional stability–instability
   b. internal–external locus of control and extraversion–introversion
   c. internal–external locus of control and emotional stability–instability
   d. melancholic–phlegmatic and choleric–sanguine

8. With regard to personality, it appears that:
   a. there is little consistency of behavior from one situation to the next and little consistency of traits over the life span.
   b. there is little consistency of behavior from one situation to the next but significant consistency of traits over the life span.
   c. there is significant consistency of behavior from one situation to the next but little consistency of traits over the life span.
   d. there is significant consistency of behavior from one situation to the next and significant consistency of traits over the life span.

9. The humanistic perspective on personality:
   a. emphasizes the driving force of unconscious motivations in personality.
   b. emphasizes the growth potential of "healthy" individuals.
   c. emphasizes the importance of interaction with the environment in shaping personality.
   d. describes personality in terms of scores on various personality scales.

10. According to Rogers, three conditions are necessary to promote growth in personality. These are:
    a. honesty, sincerity, and empathy.
    b. high self-esteem, honesty, and empathy.
    c. high self-esteem, genuineness, and acceptance.
    d. genuineness, acceptance, and empathy.

11. Regarding the self-serving bias, psychologists who study the self have found that self-affirming thinking:
    a. is generally maladaptive to the individual because it distorts reality by overinflating self-esteem.
    b. is generally adaptive to the individual because it maintains self-confidence and minimizes depression.
    c. tends to prevent the individual from viewing others with compassion and understanding.
    d. tends *not* to characterize people who have experienced unconditional positive regard.

12. Which of Freud's ideas would *not* be accepted by most contemporary psychologists?
    a. Development is essentially fixed in childhood.
    b. Sexuality is a potent drive in humans.
    c. The mind is an iceberg with consciousness being only the tip.
    d. Repression can be the cause of forgetting.

13. Projective tests such as the Rorschach inkblot test have been criticized because:
    a. their scoring system is too rigid and leads to unfair labeling.
    b. they were standardized with unrepresentative samples.
    c. they have low reliability and low validity.
    d. it is easy for people to fake answers in order to appear healthy.

14. A major criticism of trait theory is that it:
    a. places too great an emphasis on early childhood experiences.
    b. overestimates the consistency of behavior in different situations.
    c. underestimates the importance of heredity in personality development.
    d. places too great an emphasis on positive traits.

15. For humanistic psychologists, many of our behaviors and perceptions are ultimately shaped by whether our _____ is _____ or _____ .
    a. ego; strong; weak
    b. locus of control; internal; external
    c. personality structure; introverted; extraverted
    d. self-concept; positive; negative

16. In studying personality, a trait theorist would *most likely*:
    a. use a projective test.
    b. observe a person in a variety of situations.
    c. use a personality inventory.
    d. use the method of free association.

17. Id is to ego as _____ is to _____ .
    a. reality principle; pleasure principle
    b. pleasure principle; reality principle
    c. conscious forces; unconscious forces
    d. conscience; "personality executive"

18. Which of the following is the major criticism of the social-cognitive perspective?

a. It focuses too much on early childhood experiences.

b. It focuses too little on the inner traits of a person.

c. It provides descriptions but not explanations.

d. It lacks appropriate assessment techniques.

19. Recent research has provided more support for defense mechanisms such as _____ than for defense mechanisms such as _____ .

a. displacement; reaction formation

b. reaction formation; displacement

c. displacement; regression

d. displacement; projection

20. Today's personality researchers focus their work on:

a. basic dimensions of personality.

b. the interaction of persons and environments.

c. grand theories of behavior.

d. a. and b.

Matching Items

Match each definition or description with the appropriate term.

Definitions or Descriptions

_____ **1.** redirecting impulses to a less threatening object

_____ **2.** test consisting of a series of inkblots

_____ **3.** the conscious executive of personality

_____ **4.** personality inventory

_____ **5.** disguising an impulse by imputing it to another person

_____ **6.** switching an unacceptable impulse into its opposite

_____ **7.** the unconscious repository of instinctual drives

_____ **8.** a statistical technique that identifies clusters of personality traits

_____ **9.** personality structure that corresponds to a person's conscience

_____ **10.** providing self-justifying explanations for an action

_____ **11.** a projective test consisting of a set of ambiguous pictures

Terms

a. id

b. ego

c. superego

d. reaction formation

e. rationalization

f. displacement

g. factor analysis

h. projection

i. TAT

j. Rorschach

k. MMPI

PROGRESS TEST 2

Progress Test 2 should be completed during a final chapter review. Answer the following questions after you thoroughly understand the correct answers for the section reviews and Progress Test 1.

Multiple-Choice Questions

1. Which perspective on personality emphasizes the interaction between the individual and the environment in shaping personality?
   a. psychoanalytic
   c. humanistic
   b. trait
   d. social-cognitive

2. According to Freud's theory, personality arises in response to conflicts between:
   a. our unacceptable urges and our tendency to become self-actualized.
   b. the process of identification and the ego's defense mechanisms.
   c. the collective unconscious and our individual desires.
   d. our biological impulses and the social restraints against them.

3. The _____ classifies people according to Carl Jung's personality types.
   a. Myers-Briggs Type Indicator
   b. MMPI
   c. Locus of Control Scale
   d. Kagan Temperament Scale

4. Seligman has found that humans and animals who are exposed to aversive events they cannot escape may develop:
   a. an internal locus of control.
   b. a reaction formation.
   c. learned helplessness.
   d. neurotic anxiety.

5. Research has shown that individuals who are made to feel insecure are subsequently:
   a. more critical of others.
   b. less critical of others.
   c. more likely to display a self-serving bias.
   d. less likely to display a self-serving bias.

6. An example of the self-serving bias described in the text is the tendency of people to:
   a. see themselves as better than average on nearly any desirable dimension.
   b. accept more responsibility for successes than failures.
   c. be overly critical of other people.
   d. do both a. and b.

7. The Minnesota Multiphasic Personality Inventory (MMPI) is a(n):
   a. projective personality test.
   b. empirically derived and objective personality test.
   c. personality test developed mainly to assess job applicants.
   d. personality test used primarily to assess locus of control.

8. Trait theory attempts to:
   a. show how development of personality is a lifelong process.
   b. describe and classify people in terms of their predispositions to behave in certain ways.
   c. determine which traits are most conducive to individual self-actualization.
   d. explain how behavior is shaped by the interaction between traits, behavior, and the environment.

9. With which of the following statements would a social-cognitive psychologist agree?
   a. People with an internal locus of control achieve more in school.
   b. "Externals" are better able to cope with stress than "internals."
   c. "Internals" are less independent than "externals."
   d. All of the above are true.

10. Which of the following statements about self-esteem is *not* correct?
    a. People with low self-esteem tend to be negative about others.
    b. People with high self-esteem are less prone to drug addiction.
    c. People with low self-esteem tend to be non-conformists.
    d. People with high self-esteem suffer less from insomnia.

11. The Oedipus and Electra complexes have their roots in the:
    a. anal stage.
    c. latency stage.
    b. oral stage.
    d. phallic stage.

12. Which of the following is a common criticism of the humanistic perspective?
    a. Its concepts are vague and subjective.
    b. The emphasis on the self encourages selfishness in individuals.
    c. Humanism fails to appreciate the reality of evil in human behavior.
    d. All of the above are common criticisms.

13. In studying personality, a social-cognitive theorist would *most likely* make use of:
    a. personality inventories.
    b. projective tests.
    c. observing behavior in different situations.
    d. factor analyses.

14. A major difference between the psychoanalytic and trait perspectives is that:
    a. trait theory defines personality in terms of behavior; psychoanalytic theory, in terms of its underlying dynamics.
    b. trait theory describes behavior but does not attempt to explain it.
    c. psychoanalytic theory emphasizes the origins of personality in childhood sexuality.
    d. all of the above are differences.

15. The Big Five personality factors are:
    a. emotional stability, openness, introversion, sociability, locus of control.
    b. neuroticism, extraversion, openness, emotional stability, sensitivity.
    c. neuroticism, gregariousness, extraversion, impulsiveness, conscientiousness.
    d. emotional stability, extraversion, openness, agreeableness, conscientiousness.

16. Which of the following was *not* mentioned in the text as a criticism of Freud's theory?
    a. The theory is sexist.
    b. It offers few testable hypotheses.

    c. There is no evidence of anything like an "unconscious."
    d. The theory ignores the fact that human development is lifelong.

17. According to Freud, _____ is the process by which children incorporate their parents' values into their _____ .
    a. reaction formation; superegos
    b. reaction formation; egos
    c. identification; superegos
    d. identification; egos

18. Which of the following groups tend to suffer from relatively low self-esteem?
    a. women
    b. ethnic minorities
    c. disabled persons
    d. none of the above

19. In promoting personality growth, the person-centered perspective emphasizes all but:
    a. empathy.   c. genuineness.
    b. acceptance.   d. altruism.

20. Recent research on the Big Five personality factors provides evidence that:
    a. some tendencies decrease during adulthood, while others increase.
    b. these traits only describe personality in Western, individualist cultures.
    c. the heritability of individual differences in these traits generally runs about 25 percent or less.
    d. all of the above are true.

Matching Items

Match each term with the appropriate definition or description.

Terms

_____ 1. projective test
_____ 2. identification
_____ 3. collective unconscious
_____ 4. reality principle
_____ 5. psychosexual stages
_____ 6. pleasure principle
_____ 7. empirically derived test
_____ 8. reciprocal determinism
_____ 9. personality inventory
_____ 10. Oedipus complex
_____ 11. preconscious

Definitions or Descriptions

a. the id's demand for immediate gratification
b. a boy's sexual desires toward the opposite-sex parent
c. information that is retrievable but currently not in conscious awareness
d. stages of development proposed by Freud
e. questionnaire used to assess personality traits
f. the two-way interactions of behavior with personal and environmental factors
g. personality test that provides ambiguous stimuli
h. the repository of universal memories proposed by Jung
i. the process by which children incorporate their parents' values into their developing superegos
j. the process by which the ego seeks to gratify impulses of the id in nondestructive ways
k. developed by testing a pool of items and then selecting those that discriminate the group of interest

PSYCHOLOGY APPLIED

Answer these questions the day before an exam as a final check on your understanding of the chapter's terms and concepts.

Multiple-Choice Questions

1. Professor Minton believes that people strive to find meaning in life because they are terrified of their own mortality. Evidently, Professor Minton is a proponent of:
   a. terror-management theory.
   b. psychodynamic theory.
   c. the humanistic perspective.
   d. the social-cognitive perspective.

2. A psychoanalyst would characterize a person who is impulsive and self-indulgent as possessing a strong _____ and a weak _____ .
   a. id and ego; superego
   b. id; ego and superego
   c. ego; superego
   d. id; superego

3. Because Ramona identifies with her politically conservative parents, she chose to enroll in a conservative college. After four years in this environment Ramona's politics have become even more conservative. Which perspective best accounts for the mutual influences of Ramona's upbringing, choice of school, and political viewpoint?
   a. psychoanalytic
   b. trait
   c. humanistic
   d. social-cognitive

4. Jill has a biting, sarcastic manner. According to Freud, she is:
   a. projecting her anxiety onto others.
   b. fixated in the oral stage of development.
   c. fixated in the anal stage of development.
   d. displacing her anxiety onto others.

5. James attributes his failing grade in chemistry to an unfair final exam. His attitude exemplifies:
   a. internal locus of control.
   b. unconditional positive regard.
   c. the self-serving bias.
   d. reciprocal determinism.

6. The behavior of many people has been described in terms of a *spotlight effect.* This means that they
   a. tend to see themselves as being above average in ability.
   b. perceive that their fate is determined by forces not under their personal control.
   c. overestimate the extent to which other people are noticing them.
   d. do all of the above.

7. Because you have a relatively low level of brain arousal, a trait theorist would suggest that you are a(n) _____ who would naturally seek _____ .
   a. introvert; stimulation
   b. introvert; isolation
   c. extravert; stimulation
   d. extravert; isolation

8. A psychologist at the campus mental health center administered an empirically derived personality test to diagnose an emotionally troubled student. Which test did the psychologist *most likely* administer?
   a. the MMPI
   b. the TAT
   c. the Rorschach
   d. the Locus of Control Scale

9. The personality test Teresa is taking involves her describing random patterns of dots. What type of test is she taking?
   a. an empirically derived test
   b. the MMPI
   c. a personality inventory
   d. a projective test

10. Dr. Gonzalez believes that most students can be classified as "Type A" or "Type B" according to the intensities of their personalities and competitiveness. Evidently, Dr. Gonzalez is working within the _____ perspective.
    a. psychoanalytic   c. humanistic
    b. trait   d. social-cognitive

11. According to the psychoanalytic perspective, a child who frequently "slips" and calls her teacher "mom" *probably*:
    a. has some unresolved conflicts concerning her mother.
    b. is fixated in the oral stage of development.
    c. did not receive unconditional positive regard from her mother.
    d. can be classified as having a weak sense of personal control.

12. Isaiah is sober and reserved; Rashid is fun-loving and affectionate. The Eysencks would say that Isaiah _____ and Rashid _____ .
    a. has an internal locus of control; has an external locus of control
    b. has an external locus of control; has an internal locus of control
    c. is an extravert; is an introvert
    d. is an introvert; is an extravert

13. In high school, Britta and Debbie were best friends. They thought they were a lot alike, as did everyone else who knew them. After high school, they went on to very different colleges, careers, and life courses. Now, at their twenty-fifth reunion, they are shocked at how little they have in common. Bandura would suggest that their differences reflect the interactive effects of environment, personality, and behavior, which he refers to as:
    a. reciprocal determinism.
    b. personal control.
    c. identification.
    d. the self-serving bias.

14. For his class presentation, Bruce plans to discuss the Big Five personality factors used by people throughout the world to describe others or themselves. Which of the following is *not* a factor that Bruce will discuss?
    a. extraversion   c. independence
    b. openness   d. conscientiousness

15. Dayna is not very consistent in showing up for class and turning in assignments when they are due. Research studies would suggest that Dayna's inconsistent behavior:
    a. indicates that she is emotionally troubled and may need professional counseling.
    b. is a sign of learned helplessness.
    c. is not necessarily unusual.
    d. probably reflects a temporary problem in another area of her life.

16. Andrew's grandfather, who has lived a rich and productive life, is a spontaneous, loving, and self-accepting person. Maslow might say that he:
    a. has an internal locus of control.
    b. is an extravert.
    c. has resolved all the conflicts of the psychosexual stages.
    d. is a self-actualizing person.

17. The school psychologist believes that having a positive self-concept is necessary before students can achieve their potential. Evidently, the school psychologist is working within the _____ perspective.
    a. psychoanalytic   c. humanistic
    b. trait   d. social-cognitive

18. Wanda wishes to instill in her children an accepting attitude toward other people. Maslow and Rogers would probably recommend that she:
    a. teach her children first to accept themselves.
    b. use discipline sparingly.
    c. be affectionate with her children only when they behave as she wishes.
    d. do all of the above.

19. Suzy bought a used, high-mileage automobile because it was all she could afford. Attempting to justify her purchase, she raves to her friends about the car's attractiveness, good acceleration, and stereo. According to Freud, Suzy is using the defense mechanism of:
    a. displacement.   c. rationalization.
    b. reaction formation.   d. projection.

20. Nadine has a relatively high level of brain arousal. Trait theorists would probably predict that she is:
    a. an extravert.   c. an unstable person.
    b. an introvert.   d. both a. and c.

21. (Close-Up) During a class discussion, Trevor argues that "positive psychology" is sure to wane in popularity, since it suffers from the same criticisms as humanistic psychology. You counter his argument by pointing out that, unlike humanistic psychology, positive psychology:
    a. focuses on advancing human fulfillment.
    b. is rooted in science.
    c. is not based on the study of individual characteristics.
    d. has all of the above characteristics.

Essay Question

You are an honest, open, and responsible person. Discuss how these characteristics would be explained according to the major perspectives on personality. (Use the space below to list points you want to make, and organize them. Then write the essay on a separate piece of paper.)

KEY TERMS

Writing Definitions

Using your own words, on a separate piece of paper write a brief definition or explanation of each of the following terms.

1. personality
2. free association
3. psychoanalysis
4. unconscious
5. id
6. ego
7. superego
8. psychosexual stages
9. Oedipus complex
10. identification
11. fixation
12. defense mechanisms
13. repression
14. regression
15. reaction formation
16. projection
17. rationalization

18. displacement
19. collective unconscious
20. projective tests
21. Thematic Apperception Test (TAT)
22. Rorschach inkblot test
23. terror-management theory
24. self-actualization
25. unconditional positive regard
26. self-concept
27. traits
28. personality inventory
29. Minnesota Multiphasic Personality Inventory (MMPI)

30. empirically derived test
31. social-cognitive perspective
32. reciprocal determinism
33. personal control
34. external locus of control
35. internal locus of control
36. learned helplessness
37. positive psychology
38. spotlight effect
39. self-esteem
40. self-serving bias

Cross-Check

As you learned in the Prologue, reviewing and overlearning of material are important to the learning process. After you have written the definitions of the key terms in this chapter, you should complete the crossword puzzle to ensure that you can reverse the process—recognize the term, given the definition.

ACROSS

4. In Freud's theory, the area of the unconscious containing material that is retrievable into conscious awareness.
7. Locus of control that reflects the belief that one's fate is determined by forces not under personal control.
10. In Freud's theory, the personality system consisting of basic sexual and aggressive drives.
11. A person's characteristic pattern of behavior.
12. In Freud's theory, the conscious division of personality.
13. The ego's methods of unconsciously protecting itself against anxiety.

DOWN

1. Defense mechanism in which an impulse is shifted to an object other than the one that originally aroused the impulse.

2. The passive resignation a person or animal develops from repeated exposure to inescapable aversive events.

3. According to Freud, _____ occurs when development becomes arrested in an immature psychosexual stage.

4. An individual's characteristic pattern of thinking, feeling, and acting.

5. In Freud's theory, the complex developed by boys in which they are sexually attracted to their mother and resent their father.

6. In Freud's theory, the process by which the child's superego develops and incorporates the parents' values.

8. Projective test consisting of ambiguous pictures about which people are asked to make up stories.

9. A widely used test in which people are asked to interpret 10 inkblots.

14. The most widely used personality inventory.

ANSWERS

Chapter Review

Introducing Personality

1. thinking; feeling; acting
2. Sigmund Freud; humanistic; growth; self-fulfillment
3. focused

The Psychoanalytic Perspective

1. nervous
2. neurological
3. hypnosis
4. free association
5. psychoanalysis
6. unconscious; preconscious; repressed
7. unconscious; slips; manifest content; latent content
8. biological; social
9. id; ego; superego
10. unconscious; pleasure
11. after; conscious; reality

The ego is considered the executive of personality because it directs our actions as it intervenes among the impulsive demands of the id, the reality of the external world, and the ideals of the superego.

12. superego; 4 or 5
13. weak; strong
14. psychosexual; erogenous zones
15. oral; sucking (also biting, chewing)

16. anal; 18; 36
17. phallic; 3; 6; genitals; opposite; Oedipus complex; Electra complex
18. identification; gender identity

Children eventually cope with their feelings for the opposite-sex parent by repressing them and by identifying with the rival (same-sex) parent. Through this process children incorporate many of their parents' values, thereby strengthening the superego.

19. latency
20. genital
21. fixated; expulsive; retentive
22. defense mechanisms; repression
23. regression
24. reaction formation
25. projection
26. rationalization
27. displacement

Matching Items

1. e
2. d
3. b
4. c
5. a

28. unconscious
29. neo-Freudians; more; less

a. Adler emphasized the social, rather than the sexual, tensions of childhood and said that much of behavior is driven by the need to overcome feelings of inferiority.

b. Horney questioned the male bias in Freud's theory, such as the assumptions that women have weak egos and suffer "penis envy." Like Adler, she emphasized social tensions.

c. Jung emphasized an inherited collective unconscious.

30. reject; Jung; collective unconscious
31. psychodynamic; sex; unconscious; childhood; inner conflicts
32. projective
33. Thematic Apperception
34. Rorschach; inkblots; little; is not; are not
35. lifelong; earlier; is not
36. wishes; sexual; aggressive; sexual suppression
37. represses; rarer; trauma

38. unconscious; nonconscious; implicit learning

39. anxiety; terror-management; self-esteem; world-views

40. projection; false consensus; overestimate

41. after-the-fact; testable predictions

Freud drew attention to the unconscious and the irrational, to human defenses against anxiety, to the importance of human sexuality, to the tension between our biological impulses and our social well-being, and to our potential for evil.

The Humanistic Perspective

1. Maslow; Rogers

2. hierarchy; self-actualization; self-determination

For Maslow, such people were self-aware, self-accepting, open, spontaneous, loving, caring, not paralyzed by others' opinions, secure, and problem-centered rather than self-centered.

3. genuine; accepting; empathic

4. unconditional positive regard; spontaneous

5. self-concept

6. questionnaires; self-concept

7. ideally; actually

8. dehumanizing; interviews

9. counseling; education; child-rearing; management; popular; Western

10. high

Three criticisms of humanistic psychology are that its concepts are vague and subjective; the individualism it encourages can lead to self-indulgence, selfishness, and an erosion of moral restraints; and it fails to appreciate the human capacity for evil.

The Trait Perspective

1. behaviors; motives; explaining; describing

2. melancholic; sanguine; phlegmatic; choleric

3. Myers-Briggs Type Indicator; business; career

4. factor analysis; extraversion–introversion; stability–instability

5. brain arousal; frontal; extraverts; introverts

6. genes; temperament; behavioral

7. shyness; inhibition

8. are

9. personality inventories

10. Minnesota Multiphasic Personality Inventory; 10

11. empirically

Astrologers use a "stock spiel" that includes information that is generally true of almost everyone. The willingness of people to accept this type of phony information is called the "Barnum effect." A second technique used by astrologers is to "read" a person's clothing, features, reactions, etc. and build their advice from these observations.

12. a. Emotional stability: on a continuum from calm to anxious; secure to insecure
    b. Extraversion: from sociable to retiring
    c. Openness: from preference for variety to routine
    d. Agreeableness: from soft-hearted to ruthless
    e. Conscientiousness: from disciplined to impulsive

13. conscientiousness; agreeableness

14. stable; 50; describe; predict

15. traits (or dispositions); situation (or environment); person-situation

16. time; situations; correlate; not predictably consistent

17. is not

18. animation; speaking; gestures; consistent; does

At any given moment a person's behavior is powerfully influenced by the immediate situation, so that it may appear that the person does not have a consistent personality. But averaged over many situations a person's outgoingness, happiness, and carelessness, for instance, are more predictable.

The Social-Cognitive Perspective

1. environment; Bandura

2. behaviors; personal/cognitive; environmental; reciprocal determinism

Different people choose different environments partly on the basis of their dispositions. Our personality shapes how we interpret and react to events. It also helps create the situations to which we react.

3. personal control; internal locus of control; external locus of control; impulses; delay; adjustment; grades; social

4. learned helplessness

5. more

6. optimism; attributional style

7. unrealistic (illusory) optimism

8. negative states; positive
    a. positive emotions
    b. positive character
    c. positive groups, communities, and cultures

9. feedback; incompetent

10. past behavior in similar situations

11. inner traits

Exploring the Self

1. self

2. possible selves

3. spotlight effect

4. self-reference

5. self-esteem; independent of; anxiety; depression

6. hopes; think they ought to be

7. more; racial prejudice

8. do not have

9. **a.** They value the things at which they excel.
   b. They attribute problems to prejudice.
   c. They compare themselves to those in their own group.

10. high

11. self-serving

12. more

13. above

14. high

15. defensive; criticism; secure; external

16. illusions

Progress Test 1

Multiple-Choice Questions

1. **b.** is the answer. Personality is defined as patterns of response—of thinking, feeling, and acting—that are relatively consistent across a variety of situations. (p. 595)

2. **d.** is the answer. (p. 597)
   a. & b. Conscious processes are the focus of these perspectives.
   c. The trait perspective focuses on the description of behaviors.

3. **a.** is the answer. (p. 599)

4. **c.** is the answer. According to Freud, defense mechanisms reduce anxiety unconsciously, by disguising one's threatening impulses. (pp. 599–600)
   a., b., & d. Unlike these specific emotions, anxiety need not be focused. Defense mechanisms help us cope when we are unsettled but are not sure why.

5. **b.** is the answer. (p. 601)
   a. According to most neo-Freudians, Freud placed too great an emphasis on the *unconscious* mind.

   c. Freud placed great emphasis on early childhood, and the neo-Freudians basically agreed with him.
   d. The neo-Freudians accepted Freud's ideas about the basic personality structures.

6. **c.** is the answer. (p. 625)
   a. & d. In fact, just the opposite is true.
   b. Locus of control is not related to intelligence.

7. **a.** is the answer. (p. 614)
   b. & c. Locus of control is emphasized by the social-cognitive perspective.
   d. This is how the ancient Greeks described personality.

8. **b.** is the answer. Studies have shown that people do not act with predictable consistency from one situation to the next. But, over a number of situations, consistent patterns emerge, and this basic consistency of traits persists over the life span. (p. 620)

9. **b.** is the answer. (p. 609)
   a. This is true of the psychoanalytic perspective.
   c. This is true of the social-cognitive perspective.
   d. This is true of the trait perspective.

10. **d.** is the answer. (p. 610)

11. **b.** is the answer. Psychologists who study the self emphasize that for the individual, self-affirming thinking is generally adaptive (therefore, not a.); such thinking maintains self-confidence, minimizes depression, and enables us to view others with compassion and understanding (therefore, not c.); unconditional positive regard tends to promote self-esteem and thus self-affirming thinking (therefore, not d.). (p. 634)

12. **a.** is the answer. Developmental research indicates that development is lifelong. (p. 604)
   b., c., & d. To varying degrees, research has partially supported these Freudian ideas.

13. **c.** is the answer. As scoring is largely subjective and the tests have not been very successful in predicting behavior, their reliability and validity have been called into question. (p. 603)
   a. This is untrue.
   b. Unlike empirically derived personality tests, projective tests are not standardized.
   d. Although this may be true, it was not mentioned as a criticism of projective tests.

14. **b.** is the answer. In doing so, it underestimates the influence of the environment. (pp. 619–620)
   a. The trait perspective does not emphasize early childhood experiences.

c. This criticism is unlikely since trait theory does not seek to explain personality development.

d. Trait theory does not look on traits as being "positive" or "negative."

15. **d.** is the answer. (p. 610)

a. & c. Personality structure is a concern of the psychoanalytic perspective.

b. Locus of control is a major focus of the social-cognitive perspective.

16. **c.** is the answer. (p. 615)

a. & d. A psychoanalytic theorist would be most likely to use a projective test or free association.

b. This would most likely be the approach taken by a social-cognitive theorist.

17. **b.** is the answer. In Freud's theory, the id operates according to the pleasure principle; the ego operates according to the reality principle. (p. 598)

c. The id is presumed to be unconscious.

d. The superego is, according to Freud, the equivalent of a conscience; the ego is the "personality executive."

18. **b.** is the answer. The social-cognitive theory has been accused of putting so much emphasis on the situation that inner traits are neglected. (p. 630)

a. Such a criticism has been made of the psychoanalytic perspective but is not relevant to the social-cognitive perspective.

c. Such a criticism might be more relevant to the trait perspective; the social-cognitive perspective offers an explanation in the form of reciprocal determinism.

d. There are assessment techniques appropriate to the theory, namely, questionnaires and observations of behavior in situations.

19. **b.** is the answer. (p. 606)

a., c., & d. The evidence supports defenses that defend self-esteem, rather than those that are tied to instinctual energy.

20. **d.** is the answer. (p. 623)

Matching Items

1. f (p. 600)
2. j (p. 602)
3. b (p. 598)
4. k (p. 616)
5. h (p. 600)
6. d (p. 600)
7. a (p. 598)
8. g (p. 614)
9. c (p. 598)
10. e (p. 600)
11. i (p. 602)

Progress Test 2

Multiple-Choice Questions

1. **d.** is the answer. (p. 623)

a. This perspective emphasizes unconscious dynamics in personality.

b. This perspective is more concerned with *describing* than *explaining* personality.

c. This perspective emphasizes the healthy, self-actualizing tendencies of personality.

2. **d.** is the answer. (p. 598)

a. Self-actualization is a concept of the humanistic perspective.

b. Through identification, children *reduce* conflicting feelings as they incorporate their parents' values.

c. Jung, rather than Freud, proposed the concept of the collective unconscious.

3. **a.** is the answer. (p. 613)

4. **c.** is the answer. In such situations, passive resignation, called learned helplessness, develops. (p. 602)

a. This refers to the belief that one controls one's fate; the circumstances described lead to precisely the opposite belief.

b. Reaction formation is a defense mechanism in which unacceptable impulses are channeled into their opposites.

d. Seligman did not specify that neurotic anxiety occurs.

5. **a.** is the answer. Feelings of insecurity reduce self-esteem, and those who feel negative about themselves tend to feel negative about others as well. (p. 625)

6. **d.** is the answer. (p. 633)

7. **b.** is the answer. The MMPI was developed by selecting from many items those that differentiated between the groups of interest; hence, it was empirically derived. That it is an objective test is shown by the fact that it can be scored by computer. (pp. 616, 617)

a. Projective tests present ambiguous stimuli for people to interpret; the MMPI is a questionnaire.

c. Although sometimes used to assess job applicants, the MMPI was developed to assess emotionally troubled people.

d. The MMPI does not focus on control but, rather, measures various aspects of personality.

8. **b.** is the answer. Trait theory attempts to describe behavior and not to develop explanations or applications. The emphasis is more on consistency than on change. (p. 613)

9. **a.** is the answer. "Internals," or those who have a sense of personal control, have been shown to achieve more in school. Relative to externals, they also cope better with stress and are more independent. (p. 625)

10. c. is the answer. In actuality, people with *high* self-esteem are generally more independent of pressures to conform. (p. 632)

11. d. is the answer. (p. 599)

12. d. is the answer. (pp. 611–612)

13. c. is the answer. In keeping with their emphasis on interactions between people and situations, social-cognitive theorists would most likely make use of observations of behavior in relevant situations. (p. 629)
a. & d. Personality inventories and factor analyses would more likely be used by a trait theorist.
b. Projective tests would more likely be used by a psychologist working within the psychoanalytic perspective.

14. d. is the answer. Trait theory defines personality in terms of behavior and is therefore interested in describing behavior; psychoanalytic theory defines personality as dynamics underlying behavior and therefore is interested in explaining behavior in terms of these dynamics. (pp. 598, 613)

15. d. is the answer. (p. 618)

16. c. is the answer. Although many researchers think of the unconscious as information processing without awareness rather than as a reservoir of repressed information, they agree with Freud that we do indeed have limited access to all that goes on in our minds. (p. 605)

17. c. is the answer. (p. 599)
a. & b. Reaction formation is the defense mechanism by which people transform unacceptable impulses into their opposites.
d. It is the superego, rather than the ego, that represents parental values.

18. d. is the answer. (p. 633)

19. d. is the answer. (p. 610)

20. a. is the answer. Neuroticism, extraversion, and openness tend to decrease, while agreeableness and conscientiousness tend to increase. (p. 619)

b. The Big Five dimensions describe personality in various cultures reasonably well.

c. Heritability generally runs 50 percent or more for each dimension.

Matching Items

1. g (p. 602)	**5.** d (p. 598)	**9.** e (p. 615)
2. i (p. 599)	**6.** a (p. 598)	**10.** b (p. 599)
3. h (p. 601)	**7.** k (p. 617)	**11.** c (p. 597)
4. j (p. 598)	**8.** f (p. 623)	

Psychology Applied

Multiple-Choice Questions

1. a. is the answer. (p. 606)
b., c., & d. None of these theories or perspectives offers any particular explanation of this tendency.

2. d. is the answer. Impulsiveness is the mark of a strong id; self-indulgence is the mark of a weak superego. Because the ego serves to mediate the demands of the id, the superego, and the outside world, its strength or weakness is judged by its decision-making ability, not by the character of the decision—so the ego is not relevant to the question asked. (p. 598)

3. d. is the answer. The social-cognitive perspective emphasizes the reciprocal influences between people and their situations. In this example, Ramona's parents (situational factor) helped shape her political beliefs (internal factor), which influenced her choice of colleges (situational factor) and created an environment that fostered her predisposed political attitudes. (p. 623)

4. b. is the answer. Sarcasm is said to be an attempt to deny the passive dependence characteristic of the oral stage. (p. 599)
a. A person who is projecting attributes his or her own feelings to others.
c. Such a person might be either messy and disorganized or highly controlled and compulsively neat.
d. Displacement involves diverting aggressive or sexual impulses onto a more acceptable object than that which aroused them.

5. c. is the answer. (p. 634)
a. A person with an internal locus of control would be likely to *accept* responsibility for a failing grade.
b. Unconditional positive regard is an attitude of total acceptance directed toward others.
d. Reciprocal determinism refers to the mutual influences among personality, environment, and behavior.

6. c. is the answer. (p. 632)
a. This describes the self-serving bias.
b. This describes external locus of control.

7. c. is the answer. (p. 615)
a. & b. According to this theory, introverts have relatively *high* levels of arousal, causing them to crave solitude.
d. Isolation might lower arousal level even further.

8. **a.** is the answer. (pp. 616, 617)
    b. & c. The TAT and Rorschach are projective tests that were not empirically derived.
    d. A personality test that measures locus of control would not be helpful in identifying troubled behaviors.

9. **d.** is the answer. Projective tests provide ambiguous stimuli, such as random dot patterns, in an attempt to trigger in the test-taker projection of his or her personality. (p. 602)

10. **b.** is the answer. (p. 613)
    a. The psychoanalytic perspective emphasizes unconscious processes in personality dynamics.
    c. The humanistic perspective emphasizes each person's potential for healthy growth and self-actualization.
    d. The social-cognitive perspective emphasizes the reciprocal influences of personality and environment.

11. **a.** is the answer. Freud believed that dreams and such slips of the tongue reveal unconscious conflicts. (p. 597)
    b. A person fixated in the oral stage might have a sarcastic personality; this child's slip of the tongue reveals nothing about her psychosexual development.
    c. & d. Unconditional positive regard and personal control are not psychoanalytic concepts.

12. **d.** is the answer. (p. 614)
    a. & b. The traits of Isaiah and Rashid reveal nothing about their sense of personal control.

13. **a.** is the answer. Reciprocal determinism refers to the mutual influences among personal factors, environmental factors, and behavior. (p. 623)
    b. Personal control is one's sense of controlling, or being controlled by, the environment.
    c. In Freud's theory, identification is the process by which children incorporate parental values into their developing superegos.
    d. The self-serving bias describes our readiness to perceive ourselves favorably.

14. **c.** is the answer. (p. 618)

15. **c.** is the answer. (p. 620)

16. **d.** is the answer. (p. 609)
    a. & b. These are concepts used by trait theorists rather than humanistic theorists such as Maslow.
    c. This reflects Freud's viewpoint.

17. **c.** is the answer. (p. 610)
    a., b., & d. The self-concept is not relevant to the psychoanalytic, trait, or social-cognitive perspectives.

18. **a.** is the answer. (p. 610)
    b. The text does not discuss the impact of discipline on personality.
    c. This would constitute *conditional*, rather than unconditional, positive regard and would likely cause the children to be *less* accepting of themselves and others.

19. **c.** is the answer. Suzy is trying to justify her purchase by generating (inaccurate) explanations for her behavior. (p. 600)
    a. Displacement is the redirecting of impulses toward an object other than the one responsible for them.
    b. Reaction formation is the transformation of unacceptable impulses into their opposites.
    d. Projection is the attribution of one's own unacceptable thoughts and feelings to others.

20. **b.** is the answer. Introverts do not need to seek stimulation because their normal level of brain arousal is already high. (p. 615)
    c. Nadine's high level of brain arousal might imply instability but not necessarily so.

21. **b.** is the answer. (p. 628)
    a. Both positive psychology and humanistic psychology focus on advancing human fulfillment.
    c. Both perspectives focus, at least partly, on individual characteristics.

Essay Question

Since you are apparently in good psychological health, according to the psychoanalytic perspective you must have experienced a healthy childhood and successfully passed Freud's stages of psychosexual development. Freud would also say that your ego is functioning well in balancing the demands of your id with the restraining demands of your superego and reality. Freud might also say that your honest nature reflects a well-developed superego, while Jung might say it derives from a universal value found in our collective unconscious.

According to the humanistic perspective, your open and honest nature indicates that your basic needs have been met and you are in the process of self-actualization (Maslow). Furthermore, your openness indicates that you have a healthy self-concept and were likely nurtured by genuine, accepting, and empathic caregivers (Rogers). More recently, researchers who emphasize the self would also focus on the importance of a positive self-concept.

Trait theorists would be less concerned with explaining these specific characteristics than with describing them, determining their consistency, and classifying your personality type. Some trait theorists, such as Allport, Eysenck, and Kagan, attribute certain trait differences to biological factors such as autonomic reactivity and heredity.

According to the social-cognitive perspective, your personal/cognitive factors, behavior, and environmental influences interacted in shaping your personality and behaviors. The fact that you are a responsible person indicates that you perceive yourself as controlling, rather than as controlled by, your environment.

KEY TERMS

Writing Definitions

1. **Personality** is an individual's characteristic pattern of thinking, feeling, and acting. (p. 595)

2. **Free association** is the Freudian technique in which the person is encouraged to say whatever comes to mind as a means of exploring the unconscious. (p. 597)

3. In Freud's theory, **psychoanalysis** refers to the treatment of psychological disorders by seeking to expose and interpret the tensions within a patient's unconscious, using methods such as free association. (p. 597)

4. In Freud's theory, the **unconscious** is the repository of mostly unacceptable thoughts, wishes, feelings, and memories. According to contemporary psychologists, it is a level of information processing of which we are unaware. (p. 597)

5. In Freud's theory, the **id** is the unconscious system of personality, consisting of basic sexual and aggressive drives, that supplies psychic energy to personality. (p. 598)

6. In psychoanalytic theory, the **ego** is the conscious division of personality that attempts to mediate between the demands of the id, the superego, and reality. (p. 598)

7. In Freud's theory, the **superego** is the division of personality that contains the conscience and develops by incorporating the perceived moral standards of society. (p. 598)

8. Freud's **psychosexual stages** are developmental periods children pass through during which the id's pleasure-seeking energies are focused on different erogenous zones. (p. 598)

9. According to Freud, boys in the phallic stage develop a collection of feelings, known as the **Oedipus complex**, that center on sexual attraction to the mother and resentment of the father.

Some psychologists believe girls have a parallel Electra complex. (p. 599)

10. In Freud's theory, **identification** is the process by which the child's superego develops and incorporates the parents' values. Freud saw identification as crucial, not only to resolution of the Oedipus complex, but also to the development of gender identity. (p. 599)

11. In Freud's theory, **fixation** occurs when development becomes arrested, due to unresolved conflicts, in an immature psychosexual stage. (p. 599)

12. In Freud's theory, **defense mechanisms** are the ego's methods of unconsciously protecting itself against anxiety by distorting reality. (p. 600)

13. The basis of all defense mechanisms, **repression** is the unconscious exclusion of anxiety-arousing thoughts, feelings, and memories from the conscious mind. Repression is an example of motivated forgetting: One "forgets" what one really does not wish to remember. (p. 600)

14. **Regression** is the defense mechanism in which a person faced with anxiety reverts to a less mature pattern of behavior. (p. 600)

15. **Reaction formation** is the defense mechanism in which the ego converts unacceptable impulses into their opposites. (p. 600)

16. In psychoanalytic theory, **projection** is the unconscious attribution of one's own unacceptable feelings, attitudes, or desires to others. (p. 600)

    Memory aid: To project is to thrust outward. **Projection** is an example of thrusting one's own feelings outward to another person.

17. **Rationalization** is the defense mechanism in which one devises self-justifying but incorrect reasons for one's behavior. (p. 600)

18. **Displacement** is the defense mechanism in which a sexual or aggressive impulse is shifted to a more acceptable object other than the one that originally aroused the impulse. (p. 600)

19. The **collective unconscious** is Jung's concept of an inherited unconscious shared by all people and deriving from our species' history. (p. 601)

20. **Projective tests**, such as the TAT and Rorschach, present ambiguous stimuli onto which people supposedly *project* their own inner feelings. (p. 602)

21. The **Thematic Apperception Test (TAT)** is a projective test that consists of ambiguous pictures about which people are asked to make up stories. (p. 602)

22. The **Rorschach inkblot test**, the most widely used projective test, consists of 10 inkblots that people are asked to interpret. (p. 602)

23. According to **terror-management theory,** our deeply rooted fear of death causes us to act in ways that enhance our self-esteem and to adhere more strongly to worldviews that provide answers to questions about the meaning of life. (p. 606)

24. In Maslow's theory, **self-actualization** describes the process of fulfilling one's potential and becoming spontaneous, loving, creative, and self-accepting. Self-actualization is at the very top of Maslow's need hierarchy and therefore becomes active only after the more basic physical and psychological needs have been met. (p. 609)

25. **Unconditional positive regard** is, according to Rogers, an attitude of total acceptance and one of the three conditions essential to a "growth-promoting" climate. (p. 610)

26. **Self-concept** refers to one's personal awareness of "who I am." In the humanistic perspective, the self-concept is a central feature of personality; life happiness is significantly affected by whether the self-concept is positive or negative. (p. 610)

27. **Traits** are people's characteristic patterns of behavior. (p. 613)

28. **Personality inventories**, associated with the trait perspective, are questionnaires used to assess personality traits. (p. 615)

29. Consisting of 10 clinical scales, the **Minnesota Multiphasic Personality Inventory (MMPI)** is the most widely used personality inventory. (p. 616)

30. An **empirically derived test** is one developed by testing many items to see which best distinguish between groups of interest. (p. 617)

31. According to the **social-cognitive perspective,** behavior is the result of interactions between people and their social context. (p. 623)

32. According to the social-cognitive perspective, personality is shaped through **reciprocal determinism,** or the interaction between personality and environmental factors. (p. 623)

33. **Personal control** refers to a person's sense of controlling the environment. (p. 625)

34. **External locus of control** is the perception that one's fate is determined by forces not under personal control. (p. 625)

35. **Internal locus of control** is the perception that, to a great extent, one controls one's own destiny. (p. 625)

36. **Learned helplessness** is the passive resignation and perceived lack of control that a person or animal develops from repeated exposure to inescapable aversive events. (p. 625)

37. Focusing on positive emotions, character virtues such as creativity and compassion, and healthy families and neighborhoods, **positive psychology** is the scientific study of optimal human functioning. (p. 628)

38. The **spotlight effect** is the tendency of people to overestimate the extent to which other people are noticing and evaluating them. (p. 632)

39. **Self-esteem** refers to an individual's sense of self-worth. (p. 632)

40. The **self-serving bias** is the tendency to perceive oneself favorably. (p. 634)

Cross-Check

ACROSS
4. preconscious
7. external
10. id
11. trait
12. ego
13. defense mechanisms

DOWN
1. displacement
2. learned helplessness
3. fixation
4. personality
5. Oedipus
6. identification
8. TAT
9. Rorschach
14. MMPI

FOCUS ON VOCABULARY AND LANGUAGE

The Psychoanalytic Perspective

Page 596: He [Freud] had a prodigious memory and so loved reading plays, poetry, and philosophy that he once *ran up a bookstore debt* beyond his means. When he was young, Freud was a very serious student with an exceptionally good (*prodigious*) memory and an intense interest in a variety of topics. He obtained many books which he could not afford to pay for (*ran up a bookstore debt beyond his means*) in order to satisfy his curiosity about literature and the natural sciences.

Page 596: Freud's search for a cause for such disorders set his *mind running*. Patients came to Freud with strange neurological (*nervous*) disorders which had no obvious physiological explanation. Freud suspected that the problems were psychological in nature, and the questions raised by this theorizing caused him to think (*set his mind running*) in a way that changed the way we view human nature.

Page 597: He [Freud] believed he could *glimpse* the unconscious seeping not only into people's free associations, beliefs, habits, and symptoms but also into *slips of the tongue and pen*. Freud used the technique of free association to gain access to the unconscious. He also thought he got a fleeting look at (*glimpse of*) the unconscious in the content of people's dreams and in the inadvertent verbal mistakes we make in speech and writing (*slips of the tongue and pen*).

Page 598: Someone with an exceptionally strong superego may be *virtuous* yet, ironically, guilt-ridden; another with a weak superego may be *wantonly* self-indulgent and remorseless. In Freud's theory, the superego (our conscience) develops when the 4-to-5-year-old child incorporates society's values through identification with the parent of the opposite sex. A person with a well-developed superego may behave in an appropriately moral way (*virtuous*) yet still feel ashamed and anxious (*guilt-ridden*); someone with a poorly developed superego may be excessively and willfully (*wantonly*) selfish and aggressive.

Page 599: . . . *uttering biting sarcasm.* If there are unresolved conflicts at any of the psychosexual stages, the person may become stuck (**fixated**) at that stage, which will directly affect the development of a psychologically healthy personality. People fixated at the oral stage may become very dependent or may pretend to be the opposite by acting strong and independent and by using cruel and destructive humor (*biting sarcasm*) to attack the self-respect of others. In addition, this personality type may have an excessive need for oral gratification (smoking, nail biting, eating, chewing on pens, etc.).

Page 599: In such ways, Freud suggested, the *twig of personality* is *bent* at an early age. Freud believed that adult personality was formed during the first 4 or 5 years of life and was a function of the way the conflicts of the first three psychosexual stages (oral, anal, and phallic) were handled. Just as the shape of the grown tree is the result of how the young tree (*twig*) was twisted (*bent*), adult personality is a function of early childhood experiences.

Page 603: Other clinicians view it [the Rorschach inkblot test] . . . as an *icebreaker* and a revealing interview technique. Because of problems in scoring and interpreting the Rorschach inkblot test, most researchers question its validity and reliability. Some clinicians use the test to help generate hypotheses about the client's problems, and others use it as a point of departure to help get the interview under way (*as an icebreaker*).

Page 604 (margin note): . . . *linguistic flip-flops ("spoonerisms").* Professor Spooner became well known because of his habit of inadvertently twisting and distorting his sentences (*linguistic flip-flops*). For example, instead of saying "lighting a fire in the quadrangle," he said "fighting a liar in the quadrangle"; "you missed my history lecture" came out as "you hissed my mystery lecture," and "you have wasted two hours" appeared as "you have tasted two worms." Psychoanalysts call these "slips of the tongue" (Freudian slips) and believe that they represent unconscious motives and desires seeping through.

Page 605: They are *seared into the soul.* Traumatic events are likely to be remembered very well; they can occur as unwanted, persistent, and intrusive memories (*flashbacks*) that appear often (*they haunt the survivors*). In a sense, they are indelibly impressed in memory (*seared into the soul*).

Page 606: Psychologists also criticize Freud's theory for its *scientific shortcomings.* In order for a theory to be considered scientifically acceptable, it must be able to explain observations and provide testable hypotheses. Freud's theory fails on this account. In addition, his theory offers explanations only after the events or behaviors have occurred (*after-the-fact explanations*). Freud's theory does not meet acceptable or desired scientific standards (*it has scientific shortcomings*).

Page 607: Freud's most *searing* critic, Frederick Crews (1998), likens Freud to Peter Sellers' *bumbling* Inspector Clouseau, albeit with a unique talent for *bamboozling* an entire century. One harsh (*searing*) critic compares Freud to the self-important, blundering (*bumbling*) Inspector Clouseau (played by Peter Sellers in the *Pink Panther* movies) but with one difference. In contrast to the incompetent detective, Freud had a remarkable ability (*a unique talent*) for tricking and duping (*bamboozling*) people with his ideas. Others, however, note that it is unfair to criticize Freudian theory for failing to do things it never claimed to be able to do in the first place.

The Humanistic Perspective

Page 609 (caption): . . . *crippled spirits.* Abraham Maslow, a humanistic psychologist, studied healthy, motivated, creative people and came to the conclusion that once our basic needs are met, we all seek **self-actualization.** He believed that any theory of personality and motivation must be based on more than the study of psychologically impaired individuals (*crippled spirits*); rather, it should also include those who have achieved or fulfilled their innate potential (*self-actualized people*).

Page 610: Unless *thwarted* by an environment that inhibits growth, each of us is like an *acorn, primed* for growth and fulfillment. Carl Rogers was another pioneer in humanistic psychology. We are born with an innate striving (*we are primed*) for achieving our potential and like the seed (*acorn*) of the oak tree we will grow and develop unless we are blocked (*thwarted*) by an uncaring and unaccepting environment. As Rogers puts it, genuineness, acceptance, and empathy are the water, sun, and nutrients that enable people to grow like vigorous oak trees.

Page 611: Movie plots feature *rugged* individualists who, *true to themselves, buck social conventions* or take the law into their own hands. Humanistic psychology has been popular because it is consistent with Western cultural values, which emphasize strong, capable (*rugged*) individuals who follow their own beliefs and ambitions (*are true to themselves*) and oppose social norms and restrictions (*they buck social conventions*). This popular reception of the humanistic movement has elicited a strongly adverse and disapproving reaction from its critics (*set off a backlash of criticism*).

Page 612: May agreed with the critics who saw people joining the humanistic movement as seekers of "a community of like-minded persons who also are *playing possum* to the evils about us." Rollo May, a humanistic psychologist, disagreed with Carl Rogers' hopeful or optimistic viewpoint and pointed out that adopting the humanistic perspective was like joining a group of people who reinforced each other's beliefs and seemed to be oblivious to, and pretended not to notice (*played possum to*), the problems in the world.

The Trait Perspective

Page 613: Flabbergasted . . . This means to be shocked with overwhelming surprise. When Allport interviewed Freud in Vienna, he was astounded and confused (*flabbergasted*) by Freud's mistaken suggestion about the trivial story he told him. In fact, he was simply telling Freud about the events on the bus in order to start the conversation (*conversational gambit*). Nevertheless, it aroused Allport's interest in personality (*started a deep train of thought*), which finally led to his development of a trait theory.

Page 616 (Thinking Critically): . . . *scoff* . . . This means to have a contemptuously mocking attitude toward something. Astronomers who study the universe scientifically *scoff* at astrologers who believe that the planets and stars determine human affairs.

Page 616 (Thinking Critically): . . . *suckering methods* . . . To get suckered means to be easily fooled and exploited. Psychologists, such as Ray Hyman, show us how astrologers, palm (hand) readers, graphologists (who allegedly analyze handwriting to reveal personality), and others fool and exploit people by use of a few simple techniques (*suckering methods*).

Page 616 (Thinking Critically): . . . *"stock spiel"* . . . A "stock spiel" is a well-rehearsed and glib story. Astrologers, horoscope writers, and such often use statements that are generally true of almost everybody (*their "stock spiel"*), and most people find it hard to resist believing the flattering descriptions of themselves; consequently, many view astrology as an authentic art.

Page 618: Nevertheless, people have had fun *spoofing* the MMPI with their own *mock* items . . . Some items on the MMPI may appear nonsensical (*sound silly*), but they differentiated, say, depressed from nondepressed people, and so were retained in the form. Some people have created humorous but false (*mock*) items for a personality test that is a parody (*spoof*) of the MMPI.

Page 618: A slightly expanded set of factors—*dubbed* the Big Five—does a better job. . . . The Eysencks use two prime personality dimensions, or factors—extraversion–introversion and emotional stability–instability. Other researchers offer another three dimensions (openness, agreeableness, and conscientiousness), bringing the total to five factors, which they named (*dubbed*) the Big Five.

Page 620: If we remember such results, says Mischel, we will be more cautious about *labeling* and *pigeonholing* individuals. Research has shown that some behavior can be context specific (i.e., determined by the situation and not by the personality) and that personality test scores are poorly correlated with people's actual behavior on any particular occasion. Mischel warns that we should be careful about classifying individuals (*labeling*) and concluding that they belong in one particular slot (*pigeonholing*).

The Social-Cognitive Perspective

Page 624: If we expect someone to be angry with us, we may give the person a *cold shoulder, touching off* the very anger we expect. The way we are (our personalities) may influence how we are treated by others. If we believe that someone has hostile intentions toward us, we may ignore and treat the person with indifference (*give the person a cold shoulder*), and this in turn may cause (*touch off*) the angry behavior we predicted or expected from that person. As Myers notes, we are both the results (*products*) and the creators (*architects*) of our environments.

Page 625: Later placed in another situation where they *could* escape the punishment by simply *leaping a hurdle*, the dogs cowered as if without hope. In Seligman's experiments, dogs learned that nothing they did had any effect on what happened to them (**learned helplessness**), so they would not make even a minimal effort, such as jumping over a small barrier (*leaping a hurdle*), to escape being shocked. People, too, who feel they have no control over what happens to them may become depressed and feel hopeless and helpless.

Page 627: Those who *put an optimistic spin on their setbacks*—seeing them as *flukes* or as a means to learning a new approach. . . . People who view unwelcome reversals of fortune (*setbacks*) as just pure chance (*flukes*) or see them as challenges and as an opportunity to try something different (*put an optimistic spin on them*) are more likely to be successful and content. As Myers points out, positive thinking when confronted by problems (*in the face of adversity*) has many benefits (*pays dividends*).

Page 627: . . . *bombing* the upcoming exam . . . Students who are excessively optimistic and overconfident may not do as well as those who are concerned about failing (*bombing*) the exam and therefore study extremely hard. Extreme optimism may prevent us from becoming aware of potential hazards (*blind us to real risks*).

Page 629: . . . so many low-scoring students are *dumbfounded* after doing badly on an exam. People often are most overconfident when most incompetent, mainly because it is difficult for them to recognize incompetence without having competence in the first place. Consequently, many students who do not recognize that they are having problems are often astounded (*dumbfounded*) when they find they are not in the top half of the class. (As Myers notes, like pride, illusory or blind optimism may precede a negative outcome or fall.)

Exploring the Self

Page 632: Even after a blunder . . . we stick out like a sore thumb less than we imagine. A person who sticks out like a sore thumb is someone who is very noticeable to everyone as odd or different. If we make a clumsy mistake (*a blunder*), we think that everyone is paying attention to us (*we stick out like a sore thumb*), but this is often not the case. For example, students who had to wear a very unfashionable T-shirt with the picture of a lounge singer on it (*they had to don a Barry Manilow T-shirt*) thought that many people would notice their odd attire (*dorky clothes*), but very few did. This is a good illustration of the **spotlight effect.**

Page 633: Those who are *negative about themselves* also tend to be *thin-skinned* and *judgmental*. . . . People who have low self-esteem (*are negative about themselves*) are more likely to be anxious, depressed, insecure, and very sensitive to criticism (*thin-skinned*). In addition, they are also more likely to disparage and be critical (*judgmental*) of others.

Page 634: Athletes often privately credit their victories to their own *prowess* and their losses to *bad breaks, lousy officiating,* or the other team's exceptional performance. Athletes, like the rest of us, want to feel that desirable outcomes are due to their own abilities (*prowess*) and that failures are due to factors beyond their control such as poor luck (*bad breaks*), unfair refereeing (*lousy officiating*), or their opponents' unexpectedly outstanding efforts. This is called the **self-serving bias.**

Page 634: The world, it seems, is Garrison Keillor's *Lake Wobegon* writ large—a place where "all the women are strong, all the men are good-looking, and all the children are above average." Lake Wobegon is a fictional but ideal community satirized by comedian Garrison Keillor. Most abilities follow a bell-shaped distribution (the normal curve), so approximately half the population will be below average and half above on any given trait, such as strength, looks, or intelligence. The self-serving bias, which prompts most of us to rate ourselves as above average, appears to be almost universal, and the world is a magnified reflection of the Lake Wobegon community.

Page 634: Self-serving bias *flies in the face of pop psychology.* A claim of pop psychology is that we all have inferiority complexes. As is often the case, scientific psychology has clearly demonstrated that the opposite is actually true and that empirically based research findings contradict or refute the popular beliefs (*they fly in the face of pop psychology claims*).

Page 635: Moreover, *pride does often go before a fall.* Our conceit and self-important attitudes (*pride*) often precede a harsh lesson from reality (*a fall*). As Myers notes, it was nationalistic pride (the conceited belief that the Aryan race was superior) that facilitated and fostered (*fueled*) the growth of the Nazi movement and legitimized their inhumane and cruel deeds (*atrocities*).

Page 635: An adolescent or adult with a *swelled head* that gets deflated by insult or rejection is potentially dangerous. Overly self-confident people with high self-esteem (*swelled heads or large egos*) do more than retaliate in kind (*put down others*) when criticized, insulted, or rejected. Instead, they are more likely to react violently and aggressively (they are potentially dangerous). Researchers suggest that this negative aspect (*dark side*) of self-esteem is the result of threatened egotism and not low self-esteem.

Page 635 (margin): The enthusiastic claims of the self-esteem movement mostly range *from fantasy to hogwash.* The popular belief that having high self-esteem is essential to being a happy, well-adjusted, caring person is not supported by the research. Baumeister (1996) suggests that the claims of the self-esteem movement vary from being imaginative, wishful thinking (*fantasy*) to sheer nonsense (*hogwash*)—the effects of self-esteem are not very large or important.

Page 635: Sometimes self-directed *put-downs* are subtly strategic: They *elicit* reassuring *strokes.* When people disparage themselves with criticisms aimed at themselves (*self-directed put-downs*), they sometimes have an insidious or hidden purpose (*are subtly strategic*). They may want to have people reassure them that the opposite is true (*they want strokes*), or they may want to prepare for the worst possible outcome and have a rationalization for failure ready, just in case.

16 : Psychological Disorders

CHAPTER OVERVIEW

Although there is no clear-cut line between normal and abnormal behavior, we can characterize as abnormal those behaviors that are deviant, distressful, and dysfunctional. Chapter 16 discusses types of anxiety, mood disorders, dissociative disorders, schizophrenia, and personality disorders, as classified by the *Diagnostic and Statistical Manual of Mental Disorders* (DSM-IV). Although this classification system follows a medical model, in which disorders are viewed as illnesses, the chapter discusses psychological as well as physiological factors, as advocated by the current biopsychosocial approach. Thus, psychoanalytic theory, learning theory, social-cognitive theory, and other psychological perspectives are drawn on when relevant. The chapter concludes with a discussion of the incidence of serious psychological disorders in society today.

Your major task in this chapter is to learn about psychological disorders, their various subtypes and characteristics, and their possible causes. Since the material to be learned is extensive, it may be helpful to rehearse it by mentally completing the Chapter Review several times.

NOTE: Answer guidelines for all Chapter 16 questions begin on page 427.

CHAPTER REVIEW

First, skim each section, noting headings and boldface items. After you have read the section, review each objective by answering the fill-in and essay-type questions that follow it. As you proceed, evaluate your performance by consulting the answers beginning on page 427. Do not continue with the next section until you understand each answer. If you need to, review or reread the section in the textbook before continuing.

Perspectives on Psychological Disorders
(pp. 640–649)

> David Myers at times uses idioms that are unfamiliar to some readers. If you do not know the meaning of any of the following words, phrases, or expressions from the introduction and this section in the context in which they appear in the text, refer to pages 433–434 for an explanation: *eerie sense of self-recognition; draw the line; "The devil made him do it"; handy shorthand; have faulted the manual; Hinckley Insane, Public Mad; self-fulfilling prophecies.*

Objective 1: Identify the criteria for judging whether behavior is psychologically disordered.

1. Psychological disorders are persistently harmful _____ , _____ , and _____ .

2. Psychiatrists and psychologists label behavior disordered when it is _____ , _____ , and _____ .

3. This definition emphasizes that standards of acceptability for behavior are _____ (constant/variable).

4. (Thinking Critically) ADHD, or _____-_____ _____ _____ , plagues children who display one or more of three key symptoms: _____ , _____ , and _____ .

5. (Thinking Critically) ADHD is diagnosed more often in _____ (boys/girls). In

411

the past two decades, the proportion of American children being treated for this disorder _____ (increased/decreased) dramatically. Experts _____ (agree/do not agree) that ADHD is a real neuro-biological disorder.

6. (Thinking Critically) ADHD _____ (is/is not) heritable, and it _____ (is/is not) caused by eating too much sugar or poor schools. ADHD is often accompanied by a _____ disorder or with behavior that is _____ or temper-prone.

Objective 2: Contrast the medical model of psychological disorders with the biopsychosocial approach to disordered behavior.

7. The view that psychological disorders are sicknesses is the basis of the _____ model. According to this view, psychological disorders are viewed as mental _____ , or _____ , diagnosed on the basis of _____ and cured through _____ .

8. One of the first reformers to advocate this position and call for providing more humane living conditions for the mentally ill was

    _____ .

9. Today's psychologists recognize that all behavior arises from the interaction of _____ and _____ . To presume that a person is "mentally ill" attributes the condition solely to an _____ problem.

10. Major psychological disorders such as _____ and _____ are universal; others, such as _____ _____ and _____ , are culture-bound. These culture-bound disorders may share an underlying _____ , such as _____ , yet differ in their

    _____ .

11. Most mental health workers today take a _____ approach, whereby they assume that disorders are influenced by

    _____ _____

    and _____ _____ ,

inner _____ _____ , and _____ and _____ circumstances.

Objective 3: Describe the goals and content of the DSM-IV.

12. The most widely used system for classifying psychological disorders is the American Psychiatric Association manual, commonly known by its abbreviation, _____ . This manual defines a _____ process and _____ (how many?) clinical syndromes.

13. Independent diagnoses made with the current manual generally _____ (show/do not show) agreement.

14. One criticism of DSM-IV is that as the number of disorder categories has _____ (increased/decreased), the number of adults who meet the criteria for at least one psychiatric ailment has _____ (increased/decreased).

(Close-Up) Briefly describe the "unDSM."

Objective 4: Discuss the potential dangers and benefits of using diagnostic labels.

15. Studies have shown that labeling has _____ (little/a significant) effect on our interpretation of individuals and their behavior.

Outline the pros and cons of labeling psychological disorders.

Anxiety Disorders (pp. 649–658)

> If you do not know the meaning of any of the following words, phrases, or expressions in the context in which they appear in the text, refer to page 434 for an explanation: *heart palpitations . . . fidgeting; lighting up doesn't lighten up; flashbacks and nightmares; Grooming gone wild; a ruse; go fishing for multiple personalities.*

Objective 5: Define *anxiety disorders,* and explain how these conditions differ from normal feelings of stress, tension, or uneasiness.

1. Anxiety disorders are psychological disorders characterized by _____ _____ . The key to differentiating anxiety disorders from normal anxiety is in the _____ and _____ of the anxiety.

2. Four anxiety disorders discussed in the textbook are _____ _____ _____ , _____ _____ , _____ , and _____-_____ _____ .

Objective 6: Contrast the symptoms of generalized anxiety disorder and panic disorder.

3. When a person is continually tense, apprehensive, and physiologically aroused for no apparent reason, he or she is diagnosed as suffering from a _____ _____ disorder. In Freud's term, the anxiety is _____-_____ .

4. In generalized anxiety disorder, the body reacts physiologically with the arousal of the _____ nervous system. In some instances, anxiety may intensify dramatically and unpredictably and be accompanied by chest pain or choking, for example; people with these symptoms are said to have _____ _____ . This anxiety may escalate into a minutes-long episode of intense fear, or a _____ _____ .

5. People who fear situations in which escape or help might not be possible when panic strikes suffer from _____ .

Objective 7: Explain how a phobia differs from the fears we all experience.

6. When a person has an irrational fear of a specific object, activity, or situation, the diagnosis is a _____ . Although in many situations, the person can live with the problem, some _____ _____ , such as a fear of thunderstorms, are incapacitating.

7. When a person has an intense fear of being scrutinized by others, the diagnosis is a _____ _____ .

Objective 8: Describe the symptoms of obsessive-compulsive disorder.

8. When a person cannot control repetitive thoughts and actions, an _____-_____ disorder is diagnosed.

9. Older people are _____ (more/less) likely than teens and young adults to suffer from this disorder.

Objective 9: Describe the symptoms of post-traumatic stress disorder, and discuss survivor resiliency.

10. Traumatic stress, such as that associated with witnessing atrocities or combat, can produce _____-_____ _____ disorder. The symptoms of this disorder include _____ _____ , _____ , _____ _____ , _____ _____ , and _____ . Despite such symptoms, some psychologists believe this disorder is _____ .

11. Researchers who believe this disorder may be overdiagnosed point to the _____ _____ of most people who suffer

trauma. Also, suffering can lead to

_____-_____

_____ , in which people experi-

ence an increased appreciation for life.

Objective 10: Discuss the contributions of the learning and biological perspectives to our understanding of the development of anxiety disorders.

12. Freud assumed that anxiety disorders are symptoms of submerged mental energy that derives from intolerable impulses that were _____ during childhood.

13. Learning theorists, drawing on research in which rats are given unpredictable shocks, link general anxiety with _____ conditioning of _____ .

14. Some fears arise from _____ _____ , such as when a person who fears heights after a fall also comes to fear airplanes.

15. Phobias and compulsive behaviors reduce anxiety and thereby are _____ . Through _____ learning, someone might also learn fear by seeing others display their own fears.

16. Humans probably _____ (are/are not) biologically prepared to develop certain fears. Compulsive acts typically are exaggerations of behaviors that contributed to our species' _____ .

17. The anxiety response probably _____ (is/is not) genetically influenced.

18. PET scans of persons with obsessive-compulsive disorder reveal excessive activity in a brain region called the _____ _____ cortex. Some antidepressant drugs dampen fear-circuit activity in the _____ , thus reducing this behavior.

Objective 11: Describe the symptoms of dissociative disorders, and explain why some critics are skeptical about dissociative identity disorder.

19. In _____ disorders, a person experiences a sudden loss of _____ or change in _____ .

20. A person who develops two or more distinct personalities is suffering from

_____ _____

disorder.

21. Nicholas Spanos has argued that such people may merely be playing different

_____ .

22. Those who accept this as a genuine disorder point to evidence that differing personalities may be associated with distinct

_____ and _____

states.

Identify two pieces of evidence brought forth by those who do not accept dissociative identity disorder as a genuine disorder.

23. The psychoanalytic and learning perspectives view dissociative disorders as ways of dealing with _____ . Others view them as a protective response to histories of

_____ _____ .

Skeptics claim these disorders are sometimes contrived by _____-

_____ people and sometimes constructed out of the _____-

_____ interaction.

Mood Disorders (pp. 658–669)

> If you do not know the meaning of any of the following words, phrases, or expressions in the context in which they appear in the text, refer to page 435 for an explanation: *To grind temporarily to a halt; blue mood; slow motion . . . fast forward; view life through dark glasses; sour our thinking; company does not love another's misery.*

Objective 12: Define *mood disorders,* and contrast major depressive disorder and bipolar disorder.

1. Mood disorders are psychological disorders characterized by _____ _____ . They come in two forms: The experience of prolonged depression with no discernible cause is called _____ _____ disorder. When a person's mood alternates between depression and the hyperactive state of _____ , a _____ disorder is diagnosed.

2. Although _____ are more common, _____ is the number one reason that people seek mental health services. It is also the leading cause of disability worldwide.

3. In between the temporary blue moods everyone experiences and major depression is a condition called _____ _____ , in which a person feels down-in-the-dumps nearly every day for two years or more.

4. The possible signs of depression include _____ _____ .

5. Major depression occurs when its signs last _____ _____ or more with no apparent cause.

6. Depressed persons usually _____ (can/cannot) recover without therapy.

7. Symptoms of mania include _____ _____ .

8. Bipolar disorder is less common among creative professionals who rely on _____ and _____ than among those who rely on _____ expression and vivid _____ .

Objective 13: Discuss the facts that an acceptable theory of depression must explain.

9. The commonality of depression suggests that its _____ must also be common.

10. Compared with men, women are _____ (more/less) vulnerable to major depression. In general, women are most vulnerable to disorders involving _____ states, such as _____ _____ .

11. Men's disorders tend to be more _____ and include _____ .

12. It usually _____ (is/is not) the case that a depressive episode has been triggered by a stressful event. An individual's vulnerability to depression also increases following, for example, _____ .

13. With each new generation, the rate of depression is _____ (increasing/decreasing) and the disorder is striking _____ (earlier/later). In North America today, young adults are _____ times (how many?) as likely as their grandparents to suffer depression.

State the psychoanalytic explanation of depression.

Objective 14: Summarize the contributions of the biological perspective to the study of depression, and discuss the link between suicide and depression.

14. Mood disorders _____ (tend/do not tend) to run in families. Studies of _____ also reveal that genetic influences on mood disorders are _____ (weak/strong).

15. To determine which genes are involved in depression, researchers use

_____ _____ , in which they examine the _____ of both affected and unaffected family members. Using _____ studies, they also search for correlations between DNA variation and population traits.

(Close-Up) Identify several group differences in suicide rates.

16. Depression may also be caused by _____ (high/low) levels of two neurotransmitters, _____ and _____ .

17. Drugs that alleviate mania reduce _____ ; drugs that relieve depression increase _____ or _____ supplies by blocking either their _____ or their chemical _____ .

18. People with depression also have lower levels in their diet of the _____ fatty acid. Countries such as _____ , where people consume more _____ that are rich in this fatty acid, tend to have _____ (high/low) rates of depression.

19. The brains of depressed people tend to be _____ (more/less) active, especially in an area of the _____ lobe. In severely depressed patients, this brain area may also be _____ (smaller/larger) in size. The brain's _____ , which is important in processing _____ , is vulnerable to stress-related damage. Antidepressant drugs that boost _____ may promote recovery by stimulating neurons in this area of the brain.

Objective 15: Summarize the contributions of the social-cognitive perspective to the study of depression, and describe the events in the cycle of depression.

20. According to the social-cognitive perspective, depression may be linked with _____-_____ beliefs and a _____ _____ style.

21. Such beliefs may arise from _____ _____ , the feeling that can arise when the individual repeatedly experiences uncontrollable, painful events.

22. Gender differences in _____ _____ help explain why women have been twice as vulnerable to depression.

Describe how depressed people differ from others in their explanations of failure and how such explanations tend to feed depression.

23. Research studies suggest that depressing thoughts usually _____ (precede/follow/coincide with) a depressed mood.

24. Depression-prone people respond to bad events in an especially _____ , _____ way.

25. According to Susan Nolen-Hoeksema, when trouble strikes, men tend to _____ and women tend to _____ .

26. Being withdrawn, self-focused, and complaining tends to elicit social _____ (empathy/rejection).

Outline the vicious cycle of depression.

Schizophrenia (pp. 669–677)

> If you do not know the meaning of any of the following words, phrases, or expressions in the context in which they appear in the text, refer to page 435 for an explanation: *hodge-podge; flat affect.*

Objective 16: Describe the symptoms of schizophrenia, and differentiate delusions and hallucinations.

1. Schizophrenia, or "split mind," refers not to a split personality but rather to a split from

   _____ .

2. Three manifestations of schizophrenia are disorganized _____ , disturbed _____ , and inappropriate _____ and _____ .

3. The distorted, false beliefs of schizophrenia patients are called _____ .

4. Many psychologists attribute the disorganized thinking of schizophrenia to a breakdown in the capacity for _____ _____ .

5. The disturbed perceptions of people suffering from schizophrenia may take the form of _____ , which usually are _____ (visual/auditory).

6. Some victims of schizophrenia lapse into a zombielike state of apparent apathy, or _____ _____ ; others, who exhibit _____ , may remain motionless for hours and then become agitated.

Objective 17: Distinguish the five subtypes of schizophrenia, and contrast chronic and acute schizophrenia.

7. The term *schizophrenia* describes a _____ (single disorder/cluster of disorders).

8. Positive symptoms of schizophrenia include

   _____

   _____ .

   Negative symptoms include

   _____

   _____ .

9. When schizophrenia develops slowly (called _____ schizophrenia), recovery is _____ (more/less) likely than when it develops rapidly in reaction to particular life stresses (called _____ schizophrenia).

Objective 18: Outline some abnormal brain chemistry, functions, and structures associated with schizophrenia, and discuss the possible link between prenatal viral infections and schizophrenia.

10. The brain tissue of schizophrenia patients has been found to have an excess of receptors for the neurotransmitter _____ . Drugs that block these receptors have been found to _____ (increase/decrease) schizophrenia symptoms. Drugs that interfere with receptors for the neurotransmitter _____ can produce negative symptoms of schizophrenia.

11. Brain scans have shown that many people suffering from schizophrenia have abnormally _____ (high/low) brain activity in the _____ lobes.

12. Enlarged, _____-filled areas and a corresponding _____ of cerebral tissue is also characteristic of schizophrenia. Schizophrenia patients also have a smaller-than-normal _____ , which may account for their difficulty in filtering _____ _____ and focusing _____ .

13. Some scientists contend that the brain abnormalities of schizophrenia may be caused by a prenatal problem, such as _____

_____ _____ ,

birth complications such as _____

_____ , or a

_____ _____

contracted by the mother.

List several pieces of evidence for this theory.

Objective 19: Discuss the evidence for a genetic contribution to the development of schizophrenia.

14. Twin and adoptive studies _____ (support/do not support) the contention that heredity plays a role in schizophrenia.

15. The role of the prenatal environment in schizophrenia is demonstrated by the fact that identical twins who share the same _____ , and are therefore more likely to experience the same prenatal _____ , are more likely to share the disorder.

16. Adoption studies _____ (confirm/do not confirm) a genetic link in the development of schizophrenia.

Objective 20: Describe some psychological factors that may be early warning signs of schizophrenia in children.

17. It appears that for schizophrenia to develop there must be both a _____ predisposition and some _____ trigger.

List several of the warning signs of schizophrenia in high-risk children.

Personality Disorders (pp. 677–679)

> If you do not know the meaning of any of the following words, phrases, or expressions in the context in which they appear in the text, refer to page 435 for an explanation: *con artist; woven of biological as well as psychological strands.*

Objective 21: Contrast the three clusters of personality disorders, and describe the behaviors and brain activity associated with the antisocial personality disorder.

1. Personality disorders exist when an individual has character traits that are enduring and impair

_____ _____ .

2. A fearful sensitivity to rejection may predispose the _____ personality disorder. Eccentric behaviors, such as emotionless disengagement, are characteristic of the _____ personality disorder. A person with _____ personality disorder displays shallow, attention-getting emotions. A person who exaggerates his or her own importance exhibits a _____ personality disorder, and a person who has an unstable identity and unstable relationships is considered

_____ .

3. An individual who seems to have no conscience, lies, steals, is generally irresponsible, and may be criminal is said to have an _____ personality. Previously, this person was labeled a

_____ .

4. Studies of biological relatives of those with antisocial and unemotional tendencies suggest that there _____ (is/is not) a biological predisposition to such traits.

5. Some studies have detected early signs of antisocial behavior in children as young as

_____ . Antisocial adolescents tended to have been _____ ,

_____ , unconcerned with

_____ _____ ,

and low in _____ .

6. PET scans of murderers' brains reveal reduced activity in the _____ _____ .

7. As in other disorders, in antisocial personality, genetics _____ (is/is not) the whole story.

Rates of Psychological Disorders
(pp. 680–682)

Objective 22: Discuss the prevalence of psychological disorders, and summarize the findings on the link between poverty and serious psychological disorders.

1. Research reveals that approximately 1 in every _____ (how many?) Americans suffered a clinically significant mental disorder during the prior year.

2. The incidence of serious psychological disorders is _____ (higher/lower) among those below the poverty line.

3. In terms of age of onset, most psychological disorders appear by _____ (early/middle/late) adulthood. Some, such as the _____ _____ and _____ , appear during childhood.

PROGRESS TEST 1

Multiple-Choice Questions

Circle your answers to the following questions and check them with the answers beginning on page 429. If your answer is incorrect, read the explanation for why it is incorrect and then consult the appropriate pages of the text (in parentheses following the correct answer).

1. Gender differences in the prevalence of depression may be partly due to the fact that when stressful experiences occur:
   a. women tend to act, while men tend to think.
   b. women tend to think, while men tend to act.
   c. women tend to distract themselves by drinking, while men tend to delve into their work.
   d. women tend to delve into their work, while men tend to distract themselves by drinking.

2. The criteria for classifying behavior as psychologically disordered:
   a. vary from culture to culture.
   b. vary from time to time.
   c. are characterized by both a. and b.
   d. have remained largely unchanged over the course of history.

3. Most mental health workers today take the view that disordered behaviors:
   a. are usually genetically triggered.
   b. are organic diseases.
   c. arise from the interaction of nature and nurture.
   d. are the product of learning.

4. The French reformer who insisted that madness was not demon possession and who called for humane treatment of patients was:
   a. Nadel.   c. Szasz.
   b. Freud.   d. Pinel.

5. Which of the following is the most pervasive of the psychological disorders?
   a. depression
   b. schizophrenia
   c. bipolar disorder
   d. generalized anxiety disorder

6. Which of the following is *not* true concerning depression?
   a. Depression is more common in females than in males.
   b. Most depressive episodes appear not to be preceded by any particular factor or event.
   c. Most depressive episodes last less than 3 months.
   d. Most people recover from depression without professional therapy.

7. Which of the following is *not* true regarding schizophrenia?
   a. It occurs more frequently in people born in winter and spring months.
   b. It occurs less frequently as infectious disease rates have declined.
   c. It occurs more frequently in lightly populated areas.
   d. It usually appears during adolescence or early adulthood.

8. Evidence of environmental effects on psychological disorders is seen in the fact that certain disorders, such as _____ , are universal, whereas others, such as _____ , are culture-bound.
   a. schizophrenia; depression
   b. depression; schizophrenia
   c. antisocial personality; neurosis
   d. depression; anorexia nervosa

9. The effect of drugs that block receptors for dopamine is to:
   a. alleviate schizophrenia symptoms.
   b. alleviate depression.
   c. increase schizophrenia symptoms.
   d. increase depression.

10. The diagnostic reliability of DSM-IV:
   a. is unknown.
   b. depends on the age of the patient.
   c. is very low.
   d. is relatively high.

11. The early warning signs of schizophrenia, based on studies of high-risk children, include all but which of the following?
   a. having a severely schizophrenic mother
   b. having been separated from parents
   c. having a short attention span
   d. having matured physically at a very early age

12. (Thinking Critically) The term *insanity* refers to:
   a. legal definitions.
   b. psychotic disorders only.
   c. personality disorders only.
   d. both psychotic disorders and personality disorders.

13. Phobias and obsessive-compulsive behaviors are classified as:
   a. anxiety disorders.
   b. mood disorders.
   c. dissociative disorders.
   d. personality disorders.

14. According to the social-cognitive perspective, a person who experiences unexpected aversive events may develop helplessness and manifest a(n):
   a. obsessive-compulsive disorder.
   b. dissociative disorder.
   c. personality disorder.
   d. mood disorder.

15. Which of the following was presented in the text as evidence of biological influences on anxiety disorders?
   a. Identical twins often develop similar phobias.
   b. PET scans of persons with obsessive-compulsive disorder reveal unusually high activity in an area of the frontal lobes.
   c. Drugs that dampen fear-circuit activity in the amygdala also alleviate OCD.
   d. All of the above were presented.

16. Most of the hallucinations of schizophrenia patients involve the sense of:
   a. smell.   c. hearing.
   b. vision.   d. touch.

17. When expecting to be electrically shocked, people with an antisocial disorder, as compared to normal people, show:
   a. less fear and greater arousal of the autonomic nervous system.
   b. less fear and less autonomic arousal.
   c. greater fear and greater autonomic arousal.
   d. greater fear and less autonomic arousal.

18. Hearing voices would be a(n) _____ ; believing that you are Napoleon would be a(n) _____ .
   a. obsession; compulsion
   b. compulsion; obsession
   c. delusion; hallucination
   d. hallucination; delusion

19. In treating depression, a psychiatrist would probably prescribe a drug that would:
   a. increase levels of acetylcholine.
   b. decrease levels of dopamine.
   c. increase levels of norepinephrine.
   d. decrease levels of serotonin.

20. When schizophrenia is slow to develop, called _____ schizophrenia, recovery is _____ .
   a. reactive; unlikely   c. process; unlikely
   b. process; likely   d. reactive; likely

Matching Items

Match each term with the appropriate definition or description.

Terms

_____ 1. dissociative disorder
_____ 2. medical model
_____ 3. mood disorders
_____ 4. social phobia
_____ 5. biopsychosocial approach
_____ 6. mania
_____ 7. obsessive-compulsive disorder
_____ 8. schizophrenia
_____ 9. hallucination
_____ 10. panic attack

Definitions or Descriptions

a. psychological disorders marked by emotional extremes
b. an extremely elevated mood
c. a false sensory experience
d. approach that considers behavior disorders as illnesses that can be diagnosed, treated, and, in most cases, cured
e. a sudden escalation of anxiety often accompanied by a sensation of choking or other physical symptoms
f. a disorder in which conscious awareness becomes separated from previous memories, feelings, and thoughts
g. approach that considers behavior disorders to be the result of biological, psychological, and social-cultural influences
h. intense fear of being scrutinized by others
i. a group of disorders marked by disorganized thinking, disturbed perceptions, and inappropriate emotions and actions
j. a disorder characterized by repetitive thoughts and actions

PROGRESS TEST 2

Progress Test 2 should be completed during a final chapter review. Answer the following questions after you thoroughly understand the correct answers for the Chapter Review and Progress Test 1.

Multiple-Choice Questions

1. Which of the following is true concerning abnormal behavior?
   a. Definitions of abnormal behavior are culture-dependent.
   b. A behavior cannot be defined as abnormal unless it is considered harmful to society.
   c. Abnormal behavior can be defined as any behavior that is distressful.
   d. Definitions of abnormal behavior are based on physiological factors.

2. The psychoanalytic perspective would most likely view phobias as:
   a. conditioned fears.
   b. displaced responses to incompletely repressed impulses.

   c. biological predispositions.
   d. manifestations of self-defeating thoughts.

3. Many psychologists believe the disorganized thoughts of people with schizophrenia result from a breakdown in:
   a. selective attention.   c. motivation.
   b. memory storage.   d. memory retrieval.

4. Research evidence links the brain abnormalities of schizophrenia to _____ during prenatal development.
   a. maternal stress
   b. a viral infection contracted
   c. abnormal levels of certain hormones
   d. the weight of the unborn child

5. The fact that disorders such as schizophrenia are universal and influenced by heredity, whereas other disorders such as anorexia nervosa are culture-bound provides evidence for the _____ model of psychological disorders.
   a. medical   c. social-cultural
   b. biopsychosocial d. psychoanalytic

6. Our early ancestors commonly attributed disordered behavior to:
   a. "bad blood."
   b. evil spirits.
   c. brain injury.
   d. laziness.

7. In general, women are more vulnerable than men to:
   a. active disorders such as anxiety.
   b. passive disorders such as depression.
   c. active disorders such as antisocial conduct.
   d. passive disorders such as alcohol abuse.

8. Which of the following statements concerning the labeling of disordered behaviors is *not* true?
   a. Labels interfere with effective treatment of psychological disorders.
   b. Labels promote research studies of psychological disorders.
   c. Labels may create preconceptions that bias people's perceptions.
   d. Labels may influence behavior by creating self-fulfilling prophecies.

9. (Thinking Critically) Nicholas Spanos considers dissociative identity disorder to be:
   a. a genuine disorder.
   b. merely role playing.
   c. a disorder that cannot be explained according to the learning perspective.
   d. both a. and c.

10. Which neurotransmitter is present in overabundant amounts during the manic phase of bipolar disorder?
    a. dopamine
    b. serotonin
    c. epinephrine
    d. norepinephrine

11. After falling from a ladder, Joseph is afraid of airplanes, although he has never flown. This demonstrates that some fears arise from:
    a. observational learning.
    b. reinforcement.
    c. stimulus generalization.
    d. stimulus discrimination.

12. Which of the following provides evidence that human fears have been subjected to the evolutionary process?
    a. Compulsive acts typically exaggerate behaviors that contributed to our species' survival.
    b. Most phobias focus on objects that our ancestors also feared.
    c. It is easier to condition some fears than others.
    d. All of the above provide evidence.

13. Which of the following is true of the medical model?
    a. In recent years, it has been in large part discredited.
    b. It views psychological disorders as sicknesses that are diagnosable and treatable.
    c. It emphasizes the role of psychological factors in disorders over that of physiological factors.
    d. It focuses on cognitive factors.

14. (Thinking Critically) Psychoanalytic and learning theorists both agree that dissociative and anxiety disorders are symptoms that represent the person's attempt to deal with:
    a. unconscious conflicts.
    b. anxiety.
    c. unfulfilled wishes.
    d. unpleasant responsibilities.

15. Behavior is classified as disordered when it is:
    a. deviant
    b. distressful.
    c. dysfunctional.
    d. all of the above.

16. Many psychologists dislike using DSM-IV because of its:
    a. failure to emphasize observable behaviors in the diagnostic process.
    b. learning theory bias.
    c. medical model bias.
    d. psychoanalytic bias.

17. Which of the following is *not* a symptom of schizophrenia?
    a. inappropriate emotions
    b. disturbed perceptions
    c. panic attacks
    d. disorganized thinking

18. Social-cognitive theorists contend that depression is linked with:
    a. negative moods.
    b. maladaptive explanations of failure.
    c. self-defeating beliefs.
    d. all of the above.

19. According to psychoanalytic theory, memory of losses, especially in combination with internalized anger, is likely to result in:
    a. learned helplessness.
    b. the self-serving bias.
    c. weak ego defense mechanisms.
    d. depression.

20. Among the following, which is generally accepted as a possible cause of schizophrenia?
    a. an excess of endorphins in the brain
    b. being a twin
    c. extensive learned helplessness
    d. a genetic predisposition

Matching Items

Match each term with the appropriate definition or description.

Terms

_____ 1. dissociative identity disorder
_____ 2. phobia
_____ 3. dopamine
_____ 4. dysthymic disorder
_____ 5. antisocial personality
_____ 6. norepinephrine
_____ 7. serotonin
_____ 8. bipolar disorder
_____ 9. delusions
_____ 10. agoraphobia

Definitions or Descriptions

a. a neurotransmitter for which there are excess receptors in some schizophrenia patients
b. a neurotransmitter that is overabundant during mania and scarce during depression
c. an individual who seems to have no conscience
d. false beliefs that may accompany psychological disorders
e. an anxiety disorder marked by a persistent, irrational fear of a specific object or situation
f. a disorder formerly called multiple personality disorder
g. a neurotransmitter possibly linked to obsessive-compulsive behavior
h. a type of mood disorder
i. a disorder marked by chronic low energy and self-esteem
j. a fear of situations in which help might not be available during a panic attack

PSYCHOLOGY APPLIED

Answer these questions the day before an exam as a final check on your understanding of the chapter's terms and concepts.

Multiple-Choice Questions

1. Joe has an intense, irrational fear of snakes. He is suffering from a(n):
   a. generalized anxiety disorder.
   b. obsessive-compulsive disorder.
   c. phobia.
   d. mood disorder.

2. As a child, Monica was criticized severely by her mother for not living up to her expectations. This criticism was always followed by a beating with a whip. As an adult, Monica is generally introverted and extremely shy. Sometimes, however, she acts more like a young child, throwing tantrums if she doesn't get her way. At other times, she is a flirting, happy-go-lucky young lady. Most likely, Monica is suffering from:
   a. a phobia.
   b. dissociative schizophrenia.
   c. dissociative identity disorder.
   d. bipolar disorder.

3. Bob has never been able to keep a job. He's been in and out of jail for charges such as theft, sexual assault, and spousal abuse. Bob would most likely be diagnosed as having:
   a. a dissociative identity disorder.
   b. major depressive disorder.
   c. schizophrenia.
   d. an antisocial personality.

4. Julia's psychologist believes that Julia's fear of heights can be traced to a conditioned fear she developed after falling from a ladder. This explanation reflects a _____ perspective.
   a. medical
   b. psychoanalytic
   c. social-cognitive
   d. learning

5. Before he can study, Rashid must arrange his books, pencils, paper, and other items on his desk so that they are "just so." The campus counselor suggests that Rashid's compulsive behavior may help alleviate his anxiety about failing in school, which reinforces the compulsive actions. This explanation of obsessive-compulsive behavior is most consistent with which perspective?
   a. learning
   b. psychoanalytic
   c. humanistic
   d. social-cognitive

6. Sharon is continually tense, jittery, and apprehensive for no specific reason. She would probably be diagnosed as suffering a(n):
   a. phobia.
   b. major depressive disorder.
   c. obsessive-compulsive disorder.
   d. generalized anxiety disorder.

7. Jason is so preoccupied with staying clean that he showers as many as 10 times each day. Jason would be diagnosed as suffering from a(n):
   a. dissociative disorder.
   b. generalized anxiety disorder.
   c. personality disorder.
   d. obsessive-compulsive disorder.

8. Although she escaped from war-torn Bosnia two years ago, Zheina still has haunting memories and nightmares. Because she is also severely depressed, her therapist diagnoses her condition as:
   a. dissociative identity disorder.
   b. bipolar disorder.
   c. schizophrenia.
   d. post-traumatic stress disorder.

9. Claiming that she heard a voice commanding her to warn other people that eating is harmful, Sandy attempts to convince others in a restaurant not to eat. The psychiatrist to whom she is referred finds that Sandy's thinking and speech are often fragmented and incoherent. In addition, Sandy has an unreasonable fear that someone is "out to get her" and consequently trusts no one. Her condition is most indicative of:

   a. schizophrenia.
   b. generalized anxiety disorder.
   c. a phobia.
   d. obsessive-compulsive disorder.

10. Irene occasionally experiences unpredictable episodes of intense dread accompanied by chest pains and a sensation of smothering. Since her symptoms have no apparent cause, they would probably be classified as indicative of:
    a. schizophrenia.
    b. bipolar disorder.
    c. post-traumatic stress disorder.
    d. panic attack.

11. To which of the following is a person *most* likely to acquire a phobia?
    a. heights
    b. being in public
    c. being dirty
    d. All of the above are equally likely.

12. Dr. Jekyll, whose second personality was Mr. Hyde, had a(n) _____ disorder.
    a. anxiety
    b. dissociative
    c. mood
    d. personality

13. For the past 6 months, a woman has complained of feeling isolated from others, dissatisfied with life, and discouraged about the future. This woman could be diagnosed as suffering from:
    a. bipolar disorder.
    b. major depressive disorder.
    c. generalized anxiety disorder.
    d. a dissociative disorder.

14. On Monday, Matt felt optimistic, energetic, and on top of the world. On Tuesday, he felt hopeless and lethargic, and thought that the future looked very grim. Matt would *most* likely be diagnosed as having:
    a. bipolar disorder.
    b. major depressive disorder.
    c. schizophrenia.
    d. panic disorder.

15. Connie's therapist has suggested that her depression stems from unresolved anger toward her parents. Evidently, Connie's therapist is working within the _____ perspective.
    a. learning
    b. social-cognitive
    c. biological
    d. psychoanalytic

16. Ken's therapist suggested that his depression is a result of his self-defeating thoughts and negative assumptions about himself, his situation, and his future. Evidently, Ken's therapist is working within the _____ perspective.
    a. learning
    b. social-cognitive
    c. biological
    d. psychoanalytic

17. Alicia's doctor, who thinks that Alicia's depression has a biochemical cause, prescribes a drug that:
    a. reduces norepinephrine.
    b. increases norepinephrine.
    c. reduces serotonin.
    d. increases acetylcholine.

18. Wayne's doctor attempts to help Wayne by prescribing a drug that blocks receptors for dopamine. Wayne has apparently been diagnosed with:
    a. a mood disorder.
    b. an anxiety disorder.
    c. a personality disorder.
    d. schizophrenia.

19. (Thinking Critically) Thirteen-year-old Ronald constantly fidgets in his seat at school, frequently blurts out answers without being called, and is extremely distractible. A psychiatrist might diagnose Ronald with:
    a. bipolar disorder.
    b. panic disorder.
    c. attention-deficit hyperactivity disorder.
    d. obsessive-compulsive disorder.

20. Janet, whose class presentation is titled "Current Views on the Causes of Schizophrenia," concludes her talk with the statement:
    a. "Schizophrenia is caused by intolerable stress."
    b. "Schizophrenia is inherited."
    c. "Genes may predispose some people to react to particular experiences by developing schizophrenia."
    d. "As of this date, schizophrenia is completely unpredictable and its causes are unknown."

Essay Question

Clinical psychologists label people disordered if their behavior is (1) deviant, (2) distressful, and (3) dysfunctional. Demonstrate your understanding of the classification process by giving examples of behaviors that might be considered deviant, distressful, or dysfunctional but, because they do not fit all three criteria, would not necessarily be labeled disordered. (Use the space below to list the points you want to make, and organize them. Then write the essay on a separate piece of paper.)

KEY TERMS

Writing Definitions

Using your own words, on a separate piece of paper write a brief definition or explanation of each of the following terms.

1. psychological disorder

2. attention-deficit hyperactivity disorder

3. medical model

4. DSM-IV

5. anxiety disorders

6. generalized anxiety disorder

7. panic disorder

8. phobia

9. obsessive-compulsive disorder

10. post-traumatic stress disorder

11. dissociative disorders

12. dissociative identity disorder

13. mood disorders

14. major depressive disorder

15. mania

16. bipolar disorder

17. schizophrenia

18. delusions

19. personality disorders

20. antisocial personality disorder

Cross-Check

As you learned in the Prologue, reviewing and overlearning of material are important to the learning process. After you have written the definitions of the key terms in this chapter, you should complete the crossword puzzle to ensure that you can reverse the process—recognize the term, given the definition.

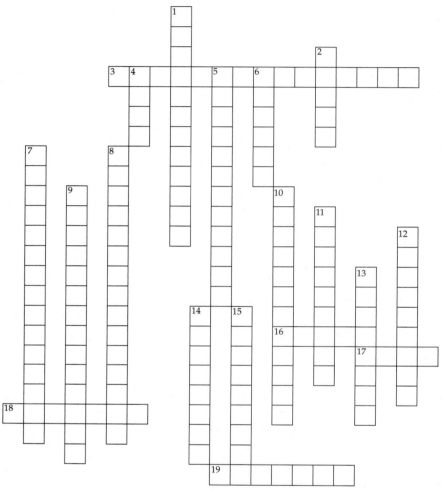

ACROSS

3. The "common cold" of psychological disorders.
16. A euphoric, hyperactive state.
17. Category of disorders that includes major depression and bipolar disorder.
18. Mood disorder in which a person alternates between depression and mania.
19. Category of disorders that includes phobias and obsessive-compulsive disorder.

DOWN

1. Subtype of schizophrenia in which emotion is flat or inappropriate.
2. A widely used system of classifying psychological disorders.
4. A psychological disorder characterized by extreme inattention, for example.
5. Disorders that involve a separation of conscious awareness from one's previous memories, thoughts, and feelings.
6. A persistent, irrational fear of a specific object or situation.
7. Biomedical research technique used to determine which genes are involved in a specific psychological disorder.
8. Approach that assumes that genes, psychological factors, and social and cultural circumstances combine and interact to produce psychological disorders.

9. False sensory experiences.
10. The viewpoint that psychological disorders are illnesses.
11. Subtype of schizophrenia in which there is immobility or excessive, purposeless movement.
12. False beliefs that often are symptoms of schizophrenia.
13. Neurotransmitter for which there are excess receptors in the brains of schizophrenia patients.
14. Category of schizophrenia symptoms that includes having a toneless voice, expressionless face, and a mute or rigid body.
15. Neurotransmitter that is scarce in depression.

ANSWERS

Chapter Review

Perspectives on Psychological Disorders

1. thoughts; feelings; actions
2. deviant; distressful; dysfunctional
3. variable
4. attention-deficit hyperactivity disorder; inattention; hyperactivity; impulsivity
5. boys; increased; agree
6. is; is not; learning; defiant
7. medical; illness; psychopathology; symptoms; therapy
8. Pinel
9. nature; nurture; internal
10. depression; schizophrenia; anorexia nervosa; bulimia; dynamic; anxiety; symptoms
11. biopsychosocial; genetic predispositions; physiological states; psychological dynamics; social; cultural
12. DSM-IV; diagnostic; 16
13. show
14. increased; increased

The "unDSM" is a new classification system that identifies 24 human strengths and virtues grouped into six clusters: wisdom and knowledge, courage, love, justice, temperance, and transcendence.

15. a significant

Psychological labels may be arbitrary. They can create preconceptions that bias our perceptions and interpretations and they can affect people's self-images. Moreover, labels can change reality, by serving as self-fulfilling prophecies. Despite these drawbacks, labels are useful in describing, treating, and researching the causes of psychological disorders.

Anxiety Disorders

1. distressing, persistent anxiety or maladaptive behaviors that reduce anxiety; intensity; persistence
2. generalized anxiety disorder; panic disorder; phobias; obsessive-compulsive disorder
3. generalized anxiety; free-floating
4. autonomic; panic disorder; panic attack
5. agoraphobia
6. phobia; specific phobias
7. social phobia
8. obsessive-compulsive
9. less
10. post-traumatic stress; haunting memories; nightmares; social withdrawal; jumpy anxiety; insomnia; overdiagnosed
11. survivor resiliency; post-traumatic growth
12. repressed
13. classical; fears
14. stimulus generalization
15. reinforced; observational
16. are; survival
17. is
18. anterior cingulate; amygdala
19. dissociative; memory; identity; personality
20. dissociative identity
21. roles
22. brain; body

Skeptics point out that the recent increase in the number of reported cases of dissociative identity disorder indicates that it has become a fad. The fact that the disorder is almost nonexistent outside North America also causes skeptics to doubt the disorder's genuineness.

23. anxiety; childhood trauma; fantasy-prone; therapist-patient

Mood Disorders

1. emotional extremes; major depressive; mania; bipolar
2. phobias; depression
3. dysthymic disorder
4. lethargy, feelings of worthlessness, and loss of interest in family, friends, and activities
5. two weeks
6. can
7. euphoria, hyperactivity, and a wildly optimistic state
8. precision; logic; emotional; imagery
9. causes
10. more; internal; depression, anxiety, and inhibited sexual desire
11. external; alcohol abuse, antisocial conduct, and lack of impulse control
12. is; a family member's death (loss of a job, a marital crisis, physical assault)
13. increasing; earlier; three

The psychoanalytic perspective suggests that adulthood depression can be triggered by losses that evoke feelings associated with earlier childhood losses. Alternatively, unresolved anger toward one's parents is turned inward and takes the form of depression.

14. tend; twins; strong

15. linkage analysis; DNA; associative

Suicide rates are higher among white Americans, the rich, older men, the nonreligious, and those who are single, widowed, or divorced. Although women more often attempt suicide, men are more likely to succeed. Suicide rates also vary widely around the world.

16. low; norepinephrine; serotonin

17. norepinephrine; norepinephrine; serotonin; reuptake; breakdown

18. omega-3; Japan; fish; low

19. less; left frontal; smaller; hippocampus; memories; serotonin

20. self-defeating; negative explanatory

21. learned helplessness

22. uncontrollable stress

Depressed people are more likely than others to explain failures or bad events in terms that are stable (it's going to last forever), global (it will affect everything), and internal (it's my fault). Such explanations lead to feelings of hopelessness, which in turn feed depression.

23. coincide with

24. self-focused; self-blaming

25. act; think (or overthink)

26. rejection

Depression is often brought on by stressful experiences. Depressed people brood over such experiences with maladaptive explanations that produce self-blame and amplify their depression, which in turn triggers other symptoms of depression. In addition, being withdrawn and complaining tends to elicit social rejection and other negative experiences.

Schizophrenia

1. reality

2. thinking; perceptions; emotions; actions

3. delusions

4. selective attention

5. hallucinations; auditory

6. flat affect; catatonia

7. cluster of disorders

8. disorganized and deluded thinking, inappropriate emotions; expressionless faces, toneless voices, mute or rigid bodies

9. chronic (or process); less; acute (or reactive)

10. dopamine; decrease; glutamate

11. low; frontal

12. fluid; shrinkage; thalamus; sensory input; attention

13. low birth weight; oxygen deprivation; viral infection

Risk of schizophrenia increases for those who undergo fetal development during a flu epidemic, or simply during the flu season. People born in densely populated areas and those born during winter and spring months are at increased risk. The months of excess schizophrenia births are reversed in the Southern Hemisphere, where the seasons are the reverse of the Northern Hemisphere's. Mothers who were sick with influenza during their pregnancy may be more likely to have children who develop schizophrenia. Blood drawn from pregnant women whose children develop schizophrenia have higher-than-normal levels of viral infection antibodies.

14. support

15. placenta; viruses

16. confirm

17. genetic; psychological

Such signs may include severe, long-lasting schizophrenia in the mother; complications at birth and low birth weight; separation from parents; short attention span and poor muscle coordination; disruptive or withdrawn behavior; emotional unpredictability; and poor peer relations and solo play.

Personality Disorders

1. social functioning

2. avoidant; schizoid; histrionic; narcissistic; borderline

3. antisocial; psychopath or sociopath

4. is

5. three to six; impulsive; uninhibited; social rewards; anxiety

6. frontal lobe

7. is not

Rates of Psychological Disorders

1. 7

2. higher

3. early; antisocial personality; phobias

Progress Test 1

Multiple-Choice Questions

1. **b.** is the answer. (p. 667)
   c. & d. Men are more likely than women to cope with stress in these ways.

2. **c.** is the answer. (p. 640)

3. **c.** is the answer. Most clinicians agree that psychological disorders may be caused by both psychological (d.) and physical (a. and b.) factors. (p. 643)

4. **d.** is the answer. (p. 642)

5. **a.** is the answer. (p. 659)

6. **b.** is the answer. Depression is often preceded by a stressful event related to work, marriage, or a close relationship. (p. 661)

7. **c.** is the answer. (p. 673)

8. **d.** is the answer. Although depression is universal, anorexia nervosa and bulimia are rare outside of Western culture. (p. 643)
   a. & b. Schizophrenia and depression are both universal.
   c. The text mentions only schizophrenia and depression as universal disorders. Furthermore, neurosis is no longer utilized as a category of diagnosis.

9. **a.** is the answer. (p. 672)
   b. & d. Thus far, only norepinephrine and serotonin have been implicated in depression and bipolar disorder.
   c. Schizophrenia has been associated with an excess of dopamine receptors. Blocking them alleviates, rather than increases, schizophrenia symptoms.

10. **d.** is the answer. (p. 644)
    b. The text does not mention DSM-IV's reliability in terms of a person's age.

11. **d.** is the answer. There is no evidence that early physical maturation is an early warning sign of schizophrenia. (p. 676)

12. **a.** is the answer. (p. 647)

13. **a.** is the answer. (p. 649)
    b. The mood disorders include major depressive disorder and bipolar disorder.
    c. Dissociative identity disorder is the only dissociative disorder discussed in the text.
    d. The personality disorders include the antisocial and histrionic personalities.

14. **d.** is the answer. Learned helplessness may lead to self-defeating beliefs, which in turn are linked with depression, a mood disorder. (pp. 665–666)

15. **d.** is the answer. (p. 655)

16. **c.** is the answer. (p. 670)

17. **b.** is the answer. Those with antisocial personality disorders show less autonomic arousal in such situations, and emotions, such as fear, are tied to arousal. (p. 678)

18. **d.** is the answer. Hallucinations are false sensory experiences; delusions are false beliefs. (pp. 669, 670)
    a. & b. Obsessions are repetitive and unwanted thoughts. Compulsions are repetitive behaviors.

19. **c.** is the answer. Drugs that relieve depression tend to increase levels of norepinephrine. (p. 664)
    a. Acetylcholine is a neurotransmitter involved in muscle contractions.
    b. It is in certain types of schizophrenia that decreasing dopamine levels is known to be helpful.
    d. On the contrary, it appears that a particular type of depression may be related to *low* levels of serotonin.

20. **c.** is the answer. (p. 671)

Matching Items

1. f (p. 656)
2. d (p. 642)
3. a (p. 658)
4. h (p. 651)
5. g (p. 643)
6. b (p. 659)
7. j (p. 651)
8. i (p. 669)
9. c (p. 670)
10. e (p. 650)

Progress Test 2

Multiple-Choice Questions

1. **a.** is the answer. Different cultures have different standards for behaviors that are considered acceptable and normal. (p. 640)
   b. Some abnormal behaviors are simply maladaptive for the individual.
   c. Many individuals who are deviant, such as Olympic gold medalists, are not considered abnormal. There are other criteria that must be met in order for behavior to be considered abnormal.
   d. Although physiological factors play a role in the various disorders, they do not define abnormal behavior. Rather, behavior is said to be abnormal if it is deviant, distressful, and dysfunctional.

2. **b.** is the answer. (pp. 653–654)
   a. This answer reflects the learning perspective.
   c. Although certain phobias are biologically predisposed, this could not fully explain phobias, nor is it the explanation offered by psychoanalytic theory.

d. Social-cognitive theorists propose self-defeating thoughts as a cause of depression.

3. **a.** is the answer. Schizophrenia sufferers are easily distracted by irrelevant stimuli, evidently because of a breakdown in the capacity for selective attention. (p. 670)

4. **b.** is the answer. (p. 673)

5. **b.** is the answer. The fact that some disorders are universal and at least partly genetic in origin implicates biological factors in their origin. The fact that other disorders appear only in certain parts of the world implicates sociocultural and psychological factors in their origin. (p. 643)

6. **b.** is the answer. (p. 642)

7. **b.** is the answer. (pp. 660–661)
   a. Anxiety is a passive disorder.
   d. Alcohol abuse is an active disorder.

8. **a.** is the answer. In fact, just the opposite is true. Labels are useful in promoting effective treatment of psychological disorders. (p. 648)

9. **b.** is the answer. (p. 656)
   c. Playing a role is most definitely a learned skill.

10. **d.** is the answer. In bipolar disorder, norepinephrine appears to be overabundant during mania and in short supply during depression. (p. 664)
    a. There is an overabundance of dopamine receptors in some schizophrenia patients.
    b. Serotonin sometimes appears to be scarce during depression.
    c. Epinephrine has not been implicated in psychological disorders.

11. **c.** is the answer. Joseph's fear has generalized from ladders to airplanes. (p. 654)
    a. Had Joseph acquired his fear after seeing someone *else* fall, observational learning would be implicated. This process would not, however, explain how his fear was transferred to airplanes.
    b. There is no indication that Joseph's phobia was acquired through reinforcement.
    d. Through stimulus discrimination, Joseph's fear would *not* have generalized from ladders to airplanes.

12. **d.** is the answer. (p. 655)

13. **b.** is the answer. (p. 642)
    a. This isn't the case; in fact, the medical model has gained credibility from recent discoveries of genetic and biochemical links to some disorders.
    c. & d. The medical perspective tends to place more emphasis on physiological factors.

14. **b.** is the answer. The psychoanalytic explanation is that these disorders are a manifestation of incompletely repressed impulses over which the person is anxious. According to the learning perspective, the troubled behaviors that result from these disorders have been reinforced by anxiety reduction. (p. 657)
    a. & c. These are true of the psychoanalytic, but not the learning, perspective.

15. **d.** is the answer. (p. 640)

16. **c.** is the answer. DSM-IV was shaped by the medical model. (p. 644)
    a. In fact, just the opposite is true. DSM-IV was revised in order to improve reliability by basing diagnoses on observable behaviors.
    b. & d. DSM-IV does not reflect a learning or a psychoanalytic bias.

17. **c.** is the answer. Panic attacks are characteristic of certain anxiety disorders, not of schizophrenia. (pp. 669–670)

18. **d.** is the answer. (pp. 665–666)

19. **d.** is the answer. A loss may evoke feelings of anger associated with an earlier loss. Such anger is turned against the self. This internalized anger results in depression. (p. 662)
    a. Learned helplessness would be an explanation offered by the social-cognitive perspective.
    b. The self-serving bias is not discussed in terms of its relationship to depression.
    c. This is the psychoanalytic explanation of anxiety.

20. **d.** is the answer. Risk for schizophrenia increases for individuals who are related to a schizophrenia victim, and the greater the genetic relatedness, the greater the risk. (p. 674)
    a. Schizophrenia victims have an overabundance of the neurotransmitter dopamine, not endorphins.
    b. Being a twin is, in itself, irrelevant to developing schizophrenia.
    c. Although learned helplessness has been suggested by social-cognitive theorists as a cause of self-defeating depressive behaviors, it has not been suggested as a cause of schizophrenia.

Matching Items

1. f (p. 656)   5. c (p. 677)   9. d (p. 669)
2. e (p. 650)   6. b (p. 664)   10. j (p. 650)
3. a (p. 672)   7. g (p. 664)
4. i (p. 659)   8. h (p. 659)

Psychology Applied

Multiple-Choice Questions

1. **c.** is the answer. An intense fear of a specific object is a phobia. (p. 650)

a. His fear is focused on a specific object, not generalized.

b. In this disorder a person is troubled by repetitive thoughts and actions.

d. Conditioned fears form the basis for anxiety rather than mood disorders.

2. **c.** is the answer. (p. 656)

a. Phobias focus anxiety on a specific object, activity, or situation.

b. There is no such disorder.

d. In this mood disorder, a person alternates between feelings of hopeless depression and overexcited mania.

3. **d.** is the answer. Repeated wrongdoing and aggressive behavior are part of the pattern associated with the antisocial personality disorder, which may also include marital problems and an inability to keep a job. (pp. 677–678)

a. Although dissociative identity disorder may involve an aggressive personality, there is nothing in the example to indicate a dissociation.

b. Nothing in the question indicates that Bob is passive and resigned and having the self-defeating thoughts characteristic of depression.

c. Bob's behavior does not include the disorganized thinking and disturbed perceptions typical of schizophrenia.

4. **d.** is the answer. In the learning perspective, a phobia, such as Julia's, is seen as a conditioned fear. (p. 654)

a. Because the fear is focused on a specific stimulus, the medical model does not easily account for the phobia. In any event, it would presumably offer an internal, biological explanation.

b. The psychoanalytic view of phobias would be that they represent incompletely repressed anxieties that are displaced onto the feared object.

c. The social-cognitive perspective would emphasize a person's conscious, cognitive processes, not reflexive conditioned responses.

5. **a.** is the answer. According to the learning view, compulsive behaviors are reinforced because they reduce the anxiety created by obsessive thoughts. Rashid's obsession concerns failing, and his desk-arranging compulsive behaviors apparently help him control these thoughts. (p. 654)

b. The psychoanalytic perspective would view obsessive thoughts as a symbolic representation of forbidden impulses. These thoughts may prompt the person to perform compulsive acts that counter these impulses.

c. & d. The text does not offer explanations of obsessive-compulsive behavior based on the hu-

manistic or social-cognitive perspectives. Presumably, however, these explanations would emphasize growth-blocking difficulties in the person's environment (humanistic perspective) and the reciprocal influences of personality and environment (social-cognitive perspective), rather than symbolic expressions of forbidden impulses.

6. **d.** is the answer. (p. 649)

a. In phobias, anxiety is focused on a specific object.

b. Major depressive disorder does not manifest these symptoms.

c. The obsessive-compulsive disorder is characterized by repetitive and unwanted thoughts and/or actions.

7. **d.** is the answer. Jason is obsessed with cleanliness; as a result, he has developed a compulsion to shower. (p. 651)

a. Dissociative disorders involve a separation of conscious awareness from previous memories and thoughts.

b. Generalized anxiety disorder does not have a specific focus.

c. This disorder is characterized by maladaptive character traits.

8. **d.** is the answer. (p. 652)

a. There is no evidence that Zheina has *lost* either her memory or her identity, as would occur in dissociative disorders.

b. Although she has symptoms of depression, Zheina does not show signs of mania, which occurs in bipolar disorder.

c. Zheina shows no signs of disorganized thinking or disturbed perceptions.

9. **a.** is the answer. Because Sandy experiences hallucinations (hearing voices), delusions (fearing someone is "out to get her"), and incoherence, she would most likely be diagnosed as suffering from schizophrenia. (pp. 669–670)

b., c., & d. These disorders are not characterized by disorganized thoughts and perceptions.

10. **d.** is the answer. (p. 650)

a. Baseless physical symptoms rarely play a role in schizophrenia.

b. There is no indication that she is exhibiting euphoric behavior.

c. There is no indication that she has suffered a trauma.

11. **a.** is the answer. Humans seem biologically prepared to develop a fear of heights and other dangers that our ancestors faced. (p. 655)

12. **b.** is the answer. (p. 656)

13. **b.** is the answer. The fact that this woman has had these symptoms for more than two weeks indicates that she is suffering from major depressive disorder. (p. 659)

14. **a.** is the answer. Matt's alternating states of the hopelessness and lethargy of depression and the energetic, optimistic state of mania are characteristic of bipolar disorder. (p. 659)
    b. Although he was depressed on Tuesday, Matt's manic state on Monday indicates that he is not suffering from major depressive disorder.
    c. Matt was depressed, not detached from reality.
    d. That Matt is not exhibiting episodes of intense dread indicates that he is not suffering from panic disorder.

15. **d.** is the answer. Freud believed that the anger once felt toward parents was internalized and would produce depression. (p. 662)
    a. & b. The learning and social-cognitive perspectives focus on environmental experiences, conditioning, and self-defeating attitudes in explaining depression.
    c. The biological perspective focuses on genetic predispositions and biochemical imbalances in explaining depression.

16. **b.** is the answer. (pp. 665–666)

17. **b.** is the answer. Norepinephrine, which increases arousal and boosts mood, is scarce during depression. Drugs that relieve depression tend to increase norepinephrine. (p. 664)
    c. Increasing serotonin, which is sometimes scarce during depression, might relieve depression.
    d. This neurotransmitter is involved in motor responses but has not been linked to psychological disorders.

18. **d.** is the answer. Schizophrenia patients sometimes have an excess of receptors for dopamine. Drugs that block these receptors can therefore reduce symptoms of schizophrenia. (p. 672)
    a., b., & c. Dopamine receptors have not been implicated in these psychological disorders.

19. **c.** is the answer. (p. 641)

20. **c.** is the answer. (p. 675)

Essay Question

There is more to a psychological disorder than being different from other people. Gifted artists, athletes, and scientists have deviant capabilities, yet are not considered psychologically disordered. Also, what is deviant in one culture may not be in another, or at another time. Homosexuality, for example, was once classified as a psychological disorder, but it is no longer. Similarly, nudity is common in some cultures

and disturbing in others. Deviant behaviors are more likely to be considered disordered when judged as distressful and dysfunctional to the individual. Prolonged feelings of depression or the use of drugs to avoid dealing with problems are examples of deviant behaviors that may signal a psychological disorder if the person is unable to function, to perform routine behaviors (become dysfunctional).

Key Terms

Writing Definitions

1. In order to be classified as a **psychological disorder**, behavior must be deviant, distressful, and dysfunctional. (p. 640)

2. **Attention-deficit hyperactivity disorder (ADHD)** is a psychological disorder characterized by one or more of three symptoms: extreme inattention, hyperactivity, and impulsivity. (p. 641)

3. The **medical model** holds that psychological disorders are illnesses that can be diagnosed, treated, and, in most cases, cured, using traditional methods of medicine and psychiatry. (p. 642)

4. **DSM-IV** is a short name for the American Psychiatric Association's *Diagnostic and Statistical Manual of Mental Disorders* (*Fourth Edition, Text Revision*), which provides a widely used system of classifying psychological disorders. (p. 644)

5. **Anxiety disorders** involve distressing, persistent anxiety or maladaptive behaviors that reduce anxiety. (p. 649)

6. In the **generalized anxiety disorder**, the person is continually tense, apprehensive, and in a state of autonomic nervous system arousal for no apparent reason. (p. 649)

7. A **panic disorder** is an episode of intense dread accompanied by chest pain, dizziness, or choking. It is essentially an escalation of the anxiety associated with generalized anxiety disorder. (p. 650)

8. A **phobia** is an anxiety disorder in which a person has a persistent, irrational fear and avoidance of a specific object or situation. (p. 650)

9. **Obsessive-compulsive disorder** is an anxiety disorder in which the person experiences uncontrollable and repetitive thoughts (obsessions) and actions (compulsions). (p. 651)

10. **Post-traumatic stress disorder (PTSD)** is an anxiety disorder characterized by haunting memories, nightmares, social withdrawal, jumpy anxiety, and/or insomnia lasting four weeks or more following a traumatic experience. (p. 652)

11. **Dissociative disorders** involve a separation of conscious awareness from one's previous memories, thoughts, and feelings. (p. 656)

Memory aid: To *dissociate* is to separate or pull apart. In the **dissociative disorders** a person becomes dissociated from his or her memories and identity.

12. The **dissociative identity disorder** is a dissociative disorder in which a person exhibits two or more distinct and alternating personalities; also called *multiple personality disorder.* (p. 656)

13. **Mood disorders** are characterized by emotional extremes. (p. 658)

14. **Major depressive disorder** is the mood disorder that occurs when a person exhibits the lethargy, feelings of worthlessness, or loss of interest in family, friends, and activities characteristic of depression for more than a two-week period and for no discernible reason. Because of its relative frequency, depression has been called the "common cold" of psychological disorders. (p. 659)

15. **Mania** is the wildly optimistic, euphoric, hyperactive state that alternates with depression in the bipolar disorder. (p. 659)

16. **Bipolar disorder** is the mood disorder in which a person alternates between depression and the euphoria of a manic state. (p. 659)

Memory aid: *Bipolar* means having two poles, that is, two opposite qualities. In **bipolar disorder,** the opposing states are mania and depression.

17. **Schizophrenia** refers to the group of severe disorders whose symptoms may include disorganized and delusional thinking, inappropriate emotions and actions, and disturbed perceptions. (p. 669)

18. **Delusions** are false beliefs that often are symptoms of psychotic disorders. (p. 669)

19. **Personality disorders** are characterized by inflexible and enduring maladaptive character traits that impair social functioning. (p. 677)

20. The **antisocial personality disorder** is a personality disorder in which the person is aggressive, ruthless, and shows no sign of a conscience that would inhibit wrongdoing. (p. 677)

Cross-Check

ACROSS
3. major depressive
16. mania
17. mood
18. bipolar
19. anxiety

DOWN
1. disorganized
2. DSM-IV
4. ADHD
6. phobia
7. linkage analysis
8. biopsychosocial
9. hallucinations
10. medical model
11. catatonia
12. delusions
13. dopamine
14. negative
15. serotonin

FOCUS ON VOCABULARY AND LANGUAGE

Page 639: It's no wonder then that studying psychological disorders may at times evoke an *eerie sense* of self-recognition, one that *illuminates* the dynamics of our own personality. When reading this chapter, you may sometimes experience the strange, uncanny feeling (*eerie sense*) that Myers is writing about you. On occasion, we all feel, think, and behave in ways similar to disturbed people, and becoming aware of how alike we sometimes are may help shed some light on (*illuminate*) the processes underlying personality.

Perspectives on Psychological Disorders

Page 640: Where should we *draw the line* between sadness and depression? Between zany creativity and bizarre irrationality? Between normality and abnormality? Myers is addressing the problem of how exactly to define psychological disorders. How do we distinguish (*draw the line*) between someone who displays unusual or absurd innovative ability (*zany creativity*) and someone who has strange and unusual reasoning (*bizarre irrationality*)? Between someone who is "abnormal" and someone who is not? For psychologists and other mental-health workers, psychological disorders involve persistently harmful thoughts, feelings, and actions that are deviant, distressful, and dysfunctional.

Page 642: "*The devil made him do it.*" Our ancestors explained strange and puzzling behavior by appealing to what they knew and believed about the nature of the world (e.g., gods, stars, demons, spirits, etc.). A person who today would be classified as psychologically disturbed because of his or her bizarre behavior in the past would have been considered to be possessed by evil spirits or demons (*the devil made him do it*). These types of nonscientific explanations persisted up until the nineteenth century.

Page 644: "Schizophrenia" provides *a handy short-hand* for describing a complex disorder. Psychology uses a classification system (DSM-IV) to describe and impose order on complicated psychological problems. When a descriptive label (diagnostic classification) is used to identify a disorder, it does not explain the problem, but it does provide a quick and useful means of communicating a great deal of information in abbreviated form (*it is a handy shorthand*).

Page 644: Some critics have *faulted* the manual for *casting too wide a net* and bringing "almost any kind of behavior within the *compass* of psychiatry." . . . The DSM-IV classification system has been received with a less-than-enthusiastic response by some practitioners (*they were not enthralled*). Many criticize (*fault*) the inclusion of a large number of behaviors as psychologically disordered (*it casts too wide a net*) and suggest that just about any behavior is now within the purview (*compass*) of psychiatry. Nevertheless, many other clinicians find DSM-IV a useful and practical tool or device.

Page 647 (Thinking Critically): "Hinckley *Insane,* Public *Mad.*" The word *mad* has a number of meanings: (a) angry, (b) insane, (c) foolish and irrational, (d) rash, (e) enthusiastic about something, (f) frantic. John Hinckley, who shot President Reagan, was not sent to prison; instead, he was confined to a mental hospital. The public was angry and upset (*mad*) because Hinckley was judged to be mad (*insane*).

Page 648: Labels can serve as *self-fulfilling prophecies.* A prophecy is a prediction about the future. When we characterize or classify (*label*) someone as a certain type of person, the very act of labeling may help bring about or create the actions described by the label (*self-fulfilling prophesy*).

Anxiety Disorders

Page 649: heart palpitations . . . ringing in the ears . . . edgy . . . jittery . . . sleeplessness . . . furrowed brows . . . twitching eyelids . . . fidgeting. These are all descriptions of the symptoms of generalized anxiety disorder. The person may may have increased heart rate (*heart palpitations*), may hear high-pitched sounds (*ringing in the ears*), may be nervous and jumpy (*edgy*), and may start trembling (*jittery*). The sufferer may worry all the time, be unable to sleep (*sleeplessness or insomnia*), and feel apprehensive, which may show in frowning (*furrowed brows*), rapidly blinking eyes (*twitching eyelids*), and restless movements (*fidgeting*).

Page 650: Because nicotine is a stimulant, *lighting up doesn't lighten up.* People who smoke cigarettes have an increased risk (*two- to fourfold*) of a first time panic attack. So, igniting and smoking a cigarette (*lighting up*) doesn't necessarily lead to an elevated mood (*it doesn't lighten up our mood*).

Page 652: Years later, images of these events intrude on him as *flashbacks* and *nightmares.* Many war veterans (*vets*) and others who experienced traumatic stressful events develop post-traumatic stress disorder. Symptoms include terrifying images of the event (*flashbacks*); very frightening dreams (*nightmares*); extreme nervousness, anxiety, or depression; and a tendency to become socially isolated.

Page 655: Grooming gone wild becomes hair pulling. The biological perspective explains our tendency to be anxious (*anxiety-prone*) in evolutionary or genetic terms. A normal behavior that once had survival value in our evolutionary past may now be distorted into compulsive action. Thus, compulsive hair pulling may be an exaggerated version of normal grooming behavior (*grooming gone wild*).

Page 656: . . . a ruse . . . Kenneth Bianchi is a convicted psychopathic murderer who pretended to be a multiple personality in order to avoid jail or the death penalty, and his cunning ploy (*ruse*) fooled many psychologists and psychiatrists. It also raised the question of the reality of dissociative identity as a genuine disorder.

Page 656: Rather, note skeptics, some therapists *go fishing for multiple personalities.* Those who doubt the existence of dissociative identity disorder (*skeptics*) find it strange that the number of diagnosed cases in North America has increased dramatically (*exploded*) in the last decade. (In the rest of the world it is rare or nonexistent; in Britain, where it is rarely diagnosed, some consider it an eccentric [*wacky*] American fad [*fashionably popular*].) In addition, the average number of personalities has multiplied (*mushroomed*) from 3 to 12 per patient. One explanation for the disorder's popularity is that many therapists expect it to be there, so they actively solicit (*go fishing for*) symptoms of dissociative identity disorder from their patients.

Mood Disorders

Page 659: To grind temporarily to a halt and *ruminate,* as depressed people do, is to reassess one's life when feeling threatened and to *redirect energy in more promising ways.* From a biological point of view, depression is a natural reaction to stress and painful events. It is like a warning signal that brings us to a complete stop (*we grind to a halt*) and allows us time to reflect on life and contemplate (*ruminate on*) the meaning of our existence and to focus more optimistically on the future.

Page 659: The difference between a *blue mood* after bad news and a mood disorder is like the difference between gasping for breath for a few minutes after a hard run and being chronically short of breath. We all feel depressed and sad (*we have blue moods*) in response to painful events and sometimes just to life in general. These feelings are points on a continuum; at the extreme end, and very distinct from ordinary depression, are the serious mood disorders (e.g., major depressive disorder) in which the signs of chronic depression (loss of appetite, sleeplessness, tiredness, low self-esteem, and a disinterest in family, friends and social activities) last two weeks or more.

Page 659: If depression is living in slow motion, mania is *fast forward.* Bipolar disorder is characterized by mood swings. While depression slows the person down (*like living in slow motion*), the hyperactivity and heightened exuberant state (*mania*) at the other emotional extreme seems to speed the person up, similar to the images you get when you press the fast forward button on the DVD player or see a "speeded-up" film.

Page 665: Depressed people *view life through dark glasses.* Social-cognitive theorists point out that biological factors do not operate independently of environmental influences. People who are depressed often have negative beliefs about themselves and about their present and future situations (*they view life through dark glasses*). These self-defeating beliefs can accentuate or amplify a nasty (*vicious*) cycle of interactions between chemistry, cognition, and mood.

Page 667: . . . even small losses can temporarily *sour* our thinking. When loyal basketball fans were depressed by their team's loss, they had a more pessimistic (*bleaker*) assessment of the outcome of future games as well as negative views of their own abilities (*the loss soured their thinking*). Depression can cause self-focused negative thinking.

Page 668: Misery may love another's company, *but company does not love another's misery.* The old saying

"*misery loves company*" means that depressed, sad people like to be with other people. The possible social consequence of being withdrawn, self-focused, self-blaming, and complaining (*depressed*), however, is rejection by others (*company does not love another's misery*).

Schizophrenia

Page 670: . . . *hodge-podge* . . . The symptoms of schizophrenia include fragmented and distorted thinking, disturbed perception, and inappropriate feelings and behaviors. Schizophrenia victims, when talking, may move rapidly from topic to topic and idea to idea so that their speech is incomprehensible (*a word salad*). This may be the result of a breakdown in selective attention, whereby an assorted mixture (*hodge-podge*) of stimuli continually distracts the person.

Page 670: Other victims of schizophrenia sometimes lapse into *flat affect,* a zombielike state of apparent apathy. The emotions of schizophrenia are frequently not appropriate for the situation. There may be laughter at a funeral, anger and tears for no apparent reason, or no expression of emotion whatsoever (*flat affect*), which resembles a half-dead, trancelike (*zombielike*) state of indifference (*apathy*).

Personality Disorders

Page 678: . . . *con artist* . . . A person who has an antisocial personality is usually a male who has no conscience, who lies, steals, cheats, and is unable to keep a job or take on the normal responsibilities of family and society. When combined with high intelligence and no moral sense, the result may be a clever, smooth talking, and deceitful trickster or confidence man (*con artist*).

Page 678: . . . the antisocial personality disorder is *woven* of biological and psychological *strands.* The analogy here is between the antisocial personality and how cloth is made (*woven*). Both psychological and biological factors (*strands*) combine to produce the disorder. If the biological predispositions are fostered (*channeled*) in more positive ways, the result may be a fearless hero; alternatively, the same disposition may produce a killer or a manipulative, calculating, self-centered, but charming and intelligent individual (*a clever con artist*). Research confirms that with antisocial behavior, as with many other things, nature and nurture interact.

17 : Therapy

CHAPTER OVERVIEW

Chapter 17 discusses the major psychotherapies and biomedical therapies for maladaptive behaviors. The various psychotherapies all derive from the personality theories discussed earlier, namely, the psychoanalytic, humanistic, behavioral, and cognitive theories. The chapter groups the therapies by perspective but also emphasizes the common threads that run through them. In evaluating the therapies, the chapter points out that, although people who are untreated often improve, those receiving psychotherapy tend to improve somewhat more, regardless of the type of therapy they receive. This section includes a discussion of several popular alternative therapies.

The biomedical therapies discussed are drug therapies, electroconvulsive therapy, and psychosurgery, which is seldom used. By far the most important of these, drug therapies are being used in the treatment of psychotic, anxiety, and mood disorders.

Because the origins of problems often lie beyond the individual, the chapter concludes with approaches that aim at preventing psychological disorders by focusing on the family or on the larger social environment as possible contributors to psychological disorders.

NOTE: Answer guidelines for all Chapter 17 questions begin on page 453.

CHAPTER REVIEW

First, skim each section, noting headings and boldface items. After you have read the section, review each objective by answering the fill-in and essay-type questions that follow it. As you proceed, evaluate your performance by consulting the answers beginning on page 453. Do not continue with the next section until you understand each answer. If you need to, review or reread the section in the textbook before continuing.

Introducing Therapy (pp. 685–686)

> David Myers at times uses idioms that are unfamiliar to some readers. If you do not know the meaning of any of the following words or expressions in the context in which they appear in the introduction, refer to page 460 for an explanation: *cracked the genetic code; gawk.*

Objective 1: Discuss some ways that *psychotherapy, biomedical therapy,* and an *eclectic approach* to therapy differ.

1. Mental health therapies are classified as either _____therapies or _____therapies.

2. Psychological therapy is more commonly called _____ . This type of therapy is appropriate for disorders that are

   _____ .

3. Biomedical therapies include the use of

   _____ _____

   and medical procedures that act directly on the patient's _____

   _____ .

4. Some therapists, particularly those who adopt a biopsychosocial view, blend several psychotherapy techniques and so are said to take an _____ approach. Closely related to this approach is _____ _____ , which attempts to combine methods into a single, coherent system.

The Psychological Therapies (pp. 686–699)

> If you do not know the meaning of any of the following words, phrases, or expressions in the context in which they appear in this section, refer to pages 460–461 for an explanation: *fueled . . . residue; aim to boost; knocks the props out from under you; lore; drinks laced with a drug; aggressive and self-abusive behaviors; colors our feelings; catastrophizing.*

Objective 2: Define *psychoanalysis,* and discuss the aims of this form of therapy.

1. The goal of Freud's psychoanalysis, which is based on his personality theory, is to help the patient gain _____ .

2. Freud assumed that many psychological problems originate in childhood impulses and conflicts that have been _____ .

3. Psychoanalysts attempt to bring _____ feelings into _____ awareness where they can be dealt with.

Objective 3: Describe some of the methods used in psychoanalysis, and list some criticisms of this form of therapy.

4. Freud's technique in which a patient says whatever comes to mind is called _____ _____ .

5. When, in the course of therapy, a person omits shameful or embarrassing material, _____ is occurring. Insight is facilitated by the analyst's _____ of the meaning of such omissions, of dreams, and of other information revealed during therapy sessions.

6. Freud referred to the hidden meaning of a dream as its _____ _____ .

7. When strong feelings, similar to those experienced in other important relationships, are developed toward the therapist, _____ has occurred.

8. Critics point out that psychoanalysts' interpretations are hard to _____ and that therapy takes a long time and is very _____ .

Objective 4: Contrast psychodynamic therapy and interpersonal therapy with traditional psychoanalysis.

9. Therapists who are influenced by Freud's psychoanalysis but who talk to the patient face to face are _____ therapists. In addition, they work with patients only _____ (how long?) and for only a few weeks or months.

10. A brief alternative to psychodynamic therapy that has proven effective with _____ patients is _____ _____ .

11. While this approach aims to help people gain _____ into their difficulties, it focuses on _____ _____ rather than on past hurts.

Objective 5: Identify the basis characteristics of the humanistic therapies, and describe the specific goals and techniques of Carl Rogers' client-centered therapy.

12. Humanistic therapies attempt to help people meet their potential for _____ .

List several ways that humanistic therapy differs from psychoanalysis.

13. The humanistic therapy based on Rogers' theory is called _____-_____ therapy, which is described as _____ therapy because the therapist _____ (interprets/does not interpret) the person's problems.

14. In order to promote growth in clients, Rogerian therapists exhibit _____ , _____ , and _____ .

15. Rogers' technique of restating and clarifying what a person is saying is called

_____ _____ .

Given a nonjudgmental environment that provides _____ _____

_____ , patients are better able to accept themselves as they are and to feel valued and whole.

16. Three tips for listening more actively in your own relationships are to _____ ,

_____ _____ ,

and _____ _____ .

Objective 6: Explain how the basic assumption of behavior therapy differs from those of traditional psychoanalytic and humanistic therapies.

17. Behavior therapy applies principles of _____ to eliminate troubling behaviors.

Contrast the assumptions of the behavior therapies with those of psychoanalysis and humanistic therapy.

Objective 7: Define *counterconditioning,* and describe the techniques used in exposure therapies and aversive conditioning.

18. One cluster of behavior therapies is based on the principles of _____

_____ , as developed in Pavlov's experiments. This technique, in which a new, incompatible response is substituted for a maladaptive one, is called _____ .

Two examples of this technique are

_____ _____

and _____ _____ .

19. The most widely used techniques of behavior therapy are the _____

_____ . The technique of systematic desensitization has been most fully developed by the therapist _____ .

The assumption behind this technique is that one cannot simultaneously be _____ and relaxed.

20. The first step in systematic desensitization is the construction of a _____ of anxiety-arousing stimuli. The second step involves training in _____

_____ . In the final step, the person is trained to associate the

_____ state with the

_____ -arousing stimuli.

21. For those who are unable to visually imagine an anxiety-arousing situation, or too afraid or embarrassed to do so, _____

_____ _____

therapy offers a promising alternative.

22. In aversive conditioning, the therapist attempts to substitute a _____ (positive/ negative) response for one that is currently _____ (positive/negative).

In this technique, a person's unwanted behaviors become associated with _____ feelings.

Objective 8: State the main premise of therapy based on operant conditioning principles, and describe the views of proponents and critics of behavior modification.

23. Reinforcing desired behaviors and withholding reinforcement for undesired behaviors are key aspects of _____

_____ .

24. Therapies that influence behavior by controlling its consequences are based on principles of _____ conditioning. One application of this form of therapy to institutional

settings is the _____

_____ , in which desired

behaviors are rewarded.

State two criticisms of behavior modification.

State some responses of proponents of behavior modification.

Objective 9: Contrast cognitive therapy and cognitive-behavior therapy, and give some examples of cognitive therapy for depression.

25. Therapists who teach people new, more constructive ways of thinking are using _____ therapy.

26. One variety of cognitive therapy attempts to reverse the _____ beliefs often associated with _____ by helping clients see their irrationalities. This therapy was developed by _____ .

27. A form of cognitive therapy developed by Adele Rabin builds on the finding that depressed people _____ (do/do not) exhibit the self-serving bias.

28. Training people to restructure their thinking in stressful situations is the goal of _____ _____ training. Students trained to _____ their negative thoughts are less likely to experience future depression.

29. Treatment that combines an attack on negative thinking with efforts to modify behavior is known as _____ - _____ therapy.

Objective 10: Discuss the rationale and benefits of group therapy, including family therapy.

List several advantages of group therapy.

30. The type of group interaction that focuses on the fact that we live and grow in relation to others is _____ _____ .

31. In this type of group, therapists focus on improving _____ within the family and helping family members to discover new ways of preventing or resolving _____ .

32. Two common types of group therapy are _____ and _____ groups for the addicted, the divorced, and those simply looking for fellowship and growth, for example. Most support groups focus on _____ and _____ - _____ - _____ illnesses.

Evaluating Psychotherapies (pp. 700–710)

> If you do not know the meaning of any of the following words, phrases, or expressions in the context in which they appear in the text, refer to pages 461–462 for an explanation: *Hang in there; testimonials; ebb and flow of events; clearcut; fertile soil for pseudotherapies; harness; empathy are hallmarks.*

1. In contrast to earlier times, most therapy today _____ (is/is not) provided by psychiatrists.

Objective 11: Explain why clients tend to overestimate the effectiveness of psychotherapy.

2. A majority of psychotherapy clients express _____ (satisfaction/dissatisfaction) with their therapy.

Give three reasons why client testimonials are not persuasive evidence for psychotherapy's effectiveness.

3. A long-term study of 500 Massachusetts boys found that those who received intensive counseling _____ (had/did not have) significantly fewer problems than a control group. Research has also shown that "Scared Straight" programs _____ (are/are not) effective in reducing criminal offenses committed by delinquent boys.

Objective 12: Give some reasons why clinicians tend to overestimate the effectiveness of psychotherapy, and describe two phenomena that contribute to clients' and clinicians' misperceptions in this area.

4. Clinicians tend to _____ (overestimate/underestimate) the effectiveness of psychotherapy.

5. One reason clinicians' perceptions of the effectiveness of psychotherapy are inaccurate is that clients justify entering therapy by emphasizing their _____ and justify leaving therapy by emphasizing their _____ .

6. (Thinking Critically) Clients' and therapists' perceptions of therapy's effectiveness may be inflated by their _____ that a treatment works. This phenomenon is called the _____ _____ .

Another phenomenon that may inflate their perceptions of therapy's effectiveness is the phenomenon called _____ _____ _____ , which is the tendency for _____ events or emotions to return to their _____ state.

Objective 13: Discuss the importance of outcome studies in judging the effectiveness of psychotherapies, and describe some of these findings.

7. In hopes of better assessing psychotherapy's effectiveness, psychologists have turned to _____ research studies.

8. The debate over the effectiveness of psychotherapy began with a study by _____ ; it showed that the rate of improvement for those who received therapy _____ (was/was not) higher than the rate for those who did not.

9. A statistical technique that makes it possible to combine the results of many different psychotherapy outcome studies is called _____-_____ . Overall, the results of such analyses indicate that psychotherapy is _____ (somewhat effective/ineffective).

10. Psychotherapy is cost-effective when compared with the greater costs of _____ care for psychological problems.

Objective 14: Summarize the findings on which psychotherapies are most effective for specific disorders.

11. Comparisons of the effectiveness of different forms of therapy reveal _____ (clear/no clear) differences, that the type of therapy provider _____ (matters greatly/does not matter), and that whether therapy is provided by an individual therapist or within a group _____ (makes a difference/does not make a difference).

12. Controlled treatment studies have demonstrated that depression may be effectively treated with _____ , _____ , and _____ therapies. In treating

anxiety, _____ and

_____ therapies and

_____ _____

training have proven effective. Cognitive-
behavior therapy has proven effective in treating
_____ , and behavior modifica-
tion in treating _____

_____ .

13. With phobias, compulsions, and other specific
    behavior problems, _____
    _____ therapies have been the
    most effective.

14. As a rule, psychotherapy is most effective with
    problems that are _____
    (specific/nonspecific).

Objective 15: Evaluate the effectiveness of eye movement desensitization and reprocessing (EMDR) and
light exposure therapies.

15. Today, many forms of _____
    _____ are touted as effective
    treatments for a variety of complaints.

16. Aside from testimonials, there is very little evi-
    dence based on _____ research
    for such therapies.

17. In one popular alternative therapy, a therapist
    triggers eye movements in patients while they
    imagine _____
    _____ . This therapy, called

    _____ _____

    _____ _____

    _____ , has proven
    _____ (completely
    ineffective/somewhat effective) as a treatment for
    nonmilitary _____-

    _____ _____

    _____ . However, skeptics point
    to evidence that _____
    _____ is just as effective as
    triggered eye movements in producing beneficial
    results. The key seems to be in the person's
    _____ traumatic memories and
    in a _____ effect.

18. For people who suffer from the wintertime form
    of depression called _____

    _____ _____ ,
    timed _____-_____
    therapy may be beneficial.

Objective 16: Describe the three benefits attributed to
all psychotherapies.

19. All forms of psychotherapy offer three benefits:
    _____ for demoralized people; a
    new _____ on oneself; and a
    relationship that is _____ ,
    _____ , and _____ .

20. Therapy outcomes vary with the
    _____ of the person seeking
    help.

21. In one study of depression treatment, the most
    effective therapists were those who were per-
    ceived as most _____ and
    _____ .

22. Several studies found that treatment for mild
    problems offered by paraprofessionals
    _____ (is/is not) as effective as
    that offered by professional therapists.

Objective 17: Discuss the role of values and cultural
differences in the therapeutic process.

23. Generally speaking, psychotherapists' personal
    values _____ (do/do not) influ-
    ence their therapy. This is particularly significant
    when the therapist and client are from
    _____ (the same/different)
    cultures.

24. In North America, Europe, and Australia, most
    therapists reflect their culture's
    _____ .

25. Differences in values may help explain the reluc-
    tance of some _____ popula-
    tions to use mental health services.

The Biomedical Therapies (pp. 711–719)

> If you do not know the meaning of any of the following words, phrases, or expressions in the context in which they appear in the text, refer to pages 462–463 for an explanation: *sluggishness, tremors, and twitches; "Popping a Xanax"; lift people up; barbaric image; jump-starting the brain.*

Objective 18: Define *psychopharmacology*, and explain how double-blind studies help researchers evaluate a drug's effectiveness.

1. The most widely used biomedical treatments are the _____ therapies. Thanks to these therapies, the number of residents in mental hospitals has _____ (increased/decreased) sharply.

2. The field that studies the effects of drugs on the mind and behavior is _____ .

3. To guard against the _____ effect and normal _____ , neither the patients nor the staff involved in a study may be aware of which condition a given individual is in; this is called a _____-_____ study.

Objective 19: Describe the characteristics of antipsychotic drugs, and discuss their use in treating schizophrenia.

4. One effect of _____ drugs such as _____ is to help those experiencing _____ (positive/negative) symptoms of schizophrenia by decreasing their responsiveness to irrelevant stimuli; schizophrenia patients who are apathetic and withdrawn may be more effectively treated with the drug _____ .

5. These drugs work by blocking the receptor sites for the neurotransmitters _____ and _____ .

6. Long-term use of first-generation antipsychotic drugs can produce _____ _____ , which involves involuntary movements of the

muscles of the _____ , _____ , and _____ .

Objective 20: Describe the characteristics of antianxiety drugs.

7. Xanax and Ativan are classified as _____ drugs.

8. These drugs depress activity in the _____ _____ .

9. When used in combination with _____ _____ , these drugs can help people cope with frightening situations.

10. Antianxiety drugs have been criticized for merely reducing _____ , rather than resolving underlying _____ . These drugs can also cause _____ _____ .

Objective 21: Describe the characteristics of antidepressant drugs, and discuss their use in treating specific disorders.

11. Drugs that are prescribed to alleviate depression are called _____ drugs. These drugs also work by increasing levels of the neurotransmitters _____ or _____ .

12. One example of this type of drug is _____ , which works by blocking the reuptake of _____ from synapses and is therefore called a _____-_____-_____ drug.

13. Equally effective in calming anxious people and energizing depressed people is _____ _____ , which has positive side effects. Even better is to use drugs, which work _____-_____ (bottom-up/top-down) in conjunction with _____-_____ therapy, which works _____-_____ (bottom-up/top-down).

14. Although people with depression often improve after one month on antidepressants, meta-analysis studies demonstrate that a large percentage of the effectiveness is due to

_____ _____

or a _____ _____ .

Objective 22: Describe the use and effects of mood-stabilizing medications.

15. In order to stabilize the mood swings of a bipolar disorder, the simple salt _____ is often prescribed.

16. Another effective drug in the control of mania was originally used to treat epilepsy; it is

_____ .

Objective 23: Describe the use of electroconvulsive therapy in treating severe depression, and describe some possible alternatives to ECT.

17. The therapeutic technique in which the patient receives an electric shock to the brain is referred to as _____ therapy, abbreviated as _____ .

18. ECT is most often used with patients suffering from severe _____ . Research evidence _____ (confirms/does not confirm) ECT's effectiveness with such patients.

19. The mechanism by which ECT works is

_____ .

20. A gentler alternative is a chest _____ that intermittently stimulates the _____ nerve.

21. Another gentler procedure called _____

_____ _____

_____ aims to treat depression by presenting pulses through a magnetic coil held close to a person's skull above the right eyebrow. Unlike ECT, this procedure produces no

_____ , _____

loss, or other side effects. This procedure may work by energizing the brain's left

_____ _____ ,

which is relatively inactive in depressed patients.

Objective 24: Summarize the history of the psychosurgical procedure known as a lobotomy, and discuss the use of psychosurgery today.

22. The biomedical therapy in which a portion of brain tissue is removed or destroyed is called

_____ .

23. In the 1930s, Moniz developed an operation called the _____ . In this procedure, the _____ lobe of the brain is disconnected from the rest of the brain.

24. Today, most psychosurgery has been replaced by the use of _____ or some other form of treatment.

Preventing Psychological Disorders
(pp. 719–720)

> If you do not know the meaning of the following expression in the context in which it appears in the text, refer to page 463 for an explanation: *upstream work.*

Objective 25: Explain the rationale of preventive mental health programs.

1. Psychotherapies and biomedical therapies locate the cause of psychological disorders within the

_____ .

2. An alternative viewpoint is that many psychological disorders are responses to

_____ .

3. According to this viewpoint, it is not just the _____ who needs treatment but also the person's _____

_____ .

4. One advocate of _____ mental health, George Albee, believes that many social stresses undermine people's sense of

_____ , _____

_____ , and _____-

_____ . These stresses include

_____ , work that is

_____ , constant _____ ,

_____ , _____ ,

and _____ .

5. Albee's views remind us that disorders are not just biological and not just environmental or psychological, because we are all an _____ _____ system.

PROGRESS TEST 1

Multiple-Choice Questions

Circle your answers to the following questions and check them with the answers beginning on page 455. If your answer is incorrect, read the explanation for why it is incorrect and then consult the appropriate pages of the text (in parentheses following the correct answer).

1. Electroconvulsive therapy is most useful in the treatment of:
   a. schizophrenia.
   b. depression.
   c. personality disorders.
   d. anxiety disorders.

2. The technique in which a person is asked to report everything that comes to his or her mind is called _____ ; it is favored by_____ therapists.
   a. active listening; cognitive
   b. spontaneous remission; humanistic
   c. free association; psychoanalytic
   d. systematic desensitization; behavior

3. Of the following categories of psychotherapy, which is known for its nondirective nature?
   a. psychoanalysis   c. behavior therapy
   b. humanistic therapy   d. cognitive therapy

4. Which of the following is *not* a common criticism of psychoanalysis?
   a. It emphasizes the existence of repressed memories.
   b. It provides interpretations that are hard to disprove.
   c. It is generally a very expensive process.
   d. It gives therapists too much control over patients.

5. Which of the following types of therapy does *not* belong with the others?
   a. cognitive therapy
   b. family therapy
   c. self-help group
   d. support group

6. Which of the following is *not* necessarily an advantage of group therapies over individual therapies?
   a. They tend to take less time for the therapist.
   b. They tend to cost less money for the client.
   c. They are more effective.
   d. They allow the client to test new behaviors in a social context.

7. Which biomedical therapy is *most* likely to be practiced today?
   a. psychosurgery
   b. electroconvulsive therapy
   c. drug therapy
   d. counterconditioning

8. The effectiveness of psychotherapy has been assessed both through clients' perspectives and through controlled research studies. What have such assessments found?
   a. Clients' perceptions and controlled studies alike strongly affirm the effectiveness of psychotherapy.
   b. Whereas clients' perceptions strongly affirm the effectiveness of psychotherapy, studies point to more modest results.
   c. Whereas studies strongly affirm the effectiveness of psychotherapy, many clients feel dissatisfied with their progress.
   d. Clients' perceptions and controlled studies alike paint a very mixed picture of the effectiveness of psychotherapy.

9. Which of the following best describes the results of the 30-year follow-up study of 500 Massachusetts boys who had been considered predelinquents?
   a. Predelinquent boys who received counseling had fewer problems as adults than untreated predelinquent boys.
   b. Predelinquent boys who did not receive counseling had slightly fewer problems as adults than boys who received counseling.
   c. Predelinquent boys who underwent behavior therapy had fewer problems as adults than boys who underwent psychoanalysis.
   d. Predelinquent boys who underwent psychoanalysis had fewer problems as adults than boys who underwent behavior therapy.

10. The results of meta-analysis of the effectiveness of different psychotherapies reveals that:
    a. no single type of therapy is consistently superior.
    b. behavior therapies are most effective in treating specific problems, such as phobias.
    c. cognitive therapies are most effective in treating depressed emotions.
    d. all of the above are true.

11. The antipsychotic drugs appear to produce their effects by blocking the receptor sites for:
    a. dopamine.
    b. epinephrine.
    c. norepinephrine.
    d. serotonin.

12. Psychologists who advocate a _____ approach to mental health contend that many psychological disorders could be prevented by changing the disturbed individual's _____ .
    a. biomedical; diet
    b. family; behavior
    c. humanistic; feelings
    d. preventive; environment

13. An eclectic psychotherapist is one who:
    a. takes a nondirective approach in helping clients solve their problems.
    b. views psychological disorders as usually stemming from one cause, such as a biological abnormality.
    c. uses one particular technique, such as psychoanalysis or counterconditioning, in treating disorders.
    d. uses a variety of techniques, depending on the client and the problem.

14. The technique in which a therapist echoes and restates what a person says in a nondirective manner is called:
    a. active listening.
    b. free association.
    c. systematic desensitization.
    d. meta-analysis.

15. Unlike traditional psychoanalytic therapy, interpersonal psychotherapy:
    a. helps people gain insight into the roots of their problems.
    b. offers interpretations of patients' feelings.
    c. focuses on current relationships.
    d. does all of the above.

16. The technique of systematic desensitization is based on the premise that maladaptive symptoms are:
    a. a reflection of irrational thinking.
    b. conditioned responses.
    c. expressions of unfulfilled wishes.
    d. all of the above.

17. The operant conditioning technique in which desired behaviors are rewarded with points or poker chips that can later be exchanged for various rewards is called:
    a. counterconditioning.
    b. systematic desensitization.
    c. a token economy.
    d. exposure therapy.

18. One variety of _____ therapy is based on the finding that depressed people often attribute their failures to _____ .
    a. humanistic; themselves
    b. behavior; external circumstances
    c. cognitive; external circumstances
    d. cognitive; themselves

19. (Thinking Critically and text) A person can derive benefits from psychotherapy simply by believing in it. This illustrates the importance of:
    a. spontaneous recovery.
    b. the placebo effect.
    c. the transference effect.
    d. interpretation.

20. Before 1950, the main mental health providers were:
    a. psychologists.
    b. paraprofessionals.
    c. psychiatrists.
    d. the clergy.

Matching Items

Match each term with the appropriate definition or description.

Terms

_____ **1.** cognitive therapy
_____ **2.** behavior therapy
_____ **3.** systematic desensitization
_____ **4.** cognitive-behavior therapy
_____ **5.** client-centered therapy
_____ **6.** regression toward the mean
_____ **7.** aversive conditioning
_____ **8.** psychoanalysis
_____ **9.** preventive mental health
_____ **10.** biomedical therapy
_____ **11.** counterconditioning

Definitions or Descriptions

a. associates unwanted behavior with unpleasant experiences
b. associates a relaxed state with anxiety-arousing stimuli
c. emphasizes the social context of psychological disorders
d. integrated therapy that focuses on changing self-defeating thinking and unwanted behavior
e. category of therapies that teach people more adaptive ways of thinking and acting
f. the tendency for unusual events to return to their average state
g. therapy developed by Carl Rogers
h. therapy based on Freud's theory of personality
i. treatment with psychosurgery, electroconvulsive therapy, or drugs
j. classical conditioning procedure in which new responses are conditioned to stimuli that trigger unwanted behaviors
k. category of therapies based on learning principles derived from classical and operant conditioning

PROGRESS TEST 2

Progress Test 2 should be completed during a final chapter review. Answer the following questions after you thoroughly understand the correct answers for the section reviews and Progress Test 1.

Multiple-Choice Questions

1. Carl Rogers was a _____ therapist who was the creator of _____ .
   a. behavior; systematic desensitization
   b. psychoanalytic; insight therapy
   c. humanistic; client-centered therapy
   d. cognitive; cognitive therapy for depression

2. Using techniques of classical conditioning to develop an association between unwanted behavior and an unpleasant experience is known as:
   a. aversive conditioning.
   b. systematic desensitization.
   c. transference.
   d. electroconvulsive therapy.

3. Which type of psychotherapy emphasizes the individual's inherent potential for self-fulfillment?
   a. behavior therapy   c. humanistic therapy
   b. psychoanalysis   d. biomedical therapy

4. Light-exposure therapy has proven useful as a form of treatment for people suffering from:
   a. bulimia.
   b. seasonal affective disorder.
   c. schizophrenia.
   d. dissociative identity disorder.

5. Which type of psychotherapy focuses on changing unwanted behaviors rather than on discovering their underlying causes?
   a. behavior therapy
   b. cognitive therapy
   c. humanistic therapy
   d. psychoanalysis

6. The techniques of counterconditioning are based on principles of:
   a. observational learning.
   b. classical conditioning.
   c. operant conditioning.
   d. behavior modification.

7. In which of the following does the client learn to associate a relaxed state with a hierarchy of anxiety-arousing situations?
   a. cognitive therapy
   b. aversive conditioning
   c. counterconditioning
   d. systematic desensitization

8. Principles of operant conditioning underlie which of the following techniques?
   a. counterconditioning
   b. systematic desensitization
   c. stress inoculation training
   d. the token economy

9. Which of the following is *not* a common criticism of behavior therapy?
   a. Clients may rely too much on extrinsic motivation for their new behaviors.
   b. Behavior control is unethical.
   c. Outside the therapeutic setting, the new behavior may disappear.
   d. All of the above are criticisms of behavior therapy.

10. Which type of therapy focuses on eliminating irrational thinking?
    a. EMDR
    b. client-centered therapy
    c. cognitive therapy
    d. behavior therapy

11. Antidepressant drugs are believed to work by affecting serotonin or:
    a. dopamine.   c. norepinephrine.
    b. lithium.   d. acetylcholine.

12. The following are some of the conclusions drawn in the text regarding the effectiveness of psychotherapy. For which of these conclusions did the Massachusetts study of predelinquent boys provide evidence?
    a. Clients' perceptions of the effectiveness of therapy usually are very accurate.
    b. Clients' perceptions of the effectiveness of therapy differ somewhat from the objective findings.
    c. Individuals who receive treatment do somewhat better than individuals who do not.

   d. Overall, no one type of therapy is a "winner," but certain therapies are more suited to certain problems.

13. Which of the following is the mood-stabilizing drug most commonly used to treat bipolar disorder?
    a. Ativan   c. Xanax
    b. chlorpromazine   d. lithium

14. The type of drugs criticized for reducing symptoms without resolving underlying problems are the:
    a. antianxiety drugs.
    b. antipsychotic drugs.
    c. antidepressant drugs.
    d. amphetamines.

15. Which form of therapy is *most* likely to be successful in treating depression?
    a. behavior modification c. cognitive therapy
    b. psychoanalysis   d. humanistic therapy

16. Although Moniz won the Nobel prize for developing the lobotomy procedure, the technique is not widely used today because:
    a. it produces a lethargic, immature personality.
    b. it is irreversible.
    c. calming drugs became available in the 1950s.
    d. of all of the above reasons.

17. A meta-analysis of research studies comparing the effectiveness of professional therapists with paraprofessionals found that:
    a. the professionals were much more effective than the paraprofessionals.
    b. the paraprofessionals were much more effective than the professionals.
    c. except in treating depression, the paraprofessionals were about as effective as the professionals.
    d. the paraprofessionals were about as effective as the professionals.

18. Among the common ingredients of the psychotherapies is:
    a. the offer of a therapeutic relationship.
    b. the expectation among clients that the therapy will prove helpful.
    c. the chance to develop a fresh perspective on oneself and the world.
    d. all of the above.

19. Family therapy differs from other forms of psychotherapy because it focuses on:
   a. using a variety of treatment techniques.
   b. conscious rather than unconscious processes.
   c. the present instead of the past.
   d. how family tensions may cause individual problems.

20. One reason that aversive conditioning may only be temporarily effective is that:
   a. for ethical reasons, therapists cannot use sufficiently intense unconditioned stimuli to sustain classical conditioning.
   b. patients are often unable to become sufficiently relaxed for conditioning to take place.
   c. patients know that outside the therapist's office they can engage in the undesirable behavior without fear of aversive consequences.
   d. most conditioned responses are elicited by many nonspecific stimuli and it is impossible to countercondition them all.

21. Cognitive-behavior therapy aims to:
   a. alter the way people act.
   b. Make people more aware of their irrational negative thinking.
   c. Alter the way people think and act.
   d. Countercondition anxiety-provoking stimuli.

Matching Items

Match each term with the appropriate definition or description.

Terms

_____ **1.** active listening
_____ **2.** token economy
_____ **3.** placebo effect
_____ **4.** lobotomy
_____ **5.** lithium
_____ **6.** meta-analysis
_____ **7.** psychopharmacology
_____ **8.** double-blind technique
_____ **9.** Xanax
_____ **10.** free association
_____ **11.** stress inoculation training

Definitions or Descriptions

a. type of psychosurgery
b. procedure for statistically combining the results of many experiments
c. mood-stabilizing drug
d. empathic technique used in person-centered therapy
e. the beneficial effect of a person's expecting that treatment will be effective
f. antianxiety drug
g. technique of psychoanalytic therapy
h. an operant conditioning procedure
i. the study of the effects of drugs on the mind and behavior
j. experimental procedure in which both the patient and staff are unaware of a patient's treatment condition
k. cognitive-behavior therapy in which people are trained to restructure their thinking in stressful situations

PSYCHOLOGY APPLIED

Answer these questions the day before an exam as a final check on your understanding of the chapter's terms and concepts.

Multiple-Choice Questions

1. During a session with his psychoanalyst, Jamal hesitates while describing a highly embarrassing thought. In the psychoanalytic framework, this is an example of:
   a. transference.
   b. insight.
   c. mental repression.
   d. resistance.

2. During psychoanalysis, Jane has developed strong feelings of hatred for her therapist. The analyst interprets Jane's behavior in terms of a _____ of her feelings toward her father.
   a. projection
   b. resistance
   c. regression
   d. transference

3. Given that Jim's therapist attempts to help him by offering genuineness, acceptance, and empathy, she is probably practicing:
   a. psychoanalysis.
   b. behavior therapy.
   c. cognitive therapy.
   d. client-centered therapy.

4. To help Sam quit smoking, his therapist blew a blast of smoke into Sam's face each time Sam inhaled. Which technique is the therapist using?
   a. exposure therapy
   b. behavior modification
   c. systematic desensitization
   d. aversive conditioning

5. After Darnel dropped a pass in an important football game, he became depressed and vowed to quit the team because of his athletic incompetence. The campus psychologist challenged his illogical reasoning and pointed out that Darnel's "incompetence" had earned him an athletic scholarship. The psychologist's response was most typical of a _____ therapist.
   a. behavior
   b. psychoanalytic
   c. client-centered
   d. cognitive

6. Seth enters therapy to talk about some issues that have been upsetting him. The therapist prescribes some medication to help him. The therapist is most likely a:
   a. clinical psychologist.
   b. psychiatrist.
   c. psychiatric social worker.
   d. clinical social worker.

7. In an experiment testing the effects of a new antipsychotic drug, neither Dr. Cunningham nor her patients know whether the patients are in the experimental or the control group. This is an example of the _____ technique.
   a. meta-analysis
   b. within-subjects
   c. double-blind
   d. single-blind

8. A close friend who for years has suffered from wintertime depression is seeking your advice regarding the effectiveness of light-exposure therapy. What should you tell your friend?
   a. "Don't waste your time and money. It doesn't work."
   b. "A more effective treatment for seasonal affective disorder is eye movement desensitization and reprocessing."
   c. "You'd be better off with a prescription for lithium."
   d. "It might be worth a try. There is some evidence that morning light exposure produces relief."

9. A relative wants to know which type of therapy works best. You should tell your relative that:
   a. psychotherapy does not work.
   b. behavior therapy is the most effective.
   c. cognitive therapy is the most effective.
   d. no one type of therapy is consistently the most successful.

10. Leota is startled when her therapist says that she needs to focus on eliminating her problem behavior rather than gaining insight into its underlying cause. Most likely, Leota has consulted a _____ therapist.
    a. behavior
    b. humanistic
    c. cognitive
    d. psychoanalytic

11. In order to help him overcome his fear of flying, Duane's therapist has him construct a hierarchy of anxiety-triggering stimuli and then learn to associate each with a state of deep relaxation. Duane's therapist is using the technique called:
    a. systematic desensitization.
    b. aversive conditioning.
    c. shaping.
    d. free association.

12. A patient in a hospital receives poker chips for making her bed, being punctual at meal times, and maintaining her physical appearance. The poker chips can be exchanged for privileges, such as television viewing, snacks, and magazines. This is an example of the:
    a. psychodynamic therapy technique called systematic desensitization.
    b. behavior therapy technique called token economy.
    c. cognitive therapy technique called token economy.
    d. humanistic therapy technique called systematic desensitization.

13. Ben is a cognitive-behavior therapist. Compared to Rachel, who is a behavior therapist, Ben is more likely to:
    a. base his therapy on principles of operant conditioning.
    b. base his therapy on principles of classical conditioning.
    c. address clients' attitudes as well as behaviors.
    d. focus on clients' unconscious urges.

14. A psychotherapist who believes that the best way to treat psychological disorders is to prevent them from developing would be *most* likely to view disordered behavior as:
    a. maladaptive thoughts and actions.
    b. expressions of unconscious conflicts.
    c. conditioned responses.
    d. an understandable response to stressful social conditions.

15. Linda's doctor prescribes medication that blocks the activity of dopamine in her nervous system. Evidently, Linda is being treated with an _____ drug.
    a. antipsychotic   c. antidepressant
    b. antianxiety   d. anticonvulsive

16. Abraham's doctor prescribes medication that increases the availability of norepinephrine or serotonin in his nervous system. Evidently, Abraham is being treated with an _____ drug.
    a. antipsychotic
    b. antianxiety
    c. antidepressant
    d. anticonvulsive

17. In concluding her talk entitled "Psychosurgery Today," Ashley states that:
    a. "Psychosurgery is still widely used throughout the world."

    b. "Electroconvulsive therapy is the only remaining psychosurgical technique that is widely practiced."
    c. "With advances in psychopharmacology, psychosurgery has largely been abandoned."
    d. "Although lobotomies remain popular, other psychosurgical techniques have been abandoned."

18. A psychiatrist has diagnosed a patient as having bipolar disorder. It is likely that she will prescribe:
    a. an antipsychotic drug.
    b. lithium.
    c. an antianxiety drug.
    d. a drug that blocks receptor sites for serotonin.

19. Which type(s) of psychotherapy would be most likely to use the interpretation of dreams as a technique for bringing unconscious feelings into awareness?
    a. psychoanalysis
    b. psychodynamic therapy
    c. cognitive therapy
    d. both a. and b.

20. Of the following therapists, who would be most likely to interpret a person's psychological problems in terms of repressed impulses?
    a. a behavior therapist
    b. a cognitive therapist
    c. a humanistic therapist
    d. a psychoanalyst

21. Nick survived a car accident in which another passenger died. Feeling anxious and guilty, he sought treatment from an alternative therapist, who used eye movement desensitization and reprocessing to help Nick return to his normally upbeat, optimistic frame of mind. After several months of treatment Nick began feeling better. Although Nick is convinced that the alternative therapy was responsible for his improvement, it is also possible that it was the result of:
    a. regression toward the mean.
    b. a placebo effect.
    c. merely seeking treatment from any practitioner who provided an empathic, trusting environment.
    d. all of the above.

Essay Question

Willie has been diagnosed as suffering from major depressive disorder. Describe the treatment he might receive from a psychoanalyst, a cognitive therapist, and a biomedical therapist. (Use the space below to list points you want to make, and organize them. Then write the essay on a separate sheet of paper.)

KEY TERMS

Writing Definitions

Using your own words, on a separate piece of paper write a brief definition or explanation of each of the following terms.

1. psychotherapy
2. biomedical therapy
3. eclectic approach
4. psychoanalysis
5. resistance
6. interpretation
7. transference
8. client-centered therapy
9. active listening
10. behavior therapy
11. counterconditioning
12. exposure therapies
13. systematic desensitization
14. virtual reality exposure therapy
15. aversive conditioning
16. token economy
17. cognitive therapy
18. cognitive-behavior therapy
19. family therapy
20. regression toward the mean
21. meta-analysis
22. psychopharmacology
23. tardive dyskinesia
24. electroconvulsive therapy (ECT)
25. repetitive transcranial magnetic stimulation (rTMS)
26. psychosurgery
27. lobotomy

Cross-Check

As you learned in the Prologue, reviewing and overlearning of material are important to the learning process. After you have written the definitions of the key terms in this chapter, you should complete the crossword puzzle to ensure that you can reverse the process—recognize the term, given the definition.

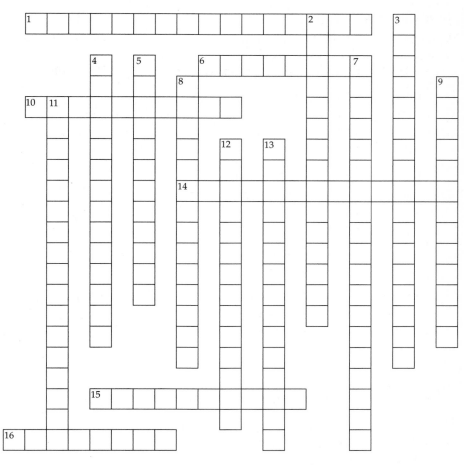

ACROSS

1. Therapy that teaches people new and more adaptive ways of thinking.
6. Approach that draws on a variety of forms of therapy to best suit clients' needs.
10. Blocking anxiety-provoking memories from consciousness.
14. Therapy that attempts to change behavior by removing or destroying brain tissue.
15. Therapy that uses prescribed medications or medical procedures to treat psychological disorders.
16. Conditioning in which an unpleasant state is associated with an unwanted behavior.

13. Therapy that applies principles of operant or classical conditioning to eliminate problem behaviors.

DOWN

2. Nondirective technique in which the listener echoes and restates, but does not interpret, clients' remarks.
3. Integrated therapy that focuses on changing self-defeating thinking and unwanted behaviors.
4. Humanistic therapy developed by Carl Rogers.
5. Statistical procedure for combining the results of many different research studies.
7. Behavior therapy in which new responses are classically conditioned to stimuli that trigger unwanted behaviors.
8. Psychoanalytic term for the analyst's helping a client to gain deeper insights into unwanted thoughts and behaviors.
9. Therapy that views problem behaviors as partially engendered by the client's environment.
11. Biomedical therapy often used to treat severe depression.
12. Therapy developed by Sigmund Freud.

ANSWERS

Chapter Review

Introducing Therapy

1. psychological; biomedical
2. psychotherapy; learned
3. prescribed medications; nervous system
4. eclectic; psychotherapy integration

The Psychological Therapies

1. self-insight
2. repressed
3. repressed; conscious
4. free association
5. resistance; interpretation
6. latent content

7. transference

8. disprove; expensive

9. psychodynamic; once a week

10. depressed; interpersonal psychotherapy

11. insight; current relationships

12. self-fulfillment

Unlike psychoanalysis, humanistic therapy is focused on the present instead of the past, on awareness of feelings as they occur rather than on achieving insights into the childhood origins of the feelings, on conscious rather than unconscious processes, on promoting growth and fulfillment instead of curing illness, and on helping clients take immediate responsibility for their feelings and actions rather than on uncovering the obstacles to doing so.

13. client-centered; nondirective; does not interpret

14. genuineness; acceptance; empathy

15. active listening; unconditional positive regard

16. paraphrase; invite clarification; reflect feelings

17. learning

Whereas psychoanalysis and humanistic therapies assume that problems diminish as self-awareness grows, behavior therapists doubt that self-awareness is the key. Instead of looking for the inner cause of unwanted behavior, behavior therapy applies learning principles to directly attack the unwanted behavior itself.

18. classical conditioning; counterconditioning; systematic desensitization; aversive conditioning

19. exposure therapies; Wolpe; anxious

20. hierarchy; progressive relaxation; relaxed; anxiety

21. virtual reality exposure

22. negative; positive; unpleasant

23. behavior modification

24. operant; token economy

Behavior modification is criticized because the desired behavior may stop when the rewards are stopped. Also, critics contend that one person should not be allowed to control another.

Proponents of behavior modification contend that some clients request this therapy. Also, control already exists.

25. cognitive

26. catastrophizing; depression; Beck

27. do not

28. stress inoculation; dispute

29. cognitive-behavior

Group therapy saves therapists time and clients money. The social context of group therapy allows people to discover that others have similar problems

and to try out new ways of behaving.

30. family therapy

31. communication; conflict

32. self-help; support; stigmatized, hard-to-discuss

Evaluating Psychotherapies

1. is not

2. satisfaction

   People often enter therapy in crisis. When the crisis passes, they may attribute their improvement to the therapy. Clients, who may need to believe the therapy was worth the effort, may overestimate its effectiveness. Clients generally find positive things to say about their therapists, even if their problems remain.

3. did not have; are not

4. overestimate

5. unhappiness; well-being

6. belief; placebo effect; regression toward the mean; unusual; average

7. controlled

8. Eysenck; was not

9. meta-analysis; somewhat effective

10. medical

11. no clear; does not matter; does not make a difference

12. cognitive; interpersonal; behavior; cognitive; exposure; stress inoculation; bulimia; bed wetting

13. behavioral conditioning

14. specific

15. alternative therapy

16. controlled

17. traumatic events; eye movement desensitization and reprocessing (EMDR); somewhat effective; post-traumatic stress disorder; finger tapping; reliving; placebo

18. seasonal affective disorder; light-exposure

19. hope; perspective; caring; trusting; empathic

20. attitude

21. empathic; caring

22. is

23. do; different

24. individualism

25. minority

The Biomedical Therapies

1. drug; decreased

2. psychopharmacology

3. placebo; recovery; double-blind

4. antipsychotic; chlorpromazine (Thorazine); positive; clozapine (Clozaril)

5. dopamine; serotonin

6. tardive dyskinesia; face; tongue; limbs

7. antianxiety

8. central nervous system

9. psychological therapy

10. symptoms; problems; physiological dependence

11. antidepressant; norepinephrine; serotonin

12. fluoxetine (Prozac); serotonin; selective-serotonin-reuptake-inhibitor

13. aerobic exercise; bottom-up; cognitive-behavior; top-down

14. spontaneous recovery; placebo effect

15. lithium

16. Depakote

17. electroconvulsive; ECT

18. depression; confirms

19. unknown

20. implant; vagus

21. repetitive transcranial magnetic stimulation (rTMS); seizures; memory; frontal lobe

22. psychosurgery

23. lobotomy; frontal

24. drugs

Preventing Psychological Disorders

1. person

2. a disturbing and stressful society

3. person; social context

4. preventive; competence; personal control; self-esteem; poverty; meaningless; criticism; unemployment; racism; sexism

5. integrated biopsychosocial

Progress Test 1

Multiple-Choice Questions

1. **b.** is the answer. Although no one is sure how ECT works, one possible explanation is that it increases release of norepinephrine, the neurotransmitter that elevates mood. (p. 715)

2. **c.** is the answer. (p. 687)
   a. Active listening is a Rogerian technique in which the therapist echoes, restates, and seeks clarification of the client's statements.

b. Spontaneous recovery refers to improvement without treatment.
d. Systematic desensitization is a process in which a person is conditioned to associate a relaxed state with anxiety-triggering stimuli.

3. **b.** is the answer. (p. 689)

4. **d.** is the answer. This is not among the criticisms commonly made of psychoanalysis. (It would more likely be made of behavior therapies.) (pp. 687–688)

5. **a.** is the answer. (pp. 697–698)
   b., c., & d. Each of these is a type of group therapy.

6. **c.** is the answer. Meta-analysis of the relative effectiveness of different therapies reveals no clear winner; the other factors mentioned are advantages of group therapies. (p. 703)

7. **c.** is the answer. (p. 711)
   a. The fact that its effects are irreversible makes psychosurgery a drastic procedure, and with advances in psychopharmacology, psychosurgery was largely abandoned.
   b. ECT is still widely used as a treatment of severe depression, but in general it is not used as frequently as drug therapy.
   d. Counterconditioning is not a biomedical therapy.

8. **b.** is the answer. Clients' testimonials regarding psychotherapy are generally very positive. The research, in contrast, seems to show that therapy is only *somewhat* effective. (pp. 700–701, 703)

9. **b.** is the answer. Although many of those who received counseling felt it had saved their lives, on a number of measures these men exhibited slightly *more* problems than those who had not received counseling. (p. 701)
   a. Boys who received counseling had slightly *more* problems as adults.
   c. & d. This study did not compare the effectiveness of different forms of psychotherapy.

10. **d.** is the answer. (pp. 703–704)

11. **a.** is the answer. By occupying receptor sites for dopamine, these drugs block its activity and reduce its production. (p. 712)

12. **d.** is the answer. (p. 719)

13. **d.** is the answer. Today, half of all psychotherapists describe themselves as eclectic—as using a blend of therapies. (p. 686)
    a. An eclectic therapist may use a nondirective approach with certain behaviors; however, a more directive approach might be chosen for other clients and problems.

b. In fact, just the opposite is true. Eclectic therapists generally view disorders as stemming from many influences.

c. Eclectic therapists, in contrast to this example, use a combination of treatments.

14. **a.** is the answer. (p. 689)

15. **c.** is the answer. (p. 688)

16. **b.** is the answer. (p. 692)
    a. This reflects a cognitive perspective.
    c. This reflects a psychoanalytic perspective.

17. **c.** is the answer. (p. 693)
    a. & b. Counterconditioning is the replacement of an undesired response with a desired one by means of aversive conditioning or systematic desensitization.
    d. Exposure therapy exposes a person, in imagination or in actuality, to a feared situation.

18. **d.** is the answer. (p. 696)

19. **b.** is the answer. (pp. 702, 707)
    a. Spontaneous recovery refers to improvement without any treatment.
    c. Transference is the psychoanalytic phenomenon in which a client transfers feelings from other relationships onto his or her analyst.
    d. Interpretation is the psychoanalytic procedure through which the analyst helps the client become aware of resistances and understand their meaning.

20. **c.** is the answer. (p. 700)

Matching Items

1. e (p. 695)
2. k (p. 690)
3. b (p. 692)
4. d (p. 697)
5. g (p. 689)
6. f (p. 702)
7. a (p. 692)
8. h (p. 686)
9. c (p. 719)
10. i (p. 686)
11. j (p. 691)

Progress Test 2

Multiple-Choice Questions

1. **c.** is the answer. (p. 689)
    a. This answer would be a correct description of Joseph Wolpe.
    b. There is no such thing as insight therapy.
    d. This answer would be a correct description of Aaron Beck.

2. **a.** is the answer. (p. 692)
    b. In systematic desensitization, a hierarchy of anxiety-provoking stimuli is gradually associated with a relaxed state.

c. Transference refers to a patient's transferring of feelings from other relationships onto his or her psychoanalyst.

d. Electroconvulsive therapy is a biomedical shock treatment.

3. **c.** is the answer. (p. 689)
    a. Behavior therapy focuses on behavior, not self-awareness.
    b. Psychoanalysis focuses on bringing repressed feelings into awareness.
    d. Biomedical therapy focuses on physical treatment through drugs, ECT, or psychosurgery.

4. **b.** is the answer. (p. 706)

5. **a.** is the answer. For behavior therapy, the problem behaviors *are* the problems. (p. 690)
    b. Cognitive therapy teaches people to think and act in more adaptive ways.
    c. Humanistic therapy promotes growth and self-fulfillment by providing an empathic, genuine, and accepting environment.
    d. Psychoanalytic therapy focuses on uncovering and interpreting repressed feelings.

6. **b.** is the answer. Counterconditioning techniques involve taking an established CS, which triggers an undesirable CR, and pairing it with a new US in order to condition a new, and more adaptive, CR. (p. 691)
    a. As indicated by the name, counterconditioning techniques are a form of conditioning; they do not involve learning by observation.
    c. & d. The principles of operant conditioning are the basis of behavior modification, which, in contrast to counterconditioning techniques, involves use of reinforcement.

7. **d.** is the answer. (p. 692)
    a. This is a confrontational therapy, which is aimed at teaching people to think and act in more adaptive ways.
    b. Aversive conditioning is a form of counterconditioning in which unwanted behavior is associated with unpleasant feelings.
    c. Counterconditioning is a general term, including not only systematic desensitization, in which a hierarchy of fears is desensitized, but also other techniques, such as aversive conditioning.

8. **d.** is the answer. (p. 693)
    a. & b. These techniques are based on classical conditioning.
    c. This is a type of cognitive therapy.

9. **d.** is the answer. (p. 694)

10. **c.** is the answer. (p. 695)
    a. This is an alternative therapy in which the

practitioner triggers eye movements in patients who are imagining traumatic events.

b. In this humanistic therapy, the therapist facilitates the client's growth by offering a genuine, accepting, and empathic environment.

d. Behavior therapy concentrates on modifying the actual symptoms of psychological problems.

11. **c.** is the answer. (p. 713)

12. **b.** is the answer. Although many of the treated men offered glowing reports of the effectiveness of their therapy, these testimonials did not accurately reflect the results. (p. 701)

a. In fact, as this study showed, clients' perceptions of the effectiveness of psychotherapy are often very positive but inaccurate.

c. On some measures, the treated men exhibited slightly *more* problems than the untreated men.

d. This study did not compare the effectiveness of different forms of psychotherapy.

13. **d.** is the answer. Lithium works as a mood stabilizer. (p. 715)

a. & c. Ativan and Xanax are antianxiety drugs.

b. Chlorpromazine is an antipsychotic drug.

14. **a.** is the answer. (p. 712)

15. **c.** is the answer. (pp. 695, 704)

a. Behavior modification is most likely to be successful in treating specific behavior problems, such as bed wetting.

b. & d. The text does not single out particular disorders for which these therapies tend to be most effective.

16. **d.** is the answer. (pp. 717–718)

17. **d.** is the answer. Even when dealing with seriously depressed adults, the paraprofessionals were as effective as the professionals. (p. 708)

18. **d.** is the answer. (pp. 707-708)

19. **d.** is the answer. (pp. 697–698)

a. This is true of most forms of psychotherapy.

b. & c. This is true of humanistic, cognitive, and behavior therapies.

20. **c.** is the answer. Although aversive conditioning may work in the short run, the person's ability to discriminate between the situation in which the aversive conditioning occurs and other situations can limit the treatment's effectiveness. (p. 693)

a., b., & d. These were not offered in the text as limitations of the effectiveness of aversive conditioning.

21. **c.** is the answer. (p. 697)

Matching Items

1. d (p. 689)   5. c (p. 715)   9. f (p. 712)
2. h (p. 693)   6. b (p. 703)   10. g (p. 687)
3. e (p. 702)   7. i (p. 711)   11. k (p. 696)
4. a (p. 717)   8. j (p. 711)

Psychology Applied

Multiple-Choice Questions

1. **d.** is the answer. Resistances are blocks in the flow of free association that hint at underlying anxiety. (p. 687)

a. In transference, a patient redirects feelings from other relationships to his or her analyst.

b. The goal of psychoanalysis is for patients to gain insight into their feelings.

c. Although such hesitation may well involve material that has been repressed, the hesitation itself is a resistance.

2. **d.** is the answer. In transference, the patient develops feelings toward the therapist that were experienced in important early relationships but were repressed. (p. 687)

a. Projection is a defense mechanism in which a person imputes his or her own feelings to someone else.

b. Resistances are blocks in the flow of free association that indicate repressed material.

c. Regression is a defense mechanism in which a person retreats to an earlier form of behavior.

3. **d.** is the answer. According to Rogers' client-centered therapy, the therapist must exhibit genuineness, acceptance, and empathy if the client is to move toward self-fulfillment. (p. 689)

a. Psychoanalysts are much more directive in providing interpretations of clients' problems than are humanistic therapists.

b. Behavior therapists focus on modifying the behavioral symptoms of psychological problems.

c. Cognitive therapists teach people to think and act in new, more adaptive ways.

4. **d.** is the answer. Aversive conditioning is the classical conditioning technique in which a positive response is replaced by a negative response. (In this example, the US is the blast of smoke, the CS is the taste of the cigarette as it is inhaled, and the intended CR is aversion to cigarettes.) (p. 692)

a. Exposure therapy exposes someone, in imagination (virtual reality exposure therapy) or actuality, to a feared situation.

b. Behavior modification applies the principles of operant conditioning and thus, in contrast to the example, uses reinforcement.

c. Systematic desensitization is used to help people overcome specific anxieties.

5. **d.** is the answer. Because the psychologist is challenging Darnel's illogical, self-defeating attitude, this response is most typical of rational-emotive therapy. (p. 695)
a. Behavior therapists treat behaviors rather than thoughts.
b. Psychoanalysts focus on helping patients gain insight into previously repressed feelings.
c. Client-centered therapists attempt to facilitate clients' growth by offering a genuine, accepting, empathic environment.

6. **b.** is the answer. Psychiatrists are physicians who specialize in treating psychological disorders. As doctors they can prescribe medications. (p. 709)
a., c., & d. These professionals cannot prescribe drugs.

7. **c.** is the answer. (p. 711)
a. This is a statistical technique used to combine the results of many different research studies.
b. In this design, which is not mentioned in the text, there is only a single research group.
d. This answer would be correct if the experimenter, but not the research participants, knew which condition was in effect.

8. **d.** is the answer. (pp. 706–707)
a. In fact, there is evidence that light-exposure therapy can be effective in treating SAD.
b. There is no evidence that EMDR is effective as a treatment for SAD.
c. Lithium is a mood-stabilizing drug that is often used to treat bipolar disorder.

9. **d.** is the answer. (p. 703)
a. Psychotherapy has proven "somewhat effective" and more cost-effective than physician care for psychological disorders.
b. & c. Behavior and cognitive therapies are both effective in treating depression, and behavior therapy is effective in treating specific problems such as phobias.

10. **a.** is the answer. (p. 690)
b. & c. These types of therapists are more concerned with promoting self-fulfillment (humanistic) and healthy patterns of thinking (cognitive) than with correcting specific problem behaviors.
d. Psychoanalysts see the behavior merely as a symptom and focus their treatment on its presumed underlying cause.

11. **a.** is the answer. (p. 692)
b. Aversive conditioning associates unpleasant states with unwanted behaviors.

c. Shaping is an operant conditioning technique in which successive approximations of a desired behavior are reinforced.
d. Free association is a psychoanalytic technique in which a patient says whatever comes to mind.

12. **b.** is the answer. (p. 693)

13. **c.** is the answer. (p. 697)
a. & b. Behavior therapists make extensive use of techniques based on both operant and classical conditioning.
d. Neither behavior therapists nor cognitive behavior therapists focus on clients' unconscious urges.

14. **d.** is the answer. (p. 719)
a. This would be the perspective of a cognitive behavior therapist.
b. This would be the perspective of a psychoanalyst.
c. This would be the perspective of a behavior therapist.

15. **a.** is the answer. (pp. 711–712)

16. **c.** is the answer. (p. 713)

17. **c.** is the answer. (p. 718)
b. Although still practiced, electroconvulsive therapy is not a form of psychosurgery.

18. **b.** is the answer. (p. 715)

19. **d.** is the answer. Both psychoanalysis and psychodynamic therapy seek insight into a patient's unconscious feelings. The analysis of dreams, slips of the tongue, and resistances are considered a window into these feelings. (pp. 687, 688)
c. Cognitive therapists avoid reference to unconscious feelings and would therefore be uninterested in interpreting dreams.

20. **d.** is the answer. A key aim of psychoanalysis is to unearth and understand repressed impulses. (p. 686)
a., b., & c. Behavior and cognitive therapists avoid concepts such as "repression" and "unconscious"; behavior and humanistic therapists focus on the present rather than the past.

21. **d.** is the answer. (pp. 702, 707–708)

Essay Question

Psychoanalysts assume that psychological problems such as depression are caused by unresolved, repressed, and unconscious impulses and conflicts from childhood. A psychoanalyst would probably attempt to bring these repressed feelings into Willie's conscious awareness and help him gain insight into them. He or she would likely try to interpret Willie's resistance during free association, the latent content of his dreams, and any emotional feelings he might transfer to the analyst.

Cognitive therapists assume that a person's emotional reactions are influenced by the person's thoughts in response to the event in question. A cognitive therapist would probably try to teach Willie new and more constructive ways of thinking in order to reverse his catastrophizing beliefs about himself, his situation, and his future.

Biomedical therapists attempt to treat disorders by altering the functioning of the patient's brain. A biomedical therapist would probably prescribe an antidepressant drug such as fluoxetine to increase the availability of norepinephrine and serotonin in Willie's nervous system. If Willie's depression is especially severe, a *psychiatrist* might treat it with several sessions of electroconvulsive therapy.

Key Terms

Writing Definitions

1. **Psychotherapy** is an emotionally charged, confiding interaction between a trained therapist and someone who suffers from psychological difficulties. (p. 685)

2. **Biomedical therapy** is the use of prescribed medications or medical procedures that act on a patient's nervous system to treat psychological disorders. (p. 686)

3. With an **eclectic approach**, therapists are not locked into one form of psychotherapy, but draw on whatever combination seems best suited to a client's needs. (p. 686)

4. **Psychoanalysis**, the therapy developed by Sigmund Freud, attempts to give clients self-insight by bringing into awareness and interpreting previously repressed feelings. (p. 686)

   Example: The tools of the **psychoanalyst** include free association, the analysis of dreams and transferences, and the interpretation of repressed impulses.

5. **Resistance** is the psychoanalytic term for the blocking from consciousness of anxiety-provoking memories. Hesitation during free association may reflect resistance. (p. 687)

6. **Interpretation** is the psychoanalytic term for the analyst's helping the client to understand resistances and other aspects of behavior, so that the client may gain deeper insights. (p. 687)

7. **Transference** is the psychoanalytic term for a patient's redirecting to the analyst emotions from other relationships. (p. 687)

8. **Client-centered therapy** is a humanistic therapy developed by Carl Rogers, in which growth and self-awareness are facilitated in an environment that offers genuineness, acceptance, and empathy. (p. 689)

9. **Active listening** is a nondirective technique of client-centered therapy, in which the listener echoes, restates, and seeks clarification of, but does not interpret, clients' remarks. (p. 690)

10. **Behavior therapy** is therapy that applies principles of operant or classical conditioning to the elimination of problem behaviors. (p. 690)

11. **Counterconditioning** is a category of behavior therapy in which new responses are classically conditioned to stimuli that trigger unwanted behaviors. (p. 691)

12. **Exposure therapies** treat anxiety by exposing people to things they normally fear and avoid. Among these therapies are systematic desensitization and virtual reality exposure therapy. (p. 691)

13. **Systematic desensitization** is a type of counterconditioning in which a state of relaxation is classically conditioned to a hierarchy of gradually increasing anxiety-provoking stimuli. (p. 692)

    Memory aid: This is a form of **counterconditioning** in which sensitive, anxiety-triggering stimuli are *desensitized* in a progressive, or **systematic**, fashion.

14. **Virtual reality exposure therapy** progressively exposes people to simulations of feared situations to treat their anxiety. (p. 692)

15. **Aversive conditioning** is a form of counterconditioning in which an unpleasant state becomes associated with an unwanted behavior. (p. 692)

16. A **token economy** is an operant conditioning procedure in which desirable behaviors are promoted in people by rewarding them with tokens, or positive reinforcers, which can be exchanged for privileges or treats. For the most part, token economies are used in hospitals, schools, and other institutional settings. (pp. 693–694)

17. **Cognitive therapy** focuses on teaching people new and more adaptive ways of thinking and acting. The therapy is based on the idea that our feelings and responses to events are strongly influenced by our thinking, or cognition. (p. 695)

18. **Cognitive-behavior therapy** is an integrated therapy that focuses on changing self-defeating thinking (cognitive therapy) and unwanted behaviors (behavior therapy). (p. 697)

19. **Family therapy** views problem behavior as partially engendered by the client's family system and environment. Therapy therefore focuses on relationships and problems among the various members of the family. (p. 697)

20. **Regression toward the mean** is the tendency for unusual events (or emotions) to return toward their average state. (p. 702)

21. **Meta-analysis** is a procedure for statistically combining the results of many different research studies. (p. 703)

22. **Psychopharmacology** is the study of the effects of drugs on mind and behavior. (p. 711)

    Memory aid: Pharmacology is the science of the uses and effects of drugs. *Psychopharmacology* is the science that studies the psychological effects of drugs.

23. **Tardive dyskinesia** is an involuntary movement of the muscles of the face, tongue, and limbs that sometimes accompanies the long-term use of certain antipsychotic drugs. (p. 712)

24. In **electroconvulsive therapy (ECT)**, a biomedical therapy often used to treat severe depression, electric shock is passed through the brain. (p. 715)

25. **Repetitive transcranial magnetic stimulation (rTMS)** is the delivery of repeated pulses of magnetic energy to stimulate or suppress brain activity. (p. 716)

26. **Psychosurgery** is a biomedical therapy that attempts to change behavior by removing or destroying brain tissue. Since drug therapy became widely available in the 1950s, psychosurgery has been infrequently used. (p. 717)

27. Once used to control violent patients, the **lobotomy** is a form of psychosurgery in which the nerves linking the emotion centers of the brain to the frontal lobes are severed. (p. 717)

Cross-Check

ACROSS
 1. cognitive therapy
 6. eclectic
10. resistance
14. psychosurgery
15. biomedical
16. aversive

DOWN
 2. active listening
 3. cognitive-behavior
 4. client-centered
 5. meta-analysis
 7. counterconditioning
 8. interpretation
 9. family therapy
11. electroconvulsive
12. psychoanalysis
13. behavior therapy

FOCUS ON VOCABULARY AND LANGUAGE

Introducing Therapy

Page 685: . . . cracked the genetic code . . . Myers notes the progress we have made in understanding the physical world—mapping (*charting*) the solar system (*heavens*), discovering the structure of DNA (*cracking the genetic code*), finding cures for many diseases, and so on. He contrasts these attainments with the many odd and strange techniques (*bewildering variety of harsh and gentle methods*) used to deal with people suffering from psychological disorders, such as cutting holes in the skull, piercing veins or attaching leeches to remove blood from the body (*bleeding*), whipping or striking people in order to force demons out of the body (*"beating the devil out of people"*), and so on.

Page 685 (caption): Visitors paid to *gawk* at the *patients* as if they were viewing zoo animals. In the past, mentally disordered people (*patients*) were confined to hospitals (*insane asylums*) and were often treated badly. For instance, some hospitals raised money by selling tickets to the public who could come and stare (*gawk*) at the inmates (*patients*), much as we do today when we visit the zoo and look at the captive animals.

The Psychological Therapies

Page 686: . . . Freud assumed that many psychological problems are *fueled* by childhood's *residue* of *repressed impulses and conflicts.* Freud's psychoanalytic techniques are used by many therapists; their fundamental tenet (*assumption*) is that mental disorders are created and kept in existence (*fueled*) by hidden (*repressed*) childhood urges and opposing psychic forces (*conflicts*). Psychoanalysis attempts to restore the patient to mental health by bringing these submerged (*buried*) feelings into conscious awareness where they can be examined and dealt with (*worked through*). As Myers puts it, psychoanalysis digs up (*unearths*) the past in the hopes of uncovering (*unmasking*) the present.

Page 689: Not surprisingly, humanistic therapists *aim to boost* self-fulfillment by helping people grow in self-awareness and self-acceptance. The most popular humanistic technique is Carl Rogers' nondirective person-centered therapy. The goal is to increase (*the aim is to boost*) the client's feelings of accomplishment and achievement (self-actualization) by providing nonthreatening opportunities for living in the present, for becoming less critical of one's self, and for becoming more self-aware.

Page 690: "And that just really knocks the props out from under you." In Carl Rogers' therapy sessions, he attempts to be genuine, accepting, and empathic; he also mirrors (*reflects*) back to the client in different words the feelings that were expressed. The client said he had been told that he was no good, and Rogers reflects the feelings he detects by saying that it must seem that the client's self-worth had been undermined (*knocked the props out from under you*).

Page 691: . . . Jones' story of Peter and the rabbit did not immediately become part of psychology's *lore.* Mary Cover Jones was the first to demonstrate **counterconditioning** (replacing a fear response with an incompatible response, such as relaxation through classical conditioning). This technique, however, did not become part of psychology's tradition and store of knowledge (*lore*) until Wolpe developed systematic desensitization more than 30 years later.

Pages 692–693: To treat alcoholism, an aversion therapist offers the client appealing drinks *laced* with a drug that produces *severe nausea.* Behavior therapists, focusing on observable behaviors, use a number of techniques based on well-established learning principles. Two counterconditioning techniques based on classical conditioning are **systematic desensitization** and **aversive conditioning.** In aversive therapy, people who regularly drink too much are given enticing alcoholic beverages which are infused (*laced*) with a substance that induces sickness (*severe nausea*). Alcohol should now be a potent conditioned stimulus that elicits unpleasant feelings; as a result, the person with alcoholism should want to avoid these drinks. Research shows some limited success with this approach.

Page 693: The combination of positively reinforcing desired behaviors and ignoring or punishing *aggressive and self-abusive* behaviors *worked wonders* for some. Another type of behavior therapy is based on operant conditioning principles and involves voluntary behavior followed by pleasant or unpleasant consequences. Socially withdrawn autistic children, treated to an intensive two-year program of positive reinforcement for desired behaviors and punishment for violent and self-injurious (*aggressive and self-abusive*) behaviors, responded extremely well (*it worked wonders for them*).

Page 695: The **cognitive therapies** assume that our thinking *colors* our feelings. . . . The underlying assumption of the cognitive approach to therapy is that thoughts precede and influence (*color*) our feelings. If certain destructive patterns of thinking are learned, then it must be possible to unlearn them and replace them with more constructive ways of viewing what happens to us.

Page 695: . . . *catastrophizing* . . . Aaron Beck, a cognitive therapist, believes that the way to help depressed people feel better is to turn around (*reverse*) their negative, distorted thinking, which tends to transform ordinary events into disasters (*catastrophizing*). The goal is to get them to think about their lives in more positive terms (*convince them to take off the dark glasses*).

Evaluating Psychotherapies

Page 700: "Hang in there until you find [a psychotherapist] *who fills the bill."* Each year in the United States about 15 percent of the population seek help for psychological and addictive disorders. Many people, including the late advice columnist Ann Landers, recommend that troubled people get professional help and that they persevere (*hang in there*) in finding the right therapist to meet their needs (*who fills the bill*).

Page 700: If clients' *testimonials* were the only measuring stick, we could strongly affirm the effectiveness of psychotherapy. The question of whether or not psychotherapy is effective is a very complex issue. If the only gauge (*measuring stick or yardstick*) we have was what clients said about their therapy (*testimonials*), then the conclusion would have to be that psychotherapy works. (Three-quarters, or more, of those surveyed were satisfied.) Myers points out that such testimonials can be misleading and invalid.

Page 700: When, with the normal *ebb and flow* of events, the crisis passes, people may attribute their improvement to the therapy. Because of some serious traumatic events (*crises*) in their lives, people may end up seeing a therapist; after many sessions they may feel much better. During the ordinary course (*ebb and flow*) of events, however, the crisis is likely to have passed; thus, their present feelings of well-being may have little to do with the psychotherapy.

Page 704: Moreover, therapy is most effective when the problem is *clear-cut* (Singer, 1981; Westen & Morrison, 2001). Psychotherapy tends to work best when the disturbances are well-defined (*clear-cut*) and explicitly stated or understood. For example, those who suffer from irrational fears (*phobias*), are timid or shy (*unassertive*), or have a psychologically caused sexual disorder respond better to therapy than those who suffer from *schizophrenia* or who want a total personality change. As Myers notes, the more specific the problem, the greater the hope.

Page 705: The tendency of abnormal states of mind to "regress" to normal, combined with the placebo effect, creates *fertile soil* for *pseudotherapies*. So-called alternative therapies may appear to be effective for a couple of reasons: worse-than-normal mental states tend to diminish and move back to more normal mental states (*regression to the average*) over time, and if people expect that a particular therapy will help them, they may get better as a result of their belief alone (*the placebo effect*). These factors provide a basis (*fertile soil*) for the growth and popularity of therapies that have not been empirically validated (*pseudotherapies*). Indeed, supported (*bolstered*) by anecdotes, exuberantly reported (*heralded*) by the media, given accolades (*praised*) on the Internet, alternative therapies can thrive and flourish (*can spread like wildfire*).

Page 707: Each therapy, in its individual way, may *harness* the client's own healing powers. Research has shown that actual therapy is better than no treatment, but that placebo-treated people improve significantly. This suggests that therapies work in part because they offer hope; each different type of therapy may be effective to the extent that it capitalizes on and uses (*harnesses*) the clients' ability for self-healing.

Page 708: Indeed, some believe that warmth and *empathy* are *hallmarks* of healers everywhere, whether psychiatrists, witch doctors, or shamans (Torrey, 1986). In general, therapies are approximately the same in effectiveness, but that does not mean that all therapists are equal in this respect. Fundamental qualities (*hallmarks*) of effective therapists are an ability to understand other people's experiences (*empathy*) and a capacity to show genuine concern and care (*warmth*). In addition, good listening skills, a reassuring manner, and concern for gaining (*earning*) the client's respect and trust help in the therapeutic process.

The Biomedical Therapies

Page 712: Antipsychotics are powerful drugs. The first-generation dopamine-blocking drugs (such as Thorazine) can produce *sluggishness, tremors, and twitches* similar to those of Parkinson's disease, which is marked by too little dopamine (Kaplan & Saddock, 1989). Because of the serious side effects of some antipsychotic drugs—tiredness and apathy (*sluggishness*), shaking limbs (*tremors*), and sudden involuntary spasms (*twitches*)—therapists have to be very careful (*they have to tread a fine line*) in selecting the dose of both first- and new-generation drugs that will relieve the symptoms but will not produce the side effects.

Page 712: "Popping a Xanax" at the first sign of tension can produce psychological dependence. The most popular antianxiety drugs (Xanax and Valium) are central nervous system depressants, and they reduce tension without causing too much drowsiness. As a consequence, they are prescribed for a variety of problems, including minor emotional stresses. If a person regularly takes an antianxiety drug (*routinely "pops a Xanax"*) whenever there is the slightest feeling of anxiety, the result can be psychological dependence on the drug. Withdrawal symptoms for heavy users include increased anxiety and an inability to sleep (insomnia).

Page 713: As the antianxiety drugs can calm people down from a state of anxiety, the antidepressants sometimes *lift people up from* a state of depression. Antidepressants work by either increasing the availability of the neurotransmitters norepinephrine or serotonin, blocking their reabsorption, or by inhibiting an enzyme that breaks them down. Thus, they tend to make depressed people feel more alive and aroused (*they lift them up*).

Page 715: ECT therefore gained a *barbaric* image, one that lingers still. **Electroconvulsive therapy (ECT)** has proven quite effective and is used mainly for chronically depressed people who have not responded to drug therapy. In 1938, when ECT was first introduced, wide-awake patients were strapped to a table to prevent them from hurting themselves during the convulsions and were shocked (*jolted*) with 100 volts of electricity to the brain. Although the procedure is different today, these inhumane (*barbaric*) images tend to remain in people's minds. As Myers points out, ECT is credited with saving many from suicide, but its Frankensteinlike image lingers on. (Note: Dr. Frankenstein is a fictional character who created a living monster from the body parts of dead people.)

Page 716: Hopes are now rising for gentler alternative for *jump-starting* the depressed brain. (Using power from another car's battery to start a car with a flat or dead battery is called *jump-starting*.) Depressed moods appear to improve when a painless procedure called repetitive transcranial magnetic stimulation (rTMS) is used on wide-awake patients. Thus, optimism is increasing (*hopes are rising*) for a better way to activate (*jump-start*) the depressed brain.

Preventing Psychological Disorders

Page 719: Preventive mental health is *upstream work*. Some psychologists believe that prevention is better than cure and they support programs that help relieve and stop poverty, racism, discrimination, and other disempowering or demoralizing situations. The attempt to prevent psychological disorders by getting rid of conditions that may cause them is extremely difficult (*upstream work*).

18 : Social Psychology

CHAPTER OVERVIEW

Chapter 18 demonstrates the powerful influences of social situations on the behavior of individuals. Central to this topic are research studies on attitudes and actions, conformity, compliance, and group and cultural influences. The social principles that emerge help us to understand how individuals are influenced by advertising, political candidates, and the various groups to which they belong. Although social influences are powerful, it is important to remember the significant role of individuals in choosing and creating the social situations that influence them.

The chapter also discusses how people relate to one another, from the negative—developing prejudice, behaving aggressively, and provoking conflict—to the positive—being attracted to people who are nearby and/or similar and behaving altruistically.

The chapter concludes with a discussion of techniques that have been shown to promote conflict resolution.

Although there is some terminology for you to learn in this chapter, your primary task is to absorb the findings of the many research studies discussed. The chapter headings, which organize the findings, should prove especially useful to you here. In addition, you might, for each main topic (conformity, group influence, aggression, etc.), ask yourself the question, "What situational factors promote this phenomenon?" The research findings can then form the basis for your answers.

NOTE: Answer guidelines for all Chapter 18 questions begin on page 481.

CHAPTER REVIEW

First, skim each section, noting headings and boldface items. After you have read the section, review each objective by answering the fill-in and essay-type questions that follow it. As you proceed, evaluate your performance by consulting the answers beginning on page 481. Do not continue with the next section until you understand each answer. If you need to, review or reread the section in the textbook before continuing.

Social Thinking (pp. 723–730)

> David Myers at times uses idioms that are unfamiliar to some readers. If you do not know the meaning of any of the following words, phrases, or expressions in the context in which they appear in the text, refer to pages 489–490 for an explanation: *typecast; tart-tongued remark; freeloaders; stand up for; "brainwashed"; chicken-and-egg spiral; heartening implication.*

Objective 1: Describe the three main focuses of social psychology.

1. Psychologists who study how we think about, influence, and relate to one another are called

   _____ _____ .

Objective 2: Contrast dispositional and situational attributions, and explain how the fundamental attribution error can affect our analyses of behavior.

2. Heider's theory of how we explain others' behavior is the _____ theory. According to this theory, we attribute behavior either to an internal cause, which is called a

   _____ _____ ,

   or to an external cause, which is called a

   _____ _____ .

3. Most people tend to_____
(overestimate/underestimate) the extent to which
people's actions are influenced by social situations because their _____ is
focused on the person. This tendency is called the

_____ _____

_____ . When explaining our
own behavior, or that of someone we know well,
this tendency is _____
(stronger/weaker). When observers view the
world from others' perspectives, attributions are
_____ (the same/reversed).

Give an example of the practical consequences of
attributions.

Objective 3: Define *attitude*.

4. Feelings, often based on our beliefs, that predispose our responses are called

_____ .

Objective 4: Describe the conditions under which
attitudes can affect actions.

List three conditions under which our attitudes do
predict our actions. Give examples.

Objective 5: Explain how the foot-in-the-door phenomenon, role-playing, and cognitive dissonance
illustrate the influence of actions on attitudes.

5. Many research studies demonstrate that our attitudes are strongly influenced by our

_____ . One example of this is
the tendency for people who agree to a small
request to comply later with a larger one. This is

the _____-_____-
_____-_____
phenomenon.

6. When you follow the social prescriptions for how
you should act as, say, a college student, you are
adopting a _____ .

7. Taking on a set of behaviors, or acting in a certain
way, generally _____
(changes/does not change) people's attitudes.

8. According to _____
_____ theory, thoughts and feel-
ings change because people are motivated to justify actions that would otherwise seem hypocriti-
cal. This theory was proposed by

_____ .

9. Dissonance theory predicts that people induced
(without coercion) to behave contrary to their
true attitudes will be motivated to reduce the
resulting _____ by changing
their _____ .

Social Influence (pp. 730–742)

> If you do not know the meaning of any of the
> following words, phrases, or expressions in the
> context in which they appear in the text, refer
> to pages 490–491 for an explanation: *"open-
> minded"; draw slips from a hat; draw back; kind-
> ness and obedience on a collision course; zap; devil-
> ish villains; tug-of-war; waffles.*

Objective 6: Describe the chameleon effect, and give
and example of it.

1. The *chameleon effect* refers to our natural tendency
to unconsciously _____
others' expressions, postures, and voice tones.
This helps us to feel what they are feeling,
referred to as _____

_____ .

2. Copycat violence is a serious example of the
effects of _____ on behavior.

3. Sociologists have found that suicides sometimes
increase following a _____
_____ suicide.

Objective 7: Discuss Asch's experiments on conformity, and distinguish between normative and informational social influence.

4. The term that refers to the tendency to adjust one's behavior to coincide with an assumed group standard is _____ .

5. The psychologist who first studied the effects of group pressure on conformity is

   _____ .

6. In this study, when the opinion of other group members was contradicted by objective evidence, subjects _____ (were/were not) willing to conform to the group opinion.

7. One reason that people comply with social pressure is to gain approval or avoid rejection; this is called _____

   _____ _____ .

   Understood rules for accepted and expected behavior are called social _____ .

8. Another reason people comply is that they have genuinely been influenced by what they have learned from others; this type of influence is called _____

   _____ _____ .

9. In one experiment, Robert Baron and colleagues found that people were more likely to conform to the group's judgments when the task was construed as _____ (important/ unimportant) and when it was _____ (easy/difficult).

10. Conformity rates tend to be lower in _____ (individualistic/collectivistic) cultures.

Objective 8: Describe Milgram's experiments on obedience, and outline the conditions in which obedience was highest.

11. The classic social psychology studies of obedience were conducted by _____ .
    When ordered by the experimenter to electrically shock the "learner," the majority of participants (the "teachers") in these studies _____ (complied/refused). More recent studies have found that women's compliance rates in similar situations were _____ (higher than/lower than/similar to) men's.

List the conditions under which obedience was highest in Milgram's studies.

Objective 9: Explain how the conformity and obedience studies can help us understand our susceptibility to social influence.

12. In getting people to administer increasingly larger shocks, Milgram was in effect applying the

    _____ - _____ -

    _____ - _____

    technique.

13. The Asch and Milgram studies demonstrate that strong _____ influences can make _____ people _____ to falsehoods and _____ orders to commit cruel acts.

Objective 10: Describe conditions in which the presence of others is likely to result in social facilitation, social loafing, or deindividuation.

14. The tendency to perform a task better when other people are present is called _____ _____ . In general, people become aroused in the presence of others, and arousal enhances the correct response on a(n) _____ (easy/difficult) task. Later research revealed that arousal strengthens the response that is most _____ in a given situation.

15. Researchers have found that the reactions of people in crowded situations are often _____ (lessened/amplified).

16. Ingham found that people worked _____ (harder/less hard) in a team tug-of-war than they had in an individual contest. This phenomenon has been called

    _____ _____ .

17. The feeling of anonymity and loss of self-restraint that an individual may develop when in a group is called _____ .

Objective 11: Discuss how group interaction can facilitate group polarization and groupthink.

18. Over time, the initial differences between groups usually _____ (increase/decrease).

19. The enhancement of each group's prevailing tendency over time is called

    _____ _____ .

    Future research studies will reveal whether electronic discussions on the _____ also demonstrate this tendency.

20. When the desire for group harmony overrides realistic thinking in individuals, the phenomenon known as _____ has occurred.

Objective 12: Identify the characteristic common to minority positions that sway majorities.

21. In considering the power of social influence, we cannot overlook the interaction of

    _____ _____

    (the power of the situation) and

    _____ _____

    (the power of the individual).

22. The power of one or two individuals to sway the opinion of the majority is called

    _____ _____ .

23. A minority opinion will have the most success in swaying the majority if it takes a stance that is _____ (unswerving/flexible).

Social Relations (pp. 742–771)

> If you do not know the meaning of any of the following words, phrases, or expressions in the context in which they appear in the text, refer to pages 491–492 for an explanation: *"horsing around"; with the toss of a coin; Ferdinand; she melts; an outlet for bottled-up impulses; diabolical images; familiarity breeds fondness; "beauty is only skin deep"; opposites retract; revved up; bystanders turns people away from the path that leads to helping; blasé; "sneaky," "smart-alecky stinkers"; down the tension ladder to a safer rung.*

Objective 13: Identify the three components of prejudice.

1. Prejudice is an _____ (and usually _____) attitude toward a group that involves overgeneralized beliefs known as _____ .

2. Like all attitudes, prejudice is a mixture of

   _____ , _____ ,

   and predispositions to _____ .

3. Prejudice is a negative _____ , and _____ is a negative

   _____ .

Objective 14: Contrast overt and subtle forms of prejudice, and give examples of each.

4. Americans today express _____ (less/the same/more) racial and gender prejudice than they did 50 years ago.

5. Blatant forms of prejudice _____ (have/have not) diminished. However, even people who deny holding prejudiced attitudes may carry negative _____ about race or gender.

6. (Close-Up) Recent studies of prejudice indicate that it is often an unconscious, or

   _____ , action. In one study, people who displayed the most _____

   _____ were the quickest to perceive apparent threat in black faces.

7. (Close-Up) Today's biopsychosocial approach has stimulated neuroscience studies that have detected implicit prejudice in people's

   _____-muscle responses and in the activation of their brain's

   _____ .

8. Worldwide, _____ (women/men) are more likely to live in poverty, and two-thirds of children without basic schooling are _____ (girls/boys). However, people tend to perceive women as being more _____ and _____ , and less _____ than men.

Objective 15: Discuss the social factors that contribute to prejudice.

9. For those with money, power, and prestige, prejudice often serves as a means of _____ social inequalities.

10. Discrimination increases prejudice through the tendency of people to _____ victims for their plight.

11. Through our _____ _____ , we associated ourselves with certain groups.

12. Prejudice is also fostered by the _____ _____ , a tendency to favor groups to which one belongs—called the _____—while excluding others, or the _____ .

Objective 16: Explain how scapegoating illustrates the emotional component of prejudice.

13. Research studies also reveal that the terror of facing _____ tends to heighten aggression toward people who threaten one's _____ .

14. That prejudice derives from attempts to blame others for one's frustration is proposed by the _____ theory.

15. People who feel loved and supported become more _____ to and _____ of those who differ from them.

Objective 17: Cite four ways that cognitive processes help create and maintain prejudice.

16. Research suggests that prejudice may also derive from _____ , the process by which we attempt to simplify our world by classifying people into groups. One by-product of this process is that people tend to _____ the similarity of those within a group.

17. Another factor that fosters the formation of group stereotypes and prejudice is the tendency to

_____ from vivid or memorable cases.

18. The belief that people get what they deserve—that the good are rewarded and the bad punished—is expressed in the _____ - _____ phenomenon. This phenomenon is based in part on _____ _____ , the tendency to believe that one would have foreseen how something turned out.

Objective 18: Explain how psychology's definition of *aggression* differs from everyday usage.

19. Aggressive behavior is defined by psychologists as _____ _____ . Thus, psychologists _____ (do/ do not) consider assertive salespeople to be aggressive.

20. Like other behaviors, aggression emerges from the interaction of _____ and _____ .

Objective 19: Describe three levels of biological influences on aggression.

21. Today, most psychologists _____ (do/do not) consider human aggression to be instinctive.

22. In humans, aggressiveness _____ (varies/does not vary) greatly from culture to culture, era to era, and person to person.

23. That there are genetic influences on aggression can be shown by the fact that many species of animals have been _____ for aggressiveness.

24. Twin studies suggest that genes _____ (do/do not) influence human aggression. One genetic marker of those who commit the most violence is the _____ chromosome. Studies of violent criminals reveal diminished activity in the brain's _____ _____ , which play an important role in controlling _____ .

25. In humans and animals, aggression is facilitated by _____ systems, which are in turn influenced by _____ and other substances in the blood.

26. The aggressive behavior of animals can be manipulated by altering the levels of the hormone _____ . When this level is _____ (increased/decreased), aggressive tendencies are reduced.

27. High levels of testosterone correlate with _____ , low tolerance for _____ , _____ , and _____ . Among teenage boys and adult men, high testosterone also correlates with _____ , hard _____ _____ , and aggressive responses to _____ . With age, testosterone levels—and aggressiveness— _____ (increase/decrease). Although testosterone heightens aggressiveness, aggression _____ (increases/ decreases) testosterone level.

28. One drug that unleashes aggressive responses to provocation is _____ .

Objective 20: Outline four psychological triggers of aggression.

29. According to the _____- _____ principle, inability to achieve a goal leads to anger, which may generate aggression.

30. Other aversive stimuli can provoke hostility, including _____ .

31. Aggressive behavior can be learned through _____ , as shown by the fact that people use aggression where they've found it pays, and through _____ of others.

32. Crime rates are higher in countries in which there is a large disparity between those who are _____ and those who are _____ . High violence rates also are typical of cultures and families in which there is minimal _____ _____ .

33. Once established, aggressive behavior patterns are _____ (difficult/not difficult) to change. However, _____- _____ programs have been successful in bringing down re-arrest rates of juvenile offenders.

34. Violence on television tends to _____ people to cruelty and _____ them to respond aggressively when they are provoked.

35. A woman's risk of rape is generally _____ (greater/less) today than it was half a century ago. Most rapes _____ (are/are not) reported.

36. Increased sexual aggression has coincided with the rise of the _____ video business, giving easier access to R- and X-rated films.

Comment on the impression of women that pornography frequently conveys and the effects this impression has on attitudes and behavior.

Summarize the findings of the Zillmann and Bryant study on the effects of pornography on attitudes toward rape.

37. Experiments have shown that it is not eroticism but depictions of _____ _____ that most directly affect men's acceptance and performance of aggression against women. Such depictions may create _____ _____ to which people respond when they are in new situations or are uncertain how to act.

Objective 21: Discuss the effects of violent video games on social attitudes and behavior.

38. Kids who play a lot of violent video games see the world as more _____ , get into more _____ and _____ , and get worse _____ .

39. Research studies of the impact of violent video games _____ (confirm/disconfirm) the idea that we feel better if we "blow of steam" by venting our emotions. This idea is the _____ _____ . Expressing anger breeds _____ .

40. Many factors contribute to aggression, including _____ factors, such as an increase in testosterone; _____ factors, such as frustration; and _____ , such as deindividuation.

Objective 22: Explain how social traps and mirror-image perceptions fuel social conflict.

41. A perceived incompatibility of actions, goals, or ideas is called _____ . This perception can take place between individuals, _____ , or _____ .

42. Two destructive social processes that contribute to conflict are _____ _____ and _____ perceptions.

43. When the "non-zero-sum game" is played, most people fall into the social trap by mistrusting the other player and pursuing their own _____ . To prevent people from falling into social traps, psychologists are exploring ways for people to operate for their mutual betterment—through agreed-upon _____ , through better _____ , and through _____ of their communal responsibilities.

44. The diabolical images people in conflict form of each other are called _____-_____ perceptions.

Objective 23: Describe the influence of proximity, physical attractiveness, and similarity on interpersonal attraction.

45. A prerequisite for, and perhaps the most powerful predictor of, attraction is _____ .

46. When people are repeatedly exposed to unfamiliar stimuli, their liking of the stimuli _____ (increases/decreases). This phenomenon is the _____ _____ effect. Robert Zajonc contends that this phenomenon was _____ for our ancestors, for whom the unfamiliar was often dangerous. One implication of this is that _____ against those who are culturally different may be a primitive, _____ , emotional response.

47. Our first impression of another person is most influenced by the person's _____ .

48. In a sentence, list several of the characteristics that physically attractive people are judged to possess: _____ _____ .

49. A person's attractiveness _____ (is/is not) strongly related to his or her self-esteem or happiness. Since 1970, the number of women unhappy with their appearance has _____ (increased/decreased/remained stable).

50. Cross-cultural research reveals that men judge women as more attractive if they have a _____ appearance, whereas women judge men who appear _____ , _____ , and _____ as more attractive.

51. People also seem to prefer physical features that are neither unusually _____ or _____ . Average faces, which tend to be _____ , are judged to be more sexually attractive.

52. Relationships in which the partners are very similar are _____ (more/less) likely to last.

53. Compared with strangers, friends and couples are more likely to be similar in terms of

_____

_____ .

Explain what a reward theory of attraction is and how it can account for the three predictors of liking—proximity, attractiveness, and similarity.

Objective 24: Describe the effect of physical arousal on passionate love, and identify two predictors of enduring companionate love.

54. Hatfield has distinguished two types of love: _____ love and _____ love.

55. According to the two-factor theory, emotions have two components: physical _____ and a _____ label.

56. When college men were placed in an aroused state, their feelings toward an attractive woman _____ (were/were not) more positive than those of men who had not been aroused.

57. Companionate love is promoted by _____—mutual sharing and giving by both partners. Another key ingredient of loving relationships is the revealing of intimate aspects of ourselves through _____ .

Objective 25: Define *altruism,* and give an example.

58. An unselfish regard for the welfare of others is called _____ .

Give an example of altruism.

Objective 26: Describe the steps in the decision-making process involved in bystander intervention.

59. According to Darley and Latané, people will help only if a three-stage decision-making process is completed: Bystanders must first _____ the incident, then _____ it as an emergency, and finally _____ _____ for helping.

60. When people who overheard a seizure victim calling for help thought others were hearing the same plea, they were _____ (more/less) likely to go to his aid than when they thought no one else was aware of the emergency.

61. In a series of staged accidents, Latané and Darley found that a bystander was _____ (more/less) likely to help if other bystanders were present. This phenomenon has been called the _____ _____ .

Identify the circumstances in which a person is most likely to offer help during an emergency.

Objective 27: Explain altruistic behavior from the perspective of social exchange theory and social norms.

62. The idea that social behavior aims to maximize rewards and minimize costs is proposed by _____ _____ theory.

63. One rule of social behavior tells us to return help to those who have helped us; this is the _____ norm.

64. Another rule tells us to help those who need our help; this is the _____-_____ norm.

Objective 28: Discuss effective ways of encouraging peaceful cooperation and reducing social conflict.

65. In most situations, establishing contact between two conflicting groups _____ (is/is not) sufficient to resolve conflict.

66. In Sherif's study, two conflicting groups of campers were able to resolve their conflicts by working together on projects in which they shared _____ goals. Shared _____ breed solidarity, as demonstrated by a surge in use of the word _____ in the weeks after 9/11.

67. When conflicts arise, a third-party _____ may facilitate communication and promote understanding.

68. Osgood has advanced a strategy of conciliation called GRIT, which stands for _____ and _____ _____ in _____-_____ . The key to this method is each side's offering of a small _____ gesture in order to increase mutual trust and cooperation.

PROGRESS TEST 1

Multiple-Choice Questions

Circle your answers to the following questions and check them with the answers beginning on page 483. If your answer is incorrect, read the explanation for why it is incorrect and then consult the appropriate pages of the text (in parentheses following the correct answer).

1. In his study of obedience, Stanley Milgram found that the majority of subjects:
   a. refused to shock the learner even once.
   b. complied with the experiment until the "learner" first indicated pain.
   c. complied with the experiment until the "learner" began screaming in agony.
   d. complied with all the demands of the experiment.

2. According to cognitive dissonance theory, dissonance is most likely to occur when:
   a. a person's behavior is not based on strongly held attitudes.
   b. two people have conflicting attitudes and find themselves in disagreement.
   c. an individual does something that is personally disagreeable.
   d. an individual is coerced into doing something that he or she does not want to do.

3. Which of the following statements is true?
   a. Groups are almost never swayed by minority opinions.
   b. Group polarization is most likely to occur when group members frequently disagree with one another.
   c. Groupthink provides the consensus needed for effective decision making.
   d. A group that is like-minded will probably not change its opinions through discussion.

4. Conformity increased under which of the following conditions in Asch's studies of conformity?
   a. The group had three or more people.
   b. The group had high status.
   c. Individuals were made to feel insecure.
   d. All of the above increased conformity.

5. Social traps are situations in which:
   a. conflicting parties realize that they have shared goals, the attainment of which requires their mutual cooperation.
   b. conflicting parties have similar, and generally negative, views of one another.
   c. conflicting parties each pursue their self-interests and become caught in mutually destructive behavior.
   d. two conflicting groups meet face-to-face in an effort to resolve their differences.

6. The phenomenon in which individuals lose their identity and relinquish normal restraints when they are part of a group is called:
   a. groupthink.   **c.** empathy.
   b. cognitive dissonance.   **d.** deindividuation.

7. Subjects in Asch's line-judgment experiment conformed to the group standard when their judgments were observed by others but not when they were made in private. This tendency to conform in public demonstrates:
   a. social facilitation.
   b. overjustification.
   c. informational social influence.
   d. normative social influence.

8. Based on findings from Milgram's obedience studies, participants would be *less* likely to follow the experimenter's orders when:
   a. they hear the "learner" cry out in pain.
   b. they merely administer the test while someone else delivers the shocks.
   c. the "learner" is an older person or mentions having some physical problem.
   d. they see another subject disobey instructions.

9. *Aggression* is defined as behavior that:
   a. hurts another person.
   b. is intended to hurt another person.
   c. is hostile, passionate, and produces physical injury.
   d. has all of the above characteristics.

10. Which of the following is true about aggression?
    a. It varies too much to be instinctive in humans.
    b. It is just one instinct among many.
    c. It is instinctive but shaped by learning.
    d. It is the most important human instinct.

11. Research studies have found a positive correlation between aggressive tendencies in animals and levels of the hormone:
    a. estrogen.　　　c. noradrenaline.
    b. adrenaline.　　d. testosterone.

12. Research studies have indicated that the tendency of viewers to misperceive normal sexuality, devalue their partners, and trivialize rape is:
    a. increased by exposure to pornography.
    b. not changed after exposure to pornography.
    c. decreased in men by exposure to pornography.
    d. decreased in both men and women by exposure to pornography.

13. Increasing the number of people that are present during an emergency tends to:
    a. increase the likelihood that people will cooperate in rendering assistance.
    b. decrease the empathy that people feel for the victim.
    c. increase the role that social norms governing helping will play.
    d. decrease the likelihood that anyone will help.

14. Which of the following was *not* mentioned in the text discussion of the roots of prejudice?
    a. people's tendency to overestimate the similarity of people within groups
    b. people's tendency to assume that exceptional, or especially memorable, individuals are unlike the majority of members of a group

c. people's tendency to assume that the world is just and that people get what they deserve
    d. people's tendency to discriminate against those they view as "outsiders"

15. The mere exposure effect demonstrates that:
    a. familiarity breeds contempt.
    b. opposites attract.
    c. birds of a feather flock together.
    d. familiarity breeds fondness.

16. In one experiment, college men were physically aroused and then introduced to an attractive woman. Compared to men who had not been aroused, these men:
    a. reported more positive feelings toward the woman.
    b. reported more negative feelings toward the woman.
    c. were ambiguous about their feelings toward the woman.
    d. were more likely to feel that the woman was "out of their league" in terms of attractiveness.

17. The deep affection that is felt in long-lasting relationships is called _____ love; this feeling is fostered in relationships in which _____ .
    a. passionate; there is equity between the partners
    b. passionate; traditional roles are maintained
    c. companionate; there is equity between the partners
    d. companionate; traditional roles are maintained

18. Which of the following is associated with an increased tendency on the part of a bystander to offer help in an emergency situation?
    a. being in a good mood
    b. having recently needed help and not received it
    c. observing someone as he or she refuses to offer help
    d. being a female

19. The belief that those who suffer deserve their fate is expressed in the:
    a. just-world phenomenon.
    b. phenomenon of ingroup bias.
    c. fundamental attribution error.
    d. mirror-image perception principle.

20. According to social exchange theory, a person's tendency toward altruistic behavior is based on:
   a. a determination of the relatedness of those who will be affected.
   b. a cost-benefit analysis of any action.
   c. social norms.
   d. all of the above.

Matching Items

Match each term with the appropriate definition or description.

Terms

_____ **1.** social facilitation
_____ **2.** social loafing
_____ **3.** bystander effect
_____ **4.** conformity
_____ **5.** ingroup bias
_____ **6.** normative social influence
_____ **7.** informational social influence
_____ **8.** group polarization
_____ **9.** stereotype
_____ **10.** attribution
_____ **11.** altruism
_____ **12.** mere exposure effect

Definitions or Descriptions

a. a causal explanation for someone's behavior
b. a generalized belief about a group of people
c. people work less hard in a group
d. performance is improved by an audience
e. the tendency to favor one's own group
f. the effect of social approval or disapproval
g. adjusting one's behavior to coincide with a group standard
h. group discussion enhances prevailing tendencies
i. the effect of accepting others' opinions about something
j. unselfish regard for others
k. the tendency that a person is less likely to help someone in need when others are present
l. the increased liking of a stimulus that results from repeated exposure to it

PROGRESS TEST 2

Progress Test 2 should be completed during a final chapter review. Answer the following questions after you thoroughly understand the correct answers for the section reviews and Progress Test 1.

Multiple-Choice Questions

1. (Close-Up) Which of the following is an example of implicit prejudice?
   a. Jake, who is white, gives higher evaluations to essays he believes to be written by black students than to white-authored essays.
   b. Carol believes that white people are arrogant.
   c. Brad earns more than Jane, despite having the same job skills, performance level, and seniority.
   d. In certain countries, women are not allowed to drive.

2. We tend to perceive the members of an ingroup as _____ and the members of an outgroup as _____ .
   a. similar to one another; different from one another
   b. different from one another; similar to one another
   c. above average in ability; below average in ability
   d. below average in ability; above average in ability

3. Regarding the influence of alcohol and testosterone on aggressive behavior, which of the following is true?
   a. Consumption of alcohol increases aggressive behavior; injections of testosterone reduce aggressive behavior.
   b. Consumption of alcohol reduces aggressive behavior; injections of testosterone increase aggressive behavior.
   c. Consumption of alcohol and injections of testosterone both promote aggressive behavior.
   d. Consumption of alcohol and injections of testosterone both reduce aggressive behavior.

4. Most people prefer mirror-image photographs of their faces. This is best explained by:
   a. the principle of equity.
   b. the principle of self-disclosure.
   c. the mere exposure effect.
   d. mirror-image perceptions.

5. Research studies have shown that frequent exposure to sexually explicit films:
   a. makes a woman's friendliness seem more sexual.
   b. diminishes the attitude that rape is a serious crime.
   c. may lead individuals to devalue their partners.
   d. may produce all of the above effects.

6. Research studies indicate that in an emergency situation, the presence of others often:
   a. prevents people from even noticing the situation.
   b. prevents people from interpreting an unusual event as an emergency.
   c. prevents people from assuming responsibility for assisting.
   d. leads to all of the above.

7. Two neighboring nations are each stockpiling weapons. Each sees its neighbor's actions as an act of aggression and its own actions as self-defense. Evidently, these nations are victims of:
   a. prejudice.
   b. groupthink.
   c. the self-serving bias.
   d. the fundamental attribution error.

8. Which of the following factors is the *most* powerful predictor of friendship?
   a. similarity in age
   b. common racial and religious background
   c. similarity in physical attractiveness
   d. physical proximity

9. Most researchers agree that:
   a. media violence is a factor in aggression.
   b. there is a negative correlation between media violence and aggressiveness.
   c. paradoxically, watching excessive pornography ultimately diminishes an individual's aggressive tendencies.
   d. media violence is too unreal to promote aggression in viewers.

10. When male students in an experiment were told that a woman to whom they would be speaking had been instructed to act in a friendly or unfriendly way, most of them subsequently attributed her behavior to:
    a. the situation.
    b. the situation *and* her personal disposition.
    c. her personal disposition.
    d. their own skill or lack of skill in a social situation.

11. Which of the following is true?
    a. Attitudes and actions rarely correspond.
    b. Attitudes predict behavior about half the time.
    c. Attitudes are excellent predictors of behavior.
    d. Attitudes predict behavior under certain conditions.

12. People with power and status may become prejudiced because:
    a. they tend to justify the social inequalities between themselves and others.
    b. those with less status and power tend to resent them.
    c. those with less status and power appear less capable.
    d. they feel proud and are boastful of their achievements.

13. Which of the following most accurately states the effects of crowding on behavior?
    a. Crowding makes people irritable.
    b. Crowding sometimes intensifies people's reactions.
    c. Crowding promotes altruistic behavior.
    d. Crowding usually weakens the intensity of people's reactions.

14. Research has found that for a minority to succeed in swaying a majority, the minority must:
    a. make up a sizable portion of the group.
    b. express its position as consistently as possible.
    c. express its position in the most extreme terms possible.
    d. be able to convince a key majority leader.

15. Which of the following conclusions did Milgram derive from his studies of obedience?
    a. Even ordinary people, without any particular hostility, can become agents in a destructive process.
    b. Most people are able, under the proper circumstances, to suppress their natural aggressiveness.
    c. The need to be accepted by others is a powerful motivating force.
    d. All of the above conclusions were reached.

16. Which of the following best summarizes the relative importance of personal control and social control of our behavior?
    a. Situational influences on behavior generally are much greater than personal influences.
    b. Situational influences on behavior generally are slightly greater than personal influences.
    c. Personal influences on behavior generally are much greater than situational influences.
    d. Situational and personal influences interact in determining our behavior.

17. Which of the following best describes how GRIT works?
    a. The fact that two sides in a conflict have great respect for the other's strengths prevents further escalation of the problem.
    b. The two sides engage in a series of reciprocated conciliatory acts.
    c. The two sides agree to have their differences settled by a neutral, third-party mediator.
    d. The two sides engage in cooperation in those areas in which shared goals are possible.

18. Which of the following is important in promoting conformity in individuals?
    a. whether an individual's behavior will be observed by others in the group
    b. whether the individual is male or female
    c. the size of the room in which a group is meeting
    d. whether the individual is of a higher status than other group members

19. Which theory describes how we explain others' behavior as being due to internal dispositions or external situations?
    a. social exchange theory
    b. reward theory
    c. two-factor theory
    d. attribution theory

20. Which of the following is most likely to promote groupthink?
    a. The group's leader fails to take a firm stance on an issue.
    b. A minority faction holds to its position.
    c. The group consults with various experts.
    d. Group polarization is evident.

True–False Items

Indicate whether each statement is true or false by placing *T* or *F* in the blank next to the item.

_____ 1. When explaining another's behavior, we tend to underestimate situational influences.
_____ 2. When explaining our own behavior, we tend to underestimate situational influences.
_____ 3. An individual is more likely to conform when the rest of the group is unanimous.
_____ 4. The tendency of people to conform is influenced by the culture in which they were socialized.
_____ 5. A bystander is more likely to offer help in an emergency if other bystanders are present.
_____ 6. Counter-attitudinal behavior (acting contrary to our beliefs) often leads to attitude change.
_____ 7. Human aggression is instinctual.
_____ 8. Group polarization tends to prevent groupthink from occurring.
_____ 9. Crowded conditions usually subdue people's reactions.
_____ 10. When individuals lose their sense of identity in a group, they often become more uninhibited.

PSYCHOLOGY APPLIED

Answer these questions the day before an exam as a final check on your understanding of the chapter's terms and concepts.

Multiple-Choice Questions

1. After waiting in line for an hour to buy concert tickets, Teresa is told that the concert is sold out. In her anger she pounds her fist on the ticket counter, frightening the clerk. Teresa's behavior is best explained by:
    a. evolutionary psychology.
    b. the reciprocity norm.
    c. social exchange theory.
    d. the frustration-aggression principle.

2. Before she gave a class presentation favoring gun control legislation, Wanda opposed it. Her present attitude favoring such legislation can best be explained by:
   a. attribution theory.
   b. cognitive dissonance theory.
   c. social exchange theory.
   d. evolutionary psychology.

3. Which of the following would most likely be subject to social facilitation?
   a. proofreading a page for spelling errors
   b. typing a letter with accuracy
   c. playing a difficult piece on a musical instrument
   d. running quickly around a track

4. Jane and Sandy were best friends as freshmen. Jane joined a sorority; Sandy didn't. By the end of their senior year, they found that they had less in common with each other than with the other members of their respective circles of friends. Which of the following phenomena most likely explains their feelings?
   a. group polarization   c. deindividuation
   b. groupthink   d. social facilitation

5. Which of the following strategies would be *most* likely to foster positive feelings between two conflicting groups?
   a. Take steps to reduce the likelihood of social traps.
   b. Separate the groups so that tensions diminish.
   c. Increase the amount of contact between the two conflicting groups.
   d. Have the groups work on a superordinate goal.

6. José is the one student member on the college board of trustees. At the board's first meeting, José wants to disagree with the others on several issues but in each case decides to say nothing. Studies on conformity suggest all except one of the following are factors in José's not speaking up. Which one is *not* a factor?
   a. The board is a large group.
   b. The board is prestigious and most of its members are well known.
   c. The board members are already aware that José and the student body disagree with them on these issues.
   d. Because this is the first meeting José has attended, he feels insecure and not fully competent.

7. Given the tendency of people to categorize information according to preformed schemas, which of the following stereotypes would Juan, a 65-year-old political liberal and fitness enthusiast, be most likely to have?
   a. "People who exercise regularly are very extraverted."
   b. "All political liberals are advocates of a reduced defense budget."
   c. "Young people today have no sense of responsibility."
   d. "Older people are lazy."

8. Ever since their cabin lost the camp softball competition, the campers have become increasingly hostile toward one camper in their cabin, blaming her for every problem in the cabin. This behavior is best explained in terms of:
   a. the ingroup bias.
   b. prejudice.
   c. the scapegoat theory.
   d. the reciprocity norm.

9. Maria recently heard a speech calling for a ban on aerosol sprays that endanger the earth's ozone layer. Maria's subsequent decision to stop using aerosol sprays is an example of:
   a. informational social influence.
   b. normative social influence.
   c. deindividuation.
   d. social facilitation.

10. Mr. and Mrs. Samuels are constantly fighting, and each perceives the other as hard-headed and insensitive. Their conflict is being fueled by:
    a. self-disclosure.
    b. stereotypes.
    c. a social trap.
    d. mirror-image perceptions.

11. Which of the following situations should produce the *greatest* cognitive dissonance?
    a. A soldier is forced to carry out orders he finds disagreeable.
    b. A student who loves animals has to dissect a cat in order to pass biology.
    c. As part of an experiment, a subject is directed to deliver electric shocks to another person.
    d. A student volunteers to debate an issue, taking the side he personally disagrees with.

12. Professor Washington's students did very poorly on the last exam. The tendency to make the fundamental attribution error might lead her to conclude that the class did poorly because:
    a. the test was unfair.
    b. not enough time was given for students to complete the test.
    c. students were distracted by some social function on campus.
    d. students were unmotivated.

13. Students at State University are convinced that their school is better than any other; this most directly illustrates:
    a. an ingroup bias.
    b. prejudice and discrimination.
    c. the scapegoat effect.
    d. the just-world phenomenon.

14. After Sandy helped Jack move into his new apartment, Jack felt obligated to help Sandy when she moved. Jack's sense of responsibility can best be explained by:
    a. evolutionary psychology.
    b. two-factor theory.
    c. the social responsibility norm.
    d. the reciprocity norm.

15. Ahmed and Monique are on a blind date. Which of the following will probably be *most* influential in determining whether they like each other?
    a. their personalities
    b. their beliefs
    c. their social skills
    d. their physical attractiveness

16. Opening her mail, Joan discovers a romantic greeting card from her boyfriend. According to the two-factor theory, she is likely to feel the most intense romantic feelings if, prior to reading the card, she has just:
    a. completed her daily run.
    b. finished reading a chapter in her psychology textbook.
    c. awakened from a nap.
    d. finished eating lunch.

17. Driving home from work, Althea saw a car run off the road and burst into flames. Althea stopped her car, ran to the burning vehicle, and managed to pull the elderly driver to safety before the car exploded. Althea's behavior can best be explained by:
    a. the social responsibility norm.
    b. the reciprocity norm.

c. two-factor theory.
d. reward theory.

18. Having read the chapter, which of the following is best borne out by research on attraction?
    a. Birds of a feather flock together.
    b. Opposites attract.
    c. Familiarity breeds contempt.
    d. Absence makes the heart grow fonder.

19. Alexis believes that all male athletes are self-centered and sexist. Her beliefs are an example of:
    a. in-group bias.
    b. groupthink.
    c. stereotypes.
    d. the fundamental attribution error.

20. Which of the following is an example of the foot-in-the-door phenomenon?
    a. To persuade a customer to buy a product a store owner offers a small gift.
    b. After agreeing to wear a small "Enforce Recycling" lapel pin, a woman agrees to collect signatures on a petition to make recycling required by law.
    c. After offering to sell a car at a ridiculously low price, a car salesperson is forced to tell the customer the car will cost $1000 more.
    d. All of the above are examples.

Essay Question

The Panhellenic Council on your campus has asked you to make a presentation on the topic "Social Psychology" to all freshmen who have signed up to "rush" a fraternity or sorority. In a fit of cynicism following your rejection last year by a prestigious fraternity or sorority, you decide to speak on the negative influences of groups on the behavior of individuals. What will you discuss? (Use the space below to list the points you want to make, and organize them. Then write the essay on a separate sheet of paper.)

KEY TERMS

Writing Definitions

Using your own words, on a separate piece of paper write a brief definition or explanation of each of the following terms.

1. social psychology
2. attribution theory
3. fundamental attribution error
4. attitudes
5. foot-in-the-door phenomenon
6. cognitive dissonance theory
7. conformity
8. normative social influence
9. informational social influence
10. social facilitation
11. social loafing
12. deindividuation
13. group polarization
14. groupthink
15. prejudice
16. stereotype
17. discrimination
18. ingroup
19. outgroup
20. ingroup bias
21. scapegoat theory
22. just-world phenomenon
23. aggression
24. frustration-aggression principle
25. conflict
26. social trap
27. mere exposure effect
28. passionate love
29. companionate love
30. equity
31. self-disclosure
32. altruism
33. bystander effect
34. social exchange theory
35. reciprocity norm
36. social-responsibility norm
37. superordinate goals
38. GRIT

Cross-Check

As you learned in the Prologue, reviewing and overlearning of material are important to the learning process. After you have written the definitions of the key terms in this chapter, you should complete the crossword puzzle to ensure that you can reverse the process— recognize the term, given the definition.

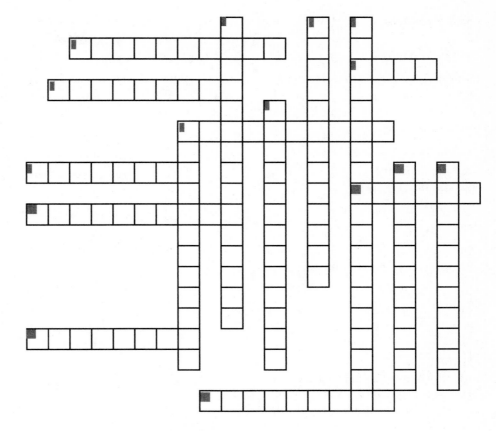

ACROSS

4. A generalized belief about a group of people.
5. A strategy of conflict resolution in which both groups make conciliatory gestures. (abbrev.)
6. Theory that proposes that prejudice provides an outlet for anger by finding someone to blame.
8. The tendency to change one's attitudes to coincide with those held by a group.
9. An unselfish regard for the welfare of others.
12. Mutual giving and receiving in a relationship.
13. Type of love that refers to an aroused state of intense positive absorption in another person.
14. Perceived incompatibility between individuals or groups.
15. Personal beliefs and feelings that influence our behavior.

DOWN

1. A person's tendency not to offer help to someone if others are present.
2. Type of social influence that results when one goes along with a group when one is unsure of what to do.
3. Psychological discomfort we experience when two of our thoughts conflict.
7. Phenomenon whereby people who agree to a small request are more likely to comply later with a larger request.
8. Type of love in which there is a deep, enduring attachment.
10. Our tendency to underestimate situational influences and overestimate dispositional influences upon the behavior of others is the _____ attribution error.
11. A causal explanation of a given behavior.

ANSWERS

Chapter Review

Social Thinking

1. social psychologists
2. attribution; dispositional attribution; situational attribution
3. underestimate; attention; fundamental attribution error; weaker; reversed

Our attributions—to individuals' dispositions or to situations—have important practical consequences. A hurtful remark from an acquaintance, for example, is more likely to be forgiven if it is attributed to a temporary situation than to a mean disposition.

4. attitudes

Attitudes predict actions when other influences on the attitudes and actions are minimized, when the attitude is specifically relevant to the behavior, and when we are especially aware of our attitudes. Thus, our attitudes are more likely to predict behavior when we are not attempting to adjust our behavior to please others, when we are in familiar situations in which we don't have to stop and think about our attitudes, and when the attitude pertains to a specific behavior, such as purchasing a product or casting a vote.

5. actions or behavior; foot-in-the-door
6. role
7. changes
8. cognitive dissonance; Festinger
9. dissonance; attitudes

Social Influence

1. mimic; mood linkage
2. suggestibility
3. highly publicized
4. conformity
5. Asch
6. were
7. normative social influence; norms
8. informational social influence
9. important; difficult
10. individualistic
11. Milgram; complied; similar to

Obedience was highest when the person giving the orders was close at hand and perceived to be a legitimate authority figure, the authority figure was supported by a prestigious institution, the victim was depersonalized, and when there were no role models for defiance.

12. foot-in-the-door
13. social; ordinary; conform; obey
14. social facilitation; easy; likely
15. amplified
16. less hard; social loafing
17. deindividuation
18. increase
19. group polarization; Internet
20. groupthink
21. social control; personal control
22. minority influence
23. unswerving

Social Relations

1. unjustifiable; negative; stereotypes
2. beliefs; emotions; action
3. attitude; discrimination; behavior
4. less
5. have; associations
6. implicit; implicit prejudice
7. facial; amygdala

8. women; girls; nurturant; sensitive; aggressive
9. justifying
10. blame
11. social identities
12. ingroup bias; ingroup; outgroup
13. death; worldview
14. scapegoat
15. open; accepting
16. categorization; overestimate
17. overgeneralize
18. just-world; hindsight bias
19. any physical or verbal behavior intended to hurt or destroy; do not
20. biology; experience
21. do not
22. varies
23. bred
24. do; Y; frontal lobes; impulses
25. neural; hormones
26. testosterone; decreased
27. irritability; frustration; assertiveness; impulsiveness; delinquency; drug use; frustration; decrease; increases
28. alcohol
29. frustration-aggression
30. physical pain, personal insults, foul odors, hot temperatures, cigarette smoke
31. rewards; observation (or imitation)
32. rich; poor; father care
33. difficult; aggression-replacement
34. desensitize; prime
35. greater; are not
36. home

Pornography tends to portray women as enjoying being the victims of sexual aggression, and this perception increases the acceptance of coercion in sexual relationships. Repeatedly watching X-rated films also makes one's partner seem less attractive, makes a woman's friendliness seem more sexual, and makes sexual aggression seem less serious.

The Zillmann and Bryant study found that after viewing sexually explicit films for several weeks, undergraduates were more likely to recommend a lighter prison sentence for a convicted rapist than were subjects who viewed nonerotic films.

37. sexual violence; social scripts

38. hostile; arguments; fights; grades

39. disconfirm; catharsis hypothesis; more anger

40. biological; psychological; social-cultural

41. conflict; groups; nations

42. social traps; distorted

43. self-interests; regulations; communication; awareness

44. mirror-image

45. proximity

46. increases; mere exposure; adaptive; prejudice; automatic

47. appearance

48. Attractive people are perceived as happier, more sensitive, more successful, and more socially skilled.

49. is not; increased

50. youthful; mature; dominant; affluent

51. large; small; symmetrical

52. more

53. attitudes, beliefs, interests, religion, race, education, intelligence, smoking behavior, economic status, age

Reward theories of attraction say that we are attracted to, and continue relationships with, those people whose behavior provides us with more benefits than costs. Proximity makes it easy to enjoy the benefits of friendship at little cost, attractiveness is pleasing, and similarity is reinforcing to us.

54. passionate; companionate

55. arousal; cognitive

56. were

57. equity; self-disclosure

58. altruism

An example of altruism is giving food and shelter to people displaced by a hurricane or other major disaster without expectation of reward.

59. notice; interpret; assume responsibility

60. less

61. less; bystander effect

People are most likely to help someone when they have just observed someone else being helpful; when they are not in a hurry; when the victim appears to need and deserve help; when they are in some way similar to the victim; when in a small town; when feeling guilty; when not preoccupied; and when in a good mood.

62. social exchange

63. reciprocity

64. social-responsibility

65. is not

66. superordinate; predicaments; "we"

67. mediator

68. Graduated; Reciprocated Initiatives; Tension-Reduction; conciliatory

Progress Test 1

Multiple-Choice Questions

1. **d.** is the answer. In Milgram's initial experiments, 63 percent of the subjects fully complied with the experiment. (p. 735)

2. **c.** is the answer. Cognitive dissonance is the tension we feel when we are aware of a discrepancy between our thoughts and actions, as would occur when we do something we find distasteful. (p. 728)
   a. Dissonance requires strongly held attitudes, which must be perceived as not fitting behavior.
   b. Dissonance is a personal cognitive process.
   d. In such a situation the person is less likely to experience dissonance, since the action can be attributed to "having no choice."

3. **d.** is the answer. In such groups, discussion usually strengthens prevailing opinion; this phenomenon is known as group polarization. (pp. 739–740)
   a. Minority opinions, especially if consistently and firmly stated, can sway the majority in a group.
   b. Group polarization, or the strengthening of a group's prevailing tendencies, is most likely in groups where members agree.
   c. When groupthink occurs, there is so much consensus that decision making becomes less effective.

4. **d.** is the answer. (p. 733)

5. **c.** is the answer. Social traps foster conflict in that two parties, by pursuing their self-interests, create a result that neither group wants. (p. 756)
   a. As Sherif's studies demonstrated, the possession of shared or superordinate goals tends to reduce conflict between groups.
   b. This is an example of mirror-image perceptions, which, along with social traps, foster conflict.
   d. Face-to-face confrontations between conflicting parties generally do not reduce conflict, nor are they social traps.

6. **d.** is the answer. (p. 739)
   a. Groupthink refers to the mode of thinking that

occurs when the desire for group harmony overrides realistic and critical thinking.

b. Cognitive dissonance refers to the discomfort we feel when two thoughts (which include the knowledge of our *behavior*) are inconsistent.

c. Empathy is feeling what another person feels.

7. **d.** is the answer. Normative social influence refers to influence on behavior that comes from a desire to look good to others. Subjects who were observed conformed because they didn't want to look like oddballs. (p. 733)

a. Social facilitation involves performing tasks better or faster in the presence of others.

b. Overjustification occurs when a person is rewarded for doing something that is already enjoyable.

c. Informational social influence is the tendency of individuals to accept the opinions of others, especially in situations where they themselves are unsure.

8. **d.** is the answer. Role models for defiance reduce levels of obedience. (p. 736)

a. & c. These did not result in diminished obedience.

b. This "depersonalization" of the victim resulted in increased obedience.

9. **b.** is the answer. Aggression is any behavior, physical or verbal, that is intended to hurt or destroy. (p. 749)

a. A person may accidentally be hurt in a nonaggressive incident; aggression does not necessarily prove hurtful.

c. Verbal behavior, which does not result in physical injury, may also be aggressive. Moreover, acts of aggression may be cool and calculated, rather than hostile and passionate.

10. **a.** is the answer. The very wide variations in aggressiveness from culture to culture indicate that aggression cannot be considered an unlearned instinct. (p. 749)

11. **d.** is the answer. (p. 750)

12. **a.** is the answer. (p. 753)

13. **d.** is the answer. This phenomenon is known as the bystander effect. (p. 766)

a. This answer is incorrect because individuals are less likely to render assistance at all if others are present.

b. Although people are less likely to assume responsibility for helping, this does not mean that they are less empathic.

c. This answer is incorrect because norms such as the social responsibility norm encourage helping others, yet people are less likely to help with others around.

14. **b.** is the answer. In fact, people tend to overgeneralize from vivid cases, rather than assume that they are unusual. (pp. 745–748)

a., c., & d. Each of these is an example of a cognitive (a. & c.) or a social (d.) root of prejudice.

15. **d.** is the answer. Being repeatedly exposed to novel stimuli increases our liking for them. (p. 759)

a. For the most part, the opposite is true.

b. & c. The mere exposure effect concerns our tendency to develop likings on the basis, not of similarities or differences, but simply of familiarity, or repeated exposure.

16. **a.** is the answer. This result supports the two-factor theory of emotion and passionate attraction, according to which arousal from any source can facilitate an emotion, depending on how we label the arousal. (p. 763)

17. **c.** is the answer. Deep affection is typical of companionate love, rather than passionate love, and is promoted by equity, whereas traditional roles may be characterized by the dominance of one sex. (pp. 763–764)

18. **a.** is the answer. (p. 766)

b. & c. These factors would most likely decrease a person's altruistic tendencies.

d. There is no evidence that one sex is more altruistic than the other.

19. **a.** is the answer. (p. 748)

b. Ingroup bias is the tendency of people to favor their own group.

c. The fundamental attribution error is the tendency of people to underestimate situational influences when observing the behavior of other people.

d. The mirror-image perception principle is the tendency of conflicting parties to form similar, diabolical images of each other.

20. **b.** is the answer. (pp. 766)

a. This is a tenet of evolutionary psychology.

c. Social exchange theory focuses on costs and benefits, rather than on norms.

Matching Items

1. d (p. 738)   5. e (p. 746)   9. b (p. 743)
2. c (p. 739)   6. f (p. 733)   10. a (p. 724)
3. k (p. 766)   7. i (p. 733)   11. j (p. 765)
4. g (p. 732)   8. h (p. 740)   12. l (p. 759)

Progress Test 2

Multiple-Choice Questions

1. **a.** is the answer. (p. 744)
   b. This is an example of prejudice.
   c. & d. These are examples of discrimination.

2. **b.** is the answer. (p. 746)
   a. We are keenly sensitive to differences within our group, less so to differences within other groups.
   c. & d. Although we tend to look more favorably on members of the ingroup, the text does not suggest that ingroup bias extends to evaluations of abilities.

3. **c.** is the answer. (p. 750)

4. **c.** is the answer. The mere exposure effect refers to our tendency to like what we're used to, and we're used to seeing mirror images of ourselves. (p. 759)
   a. Equity refers to equality in giving and taking between the partners in a relationship.
   b. Self-disclosure is the sharing of intimate feelings with a partner in a loving relationship.
   d. Although people prefer mirror images of their faces, mirror-image perceptions are often held by parties in conflict. Each party views itself favorably and the other negatively.

5. **d.** is the answer. (p. 753)

6. **d.** is the answer. (p. 765)

7. **d.** is the answer. In this case, each nation has mistakenly attributed the other's action to a *dispositional* trait, whereas its own action is viewed as a *situational* response. (p. 724)

8. **d.** is the answer. Because it provides people with an opportunity to meet, proximity is the most powerful predictor of friendship, even though, once a friendship is established, the other factors mentioned become more important. (p. 758)

9. **a.** is the answer. (pp. 753–754)

10. **c.** is the answer. In this example of the fundamental attribution error, even when given the situational explanation for the woman's behavior, students ignored it and attributed her behavior to her personal disposition. (p. 724)

11. **d.** is the answer. Our attitudes are more likely to guide our actions when other influences are minimal, when there's a specific connection between the two, and when we're keenly aware of our beliefs. The presence of other people would more likely be an outside factor that would lessen the likelihood of actions being guided by attitude. (p. 726)

12. **a.** is the answer. Such justifications arise as a way to preserve inequalities. The just-world phenomenon presumes that people get what they deserve. According to this view, someone who has less must deserve less. (p. 745)

13. **b.** is the answer. (p. 738)
    a. & c. Crowding may amplify irritability or altruistic tendencies that are already present. Crowding does not, however, produce these reactions as a general effect.
    d. In fact, just the opposite is true. Crowding often intensifies people's reactions.

14. **b.** is the answer. (p. 741)
    a. Even if they made up a sizable portion of the group, although still a minority, their numbers would not be as important as their consistency.
    c. & d. These aspects of minority influence were not discussed in the text; however, they are not likely to help a minority sway a majority.

15. **a.** is the answer. (p. 737)

16. **d.** is the answer. The text emphasizes the ways in which personal and social controls interact in influencing behavior. It does not suggest that one factor is more influential than the other. (p. 741)

17. **b.** is the answer. (p. 769)
    a. GRIT is a technique for reducing conflict through a series of conciliatory gestures, not for maintaining the status quo.
    c. & d. These measures may help reduce conflict but they are not aspects of GRIT.

18. **a.** is the answer. As Solomon Asch's experiments demonstrated, individuals are more likely to conform when they are being observed by others in the group. The other factors were not discussed in the text and probably would not promote conformity. (p. 733)

19. **d.** is the answer. (p. 724)

20. **d.** is the answer. Group polarization, or the enhancement of a group's prevailing attitudes, promotes groupthink, which leads to the disintegration of critical thinking. (p. 740)
    a. Groupthink is more likely when a leader highly favors an idea, which may make members reluctant to disagree.
    b. A strong minority faction would probably have the opposite effect: It would diminish group harmony while promoting critical thinking.
    c. Consulting experts would discourage groupthink by exposing the group to other opinions.

True–False Items

1. T (p. 724)
2. F (p. 724)
3. T (p. 733)
4. T (p. 733)
5. F (p. 766)
6. T (pp. 728–729)
7. F (p. 749)
8. F (p. 740)
9. F (p. 738)
10. T (p. 739)

Psychology Applied

1. **d.** is the answer. According to the frustration-aggression principle, the blocking of an attempt to achieve some goal—in Teresa's case, buying concert tickets—creates anger and can generate aggression. (p. 751)
   a. Evolutionary psychology maintains that aggressive behavior is a genetically based drive. Teresa's behavior clearly was a reaction to a specific situation.
   b. The reciprocity norm—that we should return help to those who have helped us—would not engender Teresa's angry reaction.
   c. Social exchange theory views behavior as an exchange process in which people try to maximize the benefits of their behavior by minimizing the costs. Teresa's behavior likely brought her few benefits while exacting some costs, including potential injury, embarrassment, and retaliation by the clerk.

2. **b.** is the answer. Dissonance theory focuses on what happens when our actions contradict our attitudes. (pp. 728–729)
   a. Attribution theory holds that we give causal explanations for others' behavior, often by crediting either the situation or people's dispositions.
   c. Social exchange theory maintains that social behaviors maximize benefits and minimize costs. It is not clear in this example whether Wanda perceives such costs and benefits.
   d. This is not a theory of social influence.

3. **d.** is the answer. Social facilitation, or better performance in the presence of others, occurs for easy tasks but not for more difficult ones. For tasks such as proofreading, typing, playing an instrument, or giving a speech, the arousal resulting from the presence of others can lead to mistakes. (p. 738)

4. **a.** is the answer. Group polarization means that the tendencies within a group—and therefore the differences among groups—grow stronger over time. Thus, because the differences between the sorority and nonsorority students have increased, Jane and Sandy are likely to have little in common. (p. 740)

   b. Groupthink is the tendency for realistic decision making to disintegrate when the desire for group harmony is strong.
   c. Deindividuation is the loss of self-consciousness and restraint that sometimes occurs when one is part of a group.
   d. Social facilitation refers to improved performance of a task in the presence of others.

5. **d.** is the answer. Sherif found that hostility between two groups could be dispelled by giving the groups superordinate, or shared, goals. (p. 767)
   a. Although reducing the likelihood of social traps might reduce mutually destructive behavior, it would not lead to positive feelings between the groups.
   b. Such segregation would likely increase in-group bias and group polarization, resulting in further group conflict.
   c. Contact by itself is not likely to reduce conflict.

6. **c.** is the answer. Prior commitment to an opposing view generally tends to work against conformity. In contrast, large group size, prestigiousness of a group, and an individual's feelings of incompetence and insecurity all strengthen the tendency to conform. (p. 733)

7. **c.** is the answer. People tend to overestimate the similarity of people within groups other than their own. Thus, Juan is not likely to form stereotypes of fitness enthusiasts (a.), political liberals (b.), or older adults (d.), because these are groups to which he belongs. (p. 746)

8. **c.** is the answer. According to the scapegoat theory, when things go wrong, people look for someone on whom to take out their anger and frustration. (p. 747)
   a. These campers are venting their frustration on a member of their *own* cabin group (although this is not always the case with scapegoats).
   b. Prejudice refers to an unjustifiable and usually negative attitude toward another group.
   d. The reciprocity norm, which refers to our tendency to help those who have helped us, was not discussed as a root of prejudice.

9. **a.** is the answer. As illustrated by Maria's decision to stop buying aerosol products, informational social influence occurs when people have genuinely been influenced by what they have learned from others. (p. 733)
   b. Had Maria's behavior been motivated by the desire to avoid rejection or to gain social approval (which we have no reason to suspect is the case), it would have been an example of normative social influence.

c. Deindividuation refers to the sense of anonymity a person may feel as part of a group.

d. Social facilitation is the improvement in performance of well-learned tasks that may result when one is observed by others.

10. **d.** is the answer. The couple's similar, and presumably distorted, feelings toward each other fuel their conflict. (p. 758)

a. Self-disclosure, or the sharing of intimate feelings, fosters love.

b. Stereotypes are overgeneralized ideas about groups.

c. Social traps are situations in which conflicting parties engage in mutually destructive behavior while pursuing their own self-interests.

11. **d.** is the answer. In this situation, the counterattitudinal behavior is performed voluntarily and cannot be attributed to the demands of the situation. (p. 728)

a., b., & c. In all of these situations, the counterattitudinal behaviors should not arouse much dissonance because they can be attributed to the demands of the situation.

12. **d.** is the answer. The fundamental attribution error refers to the tendency to underestimate situational influences in favor of this type of dispositional attribution when explaining the behavior of other people. (p. 724)

a., b., & c. These are situational attributions.

13. **a.** is the answer. (p. 746)

b. Prejudices are unjustifiable and usually negative attitudes toward other groups. They may result from an ingroup bias, but they are probably not why students favor their own university.

c. Scapegoats are individuals or groups toward which prejudice is directed as an outlet for the anger of frustrated individuals or groups.

d. The just-world phenomenon is the tendency for people to believe others "get what they deserve."

14. **d.** is the answer. (p. 766)

a. Evolutionary psychology is not discussed in terms of altruism, but it would maintain that altruistic actions are predisposed by our genes.

b. The two-factor theory holds that emotions consist of physical arousal and an appropriate cognitive label.

c. The social responsibility norm refers to the social attitude that we should help those who need our help.

15. **d.** is the answer. Hundreds of experiments indicate that first impressions are most influenced by physical appearance. (pp. 759–760)

16. **a.** is the answer. According to the two-factor theory, physical arousal can intensify whatever emotion is currently felt. Only in the situation described in a. is Joan likely to be physically aroused. (p. 763)

17. **a.** is the answer. (p. 767)

b. The reciprocity norm mandates that we help those who have helped us.

c. The two-factor theory of emotion, which assumes that emotions are based on physical arousal and a cognitive label, makes no predictions regarding altruism.

d. The reward theory, which states that social behavior is maintained by rewards, would explain Althea's altruism as being due to her having previously been rewarded for similar altruistic actions.

18. **a.** is the answer. Friends and couples are much more likely than randomly paired people to be similar in views, interests, and a range of other factors. (p. 762)

b. The opposite is true.

c. The mere exposure effect demonstrates that familiarity tends to breed fondness.

d. This is unlikely, given the positive effects of proximity and intimacy.

19. **c.** is the answer. (p. 743)

a. The ingroup bias is the tendency to favor one's own group.

b. Groupthink refers to the unrealistic thought processes and decision making that occur within groups when the desire for group harmony becomes paramount.

d. The fundamental attribution error is our tendency to underestimate the impact of situations and to overestimate the impact of personal dispositions on the behavior of others.

20. **b.** is the answer. In the foot-in-the-door phenomenon, compliance with a small initial request, such as wearing a lapel pin, later is followed by compliance with a much larger request, such as collecting petition signatures. (p. 727)

Essay Question

Your discussion might focus on some of the following topics: normative social influence; conformity, which includes suggestibility; obedience; group polarization; and groupthink.

As a member of any group with established social norms, individuals will often act in ways that enable them to avoid rejection or gain social approval. Thus, a fraternity or sorority pledge would probably be very suggestible and likely to eventually conform to the attitudes and norms projected by the group—or be rejected socially. In extreme cases of pledge haz-ing, acute social pressures may lead to atypical and antisocial individual behaviors—for example, on the part of pledges complying with the demands of senior members of the fraternity or sorority. Over time, meetings and discussions will probably enhance the group's prevailing attitudes (group polarization). This may lead to the unrealistic and irrational deci-sion making that is groupthink. The potentially nega-tive consequences of groupthink depend on the issues being discussed, but may include a variety of socially destructive behaviors.

Key Terms

Writing Definitions

1. **Social psychology** is the scientific study of how we think about, influence, and relate to one another. (p. 723)

2. **Attribution theory** deals with our causal expla-nations of behavior. We attribute behavior to the individual's disposition or to the situation. (p. 724)

3. The **fundamental attribution error** is our tenden-cy to underestimate the impact of situations and to overestimate the impact of personal disposi-tions upon the behavior of others. (p. 724)

4. **Attitudes** are feelings, often based on beliefs, that may predispose a person to respond in particular ways to objects, people, and events. (p. 726)

5. The **foot-in-the-door phenomenon** is the tenden-cy for people who agree to a small request to comply later with a larger request. (p. 727)

6. **Cognitive dissonance theory** refers to the theory that we act to reduce the psychological discom-fort we experience when our behavior conflicts with what we think and feel, or more generally, when two of our thoughts are inconsistent. This is frequently accomplished by changing our atti-tude rather than our behavior. (p. 728)

   Memory aid: *Dissonance* means "lack of harmony." **Cognitive dissonance** occurs when two thoughts, or cognitions, are at variance with one another.

7. **Conformity** is the tendency to change one's thinking or behavior to coincide with a group standard. (p. 732)

8. **Normative social influence** refers to the pressure on individuals to conform in order to avoid rejec-tion or gain social approval. (p. 733)

   Memory aid: *Normative* means "based on a norm, or pattern, regarded as typical for a specific group." **Normative social influence** is the pres-sure groups exert on the individual to behave in ways acceptable to the group standard.

9. **Informational social influence** results when one goes along with a group when one is willing to accept others' opinions about reality. (p. 733)

10. **Social facilitation** is the improvement in perfor-mance of simple or well-learned tasks that occurs when other people are present. (p. 738)

11. **Social loafing** is the tendency for individual effort to be diminished when one is part of a group working toward a common goal. (p. 739)

12. **Deindividuation** refers to the loss of self-aware-ness and self-restraint that sometimes occurs in group situations that foster arousal and anonym-ity. (p. 739)

    Memory aid: As a prefix, *de-* indicates reversal or undoing. To **deindividuate** is to undo one's indi-viduality.

13. **Group polarization** refers to the enhancement of a group's prevailing tendencies through discus-sion, which often has the effect of accentuating the group's differences from other groups. (p. 740)

    Memory aid: To *polarize* is to "cause thinking to concentrate about two poles, or contrasting posi-tions."

14. **Groupthink** refers to the unrealistic thought processes and decision making that occur within groups when the desire for group harmony over-rides a realistic appraisal of alternatives. (p. 740)

    Example: The psychological tendencies of self-justification, conformity, and group polarization foster the development of the "team spirit" men-tality known as **groupthink**.

15. **Prejudice** is an unjustifiable (and usually nega-tive) attitude toward a group and its members. (p. 743)

16. A **stereotype** is a generalized (often overgeneral-ized) belief about a group of people. (p. 743)

17. **Discrimination** is unjustifiable negative behavior toward a group or its members (p. 743)

18. The **ingroup** refers to the people and groups with whom we share a common identity. (p. 746)

19. The **outgroup** refers to the people and groups that are excluded from our ingroup. (p. 746)

20. The **ingroup bias** is the tendency to favor one's own group. (p. 746)

21. The **scapegoat theory** proposes that prejudice provides an outlet for anger by finding someone to blame. (p. 747)

22. The **just-world phenomenon** is a manifestation of the commonly held belief that good is rewarded and evil is punished. The logic is indisputable: "If I am rewarded, I must be good." (p. 748)

23. **Aggression** is any physical or verbal behavior intended to hurt or destroy. (p. 749)

24. The **frustration-aggression principle** states that aggression is triggered when people become angry because their efforts to achieve a goal have been blocked. (p. 751)

25. **Conflict** is a perceived incompatibility of actions, goals, or ideas between individuals or groups. (p. 756)

26. A **social trap** is a situation in which conflicting parties become caught up in mutually harmful behavior as they pursue their perceived best interests. (p. 756)

27. The **mere exposure effect** refers to the fact that repeated exposure to an unfamiliar stimulus increases our liking of it. (p. 759)

28. **Passionate love** refers to an aroused state of intense positive absorption in another person, especially at the beginning of a relationship. (p. 763)

29. **Companionate love** refers to a deep, enduring, affectionate attachment. (p. 763)

30. **Equity** refers to the condition in which there is mutual giving and receiving between the partners in a relationship. (p. 764)

31. **Self-disclosure** refers to a person's sharing intimate feelings with another. (p. 764)

32. **Altruism** is unselfish regard for the welfare of others. (p. 765)

33. The **bystander effect** is the tendency of a person to be less likely to offer help to someone if there are other people present. (p. 766)

34. **Social exchange theory** states that our social behavior revolves around exchanges, in which we try to minimize our costs and maximize our benefits. (p. 766)

35. The **reciprocity norm** is the expectation that people will help those who have helped them. (p. 766)

36. The **social-responsibility norm** is the expectation that people will help those who depend on them. (p. 767)

37. **Superordinate goals** are mutual goals that require the cooperation of individuals or groups otherwise in conflict. (p. 767)

38. **GRIT** (Graduated and Reciprocated Initiatives in Tension-Reduction) is a strategy of conflict resolution based on the defusing effect that conciliatory gestures can have on parties in conflict. (p. 769)

Cross-Check

ACROSS
4. stereotype
5. GRIT
6. scapegoat
8. conformity
9. altruism
12. equity
13. passionate
14. conflict
15. attitudes

DOWN
1. bystander effect
2. informational
3. cognitive dissonance
7. foot-in-the-door
8. companionate
10. fundamental
11. attribution

FOCUS ON VOCABULARY AND LANGUAGE

Social Thinking

Page 724: . . . I still assumed that the young actress was *typecast* because she was well-suited for the part. David Myers tells us about seeing a young girl play the part of a miserable old woman in a high school play and his mistaken belief that she got the part because she had the same qualities as the character she was portraying (*she was typecast*). Although he knew she was acting the part (a situational factor), he still believed that her behavior reflected her personal disposition or personality. This type of mistake is called the **fundamental attribution error.**

Page 725: Happily married couples attribute *a spouse's tart-tongued remark* to a temporary situation ("She must have had a bad day at work"). How we make attributions can have serious consequences. Couples who think that their partner's sarcastic or unkind comment (*tart-tongued remark*) was due to a cruel personality (*mean disposition*) are more likely to be dissatisfied with their marriages than couples who believe that the same remark was simply a result of some situational influence, such as a stressful day at work.

Page 725: . . . *freeloaders.* This refers to people who voluntarily live off other people. Those who believe that people are poor and/or unemployed because of personal dispositions tend to underestimate the influence of situational variables. Thus, they might call someone on welfare a *freeloader* rather than simply a victim of circumstances.

Page 726: Not only will people sometimes *stand up for* what they believe, they will also come to believe in what *they have stood up for.* Not only do people support (*stand up for*) their strong convictions by taking appropriate action, but people will also develop convictions about things that they have taken action in support of (*that they have stood up for*). Many lines (*streams*) of evidence confirm the principle that beliefs can be changed to correspond with people's actions (*attitudes follow behavior*).

Page 727: . . . *"brainwashed"* . . . This refers to a person's beliefs, values, and attitudes being changed by relentless indoctrination and mental torture. One component of this mind-changing process (*"thought-control"*) involves use of the **foot-in-the-door phenomenon**, whereby a person is first coerced into agreeing to a small request, then to complying with much greater requests. Frequently, people will change their attitudes to be consistent with their new behavior.

Page 727: This *chicken-and-egg spiral* of actions feeding attitudes feeding actions enables behavior to escalate. Whether used for good or for bad, the foot-in-the-door strategy involves starting with small requests, then slowly increasing the level of demand. The new behavior will be followed by a change in attitude which, in turn, will make the behavior more likely and that will then lead to more change in belief, etc. (*the chicken-and-egg spiral*).

Page 730: The attitudes-follow-behavior principle has another *heartening implication.* When our attitudes and behaviors are inconsistent, we feel a certain amount of tension (**cognitive dissonance**), which makes us want to do something to reduce this uncomfortable state. Thus, if we are feeling depressed (*down in the dumps*) and we behave in a more outgoing manner, talk in a more positive way, and *act* as though we are happy, we may, in fact, start feeling much better. As Myers notes, the feelings-follow-actions notion has positive ramifications (*heartening implications*).

Social Influence

Page 734: When influence supports what we approve, we applaud those who are *"open-minded"* and *"sensitive"* enough to be *"responsive."* We can be influenced by others because they provide useful knowledge (**informational influence**) or because we want them to view us favorably and not ignore us (**normative influence**). Conformity that is consistent with what we believe is true will be seen in a posi-

tive light (the conformists are *"open-minded,"* etc.), and conformity that is not will be viewed negatively (*"submissive conformity"*).

Page 734: You and another person *draw slips from a hat* to see who will be the "teacher" (which your slip says) and who will be the "learner." In Milgram's famous obedience experiments participants were deceived into believing they were randomly assigned to one of two conditions ("teacher" or "learner") by picking a piece of paper out of a container (*drawing slips from a hat*). All the subjects were actually "teachers" and were asked to "shock" the "learners" whenever they made mistakes on a memory task. A majority of the participants complied with the experimenter's request.

Page 734: When you hear these pleas, you *draw back.* But the experimenter *prods* you: "Please continue—the experiment requires that you continue." If you were a participant ("teacher") in Milgram's experiment, you would be pressured (*prodded*) by the research assistant to carry on with the experiment even though you may show great reluctance (*you draw back*) after hearing the "learner's" cries of distress at being "shocked."

Page 737: With *kindness and obedience on a collision course,* obedience usually won. Milgram's research on obedience showed that social factors that foster conformity are powerful enough to make almost any one of us behave in ways inconsistent with our beliefs. When subjects were in a conflict over (*torn between*) whether to refuse to harm an individual or to follow orders (*kindness and obedience were on a collision course*), they usually did what they were asked to do.

Page 737: Milgram did not entrap his "teachers" by asking them first to *zap* "learners" with enough electricity to make their hair stand on end. Milgram used the foot-in-the-door tactic to get his subjects to comply with his requests to shock (*zap*) the "learners" with larger and larger voltages of electricity (*enough to make their hair stand on end*). He started with a small amount (*a little tickle*) of electricity; after obtaining compliance (*obedience*), he asked them to increase the level, and so on. Subjects tended to rationalize their behavior; for some, their attitudes became consistent with their behavior over the course of the experiment.

Page 737: Contrary to images of *devilish villains,* evil does not require *monstrous characters;* all it takes is ordinary people corrupted by an evil situation. . . . We tend to think that pain and suffering (*evil*) are always caused by inhumane and cruel people (*devil-*

ish villains or *monstrous characters*), but the research in social psychology shows that almost anyone can be led to behave badly given the right (or wrong) circumstances.

Page 738: In a team *tug-of-war*, for example, do you suppose the effort that a person puts forth would be more than, less than, or the same as the effort he or she would exert in a *one-on-one tug-of-war*? In a game in which opponents pull on each end of a rope (*tug-of-war*), when two individuals compete (*one-on-one*), they work much harder (*exert more effort*) than if they were members of a group competing on the same task. This lowering of individual effort when part of a team is called **social loafing**. (Note: The term *to loaf* means *to work less hard, to slack off, to take it easy,* or *to free ride*.)

Page 741: They repeatedly found that a minority that unswervingly holds to its position is far more successful in swaying the majority than is a minority that *waffles*. Committed individuals and small groups of individuals can convince (*sway*) the majority to their point of view if they adhere strictly to their agenda and do not appear to be uncertain or unsure (*to waffle*).

Social Relations

Page 743: In one 1970s study, most white participants perceived a white man shoving a black man as *"horsing around."* Prejudices involve beliefs, emotions, and tendencies to behave in certain ways. They are a form of prejudgment that influences (*colors*) how we interpret what we see. Thus, in an experiment in which white people saw a white man pushing a black person, most interpreted the behavior as playful activity (*horsing around*); when the roles were reversed, the behavior was more likely to be described as aggressive or hostile (*violent*).

Page 746: Even arbitrarily creating an us-them distinction—by grouping people *with the toss of a coin*—leads people to show favoritism to their own group when dividing any rewards (Tajfel, 1982; Wilder, 1981). One of the factors affecting prejudice is our propensity to define ourselves through identification with a particular group (**ingroup bias**); this in turn creates an outgroup consisting of those who do not belong to our group. Even if the groups are artificially created by random assignment (*with the toss of a coin*), we will tend to see our own group as more deserving, superior, and so on.

Page 750: A raging bull will become a gentle *Ferdinand* when castration reduces its testosterone level.

Biological explanations of aggression examine the influences of genes, clusters of neurons in the brain, and biochemical agents in the blood, such as hormones and alcohol. Levels of the male sex hormone can be reduced by castration; thus, an aggressive, ferocious bull can be reduced to a playful, friendly animal similar to the fictional character (*Ferdinand*) of children's stories.

Page 753: In less graphic form, the same unrealistic script—she resists, he persists, *she melts*—is commonplace on TV and in romance novels. A common theme in certain types of films and books is the idea that if the main male character overcomes (*he persists*) the lovely female's reluctance (*she resists*) to be romantically or sexually involved, then she will be totally devoted to him (*she melts*). This depiction of male-female relationships, in both pornographic and non-pornographic media, has little to do with reality and may, in fact, promote sexual aggression.

Page 754: Contrary to much popular opinion, viewing such *depictions* does not provide *an outlet* for *bottled-up impulses*. Laboratory studies have demonstrated that watching media that show sexual violence against women does not decrease the acceptance and performance of aggression against females. In contrast to what many believe, such portrayals (*depictions*) do not allow vicarious expression (*an outlet*) for pent-up hostile urges (*bottled-up impulses*) and may have the opposite effect.

Page 758: Psychologists have noted that those in conflict have a curious tendency to form *diabolical images* of one another. We have a propensity to perceive our enemies in a very distorted manner, often categorizing them as evil, cruel, untrustworthy, and devilish (*diabolical*). They, of course, view us in the same way; the biased pictures we form of each other are called *mirror-image perceptions*.

Page 759: Within certain limits . . . *familiarity breeds fondness.* Under some circumstances, the more often we see (*become familiar with*) someone, the more likely it is that we will grow to like (*become fond of*) that person. This is called the **mere exposure effect.** This effect suggests that the popular saying "familiarity breeds contempt" may not be completely accurate.

Page 759: . . . *"beauty is only skin deep"* . . . This saying suggests that physical attractiveness (*beauty*) is only a superficial quality (*skin deep*). Research, however, has shown that how we look influences social interactions, how frequently we date, our popularity, how we are perceived by others, etc.

Page 762: In real life, *opposites retract.* The old saying *"opposites attract"* has not been supported by research in social psychology. In fact, we tend to dislike those we do not perceive as similar to ourselves (*opposites retract*). Rather than fostering *contempt,* Myers humorously suggests that similarity breeds *content.*

Page 763: To be *revved up* and to associate some of that arousal with a desirable person is to feel the pull of passion. Research has shown that one component of romantic or passionate love is physiological arousal; a second aspect is some cognitive interpretation and labeling of that feeling. So, if a person is in an aroused state (*revved up*) and this is easily linked to the presence of an attractive person, then attributions of romantic love may be made. As Myers cheerfully notes, rather than *absence, adrenaline makes the heart grow fonder* (intensifies love).

Page 765: At each step, the presence of other *bystanders turns people away from the path that leads to helping.* Darley and Latané displayed their findings in a flow diagram (See Figure 18.15, p. 765). At each decision point (i.e., noticing the event, interpreting it as an emergency, and assuming responsibility), the presence of others who appear to have observed the event (*bystanders*) causes people to be less likely to give assistance to someone in need (*they are turned away from the path that leads to helping*).

Page 765: . . . *blasé* . . . This means to be indifferent or uncaring. We arrive at the decision (especially in ambiguous situations) to help or not to help by watching the reactions of others. If they appear to be unconcerned (*blasé*), we may conclude that there is no emergency and thus may not intervene or help. This **bystander effect** means that the presence of others decreases the probability that any particular observer will provide help.

Page 767: Before long, each group became intensely proud of itself and hostile to the other group's *"sneaky," "smart-alecky stinkers."* In Sherif's experiment, competitive conditions were created in order to foster the formation of two antagonistic groups. Each group soon saw itself as superior to the other group's "dishonest and sly" (*sneaky*) "rotten know-it-alls" (*smart-alecky stinkers*). Sherif then used shared objectives and common problems (**superordinate goals**) to create reconciliation and cooperation.

Page 769: Conciliations allow both parties to begin edging *down the tension ladder to a safer rung* where communication and mutual understanding can begin. Social psychologist Charles Osgood has developed a tactic called **GRIT** (Graduated and Reciprocated Initiatives in Tension-Reduction) for increasing cooperation and trust between parties in conflict. When one side makes a small gesture or offer of goodwill (*a conciliatory act*), the other side has an opportunity to reciprocate and thus move the conflict toward some resolution (*down the tension ladder to a safer rung*) and start the process of mutual respect and understanding.

NOTES

NOTES

NOTES

NOTES

NOTES

NOTES

NOTES

NOTES

NOTES

NOTES

NOTES

NOTES

NOTES

NOTES

NOTES

NOTES

NOTES

NOTES